MALVERN £1.99

THE
OXFORD
SCHOOL
ATLAS

Acknowledgements

The publishers would like to thank the
following for permission to reproduce
photographs:

CNES,1990 Distribution Spot Image/
Science Photo Library p. 110;
Daily Telegraph Colour Library , p.4;
Dr Gene Feldman, NASAS GSFC/Science Photo Library p. 85;
Earth Satellite Corporatioon/Science Photo Library p. 89, 126;
Geospace/Science Photo Library p. 85, 86;
NOAA/Science Photo Library p. 6, 7, 29;
NRSC Ltd./Science Photo Library pp. 60, 62/3,
64/5, 67, 68, 69, 72, 70/1, 144;

Cover image:
Tom Van Sant / Geosphere Project, Santa Monica,
Science Photo Library.

The illustrations are by Chapman Bounford,
Hard Lines, Mike Saunders, and Gary Hinks.

The page design is by Adrian Smith.

Oil spillage data is from
*Oil Pollution Survey around the Coast
of the United Kingdom, 1995*
by kind permission of the publishers,
ACOPS (Advisory Committee on Protection of the Sea).

Industrial emission data for Europe is from
Environmental Factsheet No.5, December 1994, produced
by The Swedish NGO Secretariat on Acid Rain,
from data supplied by the Pollen Consultancy.

The publishers would also like to thank
the many individuals, companies, societies,
and institutions who gave assistance in the gathering of data

© Oxford University Press, 1997

© Maps copyright Oxford University Press

Oxford University Press, Great Clarendon Street, Oxford OX2 6DP

Oxford New York
Athens Auckland Bangkok Bogotá
Buenos Aires Calcutta Cape Town Chennai
Dar es Salaam Delhi Florence Hong Kong
Istanbul Karachi Kuala Lumpur Madrid
Melbourne Mexico City Mumbai Nairobi Paris
São Paulo Singapore Taipei Tokyo Toronto Warsaw

and associated companies in
Berlin Ibadan

Oxford is a registered trade mark of Oxford University Press

First published 1997
Reprinted with corrections 1998
Reprinted 1999 (twice)

ISBN 0 19 831837 5 (paperback)   ISBN 0 19 831838 3 (hardback)

Printed in Italy by G. Canale & C. S.p.A. - Borgaro T.se - Turin

Editorial Adviser

Patrick Wiegand

Oxford University Press

2 Contents

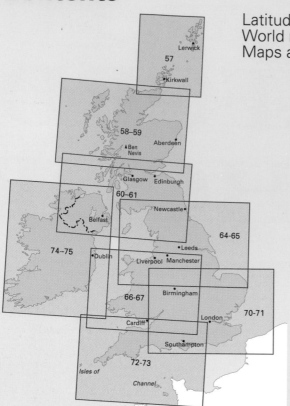

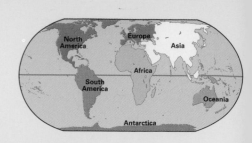

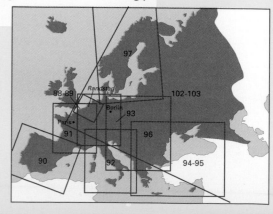

Contents 3

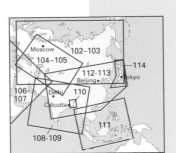
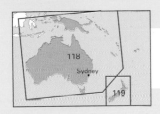
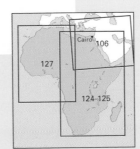

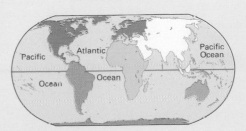
Maps that show general features of regions, countries or continents are called **topographic maps**.
These maps are shown with a light band of colour in the contents list.

For example:

South West England

4 Latitude and Longitude

The Earth is a small, blue planet.
Seen from space it has no right way up.

An imaginary grid is used
to pinpoint the position of
any place on Earth.
The grid consists of lines
called parallels of latitude
and meridians of longitude.
Both are measured in degrees.

Latitude
Parallels of latitude measure
distance north or south of the
Equator. The Equator is at
latitude 0°. The poles are at
latitudes 90°N and 90°S.

Longitude
Meridians of longitude measure
distance east or west of the
Prime Meridian. The Prime (or
Greenwich) Meridian is at
longitude 0°. The 180° line of
longitude, on the opposite side
of the Earth, is the International
Date Line.

The Equator divides the Earth
into halves : the Northern
Hemisphere and the Southern
Hemisphere. The Prime
Meridian and the 180° meridian
together also divide the Earth
into halves : the Western
Hemisphere and the Eastern
Hemisphere.

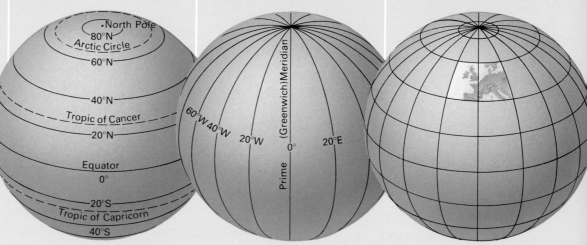

Coordinates
The position of any place on Earth can be located using
coordinates of latitude and longitude. Latitude is always
given first, then longitude.

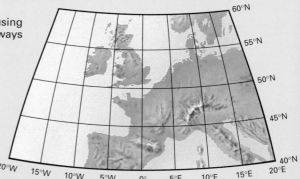

World maps
The only true representation of the Earth's surface is a globe.
World maps, however, are more convenient to use than globes.
this map has been made by unpeeling strips from the Earth's
surface. it not very satisfactory because gaps are left in the
land and sea.

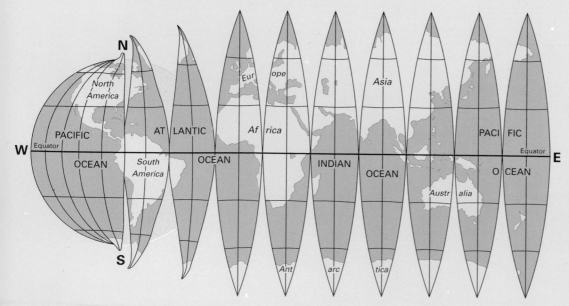

Grids of meridians and parallels,
called projections, are used to turn
the spherical surface of the Earth into
world maps. It is impossible to make
a world map that has accurate area,
shape, distance, and direction. Every
world map is distorted in at least one
of these ways.

There are very many map projections. This page shows only a few.

It is part of a cartographer's skill to select the best projection for the information that will be shown. The places shown in the centre of the map will vary according to where in the world the map is used.

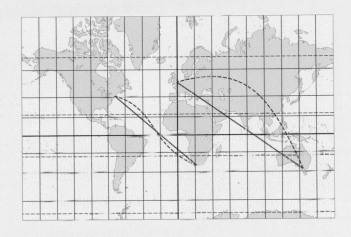

Eckert IV projection

This is the fourth map projection designed by the German cartographer Max Eckert (1868-1938).
It is an equal area projection, showing the true area of places in relation to each other. Equal area maps permit fair comparisons to be made between areas of the world.

| | tropical forest |

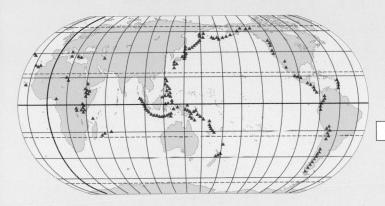

| ▲ | active volcanoes |

Mercator projection

Gerardus Mercator (1512-1594) designed this projection for navigators. It is still used for navigation today.
Any straight line on the map is a line of constant compass bearing. It is a conformal projection, which means that the shape (especially for small areas) is accurate. However, the size of the land masses is distorted. Land is shown larger the further away it is from the Equator.

------- line of constant compass bearing

——— shortest route

Gall's projection

This projection, designed by the Reverend James Gall (1868-1895), is neither conformal nor equal area but gives a reasonable compromise between accuracy of shape and area. A modified version is sometimes used in this atlas as a general purpose world map.

——— plate boundaries

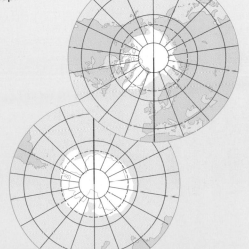

Polar projections

Most world maps do not show Antarctica or the Arctic Ocean very well. Polar projections show the world as if seen from space. Great distortion occurs near the edges of the map.

| | ice cap |

Oxford University Press

Edinburgh

Urban land use map

Urban land use maps show the general pattern of residential, industrial, and commercial areas. They also show relief and communications.

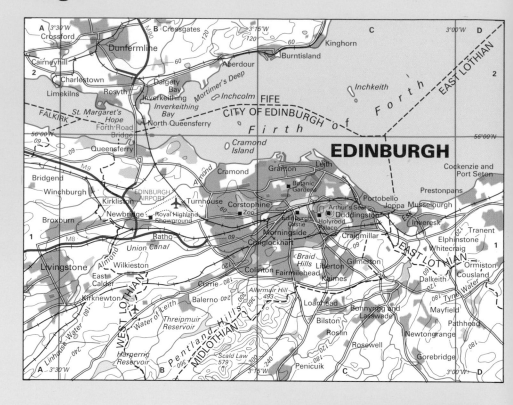

Boundaries

unitary authority

Communications

motorway

major road

other road

major railway

canal

✈ major airport

✈ other airport

Physical features

river

contours

•155 spot height in metres

Land use

central business district

other major commercial areas

industrial

residential

major parks and open spaces

non-urban

Scale 1 : 300 000

0   5 km

Satellite image

This satellite image of Edinburgh has been processed to give approximately natural colour.

Grey/light blue: urban areas
Green: grassland.
Pink/brown: arable land.
Dark blue: water.

Scale 0   5   10 km

Locator maps

Locator maps show the map or satellite image area in relation to its surroundings.

area of urban land use map

Edinburgh

area of satellite image

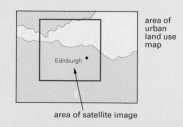

area of topographic map extract

Topographic maps

Topographic maps show the main features of the physical and human landscape.

As the scale becomes smaller maps show less detail.

Scale 1 : 1 000 000 0   10   20 km

Extract from the topographic map of South Scotland, page 61.

Scale 1 : 4 500 000

0   10   20 km

Extract from the topographic map of the British Isles, page 56.

Wales

Thematic maps

Thematic maps provide information about special topics such as industry, agriculture, population, communications, the environment and quality of life.

area of thematic map extract

Manufacturing industry

The map shows only the main centres of manufacturing for each industry.

- chemicals
- oil refining
- steel
- non-ferrous metal smelting
- metal working
- motor vehicles
- shipbuilding and repair
- mechanical engineering
- electrical engineering
- electronics and computers
- leather
- rubber
- textiles and carpets
- glass
- cement
- furniture
- pulp, paper, and board
- printing and publishing
- brewing and distilling

Regional aid to industry

- Development areas
- Intermediate areas
- previously assisted areas
- newly assisted areas
- Development Board for Rural Wales

Scale 1: 3 000 000

0   50   100 km

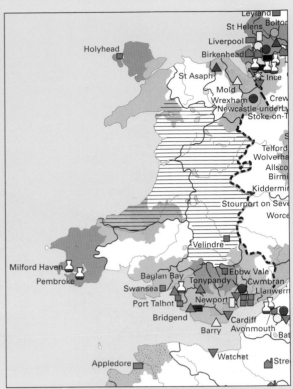

Extract from the map showing manufacturing industry in the British Isles, pages 46-47.

Agriculture

- hill-farming—mainly sheep
- barley and oats
- improved grazing
- dairying and mixed farming

• market gardening

- forest and woodland
- settlement and industry

Scale 1: 4 500 000

0   50   100 km

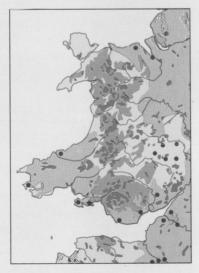

Extract from the map showing agriculture in the British Isles, page 40.

Industry

 industrial areas

Industry	Power
I iron and steel	○ nuclear power station
▲ aluminium	● hydro-electric (power station)
○ engineering	
▲ chemicals	Scale 1: 20 000 000

0   200   400 km

As the scale of the map becomes smaller thematic information is generalized.

Extract from the map showing industry in Europe, page 82.

Satellite image

This satellite image uses false colours to distinguish between different uses of the land.

Orange: rough pasture.
Red: forest.
Green: improved pasture.
Blue: urban areas.

Scale

0   50   100 km

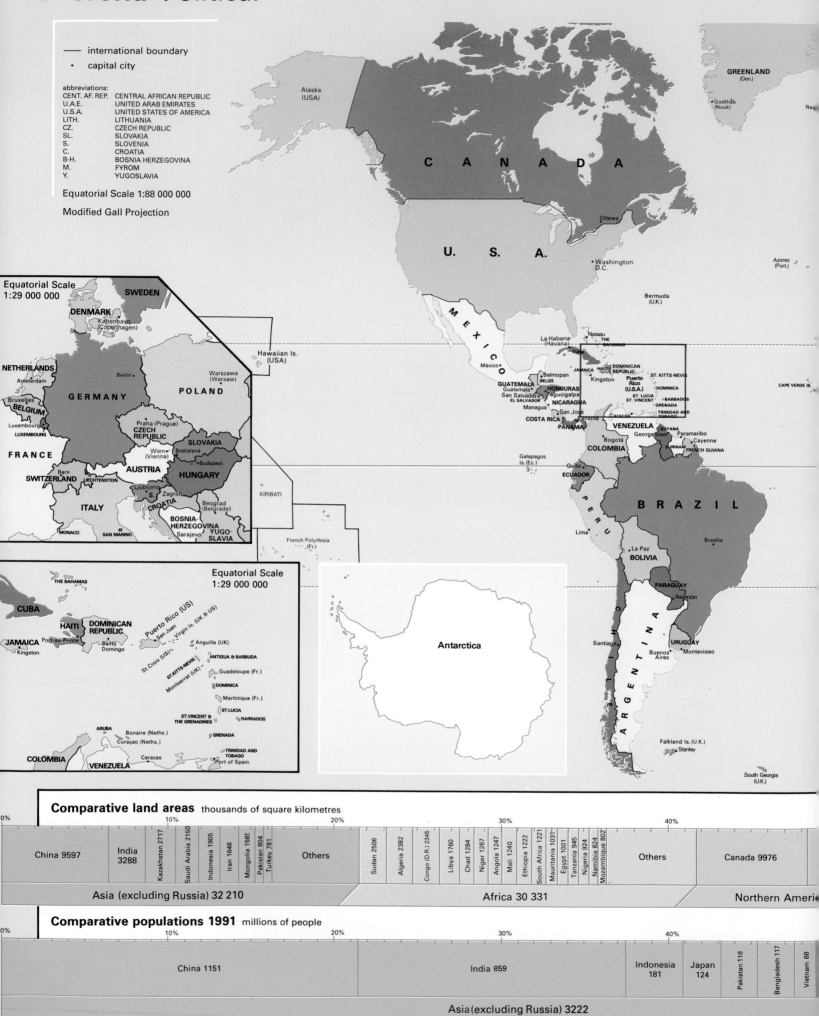

— international boundary
• capital city

abbreviations:
CENT. AF. REP. CENTRAL AFRICAN REPUBLIC
U.A.E. UNITED ARAB EMIRATES
U.S.A. UNITED STATES OF AMERICA
LITH. LITHUANIA
CZ. CZECH REPUBLIC
SL. SLOVAKIA
S. SLOVENIA
C. CROATIA
B-H. BOSNIA HERZEGOVINA
M. FYROM
Y. YUGOSLAVIA

Equatorial Scale 1:88 000 000

Modified Gall Projection

Equatorial Scale 1:29 000 000

Equatorial Scale 1:29 000 000

Comparative land areas thousands of square kilometres

| China 9597 | India 3288 | Kazakhstan 2717 | Saudi Arabia 2150 | Indonesia 1905 | Iran 1648 | Mongolia 1565 | Pakistan 804 | Turkey 781 | Others | Sudan 2506 | Algeria 2382 | Congo (D.R.) 2345 | Libya 1760 | Chad 1284 | Niger 1267 | Angola 1247 | Mali 1240 | Ethiopia 1222 | South Africa 1221 | Mauritania 1031 | Egypt 1001 | Tanzania 945 | Nigeria 924 | Namibia 824 | Mozambique 802 | Others | Canada 9976 |

Asia (excluding Russia) 32 210   Africa 30 331   Northern America

Comparative populations 1991 millions of people

| China 1151 | India 859 | Indonesia 181 | Japan 124 | Pakistan 118 | Bangladesh 117 | Vietnam 68 |

Asia (excluding Russia) 3222

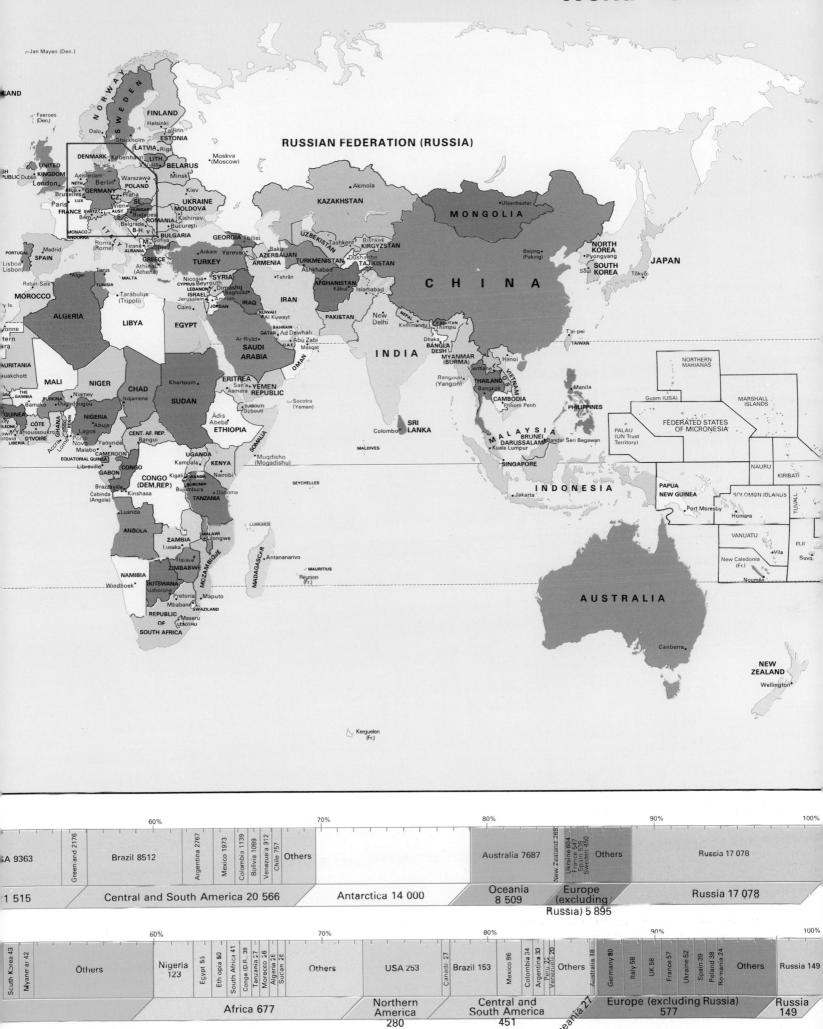

Land height and sea depth

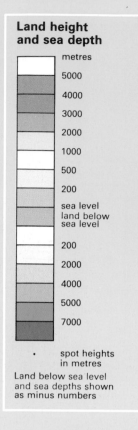

metres

5000
4000
3000
2000
1000
500
200

sea level
land below
sea level

200
2000
4000
5000
7000

• spot heights in metres

Land below sea level and sea depths shown as minus numbers

Equatorial Scale 1:88 000 000

Modified Gall Projection

Flood Risk

~~~ coast vulnerable to tsunamis (seismic sea waves)

▬ major river flood plains, some partially controlled, which are susceptible to flooding

● major floods (more than 1000 deaths, 1960-91)

Equatorial Scale 1:250 000 000

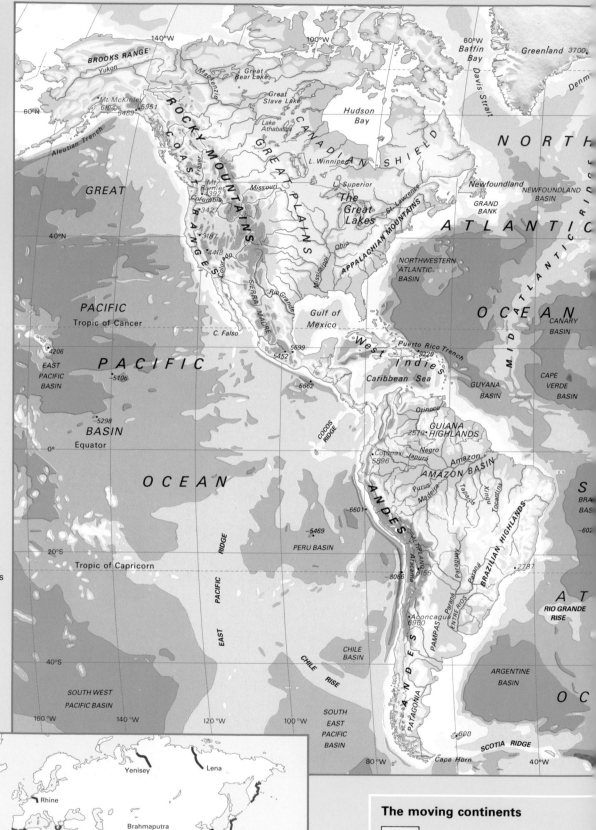

The moving continents

☐ land areas

☐ continental shelf

☐ sea areas

■ orogenic belts

········· uncertain coastline

········· uncertain continental shelf edge

Lines of latitude and longitude indicate position on the globe.

The graticules show how earlier positions of the continents compare with the present

Modified Gall Projection

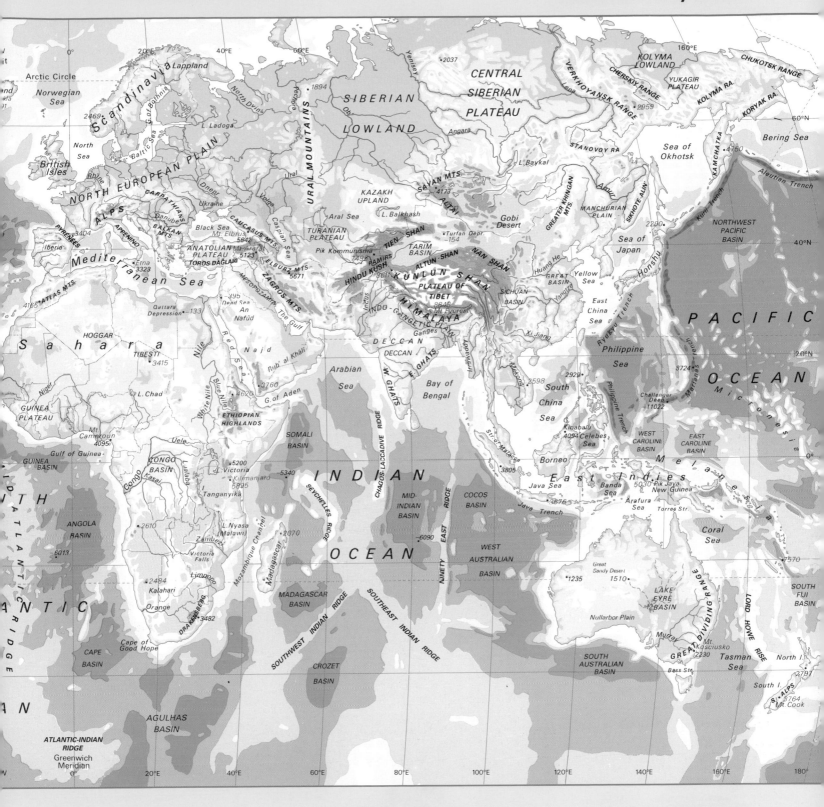

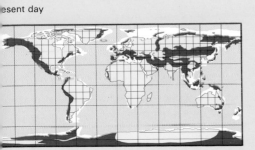

Present day

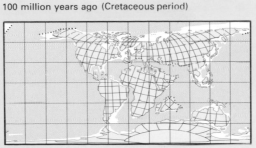

100 million years ago (Cretaceous period)

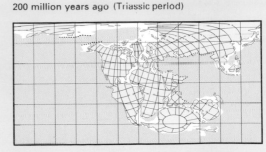

200 million years ago (Triassic period)

Oxford University Press

Rainfall
and other forms of precipitation

	mm
	over 400
	250–400
	150–250
	50–150
	25–50
	under 25

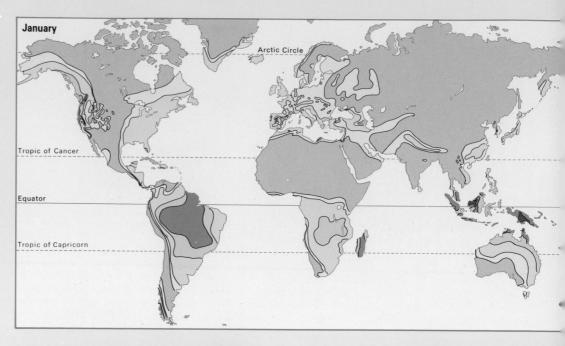

January

Temperature, ocean currents

actual temperature °C

	32
	24
	16
	8
	0
	−8
	−16
	−24

Ocean currents

cold

warm

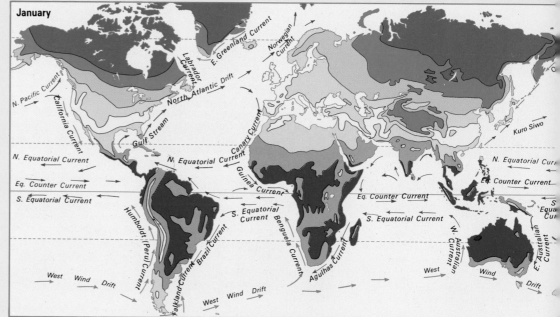

January

Pressure and winds

Pressure reduced to sea level

1035 millibars
1030
1025
1020
1015
1010
1005
1000
995

H high pressure cell

L low pressure cell

Prevailing winds
Arrows fly with the wind:
the heavier the arrow, the
more regular ('constant')
the direction of the wind

Equatorial Scale 1:218 000 000

January

Modified Gall Projection

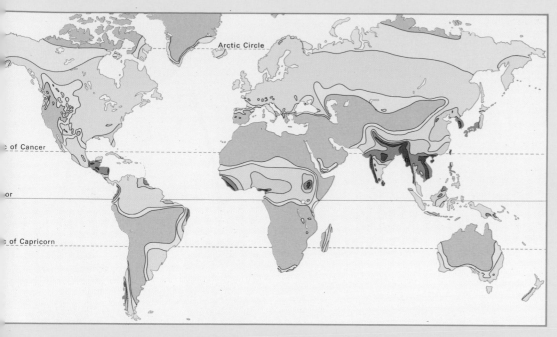

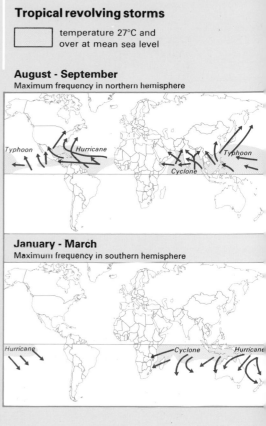

Tropical revolving storms

| temperature 27°C and over at mean sea level |

August - September
Maximum frequency in northern hemisphere

Typhoon   Hurricane   Typhoon
Cyclone

January - March
Maximum frequency in southern hemisphere

Hurricane   Cyclone   Hurricane

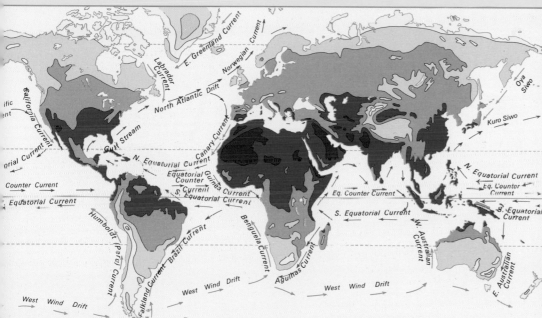

E. Greenland Current
Labrador Current
Norwegian Current
North Atlantic Drift
California Current
Gulf Stream
Canary Current
N. Equatorial Current
Equatorial Counter Current
Guinea Current
Counter Current
Equatorial Current
S. Equatorial Current
Humboldt (Peru) Current
Benguela Current
Brazil Current
Falkland Current
Agulhas Current
West Wind Drift
West Wind Drift
West Wind Drift
Oya Siwo
Kuro Siwo
N. Equatorial Current
Eq. Counter Current
Eq. Counter Current
S. Equatorial Current
S. Equatorial Current
W. Australian Current
E. Australian Current

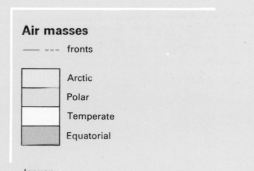

Air masses

— — — fronts

	Arctic
	Polar
	Temperate
	Equatorial

1010
1015
L
L
1015
Westerlies 1015
Westerlies
1005
Westerlies
1015
L
L
1020
H
1020
N.E. Trades
1000
L
S.W. Monsoon
1010
1015
S.E. Monsoon
N.E. Trades
S.E. Trades
S.E. Trades
S.E. Trades
S.E. Monsoon
N.E. Trades
H
1020
H
H
H
West Wind Drift
(Roaring Forties)
Westerlies
Westerlies
1015
1010
1005

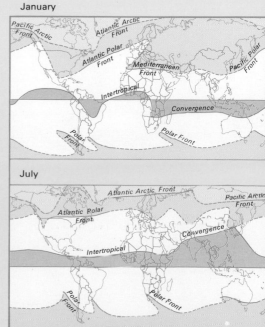

January
Pacific Arctic Front   Atlantic Arctic Front
Atlantic Polar Front
Mediterranean Front   Pacific Polar Front
Intertropical
Convergence
Polar Front
Polar Front

July
Atlantic Arctic Front
Atlantic Polar Front   Pacific Arctic Front
Convergence
Intertropical
Polar Front
Polar Front

Oxford University Press

Tropic of Cancer

Equator

Tropic of Capricorn

Arctic Circle

The Seasons

The Earth travels around the Sun once each year. The seasons happen because the Earth's axis is tilted.

For half the year, from about 21 March to 23 September, the North Pole is tilted towards the Sun. During this time, places in the northern hemisphere have spring followed by summer. At the same time, the South Pole is tilted away from the Sun and the southern hemisphere has autumn and winter.

From September to March the situation is reversed. The North Pole is tilted away from the Sun and the northern hemisphere has autumn followed by winter, while the southern hemisphere has spring and summer.

On about 21 March and 23 September, days and nights are of equal length in both hemispheres. These dates are the **equinoxes.**

On about 21 June the Sun is directly overhead at the Tropic of Cancer. This is the **summer solstice** in the northern hemisphere. At this time days are longest and nights are shortest.

On about 22 December the Sun is directly overhead at the Tropic of Capricorn. This is the **winter solstice** in the northern hemisphere, when nights are longest and days are shortest.

Northern winter
Southern summer
22 December solstice
Northern spring
Southern autumn
21 March equinox
149 597 910 km
Sun
3 months
Northern autumn
Southern spring
23 September equinox
Earth's orbit around the Sun
Northern summer
Southern winter
Earth
21 June solstice
3 months

Climate Regions

Hot tropical rainy climates
rain all year
monsoon
dry in winter

Very dry climates
with no reliable rain
with a little rain

Climates influenced by the sea: warm summers, mild winters
with dry summers (Mediterranean climate)
with dry winters
with no dry season

Cool climates
rain all year
with dry winters

Cold polar climates
no warm season and fairly dry

Mountain climates
height of the land strongly affects the climate

Equatorial scale 1 : 150 000 000

Eckert IV Projection © Oxford University Press

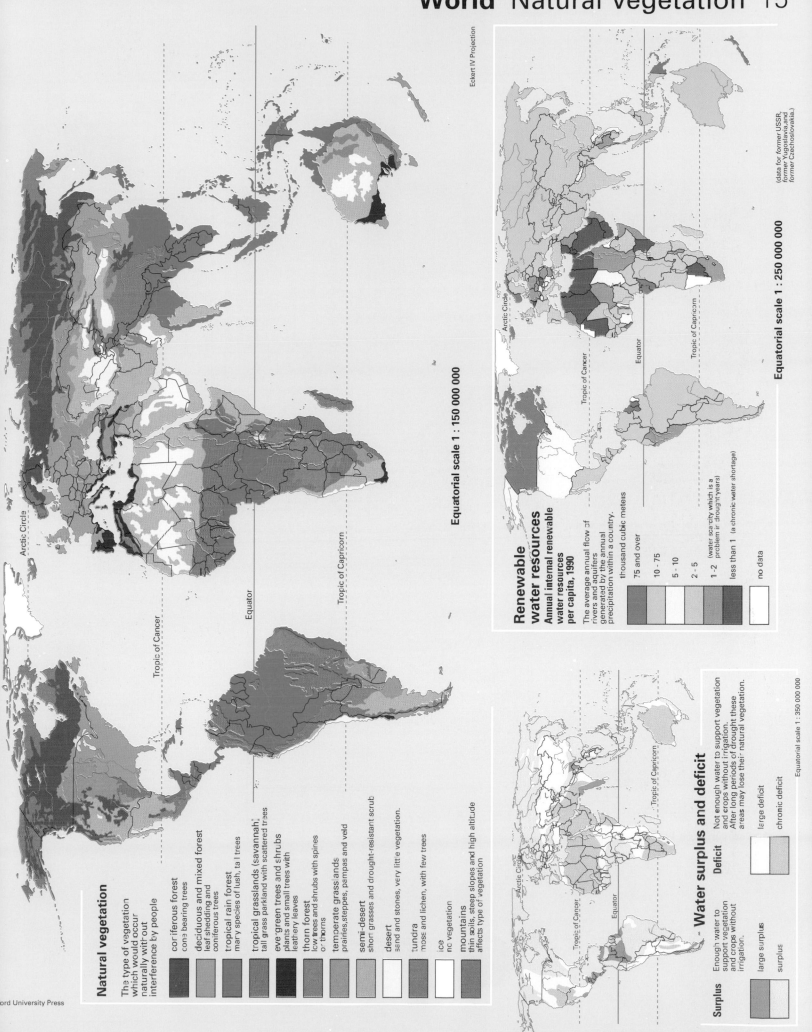

Eckert IV Projection

Equatorial scale 1 : 150 000 000

Natural vegetation

The type of vegetation which would occur naturally without interference by people

- coniferous forest
  cone bearing trees

- deciduous and mixed forest
  leaf shedding and coniferous trees

- tropical rain forest
  many species of lush, tall trees

- tropical grasslands (savannah)
  tall grass parkland with scattered trees

- evergreen trees and shrubs
  plants and small trees with leathery leaves

- thorn forest
  low trees and shrubs with spines or thorns

- temperate grasslands
  prairies, steppes, pampas and veld

- semi-desert
  short grasses and drought-resistant scrub

- desert
  sand and stones, very little vegetation

- tundra
  moss and lichen, with few trees

- ice
  no vegetation

- mountains
  thin soils, steep slopes and high altitude affects type of vegetation

Oxford University Press

Arctic Circle

Tropic of Cancer

Equator

Tropic of Capricorn

Renewable water resources

Annual internal renewable water resources per capita, 1990

The average annual flow of rivers and aquifers generated by the annual precipitation within a country.

thousand cubic metres

- 75 and over
- 10 - 75
- 5 - 10
- 2 - 5
- 1 - 2 (water scarcity which is a problem in drought years)
- less than 1 (a chronic water shortage)
- no data

(data for former USSR, former Yugoslavia, and former Czechoslovakia.)

Equatorial scale 1 : 250 000 000

Arctic Circle

Tropic of Cancer

Equator

Tropic of Capricorn

Water surplus and deficit

Surplus Enough water to support vegetation and crops without irrigation.

- large surplus
- surplus

Deficit Not enough water to support vegetation and crops without irrigation. After long periods of drought these areas may lose their natural vegetation.

- large deficit
- chronic deficit

Equatorial scale 1 : 350 000 000

Arctic Circle

Tropic of Cancer

Equator

Tropic of Capricorn

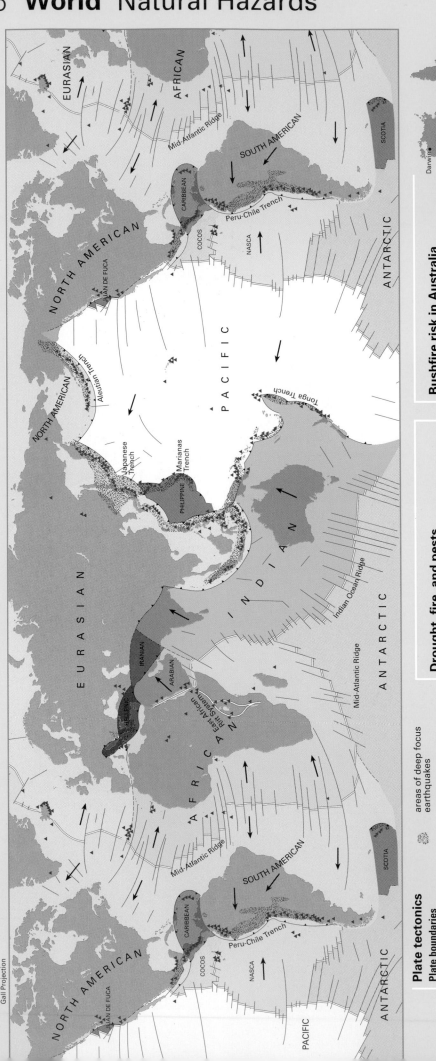

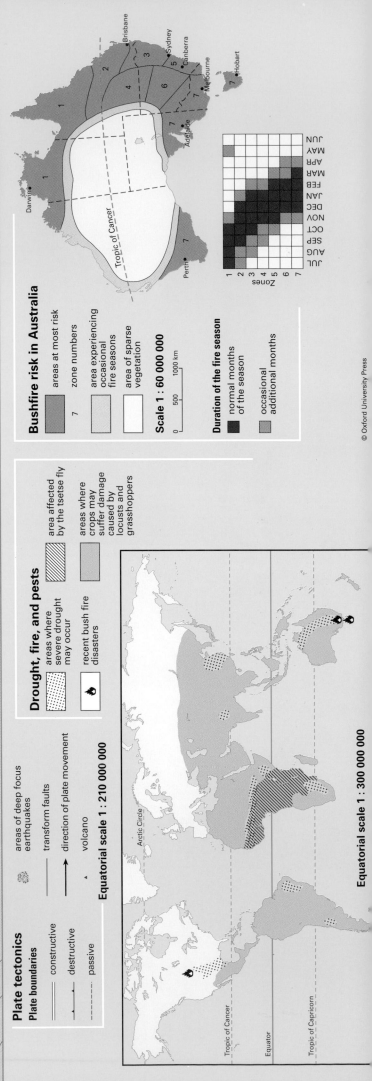

Bushfire risk in Australia

- areas at most risk
- **7** zone numbers
- area experiencing occasional fire seasons
- area of sparse vegetation

Scale 1 : 60 000 000

0 500 1000 km

Duration of the fire season

- normal months of the season
- occasional additional months

Drought, fire, and pests

- area affected by the tsetse fly
- areas where severe drought may occur
- areas where crops may suffer damage caused by locusts and grasshoppers
- recent bush fire disasters

Equatorial scale 1 : 210 000 000

Plate tectonics

Plate boundaries

- constructive
- destructive
- passive

- areas of deep focus earthquakes
- transform faults
- direction of plate movement
- volcano

Equatorial scale 1 : 300 000 000

© Oxford University Press

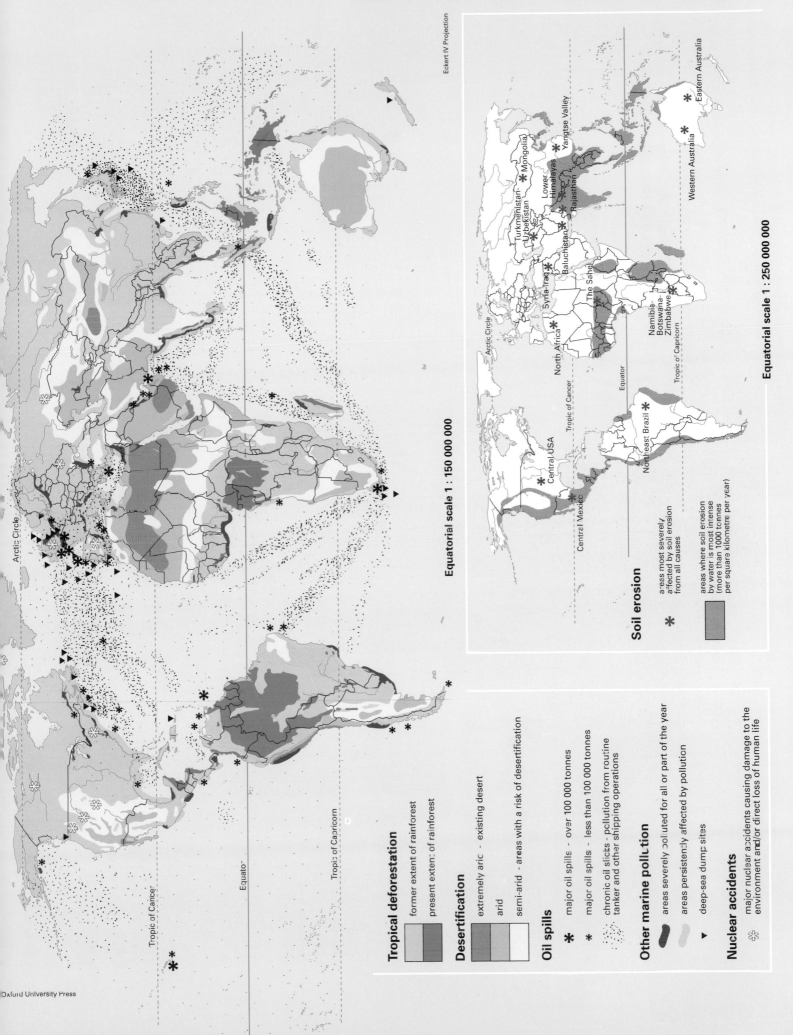

Eckert IV Projection

Equatorial scale 1 : 150 000 000

Equatorial scale 1 : 250 000 000

Mongolia

Turkmenistan
Uzbekistan

Lower Himalayas

Yangtse Valley

Rajasthan

Syria-Iraq

Baluchistan

The Sahel

North Africa

Namibia-
Botswana-
Zimbabwe

Western Australia

Eastern Australia

Central USA

Northeast Brazil

Central Mexico

Arctic Circle

Tropic of Cancer

Equator

Tropic of Capricorn

Soil erosion

* areas most severely affected by soil erosion from all causes

areas where soil erosion by water is most intense (more than 1000 tonnes per square kilometre per year)

Arctic Circle

Tropic of Cancer

Equator

Tropic of Capricorn

Tropical deforestation

former extent of rainforest

present extent of rainforest

Desertification

extremely arid - existing desert

arid

semi-arid - areas with a risk of desertification

Oil spills

* major oil spills - over 100 000 tonnes

* major oil spills - less than 100 000 tonnes

chronic oil slicks - pollution from routine tanker and other shipping operations

Other marine pollution

areas severely polluted for all or part of the year

areas persistently affected by pollution

▶ deep-sea dump sites

Nuclear accidents

major nuclear accidents causing damage to the environment and/or direct loss of human life

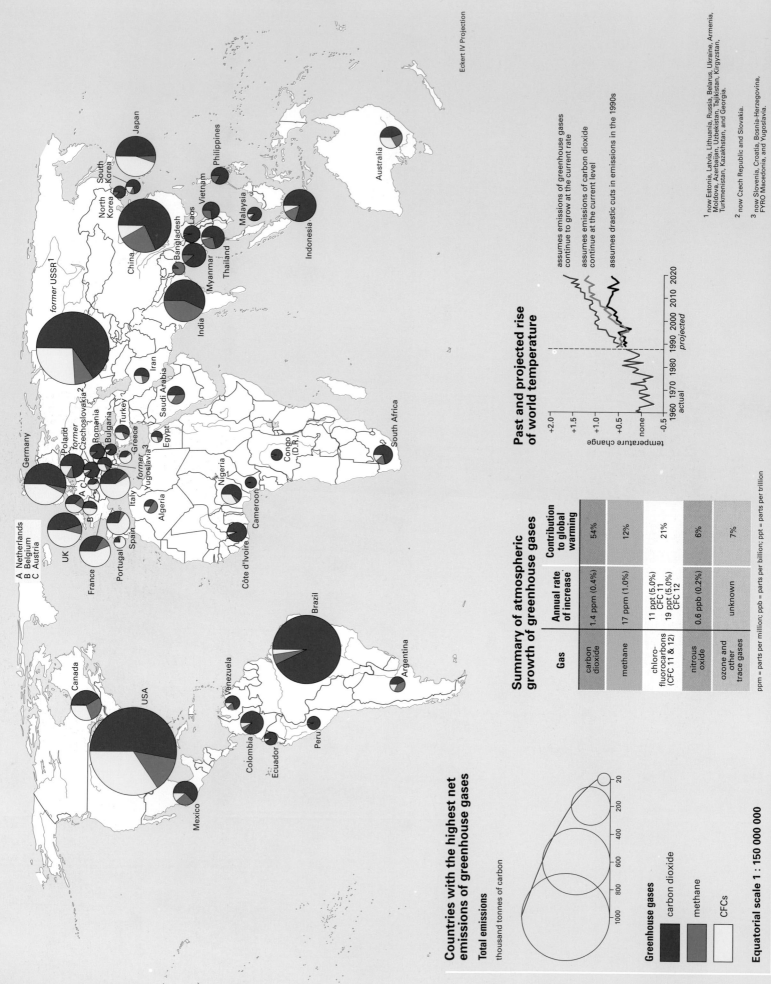

Eckert IV Projection

[1] now Estonia, Latvia, Lithuania, Russia, Belarus, Ukraine, Armenia, Moldova, Azerbaijan, Uzbekistan, Tajikistan, Kirgyzstan, Turkmenistan, Kazakhstan, and Georgia.

[2] now Czech Republic and Slovakia.

[3] now Slovenia, Croatia, Bosnia-Herzegovina, FYRO Macedonia, and Yugoslavia.

Past and projected rise of world temperature

assumes emissions of greenhouse gases continue to grow at the current rate

assumes emissions of carbon dioxide continue at the current level

assumes drastic cuts in emissions in the 1990s

temperature change

+2.0
+1.5
+1.0
+0.5
none
-0.5

1960 1970 1980 1990 2000 2010 2020
actual | projected

Summary of atmospheric growth of greenhouse gases

Gas	Annual rate of increase	Contribution to global warming
carbon dioxide	1.4 ppm (0.4%)	54%
methane	17 ppm (1.0%)	12%
chloro-fluorocarbons (CFC 11 & 12)	11 ppt (5.0%) CFC 11 / 19 ppt (5.0%) CFC 12	21%
nitrous oxide	0.6 ppb (0.2%)	6%
ozone and other trace gases	unknown	7%

Countries with the highest net emissions of greenhouse gases

Total emissions

thousand tonnes of carbon

20
200
400
600
800
1000

Greenhouse gases

carbon dioxide

methane

CFCs

Equatorial scale 1 : 150 000 000

ppm = parts per million; ppb = parts per billion; ppt = parts per trillion

© Oxford University Press

A Netherlands
B Belgium
C Austria

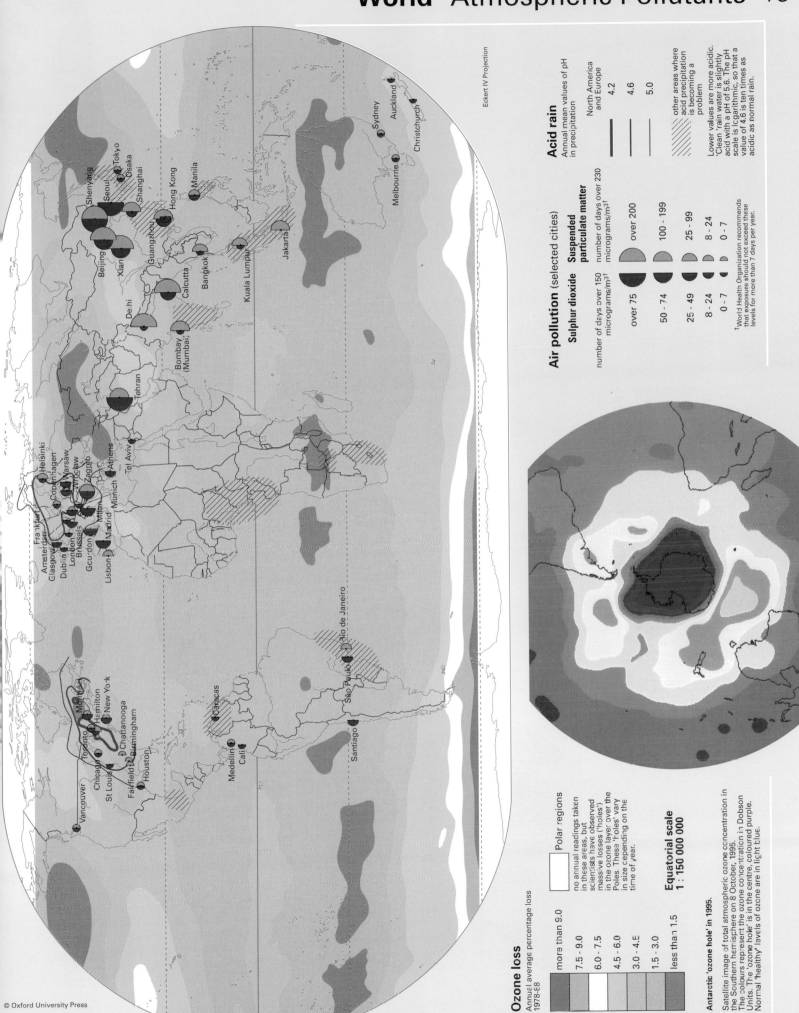

Eckert IV Projection

Air pollution (selected cities)

Sulphur dioxide	Suspended particulate matter
number of days over 150 micrograms/m³†	number of days over 230 micrograms/m³†
over 75	over 200
50 - 74	100 - 199
25 - 49	25 - 99
8 - 24	8 - 24
0 - 7	0 - 7

†World Health Organization recommends that exposure should not exceed these levels for more than 7 days per year.

Acid rain

Annual mean values of pH in precipitation

North America and Europe
4.2
4.6
5.0

other areas where acid precipitation is becoming a problem

Lower values are more acidic. 'Clean' rain water is slightly acid with a pH of 5.6. The pH scale is logarithmic, so that a value of 4.6 is ten times as acidic as normal rain.

Ozone loss

Annual average percentage loss 1978-88

more than 9.0
7.5 - 9.0
6.0 - 7.5
4.5 - 6.0
3.0 - 4.5
1.5 - 3.0
less than 1.5

Polar regions
no annual readings taken in these areas, but scientists have observed massive losses ('holes') in the ozone layer over the Poles. These 'holes' vary in size depending on the time of year.

Equatorial scale
1 : 150 000 000

Antarctic 'ozone hole' in 1995.
Satellite image of total atmospheric ozone concentration in the Southern hemisphere on 8 October, 1995. The colours represent the ozone concentration in Dobson Units. The 'ozone hole' is in the centre, coloured purple. Normal 'healthy' levels of ozone are in light blue.

© Oxford University Press

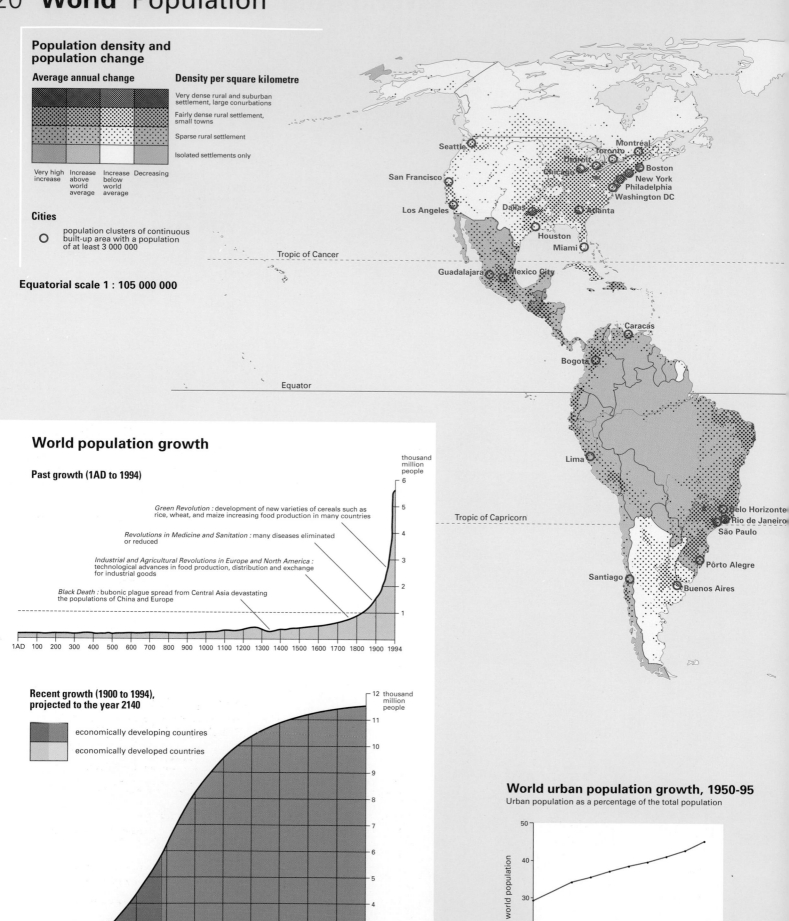

Population density and population change

Average annual change

Very high increase
Increase above world average
Increase below world average
Decreasing

Density per square kilometre

Very dense rural and suburban settlement, large conurbations

Fairly dense rural settlement, small towns

Sparse rural settlement

Isolated settlements only

Cities

O population clusters of continuous built-up area with a population of at least 3 000 000

Equatorial scale 1 : 105 000 000

World population growth

Past growth (1AD to 1994)

Green Revolution : development of new varieties of cereals such as rice, wheat, and maize increasing food production in many countries

Revolutions in Medicine and Sanitation : many diseases eliminated or reduced

Industrial and Agricultural Revolutions in Europe and North America : technological advances in food production, distribution and exchange for industrial goods

Black Death : bubonic plague spread from Central Asia devastating the populations of China and Europe

thousand million people

1AD 100 200 300 400 500 600 700 800 900 1000 1100 1200 1300 1400 1500 1600 1700 1800 1900 1994

Recent growth (1900 to 1994), projected to the year 2140

economically developing countires
economically developed countries

thousand million people

1900 1920 1940 1960 1980 2000 2020 2040 2060 2080 2100 2120 2140

projected

World urban population growth, 1950-95

Urban population as a percentage of the total population

Percent of total world population

1950 1960 1970 1980 1990 1995

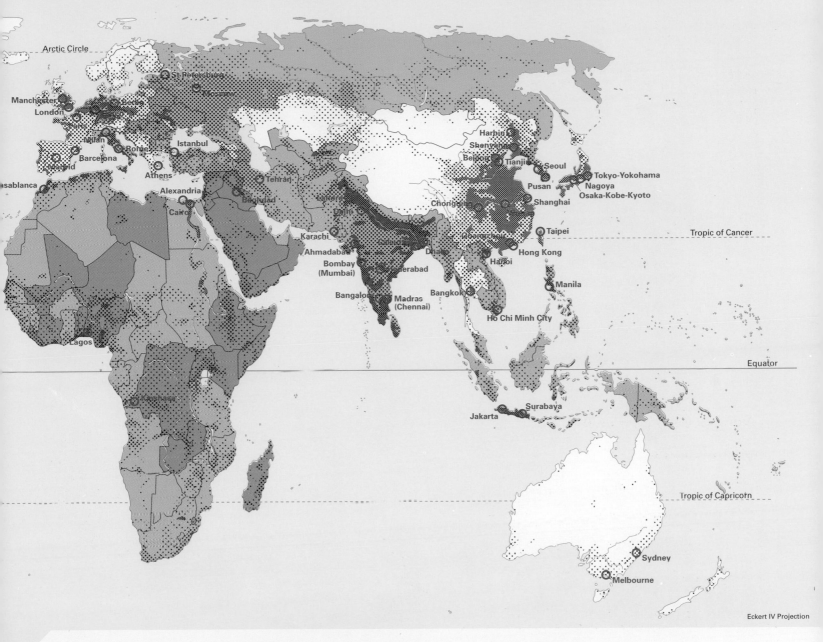

Arctic Circle

Manchester
London
Milan
Barcelona
Rome
Madrid
Athens
Casablanca
St Petersburg
Moscow
Istanbul
Tehrān
Alexandria
Baghdad
Cairo
Lahore
Delhi
Karachi
Ahmadabad
Bombay (Mumbai)
Hyderabad
Bangalore
Madras (Chennai)
Lagos

Harbin
Shenyang
Beijing
Tianjin
Seoul
Pusan
Tokyo-Yokohama
Nagoya
Osaka-Kobe-Kyoto
Shanghai
Chongqing
Taipei
Dhaka
Hong Kong
Hanoi
Bangkok
Manila
Ho Chi Minh City
Jakarta
Surabaya

Tropic of Cancer

Equator

Tropic of Capricorn

Sydney
Melbourne

Eckert IV Projection

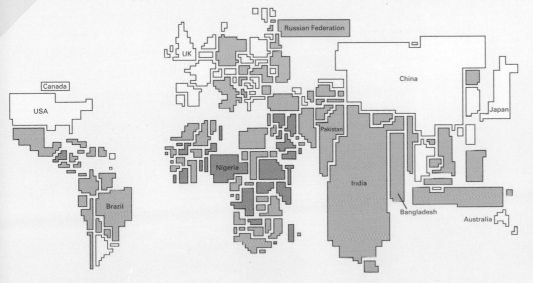

Russian Federation
UK
Canada
USA
China
Japan
Pakistan
Nigeria
India
Brazil
Bangladesh
Australia

Total population

On this map the size of each country represents the number of people living there, rather than the area of land that the country occupies.

Only those countries with at least 1 million people living in them are shown.
One small square represents 1 million people.

This represents Guatemala where eleven million people live.

Population change

The colours on this map represent the same rates of population increase or decrease shown in the legend to the main map above.

Very high increase - over 3 percent

Increase above the world average - 1.5 to 3 percent

Increase below the world average - less than 1.5 percent

Decreasing (by less than 1 percent)

Oxford University Press

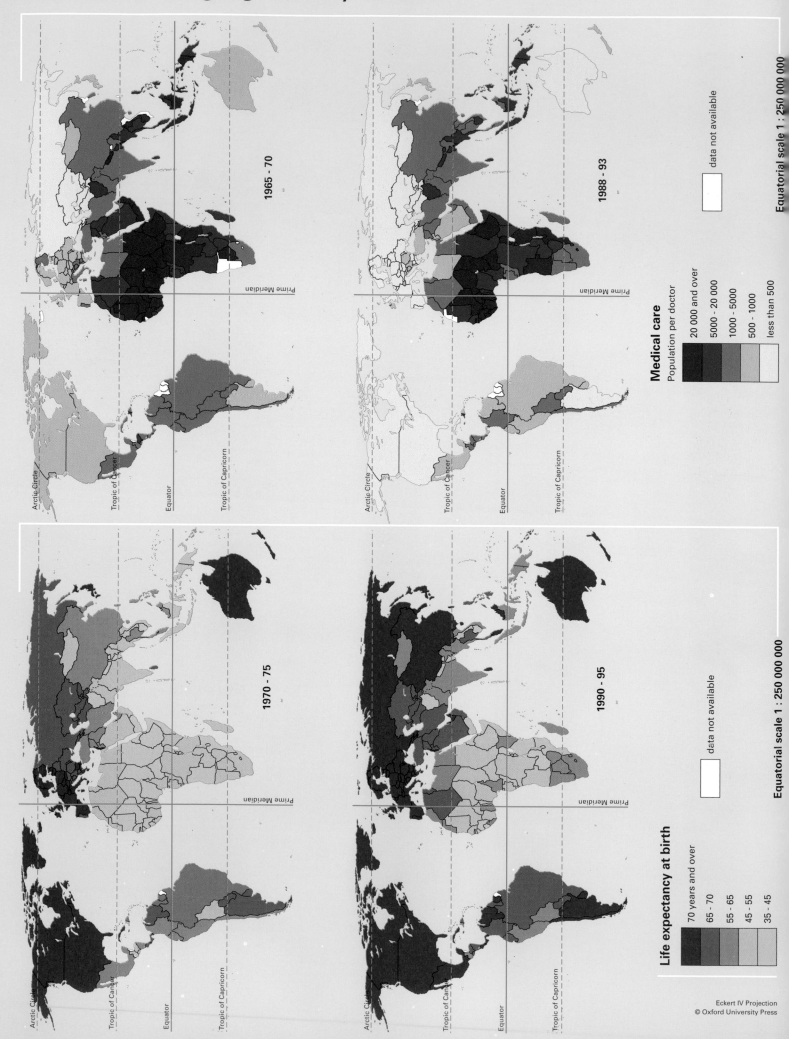

1965 - 70

1988 - 93

1970 - 75

1990 - 95

Prime Meridian

Arctic Circle

Tropic of Cancer

Equator

Tropic of Capricorn

Medical care

Population per doctor

- 20 000 and over
- 5000 - 20 000
- 1000 - 5000
- 500 - 1000
- less than 500

data not available

Equatorial scale 1 : 250 000 000

Life expectancy at birth

- 70 years and over
- 65 - 70
- 55 - 65
- 45 - 55
- 35 - 45

data not available

Equatorial scale 1 : 250 000 000

Eckert IV Projection
© Oxford University Press

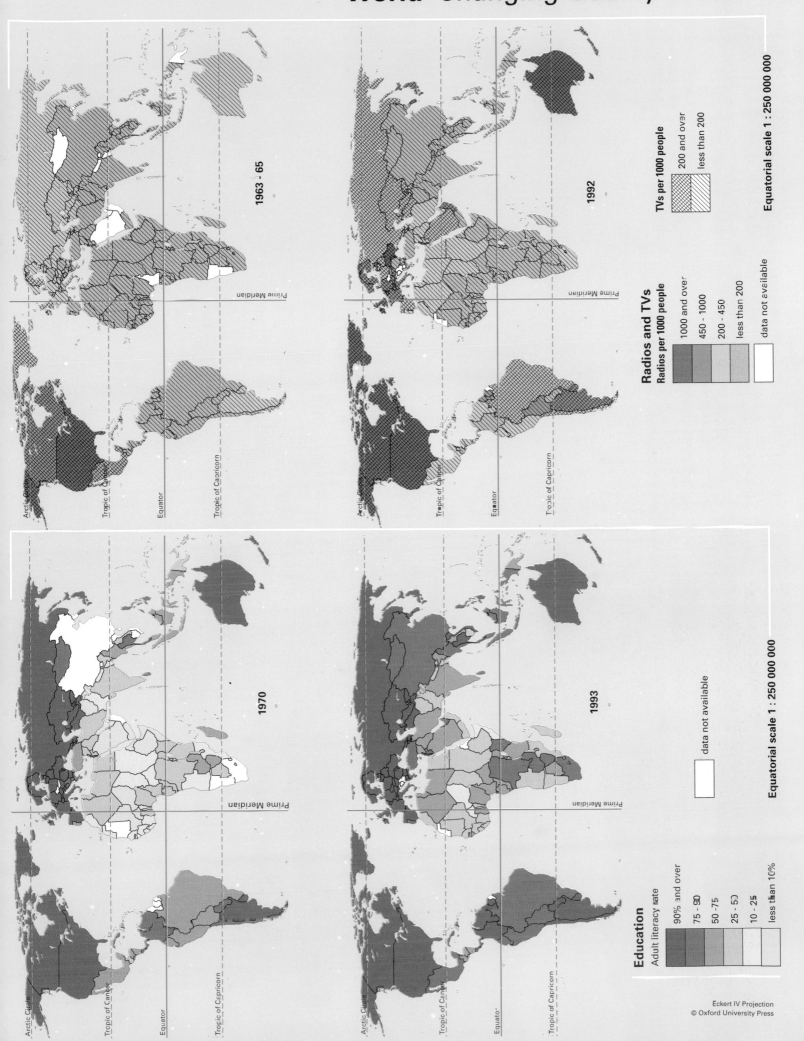

1963 - 65

1992

Radios and TVs

Radios per 1000 people

	1000 and over
	450 - 1000
	200 - 450
	less than 200
	data not available

TVs per 1000 people

	200 and over
	less than 200

Equatorial scale 1 : 250 000 000

1970

1993

data not available

Equatorial scale 1 : 250 000 000

Education

Adult literacy rate

	90% and over
	75 - 90
	50 - 75
	25 - 50
	10 - 25
	less than 10%

Eckert IV Projection
© Oxford University Press

Arctic Circle
Tropic of Cancer
Equator
Tropic of Capricorn
Prime Meridian

Gross Domestic Product (GDP)

The total value of all the goods and services produced within a country in one year.

GDP per capita ($US), 1992

15 000 and over

10 000 - 15 000

5000 - 10 000

3000 - 5000

1000 - 3000

500 - 1000

0 - 500

Industrialization

Industrialized high-income economies

The majority live in cities and enjoy high living standards based on manufacturing services, resource development, and high levels of energy consumption.

Industrializing upper-middle income economies

Manufacturing and other forms of industrial development are growing alongside traditional economies. The majority of the population have rising incomes.

Industrializing lower-middle income economies

Manufacturing and other forms of industrial development are growing alongside traditional economies. The majority of the population remain still relatively poor and rural.

Agricultural low income economies

These predominantly rural countries have made less economic progress in terms of industrializing than others, resulting in lower incomes for the majority and a greater dependence on agriculture.

• Major oil exporters

Equatorial scale 1 : 235 000 000

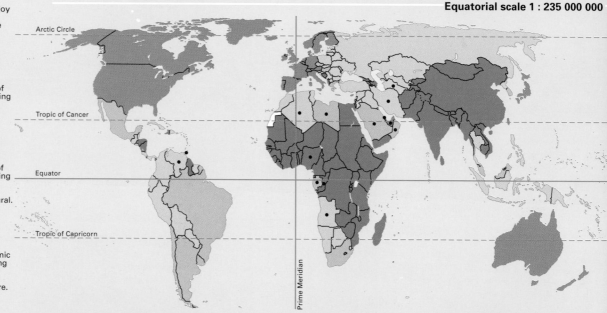

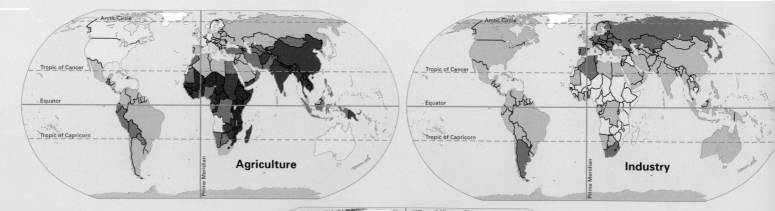

Agriculture

Industry

Employment, 1990

Percent of the labour force

over 80

60-80

30-60

10-30

less than 10

Equatorial scale 1 : 405 000 000

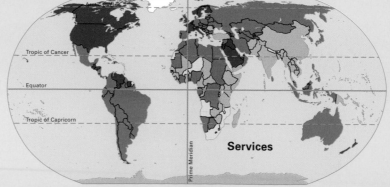

Services

Eckert IV Projection
© Oxford University Press

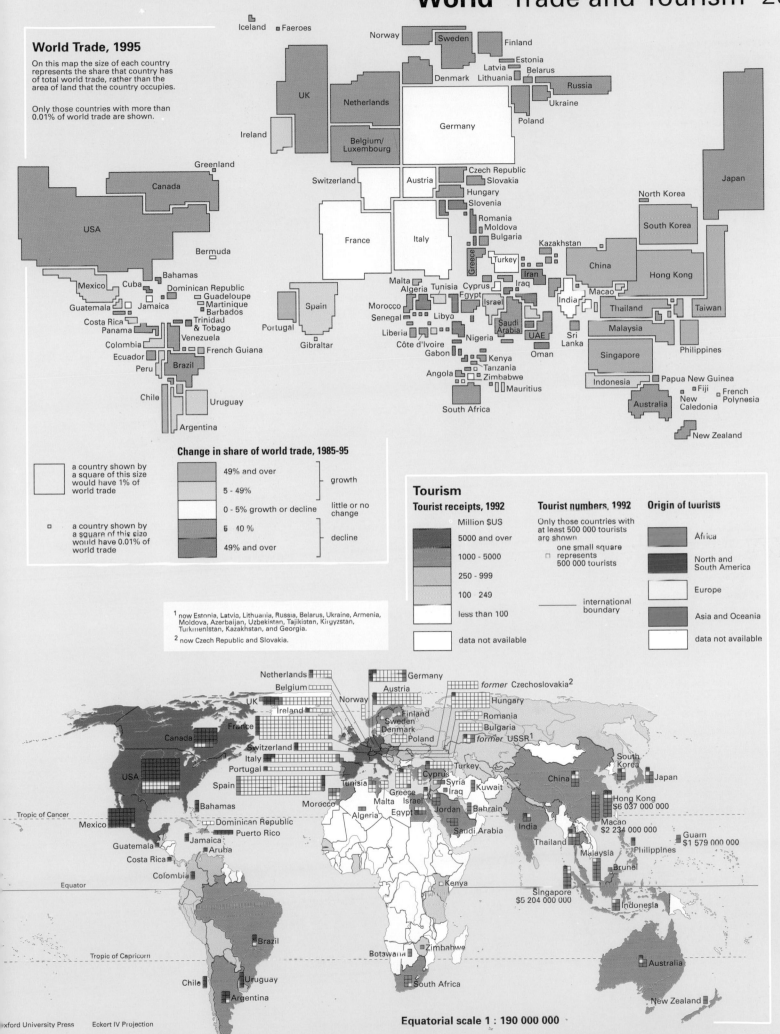

World Trade, 1995

On this map the size of each country represents the share that country has of total world trade, rather than the area of land that the country occupies.

Only those countries with more than 0.01% of world trade are shown.

Change in share of world trade, 1985-95

49% and over	growth
5 - 49%	
0 - 5% growth or decline	little or no change
5 - 49 %	decline
49% and over	

a country shown by a square of this size would have 1% of world trade

a country shown by a square of this size would have 0.01% of world trade

1 now Estonia, Latvia, Lithuania, Russia, Belarus, Ukraine, Armenia, Moldova, Azerbaijan, Uzbekistan, Tajikistan, Kirgyzstan, Turkmenistan, Kazakhstan, and Georgia.

2 now Czech Republic and Slovakia.

Tourism

Tourist receipts, 1992
Million $US

	5000 and over
	1000 - 5000
	250 - 999
	100 - 249
	less than 100
	data not available

Tourist numbers, 1992
Only those countries with at least 500 000 tourists are shown

one small square represents 500 000 tourists

international boundary

Origin of tourists

	Africa
	North and South America
	Europe
	Asia and Oceania
	data not available

Hong Kong $6 037 000 000

Macao $2 234 000 000

Guam $1 579 000 000

Singapore $5 204 000 000

Equatorial scale 1 : 190 000 000

Oxford University Press   Eckert IV Projection

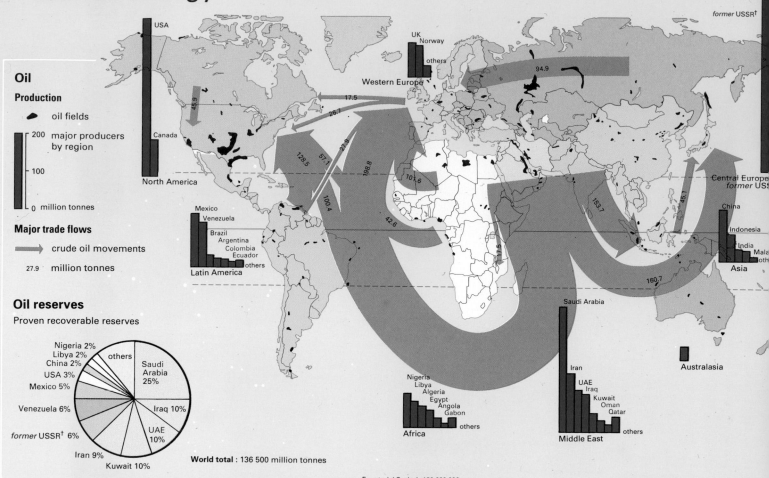

Oil

Production

- oil fields
- 200 major producers by region
  - 100
  - 0 million tonnes

Major trade flows

→ crude oil movements

27.9 million tonnes

Oil reserves

Proven recoverable reserves

Nigeria 2%
Libya 2%
China 2%
USA 3%
Mexico 5%
Venezuela 6%
former USSR† 6%
Iran 9%
Kuwait 10%
others
Saudi Arabia 25%
Iraq 10%
UAE 10%

World total : 136 500 million tonnes

Equatorial Scale 1: 180 000 000

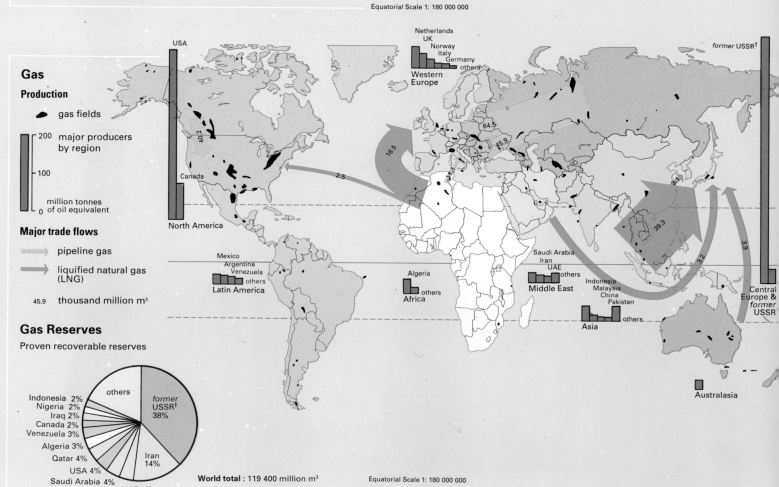

Gas

Production

- gas fields
- 200 major producers by region
  - 100
  - 0 million tonnes of oil equivalent

Major trade flows

⟶ pipeline gas

⟶ liquified natural gas (LNG)

45.9 thousand million m³

Gas Reserves

Proven recoverable reserves

Indonesia 2%
Nigeria 2%
Iraq 2%
Canada 2%
Venezuela 3%
Algeria 3%
Qatar 4%
USA 4%
Saudi Arabia 4%
UAE 4%
Iran 14%
others
former USSR† 38%

World total : 119 400 million m³

Equatorial Scale 1: 180 000 000

Modified Gall Projection

© Oxford University Press

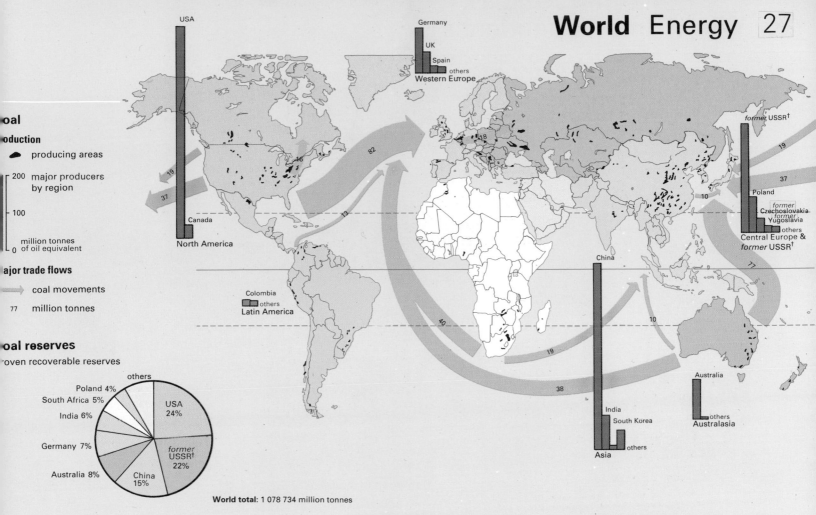

Coal

Production

- producing areas

major producers
by region

200

100

0

million tonnes
of oil equivalent

Major trade flows

coal movements

77 million tonnes

Coal reserves

Proven recoverable reserves

USA

Germany
UK
Spain
others
Western Europe

Canada
North America

former USSR†
Poland
former Czechoslovakia
former Yugoslavia
others
Central Europe &
former USSR†

82

19

37

3

10

77

40

19

38

10

China

India
South Korea
others
Asia

Australia
others
Australasia

Colombia
others
Latin America

Pie chart — Proven recoverable reserves:
- USA 24%
- former USSR† 22%
- China 15%
- Australia 8%
- Germany 7%
- India 6%
- South Africa 5%
- Poland 4%
- others

World total: 1 078 734 million tonnes

Equatorial Scale 1: 180 000 000

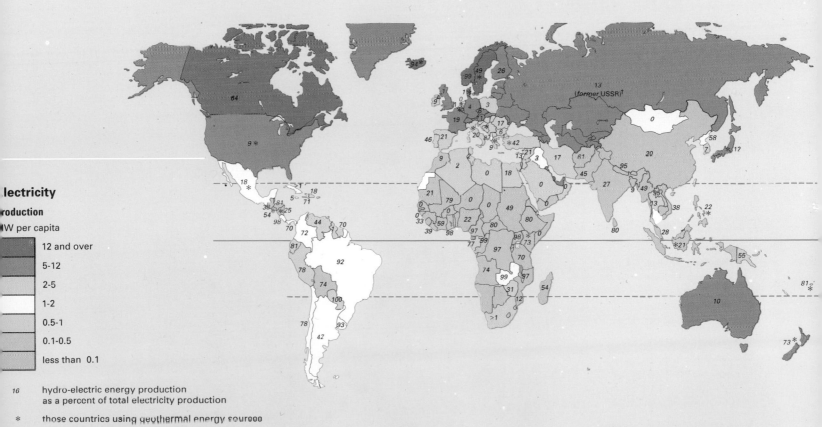

Electricity

Production

kW per capita

- 12 and over
- 5-12
- 2-5
- 1-2
- 0.5-1
- 0.1-0.5
- less than 0.1

16 hydro-electric energy production
as a percent of total electricity production

* those countries using geothermal energy sources

Equatorial Scale 1: 180 000 000

†Now the independent republics of Armenia, Azerbaijan, Belarus, Estonia, Georgia, Kazakhstan, Kirgyzstan, Latvia, Lithuania, Moldova, Russia, Tajikistan, Turkmenistan, Ukraine, and Uzbekistan.

Modified Gall Projection

Oxford University Press

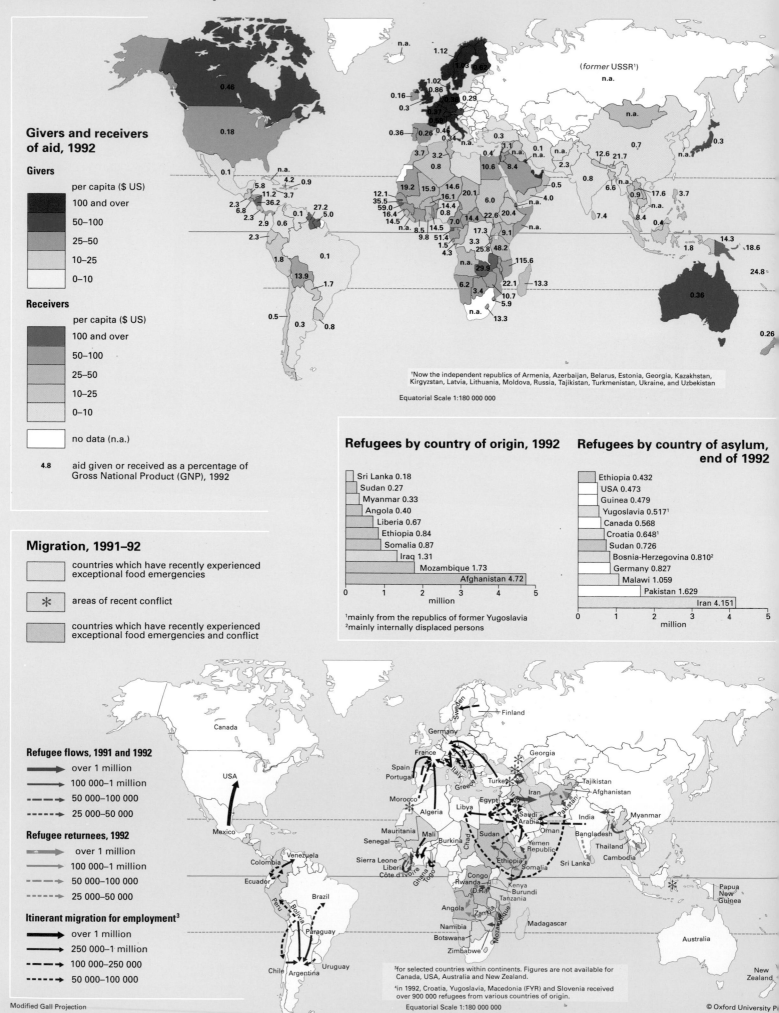

Givers and receivers of aid, 1992

Givers

per capita ($ US)

- 100 and over
- 50–100
- 25–50
- 10–25
- 0–10

Receivers

per capita ($ US)

- 100 and over
- 50–100
- 25–50
- 10–25
- 0–10

no data (n.a.)

4.8   aid given or received as a percentage of Gross National Product (GNP), 1992

Migration, 1991–92

	countries which have recently experienced exceptional food emergencies
*	areas of recent conflict
	countries which have recently experienced exceptional food emergencies and conflict

[1]Now the independent republics of Armenia, Azerbaijan, Belarus, Estonia, Georgia, Kazakhstan, Kirgyzstan, Latvia, Lithuania, Moldova, Russia, Tajikistan, Turkmenistan, Ukraine, and Uzbekistan

Equatorial Scale 1:180 000 000

Refugees by country of origin, 1992

- Sri Lanka 0.18
- Sudan 0.27
- Myanmar 0.33
- Angola 0.40
- Liberia 0.67
- Ethiopia 0.84
- Somalia 0.87
- Iraq 1.31
- Mozambique 1.73
- Afghanistan 4.72

million

[1]mainly from the republics of former Yugoslavia
[2]mainly internally displaced persons

Refugees by country of asylum, end of 1992

- Ethiopia 0.432
- USA 0.473
- Guinea 0.479
- Yugoslavia 0.517[1]
- Canada 0.568
- Croatia 0.648[1]
- Sudan 0.726
- Bosnia-Herzegovina 0.810[2]
- Germany 0.827
- Malawi 1.059
- Pakistan 1.629
- Iran 4.151

million

Refugee flows, 1991 and 1992

- over 1 million
- 100 000–1 million
- 50 000–100 000
- 25 000–50 000

Refugee returnees, 1992

- over 1 million
- 100 000–1 million
- 50 000–100 000
- 25 000–50 000

Itinerant migration for employment[3]

- over 1 million
- 250 000–1 million
- 100 000–250 000
- 50 000–100 000

[3]for selected countries within continents. Figures are not available for Canada, USA, Australia and New Zealand.

[4]in 1992, Croatia, Yugoslavia, Macedonia (FYR) and Slovenia received over 900 000 refugees from various countries of origin.

Modified Gall Projection

Equatorial Scale 1:180 000 000

© Oxford University Press

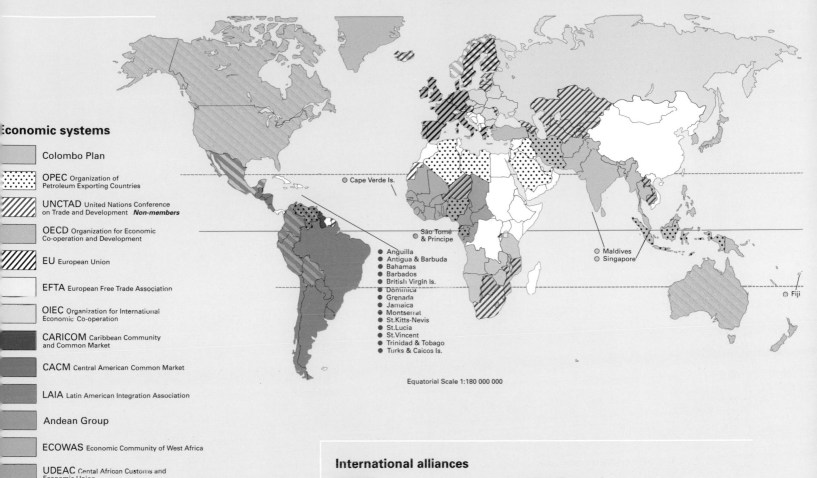

Economic systems

- **Colombo Plan**
- **OPEC** Organization of Petroleum Exporting Countries
- **UNCTAD** United Nations Conference on Trade and Development **Non-members**
- **OECD** Organization for Economic Co-operation and Development
- **EU** European Union
- **EFTA** European Free Trade Association
- **OIEC** Organization for International Economic Co-operation
- **CARICOM** Caribbean Community and Common Market
- **CACM** Central American Common Market
- **LAIA** Latin American Integration Association
- **Andean Group**
- **ECOWAS** Economic Community of West Africa
- **UDEAC** Central African Customs and Economic Union
- **SADCC** Southern African Development Co-ordination Conference

Cape Verde Is.

São Tomé & Principe

○ Anguilla
○ Antigua & Barbuda
○ Bahamas
○ Barbados
○ British Virgin Is.
○ Dominica
○ Grenada
○ Jamaica
○ Montserrat
○ St.Kitts-Nevis
○ St.Lucia
○ St.Vincent
○ Trinidad & Tobago
○ Turks & Caicos Is.

○ Maldives
○ Singapore

○ Fiji

Equatorial Scale 1:180 000 000

International alliances

- **South Pacific Forum**
- **ASEAN** Association of South East Asian Nations
- **OAS** Organization of American States
- **Commonwealth of Nations**
- **Arab League**
- **OAU** Organization of African Unity
- **NATO** North Atlantic Treaty Organization
- **Council of Europe**
- **Antarctic Treaty**

Where more than one alliance is involved, the country is shown divided by interlocking shading.

United Nations

The following countries are **non-members**

Kiribati
Nauru
Northern Marianas
Switzerland†
Taiwan
Tonga
Tuvalu
Vatican City†
Western Sahara

Information correct as of Feb 1994

† observer status

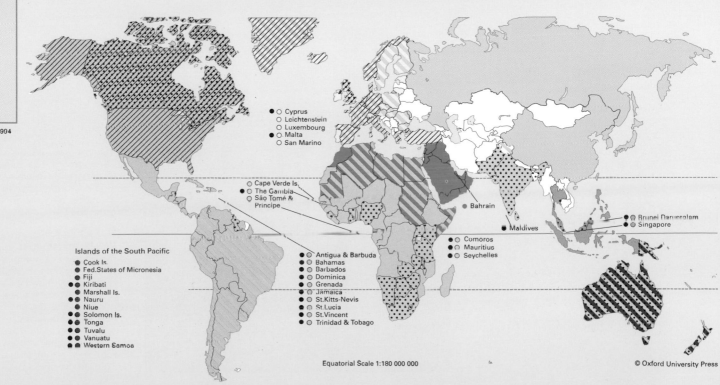

● ○ Cyprus
○ Leichtenstein
○ Luxembourg
● ○ Malta
○ San Marino

Cape Verde Is.
● The Gambia
○ São Tomé & Principe

● Bahrain

● Maldives

● ● Brunei Darussalam
● ○ Singapore

○ ● Comoros
○ Mauritius
○ ○ Seychelles

Islands of the South Pacific
● Cook Is.
○ Fed.States of Micronesia
● Fiji
● ○ Kiribati
● ○ Marshall Is.
● ○ Nauru
● Niue
● ○ Solomon Is.
● ○ Tonga
● ○ Tuvalu
● ○ Vanuatu
● ● Western Samoa

○ Antigua & Barbuda
● ○ Bahamas
● ○ Barbados
● ○ Dominica
● ○ Grenada
● ○ Jamaica
● ○ St.Kitts-Nevis
● ○ St.Lucia
● ○ St.Vincent
● ○ Trinidad & Tobago

Modified Gall Projection

Equatorial Scale 1:180 000 000

© Oxford University Press

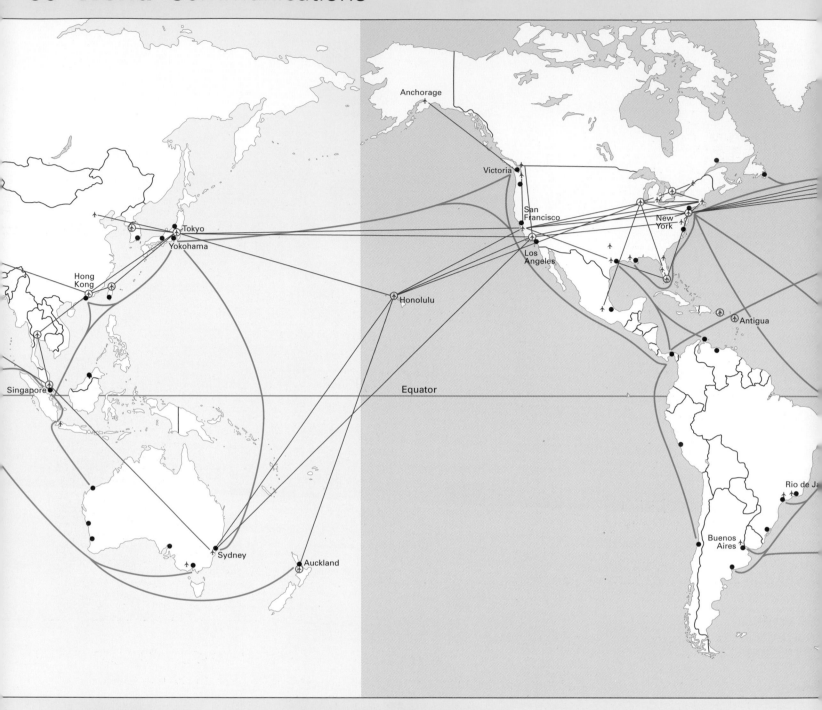

Anchorage

Victoria

San Francisco

New York

Los Angeles

Honolulu

Antigua

Tokyo

Yokohama

Hong Kong

Singapore

Equator

Rio de Ja

Buenos Aires

Sydney

Auckland

Communications

Maritime transport

— major shipping lanes

• major ports

Air transport

⊕ airports handling over 5 million passengers per year

✈ other airports on major routes

—— air routes with more than 50 direct flights per week

—— international boundary

Equatorial scale 1 : 130 000 000

Gall Projection
© Oxford University Press

sun

North Pole

dusk   **daytime**

night time   **dawn**

South Pole

Earth rotating from west to east

Earth orbiting the sun

Time

The Earth rotates on its axis once every 24 hours. The time of day is a measure of this rotation. We do not feel the Earth's rotation but, instead, see the Sun apparently move around the Earth. In one day and night the Sun will appear to have travelled the full 360° of longitude around the Earth.

In theory, all points along the same meridian of longitude will have the same time. This is not practical in everyday life, however, as the time would vary with the meridian. Instead, the Earth is divided into 24 time zones, each of 15° of longitude, in which the time is usually one hour's difference from the neighbouring zone. The edges of the time zones usually follow national boundaries rather than the lines of longitude on which they are based.

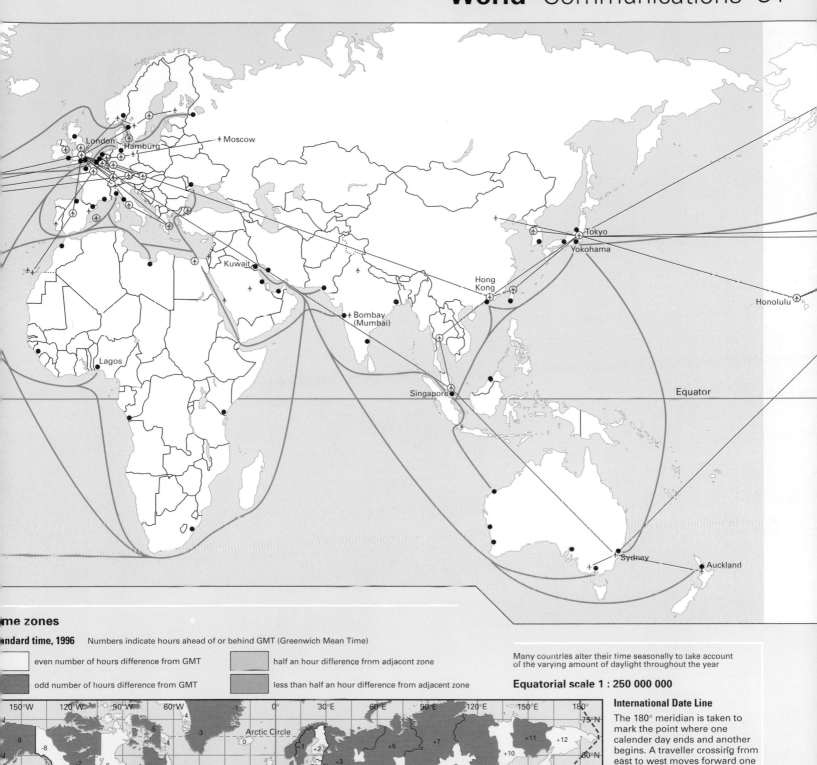

London
Hamburg
✈ Moscow
Kuwait
Bombay
(Mumbai)
Lagos
Hong Kong
Tokyo
Yokohama
Honolulu
Singapore
Equator
Sydney
Auckland

me zones

ndard time, 1996   Numbers indicate hours ahead of or behind GMT (Greenwich Mean Time)

even number of hours difference from GMT	half an hour difference from adjacent zone
odd number of hours difference from GMT	less than half an hour difference from adjacent zone

Many countries alter their time seasonally to take account of the varying amount of daylight throughout the year

Equatorial scale 1 : 250 000 000

International Date Line

The 180° meridian is taken to mark the point where one calender day ends and another begins. A traveller crossing from east to west moves forward one day. Crossing from west to east the calendar goes back one day. This line is adjusted for political convenience.

Gall Projection

150°W   120°W   90°W   60°W   30°W   0°   30°E   60°E   90°E   120°E   150°E   180°

-9
-8
-7   -6
-5
-3.5
-4
-5
-7   -6   -5
Atlantic
Ocean
-10
Tropic of Cancer
-6
-5
-4
-3
Equator
-6
-4
Atlantic
Ocean
Tropic of Capricorn
-3
-4
-5
-4
-3

Arctic Circle
-1
+1
+2
+3
+4
+5
+7
+8
+10
+11   +12
+8
+9
+4
+3
0
+2
+1
+2
+3.5   +4.5
+5.5
+5.75
+6.5
+5.5
+8
+9
+8
+5.5
+8
+7   +8
+9
+7   +8
+9   +10   +11
+8   +0.5
+10
+11   +12
+12

75°N
60°N
45°N
30°N
15°N
0°
15°S
30°S
45°S

Prime Meridian
Greenwich Mean Time

Pacific
Ocean

Indian
Ocean

International Date Line

© Oxford University Press

| -10 | -9 | -8 | -7 | -6 | -5 | -4 | -3 | -2 | -1 | 0 | +1 | +2 | +3 | +4 | +5 | +6 | +7 | +8 | +9 | +10 | +11 | +12 |

Shetland Islands

Former metropolitan counties

West Yorkshire

Bradford
Leeds
Calderdale
Kirklees
Wakefield
Barnsley
Doncaster
Sheffield
Rotherham

South Yorkshire

Newcastle upon Tyne
North Tyneside
Gateshead
South Tyne
Sunde
Tyne and Wear

Key to unitary authorities in Scotland

1	West Dunbartonshire	9	Falkirk
2	East Dunbartonshire	10	West Lothian
3	North Lanarkshire	11	City of Edinburgh
4	Glasgow City	12	Midlothian
5	East Renfrewshire	13	East Lothian
6	Renfrewshire	14	North Ayrshire
7	Inverclyde	15	East Ayrshire
8	Clackmannanshire	16	Dundee City

Orkney Islands

Greater Manchester
Rochdale
Bolton
Bury
Wigan
Sefton
St Helens
Knowsley
Salford
Oldham
Trafford
Manchester
Tameside
Liverpool
Stockport
Merseyside
Wirral

Western Isles

England, Scotland, and Wales together with Northern Ireland form the United Kingdom. England is divided into counties and unitary authorities. Scotland and Wales are divided into unitary authorities. Northern Ireland is divided into districts. The Isle of Man and Channel Islands are not included in the UK, being direct dependencies of the Crown, with their own legislative and taxation systems. The Republic of Ireland, a separate country, is divided into counties.

Northern Ireland
UNITED KINGDOM
Scotland
REPUBLIC OF IRELAND
Wales
England

SCOTLAND

Highland
Moray
Aberdeenshire
Aberdeen City
Perth and Kinross
Angus
Argyll and Bute
Stirling
Fife
Edinburgh
South Lanarkshire
Scottish Borders
South Ayrshire
Northumberland
Dumfries & Galloway
Tyne & Wear
Durham
Cumbria
Darlington
North Yorkshire

Wolverhampton
Walsall
Dudley
Sandwell
Birmingham
Solihull
Cover
West Midlands

0   25 km

Key to districts in Northern Ireland

1	Belfast	15	Omagh	21	Coleraine
2	Newtownabbey	16	Cookstown	22	Ballymoney
3	Carrickfergus	17	Magherafelt	23	Moyle
4	Castlereagh	18	Strabane	24	Ballymena
5	North Down	19	Londonderry	25	Larne
6	Ards	20	Limavady	26	Antrim
7	Down				
8	Newry & Mourne				
9	Banbridge				
10	Lisburn				
11	Craigavon				
12	Armagh				
13	Dungannon				
14	Fermanagh				

Greater London

Enfield
Harrow
Barnet
Hillingdon
Brent
Redbridge
Have
Ealing
Barking
Newham
Hounslow
Greenwich
Bexley
Merton
Bromley
Sutton
Croydon

Donegal
Belfast
Sligo
Monaghan
Cavan
Mayo
Leitrim
Roscommon
Longford
West-meath
Meath
Galway
Louth
Isle of Man
Douglas
NORTHERN IRELAND
Darlington
North Yorkshire
Blackpool
Lancashire
Blackburn with Darwen
Greater Manchester
York
West Yorkshire
South Yorkshire

0   2 (Greater London only)

Dublin
Offaly
Kildare
Laois
Clare
Tipperary
Kilkenny
Carlow
Wicklow
Wexford
Limerick
Waterford
Kerry
Cork

REPUBLIC OF IRELAND

Isle of Anglesey
Merseyside
Halton
Warrington
Cheshire
Stoke-on-Trent
Derby City
Derbyshire
Nottingham City
Nottingham-hamshire
Lincolnshire
Rutland
Peterborough
Norfolk
ENGLAND

WALES
Gwynedd
The Wrekin
Stafford-shire
West Midlands
Leicestershire
Northamptonshire
Bedford-shire
Cambridge-shire
Suffolk
Shropshire
Worcester-shire
Warwick-shire
Essex
Thurrock
Ceredigion
Powys
Herefordshire
Buckinghamshire
Hertfordshire
Southend
The Medway Towns
Pembroke-shire
Carmarthen-shire
Gloucester-shire
Oxford-shire
Slough
Greater London
Newport
Reading
West Berkshire
Bracknell Forest
Surrey
Kent
Cardiff
Wiltshire
Wokingham
Somerset
Hampshire
West Sussex
East Sussex
Devon
Southampton
Portsmouth
Isle of Wight
Brighton & Hove
Cornwall
Torbay
Dorset
Poole
Bournemouth
Plymouth

Isles of Scilly

Channel Islands

Key to unitary authorities in England

1	Hartlepool	10	Bristol
2	Stockton-on-Tees	11	North Somerset
3	Middlesbrough	12	Bath and North East Somerset
4	Redcar and Cleveland	13	Luton
5	East Riding of Yorkshire	14	Milton Keynes
6	City of Kingston upon Hull	15	Leicester City
7	North Lincolnshire	16	Swindon
8	North East Lincolnshire	17	Windsor & Maidenhead
9	South Gloucestershire		

Key to unitary authorities in Wales

1	Cardiff	8	Caerphilly
2	The Vale of Glamorgan	9	Blaenau Gwent
3	Bridgend	10	Monmouthshire
4	Swansea	11	Conwy
5	Neath Port Talbot	12	Denbighshire
6	Rhondda Cynon Taff	13	Flintshire
7	Merthyr Tydfil	14	Wrexham

Greater London key

1	City of London
2	City of Westminster
3	Camden
4	Islington
5	Haringey
6	Hackney
7	Waltham Forest
8	Tower Hamlets
9	Southwark
10	Lewisham
11	Lambeth
12	Wandsworth
13	Kensington & Chelsea
14	Hammersmith
15	Richmond upon Thames
16	Kingston upon Thames

■ capital city

Scale 1 : 4 500 000

0   50   100 km

This map includes the changes to the boundaries and names of counties and unitary authorities proposed for April 1998. The topographic and urban land use maps on pages 57-73 show those current in 1997.

Transverse Mercator Projection
© Oxford University Press

British Isles Physical

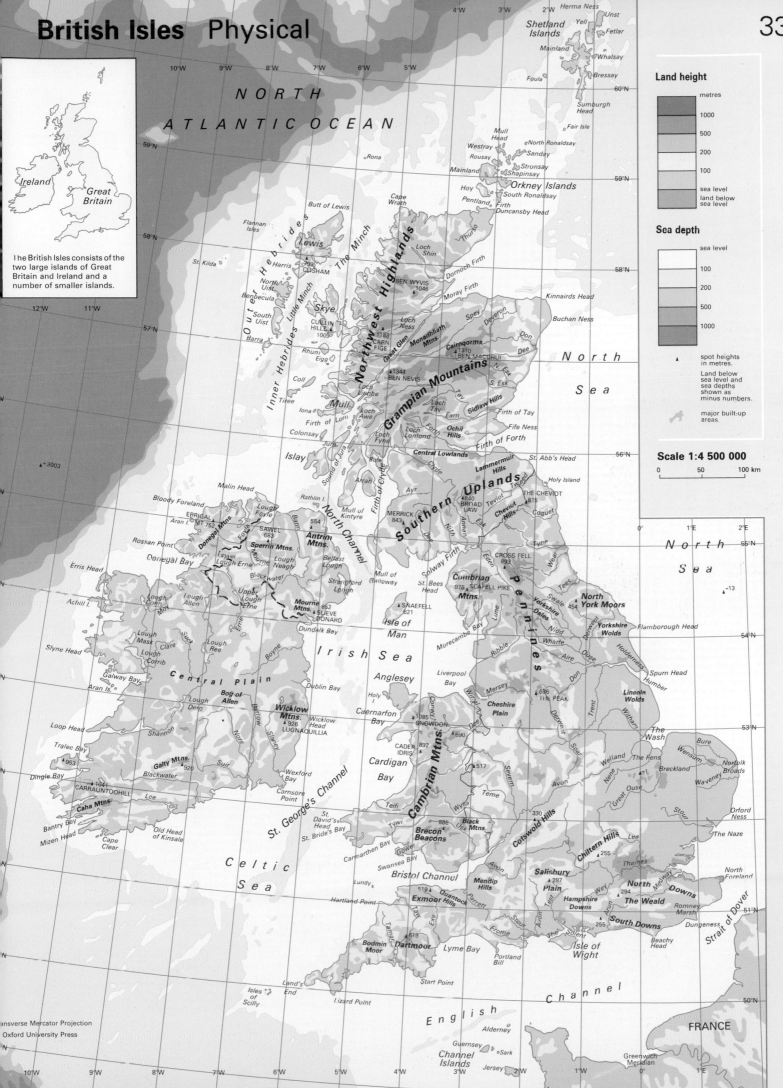

The British Isles consists of the two large islands of Great Britain and Ireland and a number of smaller islands.

Land height

metres
1000
500
200
100
sea level
land below sea level

Sea depth

sea level
100
200
500
1000

▲ spot heights in metres.

Land below sea level and sea depths shown as minus numbers.

major built-up areas.

Scale 1:4 500 000

0   50   100 km

Transverse Mercator Projection
Oxford University Press

Sedimentary	Periods	Eras	Approx. dates in millions of years before present
Alluvium	Pleistocene and Recent	Quaternary	
			2
Sands and clays	Pliocene, Oligocene and Eocene	Tertiary	
London Clay, Reading and Thanet Beds	Eocene		
			70
Chalk	Cretaceous		
Greensand and Gault Clay			
Weald Clays and Sandstones			
Purbeck and Portland Beds/ Kimmeridge and Oxford Clays	Jurassic	Mesozoic	
Oolitic Limestone			
Liassic and Rhaetic Beds			
Keuper Marl and Sandstone	Triassic		
Bunter Sandstone			
			220
Permian Marl	Permian		
Magnesian Limestone			
Coal Measures	Carboniferous	Upper Palaeozoic	
Millstone Grit and Culm Measures			
Carboniferous Limestone			
Old Red Sandstone	Devonian		
Slates and shales	Silurian	Lower Palaeozoic	
Slates and volcanic rocks	Ordovician		
Hard grits, shales and slates	Cambrian		
			600
Rough sandstones and volcanic rocks	Pre-Cambrian		

Metamorphic

Schist, gneiss, quartzite

Igneous

Extrusive rocks (volcanic)

Intrusive rocks

Major faults

Glacial deposits

Limit of the last (Devensian) glacia

Limit of maximum (Anglian) glaciatio

main areas of glacial deposition

unglaciated

Scale 1 : 14 000 000

Outer Hebrides
Skye
Mull
Arran
Moine Thrust
North-west Highlands
Great Glen Fault
Grampian Mountains
Highland Boundary Fault
Southern Uplands Fault
Southern Uplands
Cheviot Hills
Pennine Fault
Lake District
Craven Fault
Isle of Man
York Moors
Pennines
Anglesey
Lincoln Wolds
Cambrian Mtns.
Church Stretton Fault
Cotswolds
Chiltern Hills
North Downs
The Weald
South Downs
Exmoor
Dartmoor
maximum extent of glaciation

Donegal Mtns.
Antrim Mtns.
Mourne Mtns.
Connemara Mtns.
Slieve Bloom Mtns.
Wicklow Mtns.
Caha Mtns.

This map shows solid geology. Surface deposits of peat, gravels, clays and alluvium were added during late Pleistocene times and recently.

Scale 1:4 500 000

0   50   100 km

Transverse Mercator Projecti

© Oxford University Pre

...land
...eat

Lowland fen peat

Alluvial gley

Gley

Poorly drained soils

Upland peat and peat bog. Well-leached acid peat formed by high rainfall.

Lowland fen peat. Alkaline peat formed by water-logging in low areas.

Alluvial gleys. Gleying from low lying location such as flooding by sea or river.

Gleys. Gleying from underlying impermeable parent material, usually clay.

Well drained soils

Brown earths. Subsoil formed from weathering of parent material.

Argillic brown earths. Subsoil formed by the accumulation of clay leached from above.

Podzols. Subsoil has an accumulation of iron and/or aluminium.

Rendzinas and brown calcareous soils. Shallow and moderately deep soils over limestones and chalk.

major urban areas.

Brown earth

Argillic brown earth

Podzol

Rendzina

Scottish Highlands

Scottish Lowlands

Southern Uplands

Donegal Mtns.

Antrim Plateau

Mayo Mtns.

Mountains of Mourne

Lake District

The Pennines

Central Plain

Wicklow Mtns.

Welsh Uplands

Fenlands

East Anglia

Munster Mtns.

Lowlands

English Lowlands

London Basin

The Weald

Southwest Peninsula

Scale 1:4 500 000

0   50   100 km

Transverse Mercator Projection

© Oxford University Press

Actual surface temperature

°C
17
16
15
14
13
12
11
10
9
8
7
6
5
4
3
2
1
0
−1
−2

isotherms reduced to sea level

→ warm sea currents

→ cold sea currents

January

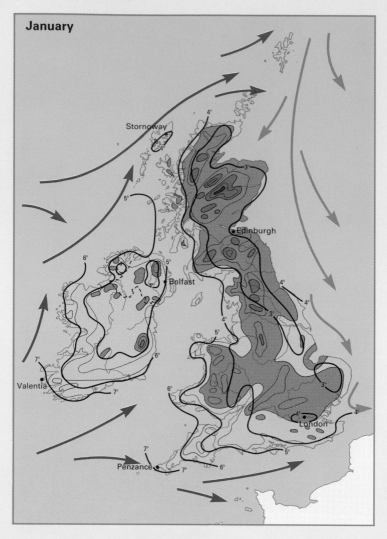

July

Scale 1 : 10 000 000

0   100   200 km

Transverse Mercator Projectie

© Oxford University Pre

Climate graphs for selected British Isles stations
(1951–80 averages)

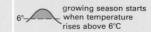

6°   growing season starts when temperature rises above 6°C

Stornoway

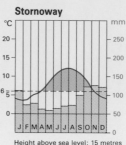

Height above sea level: 15 metres
Mean annual rainfall: 1096 mm
Mean January temperature: 4.0°C
Mean July temperature: 12.6°C

Edinburgh

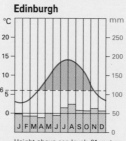

Height above sea level: 61 metres
Mean annual rainfall: 642 mm
Mean January temperature: 3.0°C
Mean July temperature: 14.3°C

Belfast

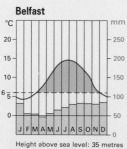

Height above sea level: 35 metres
Mean annual rainfall: 837 mm
Mean January temperature: 4.0°C
Mean July temperature: 14.6°C

London (Kew)

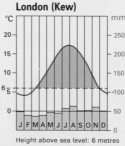

Height above sea level: 6 metres
Mean annual rainfall: 599 mm
Mean January temperature: 4.4°C
Mean July temperature: 17.4°C

Valentia

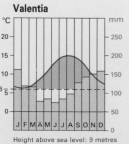

Height above sea level: 9 metres
Mean annual rainfall: 1400 mm
Mean January temperature: 6.6°C
Mean July temperature: 14.8°C

Penzance

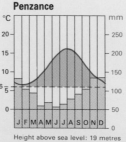

Height above sea level: 19 metres
Mean annual rainfall: 1131 mm
Mean January temperature: 6.9°C
Mean July temperature: 16.1°C

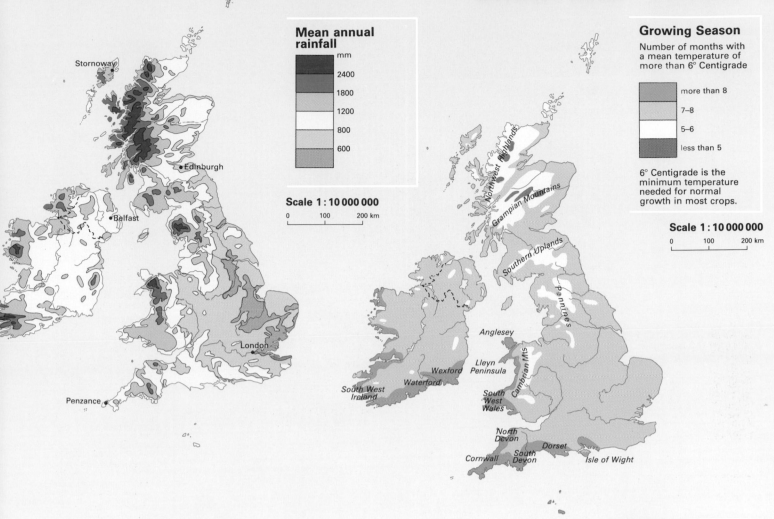

Mean annual rainfall

mm
2400
1800
1200
800
600

Scale 1 : 10 000 000

0   100   200 km

Stornoway
Edinburgh
Belfast
London
Penzance

Growing Season

Number of months with a mean temperature of more than 6° Centigrade

more than 8
7–8
5–6
less than 5

6° Centigrade is the minimum temperature needed for normal growth in most crops.

Scale 1 : 10 000 000

0   100   200 km

Northwest Highlands
Grampian Mountains
Southern Uplands
Pennines
Anglesey
Lleyn Peninsula
Cambrian Mts
Wexford
Waterford
South West Ireland
South West Wales
North Devon
South Devon
Cornwall
Dorset
Isle of Wight

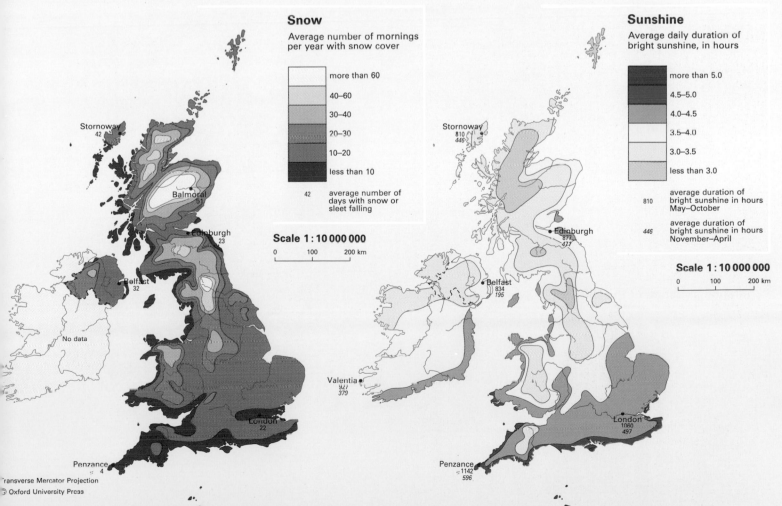

Snow

Average number of mornings per year with snow cover

more than 60
40–60
30–40
20–30
10–20
less than 10

42   average number of days with snow or sleet falling

Scale 1 : 10 000 000

0   100   200 km

Stornoway
42
Balmoral
51
Edinburgh
23
Belfast
32
London
22
No data
Penzance
4

Transverse Mercator Projection
© Oxford University Press

Sunshine

Average daily duration of bright sunshine, in hours

more than 5.0
4.5–5.0
4.0–4.5
3.5–4.0
3.0–3.5
less than 3.0

810   average duration of bright sunshine in hours May–October

446   average duration of bright sunshine in hours November–April

Scale 1 : 10 000 000

0   100   200 km

Stornoway
810
446
Edinburgh
877
471
Belfast
834
195
Valentia
927
379
London
1060
497
Penzance
1142
596

Population density, 1994

Persons per square kilometre

more than 1500
1000 - 1500
500 - 1000
250 - 500
100 - 250
50 - 100
10 - 50
0 - 10

Cities and towns

over 2 million
inhabitants

1 - 2 million
inhabitants

400 000 to 1 million
inhabitants

100 000 to 400 000
inhabitants

25 000 to 100 000
inhabitants

On this map the population of the Inner
London Boroughs is shown using one
symbol. The Outer London Boroughs
each have their own symbol.

- - - international
boundary

——— county
boundary, 1991

Scale 1 : 4 500 000

0   50   100 km

Population growth 1801-1991

Population in millions

British Isles

England & Wales

Irish Rep. & N. Ireland

Scotland

1801 '31 '61 '91 1921 '51 '81 '91

Note:
No census was taken in 1941.
Irish data available separately as Irish Republic or
Northern Ireland from 1931.

UK: birth and death rates per 1000 population, 1971-94

births

deaths

'71 '73 '75 '77 '79 '81 '83 '85 '87 '89 '91 '93

Total population, 1995

United Kingdom	58.61 million
Republic of Ireland	3.58 million
Isle of Man	0.07 million
Channel Islands	0.15 million

Population density, 1994

Average for the UK: 241 persons per km^2
Average for the Republic of Ireland:
51 persons per km^2

Population structure of the UK, 1995

Year
of birth

Age at
mid 1995

males   females

1905
1915
1925
1935
1945
1955
1965
1975
1985
1995

90
80
70
60
50
40
30
20
10
0

3   2   1   0   0   1   2   3
million people   million people

Transverse Mercator Projec

© Oxford University P

International migration, 1985-92

Thousands of people,
by origin or destination of migrants
for each Standard Statistical Region

- Old Commonwealth
- New Commonwealth and Pakistan
- EU
- USA and other

thousands of people

International in-migration

International out-migration

Scotland
Northern Ireland
North
Yorkshire & Humberside
North West
East Midlands
East Anglia
Wales
South East
South West
West Midlands

Northern Ireland
North
Wales
Yorkshire & Humberside
East Anglia
West Midlands
East Midlands
North West
Scotland
South West

Greater London
Rest of South East

Population change, 1981-91

Percentage gain, by county

- more than 20
- 10 - 15
- 5 - 10
- 1 - 5
- 0 - 1

Percentage loss, by county

- 0 - 1
- 1 - 5
- 5 - 12

Scale 1 : 10 000 000

0   100   200 km

Population of pensionable age

(women over 60, men over 65)
Percentage of total population, by district

- more than 25
- 20 - 25
- 18 - 20
- 16 - 18
- 14 - 16
- 12 - 14
- 10 - 12
- less than 10

- - - - - international boundary

——— boundary of Standard Statistical Region

Transverse Mercator Projection
© Oxford University Press

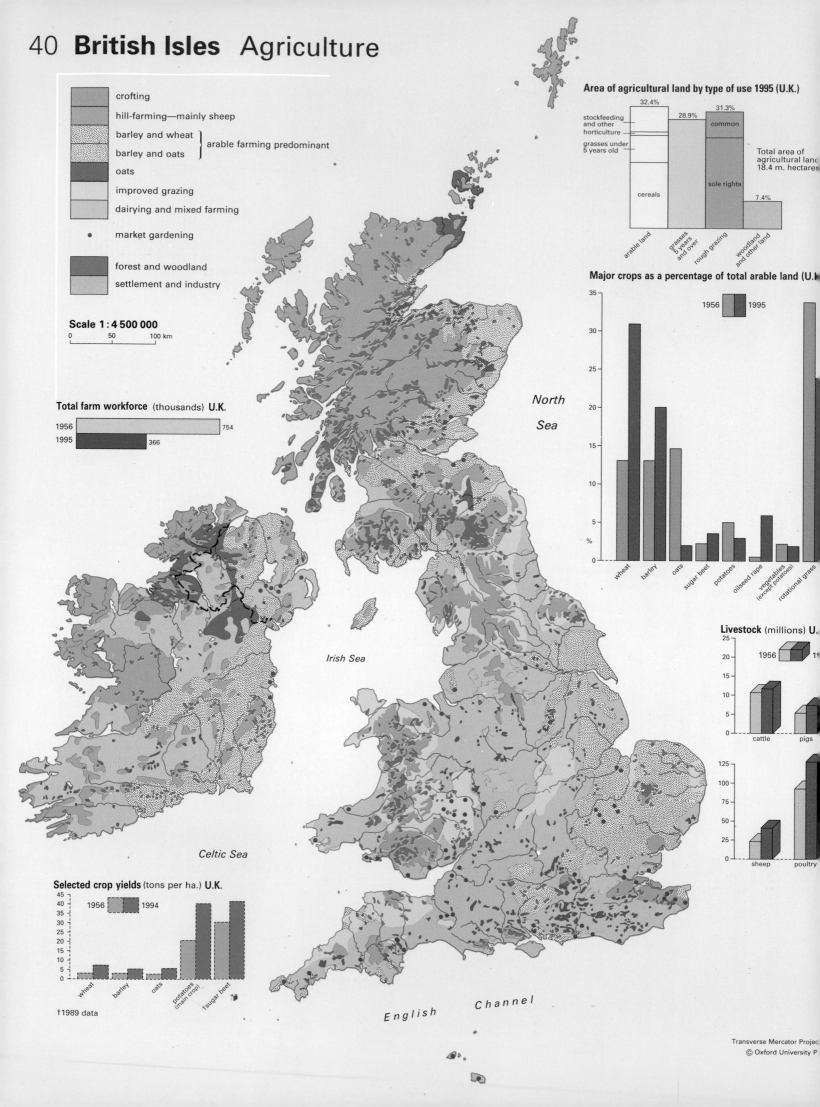

Legend
- crofting
- hill-farming—mainly sheep
- barley and wheat ⎤
- barley and oats ⎦ arable farming predominant
- oats
- improved grazing
- dairying and mixed farming
- • market gardening
- forest and woodland
- settlement and industry

Scale 1 : 4 500 000

0   50   100 km

Total farm workforce (thousands) U.K.

1956	754
1995	366

Area of agricultural land by type of use 1995 (U.K.)

32.4% — arable land
- stockfeeding and other horticulture
- grasses under 5 years old
- cereals

28.9% — grasses 5 years and over

31.3% — rough grazing
- common
- sole rights

7.4% — woodland and other land

Total area of agricultural land 18.4 m. hectares

Major crops as a percentage of total arable land (U.K.)

1956   1995

wheat, barley, oats, sugar beet, potatoes, oilseed rape, vegetables (except potatoes), rotational grass

Livestock (millions) U.K.

1956   1995

cattle, pigs, sheep, poultry

Selected crop yields (tons per ha.) U.K.

1956   1994

wheat, barley, oats, potatoes (main crop), †sugar beet

†1989 data

North Sea

Irish Sea

Celtic Sea

English Channel

Transverse Mercator Projection
© Oxford University Press

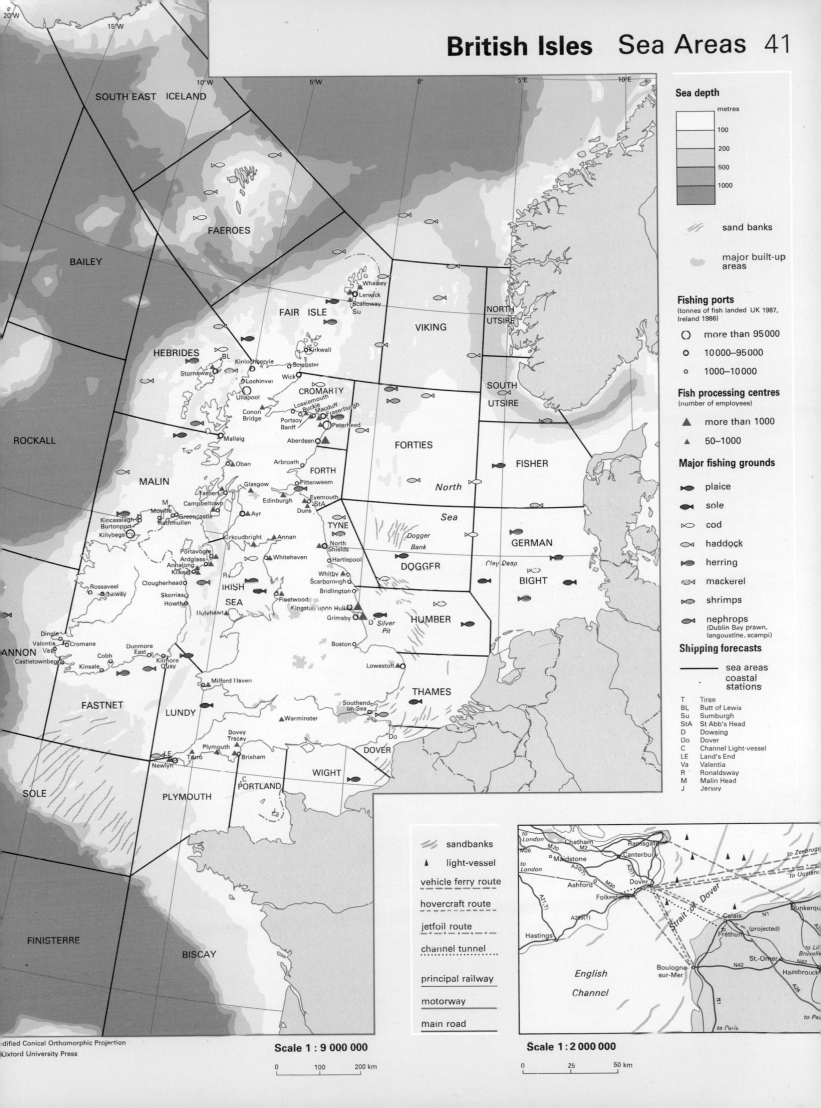

Sea depth

metres

| 100 |
| 200 |
| 500 |
| 1000 |

sand banks

major built-up areas

Fishing ports
(tonnes of fish landed UK 1987, Ireland 1986)

⊖ more than 95000

◦ 10000–95000

∘ 1000–10000

Fish processing centres
(number of employees)

▲ more than 1000

▴ 50–1000

Major fishing grounds

plaice

sole

cod

haddock

herring

mackerel

shrimps

nephrops
(Dublin Bay prawn, langoustine, scampi)

Shipping forecasts

— sea areas

• coastal stations

T	Tiree
BL	Butt of Lewis
Su	Sumburgh
StA	St Abb's Head
D	Dowsing
Do	Dover
C	Channel Light-vessel
LE	Land's End
Va	Valentia
R	Ronaldsway
M	Malin Head
J	Jersey

Sea areas on map: SOUTH EAST ICELAND, FAEROES, BAILEY, FAIR ISLE, HEBRIDES, CROMARTY, VIKING, NORTH UTSIRE, SOUTH UTSIRE, FORTIES, FISHER, ROCKALL, MALIN, FORTH, TYNE, DOGGER, GERMAN BIGHT, HUMBER, IRISH SEA, FASTNET, LUNDY, THAMES, DOVER, WIGHT, PORTLAND, PLYMOUTH, SOLE, FINISTERRE, BISCAY, SHANNON, North Sea, Dogger Bank, Silver Pit, Clay Deep

Places: Lerwick, Scalloway, Su, Whalsey, Kirkwall, Scrabster, Wick, Kinlochbervie, BL, Stornoway, Lochinver, Ullapool, Lossiemouth, Buckie, Macduff, Fraserburgh, Conon Bridge, Portsoy, Banff, Peterhead, Aberdeen, Mallaig, Oban, Arbroath, Pittenweem, Glasgow, Edinburgh, Eyemouth, StA, Duns, Tarbert, Campbeltown, M, Moville, Greencastle, Rathmullen, Kincasslagh, Burtonport, Killybegs, Ayr, Kirkcudbright, Annan, North Shields, Hartlepool, Portavogie, Ardglass, Anhalong, Kilkeel, Whitehaven, Clougherhead, Whitby, Scarborough, Bridlington, Rossaveel, Galway, Skerries, Howth, Fleetwood, Holyhead, Kingston upon Hull, Grimsby, Silver Pit, Boston, Dingle, Valentia, Va, Cromane, Cobh, Kinsale, Castletownbere, Dunmore East, Kilmore Quay, Lowestoft, Milford Haven, Southend-on-Sea, Warminster, Bovey Tracey, Plymouth, Truro, Brixham, Newlyn, LE, C

Scale 1 : 9 000 000

0   100   200 km

...dified Conical Orthomorphic Projection
Oxford University Press

Inset legend:

sandbanks

▲ light-vessel

vehicle ferry route

hovercraft route

jetfoil route

channel tunnel

principal railway

motorway

main road

Inset map places: to London, Chatham, Ramsgate, M26, M20, M2, Maidstone, Canterbury, to London, Ashford, A20(T), M20, Dover, to Zeebrug, to Oosten, Folkestone, A21(T), Strait of Dover, Hastings, A259(T), Calais, N1, Fréthun, Dunkerqu, St.-Omer, Boulogne-sur-Mer, N42, N42, Hazebrouck, English Channel, to Lil, Bruxelles, to Pa, N1, (projected), A26, to Paris

Scale 1 : 2 000 000

0   25   50 km

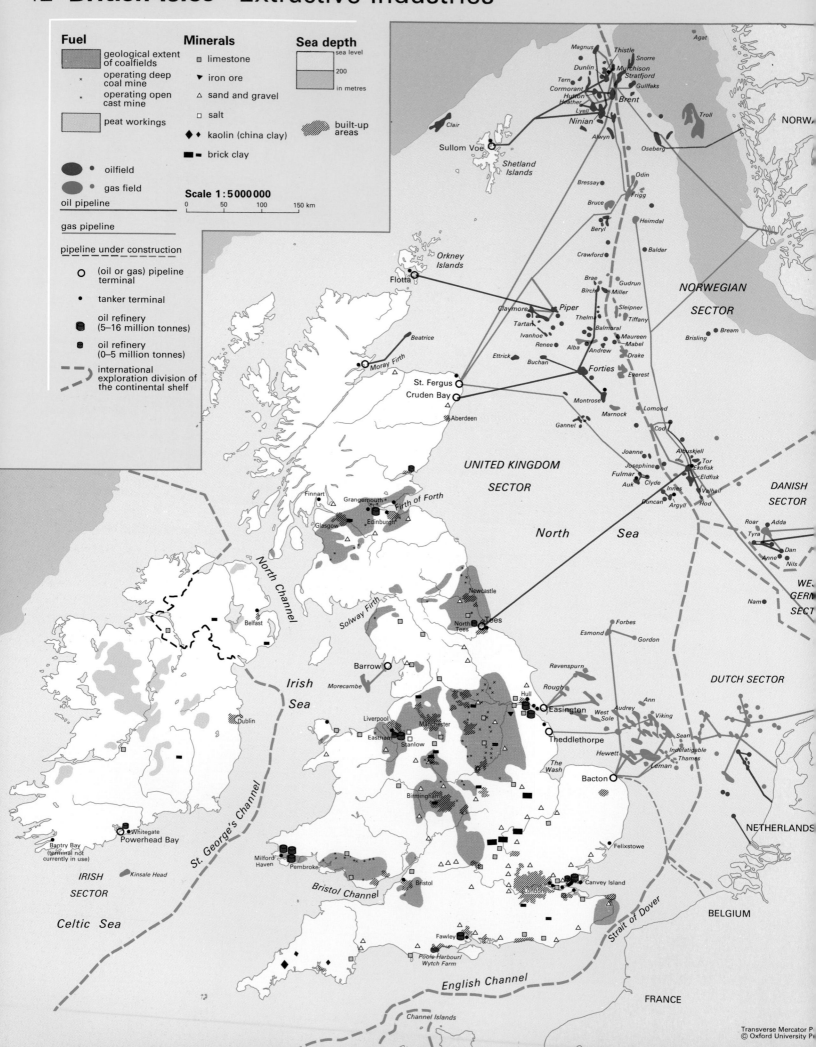

Fuel
- geological extent of coalfields
- × operating deep coal mine
- • operating open cast mine
- peat workings
- ⬤ • oilfield
- ⬤ • gas field
- oil pipeline
- gas pipeline
- pipeline under construction
- ○ (oil or gas) pipeline terminal
- • tanker terminal
- oil refinery (5–16 million tonnes)
- oil refinery (0–5 million tonnes)
- international exploration division of the continental shelf

Minerals
- ▫ limestone
- ▾ iron ore
- △ sand and gravel
- ▫ salt
- ◆ ◆ kaolin (china clay)
- ▬ ▬ brick clay
- built-up areas

Sea depth
- sea level
- 200
- in metres

Scale 1:5 000 000

0   50   100   150 km

NORWAY

Magnus Thistle Snorre Agat
Dunlin Murchison Stratfjord
Tern Cormorant Gullfaks Troll
Hutton Heather Brent
Clair Lyell Ninian
Alwyn Oseberg
Sullom Voe
Shetland Islands

Bressay Odin
Frigg
Bruce Heimdal
Beryl Balder
Crawford

Orkney Islands
Flotta

Brae Gudrun
Birch Miller
Claymore Piper Sleipner
Tartan Thelma Tiffany
Ivanhoe Balmoral
Renee Maureen Bream
Beatrice Alba Mabel Brisling
Moray Firth Andrew Drake
Ettrick Buchan
St. Fergus Forties Everest
Cruden Bay Montrose
Aberdeen Marnock Lomond
Gannet Cod
Albuskjell
Josephine Tor Ekofisk
Fulmar Eldfisk
Auk Clyde Innes Valhall
Duncan Argyll Hod

NORWEGIAN SECTOR

DANISH SECTOR
Roar Adda
Tyra Dan
Anne Nils
Nam

WEST GERMAN SECTOR

UNITED KINGDOM SECTOR

North Sea

Finnart
Grangemouth
Glasgow Firth of Forth
Edinburgh

North Channel

Solway Firth
Newcastle
North Tees Tees

Barrow
Morecambe

Irish Sea

Dublin

Belfast

IRISH SECTOR

Bantry Bay (terminal not currently in use)
Whitegate
Powerhead Bay
Kinsale Head

Celtic Sea

St. George's Channel

Ravenspurn
Rough
Hull
Liverpool Easington
Manchester
Eastham West Sole
Stanlow Theddlethorpe
The Wash
Birmingham Bacton

Forbes
Esmond Gordon

Ann
Audrey Viking
Sean
Indefatigable
Hewett Thames
Leman

DUTCH SECTOR

NETHERLANDS

Felixstowe

London Canvey Island

Bristol

Bristol Channel

Milford Haven
Pembroke

Fawley

Poole Harbour/
Wytch Farm

Strait of Dover

BELGIUM

English Channel

FRANCE

Channel Islands

Transverse Mercator Projection
© Oxford University Press

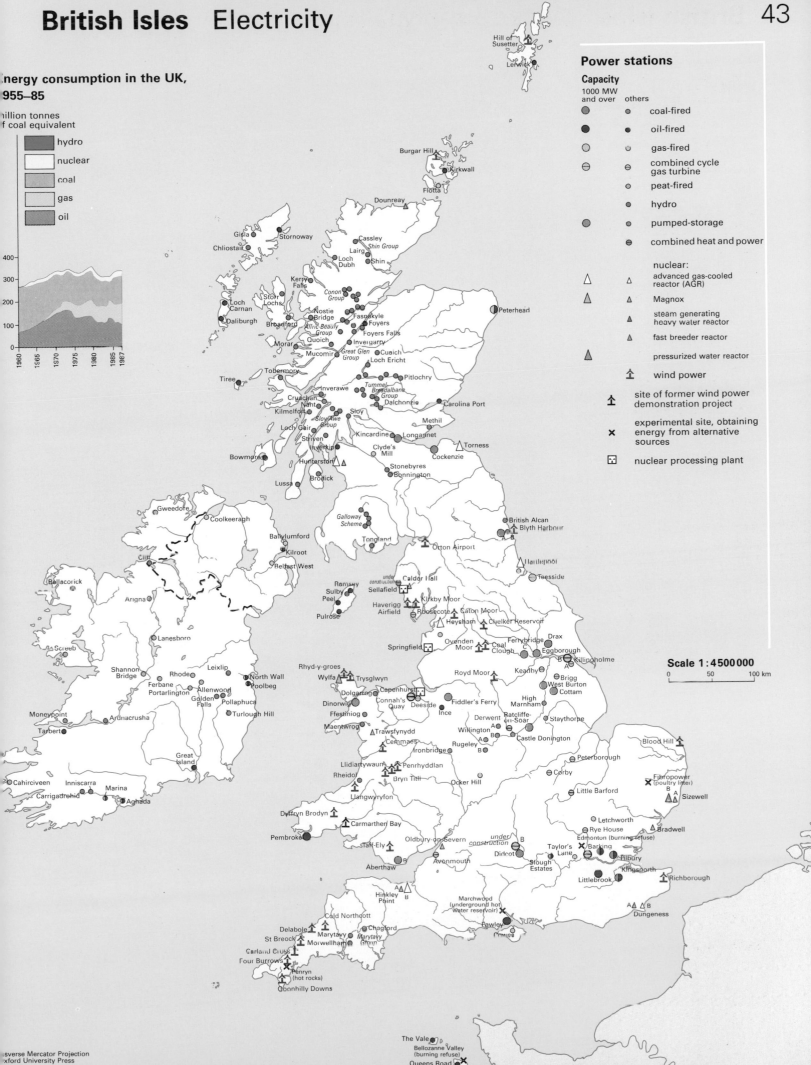

British Isles   Electricity

Legend

major built-up areas

Water

Water Authority boundary (England and Wales)

Water Authority boundary (Scotland)

Water Service Divisions (Northern Ireland)

Surface water

rivers

21 ● major reservoirs (with capacity in millions of cubic metres of water)

Groundwater

highly productive aquifers (porous rock)

highly productive aquifers (jointed rock)

NB Although chalk is slightly porous, the main groundwater flow is through fissures

▾ major public supply groundwater pumping station (more than 20000 cubic metres/day)

Scale 1 : 4 500 000

0   50   100 km

Domestic water use in England and Wales

average litres per person per day

130 ─
100 ─   flushing WC
75 ─
           baths and showers
50 ─   washing machines
25 ─
           hand washing, drinking, cooking, cleaning, outside use, etc.
0 ─

Map labels

12 Loch Calder

Loch Glass 20

26 Loch Ness

NORTH OF SCOTLAND

25 Blackwater Res.
100 Loch of Lintrathen
18
19 Loch Turret
64 Glen Finglas Res.
Loch Arklet 12
Loch Katrine
Loch Lomond 78
21
14 Carron Valley Res.
Loch Thom

EAST OF SCOTLAND

11 Portmore Loch

WEST OF SCOTLAND

12 Talla Res.
Fruid Res. 14   64 Megget Res.
23 Daer Res.

19 Loch Braden

200 Kielder Res.
NORTHUMBRIAN

22 Derwent Res.
41 Cow Green Res.
Thirlmere 15 Selset Res.
85 Haweswater   20 Balderhead Res.

NORTHERN IRELAND

Ballyshannon Res. 170

13 Silent Valley Res.

ISLE OF MAN

NORTH WEST

22 Grimwith Res.
12   YORKSHIRE
Stocks Res.

11 Covenham Res.

Rivington linked reservoirs 17
Longdendale linked reservoirs 19
28 Ladybower Res.

11 Alwen Res.   60 Llyn Brenig
Llyn Celyn 74
Lake Vyrnwy 59
WELSH
50 Llyn Clywedog
Claerwen Res. 35
48 Caban Coch Res.
Llyn Brianne Res. 61

Usk Res. 12   Talybont Res.
12
15 Taf Fechan
22 Llandegfedd Res.

Blithfield Res.
13 Foremark Res.
18
SEVERN-TRENT

Rutland Water 124

23 Pitsford Res.
18
Draycote Water   59 Grautham Water

ANGLIAN

25 Abberton Res.
27 Hanningfield Res.

THAMES

Chew Valley Lake 20
Wimbleball Lake 21
WESSEX

SOUTHERN

31 Bewl Water

SOUTH WEST
34 Roadford Res.
28 Collyford Lake Res.

Parteen Weir Res. 465

168 Pollaphuca Res.

Carrigadrohid Res. 33   57 Inishcarra Res.

Water use in England and Wales

thousand megalitres per day

40 ─
30 ─   water supply
20 ─
           Central Electricity Generating Board
10 ─
           industry   agriculture
0 ─
1976   1980   1986

Transverse Mercator Projection

© Oxford University Press

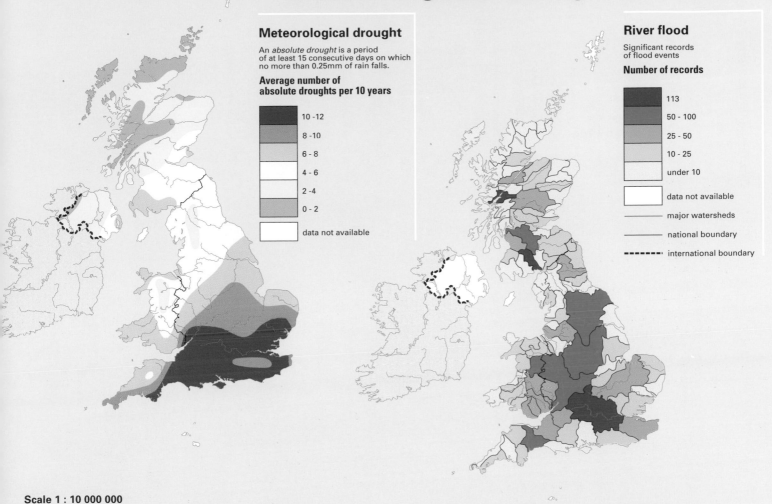

Meteorological drought

An *absolute drought* is a period of at least 15 consecutive days on which no more than 0.25mm of rain falls.

Average number of absolute droughts per 10 years

- 10 - 12
- 8 - 10
- 6 - 8
- 4 - 6
- 2 - 4
- 0 - 2
- data not available

River flood

Significant records of flood events

Number of records

- 113
- 50 - 100
- 25 - 50
- 10 - 25
- under 10
- data not available
- major watersheds
- national boundary
- international boundary

Scale 1 : 10 000 000

0   100   200km

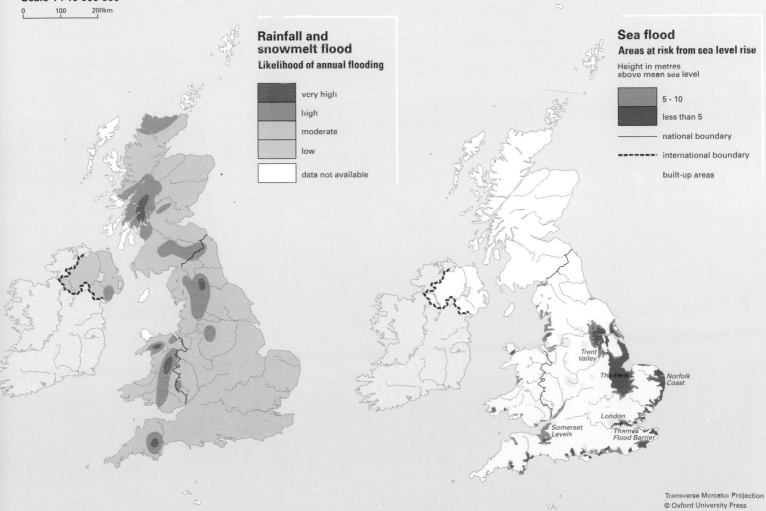

Rainfall and snowmelt flood

Likelihood of annual flooding

- very high
- high
- moderate
- low
- data not available

Sea flood

Areas at risk from sea level rise

Height in metres above mean sea level

- 5 - 10
- less than 5
- national boundary
- international boundary
- built-up areas

Trent Valley

The Fens

Norfolk Coast

London

Somerset Levels

Thames Flood Barrier

Transverse Mercator Projection

© Oxford University Press

Manufacturing industry

The map shows only the
main centres of manufacturing
for each industry.

chemicals
oil refining
nuclear fuel processing
steel
non-ferrous metal
smelting
metal working
motor vehicles
railway vehicles
aircraft and aerospace
shipbuilding and repair
mechanical engineering
electrical engineering
electronics and computers
jewellery
clothing and footwear
leather
rubber
textiles and carpets
glass
ceramics
bricks
cement
furniture
pulp, paper, and board
printing and publishing
sugar refining
brewing and distilling

Regional aid to industry, 1996

Great
Britain

Development areas
Intermediate areas
previously assisted areas
newly assisted areas
Industrial Development Board
of Northern Ireland
Isle of Man Industrial
Development Assistance
Development Board for
Rural Wales

boundary of Economic Region / Standard
Statistical Region (UK),
Planning Region (Republic of Ireland)
county, unitary authority, or district boundary
international boundary

Scale 1 : 3 000 000

0   50   100 km

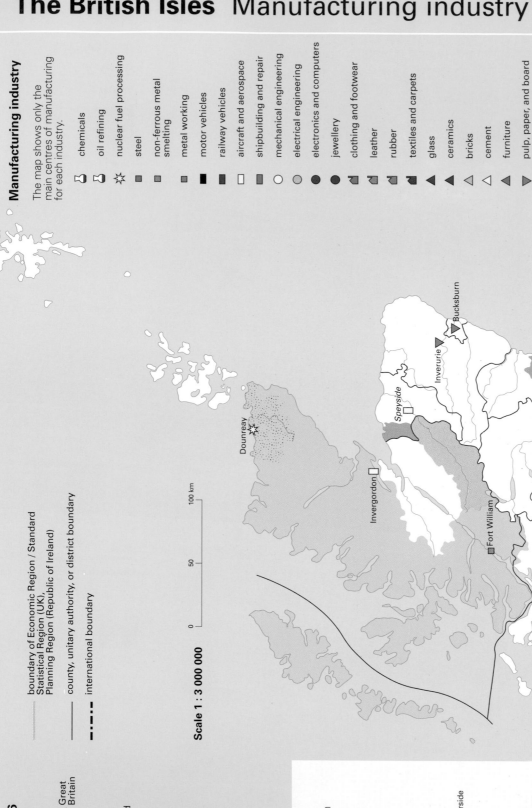

Dounreay
Invergordon
Inverurie
Bucksburn
Speyside
Markinch
Kirkcaldy
Dunbar
Leith
Edinburgh
Dundee
Kinross
Galashiels
Grangemouth
Currie
Hawick
Coatbridge
Motherwell
Selkirk
Dumbarton
Glasgow
Kilmarnock
Mauchline
Cumnock
Dumfries
Greenock
Paisley
Irvine
Prestwick
Newcastle upon Tyne/
Gateshead
Lynemouth
Girvan
Islay
Fort William
Ballymena
Larne

Job gains in the UK, 1986-96

by Economic Region/Standard Statistical Region

one small square represents 1500 jobs

Scotland
215,149

Northern Ireland
80,022

North
89,294

North West
222,759

Yorkshire & Humberside
243,292

West Midlands
242,022

East Midlands
221,702

Wales
119,988

East Anglia
115,212

South West
272,337

South East
650,174

Job losses in the UK, 1986–96

by Economic Region/Standard Statistical Region

one small square
represents 1500 jobs

Scotland
105,848

North
75,545

Yorkshire & Humberside
110,568

East Midlands
153,864

East Anglia
35,067

South East
691,633

Northern Ireland
7,565

North West
184,540

West Midlands
137,507

Wales
40,515

South West
72,336

Structure of changes in employment

primary activity and utilities agriculture, fishing, forestry; mining, and quarrying; electricity, gas, and water services

manufacturing industry manufacturing; construction

service industries wholesale and retail trade; repairs; hotels, restaurants; transport, storage; finance, property

community services public administration; education, health, and social services

Transverse Mercator Projection
© Oxford University Press

Employment in primary activity and utilities

Percentage of the workforce employed in agriculture, fishing, forestry, mining and quarrying: electricity, gas, and water services, in 1995
by Standard Statistical Region

- 0.5 - 1
- 0.3 - 0.5
- 0.2 - 0.3
- 0.1 - 0.2
- boundary of Standard Statistical Region

Employment in manufacturing industry

Percentage of the workforce employed in manufacturing industry, and construction, in 1995
by Standard Statistical Region

- 4 - 5
- 2.5 - 3
- 2 - 2.5
- 1.5 - 2
- 1 - 1.5
- 0.5 - 1

Workforce structure, UK 1995

percentage of the total workforce

2.8	females aged 60 and over; males aged 65 and over
30.7	females aged 45 - 59; males aged 45 - 64
50.5	aged 25 - 44
15.9	aged 16 - 24

Total workforce   28 520 000

Employment structure analysis, 1967-1995
by Standard Statistical Region

- primary activity and utilities
- service industries
- manufacturing industry
- community services

1995

United Kingdom

North
Yorkshire & Humberside
East Midlands
East Anglia
South East
South West
West Midlands
North West
Wales
Scotland
Northern Ireland

1981

United Kingdom

North
Yorkshire & Humberside
East Midlands
East Anglia
South East
South West
West Midlands
North West
Wales
Scotland
Northern Ireland

1967

United Kingdom

North
Yorkshire & Humberside
East Midlands
East Anglia
South East
South West
West Midlands
North West
Wales
Scotland
Northern Ireland

0   20   40   60   80   100
Percent of total workforce

Employment in service industries

Percentage of the workforce employed in wholesale and retail trade; repairs; hotels, restaurants; transport, storage; finance, and property, in 1995
by Standard Statistical Region

- 17
- 4 - 5
- 3 - 4
- 2.5 - 3
- 1.5 - 2
- 0.5 - 1

Employment in community services

Percentage of the workforce employed in public administration; education, health, and social services, in 1995
by Standard Statistical Region

- 9.85
- 3 - 4
- 2.5 - 3
- 2 - 2.5
- 1.5 - 2
- 1 - 1.5

Unemployment

Percentage of the workforce unemployed, in 1995
by Standard Statistical Region

- 15.7
- 12 - 14
- 10 - 12
- 8 - 10
- 6 - 8

Scale 1 : 14 000 000

0   100   200km

Transverse Mercator Projection
© Oxford University Press

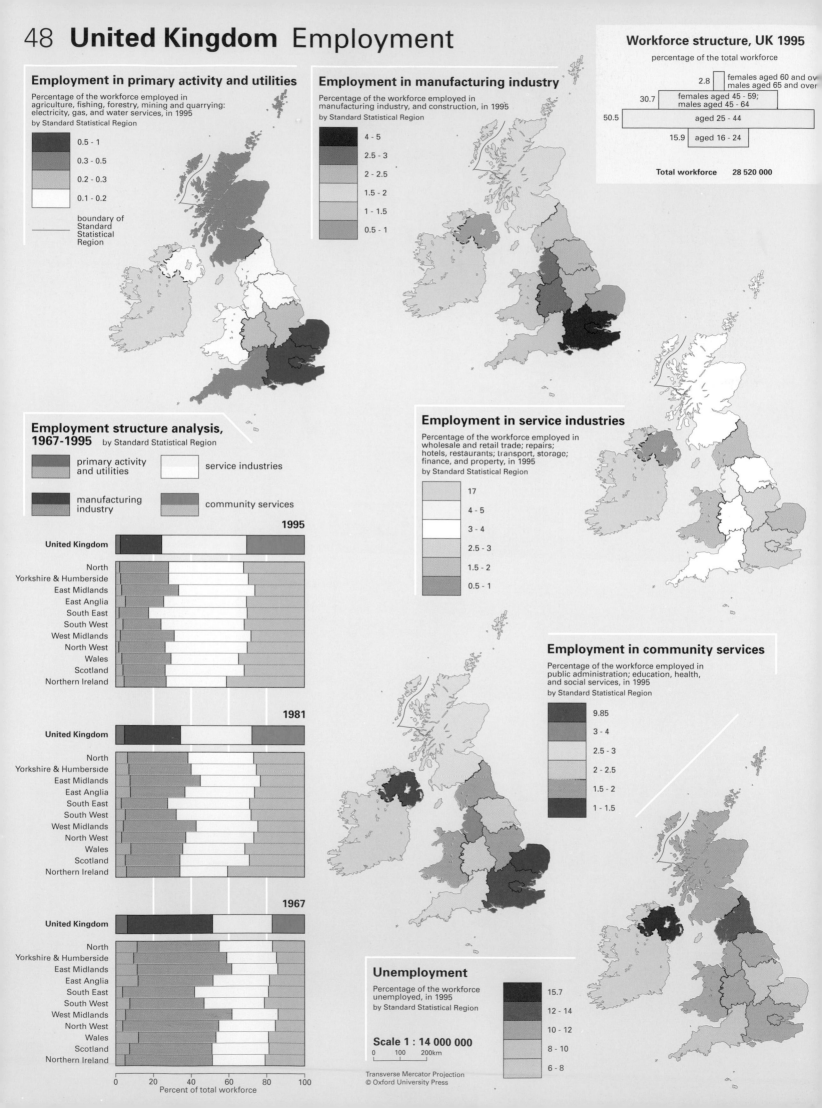

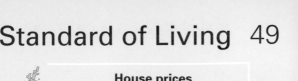

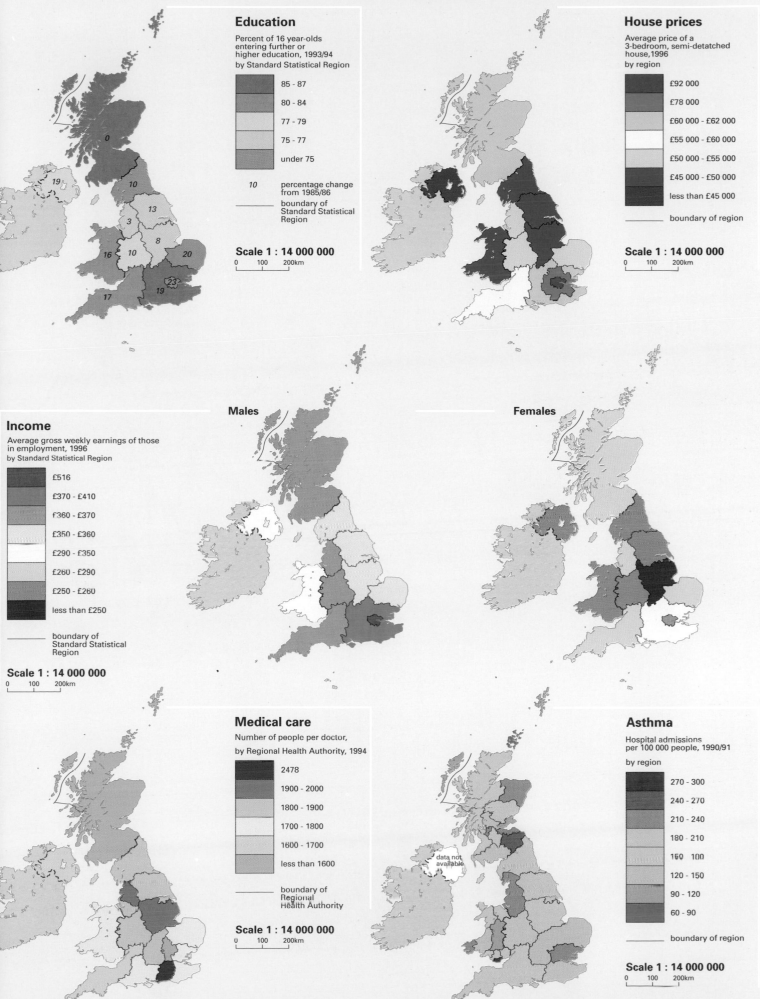

Education

Percent of 16 year-olds entering further or higher education, 1993/94 by Standard Statistical Region

- 85 - 87
- 80 - 84
- 77 - 79
- 75 - 77
- under 75

10 percentage change from 1985/86

— boundary of Standard Statistical Region

Scale 1 : 14 000 000

0   100   200km

House prices

Average price of a 3-bedroom, semi-detatched house, 1996 by region

- £92 000
- £78 000
- £60 000 - £62 000
- £55 000 - £60 000
- £50 000 - £55 000
- £45 000 - £50 000
- less than £45 000

— boundary of region

Scale 1 : 14 000 000

0   100   200km

Income

Average gross weekly earnings of those in employment, 1996 by Standard Statistical Region

- £516
- £370 - £410
- £360 - £370
- £350 - £360
- £290 - £350
- £260 - £290
- £250 - £260
- less than £250

— boundary of Standard Statistical Region

Scale 1 : 14 000 000

0   100   200km

Males

Females

Medical care

Number of people per doctor, by Regional Health Authority, 1994

- 2478
- 1900 - 2000
- 1800 - 1900
- 1700 - 1800
- 1600 - 1700
- less than 1600

— boundary of Regional Health Authority

Scale 1 : 14 000 000

0   100   200km

Asthma

Hospital admissions per 100 000 people, 1990/91 by region

- 270 - 300
- 240 - 270
- 210 - 240
- 180 - 210
- 150 - 180
- 120 - 150
- 90 - 120
- 60 - 90

— boundary of region

Scale 1 : 14 000 000

0   100   200km

data not available

Transverse Mercator Projection

© Oxford University Press

Roads, railways, waterways

motorway
main road
principal railway
Channel tunnel
vehicle ferry route
navigable rivers
canals
major freight waterways
built-up areas

Ports
Cargo handled in 1995 (tonnes)

more than 20 million
5 - 15 million
100 000 - 5 million
major container terminal

Airports
Passengers in 1995

54 million
14 - 23 million
1 - 14 million
less than 1 million

international boundary
national boundary

Scale 1 : 3 000 000

0   50   100 km

to Göteborg
to Esbjerg

to Bergen, Stavanger,
and Haugesund

Mobile phone reception

good reception offered by
at least 3 systems for
hand portable telephones, 1995

major built-up areas

Scale 1 : 10 000 000

0   50   100 km

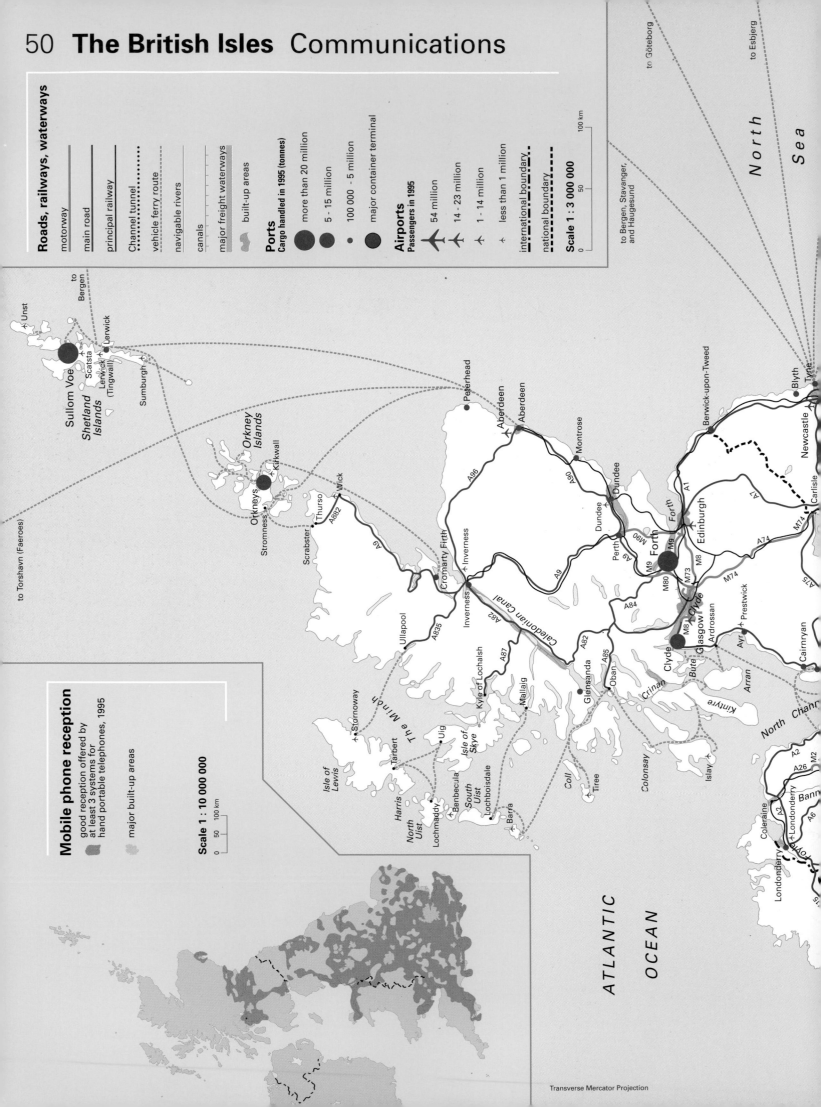

North Sea

ATLANTIC OCEAN

to Torshavn (Faeroes)

Unst
to Bergen
Sullom Voe
Shetland Islands
Scatsta
Lerwick
Lerwick (Tingwall)
Sumburgh

Orkney Islands
Kirkwall
Orkneys
Stromness
Scrabster
Thurso
Wick
A882
A9

Peterhead
Aberdeen
Aberdeen
A96
A90
Montrose
Dundee
Dundee
Cromarty Firth
Inverness
Inverness
Caledonian Canal
A84
A82
Perth
A9
Forth
M90
M9
Forth
Edinburgh
M8
Berwick-upon-Tweed
A1
A1
M74
A74
Carlisle
A7
Newcastle
Blyth
Tyne

Ullapool
A835
A82
A85
M80
M73
M74
Glensanda
Oban
M8
Clyde
Glasgow
Clyde
Bute
Arran
Kintyre
Crinan
Ardrossan
Ayr
Prestwick
Cairnryan
North Channel
Colonsay
Coll
Tiree
Islay

Stornoway
The Minch
Isle of Lewis
Harris
Tarbert
Uig
Isle of Skye
Kyle of Lochalsh
A87
Mallaig
North Uist
Benbecula
South Uist
Lochmaddy
Lochboisdale
Barra

Coleraine
Londonderry
Londonderry
A2
A6
A26
A2
Bann

Transverse Mercator Projection

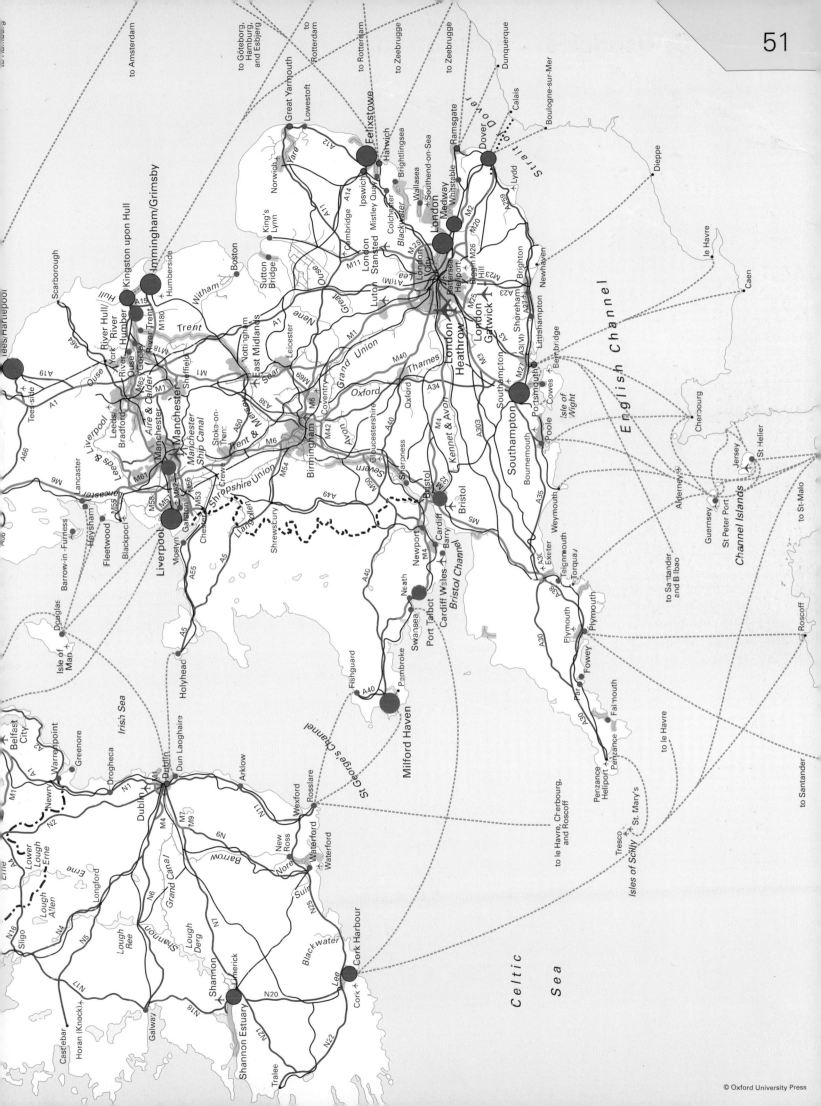

Air pollution

Ozone

Average concentrations,
April to September 1987–90,
in parts per billion

- above 32
- 28–32
- below 28

• monitoring sites
where EU guidelines
were exceeded, 1994.

• monitoring site
for both ozone and
nitrogen dioxide

Nitrogen dioxide

Average concentrations,
July to December 1993,
in parts per billion

- above 20
- 12–20
- below 12

• monitoring sites
where EU
guidelines
were exceeded
in 1993.

• monitoring site
for both ozone and
nitrogen dioxide

—— national
boundary

---- international
boundary

Acid rain

Average concentrations
of hydrogen ions, 1993.

- above 50
- 40–50
- 30–40
- 20–30
- below 20

areas most susceptible
to acid rain because
of their soils and
geological structure

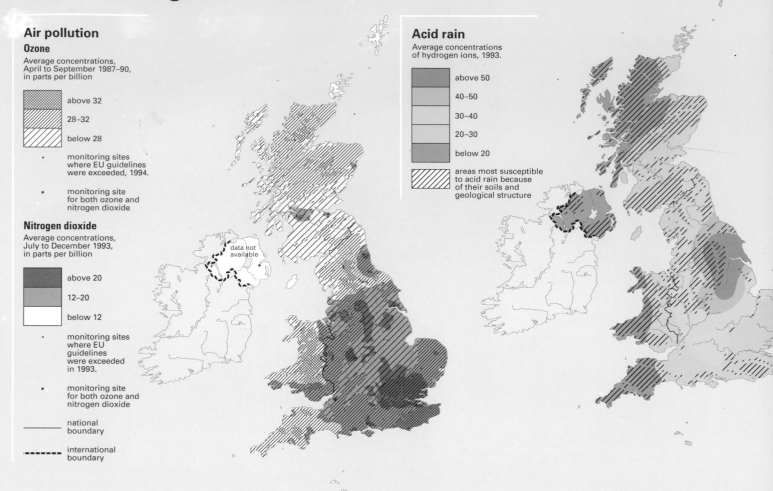

data not
available

River pollution

Rivers, lakes, and estuaries

—— heavily polluted

—— polluted

—— unpolluted

built-up areas

—— boundary of water
quality control
authorities

—— national
boundary

---- international
boundary

Coastal pollution

Bathing Beaches, 1900

· severely polluted
by sewage

· polluted by sewage

Licensed sea dumping sites

▾ sewage sludge

▾ industrial waste

□ colliery waste

◆ dredge spoil

Oil spills

✳✳ accidental oil spills, 1995

✺ specific oil tanker accidents,
which although individually
are very large, form only
a very small proportion
of the total oil spillage
in the area.

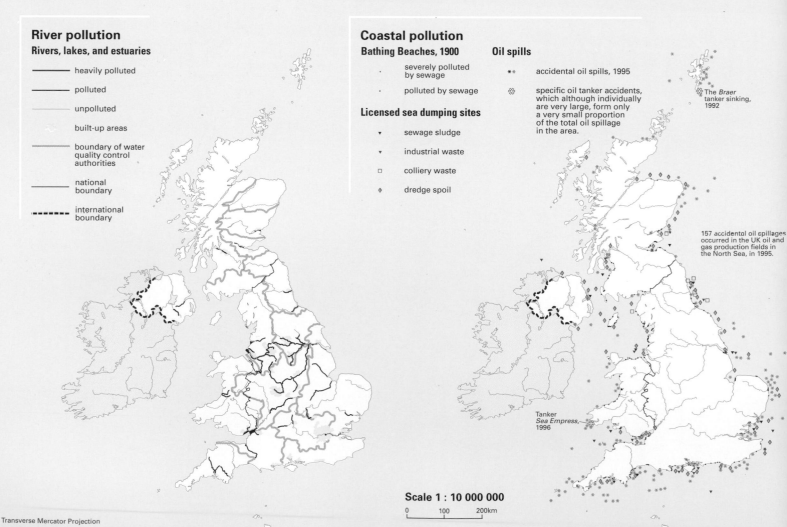

The *Braer*
tanker sinking,
1992

157 accidental oil spillages
occurred in the UK oil and
gas production fields in
the North Sea, in 1995.

Tanker
Sea Empress,
1996

Scale 1 : 10 000 000

0   100   200km

British Isles Conservation

National Parks
Areas of Outstanding Natural Beauty (England, Wales and Northern Ireland); National Scenic Areas (Scotland)
Green Belt and proposed Green Belt (United Kingdom)
Heritage Coast (defined and proposed in England and Wales); Coastal Conservation Zones (Scotland)
major reserves
internationally recognized sites (including Special Protection Areas, 'Ramsar' Sites and Biosphere Reserves)
World Heritage Sites (natural and cultural)
major built-up areas
Scale 1 : 4 500 000
0
50
100 km
The term Green Belt is now being adopted in new development plans in Northern Ireland. It is gradually replacing the Areas of Special Control, drawn around the towns and larger villages to control urban sprawl.
The National Parks were joined in 1988 by the similarly constituted Broads Authority.
Shetland
Hoy and West Mainland
Kyle of Tongue
North-west Sutherland
Assynt -Coigach
South Lewis, Harris and North Uist
St. Kilda
St Kilda
Priest Island
Dornoch Firth
Loch Eye
Trotternish
Wester Ross
Beinn Eighe
Loch Druidibeg
Loch a'Machair
Loch Stilligarry
South Uist Machair
The Cuillin Hills
Kintail
Glen Strathfarrar
Glen Affric
Rhum
The Small Isles
Knoydart
Cairngorm Mountains
Cairngorm Lochs
Loch of Skene
Aberdeen
L. Shiel
Morar, Moidart and Ardnamurchan
Claish Moss
Ben Nevis and Glen Coe
L. Tummel
Loch Lintrathen
Loch na Keal, Isle of Mull
Rannoch Moor
L. Rannoch and Glen Lyon
River Tay
Lynn of Lorn
River Earn
Scarba, Lunga and the Garvellachs
Loch Lomond
Knapdale
The Trossachs
Loch Leven
Jura
Taynish
Loch Lomond
Kyles of Bute
Glasgow
Edinburgh
North Arran
Eildon and Leaderfoot
Lindisfarne
Farne Islands
Ayr
Upper Tweeddale
Holburn Moss
Northumberland Coast
Coquet Island
Silver Flowe/ Merrick Kells
Cairnsmore of Fleet
Nith Estuary
Irthinghood Mires
Northumberland
Caerlaverock
Hadrian's Wall
Newcastle upon Tyne
Fleet Valley
East Stewartry Coast
Rockcliffe Marshes
North Pennines
Durham Cathedral/Castle
Solway Coast
Moor House/ Upper Teesdale
Lake District
North York Moors
Arnside and Silverdale
Yorkshire Dales
Fountain's Abbey/ Studley Royal Park
Leighton Moss
Nidderdale
Howardian Hills
Forest of Bowland
Leeds
York
Derwent Ings
Ribble Estuary
Martin Mere
Alt Estuary
Liverpool
Manchester
Dee Estuary
Sheffield
Lincolnshire Wolds
Rostherne Mere
Anglesey
Clwydian Range
Peak District
Castles/Town Walls of King Edward
Lleyn
Snowdonia
Stoke-on-Trent
Nottingham
North Norfolk Coast
Norfolk Coast
The Broads
Ironbridge Gorge
Cannock Chase
Cors Fochno/Dyfi
Shropshire Hills
Birmingham
Coventry
Ouse Washes
Minsmere-Walberswick
Suffolk Coast and Heaths
Cambridge
Malvern Hills
Dedham Vale
Orfordness-Havergate
Pembrokeshire Coast
Wye Valley
Blenheim Palace
Grassholm
Brecon Beacons
Cotswolds
Oxford
Abberton Reservoir
Skomer I.
Gower
Chilterns
Cardiff
London
Mendip Hills
Bristol
Bath
North Wessex Downs
The Swale
Westminster Palace/Abbey
Lundy (Marine Nature Reserve)
Bridgwater Bay
Chew Valley Lake
Surrey Hills
Kent Downs
Braunton Burrows
Exmoor
Quantock Hills
Stonehenge/Avebury
North Devon
Blackdown Hills
Cranborne Chase and West Wiltshire Downs
East Hampshire
High Weald
East Devon
Dorset
Bournemouth
Dartmoor
Chesil Beach/ Fleet
Sussex Downs
Cornwall
South Hampshire Coast
Isle of Wight
Chichester Harbour
South Devon
Isles of Scilly
Giant's Causeway
Glenveagh
Lough Barra Bog
North Derry
Antrim Coast and Glens
Sperrin
Pettigo Plateau
Lough Neagh/ Lough Beg
Belfast
Knockmoyle Sheskin
Owenboy
Owenduff Catchment
Lagan Valley
Strangford Lough
South Armagh
Lecale Coast
Mourne
Connemara
Rogerstown Estuary
Baldoyle Estuary
Mongan Bog
Dublin
North Bull Island
Keelhills, Slieve Carron
Coole Garryland
Slieve Bloom Mts.
Pollardstown Fen
Wexford Wildfowl Reserve
The Raven
Killarney
The Gearagh
Uragh Wood
Lough Hyne
Transverse Mercator Projection
© Oxford University Press

Overseas visitors to the UK
Origins, 1994 (thousands)

North America 3550
Canada 571
USA 2979
Portugal 142
Latin America 216

European Union 11 361
Republic of Ireland 1677
Netherlands 1204
France 2779
Belgium/Luxembourg 1035
Spain 681
Italy 826
Greece 166
Germany 2517
Switzerland 474
Austria 242
Denmark 333
Sweden 517
Norway 336
Finland 103

other Western Europe 1955
Finland 103
others
Gibraltar/Malta/Cyprus 159
former Yugoslavia 35
North Africa 73
South Africa 261
Africa 601

Eastern Europe 543
Middle East 602

Japan 588
Far East 1399
Australia 562
New Zealand 108
Oceania 670

Visits abroad by UK residents
Destinations, 1994 (thousands)

North America 2970
Canada 461
USA 2509
Portugal 1188
Latin America 156

European Union 28 661
Republic of Ireland 2491
Netherlands 1414
France 9009
Belgium/Luxembourg 1008
Italy 1540
Greece 2178
Spain 7705
Denmark 229
Germany 1898
Switzerland 575
Austria 590
Sweden 192
Norway 183
Finland 77

other Western Europe 3875
Gibraltar/Malta/Cyprus 1473
North Africa 511
former Yugoslavia 40
South Africa 134
Africa 1026

Eastern Europe 726
Middle East 356

Japan 80
Far East 1231
Australia 282
New Zealand 72
Oceania 354
others

Tourist attractions
Visitor numbers, 1994

○ 5 million and over
○ 2.5 - 5 million
○ 1 - 2.5 million
○ 0.5 - 1 million

Type of attraction

■ cathedrals and churches
■ other historic buildings and monuments
□ museums and galleries
■ gardens
■ wildlife attractions
■ parks and country parks
■ leisure parks and piers

Boundaries

—— county, 1994
—— Tourist Board

Inner London
Scale 1 : 400 000
0   5   10km

Madam Tussaud's
Funland & Laserbowl, Trocadero
London Zoo
British Museum
Royal Academy of Arts
Royal Albert Hall
Science Museum
Natural History Museum
Victoria & Albert Museum
St. Paul's Cathedral
Tower of London
London Dungeon
National Portrait Gallery
National Gallery
Tate Gallery
Westminster Abbey

Map labels

ISLAND AREAS

SCOTLAND
Edinburgh Zoo
Royal Botanic Gardens
Edinburgh Castle
Glasgow Art Gallery and Museum

NORTHERN IRELAND
Botanic Gardens

CUMBRIA
NORTHUMBRIA
Kielder Forest
Saltwell Park
Windermere Iron Steamboat Company

YORKSHIRE & HUMBERSIDE
National Museum of Photography
York Minster
Jorvik Viking Centre
Hornsea Pottery
Temple Newsam Country Park
Tropical World
Rother Valley
Clumber Park
Sherwood Forest Country Park
Rufford Country Park

NORTH WEST
Frontierland Morecambe
Sea Life Centre
Blackpool Pleasure Beach
Blackpool Tower
Winter Gardens
Pleasureland Southport
Camelot Theme Park
Croxteth Country Park
Wigan Pier
Walton Hall Gardens
Tate Gallery
Albert Dock
Chester Zoo
Chester Cathedral
Tatton Country Park
American Adventure Theme Park
Alton Towers

EAST MIDLANDS
Shipley Country Park
Elvaston Castle Country Park
Bradgate Park

HEART OF ENGLAND
Sandwell Valley Park
Clent Hills Country Park
Cannon Hill Park
Shakespeare's Birthplace
Drayton Manor Park
Birmingham City Museum
Warwick Castle
Wicksteed Park

WALES

EAST ANGLIA
Norwich Cathedral
Pleasure Beach, Great Yarmouth
Thetford Forest
Dunstable Downs Country Park

SOUTHERN
Black Park & Langley Country Park
Windsor Castle
Dinton Pastures Country Park
Hampton Court Gardens
Roman Baths & Pump Room

INNER LONDON
LONDON
Kew Gardens
Hampton Court Gardens
Hainault Country Park
National Maritime Museum
Leeds Castle
Canterbury Cathedral

WEST COUNTRY
Stonehenge
Salisbury Cathedral
Winchester Cathedral
Moors Valley Country Park

SOUTH EAST ENGLAND
Wisley Garden
Chessington World of Adventure
Smart's Amusement Park
Palace Pier
Eastbourne Pier
Rotunda Amusement Park

Scale 1 : 4 500 000
0   50   100km
Transverse Mercator Projection

© Oxford University Press

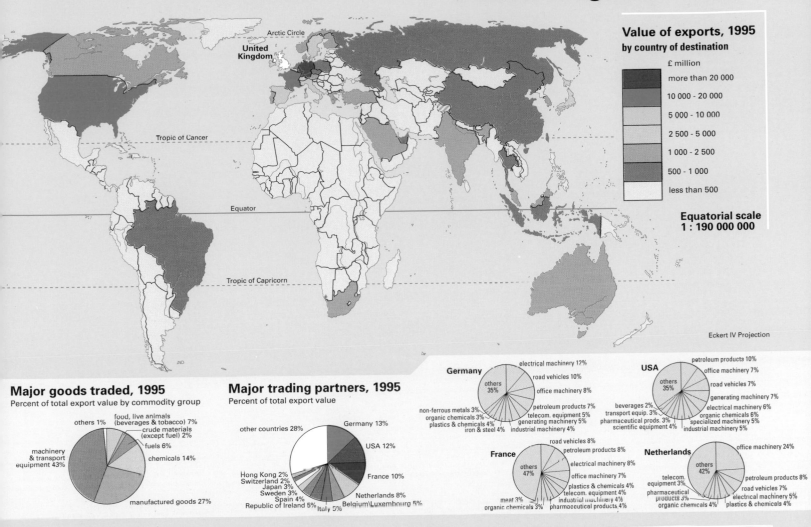

Value of exports, 1995
by country of destination

£ million

more than 20 000
10 000 - 20 000
5 000 - 10 000
2 500 - 5 000
1 000 - 2 500
500 - 1 000
less than 500

Equatorial scale
1 : 190 000 000

Eckert IV Projection

Major goods traded, 1995
Percent of total export value by commodity group

others 1%
food, live animals (beverages & tobacco) 7%
crude materials (except fuel) 2%
fuels 6%
chemicals 14%
manufactured goods 27%
machinery & transport equipment 43%

Major trading partners, 1995
Percent of total export value

other countries 28%
Germany 13%
USA 12%
France 10%
Netherlands 8%
Belgium\Luxembourg 5%
Italy 5%
Republic of Ireland 5%
Spain 4%
Sweden 3%
Japan 3%
Switzerland 2%
Hong Kong 2%

Germany
others 35%
electrical machinery 12%
road vehicles 10%
office machinery 8%
petroleum products 7%
telecom. equipment 5%
generating machinery 5%
industrial machinery 4%
iron & steel 4%
plastics & chemicals 4%
organic chemicals 3%
non-ferrous metals 3%

USA
others 35%
petroleum products 10%
office machinery 7%
road vehicles 7%
generating machinery 7%
electrical machinery 6%
organic chemicals 6%
specialized machinery 5%
industrial machinery 5%
scientific equipment 4%
pharmaceutical prods. 3%
transport equip. 3%
beverages 2%

France
others 47%
road vehicles 8%
petroleum products 8%
electrical machinery 8%
office machinery 7%
plastics & chemicals 4%
telecom. equipment 4%
industrial machinery 4%
pharmaceutical products 4%
organic chemicals 3%
meat 3%

Netherlands
others 42%
office machinery 24%
petroleum products 8%
road vehicles 7%
electrical machinery 5%
plastics & chemicals 4%
organic chemicals 4%
pharmaceutical products 3%
telecom. equipment 3%

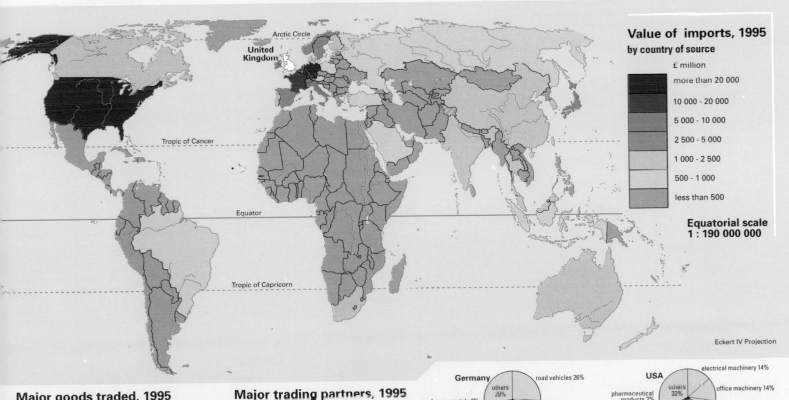

Value of imports, 1995
by country of source

£ million

more than 20 000
10 000 - 20 000
5 000 - 10 000
2 500 - 5 000
1 000 - 2 500
500 - 1 000
less than 500

Equatorial scale
1 : 190 000 000

Eckert IV Projection

Major goods traded, 1995
Percent of total import value by commodity group

others 1%
food, live animals (beverages & tobacco) 10%
crude materials (except fuel) 4%
fuels 3%
chemicals 11%
manufactured goods 30%
machinery & transport equipment 41%

Major trading partners, 1995
Percent of total import value

other countries 22%
Germany 15%
USA 12%
France 10%
Netherlands 7%
Japan 6%
Italy 5%
Belgium\Luxembourg 5%
Republic of Ireland 4%
Switzerland 3%
Sweden 3%
Norway 3%
Spain 3%
Hong Kong 2%

Germany
others 29%
road vehicles 26%
electrical machinery 8%
office machinery 6%
plastics & chemicals 6%
industrial equipment 6%
specialized machinery 5%
paper products 3%
iron & steel 3%
organic chemicals 3%
metal goods 2%
textiles 2%
non-ferrous metals 2%

USA
others 33%
electrical machinery 14%
office machinery 14%
transport equipment 7%
generating machinery 5%
scientific equipment 4%
telecommunications equipment 4%
specialized machinery 4%
industrial machinery 4%
plastics & chemicals 3%
non-ferrous metals 2%
road vehicles 2%
organic chemicals 2%
pharmaceutical products 2%

France
others 51%
road vehicles 18%
electrical machinery 7%
plastics & chemicals 6%
office machinery 4%
organic chemicals 4%
industrial machinery 4%
paper products 3%
iron & steel 3%

Netherlands
others 49%
office machinery 14%
plastics & chemicals 8%
electrical machinery 7%
road vehicles 6%
vegetables & fruit 5%
meat 4%

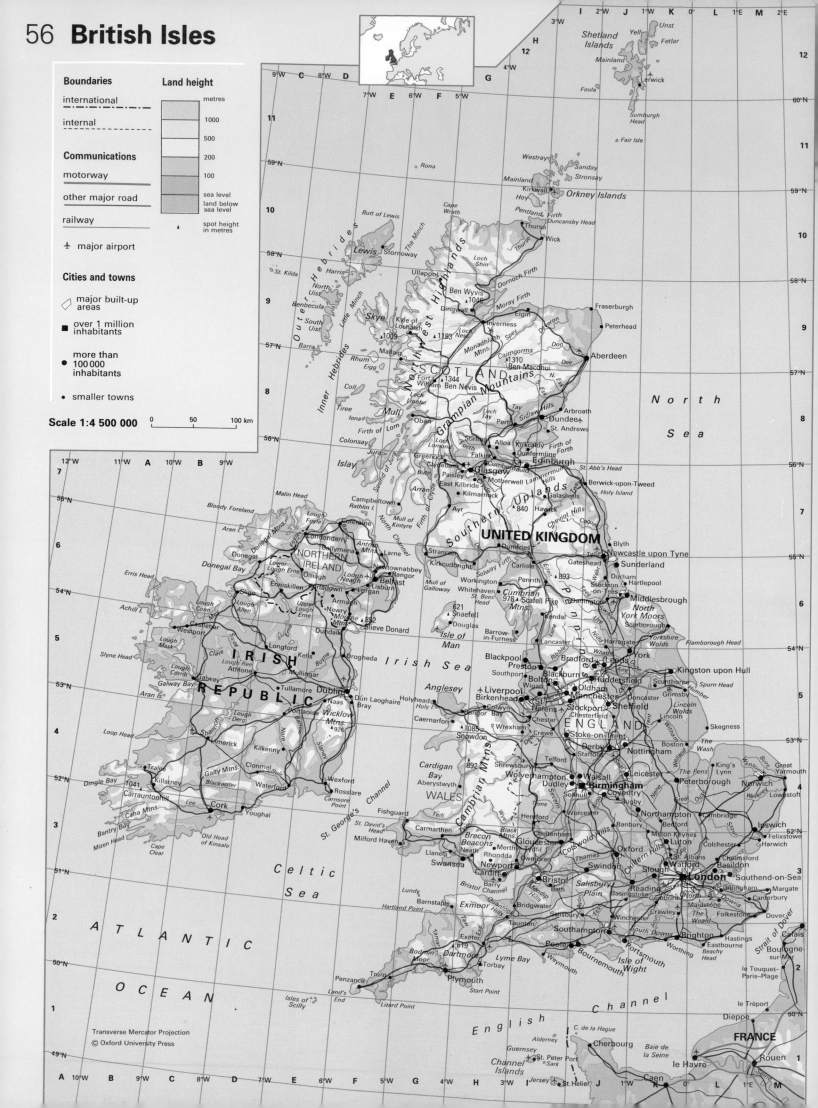

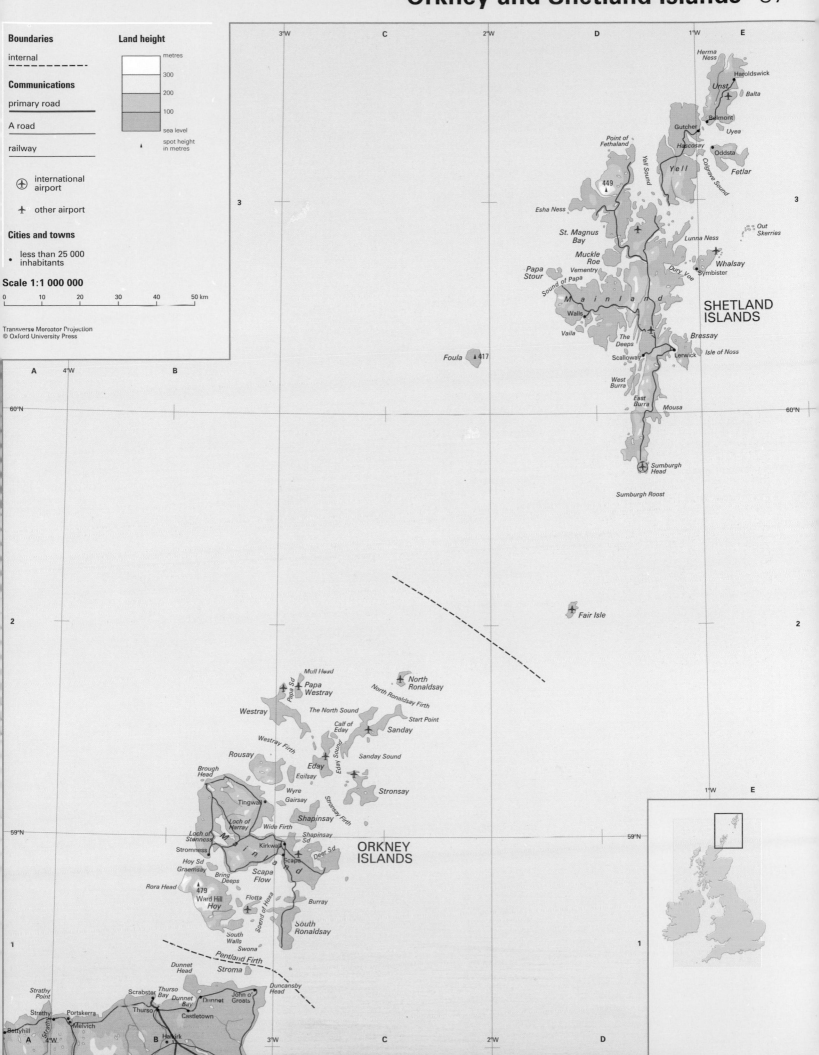

Boundaries

internal – – –

Communications

primary road

A road

railway

⊕ international airport

✈ other airport

Cities and towns

• less than 25 000 inhabitants

Scale 1:1 000 000

0   10   20   30   40   50 km

Transverse Mercator Projection
© Oxford University Press

Land height

metres
300
200
100
sea level
▲ spot height in metres

SHETLAND ISLANDS

Herma Ness
Haroldswick
Unst
Balta
Belmont
Gutcher
Uyea
Hascosay
Oddsta
Point of Fethaland
Fetlar
Yell
Colgrave Sound
Yell Sound
449
Esha Ness
Out Skerries
Lunna Ness
St. Magnus Bay
Whalsay
Muckle Roe
Symbister
Vementry
Dury Voe
Papa Stour
Sound of Papa
Mainland
Walls
Bressay
Vaila
The Deeps
Isle of Noss
Scalloway
Lerwick
West Burra
East Burra
Mousa
Sumburgh Head
Sumburgh Roost

Foula ▲ 417

Fair Isle

Mull Head
Papa Sd
Papa Westray
North Ronaldsay
North Ronaldsay Firth
Westray
The North Sound
Start Point
Calf of Eday
Sanday
Westray Firth
Rousay
Eday Sound
Sanday Sound
Brough Head
Eday
Eqilsay
Stronsay
Wyre
Gairsay
Tingwall
Shapinsay
Stronsay Firth
Loch of Harray
Wide Firth
ORKNEY ISLANDS
Loch of Stenness
Shapinsay Sd
Stromness
Kirkwall
Deer Sd
Mainland
Scapa
Hoy Sd
Graemsay
Bring Deeps
Scapa Flow
Rora Head
479
Flotta
Burray
Ward Hill
Hoy
Sound of Hoxa
South Ronaldsay
South Walls
Burray
Swona
Dunnet Head
Stroma
Pentland Firth
Duncansby Head
Strathy Point
Thurso Bay
Strathy
Scrabster
Thurso
Dunnet Bay
Dunnet
John o' Groats
Bettyhill
Portskerra
Thurso
Castletown
Melvich
Halkirk

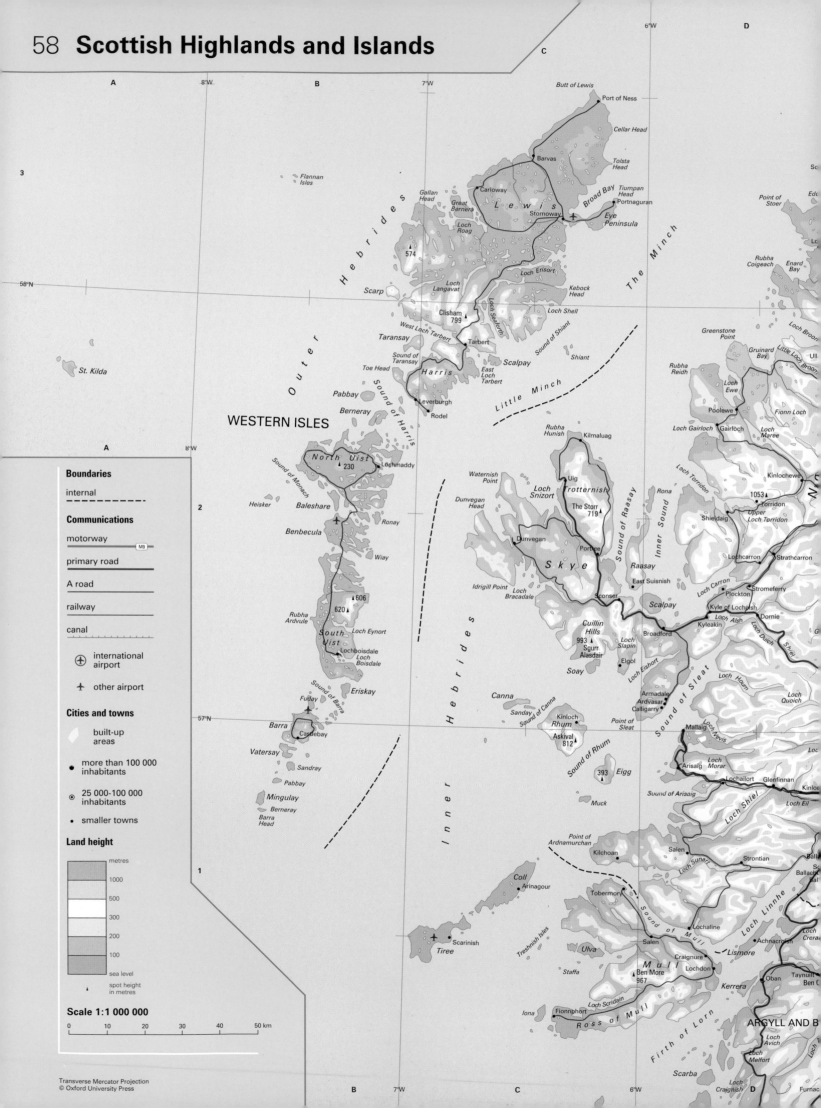

Boundaries

internal — — — —

Communications

motorway [M9]

primary road

A road

railway

canal

⊕ international airport

✈ other airport

Cities and towns

built-up areas

● more than 100 000 inhabitants

◉ 25 000–100 000 inhabitants

• smaller towns

Land height

metres
1000
500
300
200
100
sea level

▲ spot height in metres

Scale 1:1 000 000

0 10 20 30 40 50 km

Transverse Mercator Projection
© Oxford University Press

Northern Ireland. False colour satellite image.
Red : agricultural land.
Blue/green : upland vegetation.
Pale blue : urban areas and marine sediments.

Scale
0 10 20 30 40 50 km

© Oxford University Press

Scale 1:1 000 000

Boundaries	Communications	Cities and towns	Land height
international	motorway M9	built-up areas	metres 1000
national	primary road	■ over 1 million inhabitants	500
internal	A road	● more than 100 000 inhabitants	300
national park	railway	◉ 25 000–100 000 inhabitants	200
	canal	● smaller towns	100
	✈ international airport		sea level
	✈ other airport		▲ spot height in metres

0 10 20 30 40 50 km

Transverse Mercator Projection
© Oxford University Press

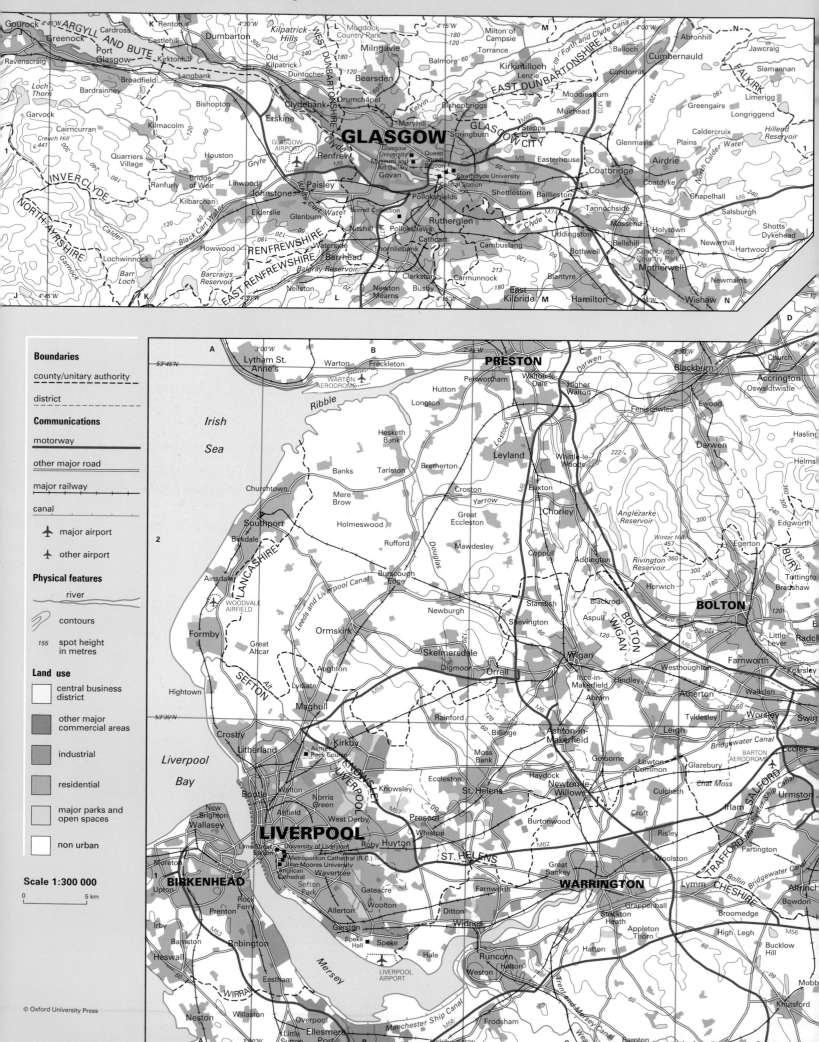

Boundaries

county/unitary authority

district

Communications

motorway

other major road

major railway

canal

✈ major airport

✈ other airport

Physical features

river

contours

155 spot height in metres

Land use

central business district

other major commercial areas

industrial

residential

major parks and open spaces

non urban

Scale 1:300 000

0   5 km

© Oxford University Press

**Manchester.
False colour satellite image.**

Red/orange : agricultural land.
Pale/green : moorland.
Dark blue : urban areas.

Scale
0   5   10   15 km

The Yorkshire Dales.
False colour satellite image.
Orange : grassland. Red : arable land.
Green : moorland. Blue : urban areas.
Scale 0 10 20 km

Boundaries
national
internal
national park

Communications
motorway M1
primary road
A road
railway
canal

⊕ international airport
✈ other airport

Cities and towns
built-up areas
■ over 1 million inhabitants
● more than 100 000 inhabitants
⊙ 25 000 - 100 000 inhabitants
• smaller towns

Land height
metres
1000
500
300
200
100
sea level
land below sea level
▲ spot height in metres

Scale 1:1 000 000
0 10 20 30 40 km

Transverse Mercator Projection

Humber Estuary and The Wash.
False colour satellite image.
Red and orange : agricultural land.
Yellow and green : rough pasture, moorland.
Dark blue : urban areas.
Scale 0 10 20 30 40 50 km

© Oxford University Press

CARDIFF

Boundaries
unitary authority

Communications
motorway

other major road

major railway

✈ major airport

Physical features
contours

Land use
central business district

other major commercial areas

industrial

residential

major parks and open spaces

non urban

Scale 1 : 300 000

0   5 km

Transverse Mercator Projection
© Oxford University Press

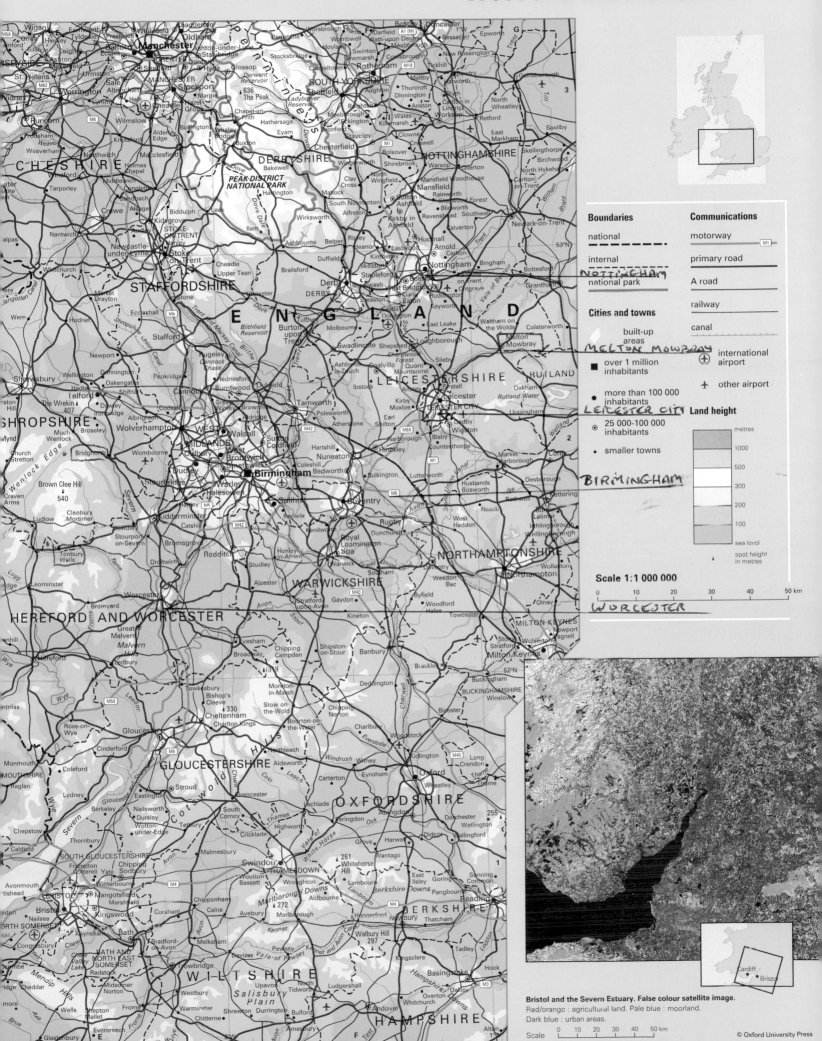

Bristol and the Severn Estuary. False colour satellite image.
Red/orange : agricultural land. Pale blue : moorland.
Dark blue : urban areas.

© Oxford University Press

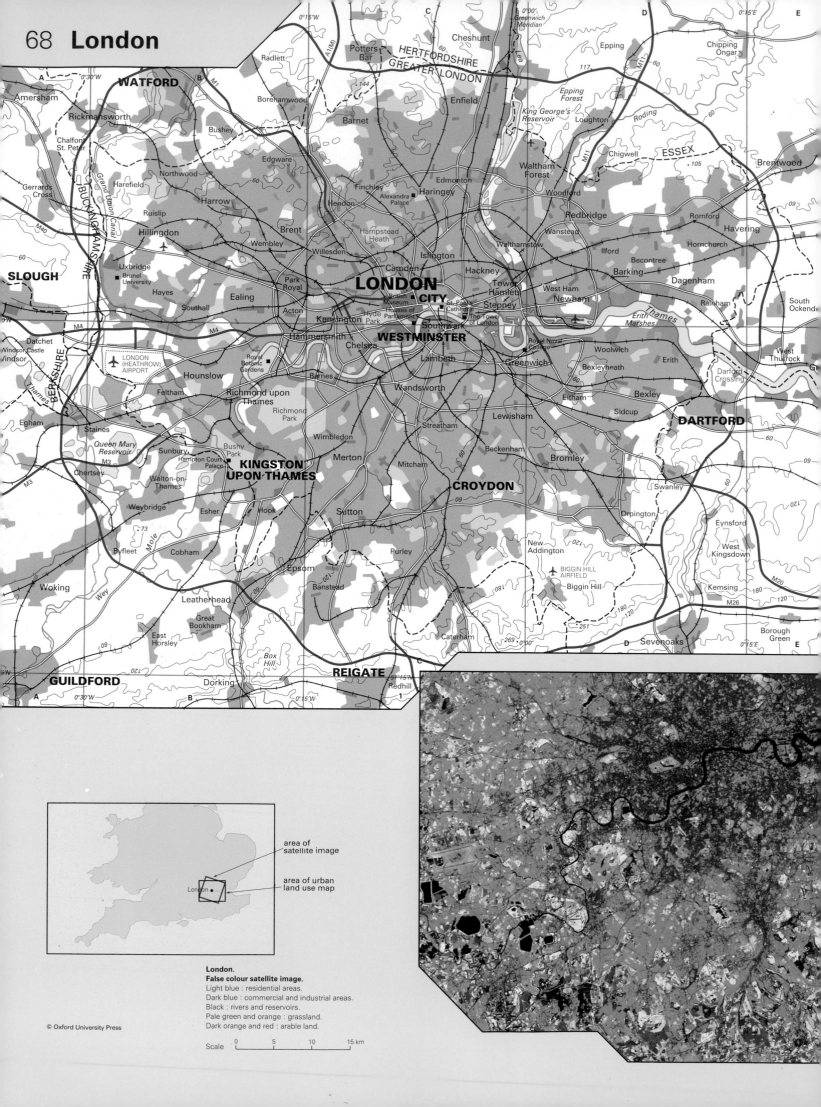

London.
False colour satellite image.
Light blue : residential areas.
Dark blue : commercial and industrial areas.
Black : rivers and reservoirs.
Pale green and orange : grassland.
Dark orange and red : arable land.

area of satellite image

area of urban land use map

© Oxford University Press

Scale 0 5 10 15 km

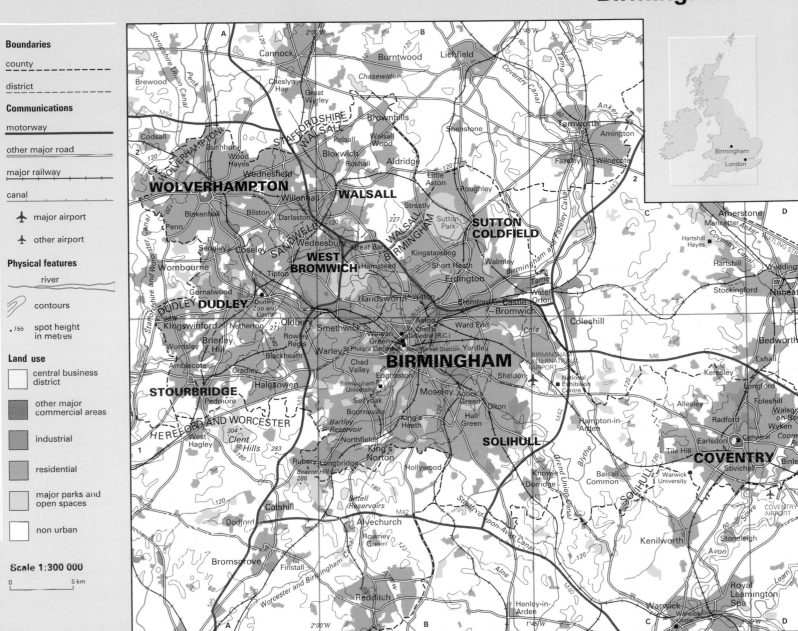

Boundaries

county ‒ ‒ ‒ ‒ ‒

district --------

Communications

motorway

other major road

major railway

canal

✈ major airport

✈ other airport

Physical features

river

contours

.155 spot height in metres

Land use

central business district

other major commercial areas

industrial

residential

major parks and open spaces

non urban

Scale 1:300 000

0 _____ 5 km

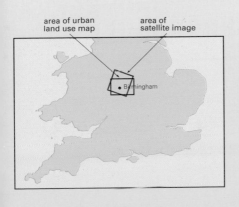

area of urban land use map

area of satellite image

• Birmingham

Oxford University Press

Birmingham and the West Midlands.
False colour satellite image.
Light blue : residential areas.
Dark blue : commercial and industrial areas.
Black : rivers and reservoirs.
Pale green and orange : grassland.
Dark orange and red : arable land.

Scale  U ___ 5 ___ 10 ___ 15 km

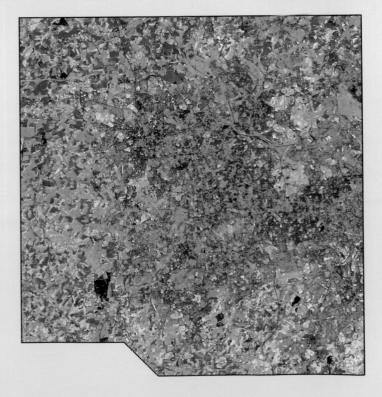

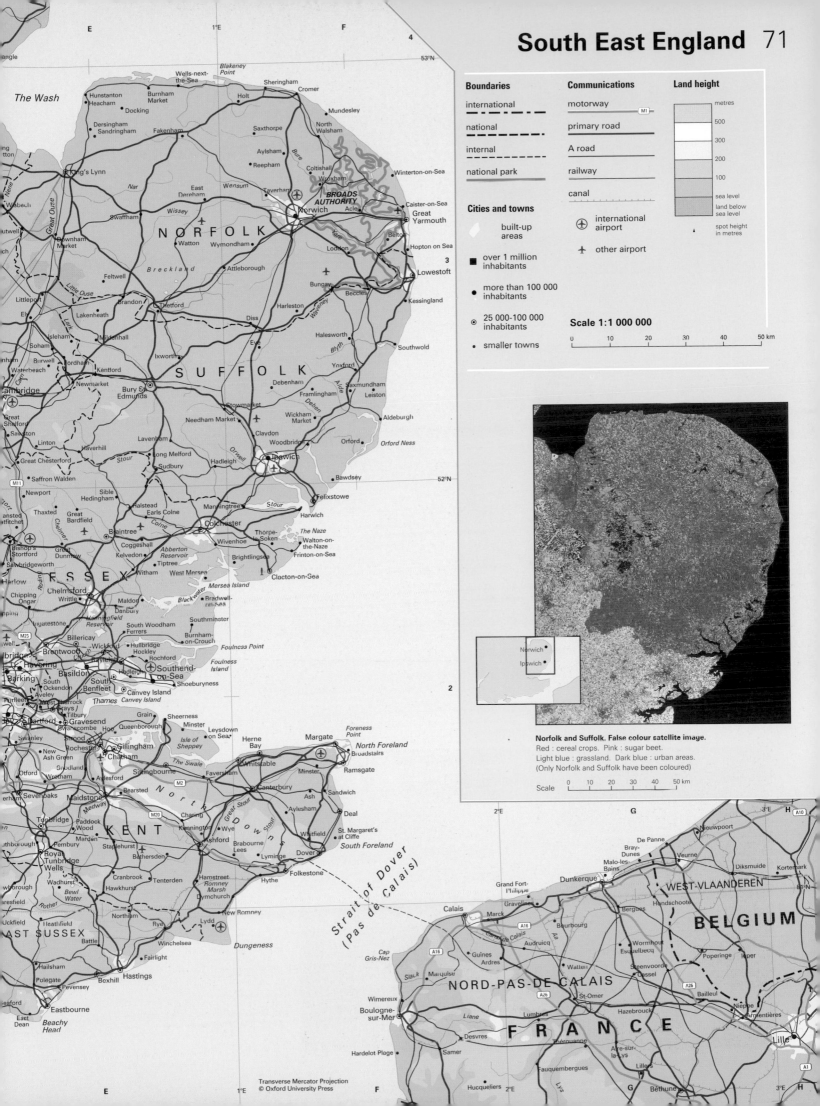

Norfolk and Suffolk. False colour satellite image.
Red : cereal crops. Pink : sugar beet.
Light blue : grassland. Dark blue : urban areas.
(Only Norfolk and Suffolk have been coloured)

Transverse Mercator Projection
© Oxford University Press

Boundaries

international

internal

national park

Communications

motorway M5

primary road

A road

railway

canal

⊕ international airport

✈ other airport

Cities and towns

built-up areas

● more than 100 000 inhabitants

◉ 25 000-100 000 inhabitants

• smaller towns

Land height

metres

500
300
200
100
sea level

▲ spot height in metres

Scale 1:1 000 000

0 10 20 30 40 50 km

Transverse Mercator Projection

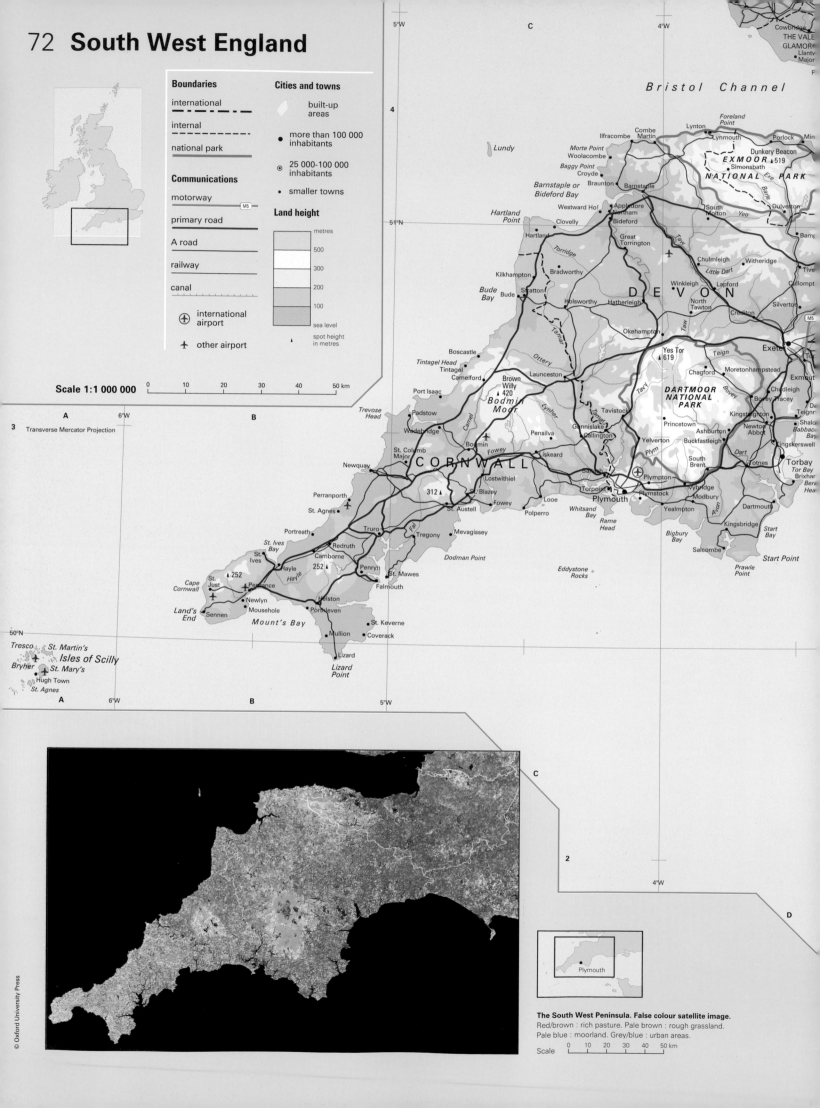

Bristol Channel

Lundy

Ilfracombe Combe Martin Lynton Foreland Point Porlock Min
Morte Point Lynmouth Dunkery Beacon ▲519 EXMOOR
Woolacombe *EXMOOR* Simonsbath NATIONAL PARK
Baggy Point Croyde Barnstaple South Dulverton
Braunton Molton Bamp
Barnstaple or Bideford Bay Barnstaple
Westward Ho! Appledore Northam
Hartland Point Bideford Witheridge Tive
Hartland Great Winkleigh Lapford Cullompt
Clovelly Torrington Chulmleigh Little Dart Silverton
Torridge Bradworthy D E V O N North Crediton
Kilkhampton Tawton
Bude Bay Stratton Holsworthy Hatherleigh Lapford M5
Bude Tamar Okehampton Teign Exeter
Ottery Yes Tor ▲619 Chagford Moretonhampstead Exmout
Boscastle Launceston DARTMOOR Chudleigh Bovey Tracey
Tintagel Head Camelford Brown NATIONAL PARK Babbaca
Tintagel Willy ▲420 *Tavy* Tavistock Kingsteignton Bay
Port Isaac *Bodmin Moor* Princetown Ashburton Newton Abbot
Trevose Head Padstow *Lynher* Gunnislake Yelverton Buckfastleigh Kingskerswell
Wadebridge *Canal* Callington South Dart Totnes Torbay
St. Columb Bodmin *Fowey* Pensilva Saltash Brent Tor Bay Brixhar
Major Liskeard Plympton Ivybridge Ber
Newquay C O R N W A L L Lostwithiel Torpoint Plymouth Modbury Head
312 ▲ St. Blazey Looe Plymstock Yealmpton Dartmouth
Perranporth Fowey Polperro *Whitsand Bay* Bigbury Kingsbridge Start Bay
St. Agnes St. Austell *Rame Head* Bay Salcombe Start Point
Portreath Truro Mevagissey Prawle Point
Redruth Tregony *Dodman Point* *Eddystone Rocks*
St. Ives Camborne 252 ▲ Penryn
St. Ives Bay Hayle St. Mawes
St. ▲252 *Hayle* Falmouth
Cape St. Just Penzance Helston
Cornwall Newlyn Porthleven
Land's End Mousehole St. Keverne
Sennen *Mount's Bay* Mullion Coverack
Lizard
Lizard Point

Tresco St. Martin's
Bryher *Isles of Scilly*
St. Mary's
Hugh Town
St. Agnes

The South West Peninsula. False colour satellite image.

Red/brown : rich pasture. Pale brown : rough grassland.
Pale blue : moorland. Grey/blue : urban areas.

Scale 0 10 20 30 40 50 km

Plymouth

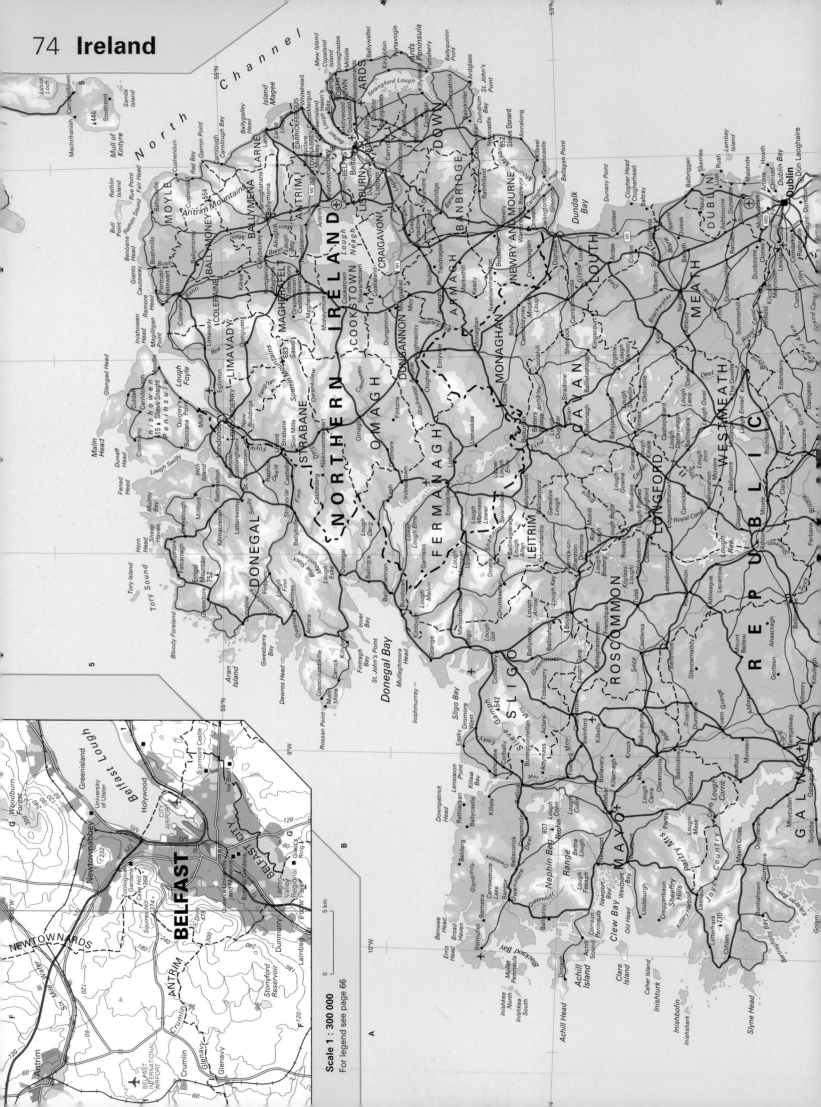

Scale 1 : 300 000
For legend see page 66

0   5 km

Boundaries

international —·—·—·—
disputed ∧∧∧∧∧∧∧∧∧
internal — — — — —

Communications

motorway
other major road
railway
canal
✈ major airport

Cities and towns

■ over 1 million inhabitants
● more than 100 000 inhabitants
• smaller towns

Land height

metres
3000
2000
1000
500
300
200
100
sea level
land below sea level
▲ spot height in metres

Conical Orthomorphic Projection

Sea depth

metres
sea level
200
3000
4000
5000
-86 sea depths shown as minus numbers

Physical features

seasonal river/lake
marsh
ice cap

Scale 1 : 16 000 000

0   160   320 km

© Oxford University Press

ATLANTIC OCEAN

Greenland Sea

ICELAND
Reykjavik
Akureyri
Hekla 1491
Höfn

Faeroe Islands
Shetland Islands
Orkney Islands
Outer Hebrides
The Minch
Cape Wrath
Inverness
Moray Firth
Aberdeen
Ben Nevis 1344m
Grampians
Glasgow
Dundee
Edinburgh
Southern Uplands
Newcastle upon Tyne
Middlesbrough
Belfast
Central Lowlands
Malin Head
Galway
REPUBLIC OF IRELAND
Dublin
Limerick
Cork
St. George's Channel
Manchester
Liverpool
Leeds
Sheffield
UNITED KINGDOM
Pennines
Birmingham
Coventry
Norwich
Cambrian Mts.
Cardiff
Bristol
London
Southampton
Plymouth
Scilly Is.
English Channel
Channel Islands

North Sea
Bergen
Stavanger
Skagerrak
Oslo
Hardanger vidda
Dovrefjell
Trondheim
Narvik
Tromsø
Lofoten Islands
Bodø
NORWAY
SWEDEN
Kjølen
Jostedalsbreen
Skerriegard
Klar
Dal
Vänern
Göteborg
Vättern
Jönköping
Norrköping
Linköping
Örebro
Västerås
Stockholm
Uppsala
Mälaren
Sundsvall
Umeå
Luleå
Skellefte
Indal
Oulu
Gulf of Bothnia
FINLAND
Vaasa
Tampere
Turku
Lappland
Inarijärvi
Torne
Kemi
Murmansk
Kola Peninsula
Kandalaksha
Petrozavodsk
Lake Ladoga
Lake Onega
St. Petersburg (Leningrad)
Novgorod
Salpausselka
Helsinki
Espoo
Vantaa
Gulf of Finland
Tallinn
ESTONIA
Tartu
Lake Peipus
Pskov
Lake Ilmen
Åland
Baltic Sea
Gotland
Öland
Bornholm
LATVIA
Riga
G. of Riga
Daugava
Liepāja
Šiauliai
Daugavpils
Vitsyebsk
LITHUANIA
Klaipėda
Kaunas
Vilnius
Kaliningrad
Minsk
BELARUS
Hrodna (Grodno)
Babruysk
Pripet Marshes
Pinsk
Pripet
Brest

DENMARK
Jylland
Ålborg
Århus
Esbjerg
Odense
Fyn
København (Copenhagen)
Sjælland
Malmö
Skåne
Kattegat
Pomeranian Bay
Kiel
Lübeck
Rostock
Gdynia
Gdańsk
Szczecin
Oder
Poznań
POLAND
Warszawa (Warsaw)
Łódź
Wrocław
Bydgoszcz
Toruń
Białystok
Vistula
Lublin
Radom
Częstochowa
Katowice
Kraków
North European Plain

NETHERLANDS
Groningen
Frisian Is.
Den Haag (The Hague)
Amsterdam
Rotterdam
Utrecht
IJsselmeer
Waal
Scheldt Est.
Maas
BELGIUM
Antwerpen (Anvers)
Gent
Bruxelles (Brussels)
Liège
Ardennes
LUXEMBOURG
Luxembourg
Hamburg
Bremen
Hannover
Bielefeld
Dortmund
Essen
Düsseldorf
Köln (Cologne)
Bonn
GERMANY
Berlin
Magdeburg
Halle
Leipzig
Dresden
Erfurt
Chemnitz
Harz Mts.
Elbe
Frankfurt
Mannheim
Nürnberg (Nuremberg)
Stuttgart
Saarbrücken
München (Munich)
Schwäbische Alb
Bodensee
Donau
Augsburg
Erzgebirge
Bohemian Massif
Plzeň
Praha (Prague)
CZECH REP.
Brno
Ostrava
Tatry
SLOVAKIA
Košice
Bratislava
Wien (Vienna)
Linz
Salzburg
Innsbruck
AUSTRIA
Graz
Tauern
Danube

France
Calais
Str. of Dover
Lille
Amiens
Le Havre
Rouen
Caen
Cotentin
Brittany Pen.
Brest
Rennes
Angers
Nantes
le Mans
Orléans
Paris
Reims
Metz
Nancy
Strasbourg
Vosges
Dijon
Saône
Loire
Tours
Limoges
Clermont-Ferrand
Massif Central
St-Étienne
Lyon
Grenoble
Bordeaux
Garonne
Dordogne
Bay of Biscay
Toulouse
Montpellier
Marseille
Avignon
Golfe du Lion
Nice
Alpes Maritimes
Toulon
Perpignan
ANDORRA
Pyrénées
Mont Blanc 4807m
Jura
Basel
Bern
SWITZERLAND
Genève
Geneva
Lausanne
LIECHTENSTEIN
Zürich
Rhine
Rhône

SPAIN
C. Finisterre
La Coruña
Vigo
Oviedo
Gijón
Santander
Cantabrian Mts.
Bilbao
San Sebastián
Bayonne
Burgos
León
Valladolid
Duero
Zaragoza
Ebro
Lérida
Barcelona
Hospitalet
Costa Brava
Balearic Islands
Menorca
Mallorca
Palma de Mallorca
Ibiza
Valencia
Albacete
Madrid
Central Cordillera
Tagus
Guadiana
Badajoz
Córdoba
Guadalquivir
Sevilla (Seville)
Jerez de la Frontera
Cádiz
Murcia
Alicante
Costa Blanca
Cartagena
Almería
Málaga
Granada
Betic Cordilleras
Str. of Gibraltar
Gibraltar (U.K.)
PORTUGAL
Porto (Oporto)
Douro
Coimbra
Lisboa (Lisbon)
Faro
Algarve

Mediterranean Sea

Tanger (Tangiers)
Tétouan
Oran
Rabat-Salé
Meknès
Fès
Casablanca
Kenitra
ALGERIA
Alger (Algiers)
Blida
Bejaïa
Sétif
Constantine
Annaba
Skikda
Bizerte
Tunis
TUNISIA
Sousse
Sfax
Gabès
Gafsa
Nabeul
El Bayadh
Djelfa
Biskra
Tébessa
Sidi Bel-Abbès
Oudja
Atlas Mountains
Bou Saâda
Ech Cheliff
Touggourt
Tozeur
Hassi Messaoud
LIBYA
Tarābulus (Tripoli)
Mişrātah (Misurata)
Surt (Sirte)
Banghāzī (Benghazi)
Beida (Al Baydā)
Darnah
Tubruq

ITALY
Torino (Turin)
Milano (Milan)
Bolzano
Bologna
Genova (Genoa)
Ligurian Sea
Modena
Verona
Venezia (Venice)
Po
Ravenna
Firenze (Florence)
Pisa
SAN MARINO
Perugia
Appennini
Roma (Rome)
Vesuvius 1277
Napoli (Naples)
Salerno
Foggia
Bari
Táranto
Gulf of Taranto
Adriatic Sea
Pescara
Corse (Corsica) (France)
Ajaccio
Bastia
Sardegna (Sardinia) (Italy)
Sássari
Cágliari
Tyrrhenian Sea
Palermo
Messina
Réggio di Calabria
Catánia
Mt Etna 3323
Sicily
Valletta
MALTA
Ionian Sea

SLOVENIA
Ljubljana
Maribor
Zagreb (Agram)
Drava
CROATIA
Rijeka
Trieste
Split
BOSNIA-HERZEGOVINA
Banja Luka
Sarajevo
Dubrovnik
MONTENEGRO
Podgorica (Titograd)
Shkodër
YUGOSLAVIA
Novi Sad
Beograd (Belgrade)
SERBIA
Kragujevac
Niš
Osijek
HUNGARY
Budapest
Pécs
Győr
Szeged
Arad
Hungarian Basin
Tisza
Debrecen
Miskolc
ROMANIA
Timişoara
Cluj Napoca
Brașov
Craiova
Ploiesti
Bucureşti (Bucharest)
Galati
Braila
Carpathians
Târgu Mureş
MOLDOVA
Chişinău (Kishinev)
Iaşi
Bălţi
Dniester
UKRAINE
Kyyiv (Kiev)
Rivne (Rovno)
L'viv (L'vov)
Zhytomyr
Vinnytsya
Chernivtsi
Dnepr
BULGARIA
Sofiya (Sofia)
Plovdiv
Ruse
Pleven
Varna
Burgas
Stara Zagora
Balkan Mts.
Danube (Donau)
FYRO MACEDONIA
Skopje
Bitola
ALBANIA
Tirana (Tirana)
Vlorë
Durrës
Pindhos Mountains
GREECE
Thessaloniki (Thessalonica)
Ioánnina
Kérkyra (Corfu)
Ionian Is.
Lárisa
Pátra
Athína (Athens)
Peiraiás (Piraeus)
Pelopónnisos
Kalamáta
Évvoia
Kykládes
Aegean Sea
Mt. Olympus 2917
Ródos
Rhodes
Kríti (Crete)
Chaniá (Khania)
Irákleio (Iráklion)
Istanbul
Edirne
Izmir
Balikesir
Larisa

Arctic Circle
North Sea

20°W 15°W 10°W 5°W 0° 5°E 10°E 15°E 20°E 25°E 30°E 35°E 40°E
70°N 65°N 60°N 55°N 50°N 45°N 40°N 35°N

Scale 1 : 350 000 000

North Atlantic Treaty Organization (NATO)

Headquarters: Brussels

member country

Headquarters of other European and World Organizations

The Hague: International Court of Justice

Geneva: World Health Organization (WHO)

Paris: United Nations Educational, Scientific, and Cultural Organization (UNESCO)

Organization for Economic Cooperation and Development (OECD)

Rome: Food and Agricultural Organization of the United Nations (FAO)

The European Union

Headquarters: Brussels

European Parliament meets in Strasbourg. European Court of Justice sits in Luxembourg.

member country of the European Union

countries that have applied to join the European Union

— — — international boundary

• national capital

+ other cities

Scale 1 : 40 000 000

0   400   800   1200km

Geological structure

Precambrian

ancient shields

sedimentary rocks

Mountain building

Caledonian

Hercynian

Alpine

Oceans and seas

continental shelf

oceanic crust (Atlantic)
deep troughs (Mediterranean)

recent volcanism

major faults

major thrusts

limit of Quaternary glaciation

international boundary

Scale 1 : 56 000 000

0   400   800km

Conical Orthomorphic Projection

© Oxford University Press

Cloud amount

○ 0   ◔ 5
◷ 1 or less   ◕ 6
◑ 2   ◕ 7 or more
◑ 3   ● 8 (oktas)
◑ 4

Weather

≡ mist
☰ fog
• drizzle
• , rain and drizzle
, rain
, * rain and snow
* snow

Air Pressure

isobars at 4mb intervals
—— 1024

Temperature

05 in degrees Celsius

Wind speed (knots)

◎ calm
○— 1–2
○⟍ 3–7
○⟍ 8–12 for each additional
○⟍ 13–17 half-feather add 5 knots

Fronts

warm
cold
occluded

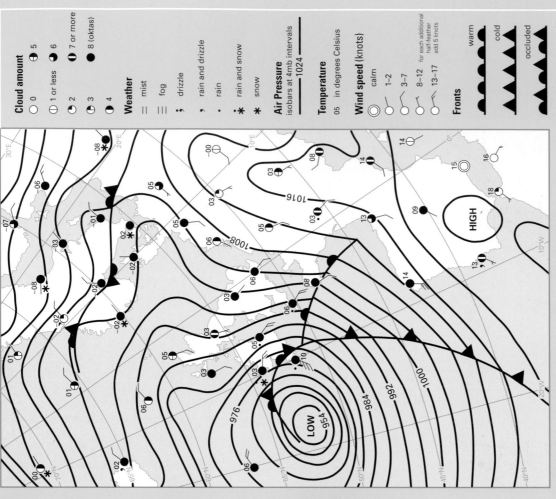

Synoptic chart for 31 January 1988 at 1800 hours GMT

The passage of a depression across Western Europe (NOAA-9 satellite images)

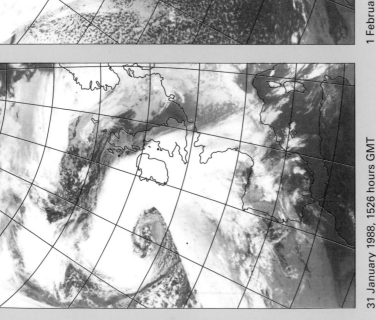

31 January 1988, 1526 hours GMT

1 February 1988, 1515 hours GMT

Weather summary for the United Kingdom, 1 February 1988

Scotland had rain or sleet overnight with snow on higher ground. By morning most places had become dry, although rain continued in the far north and extreme east. During the day, as the depression crossed from the southwest, there were patches of heavy rain with snow over the mountains.

Across Northern Ireland, England, and Wales there was heavy overnight rain with a short period of sleet and snow in the north. Daytime weather was dominated by heavy, squally showers, accompanied by hail and thunder.

Winds were very strong across England and Wales, with widespread gales and gusts of 45 to 60 knots. Around exposed western and southwestern coasts, gusts above 80 knots were reported.

Temperatures were generally above normal, notably in the southern half of Great Britain. This mildness was, however, offset by the strength of the wind.

Climate Graphs

for selected stations

⟋ average daily temperature
5°C average daily temperature
⟋ growing season (that part of the year when average daily temperature remains above 5°C
▭ average rainfall

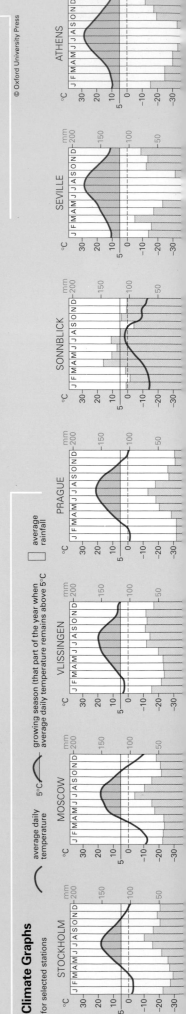

ATHENS
SEVILLE
SONNBLICK
PRAGUE
VLISSINGEN
MOSCOW
STOCKHOLM

© Oxford University Press

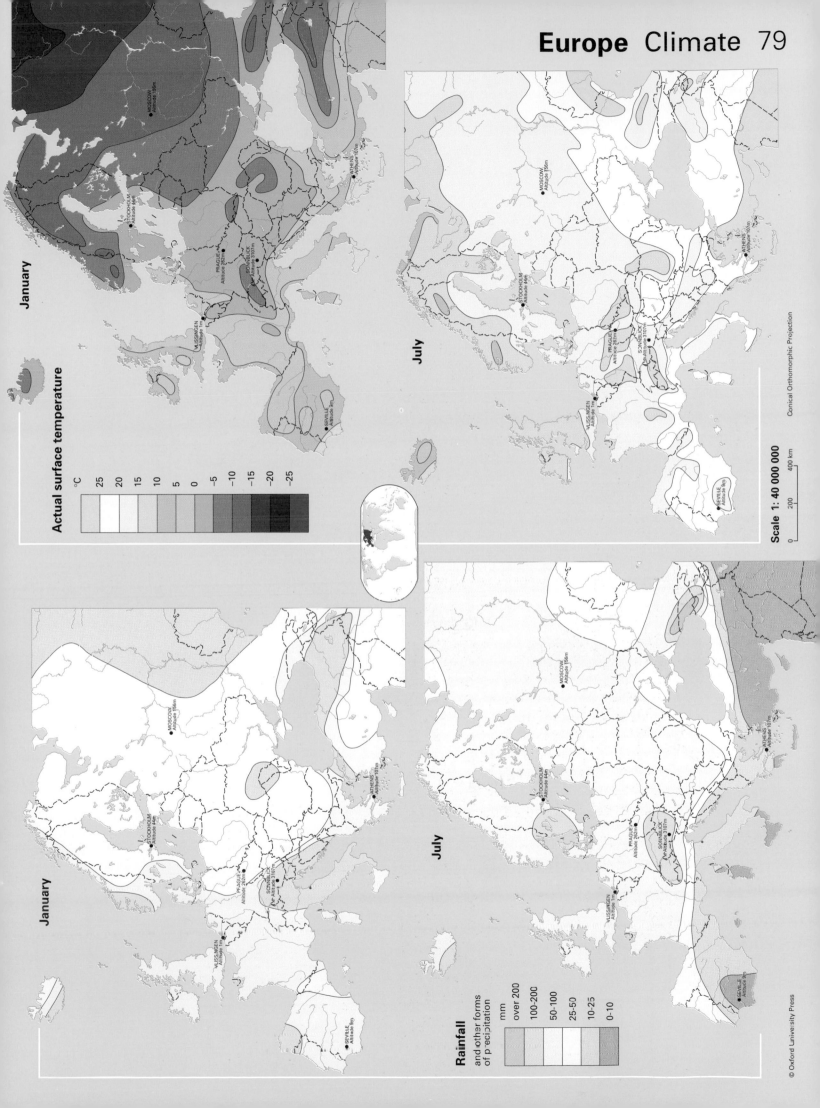

January

Actual surface temperature

°C

25
20
15
10
5
0
−5
−10
−15
−20
−25

July

Scale 1: 40 000 000

0   200   400 km

Conical Orthomorphic Projection

January

Rainfall
and other forms
of precipitation

mm

over 200
100–200
50–100
25–50
10–25
0–10

July

MOSCOW Altitude 156m

STOCKHOLM Altitude 44m

PRAGUE Altitude 262m

SONNBLICK Altitude 3107m

VLISSINGEN Altitude 1m

ATHENS Altitude 107m

SEVILLE Altitude 9m

Arctic Circle

60°N

40°N

Cash crops

wine grapes

tea

tobacco

fruit

sugar

cotton

Animal products

wool

meat

fish

little or no farming
nomadic herding
shifting cultivation
mixed subsistence
grazing and
stock rearing
mixed farming
grain farming
mediterranean
farming
specialized
horticulture
dairy farming
forestry

— international boundary

Scale 1 : 20 000 000

0   200   400 km

international boundary

industrial areas

Minerals

	iron	copper	manganese	chromium	wolfram	nickel	tin	mercury	lead	zinc	bauxite

Energy

	oil	gas	coal	lignite

oil pipeline

gas pipeline

Scale 1 : 20 000 000

0   200   400 km

Conical Orthomorphic Projection

© Oxford University Press

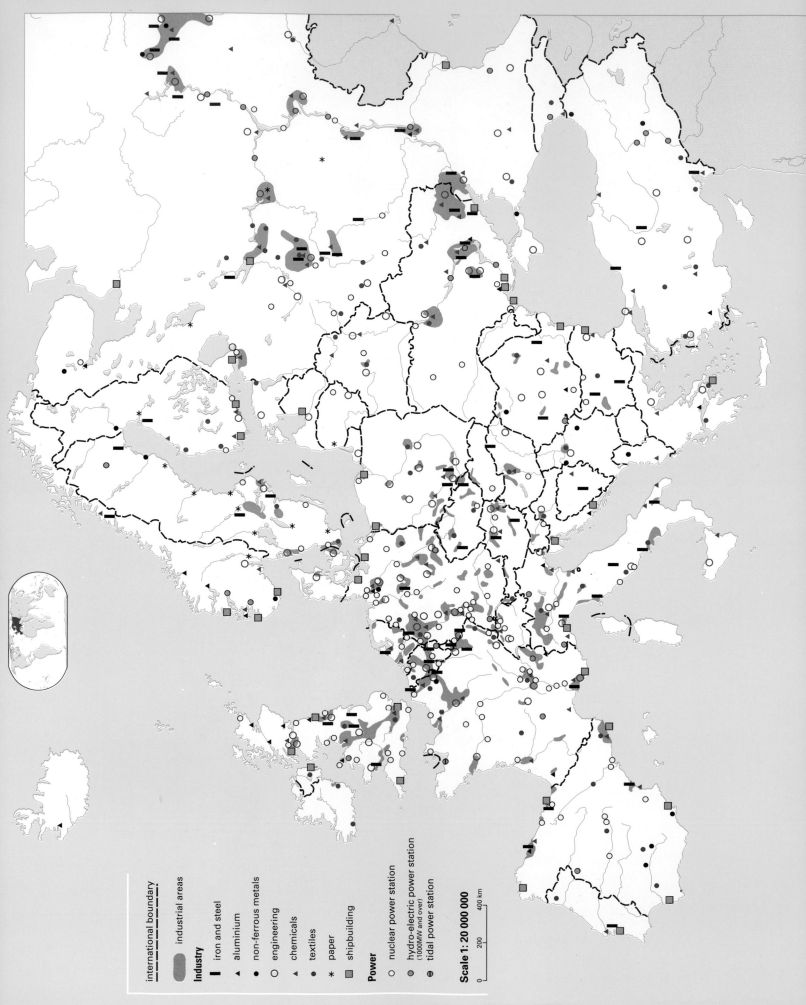

international boundary

industrial areas

Industry

▬ iron and steel

◀ aluminium

● non-ferrous metals

○ engineering

◀ chemicals

● textiles

✳ paper

■ shipbuilding

Power

○ nuclear power station

● hydro-electric power station
(1000MW and over)

◑ tidal power station

Scale 1: 20 000 000

200   400 km

Conical Orthomorphic Project
© Oxford University Press

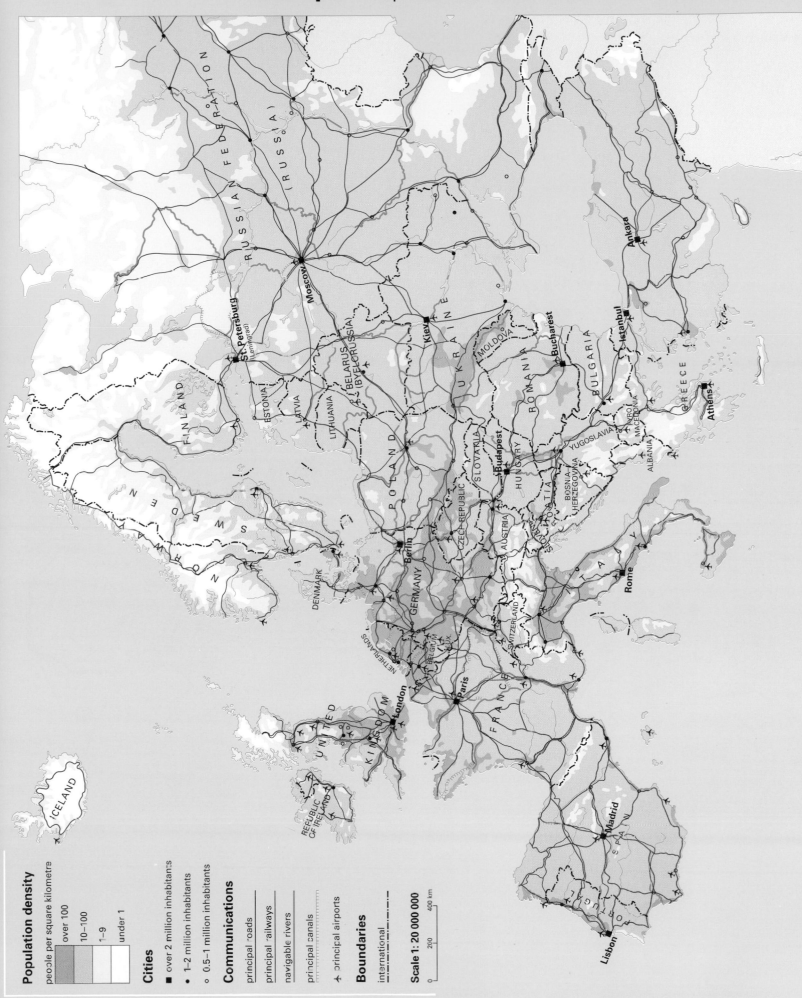

Population density

people per square kilometre

- over 100
- 10–100
- 1–9
- under 1

Cities

- ■ over 2 million inhabitants
- ● 1–2 million inhabitants
- ○ 0.5–1 million inhabitants

Communications

principal roads

principal railways

navigable rivers

principal canals

✈ principal airports

Boundaries

international

Scale 1: 20 000 000

0   200   400 km

Zapoljarnyy
Nikel
Montchegorsk

Arctic Circle

Neva
Kirishi
Helsinki
Balti

Daugava (West Dvina)

Lukomyl'

Moneypoint

Glasgow
Blyth
Ferrybridge
West Burton
Drax
Dublin
Fiddler's Ferry
Eggborough
Ironbridge
Ratcliffe-on-Soar
Thorpe Marsh
Cottam
High Marnham
Didcot
London
Kingsnorth

Copenhagen

Amsterdam
West
Brussels
Meuse/Maas
Rhine

Elbe
Odra (Oder)
Bug

Adamow
MZRP Plock
Warsaw

Gerstein
Vetschau
Lübbenau
Schwarze Pumpe
Jänschwalde
Lippendorf/Böhlen
Boxberg
Espenhain
Hagenwerder
Thierbach
Chemnitz
Chemopetrol
Prunerov
Melnik
Tisová
Počerady
Tušimice
Wrocław
Rybnik
Bełchatów
Turów
Fortuna
Frankfurt
Main
Porcheville
Seine

Kozienice

Vistula

Tripolskaya

Lodyzhinska

Burshtynskaya

Loire

Munich
Inn
Danube

Matra
Tisza

Soštanj

Oradea
Ludus
Mintia

Moldavia
Dniestr
Prut

Puentes (As Pontes)
Meirama
Compostilla

Gourdon
Garonne

Rhône
Saône

Milan
La Casella
Ostiglia
Sermide
Po
River Po
Estuary
Zagreb

Nikola Tesla
Drmno

Rovinari
Turceni
Isalnita

Douro
Madrid
Ebro
Teruel

Tagus
Lisbon
Sines
Guadiana

Tuzla

Kosovo
Bobovdol
Bitola

Kremikovtsi
Maritsa East

Varna

Gaudalquivir
Segura

Tiber

Brindisi
Sud

Rossano
Milazzo

Yeniköy (Yentes)

Som

Athens
Yatağan
(Yates)

Megalópolis/
Irini

Environmental issues

Sea pollution

| | areas severely polluted for all or part of the year |
| | areas persistently affected by pollution |

▼ deep sea dump sites

✳ major oil spills (more than 100 000 tonnes)

✳ major oil spills (less than 100 000 tonnes)

Scale 1 : 16 000 000

0   200   400 km

Acid rain

A pH scale measures acidity. Unaffected rain water is slightly acidic with a pH of 5.6

— pH of 4.2 (the most acidic)

— pH of 4.6

— pH of 5.0

Forest fires

🔥 areas where forest fires are most frequent

Rivers

rivers which are considered as severely polluted, or exceed recommended levels of more than one pollutant

Air pollution

industrial sites emitting the largest amounts of sulphur, in 1990-92 (thousand tonnes of sulphur)

◯ over 200

◯ 100 - 200

○ 50 - 100

· 30 - 50

	power station
	refinery
	smelter
	other

◇ cities where sulphur dioxide emissions are recorded, and exceed recommended levels

| | industrial areas |

- - - international boundary

Kama
Belaya
Volga
Kashira
Ryazanskaya
Cheropetskaya
Belovskaya
Volga
Zmiyivskaya
Donets
Sluv"yans'kaya
Luhanskaya
Uglegorskaya
Dniepr
Zuevskaya
Starobeshevo
Pridneprovskaya
Don
Novncherkasskaya
Zaporizhzhya
...vorozhskaya
Kurakhovskaya
Kuban

satellite image area

Kangal
...yitomer (Somtes)
Afsin-Elbistan

60 E
60 N
40 N
60 E

Algae in the Adriatic Sea.   False colour satellite image

Algae feed on pollutants such as sewage and fertilizer run-off.
The red trails in the sea show algae south of the River Po estuary.

Phytoplankton in the Mediterranean Sea.   False colour satellite image

Phytoplankton are micro-organisms that thrive in shallow, polluted sea areas.
Red, orange, and yellow show the highest densities of Phytoplankton.
Green and blue show the lowest densities.

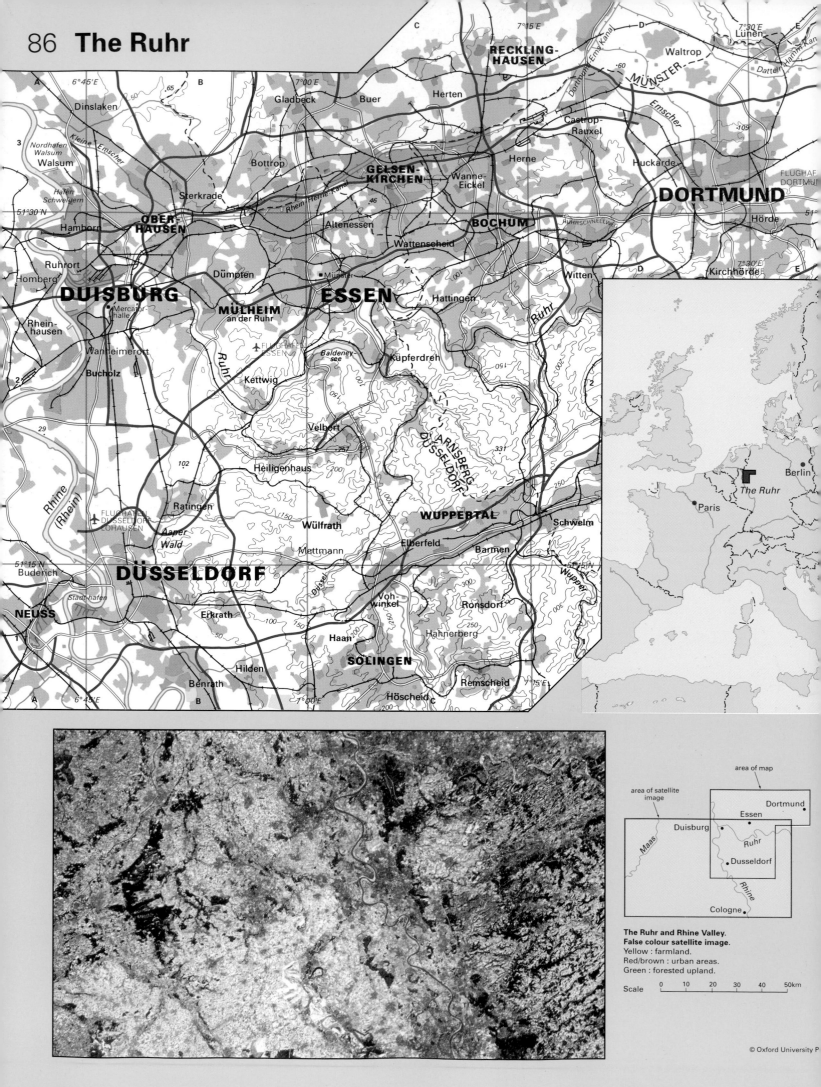

The Ruhr and Rhine Valley.
False colour satellite image.
Yellow : farmland.
Red/brown : urban areas.
Green : forested upland.

Scale 0 10 20 30 40 50km

Paris, Berlin

Boundaries

département (Paris) ‑‑‑‑

regierungsbezirk (Berlin, Ruhr) ‑‑‑‑

Communications

motorway

other major road

major railway

canal

✈ major airport

✈ other airport

central business district

other major commercial areas

industrial

residential

major parks and open spaces

non-urban

Physical features

river

contours

·155 spot height in metres

Scale 1: 300 000

0   5km

Paris map

Conflans-Ste. Honorine, Beauchamp, Herblay, Andrésy, Montmorency, Sarcelles, Écouen, Gonesse, AÉROPORT CHARLES DE GAULLE, Mitry-Mory, Cormeilles-en-Parisis, Enghien, AÉROPORT DU BOURGET, Villeparisis, Aulnay-sous-Bois, MAISONS LAFFITTE, Argenteuil, Sartrouville, Gennevilliers, ST-DENIS, le Blanc-Mesnil, POISSY, St. Germain, Colombes, Asnières, Drancy, Bobigny, Les Coudreaux, Chatou, Nanterre, Clichy, Aubervilliers, le Raincy, Faculté de Nanterre, Pantin, Noisy-le-Sec, Chelles, ST GERMAIN-en-Laye, la Défense, Neuilly, Nord Est, St Lazare, Champs-sur-Marne, Marne, Rueil-Malmaison, Arc de Triomphe, Louvre, Opéra, PARIS, Vincennes, Neuilly Plaisance, Vaucresson, St-Cloud, Bois de Boulogne, Eiffel Tower, Invalides, Notre Dame, Sorbonne, Lyon, Nogent, Metz & Nancy, VERSAILLES, Parc de St-Cloud, BOULOGNE-BILLANCOURT, Montparnasse, Austerlitz, St-Mandé, Autoroute de l'Est, Château de Versailles, Sèvres, Vanves, Montrouge, Bois de Vincennes, MARNE-LA-VALLÉE, St Cyr-l'École, Forêt de Meudon, Meudon, Ivry-s-Seine, Champigny, St Maur, Créteil, AÉRODROME DE VILLACOUBLAY, Clamart, Hay-les-Roses, Vitry-s-Seine, Villejuif, Choisy-le-Roi, Sucy-en-Brie, Forêt de Notre Dame, ST. QUENTIN-EN-YVELINES, Sceaux, Rungis, Thiais, Orly, Bièvres, Verrières, AÉROPORT D'ORLY, Villeneuve St. Georges, Brunoy, Brie-Comte-Robert, Chevreuse, Saclay, Palaiseau, Massy, Juvisy-sur-Orge, Montgeron, Draveil, Quincy-sous-Sénart, St. Rémy, Orsay, Chartres & Orléans, Longjumeau, les Ulis, Orge, Seine, Forêt de Sénart, Yerres, Évry, CORBEIL-ESSONNES, MELUN-SÉNART, Autoroute du Soleil, Sénart Ville-Nouvelle

Berlin map

Borgsdorf, Basdorf, Velten, Birkenwerder, Schönwalde, Marwitz, Bötzow, Frohnau, Schildow, Zepernick, Schwanebeck, Pausin, Glienicke, HENNIGSDORF, Berliner Forst, Hermsdorf, Buchholz, Karow, Blumberg, Schönwalde, Lindenberg, Brieselang, Reinickendorf, Blankenburg, Ahrensfelde, Altlandsberg, Falkensee, Berliner Forst Spandau, Tegel, FLUGHAFEN BERLIN-TEGEL (OTTO LILIENTHAL), Pankow, Weissensee, Jungfern heide, BERLIN, Wedding, Dallgow, Staaken, SPANDAU, Siemensstadt, Prenzlauer Berg, Friedrichshain, Hellersdorf, Neuenhagen, Fredersdorf, Charlottenburg, Brandenburger Tor, Dom, Lichtenberg, Olympiastadion, Tiergarten, Kreuzberg, Treptow, Kaulsdorf, FLUGHAFEN BERLIN-GATOW, Berliner Forst Grunewald, Schöneberg, CENTRAL FLUGHAFEN BERLIN-TEMPELHOF, Neukölln, Karlshorst, Berliner Stadtforst, Schöneiche, Kladow, Tempelhof, Steglitz, KÖPENICK, Spree, Grosser Müggelsee, Rahnsdorf, Erkner, Zehlendorf, Buckow, Königs heide, Berliner Stadtforst Köpenick, Langer See, Müggelheim, POTSDAM, Wannsee, Kleinmachnow, Rudow, Bohnsdorf, Seddin-See, Eichwalde, Babelsberg, TELTOW, Lichtenrade, Zeuthener See, Werder, Stahnsdorf, Mahlow, Schulzendorf, Drewitz, Grossbeeren, FLUGHAFEN BERLIN-SCHÖNEFELD, Blankenfelde, Wildau, Dahlewitz, Oder-Spree-Kanal, BERLINER RING

© Oxford University Press

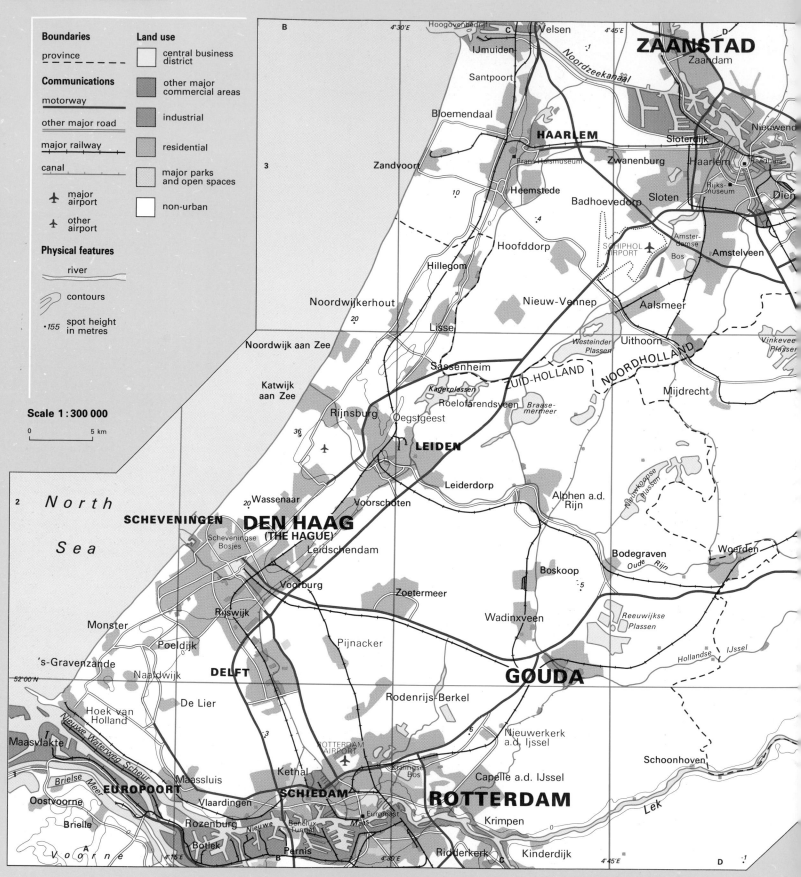

Boundaries
province

Communications
motorway
other major road
major railway
canal

✈ major airport
✈ other airport

Physical features
river
contours
·155 spot height in metres

Land use
central business district
other major commercial areas
industrial
residential
major parks and open spaces
non-urban

Scale 1 : 300 000
0   5 km

North Sea

ZAANSTAD
Zaandam
Nieuwend
Sloterdijk
Haarlem
Raadhuis
Rijks-museum
Dien
HAARLEM
Frans Halsmuseum
Zwanenburg
Badhoevedorp
Sloten
Amster-damse Bos
Amstelveen
SCHIPHOL AIRPORT
Velsen
IJmuiden
Santpoort
Bloemendaal
Zandvoort
Heemstede
Hoofddorp
Hillegom
Nieuw-Vennep
Aalsmeer
Uithoorn
Vinkevee Plasser
Noordwijkerhout
Lisse
Westeinder Plassen
ZUID-HOLLAND
NOORDHOLLAND
Mijdrecht
Noordwijk aan Zee
Sassenheim
Kagerplassen
Roelofarendsveen
Braase-mermeer
Katwijk aan Zee
Rijnsburg
Oegstgeest
LEIDEN
Leiderdorp
Alphen a.d. Rijn
Nieuwkoopse Plassen
Woerden
Wassenaar
Voorschoten
Bodegraven
Oude Rijn
SCHEVENINGEN
DEN HAAG (THE HAGUE)
Scheveningse Bosjes
Leidschendam
Boskoop
Voorburg
Zoetermeer
Wadinxveen
Reeuwijkse Plassen
Monster
Rijswijk
Poeldijk
Pijnacker
Hollandse IJssel
's-Gravenzande
Naaldwijk
DELFT
GOUDA
De Lier
Rodenrijs-Berkel
Hoek van Holland
Nieuwerkerk a.d. Ijssel
Schoonhoven
Maasvlakte
Nieuwe Waterweg Scheur
Maassluis
Kethal
ROTTERDAM AIRPORT
Gravingse Bos
Capelle a.d. IJssel
Lek
EUROPOORT
Vlaardingen
SCHIEDAM
ROTTERDAM
Brielse Meer
Oostvoorne
Rozenburg
Nieuwe
Benelux Tunnel
Maas
Euromast
Krimpen
Brielle
Botlek
Pernis
Ridderkerk
Kinderdijk
Voorne

area of satellite image

© Oxford University Press

Amsterdam and the IJsselmeer.
False colour satellite image.
Red/pink : agricultural land.
Polders have a higher percentage of blue.
Dark red/green : heathland.
Black : water.
Shallower water is shown lighter.

Scale
0   25   50 km

Boundaries
international
internal

Communications
motorway
other major road
railway
canal
✈ major airport

Physical features
marsh

Cities and towns
built-up areas
■ over 1 million inhabitants
● more than 100 000 inhabitants
• smaller towns

Land height
metres
500
300
200
100
sea level
land below sea level
▲ spot height in metres

Scale : 2 000 000
0   25   50 km

Technical Orthomorphic Projection

© Oxford University Press

Scale 1 : 5 000 000

0   50   100 km

Scale 1 : 3 000 000

0   25   50 km

Conical Orthomorphic Projection

© Oxford University Press

Balearic Islands
(Spain)

Boundaries

international

Communications

motorway

other major road

railway

canal

✈ major airport

Cities and towns

⬭ built-up areas

■ over 1 million inhabitants

● more than 100 000 inhabitants

• smaller towns

Physical features

⌇ marsh

❄ ice cap

Land height

metres
3000
2000
1000
500
300
200
100
sea level
land below sea level

▲ spot height in metres

Scale 1 : 5 000 000   0   50   100 km

Conical Orthomorphic Projection

© Oxford University Press

Scale 1 : 5 000 000

0   50   100 km

Conical Orthomorpic Projection
© Oxford University Press

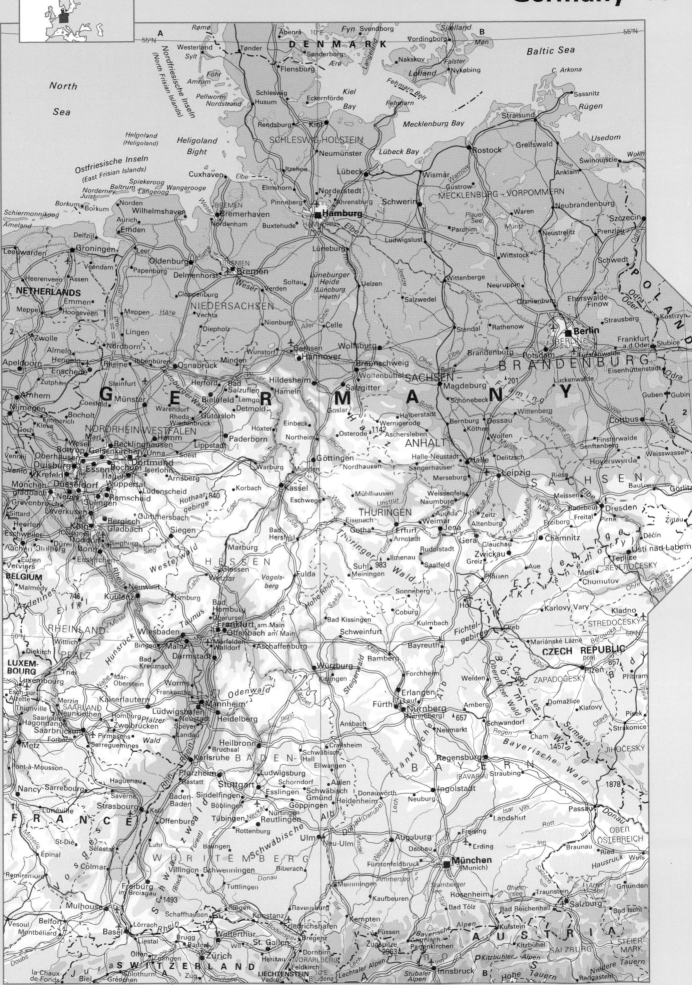

Scale 1:3 500 000   0   25   50 km

Conical Orthomorphic Projection

Boundaries
International
Internal

Communications
Motorway
Other major road
Railway
Canal
major airport

Cities and towns
built-up areas
over 1 million inhabitants
more than 100 000 inhabitants
smaller towns

Physical features
marsh
ice cap

Land height
metres
3000
2000
1000
500
300
200
100
sea level
land below sea level
▲ spot height in metres

Boundaries

international

internal

Communications

motorway

other major road

railway

canal

✈ major airport

Cities and towns

◇ built-up areas

■ over 1 million inhabitants

● more than 100 000 inhabitants

• smaller towns

+ historic sites

Physical features

seasonal river/lake

marsh

salt pan

Sea Ice

pack ice spring max.

Land height

metres
5000
3000
2000
1000
500
300
200
100
sea level
land below sea level

▲ spot height in metres

Scale 1: 5 000 000

0   50   100 km

Scale 1 : 6 250 000

0   50   100 km

Conical Orthomorphic Projection   © Oxford University Press

ICELAND

Boundaries

International

Internal

Communications

motorway

other major road

railway

canal

✈ major airport

Cities and towns

⬠ built-up area

■ over 1 million inhabitants

● more than 100 000 inhabitants

• smaller towns

Physical features

marsh

ice cap

Land height

metres

2000

1000

500

300

200

100

sea level

land below sea level

▲ spot height in metres

Scale 1:8 500 000

0   100   200 km

Modified Conical Orthomorphic Projection

© Oxford University Press

Land height | Sea depth

Land height		Sea depth
metres		sea level
5000		200
3000		3000
2000		4000
1000		5000
500		6000
300		
200		
100		
sea level land below sea level		maximum extent of glaciation
spot height in metres		ice cap
		sand desert

Land below sea level and sea depths shown as minus numbers

— · — · — international boundary

Scale 1:44 000 000   0   500   1000 km

Zenithal Equal Area Pro

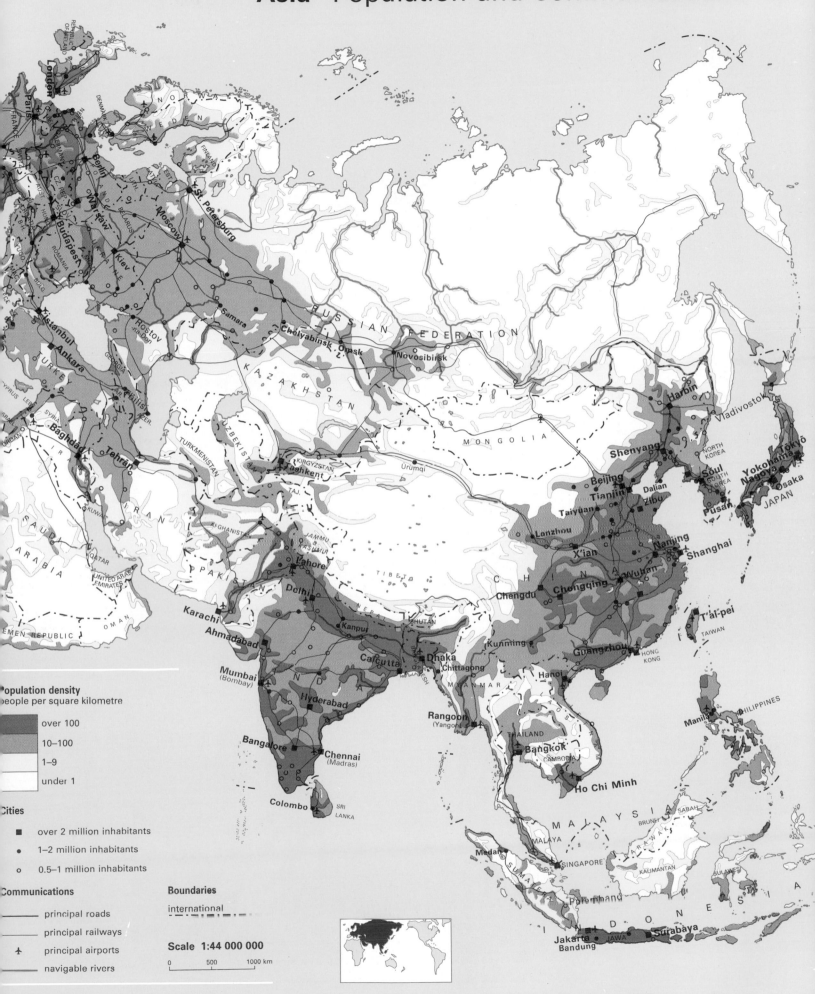

Population density
people per square kilometre

- over 100
- 10–100
- 1–9
- under 1

Cities

- ■ over 2 million inhabitants
- ● 1–2 million inhabitants
- ○ 0.5–1 million inhabitants

Communications

- —— principal roads
- —— principal railways
- ✈ principal airports
- —— navigable rivers

Boundaries

international

Scale 1:44 000 000

0   500   1000 km

Hal Equal Area Projection

xford University Press

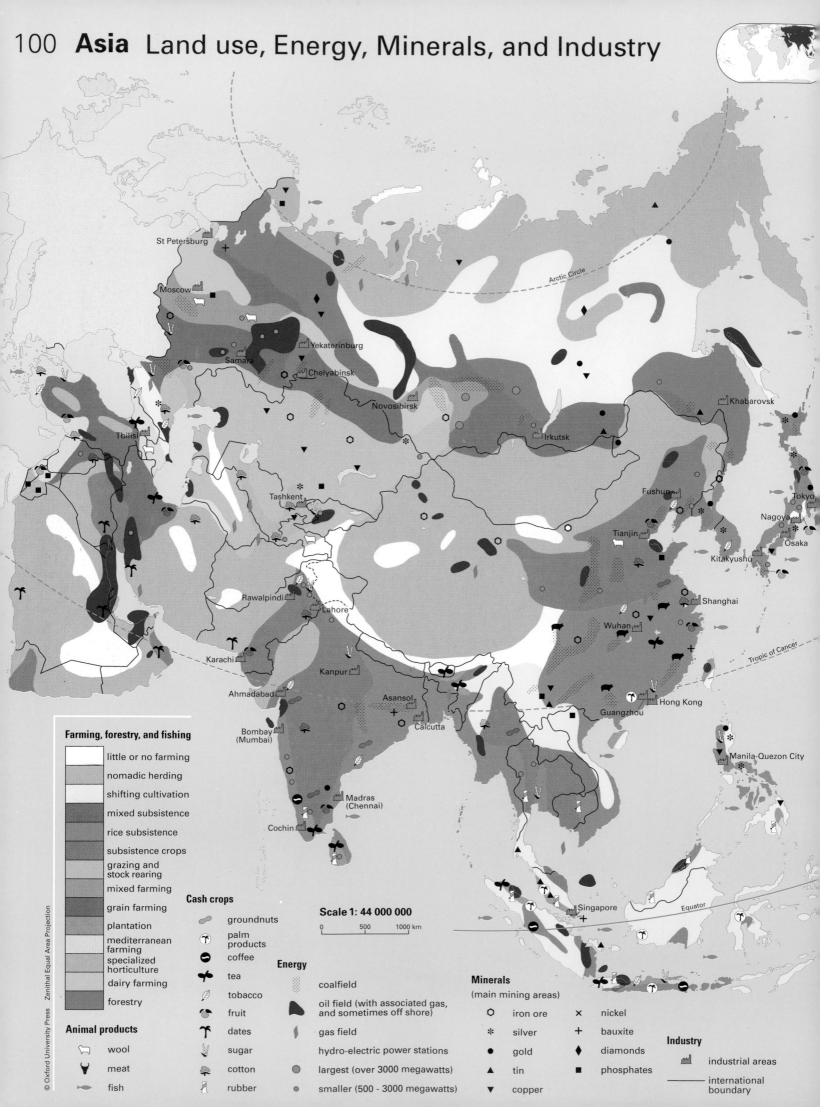

St Petersburg

Arctic Circle

Moscow

Yekaterinburg

Samara

Chelyabinsk

Novosibirsk

Khabarovsk

Irkutsk

Tbilisi

Fushun

Tokyo

Tashkent

Tianjin

Nagoya

Osaka

Kitakyushu

Shanghai

Rawalpindi

Lahore

Wuhan

Tropic of Cancer

Karachi

Kanpur

Ahmadabad

Asansol

Hong Kong

Bombay
(Mumbai)

Calcutta

Guangzhou

Madras
(Chennai)

Cochin

Manila-Quezon City

Singapore

Equator

Farming, forestry, and fishing

- little or no farming
- nomadic herding
- shifting cultivation
- mixed subsistence
- rice subsistence
- subsistence crops
- grazing and stock rearing
- mixed farming
- grain farming
- plantation
- mediterranean farming
- specialized horticulture
- dairy farming
- forestry

Cash crops

- groundnuts
- palm products
- coffee
- tea
- tobacco
- fruit
- dates
- sugar
- cotton
- rubber

Animal products

- wool
- meat
- fish

Energy

- coalfield
- oil field (with associated gas, and sometimes off shore)
- gas field
- hydro-electric power stations
- largest (over 3000 megawatts)
- smaller (500 - 3000 megawatts)

Minerals
(main mining areas)

- iron ore
- silver
- gold
- tin
- copper
- nickel
- bauxite
- diamonds
- phosphates

Industry

- industrial areas
- international boundary

Scale 1: 44 000 000

0   500   1000 km

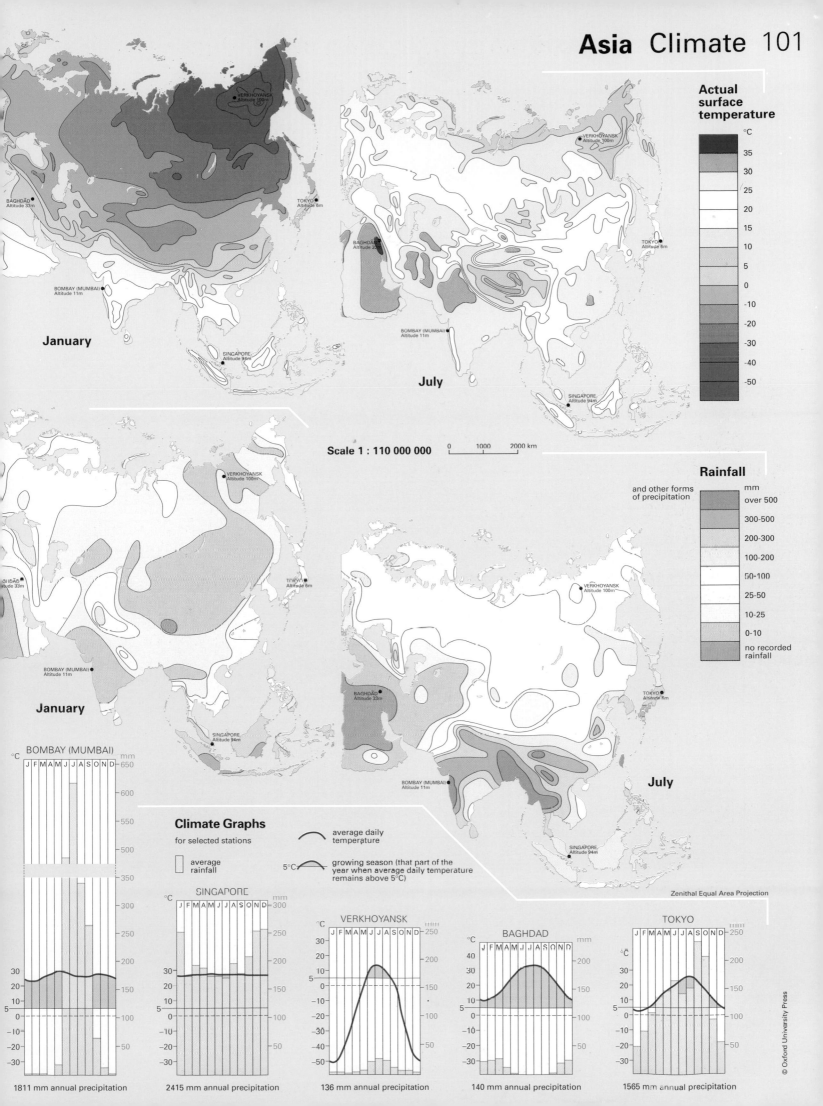

Actual surface temperature

°C
- 35
- 30
- 25
- 20
- 15
- 10
- 5
- 0
- -10
- -20
- -30
- -40
- -50

January

July

Scale 1 : 110 000 000

0   1000   2000 km

Rainfall

and other forms of precipitation

mm
- over 500
- 300-500
- 200-300
- 100-200
- 50-100
- 25-50
- 10-25
- 0-10
- no recorded rainfall

January

July

Zenithal Equal Area Projection

Climate Graphs

for selected stations

[ ] average rainfall

⌒ average daily temperature

5°C ⌒ growing season (that part of the year when average daily temperature remains above 5°C)

BOMBAY (MUMBAI)

SINGAPORE

VERKHOYANSK

BAGHDAD

TOKYO

1811 mm annual precipitation

2415 mm annual precipitation

136 mm annual precipitation

140 mm annual precipitation

1565 mm annual precipitation

© Oxford University Press

Boundaries
international
disputed
internal

Communications
motorway
other major road
railway
canal

✈ major airport

Cities and towns
■ over 1 million inhabitants
● more than 100 000 inhabitants
· smaller towns

Scale 1 : 25 000 000

0   250   500 km

Physical features
seasonal river/lake
marsh
salt pan
ice cap
sand dunes

Land height
metres
5000
3000
2000
1000
500
300
200
100
sea level
land below sea level

▲ spot height in metres

Sea Ice
unnavigable polar ice
pack ice autumn minimum
pack ice spring maximum

Boundaries
city limit/oblast

Land use
central business district
other major commercial areas
industrial
residential
major parks and open spaces
non-urban

Scale 1 : 300 000

0   5 km

Conical Orthomorphic Projection

Boundaries

international

disputed
∿∿∿∿∿∿∿∿∿

Communications

motorway

other major road

railway

canal

✈ major airport

Cities and towns

■ over 1 million
inhabitants

● more than 100 000
inhabitants

• smaller towns

Physical features

seasonal
river/lake

marsh

salt pan

ice cap

sand dunes

salt lake

Sea Ice

pack ice
spring max.

Land height

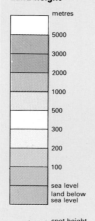

metres	
	5000
	3000
	2000
	1000
	500
	300
	200
	100
	sea level
	land below sea level

▲ spot height
in metres

Scale 1: 12 500 000

0 100 200 300 km

Conical Orthomorphic Projection

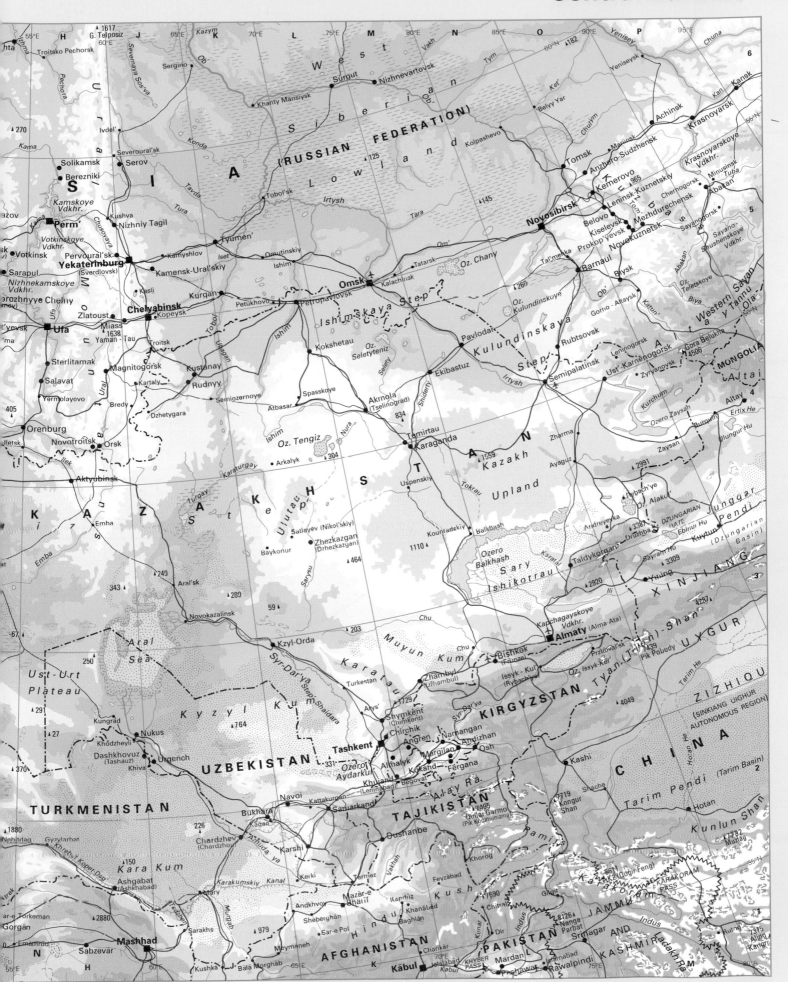

Israel & Lebanon

Scale 1:4 000 000

Conical Orthomorphic Projection

Boundaries

international
disputed
internal

Communications

motorway
other major road
railway
canal
✈ major airport

Cities and towns

■ over 1 million inhabitants
● more than 100 000 inhabitants
• smaller towns
+ historic sites

Physical features

seasonal river/lake
marsh
salt pan
ice cap
sand dunes

Land height

metres
5000
3000
2000
1000
500
300
200
100
sea level
land below sea level
▲ spot height in metres

Scale 1:12 500 000

0   125   250 km

© Oxford University Press

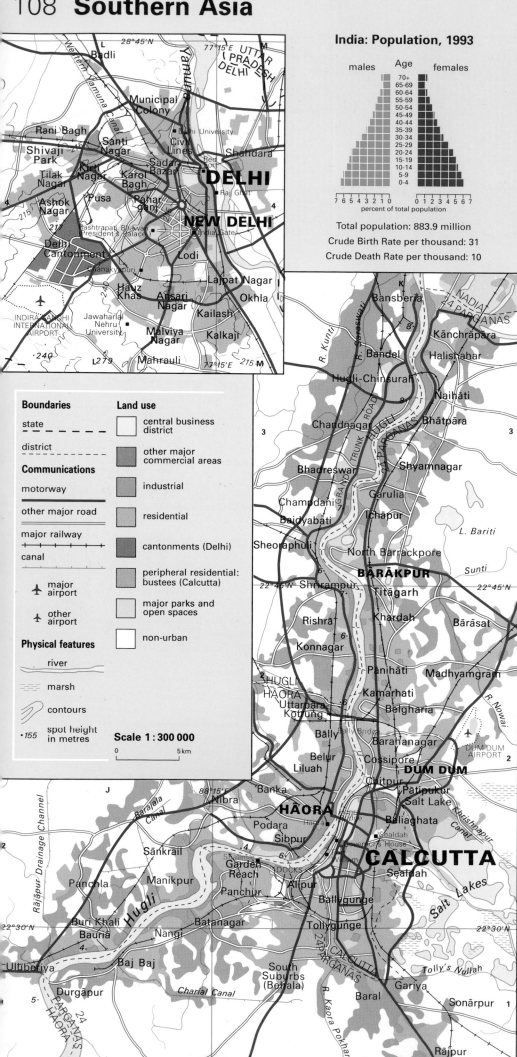

India: Population, 1993

males | Age | females
70+
65-69
60-64
55-59
50-54
45-49
40-44
35-39
30-34
25-29
20-24
15-19
10-14
5-9
0-4

7 6 5 4 3 2 1 0 | 0 1 2 3 4 5 6 7
percent of total population

Total population: 883.9 million
Crude Birth Rate per thousand: 31
Crude Death Rate per thousand: 10

Boundaries
state
district

Communications
motorway
other major road
major railway
canal

✈ major airport
✈ other airport

Physical features
river
marsh
contours
·155 spot height in metres

Land use
central business district
other major commercial areas
industrial
residential
cantonments (Delhi)
peripheral residential: bustees (Calcutta)
major parks and open spaces
non-urban

Scale 1 : 300 000
0   5km

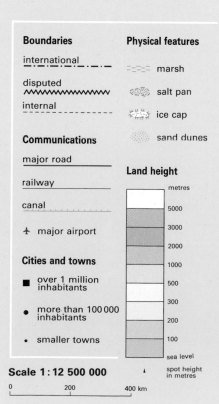

Boundaries
international
disputed
internal

Communications
major road
railway
canal
✈ major airport

Cities and towns
■ over 1 million inhabitants
● more than 100 000 inhabitants
• smaller towns

Physical features
marsh
salt pan
ice cap
sand dunes

Land height
metres
5000
3000
2000
1000
500
300
200
100
sea level
▴ spot height in metres

Scale 1 : 12 500 000
0   200   400 km

INDIA

CHINA

XIZANG ZIZHIQU (TIBET)

NEPAL

BHUTAN

BANGLA DESH

MYANMAR (BURMA)

SRI LANKA

MALDIVES

Bay of Bengal

Andaman Is. (India)

Nicobar Is. (India)

AKSHADWEEP (India)

JAMMU AND KASHMIR

HIMACHAL PRADESH

PUNJAB

HARYANA

RAJASTHAN

UTTAR PRADESH

BIHAR

WEST BENGAL

ASSAM

MEGHALAYA

NAGALAND

MANIPUR

MIZORAM

TRIPURA

ARUNACHAL PRADESH

SIKKIM

MADHYA PRADESH

GUJARAT

MAHARASHTRA

ORISSA

ANDHRA PRADESH

KARNATAKA

KERALA

TAMIL NADU

DADRA & NAGAR HAVELI

DAMAN D&D

Thar Desert

Deccan

Western Ghats

Eastern Ghats

Coromandel Coast

Malabar Coast

Vindhya Range

Satpura Range

Mahadeo Hills

Maikala Ra.

Nilgiri Hills

Cardamom Hills

Kunlun Shan

Nyainqêntanglha Shan

Tanggula Shan

Mouths of the Ganga

Mouths of the Irrawaddy

Adam's Bridge

Gulf of Mannar

Palk Str.

North Andaman

Middle Andaman

South Andaman

Little Andaman

Car Nicobar

Little Nicobar

Great Nicobar

Duncan Passage

Ten Degree Channel

Nine Degree Channel

Faisalabad · Lahore · Ludhiana · Delhi · New Delhi · Jaipur · Kanpur · Lucknow · Ahmadabad · Bhopal · Indore · Nagpur · Mumbai (Bombay) · Pune · Hyderabad · Bangalore · Chennai (Madras) · Calcutta · Patna · Varanasi · Dhaka · Chittagong · Colombo · Kandy · Mandalay

Kathmandu · Thimphu · Lhasa · Islamabad · Rawalpindi · Srinagar · Jammu · Amritsar · Chandigarh · Dehra Dun · Meerut · Agra · Gwalior · Jhansi · Allahabad · Jabalpur · Raipur · Bhubaneshwar · Cuttack · Vishakhapatnam · Vijayawada · Guntur · Nellore · Madurai · Trivandrum · Cochin · Coimbatore · Mysore · Jaffna · Trincomalee · Galle

Mt. Everest 8848 · K2 (Godwin Austen) 8611 · Nanda Devi 7816 · Kamet 7755 · Annapurna 8091 · Kangchenjunga

Indus · Ganga · Brahmaputra · Yamuna · Narmada · Tapti · Godavari · Krishna · Mahanadi · Chambal · Son · Kosi · Yarlung Zangbo Jiang (Tsangpo) · Nu Jiang (Salween) · Jinsha Jiang (Yangtze) · Lancang Jiang · Irrawaddy

Homolographic Projection

Oxford University Press

Scale 1: 3 500 000

50 km
25
0

Part of the Ganges Delta. False colour satellite image.
Blue/grey : urban areas (Dhaka is top left).
Red : vegetation. Green/yellow : sparse vegetation and bare soil.
Dark blue : water (paler blue where rich in silt and
white where silt is exposed above the water level).

area of
main map
area of
satellite
image

Dhaka

Scale

30 km
20
10
0

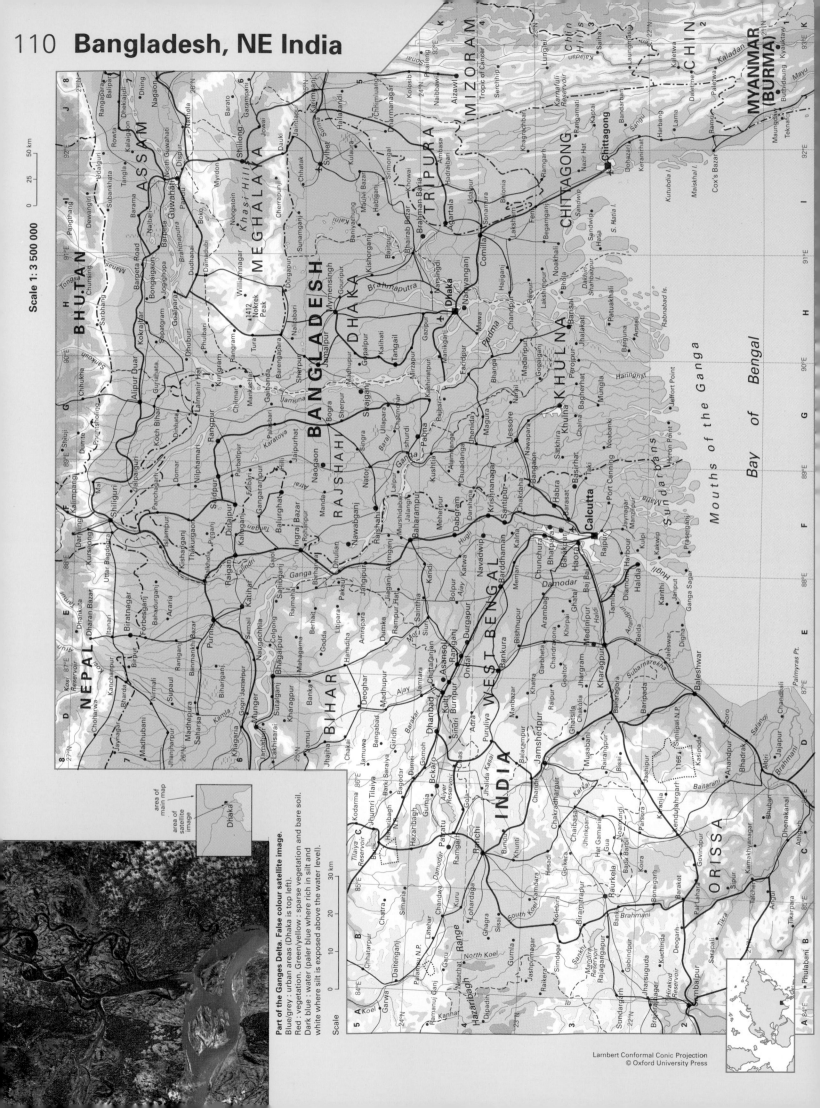

Lambert Conformal Conic Projection
© Oxford University Press

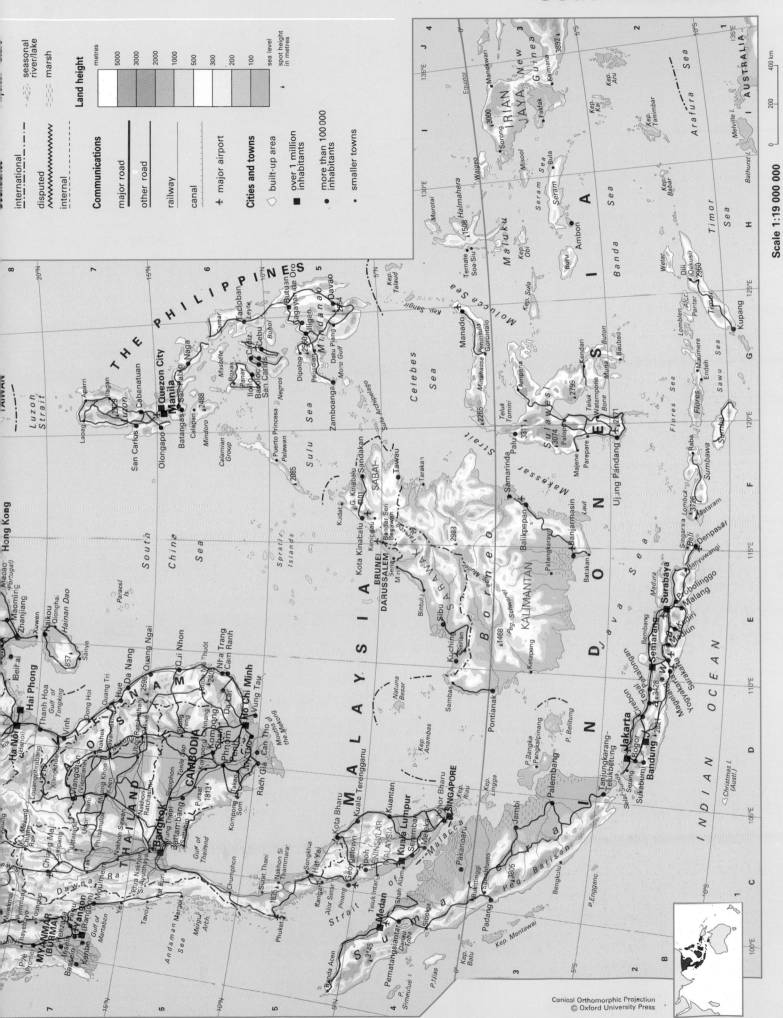

Scale 1:19 000 000

Boundaries
international
disputed
internal

Communications
motorway
motorway under construction
other major road
railway
railway tunnel
canal
✈ major airport

Cities and towns
⬠ built-up areas
■ over 1 million inhabitants
● more than 100 000 inhabitants
• smaller towns

Physical features
seasonal river/lake
marsh
salt pan
ice cap
sand dunes

Land height
metres
5000
3000
2000
1000
500
300
200
100
sea level
land below sea level
▲ spot height in metres

China scale 1 : 19 000 000
0   200   400 km

Conical Orthomorphic Projection

Hong Kong scale 1 : 500 000
0   5 km

Gauss Conformal Projection

© Oxford University

Boijing land use

- central business district
- other major commercial areas
- industrial
- residential
- major parks and open spaces
- non-urban

See page 115 for complete legend

Beijing scale 1 : 300 000

0   5 km

ford University Press

Scale 1: 2 000 000

0   25   50km

PACIFIC OCEAN

Sea of Okhotsk

Sea of Japan

PACIFIC OCEAN

Honshū

Hokkaidō

Kyūshū

Shikoku

Zenithal Equidistant Projection

© Oxford University Press

Scale 1 : 6 250 000

0   50   100 km

Boundaries
international ·—··—··—
internal ·— — — —
national park · · · · · · ·

Communications
motorway
other major road
railway
canal
✈ major airport

Cities and towns
⬭ built-up areas
■ over 1 million inhabitants
● more than 100 000 inhabitants
· smaller towns

Land height

metres
3000
2000
1000
500
300
200
100
sea level

spot height in metres

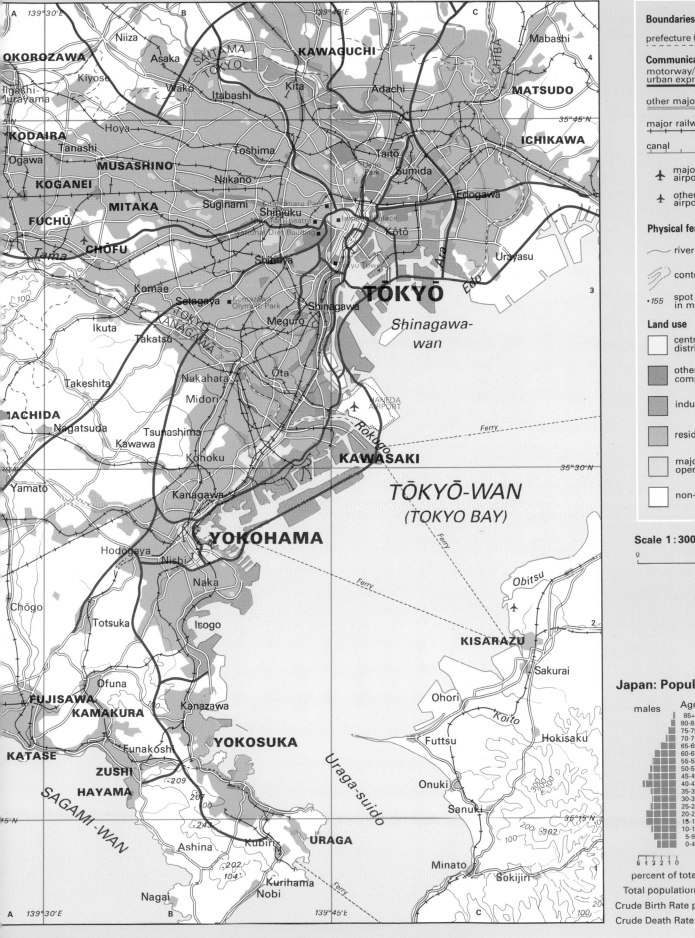

Boundaries

prefecture (Tokyo)

Communications

motorway/
urban expressway

other major road

major railway

canal

✈ major
airport

✈ other
airport

Physical features

~ river

contours

•155 spot height
in metres

Land use

central business
district

other major
commercial areas

industrial

residential

major parks and
open spaces

non-urban

Scale 1 : 300 000

0   5km

Japan: Population, 1992

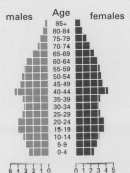

males   Age   females

85+
80-84
75-79
70-74
65-69
60-64
55-59
50-54
45-49
40-44
35-39
30-34
25-29
20-24
15-19
10-14
5-9
0-4

6 4 3 2 1 0   0 1 2 3 4 5

percent of total population

Total population: 124.5 million

Crude Birth Rate per thousand: 10

Crude Death Rate per thousand: 7

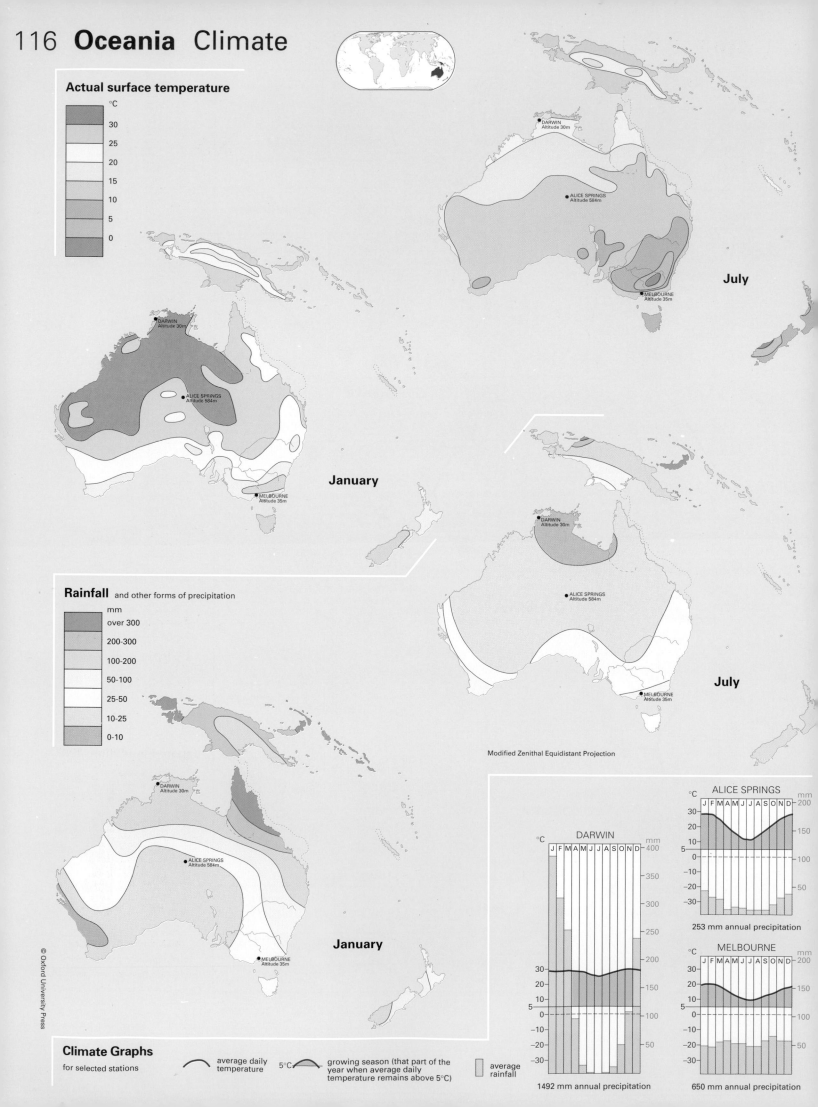

Actual surface temperature

°C
- 30
- 25
- 20
- 15
- 10
- 5
- 0

July

DARWIN
Altitude 30m

ALICE SPRINGS
Altitude 584m

MELBOURNE
Altitude 35m

DARWIN
Altitude 30m

ALICE SPRINGS
Altitude 584m

January

MELBOURNE
Altitude 35m

Rainfall and other forms of precipitation

mm
- over 300
- 200-300
- 100-200
- 50-100
- 25-50
- 10-25
- 0-10

DARWIN
Altitude 30m

ALICE SPRINGS
Altitude 584m

July

MELBOURNE
Altitude 35m

Modified Zenithal Equidistant Projection

© Oxford University Press

DARWIN
Altitude 30m

ALICE SPRINGS
Altitude 584m

MELBOURNE
Altitude 35m

January

Climate Graphs
for selected stations

— average daily temperature

5°C — growing season (that part of the year when average daily temperature remains above 5°C)

average rainfall

DARWIN

°C / mm / J F M A M J J A S O N D

1492 mm annual precipitation

ALICE SPRINGS

°C / mm

253 mm annual precipitation

MELBOURNE

°C / mm

650 mm annual precipitation

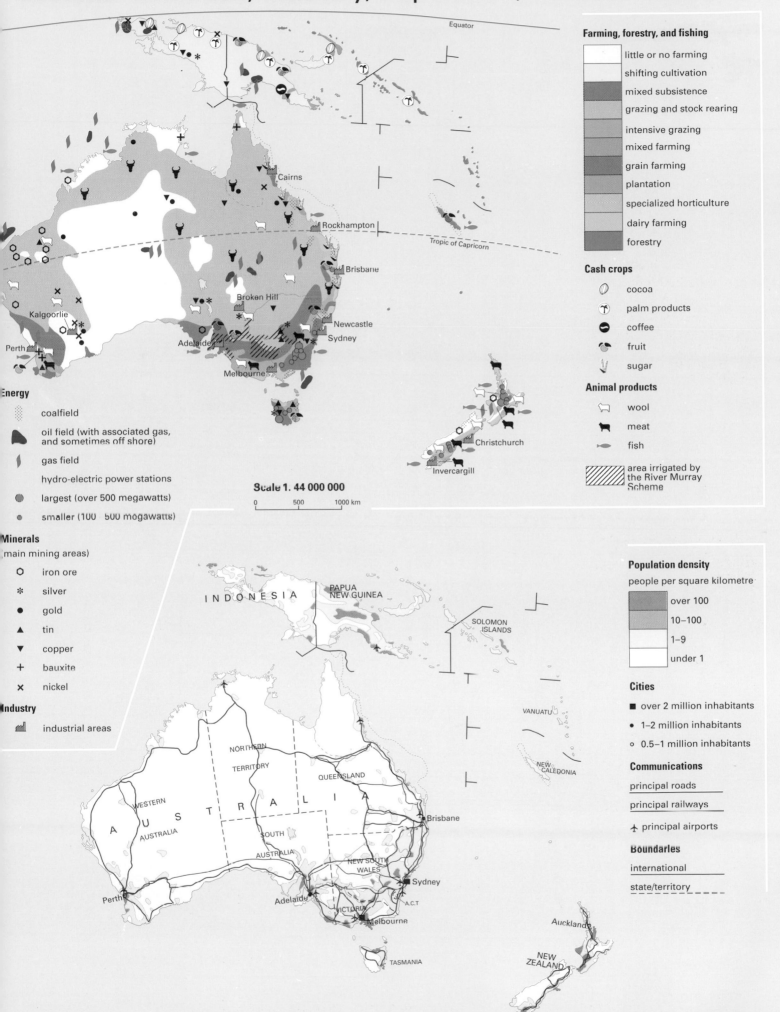

Farming, forestry, and fishing

- little or no farming
- shifting cultivation
- mixed subsistence
- grazing and stock rearing
- intensive grazing
- mixed farming
- grain farming
- plantation
- specialized horticulture
- dairy farming
- forestry

Cash crops

- cocoa
- palm products
- coffee
- fruit
- sugar

Animal products

- wool
- meat
- fish

area irrigated by the River Murray Scheme

Energy

- coalfield
- oil field (with associated gas, and sometimes off shore)
- gas field
- hydro-electric power stations
- largest (over 500 megawatts)
- smaller (100 – 500 megawatts)

Minerals

(main mining areas)

- iron ore
- silver
- gold
- tin
- copper
- bauxite
- nickel

Industry

- industrial areas

Population density

people per square kilometre

- over 100
- 10–100
- 1–9
- under 1

Cities

- over 2 million inhabitants
- 1–2 million inhabitants
- 0.5–1 million inhabitants

Communications

- principal roads
- principal railways
- principal airports

Boundaries

- international
- state/territory

Scale 1. 44 000 000

0   500   1000 km

Cairns
Rockhampton
Tropic of Capricorn
Brisbane
Broken Hill
Newcastle
Sydney
Adelaide
Melbourne
Kalgoorlie
Perth
Christchurch
Invercargill

Equator

INDONESIA
PAPUA NEW GUINEA
SOLOMON ISLANDS
VANUATU
NEW CALEDONIA

AUSTRALIA
WESTERN AUSTRALIA
NORTHERN TERRITORY
QUEENSLAND
SOUTH AUSTRALIA
NEW SOUTH WALES
VICTORIA
A.C.T
Perth
Adelaide
Melbourne
Sydney
Brisbane
TASMANIA
Auckland
NEW ZEALAND

Modified Zenithal Equidistant Projection
© Oxford University Press

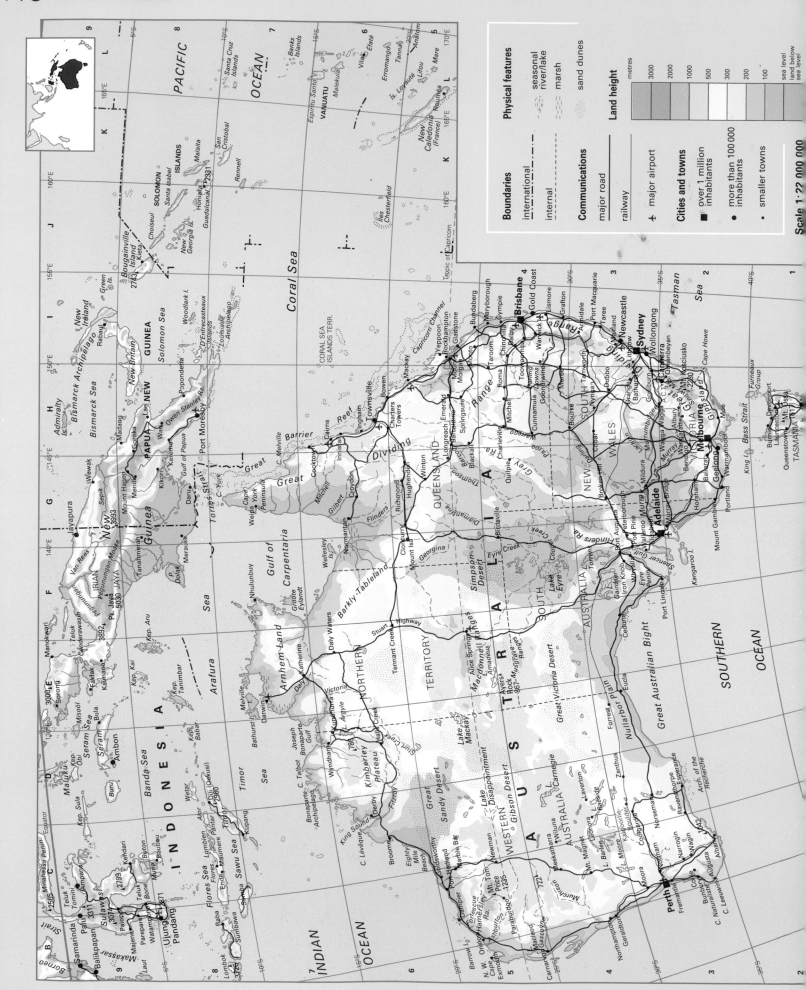

Physical features

- seasonal river/lake
- marsh
- sand dunes

Land height

metres
3000 2000 1000 500 300 200 100 sea level / land below sea level

Boundaries

- international
- internal

Communications

- major road
- railway
- ✈ major airport

Cities and towns

- ■ over 1 million inhabitants
- ● more than 100 000 inhabitants
- · smaller towns

Scale 1:22 000 000

Zenithal Equidistant Projection
© Oxford University Press

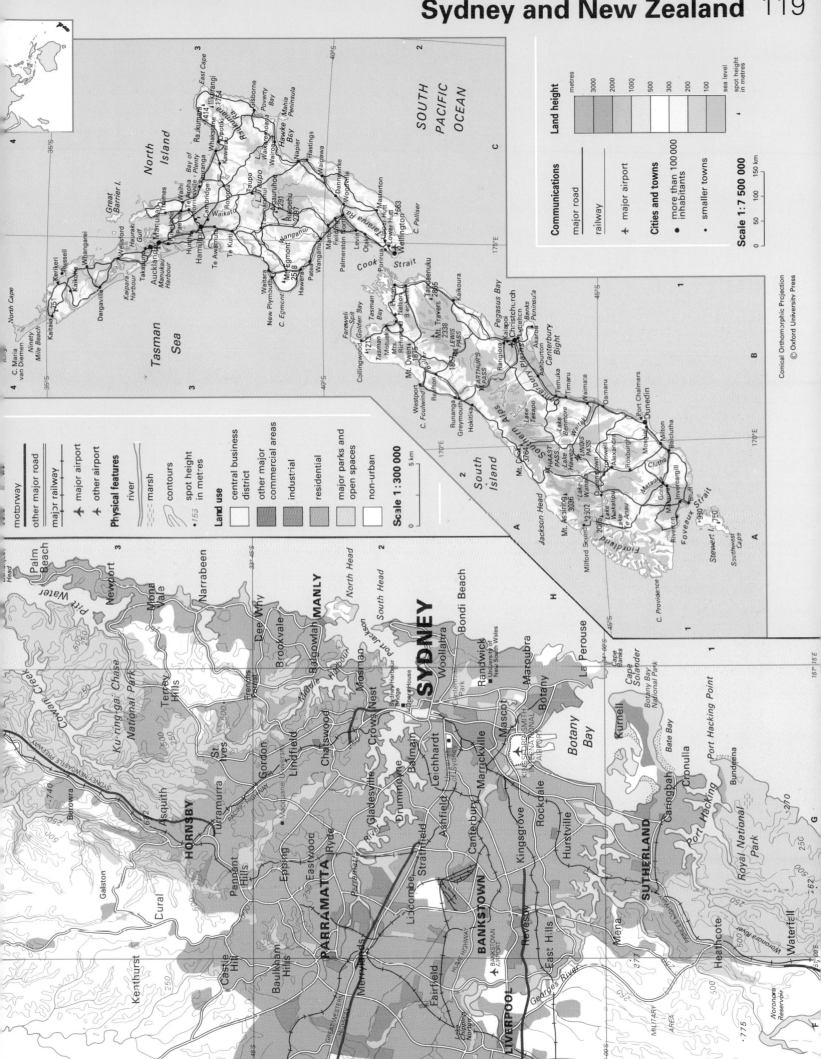

Land height

metres
3000
2000
1000
500
300
200
100
sea level
▲ spot height in metres

Communications

major road
railway
✈ major airport

Cities and towns

● more than 100 000 inhabitants
• smaller towns

Scale 1:7 500 000

0   50   100   150 km

Conical Orthomorphic Projection

© Oxford University Press

SOUTH PACIFIC OCEAN

North Island

Tasman Sea

South Island

motorway
other major road
major railway
✈ major airport
✈ other airport

Physical features

river
marsh
contours
•155 spot height in metres

Land use

central business district
other major commercial areas
industrial
residential
major parks and open spaces
non-urban

Scale 1:300 000

0   5 km

SYDNEY

HORNSBY

PARRAMATTA

BANKSTOWN

LIVERPOOL

SUTHERLAND

MANLY

Botany Bay

Port Jackson

KINGSFORD SMITH INTERNATIONAL AIRPORT

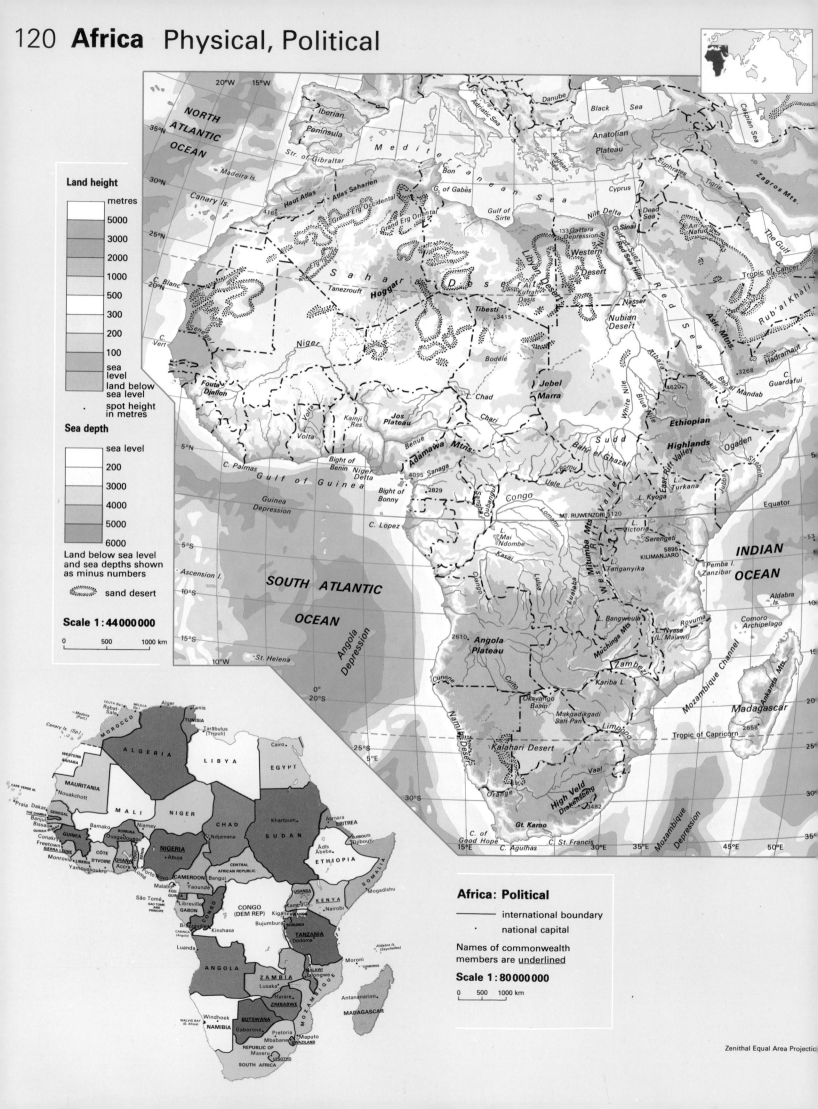

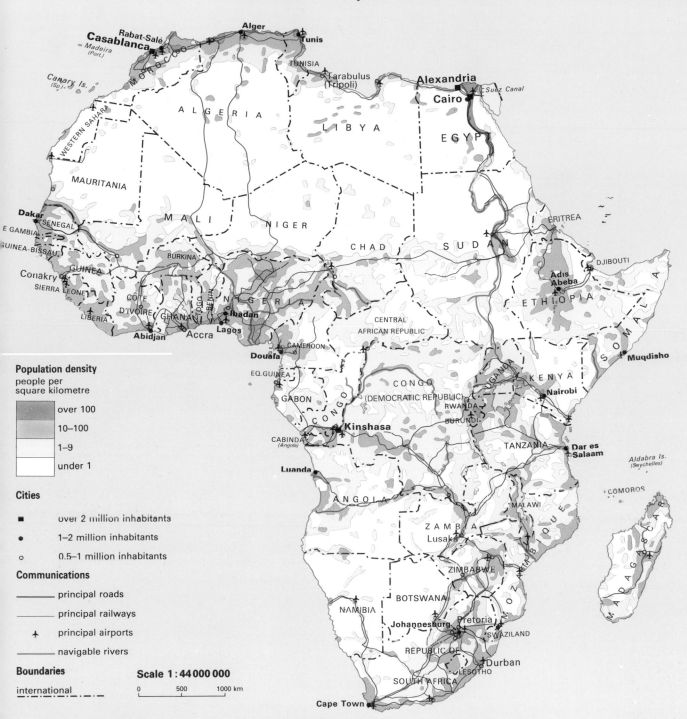

Population density

people per
square kilometre

	over 100
	10–100
	1–9
	under 1

Cities

■ over 2 million inhabitants

● 1–2 million inhabitants

○ 0.5–1 million inhabitants

Communications

—— principal roads

—— principal railways

✈ principal airports

—— navigable rivers

Boundaries

international — · —

Scale 1 : 44 000 000

0   500   1000 km

Oxford University Press

Algeria: Population, 1994

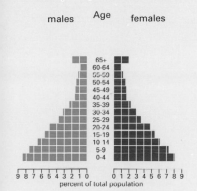

males   Age   females

percent of total population

Total population: 22.6 million

Crude Birth Rate per thousand: 30

Crude Death Rate per thousand: 6

Egypt: Population, 1992

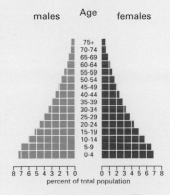

males   Age   females

percent of total population

Total population: 55.2 million

Crude Birth Rate per thousand: 30

Crude Death Rate per thousand: 8

Congo (D.R.) : Population, 1994

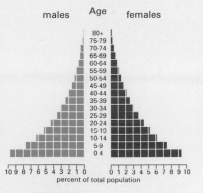

males   Age   females

percent of total population

Total population: 31.0 million

Crude Birth Rate per thousand: 48

Crude Death Rate per thousand: 16

S. Africa: Population, 1994

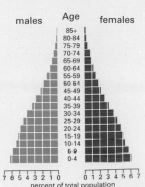

males   Age   females

percent of total population

Total population: 31.0 million

Crude Birth Rate per thousand: 31

Crude Death Rate per thousand: 8

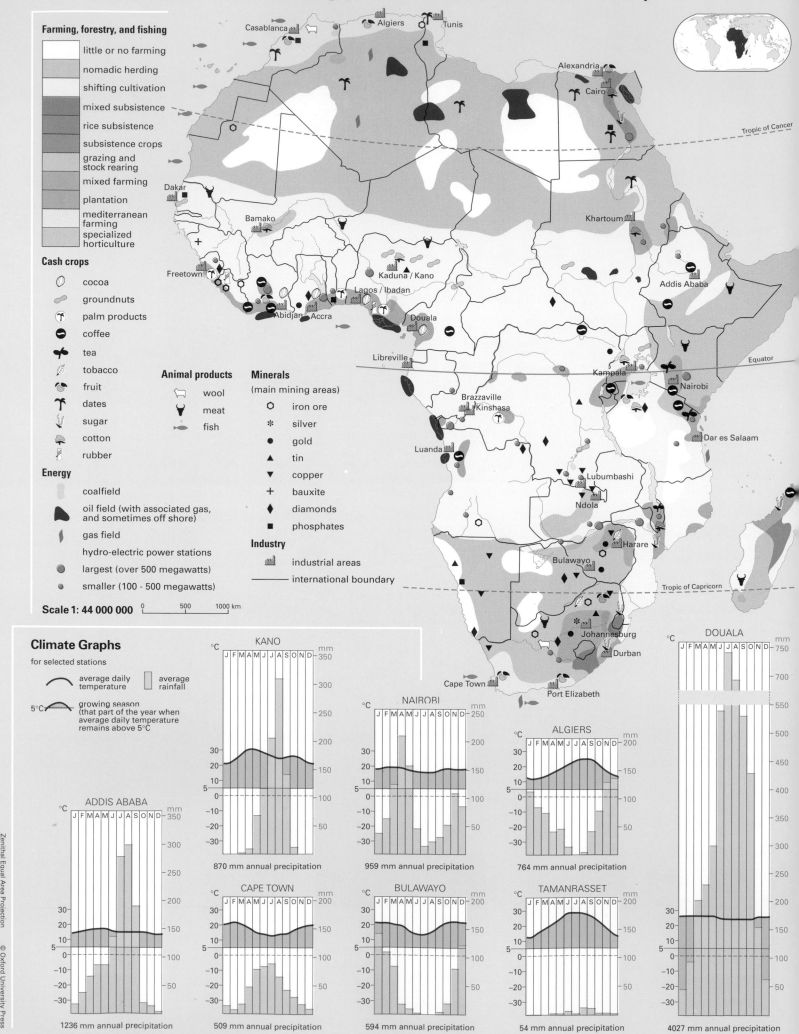

Farming, forestry, and fishing

- little or no farming
- nomadic herding
- shifting cultivation
- mixed subsistence
- rice subsistence
- subsistence crops
- grazing and stock rearing
- mixed farming
- plantation
- mediterranean farming
- specialized horticulture

Cash crops

- cocoa
- groundnuts
- palm products
- coffee
- tea
- tobacco
- fruit
- dates
- sugar
- cotton
- rubber

Animal products

- wool
- meat
- fish

Minerals (main mining areas)

- iron ore
- silver
- gold
- tin
- copper
- bauxite
- diamonds
- phosphates

Energy

- coalfield
- oil field (with associated gas, and sometimes off shore)
- gas field
- hydro-electric power stations
- largest (over 500 megawatts)
- smaller (100 - 500 megawatts)

Industry

- industrial areas
- international boundary

Scale 1: 44 000 000

0   500   1000 km

Tropic of Cancer

Equator

Tropic of Capricorn

Casablanca, Algiers, Tunis, Alexandria, Cairo, Khartoum, Addis Ababa, Dakar, Bamako, Freetown, Kaduna / Kano, Lagos / Ibadan, Abidjan, Accra, Douala, Libreville, Kampala, Nairobi, Brazzaville, Kinshasa, Dar es Salaam, Luanda, Lubumbashi, Ndola, Harare, Bulawayo, Johannesburg, Durban, Cape Town, Port Elizabeth

Climate Graphs

for selected stations

- average daily temperature
- average rainfall
- 5°C growing season (that part of the year when average daily temperature remains above 5°C)

KANO
870 mm annual precipitation

NAIROBI
959 mm annual precipitation

ALGIERS
764 mm annual precipitation

DOUALA
4027 mm annual precipitation

ADDIS ABABA
1236 mm annual precipitation

CAPE TOWN
509 mm annual precipitation

BULAWAYO
594 mm annual precipitation

TAMANRASSET
54 mm annual precipitation

Zenithal Equal Area Projection

© Oxford University Press

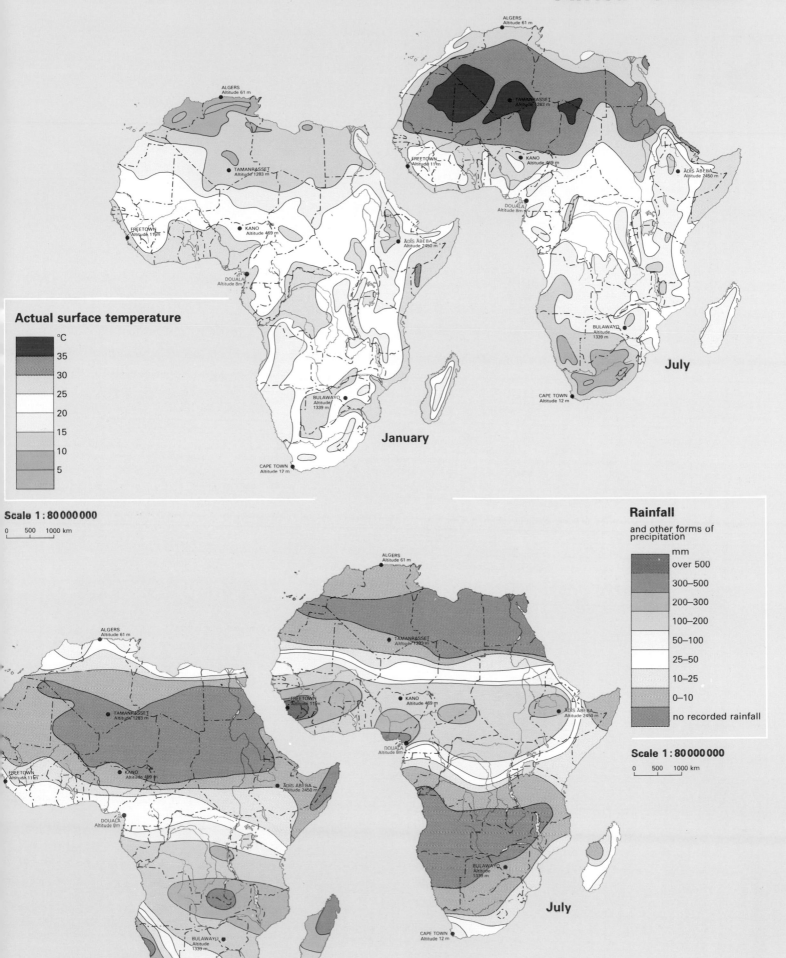

Actual surface temperature

°C
35
30
25
20
15
10
5

January

July

Scale 1 : 80 000 000

0   500   1000 km

Rainfall

and other forms of precipitation

mm
over 500
300–500
200–300
100–200
50–100
25–50
10–25
0–10
no recorded rainfall

Scale 1 : 80 000 000

0   500   1000 km

January

July

Oxford University Press

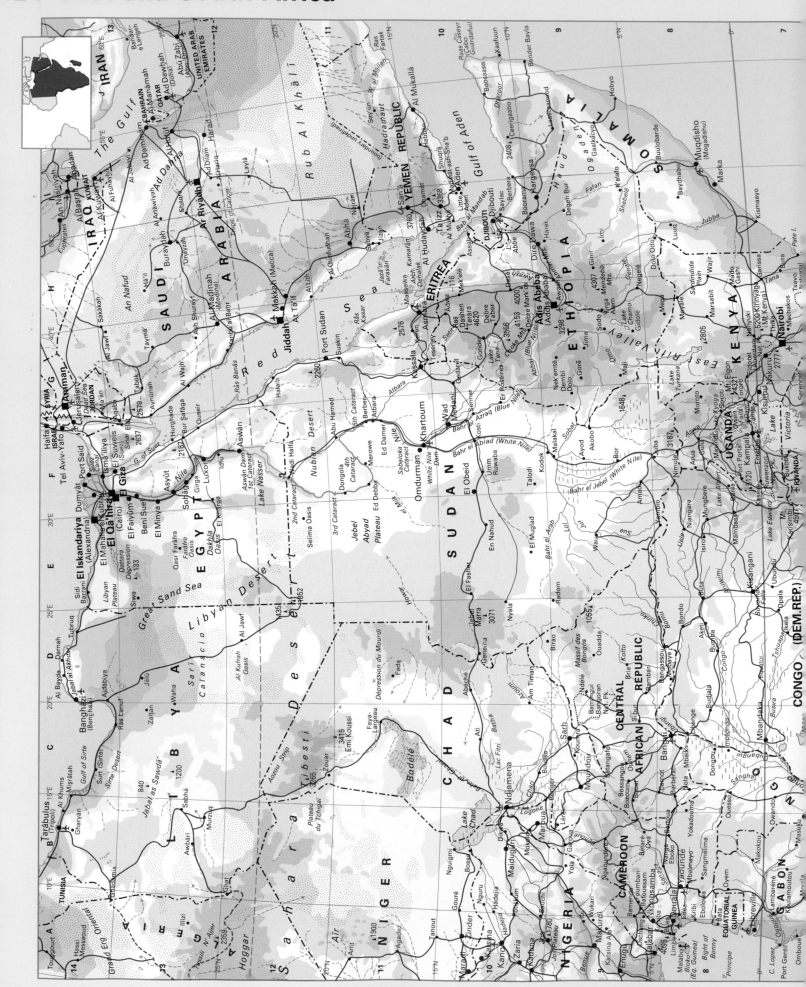

Land height

metres		
5000		
3000		
2000		
1000		
500		
300		
200		
100		
sea level		
land below sea level		

▲ spot height in metres

Physical features

seasonal river/lake
marsh
salt pan
sand dunes

Cities and towns

■ over 1 million inhabitants
● more than 100 000 inhabitants
• smaller towns

Boundaries

international
disputed
internal
national park

Communications

major road
railway
canal
✈ major airport

Scale 1:19 000 000

0   200   400 km

INDIAN OCEAN

ATLANTIC OCEAN

MADAGASCAR

MOZAMBIQUE

TANZANIA

MALAWI

ZAMBIA

ZIMBABWE

ANGOLA

NAMIBIA

BOTSWANA

REPUBLIC OF SOUTH AFRICA

LESOTHO

COMOROS

Kalahari Desert

Namib Desert

Boundaries

governorates

Communications

through routes

other major road

major railway

canal

✈ major airport

✈ other airport

Physical features

river

contours

.155 spot height in metres

Land use

central business district

other major commercial areas

industrial

residential

major parks and open spaces

non-urban

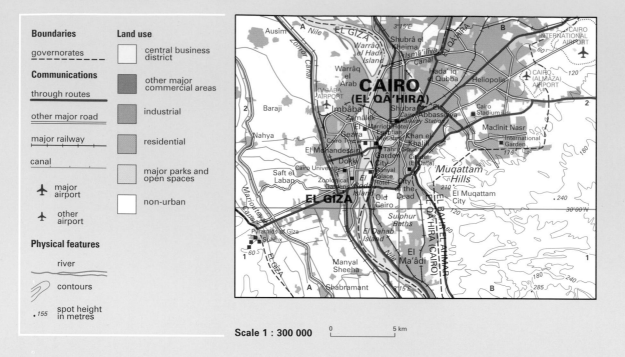

Page 124

Page 125

Scale 1 : 300 000

0   5 km

The Nile Delta and Mount Sinai.
False colour satellite image
Red: agricultural land.
Brown: desert.
Black: water.
The city of Cairo is the dark grey area
at the base of the delta

Scale: 0   50   100 km

© Oxford University Press

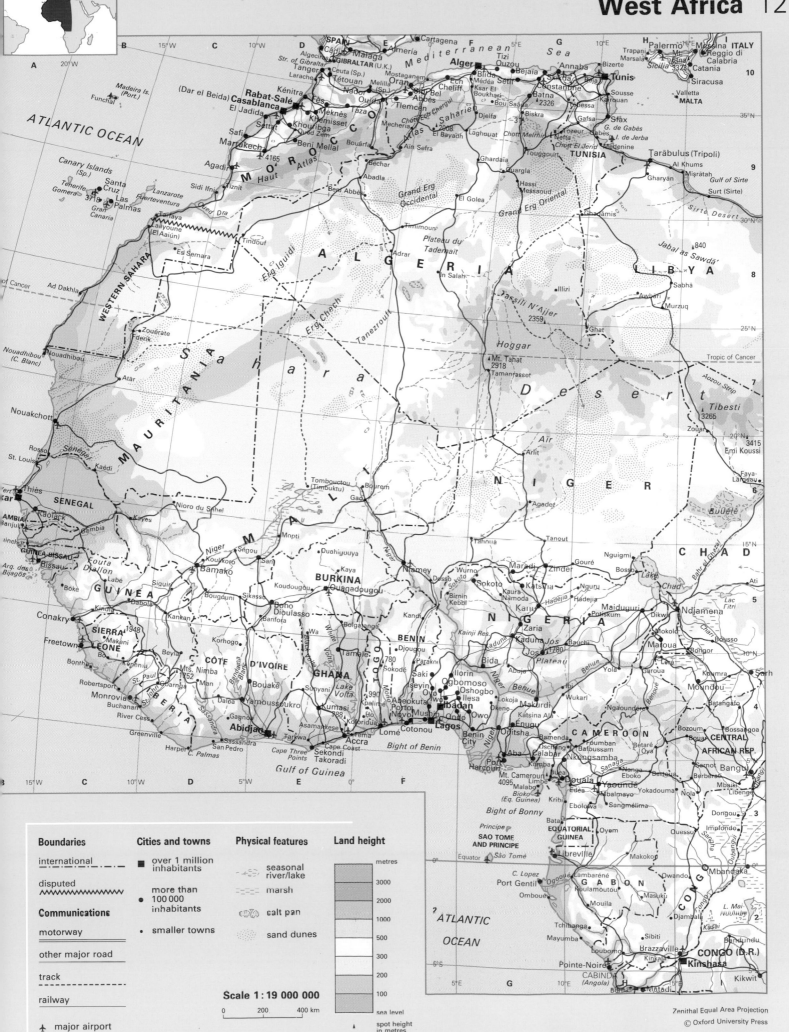

ATLANTIC OCEAN

SPAIN
GIBRALTAR (U.K.)
ITALY
Mediterranean Sea
Alger
Tunis
TUNISIA

MOROCCO
Rabat-Salé
Casablanca
Marrakech
Agadir

Madeira Is. (Port.)
Funchal

Canary Islands (Sp.)
Santa Cruz
Las Palmas
Gran Canaria

Haut Atlas

WESTERN SAHARA
Laâyoune (El Aaiún)

TARĀBULUS (Tripoli)
Gulf of Sirte
Surt (Sirte)
Sirte Desert

LIBYA

ALGERIA

Grand Erg Occidental
Grand Erg Oriental
Plateau du Tademaït
Hoggar
Mt. Tahat 2918
Tamanrasset

S a h a r a   D e s e r t

Tropic of Cancer

Tibesti 3265
Emi Koussi 3415

MAURITANIA
Nouadhibou (C. Blanc)
Nouakchott
Atar

SENEGAL
Dakar
St. Louis

MALI
Tombouctou (Timbuktu)
Gao
Bamako

NIGER
Arlit
Agadez
Niamey

CHAD
Ndjamena
Lake Chad

GAMBIA
GUINEA-BISSAU
Bissau

GUINEA
Conakry

SIERRA LEONE
Freetown

LIBERIA
Monrovia

CÔTE D'IVOIRE
Yamoussoukro
Abidjan

BURKINA
Ouagadougou

GHANA
Kumasi
Accra

TOGO
Lomé

BENIN
Porto Novo
Cotonou

NIGERIA
Kano
Kaduna
Jos
Abuja
Ibadan
Lagos
Benin City
Port Harcourt
Enugu

CAMEROON
Yaoundé
Douala
Mt. Cameroun 4095

EQUATORIAL GUINEA
Malabo
Bioko (Eq. Guinea)

SAO TOME AND PRINCIPE
Principe
São Tomé

Equator

Bight of Benin
Bight of Bonny

Gulf of Guinea

CENTRAL AFRICAN REP.
Bangui

GABON
Libreville
Port Gentil

CONGO
Brazzaville
Pointe-Noire

ATLANTIC OCEAN

CONGO (D.R.)
Kinshasa
CABINDA (Angola)

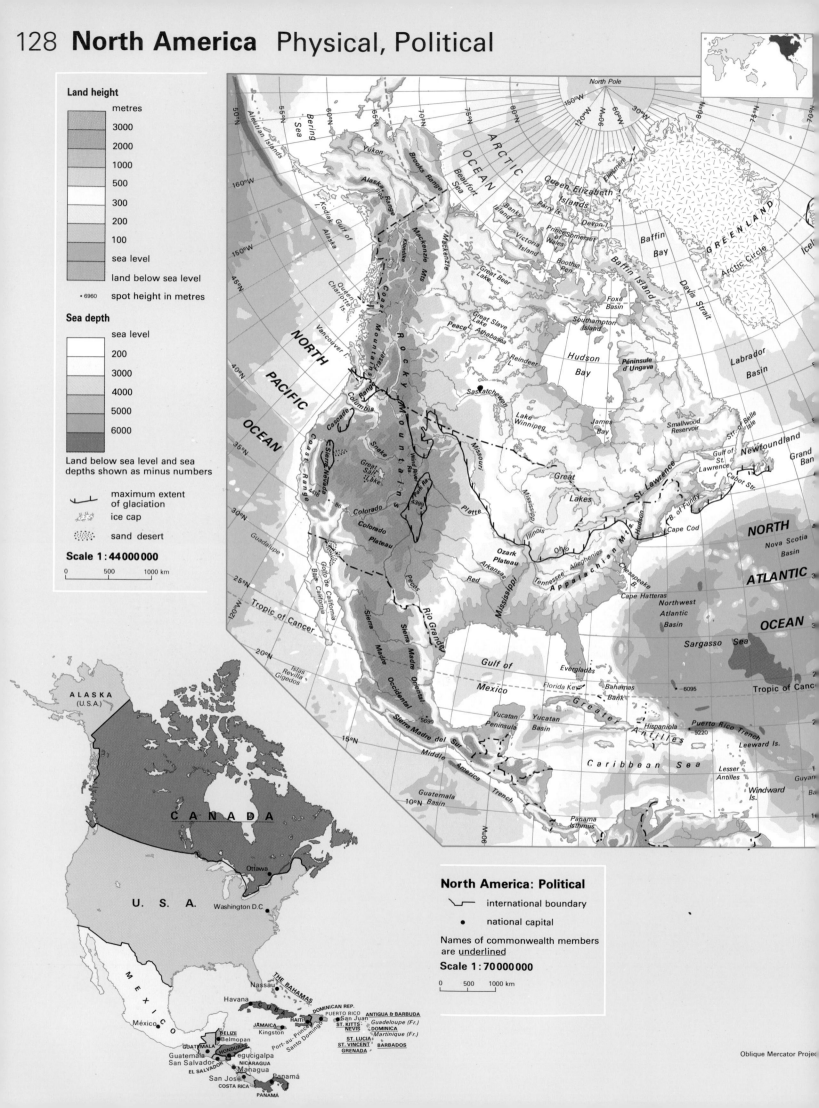

Land height

metres
3000
2000
1000
500
300
200
100
sea level
land below sea level

• 6960 spot height in metres

Sea depth

sea level
200
3000
4000
5000
6000

Land below sea level and sea depths shown as minus numbers

maximum extent of glaciation
ice cap
sand desert

Scale 1 : 44 000 000

0   500   1000 km

North America: Political

international boundary
• national capital

Names of commonwealth members are underlined

Scale 1 : 70 000 000

0   500   1000 km

Oblique Mercator Projec

ALASKA (U.S.A.)
CANADA
Ottawa
U. S. A.
Washington D.C.
M É X I C O
México
Nassau
THE BAHAMAS
Havana
CUBA
HAITI
DOMINICAN REP.
PUERTO RICO
San Juan
ANTIGUA & BARBUDA
Guadeloupe (Fr.)
ST. KITTS-NEVIS
DOMINICA
Martinique (Fr.)
ST. LUCIA
ST. VINCENT
BARBADOS
GRENADA
JAMAICA
Kingston
Port-au-Prince
Santo Domingo
BELIZE
Belmopan
GUATEMALA
Guatemala
San Salvador
HONDURAS
Tegucigalpa
NICARAGUA
EL SALVADOR
Managua
San José
COSTA RICA
PANAMÁ
Panamá

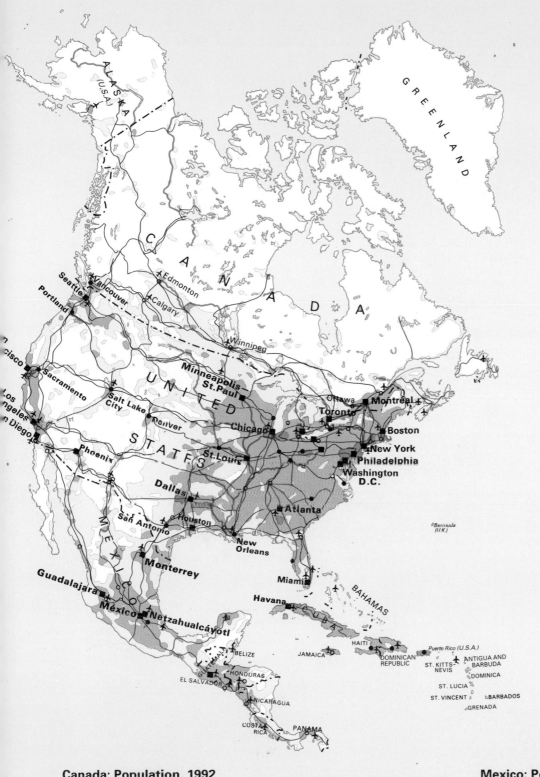

Legend

Population density
people per square kilometre

- over 100
- 10–100
- 1–9
- under 1

Cities

- ■ over 2 million inhabitants
- ● 1–2 million inhabitants
- ○ 0.5–1 million inhabitants

Communications

- —— principal roads
- —— principal railways
- ✈ principal airports
- —— navigable rivers

Boundaries

international —·—·—

Scale 1 : 44 000 000

0   500   1000 km

Jamaica: Population, 1989

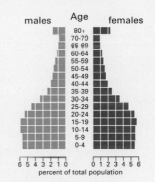

males   Age   females

80+
70-79
65-69
60-64
55-59
50-54
45-49
40-44
35-39
30-34
25-29
20-24
15-19
10-14
5-9
0-4

6 5 4 3 2 1 0   0 1 2 3 4 5 6
percent of total population

Total population: 2.4 million

Crude Birth Rate per thousand: 25

Crude Death Rate per thousand: 6

Canada: Population, 1992

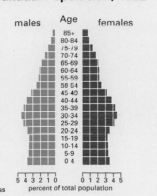

males   Age   females

85+
80-84
75-79
70-74
65-69
60-64
55-59
50-54
45-49
40-44
35-39
30-34
25-29
20-24
15-19
10-14
5-9
0-4

5 4 3 2 1 0   0 1 2 3 4 5
percent of total population

Total population: 27.4 million

Crude Birth Rate per thousand: 14

Crude Death Rate per thousand: 7

Mexico: Population, 1990

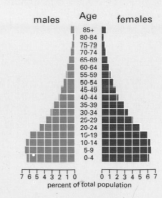

males   Age   females

85+
80-84
75-79
70-74
65-69
60-64
55-59
50-54
45-49
40-44
35-39
30-34
25-29
20-24
15-19
10-14
5-9
0-4

7 6 5 4 3 2 1 0   0 1 2 3 4 5 6 7
percent of total population

Total population: 81.2 million

Crude Birth Rate per thousand: 27

Crude Death Rate per thousand: 5

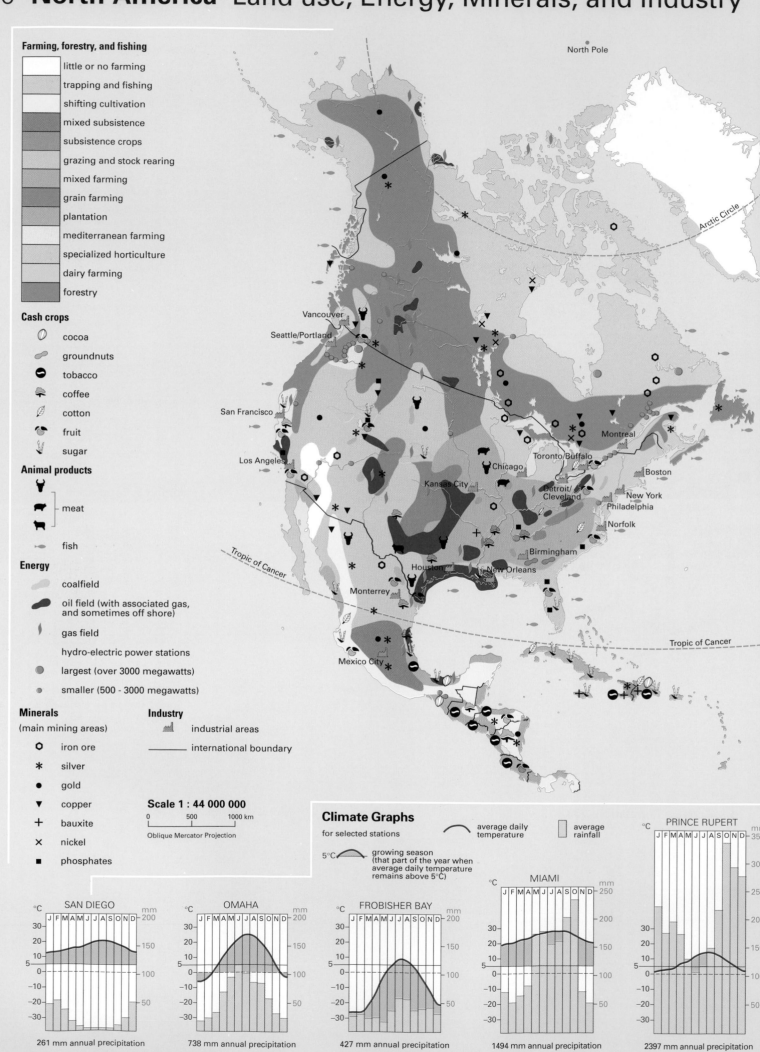

Farming, forestry, and fishing

- little or no farming
- trapping and fishing
- shifting cultivation
- mixed subsistence
- subsistence crops
- grazing and stock rearing
- mixed farming
- grain farming
- plantation
- mediterranean farming
- specialized horticulture
- dairy farming
- forestry

Cash crops

- cocoa
- groundnuts
- tobacco
- coffee
- cotton
- fruit
- sugar

Animal products

- meat
- fish

Energy

- coalfield
- oil field (with associated gas, and sometimes off shore)
- gas field
- hydro-electric power stations
- largest (over 3000 megawatts)
- smaller (500 - 3000 megawatts)

Minerals
(main mining areas)

- ◎ iron ore
- ✳ silver
- ● gold
- ▼ copper
- ✛ bauxite
- ✕ nickel
- ■ phosphates

Industry

- industrial areas
- international boundary

Scale 1 : 44 000 000

0   500   1000 km

Oblique Mercator Projection

© Oxford University Press

Climate Graphs
for selected stations

- average daily temperature
- average rainfall
- growing season (that part of the year when average daily temperature remains above 5°C)

SAN DIEGO
261 mm annual precipitation

OMAHA
738 mm annual precipitation

FROBISHER BAY
427 mm annual precipitation

MIAMI
1494 mm annual precipitation

PRINCE RUPERT
2397 mm annual precipitation

North Pole

Arctic Circle

Vancouver
Seattle/Portland
San Francisco
Los Angeles
Montreal
Toronto/Buffalo
Chicago
Kansas City
Detroit/Cleveland
Boston
New York
Philadelphia
Norfolk
Birmingham
Houston
New Orleans
Monterrey
Mexico City

Tropic of Cancer
Tropic of Cancer

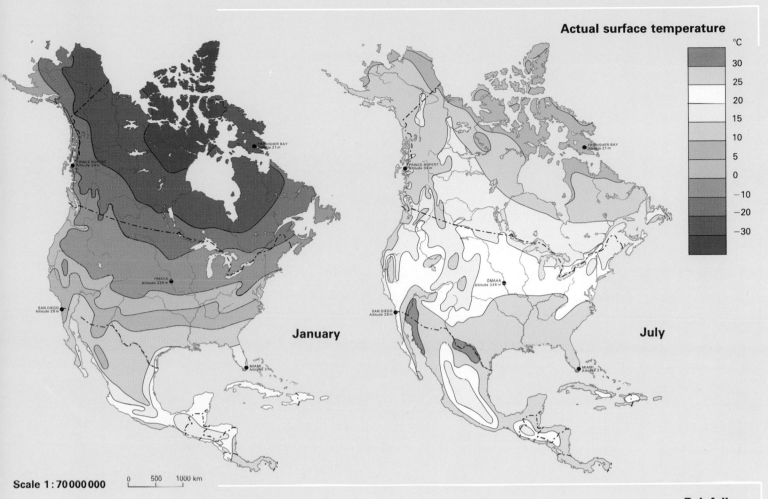

Actual surface temperature

°C
| |
| 30 |
| 25 |
| 20 |
| 15 |
| 10 |
| 5 |
| 0 |
| −10 |
| −20 |
| −30 |

January

July

Scale 1:70 000 000

0   500   1000 km

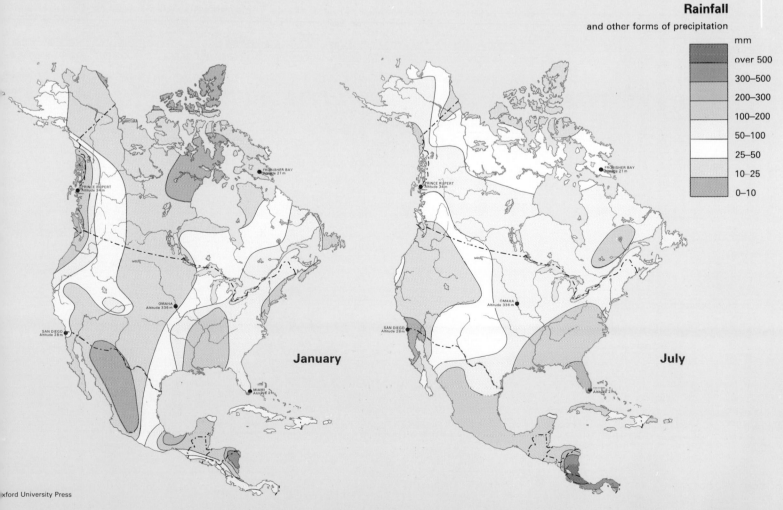

Rainfall

and other forms of precipitation

mm
| over 500 |
| 300–500 |
| 200–300 |
| 100–200 |
| 50–100 |
| 25–50 |
| 10–25 |
| 0–10 |

January

July

Boundaries

international

internal

national park

Communications

motorway

other major road

railway

canal

✈ major airport

Cities and towns

■ over 1 million inhabitants

● more than 100 000 inhabitants

• smaller towns

Physical features

marsh

ice cap

sand dunes

Land height

metres
3000
2000
1000
500
300
200
100
sea level

▲ spot height in metres

Sea Ice

unnavigable

pack ice – autumn min.

pack ice – spring maximum

Scale 1:19 000 000

0   200   400 km

Zenithal Equidistant Projec

ARCTIC OCEAN

Beaufort Sea

RUSSIA IRUSSIAN FEDERATION

Bering Strait

Bering Sea

Aleutian Islands

PACIFIC OCEAN

Gulf of Alaska

ALASKA Range

U.S.A.

YUKON TERRITORY

NORTHWEST TERRITORIES

BRITISH COLUMBIA

Rocky Mts

ALBERTA

SASKATCHEWAN

WASHINGTON

OREGON

IDAHO

MONTANA

WYOMING

NEVADA

CALIFORNIA

Vancouver

Calgary

Edmonton

Seattle

Portland

U.S.

Rocky Mountains

Cascade Ranges

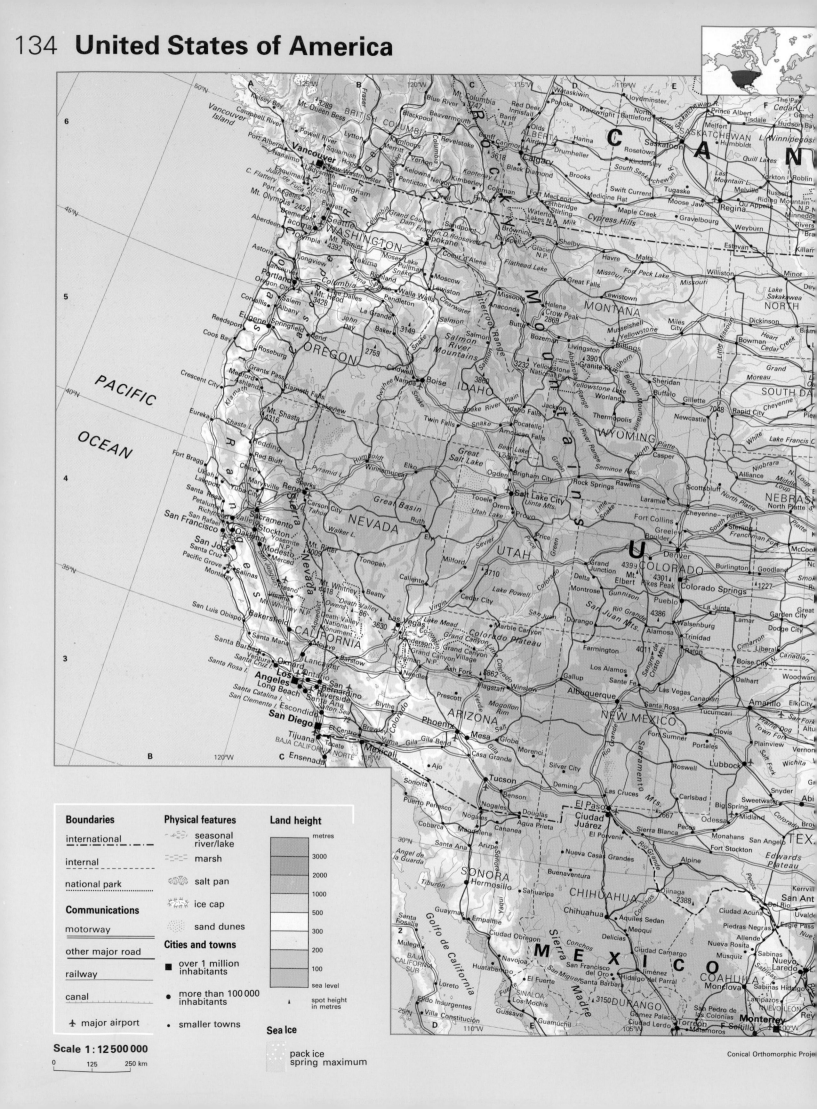

Boundaries

international

internal

national park

Communications

motorway

other major road

railway

canal

✈ major airport

Physical features

seasonal river/lake

marsh

salt pan

ice cap

sand dunes

Cities and towns

■ over 1 million inhabitants

● more than 100 000 inhabitants

• smaller towns

Land height

| metres |
| 3000 |
| 2000 |
| 1000 |
| 500 |
| 300 |
| 200 |
| 100 |
| sea level |

▲ spot height in metres

Sea Ice

pack ice spring maximum

Scale 1 : 12 500 000

0   125   250 km

Conical Orthomorphic Projection

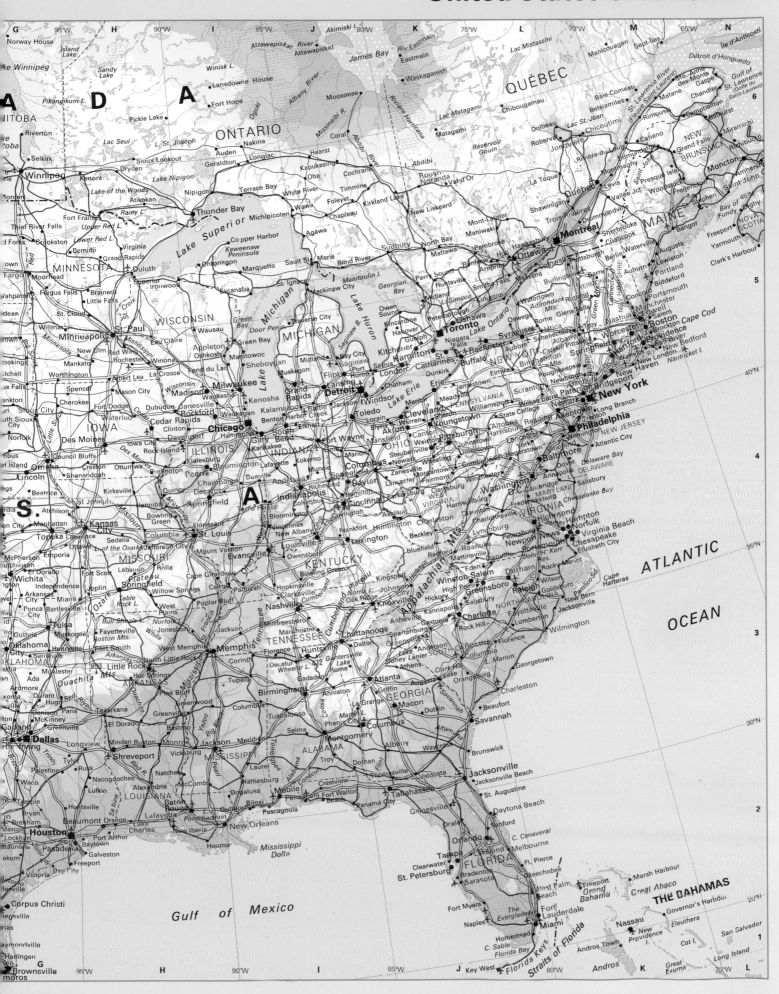

Boundaries

— international

–·–·– internal

············ national park

Communications

—— motorway

—— other major road

railway

canal

✈ major airport

Cities and towns

◇ built-up areas

■ over 1 million inhabitants

● more than 100 000 inhabitants

• smaller towns

Physical features

seasonal river/lake

marsh

Land height

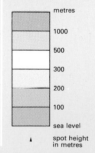

metres
1000
500
300
200
100
sea level

▲ spot height in metres

Scale 1 : 6 250 000

0   25   50 km

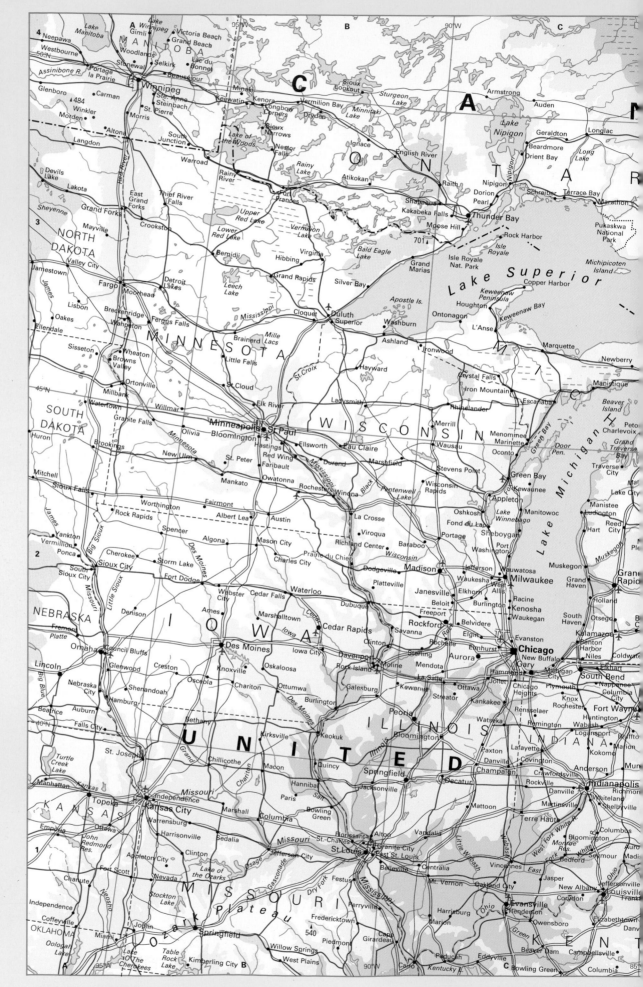

USA: Population, 1994

males   Age   females

| 85+ |
| 80-84 |
| 75-79 |
| 70-74 |
| 65-69 |
| 60-64 |
| 55-59 |
| 50-54 |
| 45-49 |
| 40-44 |
| 35-39 |
| 30-34 |
| 25-29 |
| 20-24 |
| 15-19 |
| 10-14 |
| 5-9 |
| 0-4 |

6 4 2 0   0 2 4 6

percent of total population

Total population:
260.3 million

Crude Birth Rate
per thousand: 15

Crude Death Rate
per thousand: 9

Boundaries

state —··—··—

county —·—·—

Physical features

river

marsh

contours

•155   spot height
in metres

Communications

motorway

other major road

major railway

canal

✈ major airport

✈ other airport

Land use

central business
district

other major
commercial areas

industrial

residential

major parks and
open spaces

non-urban

Scale 1 : 300 000

0   5 km

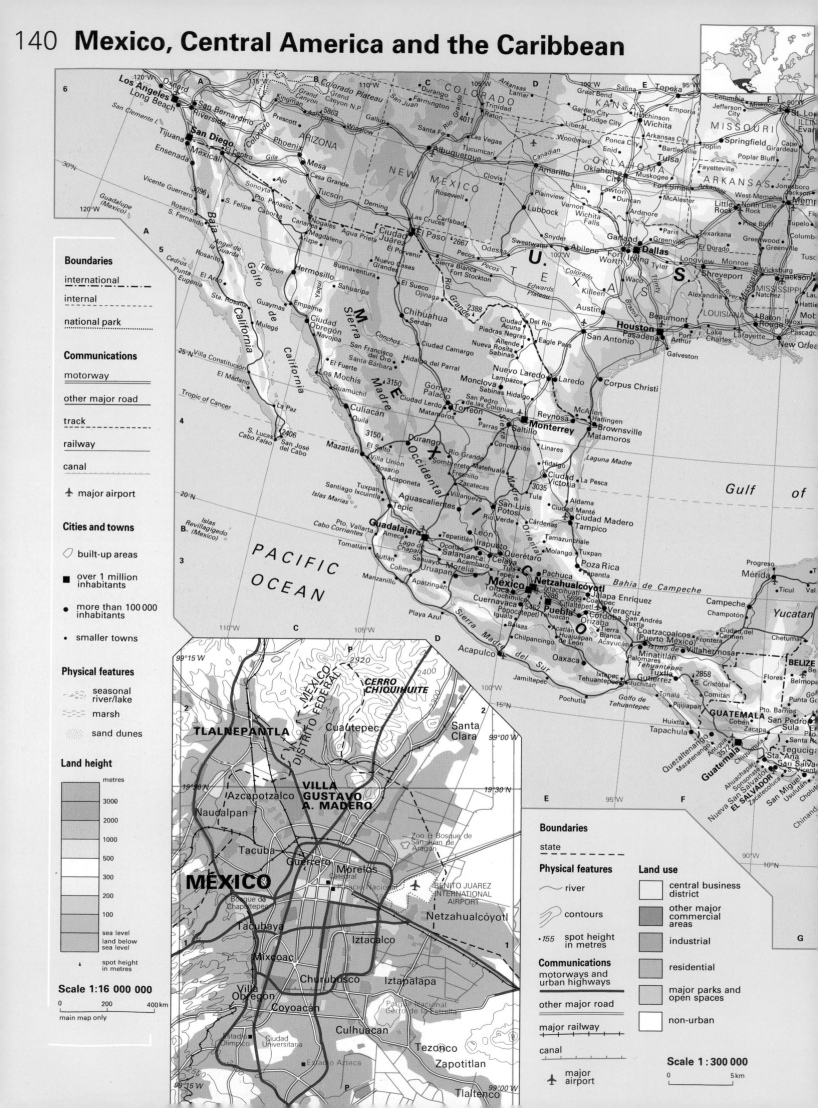

Boundaries
international
internal
national park

Communications
motorway
other major road
track
railway
canal
✈ major airport

Cities and towns
⬭ built-up areas
■ over 1 million inhabitants
● more than 100 000 inhabitants
• smaller towns

Physical features
seasonal river/lake
marsh
sand dunes

Land height

metres
3000
2000
1000
500
300
200
100
sea level
land below sea level
▲ spot height in metres

Scale 1:16 000 000
0   200   400km
main map only

Boundaries
state

Physical features
river
contours
•155 spot height in metres

Communications
motorways and urban highways
other major road
major railway
canal
✈ major airport

Land use
central business district
other major commercial areas
industrial
residential
major parks and open spaces
non-urban

Scale 1 : 300 000
0   5km

Mexico, Central America and the Caribbean

Barbados

Scale 1: 1 000 000

0   25 km

Trinidad

Trinidad Scale 1: 1 250 000

0   25 km

Jamaica

Jamaica Scale 1:3 000 000   0   25   50 km

Land height

metres

5000
3000
2000
1000
500
300
200
100
sea level
· spot height
  in metres

Sea depth

sea level
200
3000
4000
5000
6000

sea depths shown
as minus numbers

⠿ sand desert

—·—·— international
boundary

Scale 1 : 44 000 000

0   500   1000 km

Guatemala
Basin

Caribbean Sea

Windward
Is.

Guiana
Basin

50°W

40°W

Panama
Isthmus

Cord. de
Merida

Orinoco

Cocos Is.

Cocos Ridge

Cord. de Magdalena

Guiana Highlands

Mid Atlantic Ridge

0°

Galapagos
Is.

Carnegie Ridge

5896·COTOPAXI

Putumayo

Negro

Amazon

Equator

Rocas I.

Ferna
de Nore

S O U T H

Amazon

Selvas

Juruá

Tapajós

Xingu

B r a z i l i a n

10°S

P e r u

Madeira

Sierra dos Parecis

Tocantins

H i g h l a n d s

—6601

B a s i n

Titicaca

Chiquitos
Plateau

Planalto de
Mato Grosso

Goiás
Massif

São Francisco

P A C I F I C

A n d e s

Paraguay

Paraná

Brazil Plateau

Peru Chile Trench

Madeira Desert

—8066

6723

G r a n
C h a c o

Paraná

Paraná
Plateau

Trindade

Marti
Vaz

Tropic of Capric

O C E A N

ACONCAGUA
6960

Paraná

Uruguay

O C E A N

P a m p a s

Río de la Plata

90°W

Isla de Chiloé

P a t a g o n i a

Argentine Basin

—6212

S O U T H

Estrecho de
Magallanes

Falkland
Islands

A T L A N T I C

—5290

Isla Grande
de Tierra
del Fuego

Cape Horn

South
Georgia

70°W

SOUTHERN

South
Shetland
Is.

South
Orkney Is.

OCEAN

50°W

40°W

30°W

20°W

Caracas

TRINIDAD & TOBAGO
Port of Spain

VENEZUELA

Georgetown
Paramaribo
Cayenne

Bogotá

GUYANA

SURINAM

COLOMBIA

FRENCH GUIANA

Galapagos
Is. (Ec.)

Quito
ECUADOR

PERU

B R A Z I L

Lima

La Paz
BOLIVIA

· Brasília

PARAGUAY

Asunción

CHILE

ARGENTINA

URUGUAY

Santiago

Buenos
Aires

Montevideo

Stanley
Falkland
Is.(U.K.)

South America: Political

——— international boundary

· national capital

Names of commonwealth members
are <u>underlined</u>

Scale 1 : 70 000 000

0   500   1000 km

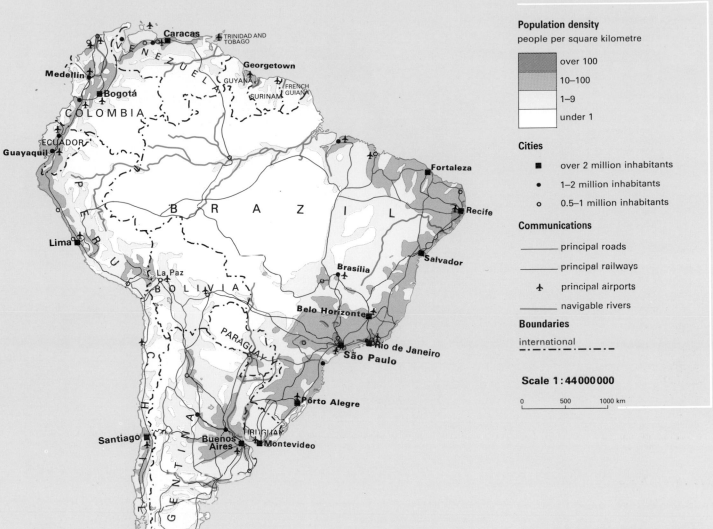

Population density

people per square kilometre

	over 100
	10–100
	1–9
	under 1

Cities

■ over 2 million inhabitants

• 1–2 million inhabitants

○ 0.5–1 million inhabitants

Communications

—— principal roads

—— principal railways

✈ principal airports

—— navigable rivers

Boundaries

international ▬ ▬ ▬ ▬ ▬

Scale 1 : 44 000 000

0   500   1000 km

Venezuela: Population, 1992

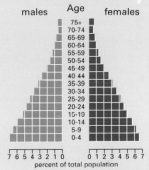

Total population: 20.2 million

Crude Birth Rate per thousand: 30

Crude Death Rate per thousand: 5

Argentina: Population, 1993

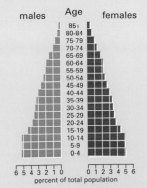

Total population: 33.7 million

Crude Birth Rate per thousand: 21

Crude Death Rate per thousand: 8

Brazil: Population, 1992

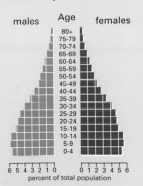

Total population: 149.2 million

Crude Birth Rate per thousand: 25

Crude Death Rate per thousand: 8

Peru: Population, 1991

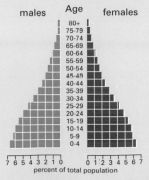

Total population: 22.0 million

Crude Birth Rate per thousand: 29

Crude Death Rate per thousand: 7

que Mercator Projection

xford University Press

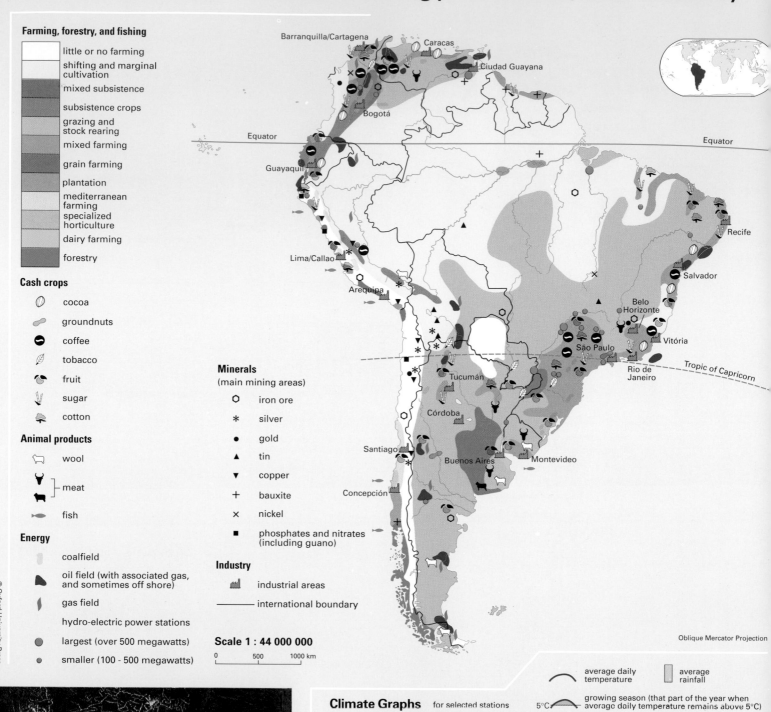

Farming, forestry, and fishing

- little or no farming
- shifting and marginal cultivation
- mixed subsistence
- subsistence crops
- grazing and stock rearing
- mixed farming
- grain farming
- plantation
- mediterranean farming
- specialized horticulture
- dairy farming
- forestry

Cash crops

- cocoa
- groundnuts
- coffee
- tobacco
- fruit
- sugar
- cotton

Animal products

- wool
- meat
- fish

Energy

- coalfield
- oil field (with associated gas, and sometimes off shore)
- gas field
- hydro-electric power stations
- largest (over 500 megawatts)
- smaller (100 - 500 megawatts)

Minerals
(main mining areas)

- iron ore
- silver
- gold
- tin
- copper
- bauxite
- nickel
- phosphates and nitrates (including guano)

Industry

- industrial areas
- international boundary

Scale 1 : 44 000 000

0   500   1000 km

Oblique Mercator Projection

Deforestation in Brazil.
Satellite image processed to give approximately natural colour.
Dark green : natural forest.
Pale green and pink : areas of forest loss.

Climate Graphs   for selected stations

- average daily temperature
- average rainfall
- 5°C — growing season (that part of the year when average daily temperature remains above 5°C)

BOGOTÁ
1061 mm annual precipitation

RIO DE JANEIRO
1086 mm annual precipitation

BUENOS AIRES
950 mm annual precipitation

LA PAZ
575 mm annual precipitation

ANTOFAGASTA
14 mm annual precipitation

PUNTA ARENAS
368 mm annual precipitation

Actual surface temperature

°C
25
20
15
10
5
0

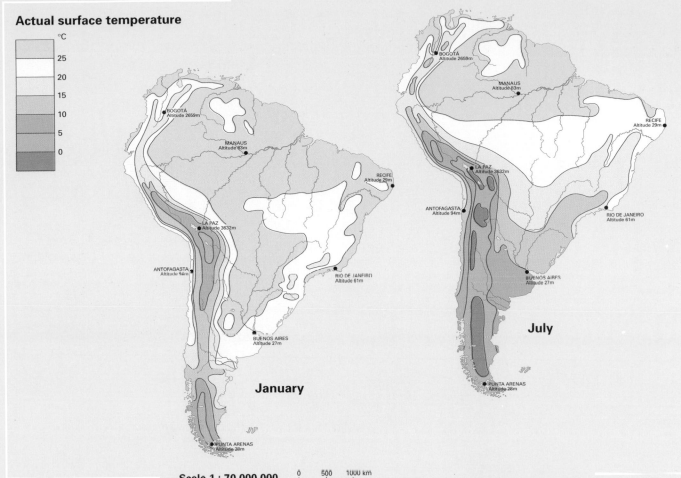

January

July

Scale 1 : 70 000 000

0   500   1000 km

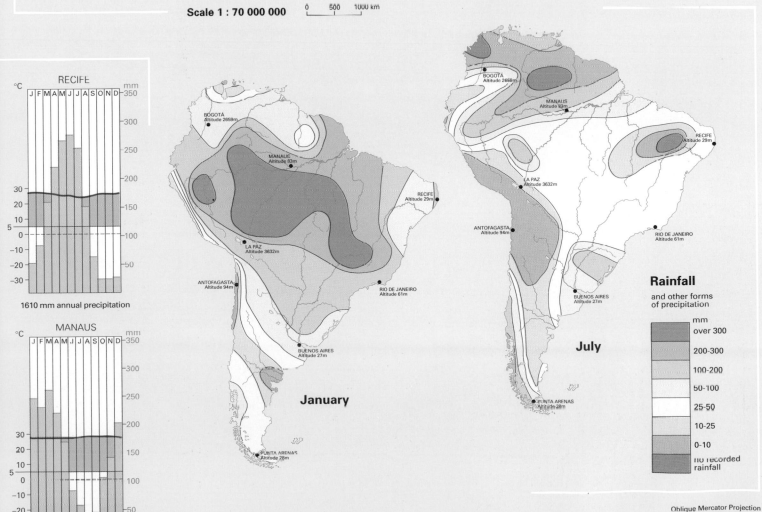

RECIFE

°C
30
20
10
5
0
−10
−20
−30

mm
350
300
250
200
150
100
50

1610 mm annual precipitation

MANAUS

°C
30
20
10
5
0
−10
−20
−30

mm
350
300
250
200
150
100
50

1811 mm annual precipitation

January

July

Rainfall

and other forms
of precipitation

mm
over 300
200-300
100-200
50-100
25-50
10-25
0-10
no recorded
rainfall

Oblique Mercator Projection

© Oxford University Press

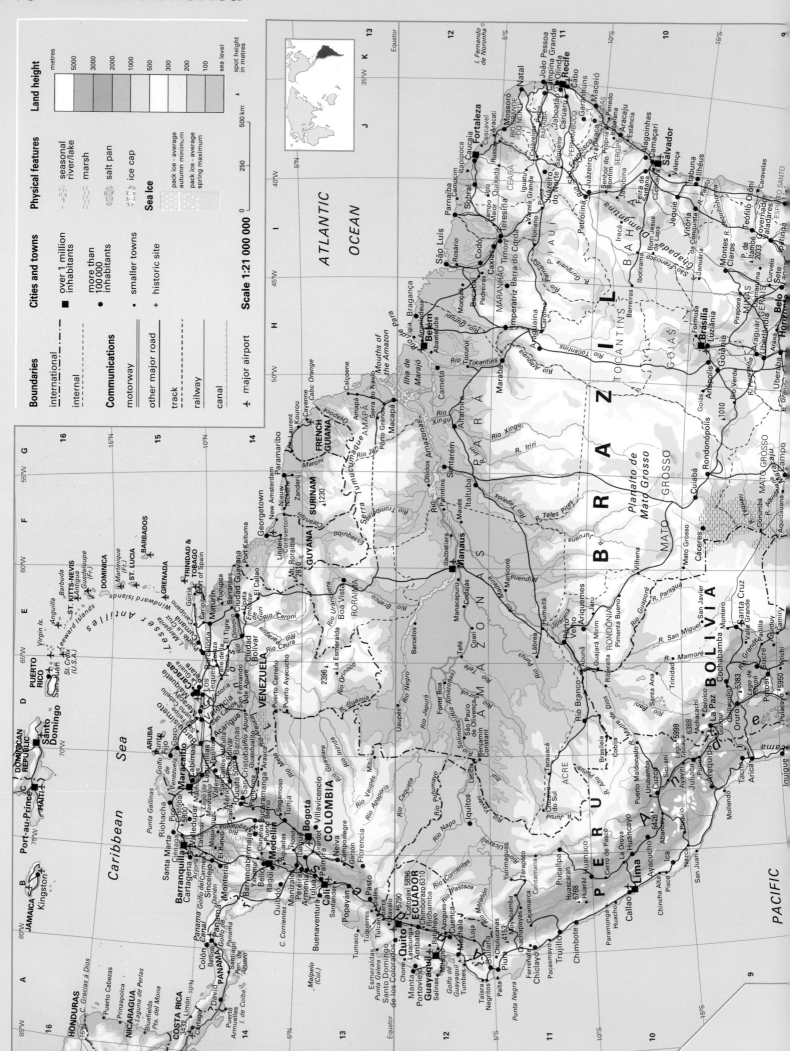

Land height

metres	
5000	
3000	
2000	
1000	
500	
300	
200	
100	
sea level	

spot height in metres

Physical features

seasonal river/lake
marsh
salt pan
ice cap

Sea ice

pack ice - average autumn minimum
pack ice - average spring maximum

Boundaries

international
internal

Communications

motorway
other major road
track
railway
canal

Cities and towns

■ over 1 million inhabitants
● more than 100 000 inhabitants
• smaller towns
+ historic site

✈ major airport

Scale 1:21 000 000

0   250   500 km

ATLANTIC OCEAN

PACIFIC

Land use

central business district
industrial
residential
favelas
major parks and open spaces
non-urban

Communications

motorway
major road
major railway
cable car
canal
major airport
other airport

Boundaries

state
district

Physical features

river
contours
•155 spot height in metres

Scale 1:300 000

0 _____ 5 km

Transverse Mercator Projection

Oxford University Press

Boundaries

international

state

Communications

major road

railway

canal

✈ major airport

Cities and towns

■ over 1 million inhabitants

● more than 100 000 inhabitants

• smaller towns

Physical features

ice cap

Land height

metres
3000
2000
1000
500
300
200
100
sea level

Sea depth

sea level
200
3000
4000
5000

▲ spot height in metres

sea depths shown as minus numbers

Sea ice

unnavigable

pack ice – autumn minimum

pack ice – spring maximum

Scale 1:25 000 000

0   250   500 km

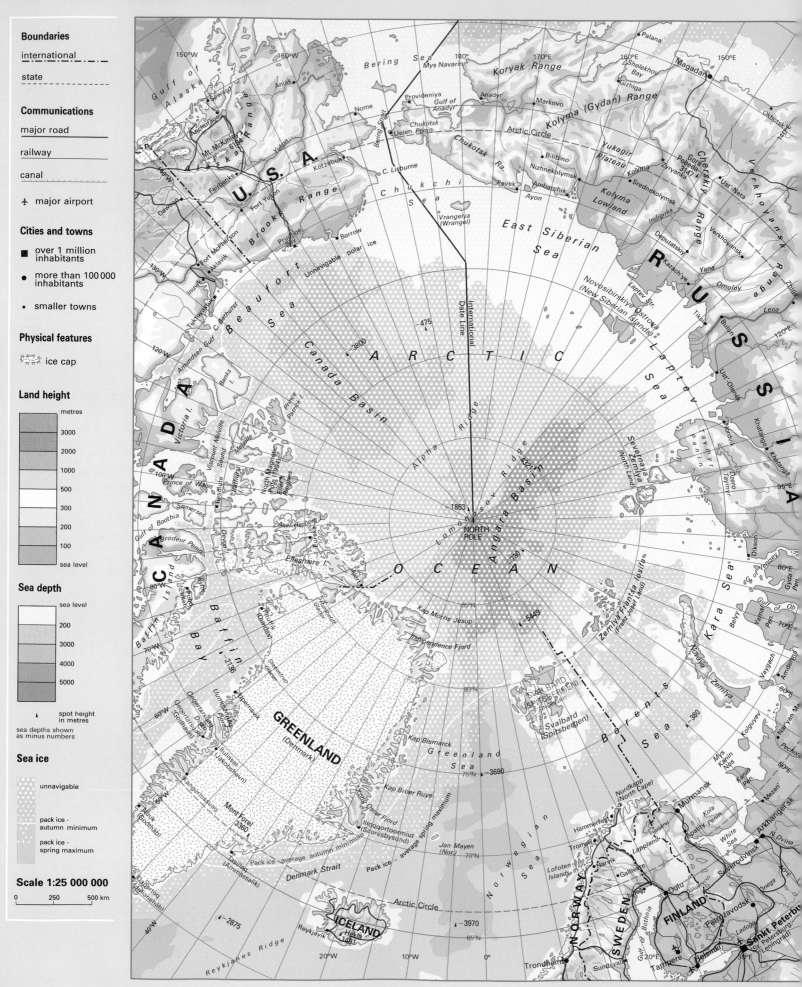

Zenithal Equidistant Projection

© Oxford University Press

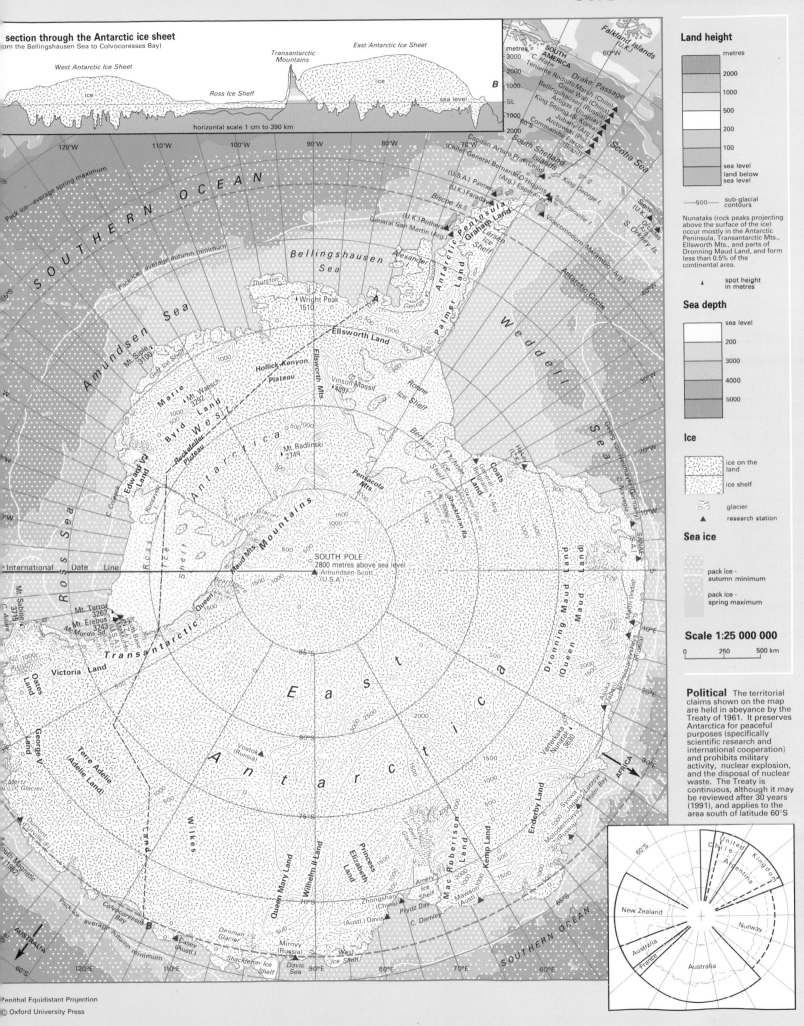

section through the Antarctic ice sheet
(from the Bellingshausen Sea to Colvocoresses Bay)

West Antarctic Ice Sheet

Transantarctic Mountains

East Antarctic Ice Sheet

ice

Ross Ice Shelf

ice

sea level

horizontal scale 1 cm to 390 km

Land height

metres	
	metres
	2000
	1000
	500
	200
	100
	sea level
	land below sea level

—500— sub-glacial contours

Nunataks (rock peaks projecting above the surface of the ice) occur mostly in the Antarctic Peninsula, Transantarctic Mts., Ellsworth Mts., and parts of Dronning Maud Land, and form less than 0.5% of the continental area.

▲ spot height in metres

Sea depth

	sea level
	200
	3000
	4000
	5000

Ice

ice on the land

ice shelf

glacier

▲ research station

Sea ice

pack ice - autumn minimum

pack ice - spring maximum

Scale 1:25 000 000

0   250   500 km

Political The territorial claims shown on the map are held in abeyance by the Treaty of 1961. It preserves Antarctica for peaceful purposes (specifically scientific research and international cooperation) and prohibits military activity, nuclear explosion, and the disposal of nuclear waste. The Treaty is continuous, although it may be reviewed after 30 years (1991), and applies to the area south of latitude 60°S

SOUTHERN OCEAN

Zenithal Equidistant Projection

© Oxford University Press

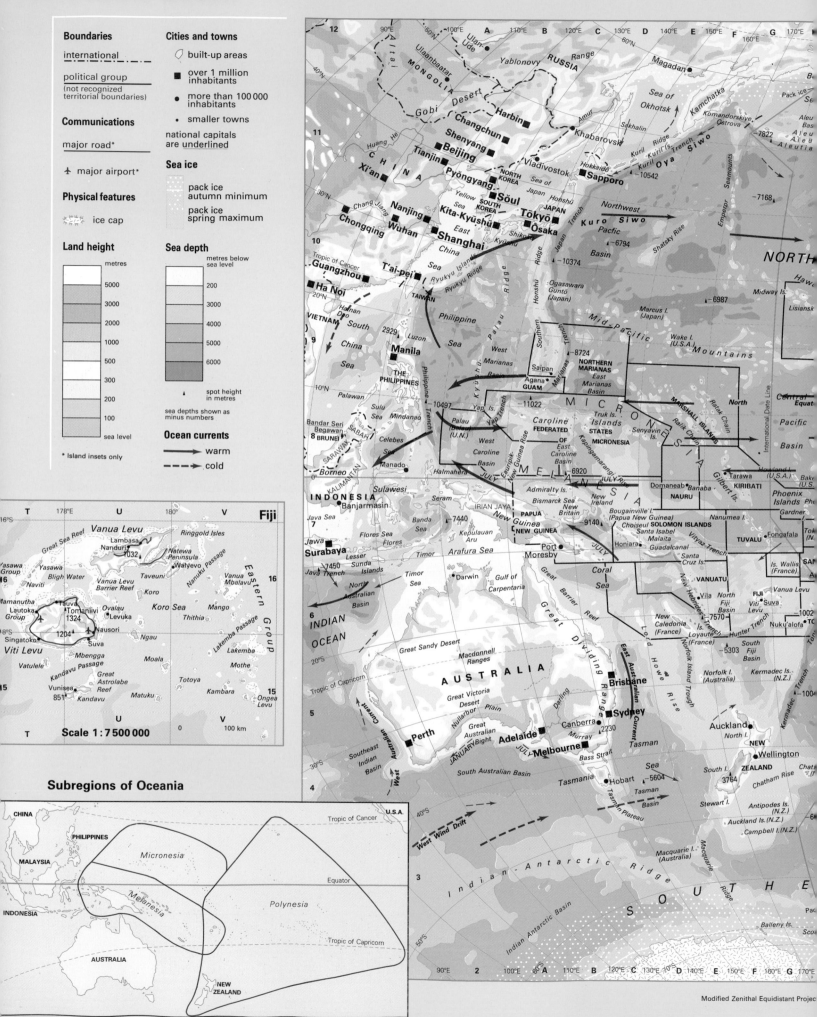

Boundaries
international
political group
(not recognized
territorial boundaries)

Communications
major road*

✈ major airport*

Physical features
ice cap

Land height
metres
5000
3000
2000
1000
500
300
200
100
sea level

Cities and towns
built-up areas
over 1 million inhabitants
more than 100 000 inhabitants
smaller towns

national capitals are underlined

Sea ice
pack ice autumn minimum
pack ice spring maximum

Sea depth
metres below sea level
200
3000
4000
5000
6000

spot height in metres

sea depths shown as minus numbers

Ocean currents
→ warm
--→ cold

* Island insets only

Fiji

Great Sea Reef
Vanua Levu
Lambasa
Nanduri
1032
Natewa Peninsula
Ringgold Isles
Yasawa Group
Yasawa
Bligh Water
Naviti
Vanua Levu Barrier Reef
Walyevo Passage
Natewa Passage
Taveuni
Koro
Nanuku Passage
Vanua Mbalavu
Mamanutha Group
Lautoka
Tauva
Tomaniivi
1324
Ovalau
Levuka
Koro Sea
Mango
Thithia
Eastern Group
Singatoko
Nausori
1204
Suva
Ngau
Lakemba Passage
Lakemba
Viti Levu
Mbengga
Vatulele
Moala
Thotoya
Kambara
Ongea Levu
Vunisea
851
Kandavu
Kandavu Passage
Great Astrolabe Reef
Matuku
Mothe

Scale 1 : 7 500 000
0   100 km

Subregions of Oceania
CHINA
PHILIPPINES
MALAYSIA
Micronesia
Tropic of Cancer
U.S.A.
INDONESIA
Melanesia
Equator
Polynesia
AUSTRALIA
Tropic of Capricorn
NEW ZEALAND

RUSSIA
MONGOLIA
Ulaanbaatar
Ulan-Ude
Yablonovy Range
Magadan
Gobi Desert
Altai
Harbin
Changchun
Shenyang
Amur
Khabarovsk
Sea of Okhotsk
Kamchatka
Sakhalin
Komandorskiye Ostrova
Pack ice
Aleu
Aleutia
CHINA
Xi'an
Tianjin
Beijing
Pyŏngyang
NORTH KOREA
Vladivostok
Hokkaido
Sapporo
Kuril Is.
Kuril Ridge
Kuril'sk
Oya Siwo
Kuril Trench
−7822
Huang He
Chang Jiang
Sŏul
SOUTH KOREA
Sea of Japan
Honshū
−10542
−7168
Nanjing
Kita-Kyūshū
Tokyō
Ōsaka
JAPAN
Northwest Pacific
Kuro Siwo
Chongqing
Wuhan
Shanghai
Yellow Sea
East China Sea
Shikoku
Kyūshū
Japan Trench
−6794
Shatsky Rise
−10374
NORTH
Emperor Seamounts
Tropic of Cancer
Guangzhou
T'ai-pei
Ryukyu Islands
Ryukyu Ridge
−6987
Midway Is.
Lisiansk
Ha Noi
Hainan Dao
TAIWAN
Philippine Sea
Palau Ridge
Honshū
Ogasawara Guntō (Japan)
Marcus I. (Japan)
Wake I. (U.S.A.)
Hawa
VIETNAM
South China Sea
2929
Luzon
Mid-Pacific Mountains
Manila
West Marianas Basin
−8724
Southern
Saipan
Northern Marianas
East Marianas Basin
THE PHILIPPINES
Palawan
Kyūshū Ridge
−10497
Yap Is.
−11022
MICRONESIA
International Date Line
Central Equat
Sulu Sea
Mindanao
Yap Trench
Palau (Belau) (U.N.)
Truk Is.
Caroline Islands
FEDERATED STATES OF MICRONESIA
MARSHALL ISLANDS
Ratak Chain
North
Pacific Basin
Bandar Seri Begawan
BRUNEI
SABAH
Celebes Sea
Manado
West Caroline Basin
East Caroline Basin
Senyavin Is.
Ralik Chain
SARAWAK
Halmahera
New Guinea Rise
−6920
JULY
Howland I. (U.S.A.)
Bake (U.S.
Borneo
KALIMANTAN
Sulawesi
JULY
Eauripik-New Guinea Rise
MELANESIA
Domaneab
Banaba
Tarawa
KIRIBATI
Phoenix Islands
Phe
INDONESIA
Banjarmasin
Seram
Admiralty Is.
New Ireland
Bismarck Sea
New Britain
Kapingamarangi Rise
NAURU
Gardner
Java Sea
Banda Sea
IRIAN JAYA
PAPUA NEW GUINEA
Bougainville I. (Papua New Guinea)
−9140
SOLOMON ISLANDS
Nanumea I.
Jawa
Flores Sea
Flores
−7440
NEW GUINEA
Choiseul
Santa Isabel
Malaita
Vityaz Trench
TUVALU
Fongafala
Tok
Surabaya
−7450
Kepulauan Aru
Arafura Sea
Port Moresby
Honiara
Guadalcanal
JULY
Java Trench
Lesser Sunda Islands
Timor
Santa Cruz Is.
Is. Wallis (France)
SA
Timor Sea
Darwin
Gulf of Carpentaria
Coral Sea
New Hebrides Trench
VANUATU
Vanua Levu
INDIAN OCEAN
North Australian Basin
Great Barrier Reef
Vila
North Fiji Basin
FIJI
Viti Levu
Suva
−1002
Great Sandy Desert
−7570
New Caledonia (France)
Loyaute (France)
Hunter Trench
South Fiji Basin
Nuku'alofa
TO
AUSTRALIA
Macdonnell Ranges
Lord Howe Rise
−5303
Norfolk I. (Australia)
Kermadec Is. (N.Z.)
−1000
Great Victoria Desert
Tropic of Capricorn
Brisbane
Norfolk Island Trough
East Australian Current
Nullarbor Plain
Darling
Sydney
Canberra
−2230
Murray
Tasman Sea
Auckland
North I.
NEW ZEALAND
Kermadec Trench
Perth
Great Australian Bight
JANUARY
Adelaide
Melbourne
Bass Strait
Tasmania
Hobart
−5604
Tasman Basin
Wellington
Chatha
Chatham Rise
3764
Southeast Indian Basin
JULY
West
South Australian Basin
South I.
Stewart I.
Antipodes Is. (N.Z.)
−6
West Wind Drift
Auckland Is. (N.Z.)
Campbell I. (N.Z.)
SOUTHE
Indian-Antarctic Ridge
Macquarie I. (Australia)
Macquarie Ridge
Indian Antarctic Basin
SOUTH
Balleny Is.
Scot
Pac

Modified Zenithal Equidistant Project

Kilanea · Kapaa · X
Lihue · Kauai
Niihau
Kaula
Kauai Channel
Kahuku Pt.
Waialua · Wahiawa · Kaneohe
Oahu · Pearl Harbor
Honolulu
Kaiwi Channel
Lanai City · Lanai
Kahoolawe
Molokai · Lahaina · Maui
Hoolehua · Halawa · 3055
Kawaihae
Alenuihaha Channel
Upolu Pt.
Honokaa
Mauna Kea 4206 · Hilo
Hawaii · Kailua
Mauna Loa 4169 · Kumukah
Napoopoo · Papa · Pahala
Kalae (South Cape)

Scale 1 : 7 500 000
0   100 km
160°W   X   158°W   Y   156°W

CANADA
Mt. McKinley 6194
Anchorage
Mt. Logan 5951
ALASKA (U.S.A.)
Kodiak I.
Gulf of Alaska
Arctic Circle
Great Slave Lake
Churchill
Hudson Bay
Rocky Mountains
Canadian Shield
Saskatchewan
Winnipeg
Queen Charlotte Is.
Vancouver I.
Vancouver
Seattle
Minneapolis St. Paul
Great Lakes
Toronto
Chicago
Missouri
Gorda Rise
Salt Lake City
UNITED STATES
Mt. Elbert 4399
Mendocino Seascarp
San Francisco
Los Angeles
Colorado
Houston
New Orleans
Rio Grande
Mississippi
Murray Seascarp
Guadalupe (Mexico)
MEXICO
Miami
THE BAHAMAS
La Habana
CUBA
Gulf of Mexico
Yucatan Basin
NORTH ATLANTIC OCEAN
Tropic of Cancer
North Equatorial Current
PACIFIC OCEAN
−6474
(U.S.A.)
Nihoa
Niihau
Honolulu
Hawaii
East
Hawaiian Ridge
−6108
California Current
Roca Alijos
Guadalajara 5452
Acapulco
Is. Revillagigedo (Mexico)
México
GUATEMALA
BELIZE
Guatemala
HONDURAS
Tegucigalpa
EL SALVADOR −6662
NICARAGUA
Managua
San José
COSTA RICA
PANAMA
Panama
Puerto Rico Trench −9220
DOMINICAN REPUBLIC
HAITI
PUERTO RICO
Cayman Trench
JAMAICA
Kingston
Leeward Is.
DOMINICA
ST. LUCIA
BARBADOS
GRENADA
TRINIDAD & TOBAGO
Venezuelan Sea
Caribbean Basin
Barranquilla
Maracaibo
Caracas
VENEZUELA
Orinoco
Llanos
Georgetown
Paramaribo
Cayenne
GUYANA
SURINAM
FRENCH GUIANA
Guyana Basin
Pacific Basin
−5106
Clarion Fracture Zone
Middle America Trench
East
Pacific
Rise
JANUARY
JULY
Clipperton I. (France)
Clipperton Fracture Zone
Equatorial Counter Current
Guatemala Basin
Cocos Ridge
I. del Coco (Costa Rica)
Medellín
COLOMBIA
Bogotá
Cali 5750
−5298
JANUARY
JULY
Palmyra Atoll (U.S.A.)
Tabuaaran I. (Kiritati)
Kiritimati I. (Kiribati)
Jarvis Is. (U.S.A.)
Line Islands
Ridge
Equatorial Current
KIRIBATI
Malden I.
Caroline I.
−6584
Marquesas Islands (France)
French Polynesia (France)
Tuamotu Archipelago (France)
Society Is. (France)
Tahiti
Tubai Is. (France)
Gambier Is. (France)
Austral Ridge
Palmerston Atoll (N.Z.)
Cook Is. (N.Z.)
Equator
Islas Galápagos (Ecuador)
Carnegie Ridge
Quito −6310
ECUADOR
Manaus
BRAZIL
Amazonas
−6768
−6001
Lima
PERU
Galápagos Rise
Peru Basin
−5469
Pacific Ridge
Nasca Ridge
Humboldt (Peru-Chile Trench)
−6388
Titicaca
La Paz
BOLIVIA
Santa Cruz
Mato Grosso
Brasília
Henderson I. (U.S.A.)
Ducie I. (France)
Oeno I.
Pitcairn Islands (U.K.)
Easter I. (Chile)
Salay Gomez (Chile)
Easter Island Fracture Zone
Islas Juan Fernández (Chile)
I. San Félix (Chile)
−8066
−6755
Chaco
Gran Chaco
C. Paraguay
Asunción
Tropic of Capricorn
Rio de Janeiro
São Paulo
SOUTH PACIFIC OCEAN
−1088
JULY
JANUARY
South West Pacific Basin
Challenger Fracture Zone
Nasca
Chile Rise
Chile Basin
Valparaíso
Córdoba −0960
Santiago
Concepción
URUGUAY
ARGENTINA
Rosario
Paraná
Buenos Aires
Montevideo
Porto Alegre
Brazil Current
Eltanin Fracture Zone
Pacific - Antarctic Ridge
West Wind Drift
South East Pacific Basin
Isla de Chiloé
Chile
Isla Wellington
PATAGONIA
Rio Gallegos
Santa Cruz
Falkland Current
Falkland Is. (U.K.)
Isla Grande de Tierra del Fuego
C. de Hornos
West Wind Drift
Argentine Basin
Rio Grande Rise
Pack ice – autumn minimum
Antarctic Circle
OCEAN

Scale 1 : 63 000 000
0   500   1000   1500 km

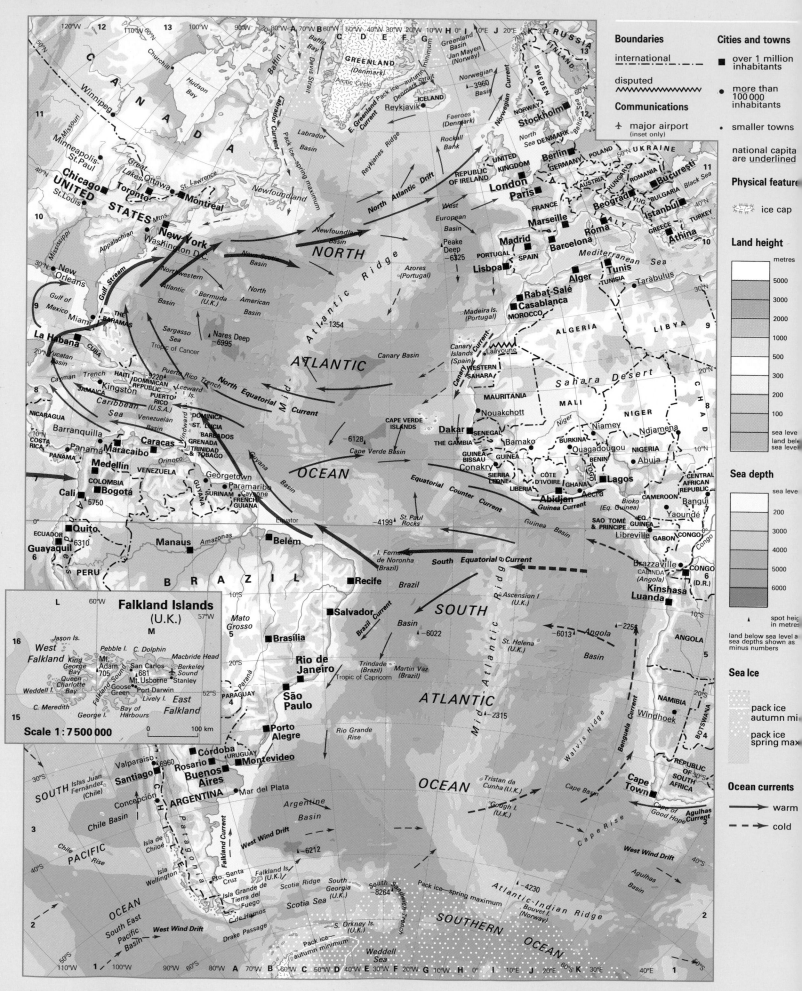

Boundaries

international

disputed

Communications

✈ major airport (inset only)

Cities and towns

■ over 1 million inhabitants

● more than 100 000 inhabitants

• smaller towns

national capital are <u>underlined</u>

Physical features

ice cap

Land height

metres
5000
3000
2000
1000
500
300
200
100
sea level
land below sea level

Sea depth

sea level
200
3000
4000
5000
6000

▲ spot height in metres

land below sea level and sea depths shown as minus numbers

Sea Ice

pack ice autumn minimum

pack ice spring maximum

Ocean currents

→ warm

--→ cold

Modified Zenithal Equidistant Projection

© Oxford University Press

Scale 1 : 63 000 000

0   500   1000   1500 km

Falkland Islands (U.K.)

Scale 1 : 7 500 000

0   100 km

Countries of the World Selected Statistics

Country	Land area	Total population	Density of population	Crude birth rate	Crude death rate	GNP per capita	Urban population	Capital city
	thousand sq.km	millions 1995	per sq.km 1995	per thousand 1995	per thousand 1995	US $ 1993	percent 1995	
Afghanistan	652	18.4	28	50	22	220	20	Kābul
Albania	29	3.5	121	23	5	340	37.3	Tiranë (Tirana)
Algeria	2382	28.4	12	30	6	1650	55.8	Alger (Algiers)
American Samoa	0.2	0.05	250	...	...	2600	...	Fagatogo*
Andorra	0.5	0.06	120	13	4	...	...	Andorra-la-Vella
Angola	1247	11.5	9	47	20	600	32.2	Luanda
Anguilla	0.16	0.009	56	25	10	...	...	The Valley
Antigua & Barbuda	0.4	0.1	250	18	5	6390	36	St John's
Argentina	2767	34.6	13	21	8	7290	87.5	Buenos Aires
Armenia	30	3.7	123	16	7	660	68	Yerevan
Aruba	0.2	0.07	350	...	...	17500	...	Oranjestad
Australia	7682	18	2	15	7	17510	85.2	Canberra
Austria	84	8.1	96	12	10	23120	60.6	Wien (Vienna)
Azerbaijan	87	7.3	84	23	7	730	55	Baki (Baku)
Bahamas, The	14	0.3	21	20	5	11500	85	Nassau
Bahrain	0.7	0.6	857	29	4	7870	89	Al'Manāmah (Manama)
Bangladesh	144	119.2	828	36	12	220	19.5	Dhaka
Barbados	0.4	0.3	750	16	9	6240	46	Bridgetown
Belarus	208	10.3	50	11	13	2840	68	Minsk
Belgium	31	10.2	329	12	11	21210	96.7	Bruxelles (Brussels)
Belize	23	0.2	9	38	5	2440	52.5	Belmopan
Benin	113	5.4	48	49	18	420	41.8	Porto Novo
Bermuda	0.05	0.061	1220	16	7	27000	100	Hamilton
Bhutan	47	0.8	17	39	15	170	6.4	Thimphu
Bolivia	1099	7.4	7	36	10	770	54.4	Sucre/La Paz*
Bosnia-Herzegovina	51	3.5	69	14	7	2500	40	Sarajevo
Botswana	582	1.5	3	31	7	2590	30.9	Gaborone
Brazil	8512	157.8	19	25	8	3020	78.7	Brasília
Brunei Darussalam	5.8	0.3	52	27	3	9000	58	Bandar Seri Begawan
Bulgaria	111	8.5	77	10	13	1160	70.7	Sofiya (Sofia)
Burkina	274	10.4	38	47	19	300	19.5	Ouagadougou
Burundi	28	6.4	229	46	16	180	6.1	Bujumbura
Cambodia	181	10.6	59	44	16	600	12.9	Phnom Penh
Cameroon	475	13.5	28	40	11	770	44.9	Yaoundé
Canada	9976	29.6	3	14	7	20670	78.1	Ottawa
Cape Verde Islands	4	0.4	100	36	9	870	49	Praia
Cayman Islands	0.3	0.03	100	15	4	...	100	George Town
Central African Republic	623	3.2	5	42	22	390	50.8	Bangui
Chad	1284	6.4	5	44	18	200	37	Ndjamena
Chile	757	14.3	19	22	6	3070	85.9	Santiago
China	9537	1218.8	128	18	6	490	30.3	Beijing (Peking)
Hong Kong	*1*	*6*	*6000*	*12*	*5*	*17860*	*94*	*Victoria*
Colombia	1139	37.7	33	24	6	1400	72.7	Bogotá
Comoros	2	0.5	250	46	11	520	29	Moroni
Congo	342	2.5	7	40	17	920	43.4	Brazzaville
Congo, Democratic Republic								
Cook Islands	0.3	0.19	63	24	5	...	...	Rarotonga
Costa Rica	51	3.3	65	26	4	2160	49.7	San José
Côte d'Ivoire	322	14.3	44	50	15	630	43.6	Yamoussoukro
Croatia	57	4.5	79	10	11	4500	52	Zagreb
Cuba	111	11.2	101	14	7	1250	76	La Habana (Havana)
Cyprus	9	0.7	78	17	8	10380	53	Nicosia
Czech Republic	79	10.4	132	12	11	2730	65	Praha (Prague)
Denmark	43	5.2	121	13	12	26510	85.5	København (Copenhagen)
Djibouti	22	0.6	27	38	16	780	82.8	Djibouti
Dominica	0.7	0.1	143	20	7	2680	41	Roseau
Dominican Republic	49	7.8	159	27	6	1080	64.6	Santo Domingo
Ecuador	284	11.5	40	28	6	1170	60.6	Quito
Egypt	1001	61.9	62	30	8	660	44.8	Cairo
El Salvador	21	5.9	281	32	6	1320	46.7	San Salvador
Equatorial Guinea	28	0.4	14	40	14	360	30.5	Malabo
Eritrea	93.7	3.5	37	42	16	500	17	Asmera
Estonia	45	1.5	33	9	14	3040	73.1	Tallinn
Ethiopia	1158	56	48	46	16	100	13.4	Ādis Ābeba (Addis Ababa)
Fiji	18	0.8	44	25	5	2140	40.7	Suva
Finland	338	5.1	15	13	10	18970	60.3	Helsinki
France	544	58.1	107	12	9	22360	72.0	Paris
French Polynesia	4	0.2	50	26	5	7000	67	Papeete
FYROM (Former Yugoslav Republic of Macedonia)	25	2.1	84	16	8	780	59	Skopje
Gabon	268	1.3	5	37	16	4050	50	Libreville
Gambia, The	11	1.1	100	48	21	360	25.5	Banjul
Georgia	70	5.4	77	12	10	560	57	T'bilisi (Tiflis)
Germany	357	81.7	229	10	11	23560	86.5	Berlin/Bonn*
Ghana	239	17.5	73	42	12	430	36.3	Accra
Greece	132	10.5	80	10	9	7390	65	Athina (Athens)
Grenada	0.3	0.1	333	29	6	2410	33	St George's
Guam	0.5	0.2	400	30	4	...	...	Agaña*
Guadeloupe	1.7	0.4	235	18	6	9000	51	Basse-Terre*
Guatemala	109	10.6	97	39	8	1110	41.5	Guatemala
Guinea	246	6.5	26	44	19	510	29.6	Conakry
Guinea Bissau	36	1.1	31	43	21	220	22.2	Bissau
Guyana	215	0.8	4	25	7	350	35.3	Georgetown
Haiti	28	7.2	257	35	12	800	31.6	Port-au-Prince
Honduras	112	5.5	49	34	6	580	47.7	Tegucigalpa
Hungary	93	10.2	110	12	14	3330	67.7	Budapest
Iceland	103	0.3	3	17	7	23620	91.6	Reykjavik
India	3287	930.6	283	29	9	290	26.8	New Delhi
Indonesia	1905	198.4	104	24	8	730	32.5	Jakarta
Iran	1648	61.3	37	36	7	4750	60.4	Tehrān
Iraq	400	20.0	47	43	7	2000	74.6	Baghdad
Ireland, Republic of	70	3.6	51	14	9	12580	58.4	Dublin
Israel	22	5.5	250	21	6	13760	92.7	Jerusalem
Italy	301	57.7	192	9	10	19620	70.5	Roma (Rome)
Jamaica	11	2.4	218	25	6	1390	55.4	Kingston
Japan	378	125.2	331	10	7	31450	77.9	Tōkyō
Jordan	98	4.1	42	38	4	1190	71.5	Amman
Kazakhstan	2717	16.9	6	19	9	1540	58	Akmola
Kenya	580	28.3	49	45	12	270	27.7	Nairobi
Kirgyzstan	199	4.4	22	26	8	830	39	Bishkek
Kiribati	0.7	0.08	114	33	12	710	39	Tarawa
Korea, North	121	23.5	194	23	6	1000	61.3	Pyŏngyang
Korea, South	99	44.9	454	15	6	7670	77.6	Sŏul (Seoul)
Kuwait	18	1.5	83	25	2	23350	97	Al Kuwayt
Laos	237	4.8	20	42	14	290	21.7	Viangchan (Vientiane)
Latvia	65	2.5	38	10	15	2030	72.9	Riga
Lebanon								

* seat of government
··· data not available

Country	Land area	Total population	Density of population	Crude birth rate	Crude death rate	GNP per capita	Urban population	Capital city
	thousand sq.km	millions 1995	per sq.km 1995	per thousand 1995	per thousand 1995	US $ 1993	percent 1995	
Lebanon	10	3.7	370	25	5	1750	87.2	Beyrouth (Beirut)
Lesotho	30	2.1	70	31	12	660	23.1	Maseru
Liberia	98	3	31	47	14	800	50.6	Monrovia
Libya	1760	5.2	3	42	8	6500	86	Tarābulus (Tripoli)
Liechtenstein	0.16	0.03	188	12	6	33510	21	Vaduz
Lithuania	65	3.7	57	13	12	1310	72.1	Vilnius
Luxembourg	3	0.4	133	13	10	35850	88	Luxembourg
Macao	0.02	0.4	20000	16	4	7500	99	Macao
Madagascar	587	14.8	25	44	12	240	27.1	Antananarivo
Malawi	118	9.7	82	47	20	220	13.5	Lilongwe
Malaysia	330	19.9	60	29	5	3160	47.2	Kuala Lumpur
Maldives	0.3	0.3	1000	43	7	820	25	Malé
Mali	1240	9.4	8	51	20	300	27	Bamako
Malta	0.32	0.4	1250	14	7	6800	88	Valletta
Marshall Islands	0.2	0.1	500	49	9	…	…	Dalap-Uliga-Darrit
Martinique	1.1	0.4	364	17	6	8500	78	Fort-de-France
Mauritania	1031	2.3	2	40	14	510	53.8	Nouakchott
Mauritius	2	1.1	550	21	7	2980	40.7	Port Louis
Mexico	1958	93.7	48	27	5	3750	75.3	México
Micronesia, Federated States of	0.7	0.1	143	38	8	…	…	Palikir
Moldova	34	4.3	126	15	12	1180	49	Chişinau
Monaco	195 hectares	0.03	15385	20	17	…	100	Monaco
Mongolia	1567	2.3	1	22	8	400	60.9	Ulaanbaatar (UlanBator)
Montserrat	0.1	0.01	100	17	10	4500	14	Plymouth
Morocco	447	29.2	65	28	6	1030	48.4	Rabat
Mozambique	799	17.4	22	45	19	80	34.3	Maputo
Myanmar (Burma)	677	44.8	66	28	9	950	26.2	Rangoon (Yangon)
Namibia	824	1.5	2	37	10	1660	30.9	Windhoek
Nauru	0.02	0.009	450	23	5	…	…	Yaren
Nepal	147	22.6	154	38	14	160	13.7	Kathmandu
Netherlands	37	15.5	419	13	9	20710	88.9	Amsterdam/The Hague*
Netherlands Antilles	0.8	0.2	250	19	6	9700	60	Willemstad
New Caledonia	19	0.2	11	26	6	6000	62	Nouméa
New Zealand	269	3.5	13	16	8	12900	84.3	Wellington
Nicaragua	130	4.4	34	33	6	360	62.9	Managua
Niger	1267	9.2	7	53	19	270	23.1	Niamey
Nigeria	924	101.2	110	43	12	310	39.3	Abuja
Northern Marianas	0.5	0.05	100	…	…	…	…	Saipan
Norway	324	4.3	13	14	11	26340	77	Oslo
Oman	212	2.2	10	53	4	5600	13.2	Masqat (Muscat)
Pakistan	796	129.7	163	39	10	430	34.7	Islamabad
Panama	77	2.6	34	29	8	2580	54.9	Panamá
Papua New Guinea	463	4.1	9	33	10	1120	17.8	Port Moresby
Paraguay	407	5	12	33	6	1500	50.7	Asunción
Peru	1285	24	19	29	7	1490	72.2	Lima
Philippines	300	68.4	228	30	9	830	45.7	Manila
Poland	313	38.6	123	12	10	2270	63.9	Warszawa (Warsaw)
Portugal	92	9.9	108	12	11	7890	36.4	Lisboa (Lisbon)
Puerto Rico	9	3.7	411	18	8	7020	77	San Juan
Qatar	11	0.5	45	19	2	15140	90	Ad Dawhah (Doha)
Réunion	2.5	0.7	280	23	6	3900	64	Saint-Denis
Romania	238	22.7	95	11	12	1120	56.2	Bucureşti (Bucharest)
Russian Federation (Russia)	17075	147.5	9	9	16	2350	75	Moskva (Moscow)
Rwanda	26	7.8	300	40	17	200	6.1	Kigali
St Kitts-Nevis	0.3	0.04	133	23	9	4470	41	Basseterre
St Lucia	0.6	0.1	167	27	6	3040	47	Castries
St Vincent & The Grenadines	0.4	0.1	250	25	7	2130	43	Kingstown
Samoa	2.8	0.2	71	34	8	980	21	Apia
San Marino	0.06	0.03	500	10	6	…	…	San Marino
São Tomé and Principe	1	0.1	100	35	9	330	44	São Tomé
Saudi Arabia	2150	18.5	9	36	4	8000	80.2	Ar Riyād (Riyadh)
Senegal	197	8.3	42	43	16	730	42.3	Dakar
Seychelles	0.4	0.1	250	23	7	6370	52	Victoria
Sierra Leone	72	4.5	63	46	19	140	36.2	Freetown
Singapore	0.6	3	5000	17	5	19310	100	Singapore City
Slovakia	49	5.4	110	14	10	1900	57	Bratislava
Slovenia	20	2	100	10	10	6310	…	Ljubljana
Solomon Islands	28	0.4	14	44	7	750	17.1	Honiara
Somalia	638	9.3	15	50	19	500	25.8	Muqdisho (Mogadishu)
South Africa, Republic of	1221	43.5	36	31	8	2900	50.8	Pretoria
Spain	505	39.1	77	10	9	13650	80.7	Madrid
Sri Lanka	66	18.2	276	21	6	600	22.4	Colombo
Sudan	2506	28.1	11	41	12	750	24.6	Khartoum
Suriname	163	0.4	2	25	6	1210	50.4	Paramaribo
Swaziland	17	1	59	43	11	1050	31.2	Mbabane
Sweden	450	8.9	20	13	12	24830	84.7	Stockholm
Switzerland	41	7	171	12	9	36410	64	Bern
Syria	185	14.7	79	41	6	5700	52.4	Dimashq (Damascus)
Taiwan	36	21.2	589	16	5	11000	75	T'ai-pei
Tajikistan	143	5.8	41	33	9	470	32	Dushanbe
Tanzania	945	28.5	30	45	15	100	24.4	Dodoma
Thailand	513	60.2	117	20	6	2040	25.4	Bangkok (Krung Thep)
Togo	57	4.4	77	47	11	330	30.8	Lomé
Tonga	0.7	0.1	143	29	4	1610	41	Nuku'alofa
Trinidad & Tobago	5	1.3	260	17	7	3730	66.6	Port-of-Spain
Tunisia	164	8.9	54	25	6	1780	59	Tunis
Turkey	779	61.4	79	23	7	2120	68.8	Ankara
Turkmenistan	448	4.5	10	33	8	1400	45	Ashgabat (Ashkhabad)
Turks & Caicos Islands	0.5	0.014	28	26	4	…	55	Grand Turk
Tuvalu	0.02	0.01	500	29	4	…	…	Fongafale (Funafuti)
Uganda	236	21.3	90	52	19	190	12.5	Kampala
Ukraine	604	52	86	11	14	1910	69	Kyyiv (Kiev)
United Arab Emirates	84	1.9	23	23	4	22470	84	Abū Zabī (Abu Dhabi)
United Kingdom (UK)	245	58.6	239	13	11	17970	89.5	London
United States of America (USA)	9373	263.2	28	15	9	24750	76.2	Washington D.C.
Uruguay	177	3.2	18	17	10	3910	90.3	Montevideo
Uzbekistan	447	22.7	51	31	7	960	41	Tashkent
Vanuatu	12	0.2	17	38	9	1230	19	Vila
Venezuela	912	21.8	24	30	5	2840	92.9	Caracas
Vietnam	330	75	227	30	7	170	20.8	Ha Nôi (Hanoi)
Western Sahara	266	0.2	1	47	18	…	…	Laayoune (El Aaiún)
Yemen Republic	528	13.2	25	50	14	800	33.6	San'a
Yugoslavia	102	10.8	106	13	10	1000	52	Beograd (Belgrade)
Zambia	753	9.1	12	47	17	370	43.1	Lusaka
Zimbabwe	391	11.3	29	39	12	540	32.1	Harare

* seat of government

… data not available

How to use the index

To find a place on an atlas map use either the grid code or latitude and longitude.

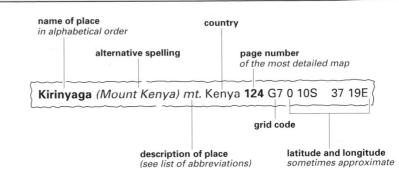

name of place *in alphabetical order*

alternative spelling

country

page number *of the most detailed map*

Kirinyaga *(Mount Kenya) mt.* Kenya **124** G7 0 10S 37 19E

grid code

description of place *(see list of abbreviations)*

latitude and longitude *sometimes approximate*

Grid code

Kirinyaga is in grid square G7

Kirinyaga *(Mount Kenya) mt.* Kenya **124** G7 0 10S 37 19E

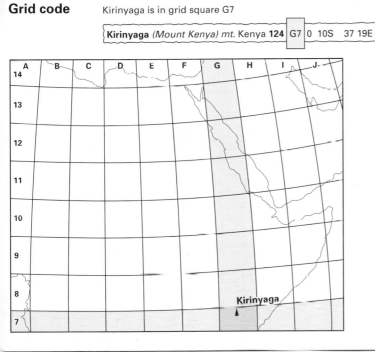

Latitude and Longitude

Kirinyaga is at latitude 0 10S longitude 37 19E

Kirinyaga *(Mount Kenya) mt.* Kenya **124** G7 0 10S 37 19E

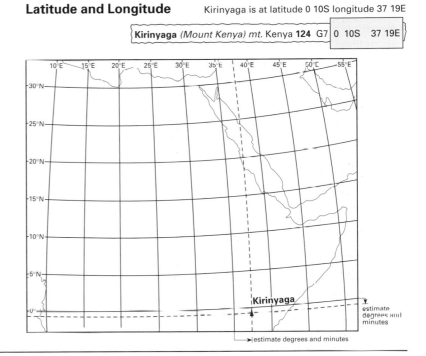

Abbreviations used in the index

admin	administrative area	*p.*	peninsula
ACT	Australian Capital Territory	*plat.*	plateau
b.	bay or harbour	*r.*	river
c.	cape, point, or headland	*r.s.*	research station
can.	canal	*reg.*	region
co.	county	*rep.*	republic
d.	desert	*res.*	reservoir
dep.	depression	*salt l.*	salt lake
D.R.	Democratic Republic	*sd.*	sound, strait, or channel
est.	estuary	*sum.*	summit
fj.	fjord	*tn.*	town or other populated place
g.	gulf	U.A.E.	United Arab Emirates
geog. reg.	geographical region	U.K.	United Kingdom
hist. site	historical site	U.S.A.	United States of America
H.K.	Hong Kong	*v.*	valley
i.	island	*vol.*	volcano
is.	islands		
ist.	isthmus		
l.	lake, lakes, lagoon		
m.s.	mission		
mt.	mountain, peak, or spot height		
mts.	mountains		
N.Z.	New Zealand		

Abbreviations used on the maps

A.C.T.	Australian Capital Territory	Pa.	Passage
Ákr.	Ákra	Peg.	Pegunungan
App.	Appenino	Pen; Penin.	Peninsula
Arch.	Archipelago	Pl.	Planina
Austl.	Australia	Port.	Portugal
C.	Cape; Cabo; Cap	proj.	projected
Ck.	Creek	Pt.	Point
Col.	Colombia	Pta.	Punta
D.C.	District of Columbia	Pte.	Pointe
Dem. Rep.	Democratic Republic	Pto.	Porto; Puerto
Den.	Denmark	R.	River; Rio
D.R.	Democratic Republic	Ra.	Range
E.	East	Res.	Reservoir
Ec.	Ecuador	Résr.	Réservoir
Eq.	Equatorial	S.	San; South
Fj	Fjord	S.A.	South Africa
Fr.	France	Sa.	Sierra
Fwy.	Freeway	Sd.	Sound
G.	Gunung; Gebel	Sev.	Severnaya
Hwy.	Highway	Sp.	Spain
I.	Island; Île; Ilha; Isla	St.	Saint
Is.	Islands; Îles; Ilhas; Islas	Ste.	Sainte
J.	Jezioro	Str.	Strait
Jez.	Jezero	Terr.	Territory
Kep.	Kepulauan	U.A.E.	United Arab Emirates
M.	Muang	u/c	under construction
Mt.	Mount; Mountains; Mont	U.K.	United Kingdom
Mte.	Monte	U.N.	United Nations
Mts.	Mountains; Monts	U.S.A.	United States of America
N.	North	U.S.S.R.	Union of Soviet Socialist Republics
Nat.Pk.	National Park	W.	West
Neths.	Netherlands		
N.P.	National Park		

A

Aa *r.* France **89** B2 50 50N 2 10E
Aachen Germany **93** A2 50 46N 6 06E
Aalen Germany **93** B1 48 50N 10 07E
Aalsmeer Netherlands **89** D4 52 16N 4 45E
Aalst Belgium **89** D2 50 57N 4 03E
Aalten Belgium **89** C3 51 56N 6 35E
Aaper Wald *hills* Germany **86** B2 51 17N 6 50E
Aare *r.* Switzerland **91** D2 47 00N 7 05E
Aarschot Belgium **89** D2 50 59N 4 50E
Aba Nigeria **127** G4 5 06N 7 21E
Ābādān Iran **107** G5 30 20N 48 15E
Abadla Algeria **127** E9 31 01N 2 45W
Abaetetuba Brazil **146** H12 1 45S 48 54W
Abakan *r.* Russia **105** O5 52 00N 88 00E
Abakan *tn.* Russia **105** P5 53 43N 91 25E
Abana Turkey **95** J4 41 58N 34 03E
Abancay Peru **146** C10 13 37S 72 52W
Abashiri Japan **114** D3 44 02N 114 17E
Abbe, Lake Ethiopia **124** H10 11 00N 44 00E
Abbert *r.* Galway Rep. of Ireland **74** C3 53 27N 8 43W
Abberton Resevoir Essex England **71** E2 51 50N 0 48E
Abbeville France **91** C3 50 06N 1 51E
Abbey Galway Rep. of Ireland **75** C3 53 06N 8 24W
Abbeyfeale Limerick Rep. of Ireland **75** B2 52 24N 9 18W
Abbeyleix Laois Rep. of Ireland **75** D2 52 55N 7 20W
Abbeytown Cumbria England **64** B3 54 51N 3 17W
Abbotsbury Dorset England **73** E3 50 40N 2 36W
Ābd al Kūri *i.* Socotra **107** H1 11 55N 52 20E
Abéché Chad **124** D10 13 49N 20 49E
Åbenrå Denmark **93** A3 55 03N 9 26E
Abeokuta Nigeria **127** F4 7 10N 3 26E
Aberaeron Ceredigion Wales **66** C2 52 49N 44 43W
Abercarn Caerphilly Wales **66** D1 51 39N 3 08W
Aberchirder Aberdeenshire Scotland **59** G2 57 33N 2 38W
Aberdare Rhondda Cynon Taff Wales **66** D1 51 43N 3 27W
Aberdare National Park Kenya **124** G7 0 30S 37 00E
Aberdaron Gwynedd Wales **66** C2 52 49N 44 43W
Aberdeen Hong Kong China **112** B1 22 14N 114 09E
Aberdeen Aberdeen City Scotland **59** G2 57 10N 2 04W
Aberdeen Maryland U.S.A. **137** E1 39 31N 76 10W
Aberdeen South Dakota U.S.A. **135** G6 45 28N 98 30W
Aberdeen Washington U.S.A. **134** B6 46 58N 123 49W
Aberdeen City *u.a.* Scotland **59** G2 57 10N 2 00W
Aberdeenshire *u.a.* Scotland **59** G2 57 10N 2 50W
Aberdyfi Gwynedd Wales **66** C2 52 33N 4 02W
Aberfeldy Perth & Kinross Scotland **59** F1 56 37N 3 54W
Aberffraw Isle of Anglesey Wales **66** C3 53 12N 4 28W
Aberfoyle Stirling Scotland **59** E1 56 11N 4 23W
Abergavenny Monmouthshire Wales **66** D1 51 50N 3 00W
Abergele Conwy Wales **66** D3 53 17N 3 34W
Aberlady East Lothian Scotland **61** G4 56 01N 2 51W
Aberporth Ceredigion Wales **66** C2 52 07N 4 34W
Abersoch Gwynedd Wales **66** C2 52 50N 4 31W
Abertillery Blaenau Gwent Wales **66** D1 51 45N 3 09W
Aberystwyth Ceredigion Wales **66** C2 52 25N 4 05W
Abhā Saudi Arabia **106** F2 18 14N 42 31E
Abidjan Côte d'Ivoire **127** E4 5 19N 4 01W
Abilene Texas U.S.A. **140** E6 32 27N 99 45W
Abingdon Oxfordshire England **70** C2 51 41N 1 17W
Abington South Lanarkshire Scotland **61** F3 55 29N 3 42W
Abitibi, Lake Canada **137** D3/E3 48 42N 79 45W
Abitibi River Ontario Canada **137** D3 50 00N 81 20W
Abovyan Armenia **95** P4 40 17N 44 36E
Aboyne Aberdeenshire Scotland **59** G2 57 05N 2 50W
Absaroka Range U.S.A. **134** D6/E5 45 00N 110 00W
Abu Dhabi *see* Abū Zaby
Abu Durba Egypt **106** N9 28 29N 33 20E
Abu Hamed Sudan **124** F11 19 32N 33 20E
Abuja Nigeria **127** G4 9 10N 7 11E
Abunā Brazil **146** D11 9 41S 65 20W
Abu Tig Egypt **106** D4 27 06N 31 17E
Abū Zaby *(Abu Dhabi)* U.A.E. **107** H3 24 28N 54 25E
Acambaro Mexico **140** D4 20 01N 100 42W
Acaponeta Mexico **140** C4 22 30N 102 25W
Acapulco Mexico **140** E3 16 51N 99 56W
Açari *r.* Brazil **147** P2 22 50S 43 22W
Acarigua Venezuela **146** D14 9 35N 69 12W
Acatlān Mexico **140** E3 18 12N 98 02W
Acayucán Mexico **140** E3 17 59N 94 58W
Accra Ghana **127** E4 5 33N 0 15W
Accrington Lancashire England **64** C2 53 46N 2 21W
Achacachi Bolivia **146** D9 16 01S 68 44W
Acharnés Greece **94** C3 38 05N 23 44E
Achill Head Mayo Rep. of Ireland **74** A3 53 59N 10 13W
Achill Island Mayo Rep. of Ireland **74** A3 53 55N 10 05W
Achill Sound Mayo Rep. of Ireland **74** B3 53 56N 9 54W
Achinsk Russia **103** L7 56 20N 90 33E
Achnacroish Argyll & Bute Scotland **58** D1 56 32N 5 30W
Achnasheen Highland Scotland **59** D2 57 35N 5 06W
Açi Göl *l.* Turkey **94** F2 37 50N 29 50E
Acklins Island The Bahamas **141** J4 22 30N 74 30W
Ackworth Moor Top West Yorkshire England **65** D2 53 39N 1 20W
Aclare Sligo Rep. of Ireland **74** C4 54 02N 8 54W
Acle Norfolk England **71** F3 52 38N 1 33E
Aconcagua *mt.* Argentina **147** C6 32 40S 70 02W
Acre *admin.* Brazil **146** C11 8 30S 71 30W
A.C.T. *see* Australian Capital Territory
Ada Oklahoma U.S.A. **135** G3 34 47N 96 41W
Adachi Japan **115** C4 35 46N 139 48E
Adaga *r.* Spain **90** B3 40 45N 4 45W
Adam, Mount Falkland Is. **152** M16 51 36S 60 00W
Adam's Bridge India/Sri Lanka **109** D1 9 10N 79 30E
Adan *(Aden)* Yemen Republic **107** G1 12 50N 45 03E
Adana Turkey **106** E6 37 00N 35 19E
Adapazari *see* Sakarya
Adare Limerick Rep. of Ireland **75** C2 52 34N 8 48W
Adare, Cape Antarctica **149** 71 30S 170 24E
Adda *r.* Italy **92** A3 46 00N 9 00E
Ad Dakhla Western Sahara **127** B7 23 50N 15 58W
Ad Dammām Saudi Arabia **107** H4 26 25N 50 06E
Ad Dawḥah *(Doha)* Qatar **107** H4 25 15N 51 36E
Ad Dilam Saudi Arabia **107** G3 23 59N 47 06E
Ad Dir'iyah Saudi Arabia **107** G3 24 45N 46 32E
Addis Ababa *see* Ādis Ābeba
Ad Dīwānīyah Iraq **106** F5 32 00N 44 57E
Addlestone Surrey England **70** D2 51 22N 0 31W
Adelaide Australia **118** F3 34 56S 138 36E
Adélie Land *see* Terre d'Adélie
Aden, Gulf of Indian Ocean **107** G1 12 30N 47 30E
Adirondack Mountains U.S.A. **137** F2 43 15N 74 40W
Ādīs Ābeba *(Addis Ababa)* Ethiopia **124** G9 9 03N 38 42E
Adiyaman Turkey **95** K2 37 46N 38 15E
Adjud Romania **96** D3 46 07N 27 10
Admiralty Islands Papua New Guinea **118** H9 2 30S 147 00E
Adoni India **109** D3 15 38N 77 16E
Adra West Bengal India **110** D4 23 31N 86 43E
Adra Spain **90** B2 36 45N 3 01W
Adrar Algeria **127** E8 27 51N 0 19W
Adrian Michigan U.S.A. **137** D2 41 55N 84 01W
Adriatic Sea Mediterranean Sea **92** B2/C2 43 00N 15 00E
Adrigole Cork Rep. of Ireland **75** B1 51 44N 9 42W
Adur *r.* West Sussex England **70** D1 50 55N 0 20W
Ādwa Ethiopia **124** G10 14 12N 38 56E
Adwick le Street South Yorkshire England **65** D2 53 34N 1 11W
Aegean Sea Mediterranean Sea **94** D3 39 00N 24 00E
Ærø *i.* Denmark **93** B2 54 52N 10 20E
Aeron *r.* Ceredigion Wales **66** C2 52 15N 4 05W
Affric *r.* Highland Scotland **59** E2 57 20N 4 52W
AFGHANISTAN 107 J5
Afognak Island U.S.A. **132** E4 58 10N 152 50W
Afşin Turkey **95** K3 38 14N 36 54E
Afyon Turkey **94** G3 38 46N 30 32E
Agadez Niger **127** G6 17 00N 7 56E
Agadir Morocco **127** D9 30 30N 9 40W
Agana Guam **150** E9 13 28N 144 45E
Agano *r.* Japan **114** C2 37 50N 139 30E
Agartala Tripura India **109** G4 23 49N 91 15E
Agawa Ontario Canada **133** S2 47 22N 84 37W
Agen France **91** C1 44 12N 0 38E
Ageo Japan **114** L2 35 57N 139 36E
Aghaville Cork Rep. of Ireland **75** B1 51 39N 9 21W
Ağin Turkey **95** L3 38 57N 38 43E
Agios Efstrátios *i.* Greece **94** D3 39 30N 25 00E
Agios Nikólaos Greece **94** D1 35 11N 25 43E
Ago Japan **114** H1 34 20N 136 50E
Agon-Coutainville France **73** F2 49 03N 1 34W
Agout *r.* France **91** C1 43 50N 1 50E
Agra India **109** D5 27 09N 78 00E
Agra *r.* Spain **90** B3 43 00N 2 50W
Agram *see* Zagreb
Ağri Turkey **95** N3 39 44N 43 04E
Agri *r.* Italy **92** C2 40 00N 16 00E
Agrigento Italy **92** B1 37 19N 13 35E
Agrínio Greece **94** B3 38 38N 21 25E
Agropoli Italy **92** B2 40 21N 14 59E
Aguadas Colombia **146** B14 5 36N 75 30W
Aguadilla Puerto Rico **141** K3 18 27N 67 08W
Agua Prieta Mexico **140** C6 31 20N 109 32W
Aguascalientes Mexico **140** D4 21 51N 102 18W
Agueda *r.* Spain **90** A3 40 50N 6 50W
Aguilas Spain **90** B2 37 25N 1 35W
Agulhas Basin Indian Ocean **152** K2 45 00S 20 00E
Agulhas, Cape Rep. of South Africa **125** D1 34 50S 20 00E
Ahascragh Galway Rep. of Ireland **74** C3 53 24N 8 20W
Ahaus Germany **89** G4 52 04N 7 01E
Aherlow *r.* Tipperary Rep. of Ireland **75** C2 52 25N 8 12W
Ahmadabad India **109** C4 23 03N 72 40E
Ahmadnagar India **109** C3 19 08N 74 48E
Ahmar Mountains Ethiopia **124** H9 9 00N 41 00E
Ahoghill Ballymena Northern Ireland **60** C2 54 51N 6 22W
Ahr *r.* Germany **89** F2 50 00N 6 00E
Ahrensburg Germany **93** B2 53 41N 10 14E
Ahrensfelde Germany **87** G2 52 35N 13 35E
Ahuachapán El Salvador **140** G2 13 57N 89 49W
Ahvāz Iran **107** G5 31 17N 48 43E
Aichi *pref.* Japan **114** J2 35 00N 137 15E
Aígina *i.* Greece **94** C2 37 45N 23 30E
Aígio Greece **94** C3 38 15N 22 05E
Ailsa Craig *i.* South Ayrshire Scotland **60** D3 55 16N 5 07W
Ain *r.* France **91** D2 46 30N 5 30E
Aïn Sefra Algeria **127** E9 32 45N 0 35W
Aïn Témouchent Algeria **90** B2 35 18N 1 09W
Aïr *mts.* Niger **127** G6 19 10N 8 20E
Airdrie Alberta Canada **132** M3 51 20N 114 00W
Airdrie North Lanarkshire Scotland **61** F3 55 52N 3 59W
Aire *r.* North Yorkshire/West Yorkshire England **65** D2 53 40N 1 00W
Aire *r.* France **89** D1 49 15N 5 00E
Aire & Calder Navigation *can.* North Yorkshire/West Yorkshire England **65** D2 53 40N 1 00W
Aire-sur-l'Adour France **91** B1 43 42N 0 15W
Aire-sur-la-Lys France **89** B2 50 40N 2 25E
Aishihik Yukon Canada **132** H5 62 00N 137 30W
Aisne *admin.* France **89** C1/D1 49 40N 4 00E
Aisne *r.* France **91** C2 49 30N 3 00E
Aiviekste *r.* Latvia **97** F2 57 00N 26 40E
Aix-en-Provence France **91** D1 43 31N 5 27E
Aix-les-Bains France **91** D2 45 41N 5 55E
Aiyer Reservoir Bihar India **110** C4 23 40N 85 45E
Aizawl Mizoram India **110** K4 23 45N 92 45E
Aizu-Wakamatsu Japan **114** C2 37 30N 139 58E
Ajaccio Corsica **91** D1 41 55N 8 43E
Ajax Ontario Canada **137** E2 43 48N 79 00W
Ajay *r.* Bihar/West Bengal India **110** D5 24 05N 86 55E
Ajdābiyā Libya **124** D14 30 46N 20 14E
Ajlūn Jordan **106** O11 32 20N 35 35E
Ajmer India **109** C5 26 29N 74 40E
Ajo Arizona U.S.A. **134** D3 32 24N 112 51W
Akabira Japan **114** D3 43 40N 141 55E
Akanthou Cyprus **95** H1 35 22N 33 45E
Akaroa N.Z. **119** B2 43 49S 172 58E
Akashi Japan **114** F1 34 39N 135 00E
Akçaabat *r.* Turkey **95** L4 40 55N 39 20E
Akçadag Turkey **95** K3 38 22N 37 58E
Akçakale Turkey **95** K2 36 44N 38 59E
Akçakoca Turkey **94** G4 41 05N 31 08E
Akechi Japan **114** J2 35 19N 137 22E
Akəti Congo (D.R.) **124** D8 2 42N 23 51E
Akhalk'alak'i Georgia **95** N4 41 26N 43 29E
Akhalts'ikhe Georgia **95** N4 41 37N 42 59E
Akhisar Turkey **94** E3 38 54N 27 50E
Ahklun Mountains U.S.A. **132** C4/5 60 00N 161 00W
Akhtubinsk Russia **104** F4 48 20N 46 10E
Akimiski Island N.W.T. Canada **133** S3 53 00N 81 00W
Akita Japan **114** D2 39 44N 140 05E
'Akko Israel **106** O11 32 55N 35 04E
Aklavik N.W.T. Canada **132** I6 68 15N 135 02W
Akmola *(Tselinograd)* Kazakhstan **105** L5 51 10N 71 28E
Akobo Sudan **124** F9 7 50N 33 05E
Akola India **109** D4 20 49N 77 05E
Ak'ordat Eritrea **106** E2 15 26N 3745E
Akpatok Island N.W.T. Canada **133** V5 60 30N 68 00W
Ákra Ákrathos *c.* Greece **94** D4 40 09N 24 23E
Ákra Akrítas *c.* Greece **94** B2 36 43N 21 52E
Ákra Kafiréas *c.* Greece **94** D3 38 10N 24 35E
Ákra Líthino *c.* Greece **94** D3 34 55N 24 44E
Ákra Maléas *c.* Greece **94** C2 36 27N 23 12E
Ákra Melékhas *c.* Greece **94** D2 35 32N 24 10E
Akranes Iceland **97** H6 64 19N 22 05W
Ákra Sideros *c.* Greece **94** E2 35 19N 26 18E
Ákra Spánta *c.* Greece **94** C1 35 42N 23 43E
Ákra Taínaro *c.* Greece **94** C2 36 23N 22 29E
Akron Ohio U.S.A. **137** D2 41 04N 81 31W
Aksaray Turkey **95** J3 38 22N 34 02E
Aksay Russia **95** L7 47 13N 39 51E
Akşehir Turkey **94** G3 38 22N 31 24E
Akşehir Gölü *l.* Turkey **94** G3 38 30N 31 25E
Akseki Turkey **94** G2 37 03N 31 46E
Aksu *r.* Turkey **94** G2 37 20N 30 45E
Āksum Ethiopia **106** E1 14 10N 38 45E
Aktau *(Shevchenko)* Kazakhstan **104** G3 43 37N 51 11E
Aktyubinsk Kazakhstan **105** H5 50 16N 57 13E
Akureyri Iceland **76** B9 65 41N 18 04W
Alabama *state* U.S.A. **135** I3 32 00N 87 00W
Alabama *r.* Alabama U.S.A. **135** I3 31 00N 88 00W
Alaca Turkey **95** J4 40 10N 34 52E
Alaçam Turkey **95** J4 41 36N 35 35E
Alagoas *admin.* Brazil **146** J11 9 30S 37 00W
Alagoinhas Brazil **146** J10 12 09S 38 21W
Alagón *r.* Spain **90** A2 40 00N 6 30W
Alajuela Costa Rica **141** H2 10 00N 84 12W
Alakanuk U.S.A. **132** C5 62 39N 164 48W
Al 'Amārah Iraq **107** G5 31 51N 47 10E
Alamdanga Khulna Bangladesh **110** F4 23 46N 88 57E
Alamosa Colorado U.S.A. **134** E4 37 28N 105 54W
Åland *is.* Finland **97** D3 60 15N 20 00E
Alanya Turkey **94** H2 36 32N 32 02E
Al Artāwīyah Saudi Arabia **107** G4 26 31N 45 21E
Ala Shan *mts.* China **113** K6/7 40 00N 102 30E
Alaska *state* U.S.A. **132** D5/F5 63 10N 157 30W
Alaska, Gulf of U.S.A. **132** F4/G4 58 00N 147 00W
Alaska Peninsula U.S.A. **132** D4 56 30N 159 00W
Alaska Range *mts.* U.S.A. **132** E5/G5 62 30N 152 30W
Alatna U.S.A. **132** E6 66 33N 152 49W
Alaverdi Armenia **95** P4 41 08N 44 40E
Al 'Ayn United Arab Emirates **107** I3 24 10N 55 43E
Alayor Balearic Islands **90** F4 39 56N 4 08E
Alay Range *mts.* Asia **105** L2 39 00N 70 00E
Albacete Spain **90** B2 39 00N 1 52W
Alba Iulia Romania **96** C3 46 04N 23 33E
ALBANIA 94 A4/B4
Albany Australia **118** B3 34 57S 117 54E
Albany Georgia U.S.A. **135** J3 31 37N 84 10W
Albany New York U.S.A. **137** F2 42 40N 73 49W
Albany Oregon U.S.A. **134** B5 44 38N 123 07W
Albany River Ontario Canada **133** S3 52 00N 84 00W
Al Başrah Iraq **107** G5 30 30N 47 50E
Al Bayḑā Libya **124** D14 32 00N 21 30E
Alberche *r.* Spain **90** B3 40 10N 4 45W
Albert France **91** C3 50 00N 2 40E
Alberta *province* Canada **132** L3 54 00N 117 30W
Albert-Kanaal *can.* Belgium **89** D3 51 10N 5 00E
Albert, Lake Uganda/Congo (D.R.) **124** F8 2 00N 31 00E
Albert Lea Minnesota U.S.A. **136** B2 43 38N 93 16W
Albertville France **91** D2 45 40N 6 24E
Albi France **91** C1 43 56N 2 08E
Al Bi'r Saudi Arabia **106** E4 28 50N 36 16E
Ålborg Denmark **97** B2 57 05N 9 50E
Albrighton Shropshire England **67** E2 52 38N 2 16W
Āl Bū Kamāl Syria **106** F5 34 29N 40 56E
Albuquerque U.S.A. **134** E4 35 05N 106 38W
Al Buraymī Oman **107** I3 24 16N 55 48E
Alcalá de Guadaira Spain **90** A2 37 20N 5 50W
Alcalá de Henares Spain **90** B3 40 28N 3 22W
Alcalá la Real Spain **90** B2 37 28N 3 55W
Alcamo Italy **92** B1 37 58N 12 58E
Alcañiz Spain **90** B3 41 03N 0 09W
Alcantarilla Spain **90** B2 37 59N 1 12W
Alcázar de San Juan Spain **90** B2 39 24N 3 12W
Alcester Warwickshire England **67** F2 52 13N 1 52W
Alchevs'k *(Kommunarsk)* Ukraine **104** D4 48 30N 38 47E
Alcira Spain **90** B2 39 10N 0 27W
Alcoy Spain **90** B2 38 42N 0 29W
Alcudia Balearic Islands **90** E4 39 51N 3 06E
Aldama Mexico **140** E4 22 54N 98 05W
Aldan Russia **103** O7 58 44N 124 22E
Aldan *r.* Russia **103** P7 59 00N 132 30E
Aldbourne Wiltshire England **70** C2 51 30N 1 37W
Aldbrough East Riding of Yorkshire England **65** E2 53 50N 0 06W
Alde *r.* Suffolk England **71** F3 52 10N 1 30E
Aldeburgh Suffolk England **71** F3 52 09N 1 35E
Alderley Edge *tn.* Cheshire England **64** C2 53 18N 2 15W
Alderney *i.* Channel Is. British Isles **73** E2 49 43N 2 12W
Aldershot Hampshire England **70** D2 51 15N 0 47W
Aldridge West Midlands England **67** F2 52 36N 1 55W
Aldsworth Gloucestershire England **70** C2 51 48N 1 46W
Alegrete Brazil **147** G7 29 45S 55 46W
Aleksandrovskoye Russia **95** N6 44 45N 42 59E
Aleksandrovsk-Sakhalinskiy Russia **103** Q6 50 55N 142 12E
Alençon France **91** C2 48 25N 0 05E
Alenuihaha Channel *sd.* Hawaiian Is. **151** Y18 20 20N 156 20W
Aleppo *see* Halab
Alert *m.s.* N.W.T. Canada **148** 80 31N 60 05W
Alès France **91** C1 44 08N 4 05E
Alessándria Italy **92** A2 44 55N 8 37E
Ålesund Norway **97** B3 62 28N 6 11E
Aleutian Basin Pacific Ocean **150** I13 54 00N 178 00W
Aleutian Islands U.S.A. **132** A3 54 00N 173 00W
Aleutian Range *mts.* U.S.A. **132** D4 56 30N 159 00W
Aleutian Ridge Pacific Ocean **150** I13 53 55N 178 00W
Aleutian Trench Pacific Ocean **150** I13 50 55N 178 00W
Alexander Archipelago *is.* U.S.A. **132** H4 57 00N 137 30W
Alexander Bay *tn.* Rep. of South Africa **125** C2 28 40S 16 30E
Alexander Island Antarctica **149** 71 00S 70 00W
Alexandra N.Z. **119** A1 45 15S 169 23E
Alexándreia Greece **94** C4 40 38N 22 28E
Alexandria Romania **96** D2 43 59N 25 19E
Alexandria West Dunbartonshire Scotland **61** E3 55 59N 4 36W
Alexandria Louisiana U.S.A. **135** H3 31 19N 92 29W
Alexandria Virginia U.S.A. **137** E1 38 49N 77 06W
Alexandria Egypt *see* El Iskandariya
Alexandria Bay *tn.* U.S.A. **137** E2 44 20N 75 55W
Alexandroúpoli Greece **94** D4 40 51N 25 53E
Alfambra *r.* Spain **90** B3 40 40N 1 00W
Al Fatḩah Iraq **95** N1 35 04N 43 34E
Alfeiós *r.* Greece **94** B2 37 30N 21 45E
Alford Lincolnshire England **65** F2 53 17N 0 11E
Alford Aberdeenshire Scotland **59** G2 57 13N 2 42W
Alfred Ontario Canada **137** F3 45 33N 74 52W
Alfreton Derbyshire England **67** F3 53 06N 1 23W
Al Fuḩayḩīl Kuwait **107** G4 29 07N 47 02E
Algarve *geog. reg.* Portugal **76** D3 37 30N 8 00W
Algeciras Spain **90** A2 36 08N 5 27W
Alger *(Algiers)* Algeria **127** F10 36 50N 3 00E
ALGERIA 127 D8/G10
Alghero Italy **92** A2 40 34N 8 19E
Algiers *see* Alger
Algona Iowa U.S.A. **136** B2 43 04N 94 11W
Al Hadīthah Iraq **106** F5 34 06N 42 25E
Alhambra California U.S.A. **139** B3 34 05N 118 10W
Al Hariq Saudi Arabia **107** G3 23 34N 46 35E
Al Hasakah Syria **106** F6 36 32N 40 44E
Al Hillah Iraq **106** F5 32 28N 44 29E
Al Hoceima Morocco **90** B2 35 14N 3 56W
Al Hudaydah Yemen Republic **106** F1 14 50N 42 58E
Al Hufūf Saudi Arabia **107** G4 25 20N 49 34E
Aliağa Turkey **94** E3 38 49N 26 59E
Aliákmonas *r.* Greece **94** C4 40 30N 22 20E
Alicante Spain **90** B2 38 21N 0 29W
Alice Texas U.S.A. **135** G2 27 45N 98 06W
Alice Springs *tn.* Australia **118** E5 23 42S 133 52E
Aligarh India **109** D5 27 54N 78 04E
Aling Kangri *mt.* China **112** F5 32 51N 81 03E
Alipur India **108** K2 22 32N 88 19E
Alipur Duar West Bengal India **110** G7 26 29N 89 38E
Aliwal North Rep. of South Africa **125** E1 30 42S 26 43E
Al Jahrah Kuwait **107** G4 29 22N 47 40E
Al Jawf Libya **124** D12 24 12N 23 18E
Al Jawf Saudi Arabia **106** E4 29 49N 39 52E
Al Jubayl Saudi Arabia **107** G4 26 59N 49 40E
Aljustrel Portugal **90** A2 37 52N 8 10W
Al Khums Libya **124** B14 32 39N 14 16E
Alkmaar Netherlands **89** D4 52 38N 4 44E
Al Kufrah Oasis Libya **124** D12 24 10N 23 15E
Al Kūt Iraq **107** G5 32 30N 45 51E
Al Kuwayt Kuwait **107** G4 29 20N 48 00E
Al Lādhiqīyah *(Latakia)* Syria **106** E6 35 31N 35 47E
Allahabad India **109** E5 25 27N 81 50E
Allegheny Mountains U.S.A. **137** E1/2 40 00N 79 00W
Allegheny Reservoir U.S.A. **137** E2 42 00N 79 00W
Allen *r.* Northumberland England **61** G2 54 50N 2 20W
Allendale Town Northumberland England **61** G2 54 54N 2 15W
Allende Mexico **140** D5 28 22N 100 50W
Allentown Pennsylvania U.S.A. **137** E2 40 37N 75 30W
Alleppey India **109** D1 9 30N 76 22E
Aller *r.* Germany **93** A2 52 00N 9 00E
Alliance Nebraska U.S.A. **134** F5 42 08N 102 54W
Allier *r.* France **91** C2 46 40N 3 00E
Alliston Ontario Canada **137** E2 44 09N 79 51W
Al Līth Saudi Arabia **106** F3 20 10N 40 20E
Alloa Clackmannanshire Scotland **61** F4 56 07N 3 49W
Allow *r.* Cork Rep. of Ireland **75** C2 52 18N 8 57W
Alma Québec Canada **137** F3 48 32N 71 41W
Alma Michigan U.S.A. **137** D2 43 23N 84 40W
Almada Portugal **90** A2 38 40N 9 09W
Almadén Spain **90** B2 38 47N 4 50W
Al Madīnah *(Medina)* Saudi Arabia **106** E3 24 30N 39 35E
Almalyk Uzbekistan **105** K3 40 50N 69 40E
Al Manāmah Bahrain **107** H4 26 12N 50 38E
Almansa Spain **90** B2 38 52N 1 06W
Almanzora *r.* Spain **90** B2 37 15N 2 10W
Almaty *(Alma-Ata)* Kazakhstan **105** M3 43 19N 76 55E
Almaty *see* Alma-Ata
Al Mawşil *(Mosul)* Iraq **106** F6 36 21N 43 08E
Almazán Spain **90** B3 41 29N 2 31W
Almelo Netherlands **89** F4 52 21N 6 40E
Almendralejo Spain **90** A2 38 41N 6 25W
Almere Netherlands **89** E4 52 22N 5 12E
Almere-Haven Netherlands **89** E3 52 21N 5 11E
Almería Spain **90** B2 36 50N 2 26W
Al'met'yevsk Russia **105** G5 54 50N 52 22E
Älmhult Sweden **97** C2 56 32N 14 10E
Al Miqdādiyah Iraq **106** F5 33 58N 44 58E
Almirós Greece **94** C3 39 11N 22 45E
Almodôvar Portugal **90** A2 37 31N 8 03W
Almond *r.* Perth & Kinross Scotland **59** F1 56 25N 3 55W
Almonte Ontario Canada **137** E3 45 13N 76 12W
Al Mubarraz Saudi Arabia **107** G4 25 26N 49 37E
Al Mukallā Yemen Republic **107** G1 14 34N 49 09E
Al Mukhā Yemen Republic **106** F1 13 20N 43 16E
Aln *r.* Northumberland England **61** H3 55 25N 1 45W
Alness Highland Scotland **59** E2 57 41N 4 15W
Alnwick Northumberland England **61** H3 55 25N 1 42W
Alónissos *i.* Greece **94** C3 39 10N 23 55E
Alor *i.* Indonesia **111** G2 8 15S 124 30E
Alor Setar Malaysia **111** C5 6 07N 100 21E
Alpena Michigan U.S.A. **137** D3 45 04N 83 27W
Alpes Maritimes *mts.* France/Italy **91** D1 44 15N 6 45E
Alpha Ridge Arctic Ocean **148** 85 00N 120 00W
Alphen aan den Rijn Netherlands **89** D4 52 08N 4 40E
Alpi Carniche *mts.* Europe **92** B3 46 00N 13 00E
Alpi Cozie *mts.* Europe **92** A2 45 00N 8 00E
Alpi Dolomitiche *mts.* Italy **92** B3 46 00N 12 00E
Alpi Graie *mts.* Europe **92** C1 45 00N 7 00E
Alpi Lepontine *mts.* Switzerland **92** A3 46 26N 8 30E
Alpine Texas U.S.A. **134** F3 30 22N 103 40W
Alpi Pennine *mts.* Italy/Switzerland **92** A3 45 55N 7 30E
Alpi Retiche *mts.* Switzerland **92** A3/B3 46 25N 9 45E
Alps *mts.* Europe **92** A3/B3 46 00N 7 30E
Al Qāmishlī Syria **95** M2 37 03N 41 15E
Al Qunfudhah Saudi Arabia **106** F2 19 09N 41 07E
Alsager Cheshire England **64** C2 53 06N 2 19W
Alsdorf Germany **89** F2 50 53N 6 10E
Alston Cumbria England **64** C3 54 49N 2 26W
Alta Norway **97** E4 69 57N 23 10E
Altadena California U.S.A. **139** B3 34 12N 118 08W
Altaelv *r.* Norway **97** E4 69 50N 23 30E
Alta Gracia Argentina **147** E6 31 42S 64 25W
Altai *mts.* Mongolia **150** Z12 47 00N 92 30E
Altamaha *r.* Georgia U.S.A. **135** J3 32 00N 82 00W
Altamira Brazil **146** G12 3 13S 52 15W
Altamura Italy **92** C2 40 49N 16 34E
Altay China **112** G8 47 48N 88 07E
Altay *mts.* Russia **103** K6 51 00N 89 00E
Altenburg Germany **93** B2 50 59N 12 27E
Altenessen Germany **86** C2 51 29N 7 02E
Altintaş Turkey **94** G3 39 04N 30 05E
Altiri Orissa India **110** D1 20 56N 86 13E
Altlandsberg Germany **87** G2 52 34N 13 45E
Altmühl *r.* Germany **93** B1 49 00N 10 00E
Altnaharra Highland Scotland **59** E3 58 16N 4 27W
Alto da Boa Vista Brazil **147** P2 22 58S 43 17W
Alto Molocue Mozambique **125** G4 15 38S 37 42E
Alton Hampshire England **70** D2 51 09N 0 59W
Alton Illinois U.S.A. **136** B1 38 55N 90 10W
Altona Manitoba Canada **136** A3 49 06N 97 35W
Altoona Pennsylvania U.S.A. **137** E2 40 32N 78 32W
Altrincham Greater Manchester England **64** C2 53 24N 2 21W
Altun Shan *mts.* China **112** G6 37 30N 86 00E
Altus Oklahoma U.S.A. **134** G3 34 39N 99 21W
Alucra Turkey **95** L4 40 20N 38 43E
Alupka Ukraine **95** J6 44 26N 34 02E
Alva Oklahoma U.S.A. **134** G4 36 48N 98 40W
Al Wajh Saudi Arabia **106** E4 26 16N 32 28E
Alwar India **109** D5 27 32N 76 35E
Alwen *r.* Wales **66** D3 53 00N 3 30W
Alwen Resevoir *res.* Wales **66** D3 53 28N 3 36W
Alyat Azerbaijan **104** F2 39 57N 49 25E
Alyth Perth & Kinross Scotland **59** F1 56 37N 3 13W
Amadeus, Lake Australia **118** E5 24 00S 132 30E
Amadi Sudan **124** F9 5 32N 30 20E
Amādīyah Iraq **95** N2 37 06N 43 29E
Amadjuak Lake N.W.T. Canada **133** U6 65 00N 71 00W
Amagasaki Japan **114** C1 34 42N 135 23E
Amakusa-shotō *is.* Japan **114** B1 32 50N 130 05E
Amaliáda Greece **94** B2 37 49N 21 22E
Amapá Brazil **146** G13 2 00N 50 50W
Amapá *admin.* Brazil **146** G13 2 00N 52 30W
Amarillo Texas U.S.A. **134** F4 35 14N 101 50W
Amasya Turkey **95** J4 40 37N 35 50E
Amatsukominato Japan **114** M2 35 08N 140 14E
Amazon *see* Rio Amazonas
Amazonas *admin.* Brazil **146** D12/F12 4 30S 65 00W
Amazon, Mouths of the *est.* Brazil **146** G13 1 00N 51 00W
Ambala India **109** D6 30 19N 76 49E
Ambarchik Russia **103** S9 69 39N 162 37E
Ambasa Tripura India **110** J4 23 56N 91 52E
Ambato Ecuador **146** B12 1 18S 78 39W
Amberg Germany **93** B1 49 26N 11 52E
Amble Northumberland England **61** H3 55 20N 1 34W
Ambleside Cumbria England **64** C3 54 26N 2 58W
Amblève *r.* Belgium **89** F2 50 22N 6 10E
Ambon Indonesia **111** H3 3 41S 128 10E
Ambovombe Madagascar **125** I2 25 10S 46 06E
Amderma Russia **103** I9 66 44N 61 35E
Amdo China **112** H5 32 22N 91 07E
Ameca Mexico **140** D4 20 34N 104 03W
Ameland *i.* Netherlands **89** E5 53 28N 5 45E
American Falls *tn.* Idaho U.S.A. **134** D5 42 47N 112 50W
American Samoa Pacific Ocean **151** J6 15 00S 170 00W
Amersfoort Netherlands **89** E4 52 09N 5 23E

Amersham Buckinghamshire England **70** D2 51 40N 0 38W
Amery Ice Shelf Antarctica **149** 70 00S 70 00E
Ames Iowa U.S.A. **136** B2 42 02N 93 33W
Amesbury Wiltshire England **70** C2 51 10N 1 47W
Amfilochía Greece **94** B3 38 52N 21 09E
Amfípoli Greece **96** C2 40 48N 23 52E
Amga Russia **103** P8 61 51N 131 59E
Amga *r.* Russia **103** P8 60 30N 130 00E
Amgun' *r.* Russia **103** P6 52 00N 137 00E
Amherst Nova Scotia Canada **133** W2 45 50N 64 14W
Amherst Virginia U.S.A. **137** E1 37 35N 79 04W
Amiens France **91** C2 49 54N 2 18E
Amik Gölü *l.* Turkey **95** K2 36 20N 36 15E
Amlia Island U.S.A. **132** A3 52 05N 173 30W
Amlwch Isle of Anglesey Wales **66** C3 53 25N 4 20W
Amman Jordan **106** O10 31 04N 46 17E
Ammanford Carmarthenshire Wales **66** D1 51 48N 3 58W
Ammassalik *see* Tasiilaq
Ammersee *l.* Germany **93** B1 48 00N 11 00E
Amorgós *i.* Greece **94** D2 36 50N 25 55E
Ampana Indonesia **111** G3 0 54S 121 35E
Amper *r.* Germany **93** B1 48 00N 11 00E
Ampthill Bedfordshire England **70** D3 52 02N 0 30W
Amrapara Bihar India **110** E5 24 33N 87 34E
Amravati India **109** D4 20 58N 77 50E
Amritsar India **109** C6 31 35N 74 56E
Amroha India **109** D5 28 54N 78 29E
Amrum *i.* Germany **93** A2 54 00N 8 00E
Amstelveen Netherlands **89** D4 52 18N 4 52E
Amsterdam Netherlands **89** D4 52 22N 4 54E
Amsterdam New York U.S.A. **137** F2 42 56N 74 12W
Amsterdam Rijnkanaal *can.* Netherlands **89** E2/3 51 15N 5 00E
Amstetten Austria **92** B3 48 08N 14 52E
Amtali Khulna Bangladesh **110** H3 22 08N 90 14E
Am Timan Chad **124** D10 10 59N 20 18E
Amund Ringnes Islands Canada **133** P8 78 00N 96 00W
Amundsen Gulf Canada **132** K7 70 30N 125 00W
Amundsen-Scott *r.s.* South Pole Antarctica **149** 90 00S
Amundsen Sea Southern Ocean **149** 72 00S 130 00W
Amungen *l.* Sweden **97** D3 61 10N 15 35E
Amur *(Heilong Jiang) r.* Asia **113** P9 52 30N 126 30E
Amudar'ya *(Oxus) r.* Asia **105** J2 39 00N 64 00E
Amursk Russia **103** P6 50 16N 136 55E
Anabar *r.* Russia **103** N10 71 30N 113 00E
Anaconda Montana U.S.A. **134** D6 46 09N 112 56W
Anadolu Dağlari *mts.* Turkey **95** K4/M4 40 30N 38 30E
Anadyr' Russia **103** T8 64 50N 178 00E
Anadyr' *r.* Russia **103** T9 65 00N 175 00E
Anadyr', Gulf of Russia **103** U8 65 00N 178 00W
Anáfi *i.* Greece **94** D2 36 20N 25 45E
Anaheim California U.S.A. **139** C2 33 50N 117 56W
Anai Mudi *mt.* India **109** D2 10 20N 77 15E
Anamur Turkey **95** H2 36 06N 32 49E
Anan Japan **114** B1 33 54N 134 40E
Anandpur Orissa India **110** D2 21 14N 86 10E
Anandpur *r.* West Bengal India **110** E3 22 10N 87 30E
Ananindeua Brazil **146** H12 1 22S 48 20W
Anantapur India **109** D2 14 42N 77 05E
Anapa Rissia **95** K6 44 54N 37 20E
Anápolis Brazil **146** H9 16 19S 48 58W
Anascaul Kerry Rep. of Ireland **75** A2 52 09N 10 04W
Anatolian Plateau Turkey **77** M3 39 00N 39 00E
Anatom *i.* Vanuatu **118** L5 20 10S 169 50E
Anchorage U.S.A. **132** F5 61 10N 150 00W
Ancona Italy **92** B2 43 37N 13 31E
Ancroft Northumberland England **61** G3 55 42N 2 00W
Anda China **113** P8 46 25N 125 20E
Andalsnes Norway **97** B3 62 33N 7 43E
Andaman Islands India **109** G2 12 00N 94 00E
Andaman Sea Indian Ocean **111** B6 13 00N 95 00E
Andenne Belgium **89** E2 50 29N 5 06E
Anderlecht Belgium **89** D2 50 50N 4 20E
Andermatt Switzerland **92** A3 46 38N 8 36E
Anderson *r.* N.W.T. Canada **132** J6 69 42N 129 01W
Anderson Indiana U.S.A. **136** C2 40 05N 85 41W
Anderson South Carolina U.S.A. **135** J3 34 30N 82 39W
Andes *mts.* South America **146** B13/C5
Andhra Pradesh *admin.* India **109** D3 16 00N 79 00E
Andizhan Uzbekistan **105** L3 40 40N 72 12E
Andkhvoy Afghanistan **107** K6 36 58N 65 00E
ANDORRA 90 C3
Andorra la Vella Andorra **90** C3 42 30N 1 30E
Andover Hampshire England **70** C2 51 13N 1 28W
Andraitx Balearic Islands **90** E4 39 35N 2 25E
Andreas Isle of Man British Isles **64** A3 54 22N 4 26W
Andreas, Cape Cyprus **95** J1 35 40N 34 35E
Andrésy France **87** A2 48 59N 2 03E
Andreyevka Kazakhstan **105** N4 45 50N 80 34E
Andreyevka Ukraine **104** D4 49 34N 36 38E
Andropov *see* Rybinsk
Andros *i.* The Bahamas **141** I4 24 00N 78 00W
Ándros Greece **94** D2 37 49N 24 54E
Ándros *i.* Greece **94** D2 37 49N 24 54E
Androscoggin River U.S.A. **137** F2 44 00N 70 00W
Andros Town The Bahamas **135** K1 24 45N 77 50W
Androth Island India **109** C2 10 51N 73 41E
Andújar Spain **90** B2 38 02N 4 03W
Andulo Angola **125** C5 11 29S 16 43E
Angara *r.* Russia **103** L7 58 00N 97 30E
Angara Basin Arctic Ocean **148** 80 00N
Angarsk Russia **103** M6 52 31N 103 55E
Angel de la Guarda *i.* Mexico **140** B5 29 00N 113 30W
Angeles National Forest U.S.A. **139** B4/C3 34 15N 118 10W
Ångermanälvern *r.* Sweden **97** D3 64 30N 16 15E
Angers France **91** B2 47 29N 0 32W
Angle Pembrokeshire Wales **66** B1 51 41N 5 06W
Anglesey *i.* Isle of Anglesey Wales **66** C3 53 18N 4 25W
Isle of Anglesey *u.a.* Isle of Anglesey Wales **66** C3 53 18N 4 25W
Angliers Québec Canada **137** E3 47 33N 79 14W
ANGOLA 125 B4/D6
Angola Basin Atlantic Ocean **152** I5 15 00S 3 00E
Angoulême France **91** C2 45 40N 0 10E
Angren Uzbekistan **105** L3 41 01N 70 10E
Anguilla *i.* Leeward Islands **141** L3 18 14N 63 05W
Angul Orissa India **110** C1 20 48N 85 04E
Angus *u.a.* Scotland **59** G1 56 45N 3 00W
Aniak U.S.A. **148** 61 32N 159 40W
Anjō Japan **114** J1 34 56N 137 05E
Ankara Turkey **95** H3 39 55N 32 50E
Ankara *r.* Turkey **94** H3 39 50N 32 10E
Ankaratra *mt.* Madagascar **125** I4 19 25S 47 12E
Anklam Germany **93** B2 53 52N 13 42E
'Annaba Algeria **127** G10 36 55N 7 47E
An Nabk Saudi Arabia **106** E5 31 21N 37 20E
An Nabk Syria **106** E5 34 02N 36 43E
An Nafud *d.* Saudi Arabia **106** F4 28 20N 40 30E
An Najaf Iraq **106** F5 31 59N 44 19E
Annalee *r.* Cavan Rep. of Ireland **74** D4 54 04N 7 13W
Annalong Newry and Mourne Northern Ireland **60** D2 54 06N 5 55W
Annan Dumfries & Galloway Scotland **61** F2 54 59N 3 16W
Annan *r.* Dumfries & Galloway Scotland **61** F3 55 05N 3 20W
Annandale *v.* Dumfries & Galloway Scotland **61** F3 55 15N 3 25W
Annapolis Maryland U.S.A. **137** E1 38 59N 76 30W
Annapurna *mt.* Nepal **109** E5 28 34N 83 50E
Ann Arbor Michigan U.S.A. **137** D2 42 18N 83 43W
Annbank South Ayrshire Scotland **61** E3 55 28N 4 30W
Ann, Cape U.S.A. **137** F2 42 39N 70 37W
Annecy France **91** D2 45 54N 6 07E
Annfield Plain Durham England **64** D3 54 52N 1 45W
Anniston Alabama U.S.A. **135** I3 33 38N 85 50W
Annotto Bay *tn.* Jamaica **141** R8 18 16N 76 47W
Anqing China **113** N5 30 46N 119 40E
Ansari Nagar India **108** L4 28 33N 77 12E
Ansbach Germany **93** B1 49 18N 10 36E
Anshan China **113** O7 41 05N 122 58E
Anshun China **113** L4 26 15N 105 51E
Anstey Leicestershire England **67** F2 52 40N 1 10W
Anston South Yorkshire England **65** D2 53 22N 1 13W
Anstruther Fife Scotland **59** G1 56 14N 2 42W
Antakya *see* Hatay
Antalya Turkey **94** G2 36 53N 30 42E
Antalya Körfezi *b.* Turkey **94** G2 36 30N 31 00E
Antananarivo *(Tananarive)* Madagascar **125** I4 18 52S 47 30E
Antarctica 149
Antarctic Peninsula Antarctica **149** 68 00S 65 00W
Antequera Spain **90** B2 37 01N 4 34W
Antibes France **91** D1 43 35N 7 07E
Antigua *i.* Antigua & Barbuda **141** L3 17 09N 61 49W
Antigua Guatemala **140** F2 14 33N 90 42W
ANTIGUA & BARBUDA 141 L3
Antipodes Islands Southern Ocean **150** H3 49 42S 178 50E
Antofagasta Chile **147** C8 23 40S 70 23W
Antrim *co.* Northern Ireland **60** C2 54 40N 6 10W
Antrim Antrim Northern Ireland **60** C2 54 43N 6 13W
Antrim Mountains Northern Ireland **60** C3 55 00N 6 10W
Antsiranana Madagascar **125** I5 12 19S 49 17E
Antwerpen *admin.* Belgium **89** C3 51 20N 4 45E
Antwerpen *(Anvers)* Belgium **89** D3 51 13N 4 25W
Antykýthira *i.* Greece **94** C1 35 52N 23 18E
Anuradhapura Sri Lanka **109** E1 8 20N 80 25E
Anvers *see* Antwerpen
Anxi China **113** J7 40 32N 95 57E
Anyang China **113** M6 36 04N 114 20E
Anzhero-Sudzhensk Russia **103** K7 56 10N 86 01E
Aomori Japan **114** D3 40 50N 140 43E
Aosta Italy **92** A3 45 43N 7 19E
Aozou Strip Chad **124** C12 23 00N 17 00E
Aparri The Philippines **111** G7 18 22N 121 40E
Apatity Russia **102** F9 67 32N 33 21E
Apatzingán Mexico **140** D3 19 05N 102 20W
Apeldoorn Netherlands **89** E4 52 13N 5 57E
Apia Samoa **150** I6 13 48S 171 45W
Ap Lei Chau *i.* H.K. China **112** B1 22 10N 114 00E
Apolda Germany **93** B2 51 02N 11 31E
Apostle Islands Wisconsin U.S.A. **136** B3 47 00N 90 00W
Appalachian Mountains U.S.A. **135** J4 37 00N 82 00W
Appennines *see* Appennini
Appennini *(Appennines) mts.* Italy **92** A2/C2 43 00N 12 30E
Appennino Abruzzese *mts.* Italy **92** B2 42 00N 14 00E
Appennino Ligure *mts.* Italy **92** A2 44 00N 9 00E
Appennino Lucano *mts.* Italy **92** C2 40 30 N 15 30E
Appennino Tosco-Emiliano *mts.* Italy **92** B2 44 00N 12 00E
Appingedam Netherlands **89** F5 53 18N 6 52E
Appleby in Westmorland Cumbria England **64** C3 53 36N 2 29W
Appledore Devon England **72** C4 51 03N 4 12W
Appleton Wisconsin U.S.A. **136** C2 44 17N 88 24W
Appleton City Missouri U.S.A. **136** B1 38 10N 94 03W
Appomattox Virginia U.S.A. **137** E1 37 12N 78 51W
Apsheronsk Russia **95** L6 44 26N 39 45E
'Aqaba Jordan **106** O9 29 32N 35 00E
'Aqaba, Gulf of Middle East **106** D4 28 40N 34 40E
Aq Chāy *r.* Iran **95** P3 38 55N 44 55E
Aquidauana Brazil **146** F8 20 27S 55 45W
Aquiles Sedan Mexico **134** E2 28 37N 105 54W
Ara India **109** E5 25 34N 84 40E
Ara *r.* Japan **115** C3 35 39N 139 51E
Ara *r.* Tipperary Rep. of Ireland **75** C2 52 30N 8 14W
Arabian Sea Indian Ocean **107** J2 17 00N 60 00E
Araç Turkey **95** H4 41 14N 33 20E
Aracaju Brazil **146** J10 10 54S 37 07W
Aracati Brazil **146** J12 4 32S 37 45W
Arad Romania **96** C3 46 10N 21 19E
Arafura Sea Australia/Indonesia **118** E8/F8 8 00S 132 00E
Aragats *mt.* Armenia **104** E3 40 32N 44 11E
Araglin *r.* Tipperary Rep. of Ireland **75** C2 52 12N 8 03W
Aragón *r.* Spain **90** B3 42 15N 1 40W
Araguaina Brazil **146** H11 7 16S 48 18W
Araguari Brazil **146** H9 18 38S 48 13W
Arak Iran **107** G5 34 05N 49 42E
Arakawa Japan **114** L2 35 58N 139 03E
Arakli Turkey **95** L4 40 58N 39 58E
Araks *see* Araxes
Aral Sea Asia **105** H3/J4 45 00N 60 00E
Aral'sk Kazakhstan **105** J4 46 56N 61 43E
Arambag West Bengal India **110** E3 22 54N 87 47E
Aranda de Duero Spain **90** B3 41 40N 3 41W
Aran Fawddwy *mt.* Gwynedd Wales **66** D2 52 47N 3 41W
Aran Island Donegal Rep. of Ireland **74** C5 55 00N 8 30W
Aran Islands Clare Rep. of Ireland **75** B3 53 10N 9 50W
Aranjuez Spain **90** B3 40 02N 3 37W
Arapiraca Brazil **146** J11 9 45S 36 40W
Ar'ar Saudi Arabia **106** F5 30 58N 41 03E
Araraquara Brazil **147** H8 21 46S 48 08W
Ararat Armenia **95** P3 39 47N 44 46E
Ararat, Mount *see* Büyük Ağri Daği
Araria Bihar India **110** E7 26 09N 87 31E
Aras *(Araks, Araxes) r.* Turkey **104** F2 40 00N 43 30E
Arauca Colombia **146** C14 7 04N 70 41W
Araure Venezuela **141** K1 9 36N 69 15W
Araxá Brazil **146** H9 19 37S 46 50W
Araxes *(Araks, Aras) r.* Iran **107** G6 38 40N 46 30E
Arbil Iraq **106** F6 36 12N 44 01E
Arbroath Angus Scotland **59** G1 56 34N 2 35W
Arc *r.* France **91** D2 45 15N 6 10E
Arcachon France **91** B1 44 40N 1 11W
Arcadia California U.S.A. **139** C3 34 09N 118 00W
Archipelago Dehalak *is.* Ethiopia **124** H11 15 45N 40 12E
Arctic Bay *tn.* N.W.T. Canada **133** R7 73 05N 85 20W
Arctic Ocean 148
Arctowski *r.s.* Antarctica **149** 62 09S 58 28W
Arcyz Moldova **94** F6 45 59N 29 26E
Arda *r.* Bulgaria **96** D2 41 30N 26 00E
Ardabil Iran **107** G6 38 15N 48 18E
Ardahan Turkey **95** N4 41 08N 42 41E
Ardara Donegal Rep. of Ireland **74** C4 54 46N 8 25W
Ardbeg Argyll & Bute Scotland **60** C3 55 39N 6 05W
Ardee Louth Rep. of Ireland **74** E3 53 52N 6 33W
Ardennes *mts.* Belgium **89** E2 50 10N 5 45E
Ardennes *admin.* France **89** D1 49 35N 4 35E
Ardeşen Turkey **95** M4 41 14N 40 00E
Ardfert Kerry Rep. of Ireland **75** B2 52 20N 9 47W
Ardglass Down Northern Ireland **60** D2 54 16N 5 37W
Ardila *r.* Spain **90** A2 38 15N 6 50W
Ardle *r.* Perth & Kinross Scotland **59** F1 56 40N 3 30W
Ardminish Argyll & Bute Scotland **60** D3 55 42N 5 44W
Ardmore Waterford Rep. of Ireland **75** D1 51 57N 7 43W
Ardmore Oklahoma U.S.A. **135** G3 34 11N 97 08W
Ardmore Point *c.* Argyll & Bute Scotland **60** C3 55 41N 6 01W
Ardnamurchan, Point of Highland Scotland **58** C1 56 44N 6 14W
Ardres France **89** A2 50 51N 1 59E
Ardrossan North Ayrshire Scotland **61** E3 55 39N 4 49W
Ards *district* Northern Ireland **60** D2 54 35N 5 35W
Ards Peninsula *p.* Ards Northern Ireland **60** D2 54 25N 5 30W
Ardvasar Highland Scotland **58** D2 57 03N 5 55W
Arendal Norway **97** B2 58 27N 8 56E
Arequipa Peru **146** C9 16 25S 71 32W
Arezzo Italy **92** B2 43 28N 11 53E
Arga *r.* Spain **91** B1 42 40N 2 10W
Argentan France **91** B2 48 45N 0 01W
Argenteuil France **87** A2 48 57N 2 14E
ARGENTINA 147 D5
Argentine Basin Atlantic Ocean **152** D2 42 00S 45 00W
Argeş *r.* Romania **96** D2 44 00N 26 00E
Árgos Greece **94** C2 37 38N 22 43E
Argostóli Greece **94** B3 38 13N 20 29E
Argun *(Ergun He) r.* Asia **113** N9 51 30N 120 00E
Argüvan Turkey **95** L3 38 46N 38 18E
Argyle, Lake Australia **118** D6 17 00S 128 30E
Argyll & Bute *u.a.* Scotland **58** D1 56 10N 5 00W
Århus Denmark **97** C2 56 15N 10 10E
Arica Chile **146** C9 18 30S 70 20W
Ariège *r.* France **91** C1 42 50N 1 40E
Arigidean *r.* Cork Rep. of Ireland **75** C1 51 41N 8 57W
Arima Trinidad and Tobago **141** T10 10 38N 61 17W
Arinagour Argyll & Bute Scotland **58** C1 56 37N 6 31W
Aripuanã *r.* Brazil **146** E11 7 00S 60 30W
Ariquemes Brazil **146** E11 9 55S 63 06W
Arisaig Highland Scotland **58** D1 56 51N 5 51W
Arisaig, Sound of Highland Scotland **58** D1 56 50N 5 50W
Arizona *state* U.S.A. **134** D3 34 00N 112 00W
Arizpe Mexico **140** B6 30 20N 110 11W
Arjeplog Sweden **97** D4 66 04N 18 00E
Arjona Colombia **146** B15 10 14N 75 22W
Arkalyk Kazakhstan **105** K5 50 17N 66 51E
Arkansas *r.* U.S.A. **135** H4 35 00N 93 00W
Arkansas *state* U.S.A. **135** H3 34 00N 93 00W
Arkansas City Kansas U.S.A. **135** G4 37 03N 97 02W
Arkhangel'sk Russia **102** G8 64 32N 40 40E
Arkítsa Greece **94** C3 38 45N 23 02E
Arklow Wicklow Rep. of Ireland **75** E2 52 48N 6 00W
Arkona, Cape Germany **93** B2 54 41N 13 26E
Arlanza *r.* Spain **90** B3 42 00N 3 30W
Arlanzón *r.* Spain **90** B3 42 00N 4 00W
Arles France **91** C1 43 41N 4 38E
Arlit Niger **127** G6 18 50N 7 00E
Arlon Belgium **89** E1 49 41N 5 49E
Armadale Falkirk Scotland **61** F3 55 54N 3 41W
Armadale Highland Scotland **58** D2 57 05N 5 54W
Armagh Armagh Northern Ireland **60** C2 54 21N 6 39W
Armagh *district* Northern Ireland **60** C2 54 20N 6 40W
Armavir Russia **102** G4 44 59N 41 40E
ARMENIA 104 E3/F2
Armenia Colombia **146** B13 4 32N 75 40W
Armentières France **91** C3 50 41N 2 53E
Armidale Australia **118** I3 30 32S 151 40E
Armstrong Ontario Canada **136** C4 50 20N 89 02W
Armthorpe South Yorkshire England **65** D2 53 32N 1 03W
Armutlu Turkey **94** F4 40 32N 28 49E
Armyans'k Ukraine **95** H7 46 05N 33 43E
Arnauti, Cape Cyprus **94** H1 35 07N 32 17E
Arnhem Netherlands **89** E3 52 00N 5 53E
Arnhem Land *geog. reg.* Australia **118** E7 13 00S 133 00E
Arno *r.* Italy **92** B2 43 00N 10 00E
Arnold Nottinghamshire England **65** D1 53 00N 1 09W
Arnprior Ontario Canada **137** E3 45 26N 76 21W
Arnsberg Germany **93** A2 51 23N 8 03E
Arnsberg *admin.* Germany **86** C2 51 20N 7 10E
Arnstadt Germany **93** B2 50 50N 10 57E
Arquipélago dos Bijagós *is.* Guinea-Bissau **127** B5 11 20N 16 40W
Ar Ramādi Iraq **106** F5 33 27N 43 19E
Ar Ramlah Jordan **106** O9 29 28N 25 58E
Arran *i.* North Ayrshire Scotland **60** D3 55 35N 5 15W
Ar Raqqah Syria **106** E6 35 57N 39 03E
Arras France **91** C3 50 17N 2 46E
Ar Rastan Syria **95** K1 34 55N 36 44E
Ar Riyād Saudi Arabia **107** G3 24 39N 46 46E
Arromanches-les-Bains France **73** G2 49 20N 0 38W
Árta Greece **94** B3 39 10N 20 59E
Artane Dublin Rep. of Ireland **74** E3 53 23N 6 12W
Artashat Armenia **95** P3 39 58N 44 34E
Arthur Ontario Canada **137** D2 43 50N 80 32W
Arthur's Pass N.Z. **119** B2 42 55S 171 34E
Arthur's Seat *sum.* City of Edinburgh Scotland **61** F3 55 57N 3 11W
Arthurstown Wexford Rep. of Ireland **75** E2 52 15N 6 57W
Artigas *r.s.* Antarctica **149** 62 11S 58 51W
Artigas Uruguay **147** F6 30 25S 56 28W
Artvin Turkey **95** M4 41 12N 41 48E
Arua Uganda **124** F8 3 02N 30 56E
ARUBA 141 K2 12 30N 70 00W
Arun *r.* England **70** D1 51 00N 0 30W
Arun *r.* Nepal **110** E8 27 05N 87 05E
Arunachal Pradesh *admin.* India **109** G5/H5 28 00N 95 00E
Arundel West Sussex England **70** D1 50 51N 0 34W
Arusha Tanzania **124** G7 3 23S 36 40E
Aruwimi *r.* Congo (D.R.) **124** E8 2 00N 25 00E
Arvika Sweden **97** C2 59 41N 12 38E
Arys' Kazakhstan **105** K3 42 26N 68 49E
Arzamas Russia **104** E6 55 24N 43 48E
Arzew Algeria **90** B2 35 50N 0 19W
Asahi Japan **114** M2 35 43N 140 38E
Asahi-dake *mt.* Japan **114** D3 43 42N 142 54E
Asahikawa Japan **114** D3 43 46N 142 23E
Asaka Japan **115** B4 35 47N 139 37E
Asamankese Ghana **127** E4 5 45N 0 45W
Asansol West Bengal India **109** F4 23 40N 86 59E
Åsarna Sweden **97** C3 62 40N 14 20E
Asbury Park *tn.* U.S.A. **137** F2 40 14N 74 00W
Ascension Island Atlantic Ocean **152** G6 7 57S 14 22W
Aschaffenburg Germany **93** A1 49 58N 9 10E
Aschersleben Germany **93** B2 51 46N 11 28E
Ascoli Piceno Italy **92** B2 42 52N 13 35E
Ascot Berkshire England **70** D2 51 25N 0 41W
Assab Eritrea **124** I10 13 01N 42 47E
Asenovgrad Bulgaria **96** C2 42 00N 24 53E
Ash Kent England **71** F2 51 17N 1 16E
Ashbourne Derbyshire England **67** F3 53 01N 1 43W
Ashbourne Meath Rep. of Ireland **74** E3 53 31N 6 24W
Ashburton *r.* Australia **118** B5 22 30S 116 00E
Ashburton Devon England **72** D3 50 31N 3 45W
Ashburton N.Z. **119** B2 43 54S 171 45E
Ashby-de-la-Zouch Leicestershire England **67** F2 52 46N 1 28W
Ashdod Israel **106** O10 31 48N 34 48E
Asheville North Carolina U.S.A. **135** J4 35 35N 82 35W
Ashfield Australia **119** G2 33 53S 151 07E
Ashford Kent England **71** E2 51 09N 0 53E
Ashfork Arizona U.S.A. **134** D4 35 13N 112 29W
Ashgabat *(Ashkhabad)* Turkmenistan **105** H2 37 58N 58 24E
Ashikaga Japan **114** C2 36 21N 139 26E
Ashina Japan **115** B1 35 13N 139 36E
Ashington Northumberland England **61** H3 55 11N 1 34W
Ashizuri-misaki *c.* Japan **114** B1 32 42N 133 00E
Ashkirk Scottish Borders Scotland **61** G3 55 29N 2 50W
Ashland Kentucky U.S.A. **137** D1 38 28N 82 40W
Ashland Oregon U.S.A. **134** B5 42 14N 122 44W
Ashland Wisconsin U.S.A. **136** B3 46 34N 90 54W
Ashok Nagar India **108** L4 28 38N 77 07E
Ashqelon Israel **106** O10 31 40N 34 35E
Ash Shadādah Syria **95** M2 36 02N 40 44E
Ash Shāriqah *(Sharjah)* U.A.E. **107** I4 25 20N 55 20E
Ashtabula Ohio U.S.A. **137** D2 41 53N 80 47W
Ashton-in-Makerfield Greater Manchester England **64** C2 53 29N 2 39W
Ashton-under-Lyne Greater Manchester England **64** C2 53 29N 2 06W
Ashwell Hertfordshire England **70** D3 52 03N 0 09W
Āsi *(Orontes) r.* Syria/Turkey **95** K2 36 00N 36 00E
Asilah Morocco **90** A2 35 32N 6 04W
Askaniya Nova Ukraine **95** H7 46 27N 33 53E
Askeaton Limerick Rep. of Ireland **75** C2 52 36N 8 58W
Askern South Yorkshire England **65** D2 53 37N 1 09W
Askival *mt.* Highland Scotland **58** C1 56 58N 6 18W
Askrigg North Yorkshire England **64** C3 54 19N 2 04W
Asmara Eritrea **124** G11 15 20N 38 58E
Åsnen *l.* Sweden **97** C2 56 45N 14 40E
Asnières France **87** B2 48 55N 2 17E
Asō Japan **114** M3 36 00N 141 29E
Aspatria Cumbria England **64** B3 54 46N 3 20W
Aspiring, Mount N.Z. **119** A2 44 23S 168 44E
Asquith Australia **119** G3 33 41S 151 07E
Assam *admin.* India **109** G5 26 20N 92 00E
As Samāwah Iraq **107** G5 31 18N 45 18E
Asse Belgium **89** D2 50 55N 4 12E
Assen Netherlands **89** F5 53 00N 6 34E
Assinibone River Canada **136** A3 49 55N 98 00W
Assis Brazil **147** G8 22 37S 50 25W
Assisi Italy **92** B2 43 04N 12 37E
As Sulaymānīyah Iraq **107** G6 35 32N 45 27E
As Suq Saudi Arabia **106** F3 21 55N 42 02E
As Suwaydāā Syria **106** P11 32 43N 36 33E
Astārā Azerbaijan **104** F2 38 27N 48 53E
Astee Kerry Rep. of Ireland **75** B2 52 33N 9 34W
Asti Italy **92** A2 44 54N 8 13E
Astorga Spain **90** A3 42 27N 6 04W
Astoria Oregon U.S.A. **134** B6 46 12N 123 50W
Astrakhan' Russia **102** G5 46 22N 48 04E
Astypálaia *i.* Greece **94** E2 36 30N 26 20E
Asuka *r.s.* Antarctica **149** 71 32S 24 08E
Asuke Japan **114** J2 35 08N 137 19E
Asunción Paraguay **147** F7 25 15S 57 40W
Aswa *r.* Uganda **124** F8 3 30N 32 30E
Aswân Egypt **124** F12 24 05N 32 56E
Aswân Dam Egypt **124** F12 23 40N 31 50E
Asyût Egypt **106** D4 27 14N 31 07E
Atacama Desert *see* Desierto de Atacama
Atami Japan **114** L2 35 07N 139 04E
Atar Mauritania **127** C7 20 32N 13 08W
Ataturk Baraji *res.* Turkey **95** L2 37 30N 38 30E
Atbara Sudan **124** F11 17 42N 34 00E
Atbara *r.* Sudan **124** G11 17 28N 34 30E
Atbasar Kazakhstan **105** K5 51 49N 68 18E
Atchison Kansas U.S.A. **135** G4 39 33N 95 09W
Ath Belgium **89** C2 50 38N 3 47E
Athabasca Alberta Canada **132** M3 54 44N 113 15W
Athabasca, Lake Canada **132** N4 59 10N 109 30W
Athabasca River Canada **132** M4 57 30N 111 00W
Athboy Meath Rep. of Ireland **74** E3 53 37N 6 55W
Athenry Galway Rep. of Ireland **74** C3 53 18N 8 45W
Athens Georgia U.S.A. **135** J3 33 57N 83 24W
Athens Ohio U.S.A. **137** D1 39 20N 82 06W
Athens Pennsylvania U.S.A. **137** E2 41 57N 76 31W
Athens Greece *see* Athínai
Atherstone Warwickshire England **67** F2 52 35N 1 31W
Athgarh Orissa India **110** C1 20 31N 85 41E
Athína *(Athens)* Greece **94** C3 38 00N 23 44E
Athleague Roscommon Rep. of Ireland **74** C3 53 34N 8 15W
Athlone Westmeath Rep. of Ireland **74** D3 53 25N 7 56W
Áthos *mt.* Greece **94** D4 40 10N 24 19E
Athy Kildare Rep. of Ireland **75** E2 52 59N 6 59W
Ati Chad **124** C10 13 11N 18 20E
Atikokan Ontario Canada **136** B3 48 45N 91 38W
Atikonak Lake Canada **133** W3 52 40N 64 35W
Atka Island U.S.A. **132** A3 52 05N 174 40W
Atlanta Georgia U.S.A. **135** J3 33 45N 84 23W
Atlantic City New Jersey U.S.A. **137** F1 39 23N 74 27W
Atlantic-Indian Ridge Atlantic Ocean **152** H1/J1 53 00S 3 00E
Atlantic Ocean 152
Atlas Mountains Morocco **76** F2 32 00N 2 00W
Atlas Saharien *mts.* Algeria **127** E9/F9 33 30N 1 00E
Atlin B.C. Canada **132** I4 59 31N 133 41W
Atlin Lake B.C. Canada **132** I4 59 31N 133 41W
Atrai *r.* India/Bangladesh **110** F6 25 10N 88 50E
Atrek *r.* Iran/Turkmenistan **107** H6 37 00N 54 50E
Atsugi Japan **114** L2 35 28N 139 22E
Atsumi Japan **114** J1 34 37N 137 06E
Atsumi-hanto *p.* Japan **114** J1 34 40N 137 15E
At Tāāif Saudi Arabia **106** F3 21 15N 40 21E
Attawapiskat Ontario Canada **133** S3 53 00N 82 30W
Attawapiskat River Canada **133** R3 53 00N 86 00W
Attersee *l.* Austria **93** B1 47 00N 13 00E
Attleborough Norfolk England **71** F3 52 31N 1 01E
Attymass Mayo Rep. of Ireland **74** B4 54 03N 9 04W
Atyrau *(Gur'yev)* Kazakhstan **104** G4 47 08N 51 59E
Auas Mountains Namibia **125** C3 23 00S 17 00E
Aubagne France **91** D1 43 17N 5 35E
Aube *r.* France **91** C2 48 40N 3 55E
Aubenas France **91** C1 44 37N 4 24E
Aubervilliers France **87** B2 48 55N 2 22E
Auburn Maine U.S.A. **137** F2 44 04N 70 27W
Auburn Nebraska U.S.A. **136** A2 40 22N 95 41W
Auburn New York U.S.A. **137** E2 42 57N 76 34W
Auch France **91** C1 43 40N 0 36E
Auchencairn Dumfries & Galloway Scotland **61** F2 54 51N 3 53W
Auchterarder Perth & Kinross Scotland **59** F1 56 18N 3 43W
Auchtermuchty Fife Scotland **59** F1 56 17N 3 15W
Auckland N.Z. **119** B3 36 51S 174 46E
Auckland Islands Southern Ocean **150** G2 50 35S 116 00E
Aude *r.* France **91** C1 43 00N 2 00E
Auden Ontario Canada **136** C4 50 14N 87 54W
Auderville France **73** F2 49 43N 1 56W
Audley Staffordshire England **67** E3 53 03N 2 20W
Audruicq France **71** G1 50 53N 2 05E
Aue Germany **93** B2 50 35N 12 42E
Augher Dungannon Northern Ireland **60** B2 54 26N 7 08W
Aughnacloy Dungannon Northern Ireland **60** C2 54 25N 6 59W
Aughrim Wicklow Rep. of Ireland **75** E2 52 52N 6 20W
Aughton South Yorkshire England **65** D2 53 22N 1 19W

Augsburg Germany **93** B1 48 21N 10 54E
Augusta Australia **118** B3 34 19S 115 09E
Augusta Georgia U.S.A. **135** J3 33 29N 82 00W
Augusta Maine U.S.A. **137** G2 44 17N 69 50W
Auldgirth Dumfries & Galloway Scotland **61** F3 55 12N 3 43W
Aulnay-sous-Bois France **87** C2 48 57N 2 31E
Aulne *r.* France **91** B2 48 10N 4 00W
Aurangābād India **109** D3 19 52N 75 22E
Aure *r.* France **73** F2 49 20N 1 00W
Aurich Germany **93** A2 53 28N 7 29E
Aurillac France **91** C1 44 56N 2 26E
Aurora Ontario Canada **137** E2 43 00N 79 28W
Aurora Illinois U.S.A. **136** C2 41 45N 88 20W
Aurora Indiana U.S.A. **136** D1 39 03N 84 55W
Au Sable *r.* Michigan U.S.A. **137** D2 45 00N 84 00W
Austin Minnesota U.S.A. **136** B2 43 40N 92 58W
Austin Texas U.S.A. **135** G3 30 18N 97 47W
AUSTRALIA 118
Australian Capital Territory *(A.C.T.) admin.* Australia **118** H2 35 00S 144 00E
Austral Ridge Pacific Ocean **151** K5 24 00S 155 30W
AUSTRIA 92 B3/C3
Autlán Mexico **140** D3 19 48N 104 20W
Autun France **91** C2 46 58N 4 18E
Auxerre France **91** C2 47 48N 3 35E
Auyuittuq National Park Canada **133** V6 67 00N 67 00W
Avallon France **91** C2 47 30N 3 54E
Avebury Wiltshire England **70** C2 51 27N 1 51W
Aveiro Portugal **90** A3 40 38N 8 40W
Aveley Essex England **71** E2 51 30N 0 15E
Avellaneda Argentina **147** F6 34 40S 58 20W
Avellino Italy **92** B2 40 49N 14 47E
Avesnes-sur-Helpe France **89** D2 50 08N 3 57E
Avesta Sweden **97** D3 60 09N 16 10E
Aveyron *r.* France **91** C1 44 30N 2 05E
Avezzano Italy **92** B2 42 02N 13 26E
Aviemore Highland Scotland **59** F2 57 12N 3 50W
Avignon France **91** C1 43 56N 4 48E
Avila Spain **90** B3 40 39N 4 42W
Avilés Spain **90** A3 43 33N 5 55W
Avoca Wicklow Rep. of Ireland **75** E2 52 52N 6 13W
Avoca *r.* Wicklow Rep. of Ireland **75** E2 52 49N 6 11W
Avon *r.* Devon England **72** D3 50 20N 3 48W
Avon *r.* S. Gloucestershire/Wiltshire/Bath and NE Somerset/Bristol England **70** B2 51 25N 2 05W
Avon *r.* Warwickshire/Hereford and Worcester England **67** F2 52 10N 1 55W
Avon *r.* Wiltshire/Hampshire/Dorset England **70** C2 51 05N 1 55W
Avon *r.* Highland/Moray Scotland **59** F2 51 27N 1 40W
Avonbeg *r.* Wicklow Rep. of Ireland **75** E2 52 57N 6 20W
Avonmore *r.* Wicklow Rep. of Ireland **75** E2 52 57N 6 15W
Avonmouth Bristol England **70** B2 51 31N 2 42W
Avranches France **91** B2 48 42N 1 21W
Avre *r.* France **91** C2 49 45N 2 30E
Awaji Japan **114** G1 34 35N 135 00E
Awaji-shima *i.* Japan **114** F1 34 30N 135 45E
Awali *r.* Lebanon **106** O11 33 35N 35 32E
Awash Ethiopia **124** H9 9 01N 41 10E
Awash *r.* Ethiopia **124** H10 10 00N 40 00E
Awa-shima *i.* Japan **114** C2 38 40N 139 15E
Awbārī Libya **124** B13 26 35N 12 46E
Awberg *r.* Cork Rep. of Ireland **75** C2 52 12N 8 27W
Axbridge Somerset England **73** E4 51 18N 2 49W
Axe *r.* Dorset/Devon England **73** E3 50 50N 2 50W
Axe *r.* Somerset England **73** E4 51 11N 2 43W
Axel Heiberg Island Canada **133** Q8 80 00N 90 00W
Axminster Devon England **73** E3 50 47N 3 00W
Ayabe Japan **114** G2 35 19N 135 16E
Ayacucho Peru **146** C10 13 10S 74 15W
Ayaguz Kazakhstan **105** N4 47 59N 80 27E
Ayamonte Spain **90** A2 37 13N 7 24W
Ayan Russia **103** P7 56 29N 138 07E
Ayancik Turkey **95** J4 41 56N 34 35E
Ayaş Turkey **95** H4 40 02N 32 21E
Ayaviri Peru **146** C10 14 53S 70 35W
Aydin Turkey **94** E2 37 51N 27 51E
Ayers Rock *mt.* Australia **118** E4 25 18S 131 18E
Aylesbury Buckinghamshire England **70** D2 51 50N 0 50W
Aylesford Kent England **71** E2 51 18N 0 30E
Aylesham Kent England **71** F2 51 12N 1 11E
Aylmer Ontario Canada **137** D2 42 47N 80 58W
Aylmer Québec Canada **137** E3 45 23N 75 51W
Aylsham Norfolk England **71** F3 52 49N 1 15E
Ayod Sudan **124** F9 8 08N 31 24E
Ayon *i.* Russia **103** S9 69 55N 169 10E
Ayr *r.* East Ayrshire/South Ayrshire Scotland **61** E3 55 30N 4 10W
Ayr South Ayrshire Scotland **61** E3 55 28N 4 38W
Ayre, Point of *c.* Isle of Man British Isles **64** A3 54 25N 4 22W
Aysgarth North Yorkshire England **64** D3 54 17N 2 00W
Aytos Bulgaria **94** E5 42 41N 27 15E
'Ayūnah Saudi Arabia **106** E4 28 06N 35 08E
Ayvalik Turkey **94** E3 39 18N 26 42E
Azcapotzalco Mexico **140** P1 19 29N 99 11W
AZERBAIJAN 104 F3
Azogues Ecuador **146** B12 2 46S 78 56W
Azores *is.* Atlantic Ocean **152** F10 38 30N 28 00W
Azoum *r.* Chad **124** D10 12 00N 21 00E
Azov Russia **95** L7 47 06N 39 26E
Azov, Sea of Asia **95** K7 46 00N 36 00E
Azuaga Spain **90** A2 38 16N 5 40W
Azuero, Peninsula de *p.* Panama **141** H1 7 40N 81 00W
Azul Argentina **147** F5 36 46S 59 50W
Azurduy Bolivia **146** E9 20 00S 64 29W
Azusa California U.S.A. **139** C3 34 08N 117 54W
Az Zabadānī Syria **106** P11 33 42N 36 03E
Az Zahrān *(Dhahran)* Saudi Arabia **107** H4 26 13N 50 02E

B

Barasat West Bengal India **110** F3 22 44N 88 31E
Ba'albek Lebanon **106** P12 34 00N 36 12E
Baarn Netherlands **89** E4 52 13N 5 16E
Baba Burun *c.* Turkey **94** E3 39 28N 26 05E
Babadag *mt.* Azerbaijan **104** F3 41 02N 48 07E
Babadag Romania **94** F6 44 53N 28 47E
Babahoyo Ecuador **146** B12 1 53S 79 31W
Babbacombe Bay Devon England **72** D3 50 30N 3 30W
Bab el Mandab *sd.* Red Sea **124** H10 12 30N 47 00E
Babelsberg Germany **87** E1 52 23N 13 05E
Babruysk *(Bobruysk)* Belarus **104** B5 53 08N 29 10E
Babushkin Russia **102** M2/N2 55 55N 37 44E
Babylon *hist. site* Iraq **106** F5 32 33N 44 25E
Bacabal Brazil **146** I12 4 15S 44 45W
Bacău Romania **96** D3 46 33N 26 58E
Back *r.* N.W.T. Canada **133** P6 66 00N 97 00W
Backbone Ranges Canada **132** J5 63 30N 127 50W
Bacolod The Philippines **111** G6 10 38N 122 58E
Bacup Lancashire England **64** C2 53 42N 2 12W
Bada Barbil Orissa India **110** C3 22 09N 85 20E
Badajoz Spain **90** A2 38 53N 6 58W
Badalona Spain **90** C3 41 27N 2 15E
Baden Austria **92** C3 48 01N 16 14E
Baden Switzerland **93** A1 47 28N 8 19E
Baden-Baden Germany **93** A1 48 45N 8 15E
Baden-Württemberg *admin.* Germany **93** A1 48 00N 9 00E
Badgastein Austria **93** B1 47 07N 13 09E
Bad Hersfeld Germany **93** A2 50 53N 9 43E
Badhoevedorp Netherlands **88** D3 52 20N 4 47E
Bad Homburg Germany **93** A2 50 13N 8 37E
Bad Honnef Germany **89** G2 50 38N 7 14E
Bad Ischl Austria **92** B3 47 43N 13 38E
Bad Kissingen Germany **93** B2 50 12N 10 05E
Bad Kreuznach Germany **93** A1 49 51N 7 52E
Badli India **108** L4 28 44N 77 09E
Bad Neuenahr-Ahrweiler Germany **89** G2 50 32N 7 06E
Bad Reichenhall Germany **93** B1 47 43N 12 53E
Bad Salzuflen Germany **93** A2 52 06N 8 45E
Bad Tölz Germany **93** B1 47 45N 11 34E
Badulla Sri Lanka **109** E1 6 59N 81 03E
Baffin Bay Canada/Greenland **133** V17 72 00N 65 00W
Baffin Island N.W.T. Canada **133** S7/V6 68 30N 70 00W
Bafoussam Cameroon **127** H4 5 31N 10 25E
Bāfq Iran **107** I5 31 35N 55 21E
Bafra Turkey **95** J4 41 34N 35 56E
Bagé Brazil **147** G6 31 22S 54 06W
Baggy Point *c.* Devon England **72** C4 51 09N 4 16W
Baghdād Iraq **106** F5 33 20N 44 26E
Bagherhat Khulna Bangladesh **110** G3 22 40N 89 48E
Baghlān Afghanistan **107** K6 36 11N 68 44E
Bagicha Madhya Pradesh India **110** A3 22 56N 83 38E
Bagodar Bihar India **110** C5 24 04N 85 50E
Bahadurganj Bihar India **110** E7 26 17N 87 49E
BAHAMAS, THE 141 I4
Baharagora Bihar India **110** D3 22 04N 86 47E
Baharampur West Bengal India **109** F4 24 00N 88 30E
Bahawalpur Pakistan **109** C5 29 24N 71 47E
Bahia *admin.* Brazil **146** I10 12 00S 42 30W
Bahía Blanca Argentina **147** E5 38 45S 62 15W
Bahía Blanca *b.* Argentina **147** E5 39 00S 61 00W
Bahia de Campeche *b.* Mexico **140** E4/F4 20 00N 95 00W
Bahia Grande *b.* Argentina **147** D2 51 30S 68 00W
Bahraich India **109** E5 27 35N 81 36E
BAHRAIN 107 H4
Bahrain, Gulf of The Gulf **107** H4 25 55N 50 30E
Bahr el Abiad *(White Nile) r.* Sudan **124** F10 14 00N 32 20E
Bahr el Arab *r.* Sudan **124** E9 10 00N 27 30E
Bahr el Azraq *(Blue Nile) r.* Sudan **124** F10 13 30N 33 45E
Bahr el Ghazal *r.* Chad **124** C10 14 00N 16 00E
Baia Mare Romania **96** C3 47 39N 23 36E
Baicheng China **113** O8 45 37N 122 48E
Baidyabati India **108** K3 22 48N 88 20E
Baie-Comeau *tn.* Canada **137** G3 49 12N 68 10W
Baie de la Seine *b.* France **91** B2 49 40N 0 30W
Baie d'Ungava *see* Ungava Bay
Baie-du-Poste *tn.* Canada **137** F4 50 20N 73 50W
Baie St. Paul *tn.* Canada **137** F3 47 27N 70 30W
Baie Trinité *tn.* Québec Canada **137** G3 49 25N 67 20W
Baildon West Yorkshire England **64** D2 53 52N 1 46W
Bailieborough Cavan Rep. of Ireland **74** E4 53 54N 6 59W
Bailleul France **89** B2 50 44N 2 44E
Baiona Spain **90** A3 42 07N 8 51W
Baird Mountains U.S.A. **132** D6 67 30N 160 00W
Baise *r.* France **91** C1 43 55N 0 25E
Baitarani *r.* Orissa India **110** D2 21 30N 86 00E
Baja Hungary **96** B3 46 11N 18 58E
Baja California *p.* Mexico **140** B5 27 30N 113 00W
Baj Baj West Bengal India **110** F3 22 29N 88 11E
Bajitpur Dhaka Bangladesh **110** H5 24 12N 90 57E
Bajram Curri Albania **94** B5 42 20N 20 05E
Baker Oregon U.S.A. **134** C5 44 46N 117 50W
Baker Lake N.W.T. Canada **133** Q5 64 00N 95 00W
Baker Lake *tn.* N.W.T. Canada **133** P5 64 20N 96 10W
Bakersfield California U.S.A. **134** C4 35 25N 119 00W
Bakewell Derbyshire England **67** F3 53 13N 1 40W
Bakı *(Baku)* Azerbaijan **104** F3 40 22N 49 53E
Baksan Russia **95** N5 43 42N 43 33E
Baksan *r.* Russia **95** N5 43 30N 43 10E
Bâlâ Turkey **95** H3 39 34N 33 07E
Bala Gwynedd Wales **66** D2 52 54N 3 35W
Balaghat India **109** E4 21 48N 80 16E
Balaghat Range *mts.* India **109** D3 18 45N 77 00E
Balaklava Ukraine **95** H6 44 31N 33 35E
Balakovo Russia **102** G6 52 04N 47 46E
Balama Mozambique **125** G5 13 19S 38 35E
Bālā Morghāb Afghanistan **107** J6 35 34N 63 20E
Balarampur West Bengal India **110** D4 23 04N 86 12E
Balashikha Russia **104** D6 55 47N 37 59E
Balashov Russia **104** E5 51 31N 43 10E
Balassagyarmat Hungary **96** B3 48 06N 19 17E
Balaton *l.* Hungary **96** B3 47 00N 17 30E
Balboa Panama **141** I2 8 57N 79 33W
Balbriggan Dublin Rep. of Ireland **74** E3 53 37N 6 11W
Balchik Bulgaria **94** F5 43 24N 28 10E
Balclutha N.Z. **119** A1 46 14S 169 44E
Balcombe West Sussex England **70** D2 51 04N 0 08W
Bald Eagle Lake U.S.A. **136** B3 47 48N 91 32W
Baldeney-see *l.* Germany **86** C2 51 24N 7 02E
Baldock Hertfordshire England **70** D2 51 59N 0 12W
Baldwin Park *tn.* U.S.A. **139** C3 34 05N 117 59W
Balearic Islands Mediterranean Sea **90** C2/3
Baleshare *i.* Western Isles Scotland **58** B2 57 32N 7 22W
Baleshwar Orissa India **110** D2 21 31N 86 5 9E
Balgowlah Australia **119** H2 33 48S 151 16E
Bali *i.* Indonesia **111** F2 8 30S 115 00E
Balikesir Turkey **94** E3 39 37N 27 51E
Balikh *r.* Syria **95** K2 36 10N 39 00E
Balikpapan Indonesia **111** F3 1 15S 116 50E
Balingen Germany **93** A1 48 17N 8 52E
Balipara Assam India **110** K7 26 50N 92 45E
Balkan Mountains Europe **76** K4 43 00N 25 00E
Balkhash Kazakhstan **105** L4 46 50N 74 57E
Balkhash, Lake *see* Ozero Balkhash
Ballachulish Highland Scotland **58** D1 56 40N 5 10W
Ballagan Point Louth Rep. of Ireland **74** E4 54 00N 6 06W
Ballaghaderreen Roscommon Rep. of Ireland **74** C3 53 55N 8 36W
Ballantrae South Ayrshire Scotland **60** D3 55 06N 5 00W
Ballarat Australia **118** G2 37 36S 143 58E
Ballater Aberdeenshire Scotland **59** F2 57 03N 3 03W
Ballaugh Isle of Man British Isles **64** A3 54 18N 4 32W
Balleny Islands Southern Ocean **150** G1 66 30S 1 64E
Balleroy France **73** G2 49 11N 0 50W
Ballina Mayo Rep. of Ireland **74** B4 54 07N 9 09W
Ballinafad Sligo Rep. of Ireland **74** C4 54 02N 8 20W
Ballinagleragh Leitrim Rep. of Ireland **74** C4 54 09N 8 01W
Ballinalack Westmeath Rep. of Ireland **74** D3 53 38N 7 28W
Ballinalee Longford Rep. of Ireland **74** D3 53 46N 7 39W
Ballinamore Leitrim Rep. of Ireland **74** D4 54 03N 7 47W
Ballinasloe Galway Rep. of Ireland **74** C3 53 20N 8 13W
Ballincollig Cork Rep. of Ireland **75** C1 51 54N 8 35W
Ballinderry *r.* Cookstown Northern Ireland **60** C2 54 40N 6 52W
Ballindine Mayo Rep. of Ireland **74** C3 53 40N 8 57W
Ballingry Fife Scotland **59** F1 56 11N 3 20W
Ballinhassig Cork Rep. of Ireland **75** C1 51 49N 8 32W
Ballinrobe Mayo Rep. of Ireland **74** B3 53 37N 9 13W
Ballinskelligs Bay Kerry Rep. of Ireland **75** A1 51 46N 10 17W
Ballintra Donegal Rep. of Ireland **74** C4 54 35N 8 07W
Ballon Carlow Rep. of Ireland **75** E2 52 44N 6 46W
Bālly India **108** K2 22 38N 88 20E
Ballybay Monaghan Rep. of Ireland **74** E4 54 08N 6 54W
Ballybofey Donegal Rep. of Ireland **74** D4 54 48N 7 47W
Ballybunnion Kerry Rep. of Ireland **75** B2 52 31N 9 40W
Ballycanew Wexford Rep. of Ireland **75** E2 52 36N 6 18W
Ballycastle Moyle Northern Ireland **60** C3 55 12N 6 15W
Ballycastle Mayo Rep. of Ireland **74** B4 54 17N 9 22W
Ballyclare Newtownabbey Northern Ireland **60** C2 54 45N 6 00W
Ballycolla Laois Rep. of Ireland **75** D2 52 52N 7 26W
Ballyconnell Cavan Rep. of Ireland **74** D4 54 07N 7 35W
Ballycotton Cork Rep. of Ireland **75** C1 51 50N 8 01W
Ballycotton Bay Cork Rep. of Ireland **75** D1 51 51N 7 57W
Ballycroy Mayo Rep. of Ireland **74** B4 54 02N 9 49W
Ballydavid Head *c.* Kerry Rep. of Ireland **75** A2 52 14N 10 21W
Ballydehob Cork Rep. of Ireland **75** B1 51 34N 9 28W
Ballydesmond Cork Rep. of Ireland **75** B2 52 10N 9 13W
Ballydonegan Cork Rep. of Ireland **75** A1 51 37N 10 12W
Ballydonegan Bay Cork Rep. of Ireland **75** A1 51 29N 10 09W
Ballyfinboy *r.* Tipperary Rep. of Ireland **75** C3 53 00N 8 11W
Ballygalley Head *c.* Larne Northern Ireland **60** D2 54 54N 5 51W
Ballygowan Ards Northern Ireland **60** D2 54 30N 5 47W
Ballygunge India **108** K2 22 31N 88 20E
Ballyhaunis Mayo Rep. of Ireland **74** C3 53 46N 8 46W
Ballyheige Kerry Rep. of Ireland **75** B2 52 24N 9 50W
Ballyheige Bay Kerry Rep. of Ireland **75** B2 52 23N 9 52W
Ballyhoura Mountains Cork Rep. of Ireland **75** C2 52 17N 8 33W
Ballyjamesduff Cavan Rep. of Ireland **74** D3 53 52N 7 12W
Ballykinler Down Northern Ireland **60** D2 54 17N 5 47W
Ballylanders Limerick Rep. of Ireland **75** C2 52 23N 8 21W
Ballylongford Kerry Rep. of Ireland **75** B2 52 33N 9 28W
Ballymacarbry Waterford Rep. of Ireland **75** D2 52 16N 7 12W
Ballymahon Longford Rep. of Ireland **74** D3 53 34N 7 45W
Ballymena Ballymena Northern Ireland **60** C2 54 52N 6 17W
Ballymena *district* Northern Ireland **60** C2 54 55N 6 20W
Ballymoe Galway Rep. of Ireland **74** C3 53 42N 8 28W
Ballymoney Ballymoney Northern Ireland **60** C3 55 04N 6 31W
Ballymoney *district* Northern Ireland **60** C3 55 00N 6 30W
Ballymore Donegal Rep. of Ireland **74** D5 55 09N 7 56W
Ballymore Westmeath Rep. of Ireland **74** D3 53 29N 7 40W
Ballymote Sligo Rep. of Ireland **74** C4 54 06N 8 31W
Ballynahinch Down Northern Ireland **60** D2 54 24N 5 54W
Ballynamona Cork Rep. of Ireland **75** C2 52 05N 8 39W
Ballynamult Waterford Rep. of Ireland **75** D2 52 13N 7 40W
Ballyquintin Point *c.* Ards Northern Ireland **60** D2 54 19N 5 30W
Ballyragget Kilkenny Rep. of Ireland **75** D2 52 47N 7 20W
Ballyshannon Donegal Rep. of Ireland **74** C4 54 30N 8 11W
Ballyteige Bay Wexford Rep. of Ireland **75** E2 52 12N 6 45W
Ballyvaghan Clare Rep. of Ireland **75** B3 53 07N 9 09W
Ballyvourney Cork Rep. of Ireland **75** B1 51 56N 9 10W
Ballywalter Ards Northern Ireland **60** D2 54 33N 5 30W
Balmaclellan Dumfries & Galloway Scotland **61** E3 55 05N 4 07W
Balmain Australia **119** G2 33 51S 151 11E
Balmoral Aberdeenshire Scotland **59** F2 57 02N 3 13W
Balrath Meath Rep. of Ireland **74** E3 53 37N 6 29W
Balsas Mexico **140** E3 18 00N 99 44W
Balta *i.* Shetland Islands Scotland **57** F3 60 44N 0 48W
Balta Ukraine **96** D3 47 58N 29 39E
Bălţi *(Bel'tsy)* Moldova **96** D3 47 44N 28 41E
Baltic Sea Europe **97** D2 55 15N 17 00E
Baltimore Cork Rep. of Ireland **75** B1 51 29N 9 22W
Baltimore Maryland U.S.A. **135** K4 39 18N 76 38W
Baltinglass Wicklow Rep. of Ireland **75** E2 52 55N 6 41W
Baltray Louth Rep. of Ireland **74** E3 53 44N 6 16W
Baltrum *i.* Germany **93** A2 53 44N 7 23E
Baluchistan *geog. reg.* Pakistan **108** A5/B5 27 30N 65 00E
Balurghat West Bengal India **110** F6 25 12N 88 50E
Balya Turkey **94** E3 39 45N 27 35E
Bam Iran **107** I4 29 07N 58 20E
Bamako Mali **127** D5 12 40N 7 59W
Bambari Central African Rep. **124** D9 5 40N 20 37E
Bamberg Germany **93** B1 49 54N 10 54E
Bamburgh Northumberland England **61** H3 55 36N 1 42W
Bamenda Cameroon **127** H4 5 55N 10 09E
Bamingui Bangoran National Park Central African Rep. **124** C9/D9 8 00N 20 00E
Bampton Devon England **72** D3 51 00N 3 29W
Banaba *i.* Nauru **150** G7 1 00S 167 00E
Banagher Offaly Rep. of Ireland **74** D3 53 11N 7 59W
Banas *r.* India **109** D5 26 00N 75 00E
Banbridge Banbridge Northern Ireland **60** C2 54 21N 6 16W
Banbridge *district* Northern Ireland **60** C2 54 15N 6 20W
Banbury Oxfordshire England **70** C3 52 04N 1 20W
Banchory Aberdeenshire Scotland **59** G2 57 30N 2 30W
Bancroft Ontario Canada **137** E3 45 03N 77 52W
Banda India **109** E5 25 28N 80 20E
Banda Aceh Indonesia **111** B5 5 30N 95 20E
Bandama Blanc *r.* Côte d'Ivoire **127** D4 8 00N 5 45W
Bandarban Bangladesh **110** K3 22 10N 92 13E
Bandar-e 'Abbās Iran **107** I4 27 12N 56 15E
Bandar-e Lengeh Iran **107** H4 26 34N 54 52E
Bandar-e Torkeman Iran **107** H6 36 55N 54 01E
Bandar Khomeyni Iran **107** G5 30 40N 49 08E
Bandar Seri Begawan Brunei Darussalam **111** F4 4 53N 114 57E
Banda Sea Indonesia **111** H2 5 50S 126 00E
Bandeirantes Beach Brazil **147** B1 23 01S 43 23W
Bandel India **108** K3 22 55N 88 23E
Bandirma Turkey **94** E4 40 21N 27 58E
Bandirma Körfezi *b.* Turkey **94** F4 40 25N 28 00E
Bandon Cork Rep. of Ireland **75** C1 51 45N 8 45W
Bandon *r.* Cork Rep. of Ireland **75** C1 51 44N 8 54W
Bandundu Congo (D.R.) **125** C7 3 20S 17 24E
Bandung Indonesia **111** D2 6 57S 107 34E
Banff Alberta Canada **132** L3 51 10N 115 34W
Banff Aberdeenshire Scotland **59** G2 57 40N 2 33W
Banff National Park Canada **132** L3 52 00N 116 00W
Banfora Burkina **127** E5 10 36N 4 45W
Bangalore India **109** D2 12 58N 77 35E
Bangaon West Bengal India **110** F4 23 01N 88 50E
Bangassou Central African Rep. **124** D8 4 41N 22 48E
Banghāzī *(Benghazi)* Libya **124** D14 32 07N 20 04E
Bangkok *(Krung Thep)* Thailand **111** C6 13 44N 100 30E
BANGLADESH 110
Bangor North Down Northern Ireland **60** D2 54 40N 5 40W
Bangor Mayo Rep. of Ireland **74** B4 54 09N 9 44W
Bangor Maine U.S.A. **137** G2 44 49N 68 47W
Bangor Gwynedd Wales **66** C3 53 13N 4 08W
Bangui Central African Rep. **124** C8 4 23N 18 37E
Bangweulu, Lake Zambia **125** E5 11 15S 29 45E
Baniyachung Bangladesh **110** J5 24 30N 91 21E
Bāniyās Syria **95** J1 35 12N 35 57E
Banja Luka Bosnia-Herzegovina **96** B2 44 47N 17 11E
Banjarmasin Indonesia **111** E3 3 22S 114 33E
Banjul The Gambia **127** B5 13 28N 16 39W
Banka India **108** K2 22 36N 88 17E
Banka Bihar India **110** D5 24 53N 86 56E
Banki Orissa India **110** B3 22 08N 84 53E
Banks Island Canada **132** K7/L7 72 30N 122 30W
Banks Islands Vanuatu **118** L7 13 40S 167 30E
Banks Peninsula N.Z. **119** B2 43 45S 173 00E
Bankstown Australia **119** G2 33 55S 151 02E
Bankura West Bengal India **110** E4 23 14N 87 05E
Banmankhi Bazar Bihar India **110** E6 25 53N 87 11E
Bann *r.* Northern Ireland **60** C3 55 05N 6 35W
Bann *r.* Wexford Rep. of Ireland **75** E2 52 39W 6 24W
Bannockburn Stirling Scotland **61** F4 56 05N 3 56W
Bannow Bay Wexford Rep. of Ireland **75** E2 52 13N 6 48W
Bannu Pakistan **107** L5 33 00N 70 40E
Bansberia India **108** K3 22 57N 88 23E
Bansha Tipperary Rep. of Ireland **75** C2 52 28N 8 04W
Banská Bystrica Slovakia **96** B3 48 44N 19 10E
Bansko Bulgaria **94** C4 41 50N 23 30E
Banstead Surrey England **70** D2 51 19N 0 12W
Banteer Cork Rep. of Ireland **75** C2 52 08N 8 54W
Bantry Cork Rep. of Ireland **75** B1 51 41N 9 27W
Bantry Bay Cork Rep. of Ireland **75** B1 51 35N 9 40W
Banyuwangi Indonesia **111** E2 8 12S 114 22E
Baoding China **113** N6 38 54N 115 26E
Baoji China **113** L5 34 23N 107 16E
Baotou China **113** L7 40 38N 109 59E
Ba'qūbah Iraq **106** F5 33 45N 44 40E
Bar Montenegro Yugoslavia **94** A5 42 05N 19 06E
Baraboo Wisconsin U.S.A. **136** C2 43 27N 89 45W
Baracaldo Spain **90** B3 43 17N 2 59W
Barahanagar India **108** K2 22 38N 88 23E
Barahona Dominican Republic **141** J3 18 13N 71 07W
Barajala Canal India **108** J2 22 35N 88 12E
Barakar *r.* India **110** D4/5 24 00N 86 30E
Barakot Orissa India **110** B2 21 35N 85 05E
Barākpur West Bengal India **110** F4 22 45N 88 22E
Baral *r.* Bangladesh **110** G5 24 20N 89 05E
Baral India **108** K1 22 27N 88 22E
Barama Assam India **110** J7 26 32N 91 20E
Baranavichy *(Baranovichi)* Belarus **104** B5 53 09N 26 00E
Baranovichi *see* Baranavichy
Bārāsat India **108** K2 22 43N 88 26E
Barato Assam India **110** K6 25 31N 92 31E
Barbacena Brazil **147** I8 21 13S 43 47W
BARBADOS 141 M2
Barbastro Spain **90** C3 42 02N 0 07E
Barbuda *i.* Antigua & Barbuda **141** L3 17 41N 61 48W
Barcaldine Australia **118** H5 23 31S 145 15E
Barcellona Italy **92** C1 38 10N 15 15E
Barcelona Spain **90** C3 41 25N 2 10E
Barcelona Venezuela **146** E15 10 08N 64 43W
Barcelonnette France **91** D1 44 24N 6 40E
Barcelos Brazil **146** E12 0 59S 62 58W
Barcoo *r.* Australia **118** G5 24 00S 144 00E
Barcs Hungary **96** B3 45 58N 17 30E
Barddhamān West Bengal India **109** F4 23 20N 88 00E
Bardsey Island *i.* Gwynedd Wales **66** C2 52 46N 4 48W
Barduelv *r.* Norway **97** D4 68 48N 18 22E
Bareilly India **109** D5 28 20N 79 24E
Barengapara Assam India **110** H6 25 16N 90 13E
Barents Sea Arctic Ocean **148** 75 00N 40 00E
Barfleur France **73** F2 49 40N 1 16W
Barga China **109** E6 30 51N 81 20E
Bargoed Caerphilly Wales **66** D1 51 43N 3 15W
Barguna Khulna Bangladesh **110** H3 22 09N 90 07E
Barharwa Bihar India **110** E5 24 52N 87 47E
Barhi Bihar India **110** C5 24 19N 85 25E
Bari Italy **92** C2 41 07N 16 52E
Barinas Venezuela **146** C14 8 36N 70 15W
Baripada Orissa India **110** D2 21 52N 86 48E
Barisal Khulna Bangladesh **110** H3 22 41N 90 20E
Bariti, Lake India **108** K3 22 48N 88 26E
Barking Greater London England **71** E2 51 33N 0 06E
Barki Saraiya Bihar India **110** C5 24 10N 85 54E
Barkly-Tableland *geog. reg.* Australia **118** F6 17 30S 137 00E
Bârlad Romania **96** D3 46 14N 27 40E
Bârlad *r.* Romania **94** E7 46 20N 27 45E
Barle *r.* Somerset England **72** D4 51 05N 3 36W
Bar-le-Duc France **91** D2 48 46N 5 10E
Barlee, Lake Australia **118** B4 28 30S 120 00E
Barletta Italy **92** C2 41 20N 16 17E
Barmen Germany **86** C2 51 16N 7 13E
Barmouth Gwynedd Wales **66** C2 52 43N 4 03W
Barnard Castle Durham England **64** D3 54 33N 1 55W
Barnatra Mayo Rep. of Ireland **74** B4 54 13N 9 50W
Barnaul Russia **103** K6 53 21N 83 45E
Barnes Ice Cap N.W.T. Canada **133** U7 70 10N 74 00W
Barnet Greater London England **70** D2 51 39N 0 12W
Barneveld Netherlands **89** E4 52 08N 5 35E
Barneville-Carteret France **73** F2 49 23N 1 45W
Barnoldswick Lancashire England **64** C2 53 56N 2 16W
Barnsley South Yorkshire England **65** D2 53 34N 1 28W
Barnstaple Devon England **72** C4 51 05N 4 04W
Barnstaple or Bideford Bay Devon England **72** C4 51 05N 4 25W
Barpeta Assam India **110** J7 26 20N 91 02E
Barpeta Road *tn.* Assam India **110** H7 26 26N 90 53E
Barquisimeto Venezuela **146** D15 10 03N 69 18W
Barra *i.* Western Isles Scotland **58** B1 57 00N 7 25W
Barra da Tijuca Brazil **147** P1 23 00S 43 20W
Barra do Corba Brazil **146** H11 5 30S 45 12W
Barra Head Western Isles Scotland **58** B1 56 47N 7 36W
Barrancabermeja Colombia **146** C14 7 06N 73 54W
Barrancas Venezuela **146** E14 8 45N 62 13W
Barrancones Point Trinidad and Tobago **141** T10 10 30N 61 28W
Barranjoey Head *c.* Australia **119** H3 33 35S 151 20E
Barranquilla Colombia **146** C15 11 10N 74 50W
Barra, Sound of Western Isles Scotland **58** B2
Barre Vermont U.S.A. **137** F2 44 13N 72 31W
Barreiras Brazil **146** I10 12 09S 44 58W
Barreiro Portugal **90** A2 38 40N 9 05W
Barreto Brazil **147** Q2 22 53S 43 07W
Barrhead Alberta Canada **132** M3 54 10N 114 22W
Barrhead East Renfrewshire Scotland **61** E3 55 48N 4 24W
Barrie Ontario Canada **137** E2 44 22N 79 42W
Barrow *r.* Loais/Carlow Rep. of Ireland **75** E2 52 38N 6 58W
Barrow U.S.A. **132** D7 71 16N 156 50W
Barrow-in-Furness Cumbria England **64** B3 54 07N 3 14W
Barrow Island Australia **118** B5 21 00S 115 00E
Barrow, Point U.S.A. **132** D7 71 05N 156 00W
Barry The Vale of Glamorgan Wales **66** D1 51 24N 3 18W
Barrys Bay *tn.* Ontario Canada **137** E3 45 30N 77 41W

Barstow California U.S.A. 134 C3 34 55N 117 01W
Bartin Turkey 94 H4 41 37N 32 20E
Bartlesville Oklahoma U.S.A. 135 G4 36 44N 95 59W
Barton Vermont U.S.A. 137 F2 44 44N 72 12W
Barton-upon-Humber North Lincolnshire England 65 E2 53 41N 0 27W
Barvas Western Isles Scotland 58 C3 58 22N 6 32W
Barysaw (Borisov) Belarus 104 B5 54 09N 28 30E
Basalt Island Hong Kong China 112 C1 22 19N 114 21E
Basarabi Romania 94 F6 44 10N 28 26E
Basdorf Germany 87 F2 52 44N 13 27E
Basel Switzerland 92 A3 47 33N 7 36E
Bashtanka Ukraine 94 H7 47 24N 32 26E
Basildon Essex England 71 E2 51 34N 0 25W
Basingstoke Hampshire England 70 C2 51 16N 1 05W
Basirhat West Bengal India 110 F3 22 38N 88 52E
Baskil Turkey 95 L3 38 38N 38 47E
Baskunchak Russia 104 F4 48 14N 46 44E
Bassas da India i. Mozambique Channel 125 G3 22 00S 40 00E
Bassein Myanmar 109 G3 16 46N 94 45E
Bassenthwaite Lake Cumbria England 64 B3 54 40N 3 13W
Basse Terre i. Lesser Antilles 141 L3 16 00N 61 20W
Basse Terre Trinidad and Tobago 141 T9 10 07N 61 17W
Bass Strait Australia 118 H1/2 40 00S 145 00E
Bastia Corsica France 91 D1 42 14N 9 26E
Bastogne Belgium 89 E2 50 00N 5 43E
Bastrop Louisiana U.S.A. 135 H3 32 49N 91 54W
Bata Equatorial Guinea 127 G3 1 51N 9 49E
Batakan Indonesia 111 E3 4 03S 114 39E
Bataklik Gölü l. Turkey 95 H2 37 30N 33 10E
Batala India 109 D6 31 48N 75 17E
Batanagar India 108 K2 22 30N 88 14E
Batang China 113 J5 30 02N 99 01E
Batangafo Central African Rep. 124 C9 7 27N 18 11E
Batangas The Philippines 111 G6 13 46N 121 01E
Batavia New York U.S.A. 137 E2 43 00N 78 11W
Bataysk Russia 95 L7 47 09N 39 46E
Bate Bay Australia 119 G1 34 03S 151 11E
Bath Bath and North East Somerset England 70 B2 51 23N 2 22W
Bath Jamaica 141 R7 17 57N 76 22W
Batha r. Chad 124 C10 13 00N 19 00E
Bath and North East Somerset u.a. England 70 B2 51 25N 2 30W
Bathgate West Lothian Scotland 61 F3 55 55N 3 39W
Bathsheba Barbados 141 V12 13 12N 59 32W
Bathurst Australia 118 H3 33 27S 149 35E
Bathurst New Brunswick Canada 133 V2 47 37N 65 40W
Bathurst, Cape N.W.T. Canada 132 J7 70 31N 127 53W
Bathurst Inlet N.W.T. Canada 132 N6 66 49N 108 00W
Bathurst Island Australia 118 E7 12 00S 130 00E
Bathurst Island N.W.T. Canada 133 P8 76 00N 100 00W
Batley West Yorkshire England 64 D2 53 44N 1 37W
Batman Turkey 95 M2 37 52N 41 02E
Batman r. Turkey 95 M2/3 38 00N 41 00E
Batna Algeria 127 G10 35 34N 6 10E
Baton Rouge Louisiana U.S.A. 135 H3 30 30N 91 10W
Batroûn Lebanon 106 O12 36 16N 35 40E
Battambang Cambodia 111 C6 13 06N 103 13E
Batticaloa Sri Lanka 109 E1 7 43N 81 42E
Battle East Sussex England 71 E1 50 55N 0 29E
Battle Creek tn. Michigan U.S.A. 136 C2 42 20N 85 21W
Battle Harbour tn. Newfoundland Canada 133 X3 51 16N 55 36W
Bat'umi Georgia 95 M4 41 37N 41 36E
Bat Yam Israel 106 O10 32 01N 34 45E
Baubau Indonesia 111 G2 5 30S 122 37E
Bauchi Nigeria 127 G5 10 16N 9 50E
Baudh Orissa India 110 B1 20 50N 84 22E
Baulkham Hills Australia 119 F2/G2 33 46S 151 00E
Bauru Brazil 147 H8 22 19S 49 07W
Bautzen Germany 93 B2 51 11N 14 29E
Bavaria see Bayern
Bawdsey Suffolk England 71 F3 52 01N 1 25E
Bawtry South Yorkshire England 65 D2 53 26N 1 01W
Bayamo Cuba 141 I4 20 23N 76 39W
Bayat Turkey 95 J4 40 34N 34 07E
Bayburt Turkey 95 M4 40 15N 40 16E
Bay City Michigan U.S.A. 137 D2 43 35N 83 52W
Bay City Texas U.S.A. 135 G2 28 59N 96 00W
Baydhabo Somalia 124 H8 3 08N 43 34E
Bayerische Alpen mts. Germany 93 B1 47 00N 11 00E
Bayerische Wald geog. reg. Germany 93 B1 49 00N 13 00E
Bayern (Bavaria) admin. Germany 93 B1 49 00N 12 00E
Bayeux France 91 B2 49 16N 0 42W
Bayfield Barbados 141 W12 13 10N 59 25W
Bayindir Turkey 94 E3 38 12N 27 40E
Baykal, Lake see Ozero Baykal
Baykonur Kazakhstan 105 K4 47 50N 66 03E
Bay of Plenty N.Z. 119 C3 37 48S 177 12E
Bayonne France 91 B1 43 30N 1 28W
Bayonne New Jersey U.S.A. 138 B1 40 39N 74 07W
Bayramiç Turkey 94 E3 39 47N 26 37E
Bayreuth Germany 93 B1 49 27N 11 35E
Bay Ridge tn. New York U.S.A. 138 B1 40 37N 74 02W
Bayston Hill tn. Shropshire England 67 E2 52 40N 2 48W
Baytown Texas U.S.A. 135 H2 29 43N 94 59W
Baza Spain 90 B2 37 30N 2 45W
Bazar-Dyuzi mt. Azerbaijan 104 F3 41 14N 47 50E
Bcharre Lebanon 106 P12 34 15N 36 00E
Beachy Head East Sussex England 71 E1 50 44N 0 16E
Beaconsfield Buckinghamshire England 70 D2 51 37N 0 39W
Beadnell Bay Northumberland England 61 H3 55 32N 1 30W
Beaminster Dorset England 73 E3 50 49N 2 45W
Beardmore Ontario Canada 136 C3 49 36N 87 59W
Beardmore Glacier Antarctica 149 84 00S 170 00E
Bear Island i. Cork Rep. of Ireland 75 B1 51 40N 9 48W
Bear Lake U.S.A. 134 D5 42 00N 111 20W
Bearsden East Dunbartonshire Scotland 61 E3 55 56N 4 20W
Bearsted Kent England 71 E2 51 17N 0 35E
Beatrice Nebraska U.S.A. 136 A2 40 17N 96 45W
Beatty Nevada U.S.A. 134 C4 36 54N 116 45W
Beauchamp France 87 A3 49 00N 2 12E
Beaufort South Carolina U.S.A. 135 J3 32 26N 80 40W
Beaufort Island H.K. China 112 C1 22 11N 114 15E
Beaufort Sea Arctic Ocean 148 72 00N 135 00W
Beaufort West Rep. of South Africa 125 D1 32 21S 22 35E
Beaulieu Hampshire England 70 C1 50 49N 1 27W
Beauly Highland Scotland 59 E2 57 29N 4 29W
Beauly r. Highland Scotland 59 E2 57 25N 4 32W
Beauly Firth Highland Scotland 59 E2 57 30N 4 20W
Beaumaris Isle of Anglesey Wales 66 C3 53 16N 4 05W
Beaumont Belgium 89 D2 50 14N 4 14E
Beaumont France 73 F2 49 40N 1 51W
Beaumont Texas U.S.A. 135 H3 30 04N 94 06W
Beaune France 91 C2 47 02N 4 50E
Beauséjour Manitoba Canada 136 A4 50 04N 96 30W
Beauvais France 91 C2 49 26N 2 05E
Beauval Saskatchewan Canada 132 N4 55 09N 107 35W
Beaver Alaska U.S.A. 132 F6 66 22N 147 30W
Beaver Dam tn. Kentucky U.S.A. 136 C1 37 42N 86 52W
Beaver Island Michigan U.S.A. 136 C3 45 00N 85 00W
Beavermouth Canada 132 L3 51 30N 117 28W
Bebington Merseyside England 64 B2 53 20N 2 59W
Beccles Suffolk England 71 F3 52 28N 1 34E
Béchar Algeria 127 E9 31 35N 2 17W
Becharof Lake U.S.A. 132 D4 58 00N 156 30W
Beckley West Virginia U.S.A. 137 D1 37 46N 81 12W
Bedale North Yorkshire England 64 D3 54 17N 1 35W
Bedford Bedfordshire England 70 D3 52 08N 0 29W
Bedford Indiana U.S.A. 136 C1 38 51N 86 30W
Bedford Levels geog. reg. Cambridgeshire England 70 D3 52 35N 0 00
Bedfordshire co. England 70 D2/D3 52 08N 0 29W
Bedlington Northumberland England 61 H3 55 08N 1 25W
Bedwas Caerphilly Wales 66 D1 51 35N 3 12W
Bedworth Warwickshire England 67 F2 52 29N 1 28W
Be'ér Sheva' Israel 106 O10 31 15N 34 47E
Beeston Nottinghamshire England 65 D1 52 56N 1 12W
Beeville Texas U.S.A. 135 G2 28 25N 97 47W
Begamganj Bangladesh 110 J3 22 59N 91 04E
Begna r. Norway 97 B3 61 00N 9 00E
Begovat Uzbekistan 105 K3 40 14N 69 14E
Behala see South Suburbs
Behbehān Iran 107 H5 30 34N 50 18E
Beht r. Morocco 90 A1 34 30N 5 50W
Bei'an China 113 P8 48 16N 126 36E
Beida (Al Baydā) Libya 76 K2 32 00N 21 30E
Beighton South Yorkshire England 65 D2 53 21N 1 21W
Beihai China 113 L3 21 29N 109 10E
Beijing (Peking) China 113 N6 39 55N 116 26E
Beinn Dearg mt. Highland Scotland 59 E2 57 47N 4 56W
Beira Mozambique 125 F4 19 49S 34 52E
Beirut see Beyrouth
Beith North Ayrshire Scotland 61 E3 55 45N 4 38W
Beius Romania 96 C3 46 40N 22 21E
Beja Portugal 90 A2 38 01N 7 52W
Béja Tunisia 127 G10 36 52N 9 13E
Bejaïa Algeria 127 G10 36 49N 5 03E
Béjar Spain 90 A3 40 24N 5 45W
Békéscsaba Hungary 96 C3 46 45N 21 09E
Bela Pakistan 108 D5 26 12N 66 20E
BELARUS 102 E6
Belau see i. Palau
Belaya Glina Russia 95 M7 46 04N 40 54E
Belda West Bengal India 110 E3 22 05N 87 21E
Belderrig Mayo Rep. of Ireland 74 B4 54 18N 9 33W
Belém Brazil 146 H12 1 27S 48 29W
Belfast co. Northern Ireland 60 C2/D2 54 40N 6 05W
Belfast Belfast Northern Ireland 60 D2 54 35N 5 55W
Belfast Maine U.S.A. 137 G2 44 26N 69 01W
Belfast Lough est. Northern Ireland 60 D2 54 40N 5 50W
Belford Northumberland England 61 H3 55 36N 1 49W
Belford Roxe Brazil 147 P2 22 45S 43 24W
Belfort France 91 D2 47 38N 6 52E
Belgaum India 109 C3 15 54N 74 36E
Belgharia India 108 K2 22 39N 88 23E
BELGIUM 89 C2/E2
Belgorod Russia 104 D5 50 38N 36 36E
Belgrade see Beograd
Beliaghata India 108 K2 22 34N 88 23E
BELIZE 140 G3
Belize Belize 140 G3 17 29N 88 10W
Bellac France 91 C2 46 07N 1 04E
Bella Coola B.C. Canada 132 J3 52 23N 126 46W
Bellacorick Mayo Rep. of Ireland 74 B4 54 07N 9 34W
Bellanagh Cavan Rep. of Ireland 74 D3 53 56N 7 24W
Bellary India 109 D3 15 11N 76 54E
Bellavary Mayo Rep. of Ireland 74 B3 53 53N 9 12W
Bella Vista Argentina 147 F7 28 31S 59 00W
Belle-Île i. France 91 B2 47 20N 3 10W
Belle Isle, Strait of Newfoundland Canada 133 X3 51 00N 57 30W
Bellen Netherlands 89 F4 52 51N 0 01E
Belleplaine Barbados 141 V12 13 14N 59 35W
Belleville Ontario Canada 137 E2 44 10N 77 22W
Belleville Illinois U.S.A. 136 C1 38 31N 89 59W
Bellflower California U.S.A. 139 B2 33 53N 118 08W
Bellingham Northumberland England 61 G3 55 09N 2 16W
Bellingham Washington U.S.A. 134 B6 48 45N 122 29W
Bellingshausen r.s. Antarctica 149 62 12S 58 58W
Bellingshausen Sea Southern Ocean 149 71 00S 85 00W
Bellinzona Switzerland 91 D2 46 12N 9 02E
Bello Colombia 146 B14 6 20N 75 41W
Bellsbank East Ayrshire Scotland 61 E3 55 19N 4 24W
Bellshill North Lanarkshire Scotland 61 E3 55 49N 4 02W
Belluno Italy 92 B3 46 08N 12 13E
Belmont Shetland Islands Scotland 57 F3 60 41N 0 58W
Belmopan Belize 140 G3 17 13N 88 48W
Belmullet Mayo Rep. of Ireland 74 B4 54 14N 10 00W
Belogorsk Russia 103 O6 50 55N 128 26E
Belo Horizonte Brazil 146 I9 19 54S 43 54W
Beloit Wisconsin U.S.A. 136 C2 42 31N 89 04W
Belonia Tripura India 110 J4 23 15N 91 25E
Belorechensk Russia 95 L6 44 46N 39 54E
Belovo Russia 105 O5 54 27N 86 19E
Belper Derbyshire England 67 F3 53 01N 1 29W
Belton Norfolk England 71 F3 52 34N 1 40E
Beltra Lough l. Mayo Rep. of Ireland 74 B3 53 55N 9 25W
Bel'tsy see Bălţi
Belturbet Cavan Rep. of Ireland 74 D4 54 06N 7 28W
Belur India 108 K2 22 37N 88 20E
Belvidere Illinois U.S.A. 136 C2 42 50N 88 50W
Belvoir, Vale of Leicestershire England 65 E1 52 58N 0 55W
Belyy i. Russia 148 73 00N 70 00E
Belyy Yar Russia 105 O6 58 28N 85 03E
Bembézar r. Spain 90 A2 38 00N 5 15W
Bembridge Isle of Wight England 70 C1 50 41N 1 05W
Bemidji Minnesota U.S.A. 136 B3 47 29N 94 52W
Ben Alder mt. Highland Scotland 59 E1 56 49N 4 28W
Benavente Spain 90 A3 42 00N 5 40W
Benbane Head c. Moyle Northern Ireland 60 C3 55 14N 6 29W
Benbecula i. Western Isles Scotland 58 B2 57 25N 7 20W
Ben Cleuch mt. Clackmannanshire Scotland 59 F1 56 11N 3 47W
Ben Cruachan mt. Argyll & Bute Scotland 58 D1 56 26N 5 09W
Bend Oregon U.S.A. 134 B5 44 04N 121 20W
Bender-Bayla Somalia 124 J9 9 30N 50 50E
Bendigo Australia 118 G2 36 48S 144 21E
Benevento Italy 92 B2 41 08N 14 46E
Benfica Brazil 147 P2 22 52S 43 16W
Bengabad Bihar India 110 D5 24 19N 86 22E
Bengal, Bay of Indian Ocean 109 F3/G3 17 00N 88 00E
Bengbu China 113 N5 32 56N 117 27E
Benghazi see Banghāzī
Bengkulu Indonesia 111 C3 3 46S 102 16E
Benguela Angola 125 B5 12 34S 13 24E
Ben Hope mt. Highland Scotland 59 E3 58 24N 4 37W
Beni Abbès Algeria 127 E9 30 11N 2 14W
Beni Boufrah Morocco 90 B2 35 05N 4 18W
Benicarló Spain 90 C3 40 25N 0 25E
Benidorm Spain 90 B2 38 33N 0 09W
Beni Mellal Morocco 127 D9 32 22N 6 29W
BENIN 127 F4/F5
Benin, Bight of b. West Africa 127 F3/4 5 50N 2 30E
Benin City Nigeria 127 G4 6 19N 5 41E
Beni Saf Algeria 90 B2 35 28N 1 22W
Beni Suef Egypt 124 F13 29 05N 31 05E
Benjamin Constant Brazil 146 C12 4 23S 69 59W
Ben Klibreck mt. Highland Scotland 59 E3 58 14N 4 22W
Ben Lawers mt. Perth & Kinross Scotland 59 E1 56 33N 4 15W
Ben Ledi mt. Stirling Scotland 59 E1 56 16N 4 20W
Benllech Isle of Anglesey Wales 66 C3 53 19N 4 15W
Ben Lomond mt. Stirling Scotland 59 E1 56 12N 4 38W
Ben Loyal mt. Highland Scotland 59 E3 58 24N 4 26W
Ben Macdui mt. Aberdeenshire Scotland 59 F2 57 04N 3 40W
Ben More mt. Argyll & Bute Scotland 58 C1 56 25N 6 02W
Ben More mt. Stirling Scotland 59 E1 56 23N 4 31W
Ben More Assynt mt. Highland Scotland 59 E3 58 07N 4 52W
Benmore, Lake N.Z. 119 B2 44 30S 170 10E
Bennettsbridge Kilkenny Rep. of Ireland 75 D2 52 35N 7 10W
Ben Nevis mt. Highland Scotland 59 E1 56 40N 5 00W
Bennington Vermont U.S.A. 137 F2 42 54N 73 12W
Bénoué (Benue) r. Cameroon 127 H4 8 10N 13 50E
Benrath Germany 86 B1 51 10N 6 53E
Benson Arizona U.S.A. 134 D3 31 58N 110 19W
Bentham's Barbados 141 V13 13 18N 59 40W
Bentley South Yorkshire England 65 D2 53 33N 1 09W
Benton Harbor tn. U.S.A. 136 C2 42 07N 86 27W
Benue (Bénoué) r. Nigeria/Cameroon 127 G4 8 00N 7 40E
Ben Venue mt. Stirling Scotland 59 E1 56 13N 4 29W
Benwee Head Mayo Rep. of Ireland 74 B4 54 21N 9 48W
Ben Wyvis mt. Highland Scotland 59 E2 57 40N 4 35W
Benxi China 113 O7 41 21N 123 45E
Beograd (Belgrade) Serbia Yugoslavia 96 C2 44 50N 20 30E
Beppu Japan 114 B1 33 18N 131 30E
Berat Albania 94 A4 40 43N 19 46E
Berber Sudan 124 F11 18 01N 34 00E
Berbera Somalia 124 I10 10 28N 45 02E
Berbérati Central African Rep. 124 C8 4 19N 15 51E
Berck France 91 C3 50 24N 1 35E
Berdyans'k Ukraine 104 D4 46 45N 36 47E
Berdychiv Ukraine 104 B4 49 54N 28 39E
Beregovo Ukraine 96 C3 48 13N 22 39E
Berezivka Ukraine 94 G7 47 12N 30 56E
Berezniki Russia 102 H7 59 26N 56 49E
Berezovo Russia 103 I8 63 58N 65 00E
Bergama Turkey 94 E3 39 08N 27 10E
Bérgamo Italy 92 A3 45 42N 9 40E
Bergen Netherlands 89 D4 52 40N 4 37E
Bergen Norway 97 B3 60 23N 5 20E
Bergenfield New Jersey U.S.A. 138 C2 40 56N 74 00W
Bergen op Zoom Netherlands 89 D3 51 30N 4 17E
Bergen Passaic Expressway U.S.A. 138 B2 40 55N 74 05W
Bergerac France 91 C1 44 50N 0 29E
Bergheim Germany 89 F2 50 57N 6 38E
Bergisch Gladbach Germany 93 A2 50 59N 7 10E
Bergues France 89 B2 50 58N 2 26E
Berhait Bihar India 110 E5 24 52N 87 37E
Bering Sea Pacific Ocean 150 H13/I13 60 00N 175 00W
Bering Strait Russia/U.S.A. 132 B6 69 00N 169 00W
Berkåk Norway 97 C3 62 48N 10 03E
Berkakit Russia 103 O7 56 36N 124 49E
Berkel r. Netherlands 89 F4 52 07N 6 30E
Berkeley Gloucestershire England 70 B2 51 42N 2 27W
Berkeley Sound Falkland Is. 152 M16 51 50S 57 50W
Berkhamsted Hertfordshire England 70 D2 51 46N 0 35W
Berkner Island Antarctica 149 80 00S 45 00W
Berkshire co. England 70 C2/D2 51 28N 1 00W
Berkshire Downs hills Berkshire England 70 C2 51 30N 1 25W
Berlevåg Norway 97 F5 70 50N 29 09E
Berlin Germany 93 B2 52 32N 13 25E
Berlin admin. Germany 93 B2 52 00N 13 00E
Berlin New Hampshire U.S.A. 137 F2 44 27N 71 13W
Bermuda i. Atlantic Ocean 152 B10 32 50N 64 20W
Bern Switzerland 92 A3 46 57N 7 26E
Bernalda Italy 92 C2 40 24N 16 44E
Bernburg Germany 93 B2 51 49N 11 43E
Berner Alpen mts. Switzerland 92 A3 46 25N 7 30E
Berneray l. Western Isles Scotland 58 B2 57 45N 7 10W
Berneray i. Western Isles Scotland 58 B1 56 47N 7 38W
Bernières-sur-Mer France 73 G2 49 19N 0 25W
Benina Pass Switzerland 92 B3 46 25N 10 02E
Berounka r. Czech Republic 93 B1 50 00N 14 00E
Berowra Australia 119 G3 33 37S 151 09E
Berriedale Highland Scotland 59 F3 58 11N 3 33W
Berriedale Water r. Highland Scotland 59 F3
Berry Head c. Devon England 72 D3 50 24N 3 29W
Bertoua Cameroon 127 H3 4 34N 13 42E
Bertraghboy Bay Galway Rep. of Ireland 74 B3 53 23N 9 50W
Berwick Nova Scotia Canada 133 W2 45 03N 64 44W
Berwick Pennsylvania U.S.A. 137 E2 41 04N 76 13W
Berwick-upon-Tweed Northumberland England 61 G3 55 46N 2 00W
Berwyn mts. Wales 66 D2 52 52N 3 25W
Besançon France 91 D2 47 14N 6 02E
Besarabeasca Moldova 94 F7 46 20N 28 59E
Beşiri Turkey 95 M2 37 56N 41 13E
Beskidy Zachodnie mts. Poland 96 C3 50 00N 20 00E
Beskudnikovo Russia 102 M2 55 54N 37 38E
Besni Turkey 95 K2 37 42N 37 53E
Bessacarr South Yorkshire England 65 D2 53 30N 1 05W
Bessbrook Newry and Mourne Northern Ireland 60 C2 54 12N 6 24W
Betanzos Spain 90 A3 43 17N 8 13W
Bétaré Oya Cameroon 127 H4 5 34N 14 09E
Bethany Missouri U.S.A. 136 B2 40 16N 94 02W
Bethel U.S.A. 132 C5 60 49N 161 49W
Bethersden Kent England 71 E2 51 07N 0 45W
Bethesda Maryland U.S.A. 137 E1 39 00N 77 05W
Bethesda Gwynedd Wales 66 C3 53 11N 4 03W
Bethlehem Middle East 106 O10 31 42N 35 12E
Bethlehem Pennsylvania U.S.A. 137 E2 40 36N 75 22W
Béthune France 91 C3 50 32N 2 38E
Betican Cordilleras mts. Spain 77 E3 37 00N 3 00W
Betroka Madagascar 125 I3 23 15S 46 07E
Betsiamites Québec Canada 137 G3 48 56N 68 40W
Betsiboka r. Madagascar 125 I4 17 00S 46 30E
Bettyhill Highland Scotland 59 E3 58 32N 4 14W
Betws-y-Coed Conwy Wales 66 D3 53 05N 3 48W
Beveren Belgium 89 D3 51 13N 4 15E
Beverley East Riding of Yorkshire England 65 E2 53 51N 0 26W
Beverly Hills tn. U.S.A. 139 A3 34 03N 118 22W
Beverwijk Netherlands 89 D4 52 29N 4 40E
Bewdley Hereford and Worcester England 67 E2 52 22N 2 19W
Bewl Water l. Essex England 71 E2 51 02N 0 23E
Bexhill East Sussex England 71 E1 50 50N 0 29E
Bexley Greater London England 71 E2 51 27N 0 09E
Beydili Turkey 94 G4 40 10N 30 56E
Beykoz Turkey 94 F4 41 08N 29 07E
Beyla Guinea 127 D4 8 42N 8 39W
Beyrouth (Beirut) Lebanon 106 O11 33 52N 35 30E
Beyşehir Turkey 94 G2 37 40N 31 43E
Beyşehir Gölü l. Turkey 94 G2 37 40N 31 43E
Beysug r. Russia 95 L6 45 45N 39 40E
Béziers France 91 C1 43 21N 3 13E
Bhadgaon Nepal 109 F5 27 41N 85 26E
Bhadrak Orissa India 110 D2 21 05N 86 36E
Bhadravati India 109 D2 13 54N 75 38E
Bhadreswar India 108 K3 22 50N 88 20E
Bhagalpur Bihar India 109 F5 25 14N 86 59E
Bhairab Bazar Dhaka Bangladesh 110 H5 24 04N 91 00E
Bhandara India 109 D4 21 10N 79 41E
Bhanga Dhaka Bangladesh 110 H4 23 90
Bharatpur India 109 D5 27 14N 77 29E
Bharda Nepal 110 D7 26 31N 86 52E
Bharuch India 109 C4 21 40N 73 02E
Bhatinda India 109 C6 30 10N 74 58E
Bhatpara West Bengal India 110 F3 22 51N 88 31E
Bhavnagar India 109 C4 21 46N 72 14E
Bhilwara India 109 C5 25 23N 74 39E
Bhima r. India 109 D3 17 00N 77 00E
Bhiwandi India 109 C3 19 21N 73 08E
Bhola Khulna Bangladesh 110 H3 22 45N 90 35E
Bhopal India 109 D4 23 17N 77 28E
Bhuban Orissa India 110 C1 20 52N 85 51E
Bhubaneshwar India 109 F4 20 13N 85 50E
Bhuj India 108 B4 23 12N 69 54E
Bhusawal India 109 D4 21 01N 75 50E
BHUTAN 109 F5/G5
Biała Podlaska Poland 96 C4 52 03N 23 05E
Białystok Poland 96 C4 53 09N 23 10E
Biarritz France 91 B1 43 29N 1 33W
Bibai Japan 114 D3 43 21N 141 53E
Biberach Germany 93 A1 48 06N 9 48E
Bicester Oxfordshire England 70 C2 51 54N 1 09W
Biche Trinidad and Tobago 141 T9 10 26N 61 07W
Bida Nigeria 127 G4 9 06N 5 59E
Bidar India 109 D3 17 56N 77 35E
Biddeford Maine U.S.A. 137 F2 43 29N 70 27W
Biddulph Staffordshire England 67 E3 53 08N 2 10W
Bideford Devon England 72 C4 51 01N 4 13W
Biebrza r. Poland 96 C4 53 00N 22 00E
Biel Switzerland 92 A3 46 27N 8 13E
Bielefeld Germany 93 A2 52 02N 8 32E
Biella Italy 92 A3 45 34N 8 04E
Bielsko-Biała Poland 96 B3 49 50N 19 00E
Bielsk Podlaski Poland 96 C4 52 47N 23 11E
Bièvres France 87 A2 48 45N 2 11E
Biferno r. Italy 92 B2 41 00N 14 00E
Biğa Turkey 94 F4 40 13N 27 14E
Big Black r. Mississippi U.S.A. 135 H3 33 00N 90 00W
Big Blue r. U.S.A. 136 A2 40 00N 98 00W
Bigbury Bay Devon England 72 D3 50 17N 4 00W
Biggar South Lanarkshire Scotland 61 F3 55 38N 3 32W
Biggleswade Bedfordshire England 70 D3 52 05N 0 17W
Bighorn r. U.S.A. 134 E6 45 00N 108 00W
Bighorn Mountains U.S.A. 134 E5 44 00N 108 00W
Big Salmon Yukon Canada 132 I5 61 52N 134 56W
Big Santa Anita Reservoir U.S.A. 139 B3 34 11N 118 01W
Big Sioux r. U.S.A. 136 A2 44 00N 96 00W
Big Spring tn. Texas U.S.A. 134 F3 32 15N 101 30W
Big Trout Lake Ontario Canada 133 R3 54 00N 89 00W
Big Tujunga Reservoir U.S.A. 139 B4 34 19N 118 11W
Bihac Bosnia-Herzegovina 96 B2 44 49N 15 53E
Bihar admin. India 109 F4 24 40N 86 00E
Biharamulo Tanzania 124 E7 2 37S 31 20E
Bihariganj Bihar India 110 D6 25 44N 86 59E
Bijapur India 109 D3 16 47N 75 48E
Bījar Iran 107 G6 35 52N 47 39E
Bijlmermeer Netherlands 88 D3 52 19N 4 58E
Bikaner India 109 C5 28 01N 73 22E
Bilaspur India 109 E4 27 51N 82 00E
Bila Tserkva Ukraine 104 C4 49 49N 30 10E
Bilbao Spain 90 B3 43 15N 2 56W
Bilboa r. Limerick Rep. of Ireland 75 B2 52 37N 8 13W
Bilecik Turkey 94 F4 40 10N 29 59E
Bilhorod-Dnistrovs'kyy Ukraine 94 G7 46 10N 30 19E
Bilibino Russia 103 S9 68 00N 166 15E
Billericay Essex England 71 E2 51 38N 0 25E
Billinge Merseyside England 64 C2 53 30N 2 42W
Billingham Stockton-on-Tees England 65 D3 54 36N 1 17W
Billings Montana U.S.A. 134 E6 45 47N 108 30W
Billingshurst West Sussex England 70 D2 51 01N 0 28W
Bill of Portland c. Dorset England 73 E3 50 31N 2 27W
Biloxi Mississippi U.S.A. 135 I3 30 24N 88 55W
Bilthoven Netherlands 89 E2 52 08N 5 09E
Binche Belgium 89 D2 50 25N 4 10E
Bingen Germany 93 A1 49 58N 7 55E
Bingham Nottinghamshire England 65 E1 52 57N 0 57W
Bingham Maine U.S.A. 137 G3 45 03N 69 53W
Binghampton New York U.S.A. 137 E2 42 06N 75 55W
Bingley West Yorkshire England 64 D2 53 51N 1 50W
Bingöl Turkey 95 M3 38 54N 40 29E
Binka Orissa India 110 A2 21 02N 83 51E
Bintulu Malaysia 111 F4 3 10N 113 02E
Bioko i. Equatorial Guinea 127 G3 3 00N 8 20E
Biramitrapur Orissa India 110 B3 22 25N 84 44E
Birao Central African Rep. 124 D10 10 11N 22 49E
Biratnagar Nepal 109 F5 26 27N 87 17E
Birchwood tn Lincolnshire England 65 E2 53 14N 0 33W
Birdsville Australia 118 F4 25 50S 139 20E
Dirjand Iran 107 I5 32 55N 59 10E
Birkenhead Merseyside England 64 B2 53 24N 3 02W
Birkenwerder Germany 87 F2 52 42N 13 17E
Birmingham West Midlands England 67 F2 52 30N 1 50W
Birmingham Alabama U.S.A. 135 I3 33 30N 86 55W
Birnin Kebbi Nigeria 127 F5 12 30N 4 11E
Birobidzhan Russia 103 P5 48 49N 132 54E
Birpur Bihar India 110 D7 26 30N 86 59E
Birr Offaly Rep. of Ireland 75 D3 53 05N 7 54W
Birstall Leicestershire England 67 F2 52 40N 1 08W
Bisai Orissa India 110 D3 22 11N 86 20E
Biscay, Bay of Atlantic Ocean 91 B2 45 30N 2 50W
Biscoe Islands Antarctica 149 66 00S 67 00W
Bishkek (Frunze) Kirgyzstan 103 J4 42 53N 74 46E
Bishnupur West Bengal India 110 E4 23 05N 87 20E
Bishop Auckland Durham England 64 D3 54 40N 1 40W
Bishopbriggs East Dunbartonshire Scotland 61 E3 55 54N 4 14W
Bishop's Castle tn. Shropshire England 66 D2 52 29N 3 00W
Bishop's Cleeve Gloucestershire England 70 B2 51 57N 2 04W
Bishop's Lydeard Somerset England 73 D4 51 04N 3 12W
Bishop's Stortford Hertfordshire England 71 E2 51 53N 0 09E
Bishopston Swansea Wales 66 C1 51 35N 4 03W
Bishop's Waltham Hampshire England 70 C1 50 58N 1 12W
Bishopton Renfrewshire Scotland 61 E3 55 54N 4 31W
Biskra Algeria 127 G9 34 50N 5 41E
Bismarck North Dakota U.S.A. 134 F6 46 50N 100 48W
Bismarck Archipelago is. Papua New Guinea 118 H9/I9 2 00S 146 00E
Bismarck Sea Papua New Guinea 118 H9 3 30S 148 00E
Bissau Guinea-Bissau 127 B5 11 52N 15 39W
Bistrița Romania 96 C3 47 08N 24 30E
Bistrița r. Romania 96 D3 47 00N 25 00E
Bitburg Germany 89 F1 49 58N 6 32E
Bitlis Turkey 95 N3 38 23N 42 04E
Bitola FYROM 94 B4 41 01N 21 21E
Bitterroot Range mts. U.S.A. 134 D6 46 00N 114 00W
Biwa-ko l. Japan 114 C2 35 20N 135 20E
Biwa-ko l. Japan 114 H2 35 10N 136 00E
Biya r. Russia 105 O5 51 00N 88 00E
Biysk Russia 103 K6 52 35N 85 16E
Bizerte Tunisia 127 G10 37 18N 9 52E

Bruton Somerset England 73 E4 51 07N 2 27W
Bruxelles (Brussel, Brussels) Belgium 89 D2 50 50N 4 21E
Bryan Texas U.S.A. 135 G3 30 41N 96 24W
Bryansk Russia 102 F6 53 15N 34 09E
Bryher i. Isles of Scilly England 72 A2 49 57N 6 21W
Brymbo Wrexham Wales 66 D3 53 05N 3 03W
Brynamman Carmarthenshire Wales 66 D1 51 49N 3 52W
Brynmawr Blaenau Gwent Wales 66 D1 51 49N 3 11W
Brzeg Poland 96 B4 50 52N 17 27E
Bucak Turkey 94 G2 37 28N 30 37E
Bucaramanga Colombia 146 C14 7 08N 73 10W
Buchanan Liberia 127 C4 5 57N 10 02W
Buchan Ness c. Aberdeenshire Scotland 59 H2 57 28N 1 47W
Bucharest see Bucureşti
Bucholz Germany 86 B2 51 25N 6 45E
Buckfastleigh Devon England 72 D3 50 29N 3 46W
Buckhaven Fife Scotland 59 F1 56 11N 3 03W
Buckie Moray Scotland 59 G2 57 40N 2 58W
Buckingham Québec Canada 137 E3 45 35N 75 25W
Buckingham Buckinghamshire England 70 D2 52 00N 1 00W
Buckinghamshire co. England 70 D2 51 50N 0 50W
Buckley Flintshire Wales 66 D3 53 10N 3 05W
Buckow Germany 87 F1 52 24N 1324E
Bucksport Maine U.S.A. 137 G2 44 35N 68 47W
Bucureşti (Bucharest) Romania 96 D2 44 25N 26 07E
Budapest Hungary 96 B3 47 30N 19 03E
Buddon Ness Angus Scotland 59 G1 56 27N 2 45W
Bude Cornwall England 72 C3 50 50N 4 33W
Bude Bay b. Cornwall England 72 C3 50 50N 4 40W
Budennovsk Russia 95 P6 44 46N 44 10E
Büderlich Germany 86 A1 51 15N 6 20E
Budjala Congo (D.R.) 124 C8 2 38N 19 48E
Budleigh Salterton Devon England 73 D3 50 38N 3 20W
Buea Cameroon 127 G3 4 09N 9 13E
Buena Park tn. California U.S.A. 139 B2 33 52N 118 02W
Buenaventura Colombia 146 B13 3 54N 77 02W
Buenaventura Mexico 140 C5 29 50N 107 30W
Buenos Aires Argentina 147 F6 34 40S 58 30W
Buenos Aires, Lake Argentina/Chile 147 C3 47 00S 72 00W
Buer Germany 86 C3 51 35N 7 05E
Buffalo New York U.S.A. 137 E2 42 52N 78 55W
Buffalo Wyoming U.S.A. 134 E5 44 21N 106 40W
Buffalo Lake N.W.T. Canada 132 L5 60 40N 115 30W
Buffalo Narrows tn. Canada 132 N4 55 52N 108 28W
Buff Bay tn. Jamaica 141 R8 18 18N 76 40W
Bug r. Ukraine 76 M5 48 00N 30 30 E
Bugul'ma Russia 105 G5 54 32N 52 46E
Buḩayrat al Asad l. Syria 95 L1 35 55N 38 15E
Buhuşi Romania 96 D3 46 41N 26 45E
Builth Wells Powys Wales 66 D2 52 09N 3 24W
Bujanovac Serbia Yugoslavia 94 B5 42 27N 21 46E
Bujumbura Burundi 125 E7 3 22S 29 19E
Bukachacha Russia 103 N6 53 00N 116 58E
Bukama Congo (D.R.) 125 E6 9 13S 25 52E
Bukavu Congo (D.R.) 124 E7 2 30S 28 50E
Bukhara Uzbekistan 105 J2 39 47N 64 26E
Bukittinggi Indonesia 111 C3 0 18S 100 20E
Bukoba Tanzania 124 F7 1 19S 31 49E
Bula Indonesia 118 E9 3 07S 130 27E
Bulandshahr India 109 D5 28 30N 77 49E
Bulanik Turkey 95 N3 39 04N 42 16E
Bulawayo Zimbabwe 125 E3 20 10S 28 43E
Buldan Turkey 94 F3 38 03N 28 50E
Bulford Wiltshire England 70 C2 51 12N 1 40W
BULGARIA 96 C2
Bulkington Warwickshire England 67 F2 52 28N 1 25W
Buller r. N.Z. 119 B2 41 50S 171 35E
Bull Point c. Moyle Northern Ireland 60 C3 55 10N 6 16W
Bull Shoals Lake U.S.A. 135 H4 36 00N 93 00W
Bulun Russia 103 O10 70 45N 127 20E
Bumba Congo (D.R.) 124 D8 2 10N 22 30E
Bunbury Australia 118 B3 33 20S 115 34E
Bunclody Wexford Rep. of Ireland 75 E2 52 38N 6 40W
Buncrana Donegal Rep. of Ireland 74 D5 55 08N 7 27W
Bundaberg Australia 118 I5 24 50S 152 21E
Bundeena Australia 119 G1 34 06S 151 07E
Bundoran Donegal Rep. of Ireland 74 C4 54 28N 8 17W
Bundu Bihar India 110 C4 23 08N 85 19E
Bungay Suffolk England 71 F3 52 28N 1 26E
Bungo-suidō sd. Japan 114 B1 33 00N 132 30E
Bunia Congo (D.R.) 124 F8 1 33N 30 13E
Bunmahon Waterford Rep. of Ireland 75 D2 52 08N 7 23W
Bunnahown Galway Rep. of Ireland 74 B3 53 24N 9 47W
Bunnyconnellan Mayo Rep. of Ireland 74 B4 54 06N 9 01W
Bünyan Turkey 95 J3 38 51N 35 50E
Buôn Mê Thuôt Vietnam 111 D6 12 41N 108 02E
Bura Kenya 124 G7 1 06S 39 58E
Buraolt Romania 96 D3 46 04N 25 36E
Buraydah Saudi Arabia 106 F4 26 20N 43 59E
Burbank California U.S.A. 139 A3 34 10N 118 25W
Burdur Turkey 94 G2 37 44N 30 17E
Burdur Gölü l. Turkey 94 G2 37 40N 30 10E
Bure r. Norfolk England 71 F3 52 47N 1 20E
Bureya r. Russia 103 P6 52 00N 133 00E
Burg Germany 93 B2 52 17N 11 51E
Burgas Bulgaria 96 D2 42 30N 27 29E
Burgess Hill tn. West Sussex England 70 D1 50 58N 0 08W
Burghead tn. Moray Scotland 59 F2 57 42N 3 30W
Burghead Bay Moray Scotland 59 F2 57 41N 3 32W
Burgh le Marsh Lincolnshire England 65 F2 53 10N 0 15E
Burgos Spain 90 B3 42 21N 3 41W
Burhaniye Turkey 94 E3 39 29N 26 59E
Burhanpur India 109 D4 21 18N 76 08E
Buri Khali India 108 J1 22 30N 88 10E
BURKINA 127 E5
Burk's Falls tn. Ontario Canada 137 E3 45 37N 79 25W
Burley-in-Wharfedale West Yorkshire England 64 D2 53 55N 1 45W
Burlington Ontario Canada 137 F2 43 19N 79 48W
Burlington Colorado U.S.A. 134 F4 39 17N 102 17W
Burlington Iowa U.S.A. 136 B2 40 50N 91 07W
Burlington Vermont U.S.A. 137 F2 44 28N 73 14W
Burlington West Virginia U.S.A. 137 E1 39 20N 78 56W
Burlington Wisconsin U.S.A. 136 C2 42 41N 88 17W
BURMA see MYANMAR
Burnham Market Norfolk England 71 E3 52 57N 0 44E
Burnham-on-Crouch Essex England 71 E2 51 38N 0 49E
Burnham-on-Sea Somerset England 73 E4 51 15N 3 00W
Burnie Australia 118 H1 41 03S 145 55E
Burnley Lancashire England 64 C2 53 48N 2 14W
Burnmouth Scottish Borders Scotland 61 G3 55 50N 2 04W
Burnpur West Bengal India 110 D4 23 41N 86 55E
Burnsall North Yorkshire England 64 D3 54 03N 1 57W
Burntisland tn. Fife Scotland 61 F4 56 03N 3 15W
Burntwood Staffordshire England 67 F2 52 40N 1 56W
Burquin China 105 O4 47 44N 86 55E
Burray i. Orkney Islands Scotland 57 C1 58 51N 2 54W
Burrel Albania 94 B4 41 36N 20 01E
Burrow Head c. Dumfries & Galloway Scotland 61 E2 54 41N 4 24W
Burry Port Carmarthenshire Wales 66 C1 51 42N 4 15W
Bursa Turkey 94 F4 40 12N 29 04E
Būr Safāga Egypt 124 F13 25 43N 33 55E
Būr Sa'īd see Port Said
Burscough Bridge tn. Lancashire England 64 C2 53 37N 2 51W
Burton Agnes East Riding of Yorkshire England 65 E3 54 03N 0 19W
Burton Latimer Northamptonshire England 70 D3 52 22N 0 40W
Burton upon Trent Staffordshire England 67 F2 52 48N 1 36W
Buru i. Indonesia 111 H3 3 30S 126 30E
BURUNDI 125 E7
Burwell Cambridgeshire England 71 E3 52 16N 0 19E
Burwell Nebraska U.S.A. 134 G5 41 48N 99 09W
Bury Greater Manchester England 64 C2 53 36N 2 17W
Bury St. Edmunds Suffolk England 71 E3 52 15N 0 43E
Bush r. Ballymoney/Moyle Northern Ireland 60 C3 55 10N 6 30W
Būshehr Iran 107 H4 28 57N 50 52E
Bushey Hertfordshire England 70 D2 51 39N 0 22W
Bushmills Moyle Northern Ireland 60 C3 55 12N 6 32W
Busira r. Congo (D.R.) 124 C7 1 20S 20 00E
Bussum Netherlands 89 E4 52 16N 5 09E
Busto Arsizio Italy 92 A3 45 37N 8 51E
Buta Congo (D.R.) 124 D8 2 49N 24 50E
Butare Rwanda 124 E7 2 35S 29 44E
Bute i. Argyll & Bute Scotland 60 D3 55 50N 5 05W
Bute, Sound of Argyll & Bute/North Ayrshire Scotland 60 D3 55 45N 5 10W
Buthidaung Myanmar 110 K1 20 50N 92 35E
Butler Pennsylvania U.S.A. 137 E2 40 51N 79 55W
Butler's Bridge Cavan Rep. of Ireland 74 D4 54 03N 7 22W
Buton i. Indonesia 111 G3 5 00S 122 45E
Butovo Russia 102 M1 55 30N 37 32E
Butte Montana U.S.A. 134 D6 46 00N 112 31W
Buttermere l. Cumbria England 64 B3 54 32N 3 16W
Buttevant Cork Rep. of Ireland 75 C2 52 14N 8 40W
Butt of Lewis c. Western Isles Scotland 58 C3 58 30N 6 20W
Butuan The Philippines 111 H5 8 56N 125 31E
Buulobarde Somalia 124 I8 3 50N 45 33E
Buxtehude Germany 93 A2 53 29N 9 42E
Buxton Derbyshire England 67 F3 53 15N 1 55W
Büyük Ağri Daği (Mt. Ararat) Turkey 95 P3 39 44N 44 15E
Büyük Menderes r. Turkey 94 E2 37 45N 27 30E
Buzău Romania 96 D3 45 09N 26 49E
Byarezina r. Belarus 104 B5 54 00N 29 00E
Bydgoszcz Poland 96 B4 53 16N 18 00E
BYELORUSSIA see BELARUS
Byfield Northamptonshire England 70 C3 52 11N 1 14W
Bygland Norway 97 B2 58 50N 7 49E
Bylot Island N.W.T. Canada 133 T7 73 30N 79 00W
Byrranga Mountains Russia 103 L10 75 00N 100 00E
Bytom Poland 96 B4 50 21N 18 51E

C

Cabanatuan The Philippines 111 G7 15 30N 120 58E
Caban-coch Resevoir res. Wales 66 D2 52 15N 3 35W
Cabano Québec Canada 137 G3 47 40N 68 56W
Cabimas Venezuela 146 C15 10 26N 71 27W
Cabinda admin. Angola 125 B6 5 30S 12 20E
Cabo Brazil 146 J11 8 16S 35 00W
Cabo Blanco c. Costa Rica 141 G1 9 36N 85 06W
Cabo Caballeria c. Balearic Islands 90 F5 40 05N 4 05E
Cabo Catoche c. Mexico 141 G4 21 38N 87 08W
Cabo Corrientes c. Colombia 146 B14 5 29N 77 36W
Cabo Corrientes c. Mexico 140 C4 20 25N 105 42W
Cabo d'Artrutx c. Balearic Islands 90 E4 39 55N 3 49E
Cabo de Barberia c. Balearic Islands 90 D4 30 40N 1 20E
Cabo de Cala Figuera c. Balearic Is. 90 E4 39 27N 2 31E
Cabo de Creus c. Spain 90 C3 42 19N 3 19E
Cabo de Formentor c. Balearic Is. 90 E4 39 58N 3 13E
Cabo de Gata c. Spain 90 B2 36 44N 2 10W
Cabo de Hornos (Cape Horn) Chile 147 D1 56 00S 67 15W
Cabo de la Nao c. Spain 90 C2 38 44N 0 14E
Cabo Delgado c. Mozambique 125 H5 10 45S 40 45E
Cabo de Palos c. Spain 90 B2 37 38N 0 40W
Cabo de Peñas c. Spain 90 A3 43 39N 5 50W
Cabo de Salinas c. Balearic Islands 90 E4 39 16N 3 04E
Cabo de São Vicente c. Portugal 90 A2 37 01N 8 59W
Cabo de Tortosa c. Spain 90 C3 40 44N 0 54E
Cabo Dos Bahías c. Argentina 147 D4 45 00S 65 30W
Cabo Espichel c. Portugal 90 A2 38 24N 9 13W
Cabo Falso c. Mexico 140 B4 22 50N 110 00W
Cabo Finisterre c. Spain 90 A3 42 52N 9 16W
Cabo Freu c. Balearic Islands 90 E4 39 45N 3 27E
Cabo Gracias á Dios c. Nicaragua 141 H3 15 00N 83 10W
Cabo Guardafui see Raas Caseyr
Cabo Orange c. Brazil 146 G13 4 25N 51 32W
Cabo Ortegal c. Spain 90 A3 43 46N 7 54W
Cabora Bassa Dam Mozambique 125 F4 16 00S 33 00E
Caborca Mexico 140 B6 30 42N 112 10W
Cabo San Juan c. Argentina 147 E2 54 45S 63 46W
Cabo Santa Elena c. Costa Rica 141 G2 10 54N 85 56W
Cabot Strait Canada 133 W2 47 10N 59 30W
Cabo Vírgenes c. Argentina 147 D2 52 20S 68 00W
Cabrera i. Balearic Islands 90 E4 39 00N 2 59E
Cabriel r. Spain 90 B2 39 20N 1 15W
Čačak Serbia Yugoslavia 96 C2 43 54N 20 22E
Cáceres Brazil 146 F9 16 05S 57 40W
Cáceres Spain 90 A2 39 29N 6 23W
Cachoeira Brazil 146 J10 12 35S 38 59W
Cachoeira do Sul Brazil 147 G7 30 03S 52 52W
Cachoeiro de Itapemirim Brazil 147 I8 20 51N 41 07W
Cadair Idris mt. Gwynedd Wales 66 D2 52 42N 3 54W
Cádiz Spain 90 A2 36 32N 6 18W
Cadiz The Philippines 111 G6 10 57N 123 18E
Cádiz, Gulf of Spain 90 A2 36 30N 7 15W
Caen France 91 B2 49 11N 0 22W
Caerleon Newport Wales 66 E1 51 37N 2 57W
Caernarfon Gwynedd Wales 66 C3 53 08N 4 16W
Caernarfon Bay Gwynedd Wales 66 C3 53 05N 4 30W
Caerphilly u.a. Wales 66 D1 51 37N 3 5W
Caerphilly Caerphilly Wales 66 D1 51 35N 3 14W
Caersws Powys Wales 66 D2 52 31N 3 26W
Cagayan de Oro The Philippines 111 G5 8 29N 124 40E
Cagliari Italy 92 A1 39 13N 9 08E
Caguas Puerto Rico 141 K3 18 41N 66 04W
Caha Mountains Kerry/Cork Rep. of Ireland 75 B1 51 40N 9 40W
Caher Tipperary Rep. of Ireland 75 D2 52 21N 7 56W
Caher Island Mayo Rep. of Ireland 74 A3 53 43N 10 01W
Cahersiveen Kerry Rep. of Ireland 75 A1 51 57N 10 13W
Cahore Point c. Wexford Rep. of Ireland 75 E2 52 34N 6 11W
Cahors France 91 C1 44 28N 0 26E
Cahul Moldova 94 F6 45 58N 28 10E
Caicos Passage sd. West Indies 141 J4 22 20N 72 30W
Cairn Gorm mt. Moray Scotland 59 F2 57 07N 3 40W
Cairngorms mts. Highland/Moray Scotland 59 F2 57 10N 3 30W
Cairnryan Dumfries & Galloway Scotland 60 D2 54 58N 5 02W
Cairns Australia 118 H6 16 51S 145 43E
Cairnsmore of Fleet mt. Dumfries & Galloway Scotland 61 E2 54 58N 4 21W
Cairo Illinois U.S.A. 136 C1 37 01N 89 09W
Cairo Egypt see El Qâ'hira
Caister-on-Sea Norfolk England 71 F3 52 39N 1 44E
Caistor Lincolnshire England 65 E2 53 30N 0 20W
Cajamarca Peru 146 B11 7 09S 78 32W
Cajàzeiras Brazil 146 J11 6 52S 38 31W
Caju Brazil 147 Q2 22 53S 43 13W
Cakerek Irmak r. Turkey 95 J3/H4 40 00N 36 00E
Çakırgöl Dağı mt. Turkey 95 L4 40 33N 39 40E
Čakovec Croatia 92 C4 46 24N 16 26E
Çal Turkey 94 F3 38 05N 29 22E
Calabar Nigeria 127 G3 4 56N 8 22E
Calabozo Venezuela 141 K1 8 58N 67 28W
Calahorra Spain 90 B3 46 19N 1 58W
Calais France 91 C3 50 57N 1 52E
Calama Chile 147 D8 22 30S 68 55W
Calamar Colombia 146 C15 10 16N 74 55W
Calamian Group is. The Philippines 111 G6 12 00N 120 00E
Calamocha Spain 90 B3 40 54N 1 18W
Calapan The Philippines 111 G6 13 23N 121 10E
Călăraşi Moldova 94 F7 47 18N 28 16E
Călăraşi Romania 96 D2 44 12N 27 22E
Calatayud Spain 90 B3 41 21N 1 39W
Calçoene Brazil 146 G13 20 30N 50 55W
Calcutta admin. India 108 K1 22 28N 88 20E
Calcutta West Bengal India 109 F4 22 30N 88 20E
Caldas da Rainha Portugal 90 A2 39 24N 9 08W
Caldew r. Cumbria England 64 C3 54 45N 3 00W
Caldey Island Pembrokeshire Wales 66 C1 51 38N 4 42W
Caldicot Monmouthshire Wales 67 E1 51 36N 2 45W
Caldwell Idaho U.S.A. 134 C5 43 39N 116 40W
Caldwell New Jersey U.S.A. 138 A2 40 49N 74 16W
Caldwell Wright Airport U.S.A. 138 A2 40 51N 74 16W
Calf of Eday i. Orkney Is. Scotland 57 C2 59 14N 2 44W
Calf of Man i. Isle of Man British Isles 64 A3 54 03N 4 49W
Calgary Alberta Canada 132 M3 51 05N 11 05W
Cali Colombia 146 B13 3 24N 76 30W
Calicut India 109 D2 11 15N 75 45E
Caliente Nevada U.S.A. 134 D4 37 36N 114 31W
California Trinidad and Tobago 141 T9 10 24N 61 28W
California state U.S.A. 134 C4 35 00N 119 00W
Callan Kilkenny Rep. of Ireland 75 D2 52 33N 7 23W
Callander Stirling Scotland 59 E1 56 15N 4 13W
Callao Peru 146 B10 12 05S 77 08W
Calligarry Highland Scotland 58 D2 57 02N 5 58E
Callington Cornwall England 72 C3 50 30N 4 18W
Calne Wiltshire England 70 B2 51 27N 2 00W
Caltanissetta Italy 92 B1 37 29N 14 04E
Calverton Nottinghamshire England 65 D2 53 03N 1 05W
Calvi Corsica 91 D1 42 34N 8 44E
Calvia Balearic Islands 90 E4 39 33N 2 29E
Calvinia Rep. of South Africa 125 C1 31 25S 19 47E
Cam r. Cambridgeshire England 71 E3 52 15N 0 11E
Camaçari Brazil 146 J10 12 44S 38 16W
Camacupa Angola 125 C5 12 03S 17 50E
Camagüey Cuba 141 I4 21 25N 77 55W
Çamardi Turkey 95 J2 37 49N 35 00E
Camberley Surrey England 70 D2 51 21N 0 45W
CAMBODIA 111 C6/D6
Camborne Cornwall England 72 B3 50 12N 5 19W
Cambrai France 91 C3 50 10N 3 14E
Cambrian Mountains mts. Wales 66 D2 52 15N 3 45W
Cambridge Ontario Canada 137 D2 43 22N 80 20W
Cambridge Cambridgeshire England 71 E3 52 12N 0 07E
Cambridge Jamaica 141 Q8 18 18N 77 54W
Cambridge N.Z. 119 C3 37 53S 175 28E
Cambridge Maryland U.S.A. 135 K4 38 34N 76 04W
Cambridge Ohio U.S.A. 137 D2 40 02N 81 36W
Cambridge Bay tn. Canada 133 N6 69 09N 105 00W
Cambridgeshire co. England 70 D3 52 30N 0 00
Çam Burun c. Turkey 95 K4 41 09N 37 48E
Camden New Jersey U.S.A. 137 E1 39 57N 75 06W
Cameia National Park Angola 125 D5 12 00S 22 00E
Camel r. Cornwall England 72 C3 50 31N 4 44W
Çameli Turkey 94 F2 37 05N 29 24E
Camelford Cornwall England 72 D3 50 37N 4 41W
CAMEROON 127 H3/4
Cametá Brazil 146 H12 2 12S 49 30W
Camiri Bolivia 146 F8 20 08S 63 33W
Çamlıdere Turkey 94 H4 40 28N 32 25E
Camlin r. Longford Rep. of Ireland 74 D3 53 46N 7 35W
Camocin Brazil 146 I12 2 55S 40 50W
Camoge r. Limerick Rep. of Ireland 75 B2 52 32N 8 34W
Camorta i. Nicobar Islands 109 G1 7 30N 93 30E
Campbell Island Southern Ocean 150 G2 52 30S 169 10E
Campbell River tn. Canada 132 J2 50 00N 125 18W
Campbellsville Kentucky U.S.A. 136 C1 37 20N 85 21W
Campbellton Canada 133 V2 48 00N 66 30W
Campbeltown Argyll & Bute Scotland 60 D3 55 26N 5 36W
Campeche Mexico 140 F3 19 50N 90 30W
Câmpina Romania 96 D3 45 08N 25 44E
Campina Grande Brazil 146 J11 7 15S 35 50W
Campinas Brazil 147 H8 22 54S 47 06W
Campines see Kempenland
Campoalegre Colombia 146 B13 2 49N 75 19W
Campobasso Italy 96 A2 41 33N 14 39E
Campo Grande Brazil 146 G8 20 24S 54 35W
Campo Maior Brazil 146 I12 4 50S 42 12W
Campo Mourão Brazil 147 G8 24 01S 52 24W
Campos Brazil 147 I8 21 46S 41 21W
Campos del Puerto Balearic Is. 90 E4 39 26N 3 01E
Campos Elyseos Brazil 147 P3 22 42S 43 16W
Campsie Fells hills Scotland 61 E4 56 00N 4 15W
Câmpulung Romania 96 D3 45 16N 25 02E
Cam Rahn Vietnam 111 D6 11 54N 109 14E
Çan Turkey 94 E4 40 03N 27 03E
CANADA 132/133
Canada Basin Arctic Ocean 148 80 00N 140 00W
Canadian r. U.S.A. 134 F4 35 00N 104 00W
Canadian Shield mts. Canada 151 Q13/S12 50 00N 90 00W
Canakkale Turkey 94 E4 40 09N 26 25E
Canal de Calais can. France 91 F1/G1 50 54N 2 00E
Canal de l'Ourcq can. France 87 C2 48 55N 2 32E
Canal des Ardennes France 89 D1 49 50N 4 30E
Canal du Midi France 91 C1 43 20N 2 00E
Cananea Mexico 140 B6 30 59N 110 20W
Canary Basin Atlantic Ocean 152 E9/F9 26 20N 30 00W
Canary Islands Spain 127 B8/C8 28 30N 15 10W
Canaveral, Cape Florida U.S.A. 135 J2 28 28N 80 28W
Canberra Australia 118 H2 35 18S 149 08E
Cancún Mexico 141 G4 21 09N 86 45W
Cangamba Angola 125 C5 13 40S 19 47E
Cangrejos Point Trinidad & Tobago 141 T9 10 25N 61 29W
Cangzhou China 113 N6 38 19N 116 54E
Caniapiscau r. Québec Canada 133 V4 57 30N 68 40W
Canisp mt. Highland Scotland 59 D3 58 07N 5 03W
Çankaya Turkey 95 H3 39 52N 32 52E
Çankiri Turkey 95 H4 40 35N 33 37E
Canmore Alberta Canada 132 L3 51 07N 115 18W
Canna i. Highland Scotland 58 C2 57 05N 6 35W
Cannanore India 109 D2 11 53N 75 23 E
Canna, Sound of Highland Scotland 58 C2
Cannes France 91 D1 43 33N 7 00E
Cannich Highland Scotland 59 E2 57 12N 4 46W
Cannington Somerset England 73 D4 51 09N 3 04E
Cannock Staffordshire England 67 E2 52 42N 2 01W
Cannock Chase Staffordshire England 67 E2/F2 52 45N 2 04W
Canōas Brazil 147 G7 28 55S 51 10W
Canonbie Dumfries & Galloway Scotland 61 G3 55 05N 2 57W
Canso Nova Scotia Canada 133 W2 45 20N 61 00W
Cantabrian Mountains see Cordillera Cantabrica
Cantaro Trinidad and Tobago 141 T10 10 42N 61 28W
Canterbury Australia 119 G2 33 55S 151 07E
Canterbury Kent England 71 F2 51 17N 1 05E
Canterbury Bight N.Z. 119 B2 44 00S 172 00E
Canterbury Plains N.Z. 119 B2 43 45S 171 56E
Can Tho Vietnam 111 D5 10 03N 105 46E
Canton Ohio U.S.A. 137 D2 40 48N 81 23W
Canton see Guangzhou
Canvey Island tn. Essex England 71 E2 51 32N 0 33E
Canvey Island i. Essex England 71 E2 51 32N 0 33E
Caparo Trinidad and Tobago 141 T9 10 27N 61 19W
Caparo r. Trinidad and Tobago 141 T9 10 31N 61 25W
Cap Blanc see Ras Nouadhibou
Cap Bon c. Tunisia 92 B1 37 08N 11 00E
Cap Corse c. Corsica 91 D1 43 00N 9 21E
Cap d'Ambre c. Madagascar 125 I5 12 00S 49 15E
Cap de Carteret c. France 73 F2 49 22N 1 53W
Cap de Flamanville c. France 73 F2 49 32N 1 53W
Cap de la Hague c. France 91 B2 49 44N 1 56W
Cap de la Madeleine tn. Canada 137 F3 46 22N 72 31W
Cap de le Hague c. France 73 F2 49 45N 1 52W
Cap des Trois Fourches c. Morocco 90 B2 35 26N 2 57W
Cape Basin Atlantic Ocean 152 I3 36 00S 6 00E
Cape Breton Island Canada 133 W2 46 45N 60 00W
Cape Charles tn. Virginia U.S.A. 137 E1 37 17N 76 01W
Cape Clear Cork Rep. of Ireland 75 B1 51 30N 9 30W
Cape Coast tn. Ghana 127 E4 5 10N 1 13W
Cape Cod Bay U.S.A. 137 F2 41 00N 70 00W
Cape Cornwall Cornwall England 72 B3 50 07N 5 44W
Cape Dorset tn. N.W.T. Canada 133 T5 64 10N 76 40W
Cape Dyer tn. N.W.T. Canada 133 W6 66 30N 61 20W
Cape Girardeau tn. U.S.A. 136 C1 37 19N 89 31W
Capel Surrey England 70 D2 51 10N 0 20W
Capelle aan den IJssel Netherlands 89 D3 51 56N 4 36E
Cape May tn. New Jersey U.S.A. 137 F1 38 56N 74 54W
Cape Province admin. Rep. of South Africa 125 D1 31 00S 22 00E
Cape Rise Atlantic Ocean 152 J2 42 00S 11 00E
Cape Town Rep. of South Africa 125 C1 33 56S 18 28E
Cape Verde Basin Atlantic Ocean 152 E8 11 00N 35 00W
Cape Verde Islands Atlantic Ocean 152 F8 16 00N 24 00W
Cape York Peninsula Australia 118 G7 12 30S 142 30E
Cap Ferret c. France 91 B1 44 42N 1 16W
Cap Gris Nez c. France 89 A2 50 52N 1 35E
Cap-Haïtien Haiti 141 J3 19 47N 72 17W
Capitán Arturo Prat r.s. Antarctica 149 62 30S 59 41W
Cap Lévy c. France 73 F2 49 42N 1 58W
Capo Carbonara c. Italy 92 A1 39 07N 9 33E
Capo Passero c. Italy 92 C1 36 42N 15 09E
Capo Santa Maria di Leuca c. Italy 92 C1 39 47N 18 22E
Capo San Vito c. Italy 92 B1 38 12N 12 43E
Capo Spartivento c. Italy 92 C1 37 45N 15 30E
Cappagh White Tipperary Rep. of Ireland 75 C2 52 40N 8 10W
Cappamore Limerick Rep. of Ireland 75 C2 52 37N 8 20W
Cappoquin Waterford Rep. of Ireland 75 D2 52 08N 7 50W
Capri i. Italy 92 B2 40 33N 14 15E
Capricorn Channel Australia 118 I5 23 00S 152 30E
Caprivi Strip Namibia 125 D4 17 00S 27 50E
Cap Ste. Marie c. Madagascar 125 I2 25 34S 45 10E
Cap Vert c. Senegal 127 B5 14 43N 17 33W
Caracal Romania 96 C2 44 07N 24 18E
Caracas Venezuela 146 D15 10 35N 66 56W
Caransebeş Romania 96 C3 45 23N 22 13E
Caratinga Brazil 146 I9 19 50S 42 06W
Caravelas Brazil 146 J9 17 45S 39 15W
Carbondale Pennsylvania U.S.A. 137 E2 41 35N 75 31W
Carcassonne France 91 C1 43 13N 2 21E
Carcross Yukon Canada 132 I5 60 11N 134 41W
Cardak Turkey 94 F2 37 51N 29 39E
Cardamom Hills India 109 D1 9 50N 77 00E
Cárdenas Mexico 140 E4 22 00N 99 41W
Cardiff u.a. Wales 66 D1 51 32N 3 14W
Cardiff Cardiff Wales 66 D1 51 30N 3 13W
Cardigan Ceredigion Wales 66 C2 52 06N 4 40W
Cardigan Bay Wales 66 C2 52 30N 4 30W
Carei Romania 96 C3 47 40N 22 28E
Cargenbridge Dumfries & Galloway Scotland 61 F3 55 05N 3 41W
Cariacica Brazil 146 I9 20 15S 40 23W
Caribbean Sea Central America 141 I3 15 00N 75 00W
Caribou Mountains Canada 132 L4 59 00N 115 30W
Caringbah Australia 119 G1 34 03S 151 07E
Caripito Venezuela 146 E15 10 07N 63 07W
Carleton Place Ontario Canada 137 E3 45 08N 76 09W
Carlingford Louth Rep. of Ireland 74 E4 54 02N 6 11W
Carlingford Lough b. Northern Ireland/Rep. of Ireland 60 C2 54 05N 6 10W
Carlisle Cumbria England 64 C3 54 54N 2 55W
Carlisle Bay Barbados 141 V12 13 05N 59 37W
Carlow co. Rep. of Ireland 75 E2 52 40N 6 55W
Carlow Carlow Rep. of Ireland 75 E2 52 50N 6 55W
Carloway Western Isles Scotland 58 C3 58 17N 6 48W
Carlsbad U.S.A. 134 F3 32 25N 104 14W
Carlton in Lindrick Nottinghamshire England 65 D2 53 22N 1 06W
Carlton-on-Trent Nottinghamshire England 65 E2 53 10N 0 48W
Carluke South Lanarkshire Scotland 61 F3 55 45N 3 51W
Carmacks Yukon Canada 132 H5 62 04N 136 21W
Carman Manitoba Canada 136 A3 49 32N 97 59W
Carmarthen Carmarthenshire Wales 66 C1 51 51N 4 20W
Carmarthen Bay Carmarthenshire Wales 66 C1 51 40N 4 30W
Carmarthenshire u.a. Wales 66 C1/D1 51 55N 4 00W
Carmel Head Isle of Anglesey Wales 66 C3 53 24N 4 34W
Carmen Colombia 146 B14 9 46N 75 06W
Carnarvon Australia 118 A5 24 51S 113 45E
Carndonagh Donegal Rep. of Ireland 74 D5 55 15N 7 15W
Carnedd Llewelyn mt. Conwy Wales 66 D3 53 10N 3 58W
Carnegie, Lake Australia 118 C4 27 00S 124 00E
Carnegie Ridge Pacific Ocean 151 R7 1 30S 95 00W
Carn Eige mt. Highland Scotland 59 D2 57 22N 5 07W
Carnforth Lancashire England 64 C3 54 08N 2 46W
Car Nicobar i. Nicobar Islands 109 G1 9 00N 93 00E
Carnlough Larne Northern Ireland 60 D2 54 59N 5 59W
Carnlough Bay b. Larne Northern Ireland 60 D2 54 59N 5 57W
Carnot Central African Rep. 124 C8 4 59N 15 56E
Carnoustie Angus Scotland 59 G1 56 30N 2 44W
Carnowen r. Omagh Northern Ireland 60 B2 54 34N 7 07W
Carnsore Point Wexford Rep. of Ireland 75 E2 52 10N 6 22W
Carolina Brazil 146 H11 7 20S 47 25W
Caroline Island Pacific Ocean 151 L7 10 00S 150 00W
Caroline Islands Pacific Ocean 150 E8/F8 8 00N 148 00E
Carona Arena Dam Trinidad and Tobago 141 T10
Caroni Trinidad and Tobago 141 T10 10 36N 61 22W
Caroni r. Trinidad and Tobago 141 T10 10 35N 61 20W

DOMINICAN REPUBLIC 141 K3
Don *r.* South Yorkshire England **65** D2 53 37N 1 02W
Don *r.* Russia **102** G6 50 00N 41 00E
Don *r.* Aberdeenshire/Aberdeen City Scotland **59** G2 57 15N 2 15W
Donabate Dublin Rep. of Ireland **74** E3 53 30N 6 09W
Donaghadee Ards Northern Ireland **60** D2 54 39N 5 33W
Donau *(Danube) r.* Germany/Austria **93** B1 48 00N 13 00E
Donauwörth Germany **93** B1 48 44N 10 48E
Don Benito Spain **90** A2 38 57N 5 52W
Doncaster South Yorkshire England **65** D2 53 32N 1 07W
Donegal *co.* Rep. of Ireland **74** C4/D4 54 55N 8 00W
Donegal Donegal Rep. of Ireland **74** C4 54 39N 8 07W
Donegal Bay Donegal/Leitrim/Sligo Rep. of Ireland **74** C4 54 30N 8 30W
Donegal Point Clare Rep. of Ireland **75** B2 52 44N 9 38W
Donets *r.* Asia **77** N5 49 00N 30 00E
Donets'k Ukraine **104** D4 48 00N 37 50E
Dongchuan China **113** K4 26 07N 103 05E
Dongen Netherlands **89** D3 51 38N 4 56E
Dông Hôi Vietnam **111** D7 17 32N 106 35E
Dongola Sudan **124** F11 19 10N 30 27E
Dongou Congo **127** I3 2 02N 18 02E
Donington Lincolnshire England **65** E1 52 55N 0 12W
Dønna *i.* Norway **97** C4 66 05N 12 30E
Donnacona Québec Canada **137** F3 46 41N 71 45W
Donnington Shropshire England **67** E2 52 43N 2 25W
Donoughmore Cork Rep. of Ireland **75** C1 51 57N 8 45W
Donting Hu *l.* China **113** M4 29 00N 112 30E
Dooagh Mayo Rep. of Ireland **74** A3 53 58N 10 07W
Doon *r.* East Ayrshire/South Ayrshire Scotland **61** E3 55 20N 4 30W
Doonbeg Clare Rep. of Ireland **75** B2 52 44N 9 32W
Doonbeg *r.* Clare Rep. of Ireland **75** B2 52 43N 9 26W
Door Peninsula U.S.A. **136** C2/3 45 00N 87 00W
Dora Báltea *r.* Italy **91** D2 45 00N 7 00E
Dora Riparia *r.* Italy **92** A3 45 00N 7 00E
Dorchester Dorset England **73** E3 50 43N 2 26W
Dorchester Oxfordshire England **70** C2 51 39N 1 10W
Dordogne *r.* France **91** C1 44 55N 0 30E
Dordrecht Netherlands **89** D3 51 48N 4 40E
Dore *r.* France **91** C2 45 40N 3 30E
Dori *r.* Afghanistan **107** K5 31 20N 65 30E
Dorion Ontario Canada **136** C3 48 49N 88 33W
Dorking Surrey England **70** D2 51 14N 0 20W
Dormagen Germany **89** F3 51 06N 6 50E
Dornbirn Austria **92** A3 47 25N 9 46E
Dornie Highland Scotland **58** D2 57 17N 5 31W
Dornoch Highland Scotland **59** E2 57 52N 4 02W
Dornoch Firth *est.* Highland Scotland **59** E2/F2 57 55N 3 55W
Dorohoi Romania **96** D3 47 57N 26 31E
Dorset *co.* England **73** E3 50 50N 2 20W
Dorsten Germany **89** F3 51 38N 6 58E
Dortmund Germany **93** A2 51 32N 7 27E
Dortmund-Ems-Kanal *can.* Germany **86** D3 51 40N 7 20E
Dos Hermanas Spain **90** A2 37 16N 5 55W
Dosso Niger **127** F5 13 03N 3 10E
Dothan Alabama U.S.A. **135** I3 31 12N 85 25W
Douai France **91** C3 50 22N 3 05E
Douala Cameroon **127** G3 4 04N 9 43E
Douarnenez France **91** B2 48 05N 4 20W
Double Island Hong Kong China **112** C3 22 31N 114 08E
Doubs *r.* France **91** D2 47 20N 6 25E
Douglas *r.* Lancashire England **64** C2 53 38N 2 48W
Douglas Isle of Man British Isles **64** A3 54 09N 4 29W
Douglas South Lanarkshire Scotland **61** F3 55 33N 3 51W
Douglas Alaska U.S.A. **132** I4 58 15N 134 24W
Douglas Arizona U.S.A. **134** F3 31 21N 109 34W
Doullens France **91** C3 50 09N 2 21E
Doulus Head Kerry Rep. of Ireland **75** A1 51 57N 10 19W
Doune Stirling Scotland **59** E1 56 11N 4 04W
Dourados Brazil **147** G0 22 09S 54 52W
Douro *(Duero) r.* Portugal/Spain **90** A3 41 00N 8 30W
Douve *r.* France **73** F2 49 32N 1 30W
Dove *r.* Derbyshire/Staffordshire England **67** F2 52 55N 1 50W
Dove Dale *v.* Derbyshire England **67** F3 53 10N 1 45W
Dover Kent England **71** F2 51 08N 1 19E
Dover Delaware U.S.A. **137** E1 39 10N 75 32W
Dover New Hampshire U.S.A. **137** F2 43 12N 70 55W
Dover Foxcroft Maine U.S.A. **137** G3 45 12N 69 16W
Dover, Strait of *(Pas de Calais) sd.* English Channel **71** F1/F2 51 00N 1 20W
Dovrefjell *mts.* Norway **97** B3 62 15N 9 10E
Down *district* Northern Ireland **60** D2 54 25N 5 55W
Downey California U.S.A. **139** B2 33 56N 118 25W
Downham Market Norfolk England **71** E3 52 36N 0 23E
Downpatrick Down Northern Ireland **60** D2 54 20N 5 43W
Downpatrick Head *c.* Mayo Rep. of Ireland **74** B4 54 20N 9 15W
Downton Wiltshire England **70** A2 51 00N 1 44W
Dowra Cavan Rep. of Ireland **74** C4 54 11N 8 02W
Dōzen *is.* Japan **114** B2 36 05N 133 00E
Drachten Netherlands **89** F5 53 07N 6 06E
Dragan *l.* Sweden **97** D3 64 05N 15 20E
Dragons Mouths, The *(Bocas del Dragons)* Trinidad & Tobago **141** S10 10 37N 61 50W
Draguignan France **91** D1 43 32N 6 28E
Drakensberg *mts.* Rep. of South Africa **125** E1/2 30 00S 28 00E
Drake Passage *sd.* Southern Ocean **147** C1/E1 58 00S 66 00W
Dráma Greece **94** D4 41 10N 24 11E
Drammen Norway **97** C2 59 45N 10 15E
Drancy France **87** B2 48 55N 2 28E
Draperstown Magherafelt Northern Ireland **60** C2 54 48N 6 47W
Drau *r.* Austria **92** B3 46 00N 14 00E
Drava *r.* Europe **92** C3 46 00N 18 00E
Draveil France **87** B1 48 40N 2 25E
Dreghorn North Ayrshire Scotland **61** E3 55 37N 4 37W
Drenthe *admin.* Netherlands **89** F4 52 55N 6 45E
Dresden Germany **93** B2 51 03N 13 45E
Dreswick Point *c.* Isle of Man British Isles **64** A3 54 03N 4 37W
Dreux France **91** C2 48 44N 1 23E
Drewitz Germany **87** E1 52 20N 13 08E
Drimoleague Cork Rep. of Ireland **75** B1 51 40N 9 15W
Drin *r.* Albania **94** A4 42 00N 20 00E
Drina *r.* Europe **92** C2 44 00N 19 30E
Drobeta-Turnu-Severin Romania **96** C2 44 36N 22 39E
Drogheda Louth Rep. of Ireland **74** E3 53 43N 6 21W
Drohobyč Ukraine **96** C3 49 22N 23 33E
Droichead Nua Kildare Rep. of Ireland **74** E3 53 11N 6 45W
Droitwich Hereford and Worcester England **67** E2 52 16N 2 09W
Dromcolliher Limerick Rep. of Ireland **75** C2 52 20N 8 55W
Drôme *r.* Drôme France **91** D1 44 50N 5 00E
Drôme *r.* Basse-Normandie France **73** G2 49 13N 0 34W
Dromore Banbridge Northern Ireland **60** C2 54 25N 6 09W
Dromore Omagh Northern Ireland **60** B2 54 31N 7 28W
Dromore West Sligo Rep. of Ireland **74** C4 54 15N 8 53W
Dronfield Derbyshire England **67** F3 53 19N 1 27W
Drongan East Ayrshire Scotland **61** E3 55 29N 4 30W
Dronning Maud Land *(Queen Maud Land) geog. reg.* Antarctica **149** 73 00S 10 00E
Dronten Netherlands **89** E4 53 21N 5 41E
Drumheller Alberta Canada **132** M3 51 28N 112 40W
Drumkeeran Leitrim Rep. of Ireland **74** C4 54 10N 8 08W
Drummondville Québec Canada **137** F3 45 52N 72 30W
Drummond Island U.S.A. **137** D3 46 00N 84 00W
Drummore Dumfries & Galloway Scotland **60** E2 54 42N 4 54W
Drummoyne Australia **119** G2 33 51S 151 09E
Drumnadrochit Highland Scotland **59** E2 57 20N 4 30W
Drumshanbo Leitrim Rep. of Ireland **74** C4 54 03N 8 02W
Drumsna Leitrim Rep. of Ireland **74** C3 53 56N 8 00W
Druzhba Kazakhstan **105** N4 45 18N 82 29E
Dryden Ontario Canada **136** B3 49 48N 92 48W
Dry Fork *r.* Missouri U.S.A. **136** B1 38 00N 91 00W
Dschang Cameroon **127** H4 5 28N 10 02E
Dubai *see* Dubayy
Dubăsari Moldova **94** F7 47 18N 29 08E
Dubawnt Lake Canada **133** O5 63 15N 102 00W
Dubayy *(Dubai)* United Arab Emirates **107** I4 25 14N 55 17E
Dubbo Australia **118** H3 32 16S 148 41E
Dublin *co.* Rep. of Ireland **74** E3 53 25N 6 10W
Dublin Dublin Rep. of Ireland **74** E3 53 20N 6 15W
Dublin Georgia U.S.A. **135** J3 32 31N 82 54W
Dublin Bay Dublin Rep. of Ireland **74** E3 53 20N 6 05W
Dubno Ukraine **104** B5 50 28N 25 40E
Dubrovnik Croatia **92** C2 42 40N 18 07E
Dubuque Iowa U.S.A. **136** B2 42 31N 90 41W
Ducie Island Pitcairn Islands **151** N5 24 40S 124 48W
Duddon *r.* Cumbria England **64** B3 54 20N 3 20W
Dudelange Luxembourg **89** F1 49 28N 6 05E
Dudhanai Assam India **110** H6 25 59N 90 48E
Dudinka Russia **103** K9 69 27N 86 13E
Dudley Tyne and Wear England **64** D4 55 10N 1 20W
Dudley West Midlands England **67** E2 52 30N 2 05W
Duero *see* Douro
Duffield Derbyshire England **67** F2 52 59N 1 29W
Dufftown Moray Scotland **59** F2 57 26N 3 08W
Dugi Otok *i.* Croatia **96** B2 44 00N 15 00E
Duisburg Germany **93** A2 51 26N 6 45E
Duiveland *i.* Netherlands **89** C3 51 37N 4 00E
Duleek Meath Rep. of Ireland **74** E3 53 39N 6 25W
Dülmen Germany **89** G3 51 49N 7 17E
Dulnain *r.* Highland Scotland **59** F2 57 20N 3 57W
Dulovo Bulgaria **94** E5 43 48N 27 09E
Duluth Minnesota U.S.A. **136** B3 46 45N 92 10W
Dulverton Somerset England **72** D4 51 03N 3 33W
Dumbarton West Dunbartonshire Scotland **61** E3 55 57N 4 35W
Dum Dum India **108** K2 22 37N 88 24E
Dumfries Dumfries & Galloway Scotland **61** F3 55 04N 3 37W
Dumfries & Galloway *reg.* Scotland **61** E3/F3 55 10N 4 10W
Dumka Bihar India **110** E5 24 17N 87 15E
Dumont d'Urville *r.s.* Antarctica **149** 66 40S 140 01E
Dümpten Germany **86** B2 51 28N 6 50E
Dumri Bihar India **110** D4 23 59N 86 03E
Dumte Bhutan **110** G7 26 59N 89 15E
Dumyât *(Damietta)* Egypt **106** D5 31 26N 31 48E
Duna *(Danube) r.* Hungary **96** B3 46 00N 19 00E
Dunaff Head *c.* Donegal Rep. of Ireland **74** D5 55 17N 7 31W
Dunalastair Reservoir Perth & Kinross Scotland **59** E1 56 40N 4 10W
Dunany Point Louth Rep. of Ireland **74** E3 53 51N 6 14W
Dunărea *(Danube) r.* Romania **96** D2 44 00N 28 00E
Dunaújváros Hungary **96** B3 47 00N 18 55E
Dunav *(Danube) r.* Serbia/Bulgaria **92** C3 45 00N 19 00E
Dunbar East Lothian Scotland **61** G3 56 00N 2 31W
Dunbeath Highland Scotland **59** F3 58 15N 3 25W
Dunbeath Water *r.* Highland Scotland **57** B1 58 15N 3 35W
Dunblane Stirling Scotland **59** F1 56 12N 3 59W
Dunboyne Meath Rep. of Ireland **74** E3 53 25N 6 29W
Duncan Oklahoma U.S.A. **135** G3 34 30N 97 57W
Duncannon Wexford Rep. of Ireland **75** E2 51 13N 6 55W
Duncan Passage *sd.* Andaman Is. **109** G2 11 00N 93 00E
Duncansby Head Highland Scotland **59** F3 58 39N 3 01W
Dunchurch Warwickshire England **67** F2 52 20N 1 16W
Dundalk Louth Rep. of Ireland **74** E4 54 01N 6 25W
Dundalk Bay Louth Rep. of Ireland **74** E3 53 55N 6 15W
Dundas Ontario Canada **137** E2 43 16N 79 57W
Dundas *see* Pituffik
Dundee Dundee City Scotland **59** G1 56 28N 3 00W
Dundee City *u.a.* Scotland **59** F1/G1 56 30N 2 55W
Dundonald Castlereagh Northern Ireland **60** D2 54 36N 5 48W
Dundrennan Dumfries & Galloway Scotland **61** F2 54 49N 3 57W
Dundrum Dublin Rep. of Ireland **74** E3 53 17N 6 15W
Dundrum Bay Down Northern Ireland **60** D2 54 13N 5 45W
Dunedin N.Z. **119** B1 45 53S 170 30E
Dunfermline Fife Scotland **61** F4 56 04N 3 29W
Dungannon *district* Northern Ireland **60** B2/C2 54 30N 7 05W
Dungannon Dungannon Northern Ireland **60** B2 54 31N 6 46W
Dungarvan Waterford Rep. of Ireland **75** D2 52 05N 7 37W
Dungarvan Harbour *b.* Waterford Rep. of Ireland **75** D2 52 04N 7 35W
Dungeness *c.* Kent England **71** E1 50 55N 0 58E
Dungiven Limavady Northern Ireland **60** C2 54 55N 6 56W
Dunglow Donegal Rep. of Ireland **74** C4 54 57N 8 22W
Dungourney Cork Rep. of Ireland **75** C1 51 58N 8 05W
Dunholme Lincolnshire England **65** E2 53 18N 0 29W
Dunkeld Perth & Kinross Scotland **59** F1 56 34N 3 35W
Dunkellin *r.* Galway Rep. of Ireland **74** C3 53 13N 8 47W
Dunkerque *(Dunkirk)* France **91** C3 51 02N 2 23E
Dunkery Beacon *sum.* Somerset England **72** D4 51 11N 3 35W
Dunkirk New York U.S.A. **137** E2 42 29N 79 21W
Dunkirk France *see* Dunkerque
Dún Laoghaire Dublin Rep. of Ireland **74** E3 53 17N 6 08W
Dunleer Louth Rep. of Ireland **74** E3 53 50N 6 24W
Dunmanus Bay Cork Rep. of Ireland **75** B1 51 30N 9 50W
Dunmanway Cork Rep. of Ireland **75** B1 51 43N 9 06W
Dunmore Galway Rep. of Ireland **74** C3 53 37N 8 44W
Dunmurry Antrim Northern Ireland **60** C2 54 33N 6 00W
Dunnamaggan Kilkenny Rep. of Ireland **75** D2 52 29N 7 17W
Dunnet Highland Scotland **59** F3 58 37N 3 21W
Dunnet Bay Highland Scotland **59** F3 58 36N 3 23W
Dunnett Head Highland Scotland **59** F3 58 40N 3 25W
Dunoon Argyll & Bute Scotland **60** E3 55 57N 4 56W
Dun Rig *mt.* Scottish Borders Scotland **61** F3 55 33N 3 11W
Duns Scottish Borders Scotland **61** G3 55 47N 2 20W
Dunshaughlin Meath Rep. of Ireland **74** E3 53 31N 6 33W
Dunstable Bedfordshire England **70** D2 51 53N 0 32W
Dunvegan Highland Scotland **58** C2 57 26N 6 35W
Dunvegan Head Highland Scotland **58** C2 57 30N 6 43W
Duque de Caxias Brazil **147** P2 22 46S 43 18W
Duque de Caxias *admin.* Brazil **147** P2 22 48N 43 18W
Duroğan Turkey **95** J4 41 26N 35 03E
Dural Australia **119** G3 33 41S 151 02E
Durance *r.* France **91** D1 43 50N 5 15E
Durand Wisconsin U.S.A. **136** B2 44 37N 91 56W
Durango Mexico **140** D4 24 01N 104 40W
Durango *admin.* Mexico **134** E2 25 00N 105 00W
Durango Spain **90** B3 43 10N 2 38W
Durango Colorado U.S.A. **134** E4 37 16N 107 53W
Durankulak Bulgaria **94** F5 43 41N 28 32E
Durant Oklahoma U.S.A. **135** G3 33 59N 96 24W
Durazno Uruguay **147** F6 33 22S 56 31W
Durban Rep. of South Africa **125** F2 29 53S 31 00E
Düren Germany **93** A2 50 48N 6 30E
Durgāpur Calcutta India **108** J1 22 47N 87 44E
Durgapur Dhaka Bangladesh **110** H6 25 08N 90 41E
Durgapur West Bengal India **109** F4 24 47N 87 44E
Durg-Bhilai India **109** E4 21 12N 81 20E
Durham Durham England **64** D3 54 47N 1 34W
Durham North Carolina U.S.A. **135** K4 36 00N 78 54W
Durlston Head *c.* Dorset England **73** E3 50 35N 1 57W
Durness Highland Scotland **59** E3 58 33N 4 45W
Durrës Albania **94** A4 41 18N 19 28E
Durrington Wiltshire England **70** C2 51 12N 1 48W
Durrow Laois Rep. of Ireland **75** D2 52 51N 7 23W
Dursey Head Cork Rep. of Ireland **75** A1 51 20N 10 10W
Dursey Island Cork Rep. of Ireland **75** A1 51 36N 10 12W
Dursley Gloucestershire England **70** B2 51 42N 2 21W
Dursunbey Turkey **94** F3 39 35N 28 37E
Dury Voe *inlet* Shetland Islands Scotland **57** D3 60 20N 1 08W
Dushanbe Tajikistan **105** K2 38 38N 68 51E
Düssel *r.* Germany **86** C1 51 14N 7 01E
Düsseldorf Germany **93** A2 51 13N 6 47E
Düsseldorf *admin.* Germany **86** C2 51 20N 7 10E
Dutch Harbor *tn.* U.S.A. **132** B3 53 55N 166 36W
Duyun China **113** L4 26 16N 107 29E
Düzce Turkey **94** G4 40 51N 31 09E
Dyce Aberdeen City Scotland **59** G2 57 12N 2 11W
Dye Water *r.* Scottish Borders Scotland **61** G3 55 49N 2 35W
Dyfi *r.* Powys Wales **66** D2 52 38N 3 50W
Dyfrdwy *r.* Wales/England **66** D2 53 00N 2 50W
Dyke *r.* Highland Scotland **57** B1 58 25N 4 00W
Dymchurch Kent England **71** E2 51 02N 1 00E
Dysart Fife Scotland **61** F4 56 08N 3 08W
Dzhankoy Ukraine **95** J6 45 42N 34 23E
Dzhetygara Kazakhstan **105** J5 52 14N 61 10E
Dzhugdzhur Range Russia **103** P7 57 00N 137 00E
Dzungarian Basin *see* Junggar Pendi
Dzungarian Gate *pass* Kazakhstan/China **105** N4 45 00N 83 00E
Dzyarzhynsk Belarus **104** B5 55 40N 27 01E

E

Eagle Alaska U.S.A. **132** G5 64 46N 141 20W
Eagle Lake Maine U.S.A. **137** G3 46 00N 69 00W
Eagle Pass *tn.* Texas U.S.A. **134** F2 28 44N 100 31W
Eaglescliffe Stockton-on-Tees England **65** D3 54 31N 1 22W
Eaglesfield Dumfries & Galloway Scotland **61** F3 55 04N 3 12W
Ealing Greater London England **70** D2 51 31N 0 18W
Earby Lancashire England **64** C2 53 56N 2 08W
Earls Colne Essex England **71** E2 51 56N 0 42E
Earl Shilton Leicestershire England **67** F2 52 35N 1 18W
Earlston Scottish Borders Scotland **61** G3 55 39N 2 40W
Earn *r.* Perth & Kinross Scotland **59** F1 56 20N 3 40W
Easington Durham England **65** D3 54 47N 1 21W
Easington East Riding of Yorkshire England **65** F2 53 40N 0 07E
Easingwold North Yorkshire England **65** D3 54 07N 1 11W
Easky Sligo Rep. of Ireland **74** C4 54 17N 8 58W
Easky *r.* Sligo Rep. of Ireland **74** C4 54 13N 8 56W
East Antarctica *geog. reg.* Antarctica **149**
East Ayrshire *u.a.* Scotland **61** E3 55 30N 4 30W
Eastbourne East Sussex England **71** E1 50 46N 0 17E
East Burra *i.* Shetland Is. Scotland **57** D3 60 04N 1 19W
East Cape N.Z. **119** C3 37 41S 178 33E
East Caroline Basin Pacific Ocean **150** E8 4 00N 148 00E
East China Sea China/Japan **113** P5 32 00N 126 00E
East Cowes Isle of Wight England **70** C1 50 45N 1 16W
East Dean East Sussex England **71** E1 50 45N 0 13E
East Dereham Norfolk England **71** E3 52 41N 0 56E
East Dunbartonshire *u.a.* Scotland **61** E3 55 55N 4 15W
Easter Island Pacific Ocean **151** P5 27 05S 109 20W
Easter Island Fracture Zone Pacific Ocean **151** Q5/R5 24 00S 100 00W
Eastern Ghats *mts.* India **109** D2/E3 15 00N 80 00E
Eastern Group *is.* Fiji **150** V15/16 17 40S 178 30W
Eastern Sayan *mts.* Russia **103** L6 53 00N 97 30E
East Falkland *i.* Falkland Is. **152** M15/16 52 00S 58 50W
Eastfield North Yorkshire England **65** E3 54 15N 0 25W
East Fork White River U.S.A. **136** C1 39 00N 87 00W
East Frisian Islands *see* Ostfriesische Inseln
East Grand Forks *tn.* U.S.A. **136** A3 47 56N 96 59W
East Grinstead West Sussex England **70** D2 51 08N 0 01W
East Hills *tn.* Australia **119** G2 33 58S 150 59E
East Ilsley Berkshire England **70** C2 51 32N 1 17W
Eastington Gloucestershire England **70** B2 51 45N 2 20W
East Kilbride South Lanarkshire Scotland **61** E3 55 46N 4 10W
East Lamma Channel H.K. China **112** B1 22 14N 114 08E
East Leake Nottinghamshire England **65** D1 52 50N 1 11W
Eastleigh Hampshire England **70** C1 50 58N 1 22W
East Linton East Lothian Scotland **61** G3 55 59N 2 39W
East Liverpool Ohio U.S.A. **137** D2 40 38N 80 36W
East Loch Tarbert Western Isles Scotland **58** C2 57 50N 6 45W
East London Rep. of South Africa **125** E1 33 00S 27 54E
East Los Angeles U.S.A. **139** B3 34 02N 118 12W
East Lothian *u.a.* Scotland **61** G3 55 56N 2 42W
Eastmain Québec Canada **133** T3 52 10N 78 30W
East Marianas Basin Pacific Ocean **150** F9 13 00N 153 00E
East Markham Nottinghamshire England **65** E2 53 15N 0 54W
Easton Dorset England **73** E3 50 32N 2 26W
Easton Maryland U.S.A. **137** E1 38 46N 76 05W
Easton Pennsylvania U.S.A. **137** E2 40 41N 75 13W
East Pacific Basin Pacific Ocean **151** K9 16 00N 153 00E
East Pacific Ridge Pacific Ocean **151** O6 20 00S 113 00W
East Pacific Rise Pacific Ocean **151** P9 13 00N 103 00W
East Renfrewshire *u.a.* Scotland **61** E3 55 45N 4 25W
East Riding of Yorkshire *u.a.* England **65** E2 53 54N 0 40W
East Rift Valley East Africa **124** G8/9 6 00N 37 00E
Eastriggs Dumfries & Galloway Scotland **61** F2 54 59N 3 10W
East River New York U.S.A. **138** B1 40 43N 74 00W
East St. Louis Illinois U.S.A. **136** B1 38 34N 90 04W
East Siberian Sea Arctic Ocean **148** 72 00N 165 00E
East Suisnish Highland Scotland **58** C2 57 21N 6 03W
East Sussex *co.* England **71** E1/E2 50 55N 0 10E
East Wittering West Sussex England **70** D1 50 41N 0 53W
Eastwood Australia **119** G2 33 48S 151 05E
Eastwood Nottinghamshire England **65** D2 53 01N 1 18W
Eaton Socon Cambridgeshire England **70** D3 52 13N 0 18W
Eaton Wash Reservoir U.S.A. **139** B3 34 10N 118 05W
Eau Claire *tn.* Wisconsin U.S.A. **136** B2 44 50N 91 30W
Eauripik-New Guinea Rise Pacific Ocean **150** E8 2 00N 142 00E
Ebbw Vale Blaenau Gwent Wales **66** D1 51 47N 3 12W
Ebensburg Pennsylvania U.S.A. **137** E2 40 28N 78 44W
Eberswalde-Finow Germany **93** B2 52 50N 13 53E
Ebinur Hu *l.* China **112** F7 45 00N 83 00E
Ebolowa Cameroon **127** H3 2 56N 11 11E
Ebro *r.* Spain **90** C3 41 00N 0 30E
Ecclefechan Dumfries & Galloway Scotland **61** F3 55 03N 3 17W
Eccles Greater Manchester England **64** C2 53 29N 2 21W
Eccleshall Staffordshire England **67** E2 52 52N 2 15W
Ech Cheliff Algeria **127** F10 36 05N 1 15E
Echo Bay *tn.* N.W.T. Canada **132** L6 65 50N 117 30W
Echternach Luxembourg **89** F1 49 49N 6 25E
Ecija Spain **90** A2 37 33N 5 04W
Eckernförde Germany **93** A2 54 28N 9 50E
Eckington Derbyshire England **67** F3 53 19N 1 21W
Écouen France **87** B3 49 01N 2 22E
ECUADOR **146** B12
Edam Netherlands **89** E4 52 30N 5 02E
Eday *i.* Orkney Islands Scotland **57** C2 59 11N 2 47W
Eday Sound Orkney Is. Scotland **57** C2 59 10N 2 43W
Ed Damer Sudan **124** F11 17 37N 33 59E
Ed Debba Sudan **124** F11 18 02N 30 56E
Eddrachillis Bay Highland Scotland **58** D3 58 25N 5 15W
Eddystone Rocks English Channel **72** B3 50 10N 4 16W
Eddyville Kentucky U.S.A. **136** C1 37 03N 88 02W
Ede Netherlands **89** E4 52 03N 5 40E
Edéa Cameroon **127** H3 3 47N 10 13E
Eden *r.* Cumbria England **64** C3 54 50N 2 45W
Eden *r.* Kent/East Sussex England **71** E2 51 12N 0 06E
Eden *r.* Scotland **59** F1 56 17N 3 10W
Eden North Carolina U.S.A. **135** K4 36 30N 79 46W
Edenbridge Kent England **70** E2 51 12N 0 04E
Edenderry Offaly Rep. of Ireland **74** D3 53 21N 7 35W
Eden Mouth Fife Scotland **59** G1 56 22N 2 50W
Eder *r.* Germany **93** A2 51 00N 9 00E
Édessa Greece **94** C4 40 48N 22 03E
Edgewood Maryland U.S.A. **137** E1 39 25N 76 18W
Edgeworthstown Longford Rep. of Ireland **74** D3 53 42N 7 36W
Edinboro Pennsylvania U.S.A. **137** D2 41 53N 80 08W
Edinburgh City of Edinburgh Scotland **61** F3 55 57N 3 13W
Edirne Turkey **94** E4 41 40N 26 34E
Edmonton Alberta Canada **132** M3 53 34N 113 25W
Edmundston N.B. Canada **133** V2 47 22N 68 20W
Edogawa Japan **115** C3 35 41N 139 51E
Edremit Turkey **94** E3 39 34N 27 01E
Edremit Körfezi *b.* Turkey **94** F3 39 25N 26 45E
Edward, Lake Congo (D.R.)/Uganda **124** E7 0 30S 29 00E
Edwards Plateau Texas U.S.A. **134** F3 31 00N 100 00W
Edward VII Land *geog. reg.* Antarctica **149** 75 00S 150 00W
Eeklo Belgium **89** C3 51 11N 3 34E
Eems *(Ems) est.* Netherlands/Germany **89** F5 53 25N 6 55E
Éfaté *(Vaté) i.* Vanuatu **118** L6 17 30S 168 00E
Eflani Turkey **95** H4 41 25N 32 55E
Eforie Romania **96** D2 44 04N 28 38E
Efyrnwy *r.* Powys Wales **66** D2 52 40N 3 15W
Eger Hungary **92** D3 47 53N 20 28E
Eggerness Point *c.* Dumfries & Galloway Scotland **61** E2 54 48N 4 21W
Egham Surrey England **70** D2 51 26N 0 34W
Egilsay *i.* Orkney Is. Scotland **57** C2 59 09N 2 56W
Eğirdir Turkey **94** G2 37 52N 30 51E
Eğirdir Gölü *l.* Turkey **94** G2 37 52N 30 51E
Eglinton Londonderry Northern Ireland **60** B3 55 01N 7 11W
Egmont, Cape N.Z. **119** B3 39 17S 173 45E
Egmont, Mount *(Mount Taranaki)* N.Z. **119** B3 39 18S 174 04E
Egremont Cumbria England **64** B3 54 29N 3 33W
EGYPT **124** E13/F13
Eichwalde Germany **87** G1 52 23N 13 37E
Eifel *plat.* Germany **93** A2 50 00N 7 00E
Eigg *i.* Highland Scotland **58** C1 56 55N 6 10W
Eight Degree Channel Indian Ocean **109** C1 8 00N 73 30E
Eighty Mile Beach Australia **118** C6 19 00S 121 00E
Einbeck Germany **93** A2 51 49N 9 53E
Eindhoven Netherlands **89** E3 51 26N 5 30E
Eisenach Germany **93** B2 50 59N 10 19E
Eisenhüttenstadt Germany **93** B2 52 10N 14 42E
Eisenstadt Austria **92** C3 47 51N 16 31E
Ejmiadzin Armenia **95** P4 40 11N 44 17E
Ekibastuz Kazakhstan **105** M5 51 50N 75 10E
El Aaiún *see* Laayoune
El Arco Mexico **140** B5 28 00N 113 25W
El 'Arîsh Egypt **106** N10 31 08N 33 48E
Elassóna Greece **94** C3 39 53N 22 11E
Elat Israel **106** O9 29 33N 34 57E
Elaziğ Turkey **95** L3 38 41N 39 14E
El Banco Colombia **146** C14 9 04N 73 59W
Elbasan Albania **94** B4 41 07N 20 05E
El Bayadh Algeria **127** F9 33 40N 1 00E
Elbe *(Labe) est.* Europe **93** A2 54 00N 9 00E
Elberfeld Germany **86** C2 51 17N 7 09E
Elbert, Mount U.S.A. **134** E4 39 05N 106 27W
Elbeuf France **91** C2 49 17N 1 01E
Elbistan Turkey **95** K3 38 14N 37 11E
Elbląg Poland **96** B4 54 10N 19 25E
El'brus *mt.* Russia **104** E3 43 21N 42 29E
El'brusskiy Russia **95** N5 43 35N 42 08E
Elburg Netherlands **89** E4 52 27N 5 50E
Elburz Mountains Iran **107** H6 36 15N 51 00E
El Callao Venezuela **146** E14 7 18N 61 50W
El Centro California U.S.A. **134** C3 32 47N 115 33W
El Cerro del Aripo *mt.* Trinidad and Tobago **141** T10 10 49N 61 14W
Elche Spain **90** B2 38 16N 0 41W
Elda Spain **90** B2 38 29N 0 47W
El Dorado Arkansas U.S.A. **135** H3 33 12N 92 40W
El Dorado Kansas U.S.A. **135** G4 37 51N 96 52W
Eldoret Kenya **124** G0 0 31N 35 17E
Elefsina Greece **94** C3 38 02N 23 33E
Elektrostal' Russia **104** D6 55 46N 38 30E
Elephant Island South Shetland Is. **147** F0 62 00S 55 00W
Eleuthera *i.* The Bahamas **141** I5 25 05N 76 30W
El Faiyûm Egypt **124** F13 29 19N 30 50E
El Fasher Sudan **124** E10 13 37N 25 22E
El Ferrol del Caudillo Spain **90** A3 43 29N 8 14W
El Fuerte Mexico **140** C5 26 28N 108 35W
Elgin Moray Scotland **59** F2 57 39N 3 20W
Elgin Illinois U.S.A. **136** C2 42 03N 88 19W
El Gîza *(Giza)* Egypt **124** F13 30 01N 31 12E
Elgol Highland Scotland **58** C2 57 09N 6 06W
El Golea Algeria **127** F9 30 35N 2 51E
Elgon, Mount Uganda/Kenya **124** F8 1 07N 34 35E
Elido Insurgentes Mexico **134** D2 25 00N 110 45W
Elie Fife Scotland **59** G1 56 12N 2 50W
El Iskandarîya *(Alexandria)* Egypt **106** C5 31 13N 29 55E
Elista Russia **102** G6 46 10N 44 14E
Elizabeth Australia **118** F3 34 45S 138 39E
Elizabeth New Jersey U.S.A. **138** B1 40 39N 74 13W
Elizabeth City U.S.A. **135** K4 36 18N 76 16W
Elizabethtown Kentucky U.S.A. **136** C1 37 41N 85 51W
El Jadida Morocco **127** D9 33 19N 8 35W
El Jafr Jordan **106** O10 30 16N 36 11E

Ełk Poland 96 C4 53 51N 22 20E
Elk City Oklahoma U.S.A. 134 G4 34 25N 99 26W
El Khârga Egypt 124 F13 25 27N 30 32E
Elkhart Indiana U.S.A. 136 C2 41 52N 85 56W
Elkhorn *r.* Nebraska U.S.A. 135 G5 42 00N 98 00W
Elkhorn Wisconsin U.S.A. 136 C2 42 40N 88 34W
Elkhovo Bulgaria 94 E5 42 09N 26 36E
Elkins West Virginia U.S.A. 137 E1 38 56N 79 53W
Elko Nevada U.S.A. 134 C5 40 50N 115 46W
Elk River *tn.* Minnesota U.S.A. 136 B3 45 19N 93 31W
Elk River West Virginia U.S.A. 137 D1 38 00N 81 00W
Elland West Yorkshire England 64 D2 53 41N 1 50W
Ellef Ringnes Island Canada 133 O8 78 30N 102 00W
Ellen *r.* Cumbria England 64 B3 54 45N 3 25W
Ellendale North Dakota U.S.A. 136 A3 46 00N 98 31W
Ellesmere Shropshire England 67 E2 52 54N 2 54W
Ellesmere Island Canada 133 S8 77 30N 82 30W
Ellesmere Port Cheshire England 64 C2 53 17N 2 54W
Ellis Island New Jersey U.S.A. 138 B1 40 42N 74 02W
Ellon Aberdeenshire Scotland 59 G2 57 22N 2 05W
Ellsworth Maine U.S.A. 137 G2 44 34N 68 24W
Ellsworth Wisconsin U.S.A. 136 B2 44 44N 92 29W
Ellsworth Land *geog. reg.* Antarctica 149 75 00S 80 00W
Ellsworth Mountains Antarctica 149 80 00S 90 00W
Ellwangen Germany 93 B1 47 58N 9 55E
El Mahalla El Kubra Egypt 124 F14 30 59N 31 10E
Elmali Turkey 94 F2 36 44N 29 57E
El Médano Mexico 140 B4 24 35N 111 29W
Elmhurst Illinois U.S.A. 136 C2 41 54N 87 56W
El Milk *r.* Sudan 124 E11 17 00N 29 00E
El Minya Egypt 124 F13 28 06N 30 45E
Elmira New York U.S.A. 137 E2 42 06N 76 50W
El Monte California U.S.A. 139 B3 34 04N 118 01W
Elmshorn Germany 93 A2 53 46N 9 40E
El Muglad Sudan 124 E10 11 01N 27 50E
El Obeid Sudan 124 F10 13 11N 30 10E
El Paso Texas U.S.A. 134 E3 31 45N 106 30W
El Porvenir Mexico 140 C6 31 15N 105 48W
El Progreso Honduras 140 G3 15 20N 87 50W
El Puerto de Santa Maria Spain 90 A2 36 36N 6 14W
El Qâ'hira *(Cairo)* Egypt 124 F13 30 03N 31 15E
El Qunaytirah Syria 106 O11 33 08N 35 49E
El Reno Oklahoma U.S.A. 135 G4 35 32N 97 57W
El Salto Mexico 140 C4 23 47N 105 22W
EL SALVADOR 140 G2
El Sueco Mexico 140 C5 29 54N 106 22W
El Suweis *(Suez)* Egypt 106 D5 29 59N 32 33E
Eltanin Fracture Zone Pacific Ocean 151 L2/N2 52 00S 135 00W
El Tigre Venezuela 146 E14 8 44N 64 18W
El Tucuche *mt.* Trinidad and Tobago 141 T10 10 44N 61 25W
El Tûr Egypt 106 N9 28 14N 33 37E
Eluru India 109 E3 16 45N 81 10E
Elvas Portugal 90 A2 38 53N 7 10W
Ely Cambridgeshire England 71 E3 52 24N 0 16E
Ely Nevada U.S.A. 134 D4 39 15N 114 53W
Elyria Ohio U.S.A. 137 D2 41 22N 82 06W
Elysian Park California U.S.A. 139 A3 34 05N 118 15W
Emāmrūd Iran 107 H6 36 15N 54 59E
Emba Kazakhstan 102 H5 48 47N 58 05E
Emba *r.* Kazakhstan 105 H4 47 30N 56 00E
Embalse de Guri *l.* Venezuela 146 E14 7 30N 62 30W
Embleton Northumberland England 61 H3 55 30N 1 37W
Embrun France 91 D1 44 33N 6 30E
Emden Germany 93 A2 53 23N 7 13E
Eme *r.* Cavan Rep. of Ireland 74 D3 53 55N 7 29W
Emerald Australia 118 H5 23 30S 148 08E
Emet Turkey 94 F3 39 22N 29 15E
Emi Koussi *mt.* Chad 124 C11 19 52N 18 31E
Emirdağ Turkey 94 G3 39 01N 31 09E
Emmeloord Netherlands 89 E4 52 43N 5 46E
Emmen Netherlands 89 F4 52 47N 6 55E
Emmerich Germany 93 A2 51 49N 6 16E
Empalme Mexico 140 B5 28 00N 110 49W
Emperor Seamounts Pacific Ocean 150 G12 42 00N 169 00E
Emporia Kansas U.S.A. 136 A1 38 24N 96 10W
Ems *r.* Germany 93 A2 53 00N 7 00E
Ems *see* Eems
Emscher *r.* Germany 86 D3 51 35N 7 25E
Emsworth Hampshire England 70 D1 50 51N 0 56W
Emyvale Monaghan Rep. of Ireland 74 E4 54 21N 6 58W
Ena Japan 114 J2 35 28N 137 25E
Enard Bay Highland Scotland 58 D3 58 10N 5 25W
Encantado Brazil 147 P2 22 54S 43 18W
Encarnación Paraguay 147 F7 27 20S 55 50W
Endeh Indonesia 111 G2 8 51S 121 40E
Enderby Land *geog. reg.* Antarctica 149 65 00S 45 00E
Endicott Mountains U.S.A. 132 E6 67 35N 154 00W
Enez Turkey 94 E4 40 44N 26 05E
Enfield *bor.* Greater London England 70 D2 51 39N 0 05W
Engel's Russia 102 G6 51 30N 46 07E
Engenho Novo Brazil 147 P2 22 54S 43 16W
Enghien France 87 B2 48 58N 2 19E
England 56 I5
Englehart Ontario Canada 137 E3 47 50N 79 52W
Englewood New Jersey U.S.A. 138 C2 40 53N 73 58W
English Channel *(La Manche)* England/France 56 H1 50 00N 2 00W
English River *tn.* Canada 136 B3 49 14N 90 58W
Enguri Georgia 95 N5 43 00N 42 10E
Enid Oklahoma U.S.A. 135 G4 36 24N 97 54W
Enkhuizen Netherlands 89 E4 52 42N 5 17E
Enna Italy 92 B1 37 34N 14 16E
En Nahud Sudan 124 E10 12 41N 28 28E
Ennerdale Water *l.* Cumbria England 64 B3 54 31N 3 22W
Ennis Clare Rep. of Ireland 75 C2 52 50N 8 59W
Enniscorthy Wexford Rep. of Ireland 75 E2 52 30N 6 34W
Enniskean Cork Rep. of Ireland 75 C1 51 44N 8 56W
Enniskerry Wicklow Rep. of Ireland 74 E3 53 12N 6 10W
Enniskillen Fermanagh Northern Ireland 60 B2 54 21N 7 38W
Ennistimon Clare Rep. of Ireland 75 B2 52 57N 9 15W
Enns *r.* Austria 92 B3 48 00N 14 40E
Enontekiö Finland 97 E4 68 25N 23 40E
Enschede Netherlands 89 F4 52 13N 6 55E
Ensenada Mexico 140 A6 31 53N 116 38W
Entebbe Uganda 124 F8 0 04N 32 27E
Enugu Nigeria 127 G4 6 20N 7 29E
Epe Netherlands 89 E4 52 21N 5 59E
Épernay France 91 C2 49 02N 3 58E
Épinal France 91 D2 48 10N 6 28E
Epping Australia 119 G2 33 46S 151 05E
Epping Essex England 71 E2 51 42N 0 08E
Epsom Surrey England 70 D2 51 20N 0 16W
Epworth North Lincolnshire England 65 E2 53 31N 0 50W
EQUATORIAL GUINEA 127 G3/H3
Erbaa Turkey 95 K4 40 42N 36 37E
Erbes Kopf *mt.* Germany 89 F1 49 42N 7 07E
Erciş Turkey 95 N3 39 00N 43 20E
Erciyas Daği *mt.* Turkey 95 J3 38 32N 35 27E
Erdek Turkey 94 E4 40 25N 27 50E
Erdek Körfezi *b.* Turkey 94 E4 40 20N 27 30E
Erdenet Mongolia 113 K8 49 12N 104 05E
Erding Germany 93 B1 48 17N 11 55E
Erebus, Mount Antarctica 149 77 40S 167 20E
Erechim Brazil 147 G7 27 35S 52 15W
Ereğli Turkey 94 G4 41 17N 31 26E
Ereğli Turkey 95 J2 37 30N 34 02E
Erenhot China 113 M7 43 50N 112 00E
Erft *r.* Germany 89 F2 50 00N 6 00E
Erfurt Germany 93 B2 50 58N 11 02E
Erg Chech *geog. reg.* Algeria 127 E7 24 30N 3 00W
Ergene *r.* Turkey 94 E4 41 15N 26 45E
Erg Iguidi *geog. reg.* Algeria 127 D8 26 00N 6 00W
Ergun He *see* Argun
Erie Pennsylvania U.S.A. 137 D2 42 07N 80 05W
Erie, Lake Canada/U.S.A. 137 D2 42 15N 81 00W
Erimo-misaki *c.* Japan 114 D3 41 55N 143 13E
Erin Point Trinidad and Tobago 141 S9 10 03N 61 39W
Eriskay *i.* Western Isles Scotland 58 B2 57 05N 7 10W
ERITREA 124 G10 14 40N 40 15E
Erkelenz Germany 89 F3 51 05N 6 18E
Erkina *r.* Loais Rep. of Ireland 75 D2 52 50N 7 30W
Erkner Germany 87 H1 52 25N 13 46E
Erkrath Germany 86 B1 51 13N 6 54E
Erlangen Germany 93 B1 49 36N 11 02E
Ermelo Netherlands 89 E4 52 18N 5 38E
Ermenek Turkey 95 H2 36 38N 32 55E
Ermoúpoli Greece 94 D2 37 25N 24 56E
Erne *r.* Cavan Rep. of Ireland 74 D4 54 05N 7 25W
Erode India 109 D2 11 21N 77 43E
Errigal Mountain Rep. of Ireland 74 C5 55 02N 8 07W
Errill Laois Rep. of Ireland 75 D2 52 52N 7 40W
Erris Head Mayo Rep. of Ireland 74 A4/B4 54 20N 10 00W
Errol New Hampshire U.S.A. 137 F2 44 47N 71 10W
Erromango *i.* Vanuatu 118 L6 19 00S 169 00E
Er Roseires Sudan 124 F10 11 52N 34 23E
Ertix He *r.* China 105 O4 47 30N 88 00E
Erzgebirge *(Krušnéhory) mts.* Europe 93 B2 50 00N 13 00E
Erzincan Turkey 95 L3 39 44N 39 30E
Erzurum Turkey 95 M3 39 57N 41 17E
Esashi Japan 114 D3 41 54N 140 09E
Esbjerg Denmark 97 B2 55 20N 8 20E
Escanaba Michigan U.S.A. 136 C3 45 47N 87 04W
Escaut *r.* France 89 C2 50 30N 3 28E
Esch-sur-Alzette Luxembourg 89 E1 49 30N 5 59E
Eschwege Germany 93 B2 51 11N 10 03E
Eschweiler Germany 93 A2 50 49N 6 16E
Escondido California U.S.A. 134 C3 33 07N 117 05W
Eşfahān Iran 107 H5 32 41N 51 41E
Esha Ness *c.* Shetland Is. Scotland 57 D3 60 29N 1 37W
Esher Surrey England 70 D2 51 22N 0 22W
Esk *r.* Cumbria England 64 B3 54 25N 3 10W
Esk *r.* North Yorkshire England 65 E3 54 25N 0 40W
Esk *r.* Scotland/England 61 F3 55 10N 3 05W
Eskilstuna Sweden 97 D2 59 22N 16 31E
Eskimo Lakes Canada 132 I6 68 30N 132 30W
Eskimo Point *tn.* Canada 133 Q5 61 10N 84 15W
Eskipazar Turkey 95 H4 40 58N 32 33E
Eskişehir Turkey 94 G3 39 46N 30 30E
Esmeraldas Ecuador 146 B13 0 56N 79 40W
Espanola Ontario Canada 137 D3 46 15N 81 46W
Esperance Australia 118 C3 33 49S 121 52E
Esperanza *r.s.* Antarctica 149 63 24S 57 00W
Espírito Santo *admin.* Brazil 146 J9 18 40S 40 00W
Espiritu Santo *i.* Vanuatu 118 L6 15 10S 167 00E
Espiye Turkey 95 L4 40 56N 38 43E
Espoo Finland 97 E3 60 10N 24 40E
Esquel Argentina 147 C4 42 55S 71 20W
Esquelbecq France 71 G1 50 53N 2 26E
Esquimalt B.C. Canada 132 K2 48 25N 123 29W
Es Semara Western Sahara 127 C8 26 25N 11 30W
Essen Belgium 89 D3 51 28N 4 28E
Essen Germany 93 A2 51 27N 6 57E
Essequibo *r.* Guyana 146 F13 2 30N 58 00W
Essex *co.* England 71 E2 51 46N 0 30E
Essex County *admin.* New Jersey U.S.A. 138 B2
Esslingen Germany 93 A1 48 45N 9 19E
Essonne *admin.* France 87 A1 48 42N 2 05E
Estância Brazil 146 J10 11 15S 37 28W
Estevan Canada 133 O2 49 09N 103 00W
Eston Redcar & Cleveland England 65 D3 54 34N 1 07W
ESTONIA 97 F2
Estrecho de Magallanes *sd.* Chile 147 C2 53 00S 71 00W
Estrela *r.* Brazil 147 Q3 22 42S 43 14W
Estremoz Portugal 90 A2 38 50N 7 35W
Esztergom Hungary 96 B3 47 46N 18 44E
Étampes France 91 C2 48 26N 2 10E
Étaples France 91 C3 50 31N 1 39E
Etawah India 109 D5 26 46N 79 01E
ETHIOPIA 124 G9/H9
Etna, Mount Italy 92 C1 37 45N 15 00E
Eton Berkshire England 70 D2 51 31N 0 37W
Etosha National Park Namibia 125 C4 18 30S 16 00E
Etosha Pan *salt l.* Namibia 125 C4 18 30S 16 30E
Ettelbruck Luxembourg 89 F1 49 51N 6 06E
Etten-Leur Netherlands 89 D3 51 34N 4 27E
Ettrick Scottish Borders Scotland 61 F3 55 25N 3 05W
Ettrickbridge Scottish Borders Scotland 61 G3 55 30N 2 58W
Ettrick Water *r.* Scottish Borders Scotland 61 F3 55 25N 3 13W
Euboea *see* Evvoia
Eucla Australia 118 D3 31 40S 128 51E
Euclid Ohio U.S.A. 137 D2 41 34N 81 33W
Eugene Oregon U.S.A. 134 B5 44 03N 123 04W
Eupen Belgium 89 F2 50 38N 6 02E
Euphrates *see* Firat
Eure *r.* France 91 C2 48 45N 1 30E
Eureka *m.s.* N.W.T. Canada 148 79 59N 85 57W
Eureka California U.S.A. 134 B5 40 49N 124 10W
Europoort Netherlands 89 D3 51 55N 4 10E
Euskirchen Germany 93 A2 50 40N 6 47E
Eutsuk Lake B.C. Canada 132 J3 54 10N 126 50W
Evans Strait N.W.T. Canada 133 S5 63 15N 82 30W
Evanston Illinois U.S.A. 136 C2 42 02N 87 41W
Evansville Indiana U.S.A. 136 C1 38 00N 87 33W
Evanton Highland Scotland 59 E2 57 40N 4 20W
Evelix *r.* Highland Scotland 59 E2 57 55N 4 15W
Evenlode *r.* Oxfordshire England 70 C2 51 50N 1 30W
Evercreech Somerset England 73 E4 51 09N 2 30W
Everest, Mount China/Nepal 109 F5 27 59N 86 56E
Everett Washington U.S.A. 134 B6 47 59N 122 14W
Evesham Hereford and Worcester England 67 F2 52 06N 1 56W
Evora Portugal 90 A2 38 46N 7 41W
Evreux France 91 C2 49 03N 1 11E
Evry France 87 B1 48 38N 2 27E
Évvoia *(Euboea) i.* Greece 94 D3 38 00N 24 00E
Ewarton Jamaica 141 Q8 18 11N 77 06W
Exe *r.* Somerset England 72 D4 51 08N 3 36
Exeter Devon England 72 D3 50 43N 3 31W
Exmoor National Park Devon/Somerset England 72 D4 51 08N 3 40W
Exmouth Australia 118 A5 21 54S 114 10E
Exmouth Devon England 72 D3 50 37N 3 25W
Eyam Derbyshire England 67 F3 53 24N 1 42W
Eyasi, Lake Tanzania 125 G7 4 00S 35 00E
Eye Suffolk England 71 F3 52 19N 1 09E
Eyemouth Scottish Borders Scotland 61 G3 55 25N 2 06W
Eye Peninsula Western Isles Scotland 58 C3 58 10N 6 10W
Eyeries Cork Rep. of Ireland 75 B1 51 41N 9 57W
Eye Water *r.* Scottish Borders Scotland 61 G3 55 52N 2 18W
Eynsham Oxfordshire England 70 C2 51 46N 1 28W
Eyre Creek Australia 118 F4 26 00S 138 00E
Eyre, Lake Australia 118 F4 28 00S 136 00E
Eyre Peninsula Australia 118 F3 34 00S 136 00E
Ezine Turkey 94 E3 39 46N 26 20E

F

Fada Chad 124 D11 17 14N 21 32E
Faeroe Islands Atlantic Ocean 76 D8 62 00N 7 00W
Faeroes *is.* Atlantic Ocean 152 H13 62 00N 7 00W
Fafan *r.* Ethiopia 124 H9 7 30N 44 00E
Făgăraş Romania 96 C3 45 50N 24 59E
Fairbanks Alaska U.S.A. 132 F5 64 50N 147 50W
Fairbourne Gwynedd Wales 66 C2 52 41N 4 03W
Fairfield Australia 119 F2 33 52S 150 57E
Fair Head Moyle Northern Ireland 60 C3 55 15N 6 10W
Fair Isle *i.* Shetland Islands 57 C3 59 32N 1 38W
Fair Lawn New Jersey U.S.A. 138 B2 40 57N 74 06W
Fairlight East Sussex England 71 E1 50 52N 0 38E
Fairmont Minnesota U.S.A. 136 B2 43 39N 94 27W
Fairmont West Virginia U.S.A. 135 J4 39 28N 80 08W
Fairview Alberta Canada 132 L4 56 03N 118 28W
Fairview Park *tn.* H.K. China 112 B2 22 29N 114 03E
Faisalabad Pakistan 109 C6 31 25N 73 09E
Faizabad India 109 E5 26 46N 82 08E
Fakenham Norfolk England 71 E3 52 50N 0 51E
Fakfak Indonesia 111 I3 2 55S 132 17E
Fal *r.* Cornwall England 72 B3 50 08N 5 21W
Falam Myanmar 109 G4 22 58N 93 45E
Falcarragh Donegal Rep. of Ireland 74 C5 55 08N 8 06W
Falconara Marittima Italy 92 B2 43 37N 13 23E
Falfurrias Texas U.S.A. 135 G2 27 17N 98 10W
Falkensee *l.* Germany 87 E2 52 35N 13 08E
Falkirk Falkirk Scotland 61 F3 55 59N 3 48W
Falkirk *u.a.* Scotland 61 F3 55 55N 3 45W
Falkland Fife Scotland 59 F1 56 15N 3 13W
Falkland Islands South Atlantic Ocean 147 E2/F2 52 30S 60 00W
Falkland Sound Falkland Is. 152 M16 52 00S 60 00W
Fall River *tn.* U.S.A. 137 F2 41 41N 71 08W
Falls City Nebraska U.S.A. 136 A2 40 03N 95 36W
Falmouth Cornwall England 72 B3 50 08N 5 04W
Falmouth Jamaica 141 Q8 18 29N 77 39W
Falmouth Massachusetts U.S.A. 137 F2 41 33N 70 37W
Falster *i.* Denmark 93 B2 54 00N 12 00E
Falun Sweden 97 D3 60 37N 15 40E
Famagusta Cyprus 95 H1 35 07N 33 57E
Famagusta Bay Cyprus 95 H1 35 10N 34 00E
Fanad Head Donegal Rep. of Ireland 74 D5 55 17N 7 38W
Fane *r.* Louth Rep. of Ireland 74 E3 53 58N 6 28W
Fan Lau Hong Kong China 112 A1 22 12N 113 51E
Fanling Hong Kong China 112 B2 22 29N 114 07E
Fano Italy 92 B2 43 51N 13 01E
Faraday *r.s.* Antarctica 149 65 15S 64 16W
Farafangana Madagascar 125 I3 22 50S 47 50E
Farâfra Oasis Egypt 124 E13 27 00N 27 30E
Farāh Afghanistan 107 J5 32 22N 62 07E
Farah Rud *r.* Afghanistan 107 J5 32 00N 62 00E
Fareham Hampshire England 70 C1 50 51N 1 10W
Farewell *see* Kap Farvel
Farewell Spit N.Z. 119 B2 40 30S 172 50E
Fargo North Dakota U.S.A. 136 A3 46 52N 96 49W
Faribault Minnesota U.S.A. 136 B2 44 19N 93 15W
Faridabad India 109 D5 28 24N 77 18E
Faridpur Dhaka Bangladesh 110 G4 23 29N 89 31E
Faringdon Oxfordshire England 70 C2 51 40N 1 35W
Farmington U.S.A. 134 E4 36 43N 108 12W
Farmville Virginia U.S.A. 137 E1 37 17N 78 25W
Farnborough Hampshire England 70 D2 51 17N 0 46W
Farne Islands Northumberland England 61 H3 55 38N 1 38W
Farnham Surrey England 70 D2 51 13N 0 49W
Farnham Royal Buckinghamshire England 70 D2 51 33N 0 38W
Farnworth Greater Manchester England 64 C2 53 33N 2 24W
Faro Yukon Canada 132 I5 62 30N 133 00W
Faro Portugal 90 A2 37 01N 7 56W
Fårön *i.* Sweden 97 D2 58 00N 19 10E
Farquhar Islands Seychelles 125 J6 9 00N 50 00E
Farranfore Kerry Rep. of Ireland 75 B2 52 10N 9 33W
Farrar *r.* Highland Scotland 59 E2 57 25N 4 45W
Fastov Ukraine 96 D4 50 08N 29 59E
Fatehgarh India 109 D5 27 22N 79 38E
Fatsa Turkey 95 K4 41 02N 37 31E
Faughan *r.* Londonderry Northern Ireland 60 B2 54 54N 7 09W
Fauquembergues France 71 G1 50 35N 2 06E
Faversham Kent England 71 E2 51 20N 0 53E
Fawley Hampshire England 70 C1 50 49N 1 20W
Faxaflói *b.* Iceland 97 H6 64 20N 23 00W
Faya-Largeau Chad 124 C11 17 58N 19 06E
Fayetteville Arkansas U.S.A. 135 H4 36 03N 94 10W
Fayetteville North Carolina U.S.A. 135 K4 35 03N 78 53W
Fderik Mauritania 127 C7 22 30N 12 30W
Feale *r.* Kerry/Limerick Rep. of Ireland 75 B2 52 20N 9 16W
Featherstone West Yorkshire England 65 D2 53 41N 1 21W
Fécamp France 91 C2 49 45N 0 23E
FEDERATED STATES OF MICRONESIA 150 E8/F8
Fehmarn *i.* Germany 93 B2 54 00N 11 00E
Fehmarn Belt *sd.* Denmark 93 B2 54 00N 11 00E
Feilding N.Z. 119 C2 40 14S 175 34E
Feira de Santana Brazil 146 J10 12 17S 38 53W
Felanitx Balearic Islands 90 E4 39 28N 3 08E
Feldkirch Austria 93 A1 47 15N 9 38E
Felixstowe Suffolk England 71 F2 51 58N 1 20E
Felling *tn.* Tyne and Wear England 64 D3 54 57N 1 33W
Felton Northumberland England 61 H3 55 18N 1 42W
Feltwell Norfolk England 71 E3 52 29N 0 33E
Femund *l.* Norway 97 C3 62 30N 11 50E
Fens, The *geog. reg.* Norfolk/Lincolnshire/Cambridgeshire England 65 E1/F1 52 45N 0 05E
Feodosiya Ukraine 95 J6 45 03N 35 23E
Feolin Ferry *tn.* Argyll & Bute Scotland 60 C3 55 51N 6 06W
Ferbane Offaly Rep. of Ireland 74 D3 53 15N 7 49W
Fergana Uzbekistan 105 L3 40 23N 71 19E
Fergus *r.* Clare Rep. of Ireland 75 B2 52 45N 8 57W
Fergus Falls *tn.* U.S.A. 136 A3 46 18N 96 07W
Fermanagh *district* Northern Ireland 60 B2 54 25N 7 45W
Fermo Italy 92 B2 43 09N 13 44E
Fermoy Cork Rep. of Ireland 75 C2 52 08N 8 16W
Ferndown Dorset England 73 F3 50 48N 1 55W
Fernie B.C. Canada 132 L2 49 30N 115 00W
Ferns Wexford Rep. of Ireland 75 E2 52 35N 6 30W
Ferrara Italy 92 B2 44 50N 11 38E
Ferreñafe Peru 146 B11 6 42S 79 45W
Ferryhill *tn.* Durham England 64 D3 54 41N 1 33W
Ferryland Canada 133 Y2 47 01N 52 53W
Fès Morocco 127 D9 34 05N 5 00W
Festus Missouri U.S.A. 136 B1 38 12N 90 24W
Feteşti Romania 94 E6 44 22N 27 51E
Fethaland, Point of Shetland Islands Scotland 57 D3 60 35N 1 18W
Fethard Tipperary Rep. of Ireland 75 D2 52 27N 7 41W
Fethard Wexford Rep. of Ireland 75 E2 52 11N 6 50W
Fethiye Turkey 94 F2 36 37N 29 06E
Fethiye Körfezi *b.* Turkey 94 F2 36 40N 29 00E
Fetlar *i.* Shetland Is. Scotland 57 F3 60 37N 0 52W
Fettercairn Aberdeenshire Scotland 59 G1 56 51N 2 34W
Feyzābad Afghanistan 107 L6 37 06N 70 34E
Ffestiniog Gwynedd Wales 66 D2 52 58N 3 55W
Fforest Fawr Powys Wales 66 D1 51 50N 3 40W
Ffostrasol Ceredigion Wales 66 C2 52 06N 4 23W
Fianarantsoa Madagascar 125 I3 21 27S 47 05E
Fichtel-gebirge *mts.* Germany 93 B2 50 00N 12 00E
Fiddown Kilkenny Rep. of Ireland 75 D2 52 20N 7 19W
Fidenza Italy 92 B3 44 52N 10 04E
Fier Albania 94 A4 40 44N 19 33E
Fife *u.a.* Scotland 59 F1/G1 56 10N 3 00W
Fife Ness *c.* Fife Scotland 59 G1 56 17N 2 35W
Figeac France 91 C1 44 32N 2 01E
Figueira da Foz Portugal 90 A3 40 09N 8 51W
Figueres Spain 90 C3 42 16N 2 57E
FIJI 150 H6
Filchner Ice Shelf Antarctica 149 80 00S 37 00W
Filey North Yorkshire England 65 E3 54 12N 0 17W
Filton South Gloucestershire England 70 B2 51 31N 2 35W
Findhorn *r.* Highland/Moray Scotland 59 F2 57 25N 3 55W
Findhorn Moray Scotland 59 F2 57 39N 3 36W
Findhorn Bay Moray Scotland 59 F2 57 38N 3 36W
Findikli Turkey 95 M4 41 17N 41 07E
Findlay Ohio U.S.A. 137 D2 41 02N 83 40W
Findochty Moray Scotland 59 G2 57 42N 2 55W
Finglas Dublin Rep. of Ireland 74 E3 53 24N 6 18W
Finike Turkey 94 G2 36 18N 30 08E
Finisterre, Cape Spain 76 D4 42 52N 9 16W
FINLAND 97 F3
Finland, Gulf of Finland/Russia 97 E2 59 40N 23 30E
Finlay *r.* B.C. Canada 132 J4 57 30N 126 00W
Finn *r.* Donegal Rep. of Ireland 74 D4 54 47N 7 41W
Finnea Westmeath Rep. of Ireland 74 D3 53 47N 7 23W
Finsterwalde Germany 93 B2 51 38N 13 43E
Fintagh Bay Donegal Rep. of Ireland 74 C4 54 35N 8 33W
Fintona Omagh Rep. of Ireland 60 B2 54 30N 7 19W
Fintown Donegal Rep. of Ireland 74 C4 54 52N 8 07W
Fionn Loch *l.* Highland Scotland 58 D2 57 45N 5 44W
Fionnphort Argyll & Bute Scotland 58 C1 56 19N 6 23W
Fiordland N.Z. 119 A1 45 09S 167 18E
Firat *(Euphrates) r.* Turkey/Syria/Iraq 106 E6 37 30N 38 00E
Firenze *(Florence)* Italy 92 B2 43 47N 11 15E
Firozabad India 109 D5 27 09N 78 24E
Firozpur India 109 C6 30 55N 74 38E
Firth of Clyde *est.* North Ayrshire/Argyll & Bute Scotland 60 D3/E3 55 30N 5 00W
Firth of Forth *est.* Scotland 61 F4/G4 56 05N 3 00W
Firth of Lorn *est.* Argyll & Bute Scotland 58 D1 56 15N 6 00W
Firth of Tay *est.* Scotland 59 F1 56 25N 3 00W
Fish *r.* Namibia 125 C2 26 30S 17 30E
Fishbourne Isle of Wight England 70 C1 50 44N 1 12W
Fisher Strait N.W.T. Canada 133 S5 63 00N 84 00W
Fishguard Pembrokeshire Wales 66 C1 51 59N 4 59W
Fitchburg Massachusetts U.S.A. 137 F2 42 35N 71 50W
Fitzroy *r.* Australia 118 C6 18 00S 124 00E
Flagstaff Arizona U.S.A. 134 D4 35 12N 111 38W
Flamborough East Riding of Yorkshire England 65 E3 54 07N 0 07W
Flamborough Head *c.* East Riding of Yorkshire England 65 E3 54 06N 0 04W
Flamengo Brazil 147 Q2 22 56S 43 10W
Fläming *geog. reg.* Germany 93 B2 52 00N 12 00E
Flannan Islands Western Isles Scotland 58 B3 58 16N 7 35W
Flatbush New York U.S.A. 138 C1 40 38N 73 56W
Flathead Lake U.S.A. 134 D6 47 55N 114 05W
Flatlands New York U.S.A. 138 C1 40 37N 73 54W
Flattery, Cape U.S.A. 134 B6 48 24N 124 43W
Fleet Hampshire England 70 D2 51 16N 0 50W
Fleetwood Lancashire England 64 B2 53 56N 3 01W
Flekkefjord Norway 97 B2 58 17N 6 40E
Flensburg Germany 93 A2 54 47N 9 27E
Flers France 91 B2 48 45N 0 34W
Fleuve St-Laurent *see* St. Lawrence River
Flimby Cumbria England 64 B3 54 41N 3 31W
Flinders *r.* Australia 118 G6 19 00S 141 30E
Flinders Range *mts.* Australia 118 F3 32 00S 138 00E
Flin Flon Manitoba Canada 133 O3 54 50N 102 00W
Flint *r.* Georgia U.S.A. 135 J3 31 00N 84 00W
Flint Michigan U.S.A. 137 D2 43 03N 83 40W
Flint Flintshire Wales 66 D3 53 15N 3 07W
Flintshire *u.a.* Wales 66 D3 53 15N 3 10W
Flitwick Bedfordshire England 70 D2 52 00N 0 29W
Florence Alabama U.S.A. 135 I3 34 48N 87 40W
Florence California U.S.A. 139 A2/B2 33 58N 118 15W
Florence South Carolina U.S.A. 135 K3 34 12N 79 44W
Florence Italy *see* Firenze
Florencia Colombia 146 B13 1 37N 75 37W
Flores Guatemala 140 G3 16 58N 89 50W
Flores *i.* Indonesia 111 G2 8 30S 121 00E
Flores Sea Indonesia 111 F2/G2 7 00S 119 00E
Floresti Moldova 96 D3 47 52N 28 12E
Floriano Brazil 146 I11 6 45S 43 00W
Florianópolis Brazil 147 H7 27 35S 48 31W
Florida *state* U.S.A. 135 J2 28 00N 82 00W
Florida Uruguay 147 F6 34 04S 56 14W
Florida Bay Florida U.S.A. 135 J2 25 00N 81 00W
Florida Keys *is.* Florida U.S.A. 135 J1 25 00N 80 00W
Florida, Straits of *sd.* Cuba/U.S.A. 141 H4 24 00N 81 00W
Flórina Greece 94 B4 40 48N 21 26E
Florissant Missouri U.S.A. 136 B1 38 49N 90 24W
Florø Norway 97 B3 61 36N 5 04E
Flotta *i.* Orkney Islands Scotland 57 B1 58 49N 3 07W
Floyd Bennet Field New York U.S.A. 138 C1 40 36N 73 54W
Flushing New York U.S.A. 138 B2 40 45N 73 49W
Flushing Meadow Park New York U.S.A. 138 C1/2 40 45N 73 50W
Foça Turkey 94 E3 38 40N 26 45E
Fochabers Moray Scotland 59 F2 57 37N 3 05W
Focşani Romania 96 D3 45 41N 27 12E
Foel Wen *hill* Powys/Wrexham Wales 66 D2 52 53N 3 22W
Fóggia Italy 92 C2 41 28N 15 33E
Fohnsdorf Austria 92 B3 47 13N 14 40E
Föhr *i.* Germany 93 A2 54 00N 8 00E
Foix France 91 C1 42 57N 1 35E
Folda *sd.* Norway 97 C3 64 42N 10 30E
Folégandros *i.* Greece 94 D2 36 35N 24 55E
Foleyet Ontario Canada 133 S2 48 05N 82 26W
Foligno Italy 92 B2 42 57N 12 43E
Folkestone Kent England 71 F2 51 05N 1 11E
Folkingham Lincolnshire England 65 E1 52 54N 0 24W
Fond du Lac Wisconsin U.S.A. 136 C2 43 48N 88 27W
Fongafala Tuvalu 150 H7 8 00S 178 30E
Fontainebleau France 91 C2 48 24N 2 42E
Fonte Boa Brazil 146 D12 2 33S 65 59W
Fontstown Kildare Rep. of Ireland 75 E3 53 03N 6 53W
Forbach France 91 D2 49 11N 6 54E
Forbesganj Bihar India 110 E7 26 18N 87 16E
Forchheim Germany 93 B1 49 43N 11 05E
Fordham Cambridgeshire England 71 E3 52 19N 0 24E
Fordingbridge Hampshire England 70 C1 50 56N 1 47W

Gloucester Gloucestershire England **70** B2 51 53N 2 14W
Gloucester and Sharpness Canal Gloucestershire England **70** B2 51 45N 2 21W
Gloucestershire *co.* England **70** B2 51 50N 2 20W
Gloversville New York U.S.A. **137** F2 43 03N 74 21W
Glovertown Canada **133** Y2 48 40N 54 03W
Glusburn North Yorkshire England **64** C2 53 55N 2 01W
Glydar Fawr *mt.* Conwy/Gwynedd Wales **66** C3 53 05N 4 03W
Glyde *r.* Louth Rep. of Ireland **74** E3 53 56N 6 34W
Glyncorrwg Neath Port Talbot Wales **66** D1 51 41N 3 38W
Glyn-neath Neath Port Talbot Wales **66** D1 51 46N 3 38W
Gmunden Austria **92** B3 47 56N 13 48E
Gniezno Poland **96** B4 52 32N 17 32E
Goa, Damān & Diu *admin.* India **109** C3 15 00N 74 00E
Goalpara Assam India **109** G5 26 10N 90 38E
Goaltor West Bengal India **110** E3 22 43N 87 09E
Goat Fell *mt.* North Ayrshire Scotland **60** D3 55 39N 5 11W
Gobabis Namibia **125** C3 22 30S 18 58E
Gobi Desert Mongolia **113** J7/L7 48 30N 100 00E
Gobindpur Orissa India **110** B3 22 05N 84 16E
Goch Germany **93** A2 51 40N 6 10E
Godalming Surrey England **70** D2 51 11N 0 37W
Godāvari *r.* India **109** E3 18 00N 80 30E
Godda Bihar India **110** E5 24 50N 87 13E
Goderich Ontario Canada **137** D2 43 43N 81 43W
Godhavn *see* Qeqertarsuaq
Godhra India **109** C4 22 49N 73 40E
Godmanchester Cambridgeshire England **70** D3 52 19N 0 11W
Gödöllö Hungary **96** B3 47 36N 19 20E
Gods Lake Manitoba Canada **133** Q3 54 40N 94 20W
Godthåb *see* Nuuk
Goes Netherlands **89** C3 51 30N 3 54E
Gogri Jamalpur Bihar India **110** D6 25 26N 86 35E
Goiânia Brazil **146** H9 16 43S 49 18W
Goiás Brazil **146** G9 15 57S 50 07W
Goiás *admin.* Brazil **146** H10 14 00S 48 00W
Goikera Bihar India **110** C3 22 35N 85 23E
Gojō Japan **114** G1 34 21N 135 42E
Gökçeada Turkey **94** D4 40 12N 25 43E
Gökçeada *i.* Turkey **94** D4 40 10N 25 50E
Gökdore *r.* Turkey **95** H2 36 30N 32 45E
Gökirmak *r.* Turkey **95** J4 41 30N 34 15E
Gökova Körfezi *b.* Turkey **94** E2 37 00N 27 50E
Göksu *r.* Turkey **95** J2 37 45N 35 45E
Göksun Turkey **95** K3 38 03N 36 30E
Gola Bihar India **110** C4 23 32N 85 44E
Golam Head Galway Rep. of Ireland **74** B3 53 14N 9 44W
Golan Heights *territory* Israel **106** O11 33 00N 35 50E
Gölbaşi Turkey **95** K2 37 48N 37 37E
Gölcük Turkey **94** F4 40 44N 29 50E
Gold Coast *tn.* Australia **118** I4 27 59S 153 22E
Golden Bay N.Z. **119** B2 40 40S 172 49E
Golden State Freeway U.S.A. **139** A3/4 34 15N 118 25W
Golden Vale Tipperary/Limerick Rep. of Ireland **75** C2 52 30N 8 05W
Goldsboro North Carolina U.S.A. **135** K4 35 23N 78 00W
Goldsworthy Australia **118** B5 20 20S 119 31E
Göle Turkey **95** N4 40 47N 42 36E
Golfe de Gabès *g.* Tunisia **127** H9 34 20N 10 30E
Golfe de St-Malo *g.* France **91** B2 48 55N 2 30W
Golfe du Lion *g.* France **91** C1 43 10N 4 00E
Golfo de California *g.* Mexico **140** B5 27 00N 111 00W
Golfo de Guayaquil *g.* Ecuador **146** A12 3 00S 81 30W
Golfo de Honduras *g.* Caribbean Sea **140/141** G3 17 00N 87 30W
Golfo del Darién *g.* Colombia/Panama **141** I1 9 00N 77 00W
Golfo de Panamá *g.* Panama **141** I1 8 00N 79 00W
Golfo de San Jorge *g.* Argentina **147** D3 47 00S 66 00W
Golfo de Tehuantepec *g.* Mexico **140** E3/F3 15 30N 95 00W
Golfo de Venezuela *g.* Venezuela **146** C15 12 00N 71 30W
Golfo di Cágliari *g.* Italy **92** A1 39 00N 9 00E
Golfo di Catania *g.* Italy **92** C1 37 30N 15 20E
Golfo di Gaeta *g.* Italy **92** B2 41 00N 13 00E
Golfo di Genova *g.* Italy **92** A2 44 00N 9 00E
Golfo di Squillace *g.* Italy **92** C1 38 30N 17 00E
Golfo di Táranto *g.* Italy **92** C1/2 40 00N 17 00E
Golfo di Venézia *g.* Adriatic Sea **92** B3 45 00N 13 00E
Golfo San Matías *g.* Argentina **147** E4 42 00S 64 00W
Golmud China **112** H6 36 22N 94 55E
Golo *r.* Corsica **91** D1 42 30N 9 10E
Gölpazari Turkey **94** G4 40 16N 30 18E
Golspie Highland Scotland **59** F2 57 58N 3 58W
Gomel' *see* Homyel'
Gomera *i.* Canary Islands **127** B8 28 08N 17 14W
Gómez Palacio Mexico **140** D5 25 39N 103 30W
Gomoh Bihar India **110** D4 23 52N 86 10E
Gonder Ethiopia **124** G10 12 39N 37 29E
Gondia India **109** E4 21 23N 80 14E
Gönen Turkey **94** E4 40 06N 27 39E
Gonesse France **87** B2 48 59N 2 27E
Gongzhuling China **113** O7 43 30N 124 48E
Good Hope, Cape of Rep. of South Africa **125** C1 34 30S 19 00E
Goodland Kansas U.S.A. **134** F4 39 20N 101 43W
Goodwick Pembrokeshire Wales **66** C1 52 00N 5 00W
Gooimeer *l.* Netherlands **89** E3 52 18N 5 08E
Goole East Riding of Yorkshire England **65** E2 53 42N 0 52W
Goondiwindi Australia **118** I4 28 30S 150 17E
Goose Green *tn.* Falkland Is. **152** M16 51 52S 59 00W
Gopalganj Dhaka Bangladesh **110** G3 22 89
Gopalpur Rajshahi Bangladesh **110** G5 24 33N 89 56E
Göppingen Germany **93** A1 48 43N 9 39E
Gora Belukha *mt.* Russia/Kazakhstan **105** O4 49 50N 86 44E
Gora Kamen' *mt.* Russia **103** L9 69 06N 94 59E
Gorakhpur India **109** E5 26 45N 83 23E
Gora Narodnaya *mt.* Russia **103** I9 65 02N 60 01E
Gora Pobeda *mt.* Russia **103** Q9 65 10N 146 00E
Gora Tebulos-mta *mt.* Georgia/Russia **104** F3 42 32N 45 28E
Gora Telposiz *mt.* Russia **105** H7 63 59N 59 02E
Gorda Rise Pacific Ocean **151** M12/N12 43 00N 130 00W
Gordon Australia **119** G2 33 46S 151 09E
Gordon Landing *tn.* Canada **132** H5 63 38N 135 27W
Gorē Ethiopia **124** G9 8 10N 35 29E
Gore N.Z. **119** A1 46 06S 168 56E
Gore Bay *tn.* Ontario Canada **137** D3 45 54N 82 28W
Gorebridge Midlothian Scotland **61** F3 55 51N 3 02W
Gorey Wexford Rep. of Ireland **75** E2 52 40N 6 18W
Gorgān Iran **107** H6 36 50N 54 29E
Gori Georgia **95** P4 41 59N 44 05E
Gorinchem Netherlands **89** D3 51 50N 4 59E
Goring Oxfordshire England **70** C2 51 32N 1 09W
Gorizia Italy **92** B3 45 57N 13 37E
Gor'kiy *see* Nizhniy Novgorod
Gorkiy Park Russia **102** M1 55 44N 37 37E
Görlitz Germany **93** B2 51 09N 15 00E
Gorno-Altaysk Russia **105** O5 51 59N 85 56E
Gorodovikovsk Russia **95** M7 46 06N 41 57E
Goroka Papua New Guinea **118** H8 6 02S 145 22E
Gorontalo Indonesia **111** G4 0 33N 123 05E
Gorseinon Swansea Wales **66** C1 51 41N 4 02W
Gort Galway Rep. of Ireland **75** C3 53 04N 8 50W
Gorteen Galway Rep. of Ireland **74** C3 53 22N 8 35W
Gortmore Galway Rep. of Ireland **74** B3 53 36N 9 36W
Gorumna Island Galway Rep. of Ireland **74** B3 53 15N 9 55W
Goryachiy Klyuch Russia **95** L6 44 36N 39 08E
Goryn' *r.* Ukraine **96** D4 51 00N 26 00E
Gorzów Wielkopolski Poland **96** B4 52 42N 15 12E
Gosforth Tyne and Wear England **61** H3 55 01N 1 37W
Goslar Germany **93** B2 51 55N 10 25E
Gosport Hampshire England **70** C1 50 48N 1 08W
Gostivar FYROM **94** B4 41 47N 20 55E
Göta älv *r.* Sweden **97** C2 58 00N 12 00E
Göteborg Sweden **97** C2 57 45N 12 00E
Gotemba Japan **114** K2 35 20N 138 58E
Gotha Germany **93** B2 50 57N 10 43E
Gotland *i.* Sweden **97** D2 57 30N 18 40E
Gotse Delchev Bulgaria **94** C4 41 33N 23 45E
Göttingen Germany **93** A2 51 32N 9 57E
Gottwaldov *see* Zlín
Gouda Netherlands **89** D4 52 00N 4 42E
Gough Island Atlantic Ocean **152** H2 40 20S 10 00W
Goulburn Australia **118** H3 34 47S 149 43E
Gourde, Point Trinidad & Tobago **141** S10 10 40N 61 36W
Gouré Niger **127** H5 13 59N 10 15E
Gouripur Dhaka Bangladesh **110** H5 24 46N 90 34E
Gourock Inverclyde Scotland **61** E3 55 58N 4 49W
Governador Valadares Brazil **146** I9 18 51S 41 57W
Governor's Harbour The Bahamas **135** K2 25 20N 76 20W
Govind Ballash Pant Sagar *l.* India **109** E4 24 30N 82 30E
Govindpur Orissa India **110** C2 21 29N 85 19E
Gower *p.* Swansea Wales **66** C1 51 35N 4 10W
Gowran Kilkenny Rep. of Ireland **75** D2 52 38N 7 04W
Göynük Turkey **94** G4 40 24N 30 45E
Gozo *i.* Malta **92** B1 35 00N 14 00E
Gracefield Québec Canada **137** E3 46 05N 76 05W
Graemsay *i.* Orkney Is. Scotland **57** B1 58 56N 3 17W
Grafham Water *l.* Cambridgeshire England **70** D3 52 18N 0 20W
Grafton Australia **118** I4 29 40S 152 56E
Grafton West Virginia U.S.A. **137** D1 39 21N 80 03W
Graham Texas U.S.A. **134** G3 33 07N 98 36W
Graham Island B.C. Canada **132** I3 53 50N 133 00W
Graham Land *geog. reg.* Antarctica **149** 67 00S 64 00W
Grahamstown Rep. of South Africa **125** E1 33 18S 26 32E
Graignes France **73** F2 49 14N 1 12W
Graiguenamanagh Carlow Rep. of Ireland **75** E2 52 32N 6 56W
Graiguenamanagh Kilkenny Rep. of Ireland **75** D2 52 32N 6 56W
Grain Kent England **71** E2 51 28N 0 43E
Gramatikovo Bulgaria **94** E5 42 03N 27 38E
Grampian Mountains Scotland **59** E1/F1 56 45N 4 00W
Granada Nicaragua **141** G2 11 58N 85 59W
Granada Spain **90** B2 37 10N 3 35W
Granard Longford Rep. of Ireland **74** D3 53 47N 7 30W
Granby Québec Canada **137** F3 45 23N 72 44W
Gran Canaria *i.* Canary Islands **127** B8 28 00N 15 35W
Gran Chaco *geog. reg.* Argentina **147** E8 25 00S 62 30W
Gran Couva Trinidad & Tobago **141** T9 10 24N 61 23W
Grand *r.* U.S.A. **136** B1 40 00N 94 00W
Grand Bahama *i.* The Bahamas **141** I5 27 00N 78 00W
Grand Beach *tn.* Canada **136** A4 50 34N 96 38W
Grandcamp-Maisy France **73** F2 49 23N 1 01W
Grand Canal Kildare Rep. of Ireland **74** E3 53 16N 6 50W
Grand Canyon U.S.A. **134** D4 36 04N 112 07W
Grand Canyon National Park Arizona/Nevada U.S.A. **134** D4 34 00N 114 00W
Grand Canyon Village U.S.A. **134** D4 36 02N 112 09W
Grand Cayman *i.* Caribbean Sea **141** H3 19 20N 81 15W
Grand Coulee Dam U.S.A. **134** C6 47 59N 118 58W
Grande Cache Alberta Canada **132** L3 53 50N 118 30W
Grande Prairie *tn.* Canada **132** L4 55 10N 118 52W
Grand Erg Occidental *geog. reg.* Algeria **127** F9 30 35N 0 30E
Grand Erg Oriental *geog. reg.* Algeria **127** G9 30 15N 6 45E
Grande Rivière *tn.* Trinidad and Tobago **141** T10 10 50N 61 03W
Grande Rivière de la Baleine *r.* Québec Canada **133** T4 55 15N 77 00W
Grande Terre *i.* Lesser Antilles **141** L3 17 00N 61 40W
Grand Falls *tn.* Canada **133** V2 47 02N 67 46W
Grand Falls-Windsor Canada **133** Y2 48 57N 55 40W
Grand Forks U.S.A. **136** A3 47 57N 97 05W
Grand Fort-Philippe France **71** G2 51 00N 2 06E
Grand Haven Michigan U.S.A. **136** C2 43 04N 86 13W
Grand Island *tn.* U.S.A. **135** G5 40 56N 98 21W
Grand Junction *tn.* U.S.A. **134** E4 39 04N 108 33W
Grand Lake Canada **133** X2 49 00N 57 20W
Grand Marias U.S.A. **136** B3 47 45N 90 20W
Grand Rapids *tn.* Manitoba Canada **133** P3 53 12N 99 19W
Grand Rapids *tn.* Michigan U.S.A. **136** C2 42 57N 86 40W
Grand Rapids *tn.* Minnesota U.S.A. **136** B3 47 13N 93 31W
Grand Traverse Bay U.S.A. **136** C2 45 00N 85 00W
Grand Union Canal Leicestershire/Northamptonshire England **67** F2 52 30N 1 25W
Grane Norway **97** C4 65 35N 13 25E
Grange *r.* Galway Rep. of Ireland **74** C3 53 31N 8 41W
Grange Sligo Rep. of Ireland **74** C4 54 24N 8 31W
Grange Hill *tn.* Jamaica **141** P8 18 19N 78 11W
Grangemouth Falkirk Scotland **61** F4 56 01N 3 44W
Grange-over-Sands *tn.* Cumbria England **64** C3 54 33N 3 09W
Granite City Illinois U.S.A. **136** B1 38 43N 90 04W
Granite Falls *tn.* Minnesota U.S.A. **136** A2 44 49N 95 31W
Granite Peak Montana U.S.A. **134** E6 45 10N 109 50W
Grantham Lincolnshire England **65** E1 52 55N 0 39W
Grantown-on-Spey Highland Scotland **59** F2 57 20N 3 58W
Grants Pass *tn.* Oregon U.S.A. **134** B5 42 26N 123 20W
Granville France **91** B2 48 50N 1 35W
Granville Lake Canada **133** O4 56 00N 101 00W
Grasmere Cumbria England **64** B3 54 28N 3 02W
Grasse France **91** D1 43 40N 5 56E
Grassington North Yorkshire England **64** D3 54 04N 1 59W
Grass Island Hong Kong China **112** D2 22 29N 114 22E
Grassy Hill *mt.* Hong Kong China **112** B2 22 25N 114 10E
Gravelbourg Canada **132** N2 49 53N 106 33W
Gravelines France **89** B2 50 59N 2 08E
Gravenhurst Ontario Canada **137** E2 44 55N 79 22W
Gravesend Kent England **71** E2 51 27N 0 24E
Gravesend New York U.S.A. **138** C1 40 36N 73 58W
Gray France **91** D2 47 27N 5 35E
Grayling Michigan U.S.A. **137** D2 44 40N 84 43W
Grays Essex England **71** E2 51 29N 0 20E
Graz Austria **92** C3 47 05N 15 22E
Greasby Merseyside England **64** B2 53 23N 3 10W
Great Abaco *i.* The Bahamas **141** I5 26 40N 77 00W
Great Astrolabe Reef Fiji **150** U15 18 45S 178 50E
Great Australian Bight *b.* Australia **118** D3/E3 33 00S 130 00E
Great Bardfield Essex England **71** E2 51 57N 0 26E
Great Barrier Island N.Z. **119** C3 36 13S 175 24E
Great Barrier Reef Australia **118** G7/I5 15 00S 146 00E
Great Basin Nevada U.S.A. **134** C4 40 00N 117 00W
Great Bear Lake Canada **132** K6 66 00N 120 00W
Great Bend Kansas U.S.A. **134** G4 38 22N 98 47W
Great Bernera *i.* Western Isles Scotland **58** C3 58 13N 6 49W
Great Blasket Island Rep. of Ireland **75** A1 52 05N 10 30W
Great Broughton North Yorkshire England **65** D3 54 27N 1 110W
Great Chesterford Essex England **71** E3 52 04N 0 11E
Great Coates North East Lincolnshire England **65** E2 53 35N 0 08W
Great Cumbrae *i.* Argyll & Bute Scotland **60** E3 55 46N 4 55W
Great Dividing Range *mts.* Australia **118** G7/H2 34 00S 150 00E
Great Driffield East Riding of Yorkshire England **65** E3 54 01N 0 26W
Great Dunmow Essex England **71** E2 51 53N 0 22E
Great Eccleston Lancashire England **64** C2 53 51N 2 53W
Greater Antilles *is.* West Indies **141** H4/K3
Greater Khingan Range *see* Da Hinggan Ling
Greater London *co.* England **70** D2 51 30N 0 10W
Greater Manchester *co.* England **64** C2 53 30N 2 15W
Great Exuma *i.* The Bahamas **141** I4 23 30N 76 00W
Great Falls *tn.* Montana U.S.A. **134** D6 47 30N 111 16W
Great Harwood Lancashire England **64** C2 53 48N 2 24W
Great Inagua *i.* The Bahamas **141** J4 21 40N 73 00W
Great Karoo *mts.* Rep. of South Africa **125** D1 32 30S 22 30E
Great Kills Park New York U.S.A. **138** B1 40 33N 74 12W
Great Lakes North America **152** 45 00N 90 00W
Great Malvern Hereford and Worcester England **67** E2 52 07N 2 19W
Great Missenden Buckinghamshire England **70** D2 51 43N 0 43W
Great Neck *tn.* U.S.A. **138** D2 40 48N 72 44W
Great Nicobar *i.* Nicobar Islands **109** G1 6 30N 94 00E
Great Oasis, The *geog. reg.* Egypt **106** D3 25 00N 30 30E
Great Ormes Head *c.* Conwy Wales **66** D3 53 21N 3 53W
Great Ouse *r.* Cambridgeshire/Norfolk England **71** E3 52 40N 0 20E
Great Pedro Bluff *c.* Jamaica **141** Q7 17 51N 77 45W
Great Salt Lake Utah U.S.A. **134** D5 41 10N 112 40W
Great Sand Sea Sahara Desert **124** D13/E13 27 00N 25 00E
Great Sandy Desert Australia **118** C5/D5 21 00S 124 00E
Great Sea Reef Fiji **150** T16/U16 16 30S 178 00E
Great Shelford Cambridgeshire England **71** E3 52 08N 0 09E
Great Slave Lake Canada **132** M5 62 00N 114 00W
Great Stour *r.* Kent England **71** E2/F2 51 15N 1 00E
Great Torrington Devon England **72** C3 51 57N 4 09W
Great Victoria Desert Australia **118** D4/E4 28 00S 130 00E
Great Wall China **113** M6 40 00N 111 00E
Great Wall *(Chang Cheng)* *r.s.* Antarctica **149** 62 13S 58 58W
Great Whernside *sum.* North Yorkshire England **64** D3 54 10N 1 59W
Great Wyrley Staffordshire England **67** E2 52 27N 2 02W
Great Yarmouth Norfolk England **71** F3 52 37N 1 44E
Great Zab *r.* Iraq **104** E2 36 00N 44 00E
Greco, Cape Cyprus **95** J1 34 57N 34 05E
GREECE 94 B3
Greeley Colorado U.S.A. **134** F5 40 26N 104 43W
Green *r.* U.S.A. **134** D5 42 00N 110 00W
Green *r.* Kentucky U.S.A. **136** C1 37 00N 87 00W
Green Bay Wisconsin U.S.A. **136** C2/3 45 00N 87 00W
Green Bay *tn.* Wisconsin U.S.A. **136** C2 44 32N 88 00W
Greenbrier *r.* West Virginia U.S.A. **137** E1 38 00N 80 00W
Greencastle Newry and Mourne Northern Ireland **60** C2 54 02N 6 06W
Greenfield Massachusetts U.S.A. **137** F2 42 36N 72 37W
Green Island Hong Kong China **112** B1 22 17N 114 06E
Greenisland *tn.* Carrickfergus Northern Ireland **60** D2 54 42N 5 52W
Green Islands Papua New Guinea **118** I9 4 30S 154 15E
GREENLAND 133 AA6
Greenland Basin Atlantic Ocean **152** H13 72 00N 0 00
Greenland Sea Arctic Ocean **148** 76 00N 5 00W
Greenlaw Scottish Borders Scotland **61** G3 55 43N 2 28W
Green Mountains Vermont U.S.A. **137** F2 43 00N 73 00W
Greenock Inverclyde Scotland **61** E3 55 57N 4 45W
Greenore Louth Rep. of Ireland **74** E4 54 02N 6 08W
Greenore Point *c.* Wexford Rep. of Ireland **75** E2 52 15N 6 18W
Greensboro North Carolina U.S.A. **135** K4 36 03N 79 50W
Greenstone Point Highland Scotland **58** D2 57 55N 5 37W
Greenville Liberia **127** D3 5 01N 9 03W
Greenville Maine U.S.A. **137** G3 45 28N 69 36W
Greenville Mississippi U.S.A. **135** H3 33 23N 91 03W
Greenville Ohio U.S.A. **137** D2 40 06N 84 37W
Greenville South Carolina U.S.A. **135** J3 34 52N 82 25W
Greenville Texas U.S.A. **135** G3 33 09N 97 06W
Greenwood Mississippi U.S.A. **135** H3 33 31N 90 10W
Greese *r.* Kildare Rep. of Ireland **75** E2 52 56N 6 54W
Greifswald Germany **93** B2 54 06N 13 24E
Greiz Germany **93** B2 50 40N 12 11E
GRENADA 141 L2
Grenchen Switzerland **92** A3 47 13N 7 24E
Grenoble France **91** D2 45 11N 5 43E
Greta *r.* North Yorkshire/Lancashire England **64** C3 54 10N 2 30W
Gretna Green Dumfries & Galloway Scotland **61** F2 55 00N 3 04W
Grevenå Greece **94** B4 40 05N 21 26E
Grevenbroich Germany **93** A2 51 06N 6 36E
Greymouth N.Z. **119** B2 42 27S 171 12E
Grey Range *mts.* Australia **118** G4 27 00S 144 00E
Greystones Wicklow Rep. of Ireland **74/75** E3 53 09N 6 04W
Griffin Georgia U.S.A. **135** J3 33 15N 84 17W
Griffith Park California U.S.A. **139** A3 34 07N 118 20W
Grimethorpe South Yorkshire England **65** D2 53 34N 1 23W
Grimsby North East Lincolnshire England **65** E2 53 35N 0 05W
Grimsey *i.* Iceland **97** I7 66 33N 18 00W
Grodno *see* Hrodna
Gronau Germany **89** G4 52 13N 7 02E
Groningen Netherlands **89** F5 53 13N 6 35E
Groningen *admin.* Netherlands **89** F5 53 30N 6 45E
Grønnedal *see* Kangilinnguit
Groote Eylandt *i.* Australia **118** F7 14 00S 137 00E
Grootfontein Namibia **125** C4 19 32S 18 05E
Grossbeeren Germany **87** F1 52 20N 13 19E
Grosser Müggelsee *l.* Germany **87** G1 52 26N 13 39E
Grosser Zernsee *l.* Germany **87** D1 52 22N 12 57E
Grosseto Italy **92** B2 42 46N 11 07E
Groß Glockner *mt.* Austria **92** B3 47 05N 12 44E
Groundhog *r.* Ontario Canada **137** D3 49 00N 82 00W
Grove Oxfordshire England **70** C2 51 37N 1 26W
Groznyy Russia **102** G4 43 21N 45 42E
Grudovo Bulgaria **94** E5 42 21N 27 10E
Grudziądz Poland **96** B4 53 29N 18 45E
Gruinard Bay Highland Scotland **58** D2 57 55N 5 30W
Gua Orissa India **110** C3 22 18N 85 20E
Guadalajara Mexico **140** D4 20 40N 103 20W
Guadalajara Spain **90** B3 40 37N 3 10W
Guadalcanal *i.* Solomon Is. **118** J8/K8 9 30S 160 00E
Guadalhorce *r.* Spain **90** B2 36 45N 4 45W
Guadalope *r.* Spain **90** B3 40 50N 0 30W
Guadalquivir *r.* Spain **90** A2 37 45N 5 30W
Guadalupe Brazil **147** P2 22 50S 43 23W
Guadalupe *i.* Mexico **140** A5 29 00N 118 24W
Guadeloupe *i.* Lesser Antilles **141** L3 16 30N 61 30W
Guadiana *r.* Spain/Portugal **90** A2 38 30N 7 30W
Guadix Spain **90** B2 37 19N 3 08W
Guaico Trinidad and Tobago **141** T10 10 35N 61 09W
Guajará Mirim Brazil **146** D10 10 50S 65 21W
GUAM 150 E9
Guamúchil Mexico **140** C5 25 28N 108 10W
Guanabara Bay Brazil **147** Q2/3 22 45S 43 10W
Guanabara State *admin.* Brazil **147** Q2/3 22 45S 43 10W
Guanare Venezuela **141** K1 9 04N 69 45W
Guangzhou *(Canton)* China **113** M3 23 08N 113 20E
Guantánamo Cuba **141** I4 20 09N 75 14W
Guapo Bay Trinidad & Tobago **141** S9 10 12N 61 40W
Guaqui Bolivia **146** D9 16 38S 68 50W
Guarapuava Brazil **147** G7 25 22S 51 28W
Guarda Portugal **90** A3 40 32N 7 17W
Guardiana *r.* Spain **90** B2 39 00N 4 00W
Guasave Mexico **134** E2 25 33N 108 30W
Guasdualito Venezuela **146** C14 7 15N 70 40W
GUATEMALA 140 F3
Guatemala Guatemala **140** F2 14 38N 90 22W
Guatemala Basin Pacific Ocean **151** Q9 12 00N 95 00W
Guatuaro Point Trinidad &Tobago **141** U9 10 20N 60 58W
Guayaguayare Trinidad & Tobago **141** T9 10 09N 61 01W
Guayaguayare Bay Trinidad and Tobago **141** T9 10 07N 61 03W
Guayaquil Ecuador **146** A12 2 13S 79 54W
Guaymas Mexico **140** B5 27 59N 110 54W
Guben Germany **93** B2 51 59N 14 42E
Gubin Poland **93** B2 51 59N 14 43E
Gudaut'a Georgia **95** M5 43 08N 40 10E
Gudbrandsdalen *v.* Norway **97** B3 62 00N 58 50E
Gudri *r.* Pakistan **108** A5 26 00N 63 20E
Guelph Ontario Canada **137** D2 43 34N 80 16W
Guéret France **91** C2 46 10N 1 52E
Guernsey *i.* Channel Is. British Isles **73** E2 46 27N 2 35W
Guerrero Mexico **140** P1 19 27N 99 09W
Guia de Pacobaíba Brazil **147** Q3 22 42S 43 10W
Guide Post Northumberland England **61** H3 55 10N 1 36W
Guildford Surrey England **70** D2 51 14N 0 35W
Guilin China **113** M4 25 21N 110 11E
Guimarães Portugal **90** A3 41 26N 8 19W
GUINEA 127 C5
Guinea Basin Atlantic Ocean **152** H6/7 1 00N 8 00W
GUINEA-BISSAU 127 B5/C5
Güines Cuba **141** H4 22 50N 82 02W
Guînes Nord-Pas-de-Calais France **89** A2 50 51N 1 52E
Güiria Venezuela **146** E15 10 37N 62 21W
Guisborough Redcar and Cleveland England **65** D3 54 32N 1 04W
Guiseley West Yorkshire England **64** D2 53 53N 1 42W
Guiyang China **113** L4 26 35N 106 40E
Gujarat *admin.* India **109** C4 23 20N 72 00E
Gujranwala Pakistan **109** C6 32 06N 74 11E
Gujrat Pakistan **109** C6 32 35N 74 06E
Gulbarga India **109** D3 17 22N 76 47E
Gulfport Mississippi U.S.A. **135** I3 30 21N 80 08W
Gulf, The Middle East **107** H4 27 20N 51 00E
Gullane East Lothian Scotland **61** G4 56 02N 2 50W
Gülluk Körfezi *b.* Turkey **94** E2 37 10N 27 15E
Gülnar Turkey **95** H2 36 18N 33 24E
Gulrip'shi Georgia **95** M5 42 56N 41 08E
Gulu Uganda **124** F8 2 46N 32 21E
Gülübovo Bulgaria **94** D5 42 08N 25 51E
Gumia Bihar India **110** C4 23 48N 85 50E
Gumla Bihar India **110** B4 23 03N 84 36E
Gumma *pref.* Japan **114** K3 36 10N 138 27E
Gummersbach Germany **93** A2 51 02N 7 34E
Gümüşhane Turkey **95** L4 40 26N 39 26E
Güney Turkey **94** F3 38 10N 29 04E
Gunnislake Cornwall England **72** C3 50 31N 4 12W
Gunnison *r.* Colorado U.S.A. **134** E4 38 00N 107 00W
Guntersville, Lake U.S.A. **135** I3 34 20N 86 00W
Guntur India **109** E3 16 20N 80 27E
Gunung Kinabalu *mt.* Malaysia **111** F5 6 03N 116 32E
Guriahata West Bengal India **110** G7 26 17N 89 37E
Gurjaani Georgia **95** P4 41 45N 45 49E
Gürün Turkey **95** K3 38 44N 37 15E
Gusev Russia **96** C4 54 32N 22 12E
Güstrow Germany **93** B2 53 48N 12 11E
Gutcher Shetland Is. Scotland **57** D3 60 40N 1 00W
Gütersloh Germany **93** A2 51 54N 8 22E
Guthrie Oklahoma U.S.A. **135** G4 35 53N 97 26W
Guwahati Assam India **109** G5 26 10N 91 45E
Guwēr Iraq **95** N2 36 02N 43 03E
GUYANA 146 F13
Guyana Basin Atlantic Ocean **152** D7 8 00N 50 00W
Guyandotte *r.* U.S.A. **137** D1 38 00N 82 00W
Gwalior India **109** D5 26 12N 78 09E
Gweebarra *r.* Donegal Rep. of Ireland **74** C4 54 54N 8 14W
Gweebarra Bay Donegal Rep. of Ireland **74** C4 54 55N 8 30W
Gweedore Donegal Rep. of Ireland **74** C5 55 03N 8 14W
Gweru Zimbabwe **125** E4 19 27S 29 49E
Gwynedd *u.a.* Wales **66** D2 52 45N 3 55W
Gyangze China **109** F5 28 53N 89 35E
Gyaring Co *l.* China **109** F6 31 05N 88 00E
Gyda Peninsula Russia **103** J10 70 00N 77 30E
Gympie Australia **118** I4 26 10S 152 35E
Gymri Armenia **106** F7 40 47N 43 49E
Gyōda Japan **114** L3 36 10N 139 27E
Gyöngyös Hungary **96** B3 47 46N 20 00E
Györ Hungary **96** B3 47 41N 17 40E
Gyumri *(Leninakan)* Armenia **104** E3 40 47N 43 49E
Gyzylarbat Turkmenistan **105** H2 39 00N 56 23E

H

Haaksbergen Netherlands **89** F4 52 09N 6 45E
Haan Germany **86** C1 51 11N 7 01E
Haapsalu Estonia **97** E2 58 58N 23 32E
Haarlem Netherlands **89** D4 52 23N 4 39E
Haast Pass N.Z. **119** A2 44 06S 169 21E
Hab *r.* Pakistan **108** B5 25 20N 67 00E
Habbān Yemen Republic **107** G1 14 21N 47 04E
Habiganj Bangladesh **110** J5 24 24N 91 25E
Haboro Japan **114** D3 44 23N 141 43E
Habra West Bengal India **110** F3 22 49N 88 38E
Hachinohe Japan **114** D3 40 30N 141 30E
Hachioji Japan **114** L2 35 40N 139 20E
Hacienda Heights U.S.A. **139** B3 33 58N 118 01W
Hackensack New Jersey U.S.A. **138** B2/C2 40 53N 74 01W
Hackensack River New Jersey U.S.A. **138** B2 40 47N 74 06W
Hacketstown Carlow Rep. of Ireland **75** E2 52 52N 6 33W
Hadano Japan **114** L2 35 25N 139 10E
Haddington East Lothian Scotland **61** G3 55 58N 2 47W
Hadejia Nigeria **127** H5 12 30N 10 03E
Hadejia *r.* Nigeria **127** G5 12 10N 9 30E
Hadera Israel **106** O11 32 26N 34 55E
Hadhramaut *geog. reg.* Yemen Republic **107** G2 15 40N 47 30E
Hadibōh Yemen Republic **107** H1 12 36N 53 59E
Hadleigh Essex England **71** E2 51 34N 0 36E
Hadleigh Suffolk England **71** E3 52 02N 0 57E
Hadley Shropshire England **67** E2 52 43N 2 28W

Hadraibari Tripura India **110** J4 23 49N 91 40E
Haeju North Korea **113** P6 38 04N 125 40E
Hafik Turkey **95** K3 39 53N 37 24E
Hafnarfjördur Iceland **97** H6 64 04N 21 58W
Hagen Germany **93** A2 51 22N 7 27E
Hagerstown Maryland U.S.A. **135** K4 39 39N 77 44W
Ha Giang Vietnam **113** K3 22 50N 104 58E
Hagley Hereford and Worcester England **67** E2 52 26N 2 08W
Hagondange France **91** D2 49 16N 6 11E
Hags Head *c.* Clare Rep. of Ireland **75** B2 52 56N 9 30W
Haguenau France **91** D2 48 49N 7 47E
Hahnerberg Germany **86** C1 51 12N 7 10E
Haifa Israel **106** O11 32 49N 34 59E
Haikou China **113** M3 20 05N 110 25E
Hāāil Saudi Arabia **106** F4 27 31N 41 45E
Hailakandi Manipur India **110** K5 24 40N 92 34E
Hailar China **113** N8 49 15N 119 41E
Hailsham East Sussex England **71** E1 50 52N 0 16E
Hailuoto *i.* Finland **97** E3 65 01N 24 45E
Hainan Dao *i.* China **113** L2/M2 18 50N 109 50E
Hainaut *admin.* Belgium **89** C2/D2 50 30N 4 00E
Haines Alaska U.S.A. **132** H4 59 11N 135 23W
Haines Junction Canada **132** H5 60 45N 137 21W
Hai Phong Vietnam **111** D8 20 50N 106 41E
HAITI **141** J3
Hajiganj Bangladesh **110** H4 23 15N 90 50E
Hakkari Turkey **95** N2 37 36N 43 45E
Hakodate Japan **114** D3 41 46N 140 44E
Hakusan Japan **114** H1 34 38N 136 20E
Halab *(Aleppo)* Syria **95** K2 36 14N 37 10E
Halawa, Cape Hawaiian Is. **151** Y18 21 09N 157 15W
Halba Lebanon **106** P12 34 33N 36 04E
Halberstadt Germany **93** B2 51 54N 11 04E
Haldi *r.* West Bengal India **110** E3 22 20N 87 30E
Haldia West Bengal India **110** F3 22 05N 88 03E
Hale Greater Manchester England **64** C2 53 22N 2 20W
Halesowen West Midlands England **67** E2 52 26N 2 05W
Halesworth Suffolk England **71** F3 52 21N 1 30E
Halfeti Turkey **95** K2 37 16N 37 53E
Halifax West Yorkshire England **64** D2 53 44N 1 52W
Halifax Nova Scotia Canada **133** W1 44 38N 63 35W
Halishahar India **108** K3 22 55N 88 25E
Halkirk Highland Scotland **59** F3 58 30N 3 30W
Halladale *r.* Highland Scotland **59** F3 58 30N 3 55W
Halle Belgium **89** D2 50 44N 4 14E
Halle Germany **93** B2 51 28N 11 58E
Hallein Austria **92** B3 47 41N 13 06E
Halley *r.s.* Antarctica **149** 75 35S 26 15W
Hall Peninsula N.W.T. Canada **133** V5 66 00N 66 00W
Halls Creek *tn.* Australia **118** D6 18 17S 127 38E
Halmahera *i.* Indonesia **111** H4 0 30S 127 00E
Halmstad Sweden **97** C2 56 41N 12 55E
Halstead Essex England **71** E2 51 57N 0 38E
Haltern Germany **89** G3 51 45N 7 10E
Haltwhistle Northumberland England **61** G2 54 58N 2 27W
Halvø *(Hayes) p.* Greenland **133** V8 76 00N 67 30W
Hamada Japan **114** B1 34 56N 132 04E
Hamadān Iran **107** G5 34 46N 48 35E
Ḩamāh Syria **106** E6 35 10N 36 45E
Hamamatsu Japan **114** C1 34 42N 137 42E
Hambantota Sri Lanka **109** E1 6 07N 81 07E
Hamble-le-Rice Hampshire England **70** C1 50 52N 1 19W
Hambleton Hills North Yorkshire England **65** D3 54 15N 1 15W
Hamborn Germany **86** A2 51 29N 6 45E
Hamburg Germany **93** B2 53 33N 10 00E
Hamburg *admin.* Germany **93** A2/B2 53 00N 10 00E
Hamburg Iowa U.S.A. **136** A2 40 36N 95 40W
Hamburg Pennsylvania U.S.A. **137** E2 40 33N 75 59W
Hamden Connecticut U.S.A. **137** F2 41 23N 72 55W
Hämeenlinna Finland **97** E3 61 00N 24 25E
Hameln Germany **93** A2 52 07N 9 22E
Hamersley Range *mts.* Australia **118** B5 22 00S 117 00E
Hamhŭng North Korea **113** P6 39 54N 127 35E
Hami *(Kumul)* China **112** H7 42 37N 93 32E
Hamilton Ontario Canada **137** E2 43 15N 79 50W
Hamilton N.Z. **119** C3 37 47S 175 17E
Hamilton South Lanarkshire Scotland **61** E3 55 47N 4 03W
Hamilton Ohio U.S.A. **137** D1 39 23N 84 33W
Hamilton Inlet Canada **133** X3 54 18N 57 42W
Hamm Germany **93** A2 51 40N 7 49E
Hammerdal Sweden **97** D3 63 35N 15 20E
Hammerfest Norway **97** E5 70 40N 23 44E
Hamminkeln Germany **89** F3 51 43N 6 36E
Hammond Indiana U.S.A. **136** C2 41 36N 87 30W
Hampshire *co.* England **70** C2 51 10N 1 15W
Hampshire Downs *hills* Hampshire England **70** C2 51 15N 1 10W
Hampton Virginia U.S.A. **137** E1 37 02N 76 23W
Hamstreet Kent England **71** E2 51 05N 0 52E
Hanazono Japan **114** G1 34 09N 135 31E
Hâncesti Moldova **94** F7 46 50N 28 34E
Hancock New York U.S.A. **137** E2 41 58N 75 17W
Handa Japan **114** H1 34 52N 136 57E
Handan China **113** M6 36 35N 114 31E
Hangzhou China **113** O5 30 18N 120 07E
Hani Turkey **95** M3 38 26N 40 23E
Hanko Finland **97** E2 50 50N 23 00E
Hanley Stoke-on-Trent England **67** E3 53 01N 2 10W
Hanna Alberta Canada **132** M3 51 38N 111 56W
Hannibal Missouri U.S.A. **136** B1 39 41N 91 20W
Hanningfield Reservoir Essex England **71** E2 51 41N 0 29E
Hanno Japan **114** L2 35 52N 139 19E
Hannover Germany **93** A2 52 23N 9 44E
Hannut Belgium **89** E2 50 40N 5 05E
Hanöbukten *b.* Sweden **97** C2 55 50N 14 30E
Ha Nôi *(Hanoi)* Vietnam **111** D8 21 01N 105 52E
Hanover Ontario Canada **137** D2 44 10N 81 03W
Hanover New Hampshire U.S.A. **137** F2 43 42N 71 17W
Hanover Pennsylvania U.S.A. **137** E1 39 47N 76 59W
Hansdiha Bihar India **110** E5 24 36N 87 05E
Haora India **108** K2 22 35N 88 19E
Haora *admin.* India **108** K2
Haora West Bengal India **109** F4 22 35N 88 19E
Happy Valley Hong Kong China **112** C1 22 16N 114 11E
Happy Valley-Goose Bay *tn.* Newfoundland Canada **133** W3 53 15N 60 20W
Haql Saudi Arabia **106** D4 29 14N 34 56E
Harad Saudi Arabia **107** G3 24 12N 49 12E
Harare Zimbabwe **125** F4 17 50S 31 03E
Harbang Chittagong Bangladesh **110** J2 21 54N 92 08E
Harbin China **113** P8 45 45N 126 41E
Harbor Beach *tn.* U.S.A. **137** D2 43 51N 83 40W
Harbor Freeway U.S.A. **139** A2 33 55N 118 17W
Harbour Breton *tn.* Canada **133** X2 47 29N 55 50W
Harbours, Bay of Falkland Is. **152** M15 52 30S 59 30W
Hardangerfjorden *fj.* Norway **97** B2 60 45N 5 20E
Hardangervidda *plat.* Norway **97** B3 60 10N 7 00E
Hardelot-Plage France **71** F1 50 38N 1 35E
Hardenberg Netherlands **89** F4 52 34N 6 38E
Harderwijk Netherlands **89** E4 52 21N 5 37E
Härer Ethiopia **124** H9 9 20N 42 10E
Hargeysa Somalia **124** H9 9 31N 44 02E
Haridwar India **109** D5 29 58N 78 09E
Harima-nada *sea* Japan **114** B1 34 30N 134 30E
Haringhat *r.* Khulna Bangladesh **110** G3 22 10N 89 55E
Haringvliet *est.* Netherlands **88** A1 51 50N 4 05E
Hari Rud *r.* Afghanistan **107** J5 34 00N 64 00E
Harlech Gwynedd Wales **66** C2 52 52N 4 07W
Harlem New York U.S.A. **138** B2 40 48N 73 56W
Harleston Norfolk England **71** F3 52 24N 1 18E
Harlingen Netherlands **89** E5 53 10N 5 25E
Harlingen Texas U.S.A. **135** G2 26 12N 97 43W
Harlow Essex England **71** E2 51 47N 0 08E
Härnösand Sweden **97** D3 62 37N 17 55E
Haroldswick Shetland Is. Scotland **57** F3 60 47N 0 50W
Harpenden Hertfordshire England **70** D2 51 49N 0 22W
Harper Liberia **127** D3 4 25N 7 43W
Harricanaw River Canada **137** E4 50 00N 79 50W
Harrington Harbour *tn.* Canada **133** X3 50 31N 59 30W
Harris *i.* Western Isles Scotland **58** C2 57 50N 6 55W
Harrisburg Illinois U.S.A. **136** C1 37 40N 88 10W
Harrisburg Pennsylvania U.S.A. **137** E2 40 17N 76 54W
Harrisonburg Virginia U.S.A. **137** E1 38 27N 78 54W
Harrisonville Missouri U.S.A. **136** B1 38 04N 94 21W
Harris, Sound of Western Isles Scotland **58** B2 57 45N 7 10W
Harrisville Michigan U.S.A. **137** D2 44 41N 83 19W
Harrogate North Yorkshire England **64** D2 54 00N 1 33W
Harrow *bor.* Greater London England **70** D2 51 34N 0 20W
Harşit *r.* Turkey **95** L4 40 45N 39 00E
Hârşova Romania **94** E6 44 40N 27 59E
Hart Michigan U.S.A. **136** C2 43 43N 86 22W
Hartford Connecticut U.S.A. **137** F2 41 00N 72 00W
Hartington Derbyshire England **67** F3 53 09N 1 48W
Hartland Devon England **72** C3 50 59N 4 29W
Hartland Point *c.* Devon England **72** C4 51 02N 4 31W
Hartlepool Hartlepool England **65** D3 54 41N 1 13W
Hartlepool *u.a.* England **65** D3 54 41N 1 13W
Hartshill Warwickshire England **67** F2 52 33N 1 30W
Harwell Oxfordshire England **70** C2 51 37N 1 18W
Harwich Essex England **71** F2 51 57N 1 17E
Harworth Nottinghamshire England **65** D2 53 26N 1 04W
Haryana *admin.* India **109** D5 29 20N 75 30E
Harz *mts.* Europe **93** B2 51 40N 10 00E
Hasaki Japan **114** M2 35 46N 140 50E
Hascosay *i.* Shetland Is. Scotland **57** D3 60 36N 1 00W
Hase *r.* Germany **93** A2 52 00N 0 00E
Hashima Japan **114** H2 35 19N 136 43E
Hashimoto Japan **114** G1 34 19N 135 33E
Haslemere Surrey England **70** D2 51 06N 0 43W
Haslingden Lancashire England **64** C2 53 43N 2 18W
Hassa Turkey **95** K2 36 48N 36 30E
Hassan India **109** D2 13 01N 76 03E
Hasselt Belgium **89** E2 50 56N 5 20E
Hassi Messaoud Algeria **127** G9 31 52N 5 43E
Hastings Barbados **141** V12 13 05N 59 36W
Hastings East Sussex England **71** E1 50 51N 0 36E
Hastings Minnesota U.S.A. **136** B2 44 43N 92 50W
Hastings Nebraska U.S.A. **135** G5 40 37N 98 22W
Hatay *(Antakya)* Turkey **95** K2 36 12N 36 10E
Hatfield Hertfordshire England **70** D2 51 46N 0 13W
Hatfield South Yorkshire England **65** E2 53 36N 0 59W
Hat Gamaria Bihar India **110** C3 22 18N 85 44E
Hatherleigh Devon England **72** C3 50 49N 4 04W
Hathersage Derbyshire England **67** F3 53 19N 1 38W
Hatia Chittagong Bangladesh **110** J3 22 30N 91 05E
Ha Tsuen Hong Kong China **112** A2 22 26N 113 59E
Hatteras, Cape U.S.A. **135** K4 35 14N 75 31W
Hattiesburg Mississippi U.S.A. **135** I3 31 20N 89 19W
Hattingen Germany **86** C2 51 24N 7 10E
Hatton Aberdeenshire Scotland **59** H2 57 25N 1 55W
Hat Yai Thailand **111** C5 7 00N 100 25E
Haud *geog. reg.* Africa **124** H9/I9 8 00N 50 00E
Haugesund Norway **97** B2 59 25N 5 16E
Haukivesi *l.* Finland **97** F3 62 10N 28 30E
Hauraki Gulf N.Z. **119** B3/C3 36 38S 175 04E
Hausruck *mts.* Austria **93** B1 47 00N 14 00E
Haut Atlas *mts.* Morocco **127** D9 30 45N 6 50W
Hautes Fagnes *moor* Belgium **89** F2 50 29N 6 08E
Hauteurs de Gatine *hills* France **91** B2 46 38N 0 38W
Hauts de Meuse *hills* France **91** D2 49 15N 5 20E
Hauts-de-Seine *admin.* France **87** A2/B1 48 45N 2 18E
Hauz Khas India **108** L4 28 34N 77 11E
Havana *see* La Habana
Havant Hampshire England **70** D1 50 51N 0 59W
Havel *r.* Germany **93** B2 52 00N 12 00E
Havelkanal *can.* Germany **87** E2 52 38N 13 02E
Havelock Ontario Canada **137** E2 44 26N 77 53W
Haverfordwest Pembrokeshire Wales **66** C1 51 49N 4 58W
Haverhill Suffolk England **71** E3 52 05N 0 26E
Haverhill Massachusetts U.S.A. **137** F2 42 47N 71 07W
Havering Greater London England **71** E2 51 34N 0 14E
Havran Turkey **94** E3 39 33N 27 05E
Havre Montana U.S.A. **134** E6 48 34N 109 40W
Havza Turkey **95** J4 40 57N 35 40E
Hawaii *i.* Hawaiian Islands **151** Z17 19 50N 157 50W
Hawaiian Islands Pacific Ocean **150** I10/K10 25 00N 166 00W
Hawaiian Ridge Pacific Ocean **151** J10 23 00N 166 00W
Hawarden Flintshire Wales **66** D3 53 11N 3 02W
Hawea, Lake N.Z. **119** A2 44 28S 169 17E
Hawera N.Z. **119** B3 39 35S 174 17E
Hawes North Yorkshire England **64** C3 54 18N 2 12W
Haweswater Reservoir Cumbria England **64** C3 54 31N 2 49W
Hawick Scottish Borders Scotland **61** G3 55 25N 2 47W
Hawke Bay N.Z. **119** C3 39 23S 177 12E
Hawkesbury Ontario Canada **133** U2 45 36N 74 38W
Hawkhurst Kent England **71** E2 51 02N 0 30E
Haworth West Yorkshire England **64** D2 53 50N 1 57W
Hawthorne California U.S.A. **139** A2 33 54N 118 21W
Hawthorne New Jersey U.S.A. **138** B2 40 57N 74 10W
Haxby York England **65** D3 54 01N 1 05W
Hay *r.* Alberta/N.W.T. Canada **132** L5 61 00N 115 30W
Hayama Japan **115** B2 35 16N 139 35E
Haydon Bridge *tn.* Northumberland England **61** G2 54 58N 21 4W
Hayes *r.* Manitoba Canada **133** Q4 56 00N 94 00W
Hayes *see* Halvø
Hayle Cornwall England **72** B3 50 10N 5 25W
Hay-on-Wye Powys Wales **66** D2 52 04N 3 07W
Hay River *tn.* N.W.T. Canada **132** L5 60 51N 115 42W
Hayward Wisconsin U.S.A. **136** B3 46 02N 91 26W
Haywards Heath West Sussex England **70** D2 51 00N 0 08W
Hazar Turkey **95** L3 38 26N 39 32E
Hazard Kentucky U.S.A. **137** D1 37 14N 83 11W
Hazaribagh Bihar India **110** C4 24 00N 85 23E
Hazaribagh National Park India **110** C5 24 10N 85 20E
Hazaribagh Range India **110** A4/B4 23 25N 84 00N
Hazel Grove *tn.* Greater Manchester England **64** C2 53 23N 2 08W
Hazelmere Buckinghamshire England **70** D2 51 38N 0 44W
Hazelton Canada **132** J4 55 16N 127 18W
Hazro Turkey **96** M3 38 16N 40 14E
Heacham Norfolk England **71** E3 52 55N 0 30E
Headford Galway Rep. of Ireland **74** B3 53 28N 9 06W
Heanor Derbyshire England **67** F3 53 01N 1 22W
Hearst Ontario Canada **137** D3 49 42N 83 40W
Heart *r.* North Dakota U.S.A. **134** F6 47 00N 102 00W
Heathcote Australia **119** G1 34 05S 151 00E
Heathfield East Sussex England **71** E1 50 58N 0 15E
Hebden Bridge West Yorkshire England **64** C2 53 45N 2 00W
Hebi China **113** M6 35 57N 114 08E
Hebron Middle East **106** O10 31 32N 35 06E
Hecate Strait B.C. Canada **132** I3 53 00N 131 00W
Hechuan China **113** L5 30 02N 106 5E
Heckington Lincolnshire England **65** E1 52 59N 0 18W
Heckmondwike West Yorkshire England **64** D2 53 43N 1 45W
Heda Japan **114** K1 34 58N 138 46E
Hedesundafjärdarna *l.* Sweden **97** D3 60 20N 17 00E
Hedge End Hampshire England **70** C1 50 55N 1 18W
Hednesford Staffordshire England **67** E2 52 43N 2 00W
Hedon East Riding of Yorkshire England **65** E2 53 44N 0 12W
Heemstede Netherlands **89** D4 52 21N 4 37E
Heerenveen Netherlands **89** E4 52 57N 5 55E
Heerhugowaard Netherlands **89** D4 52 40N 4 50E
Heerlen Netherlands **89** E2 50 53N 5 59E
Hefei China **113** N5 31 55N 117 18E
Hegang China **113** Q8 47 36N 130 30E
Hegura-jima *i.* Japan **114** C2 37 52N 136 56E
Heidelberg Germany **93** A1 49 25N 8 42E
Heidenheim Baden-Württemberg Germany **93** B1 48 41N 10 10E
Heighington Lincolnshire England **65** E2 54 36N 1 37W
Heilbronn Germany **93** A1 49 08N 9 14E
Heiligenhaus Germany **86** B2 52 20N 6 49E
Hei Ling Chau *i.* H.K.China **112** B1 22 15N 114 02E
Heiloo Netherlands **89** D4 52 36N 4 43E
Heisker *is.* Western Isles Scotland **58** B2 57 30N 7 40W
Heist op den Berg Belgium **89** D3 51 05N 4 44E
Hekimhan Turkey **95** K3 38 50N 37 56E
Hekla *mt.* Iceland **97** I6 64 00N 19 41W
Hekou China **113** K3 22 30N 104 00E
Helan Shan *mts.* China **113** L6 38 00N 106 00E
Helchteren Belgium **89** E3 51 03N 5 23E
Helena Montana U.S.A. **134** D6 46 35N 112 00W
Helen's Bay *tn.* North Down Northern Ireland **60** D2 54 41N 5 50W
Helensburgh Argyll & Bute Scotland **61** E4 56 01N 4 44W
Helgeland *geog. reg.* Norway **97** C4 64 45N 13 00E
Helgoland *(Heligoland) i.* Germany **93** A2 54 00N 8 00E
Heligoland Bight *b.* Germany **93** A2 54 00N 8 00E
Heilong Jiang *see* Amur
Hellendoorn Netherlands **89** F4 52 23N 6 27E
Hellersdorf Germany **87** G2 52 32N 13 35E
Hellevoetsluis Netherlands **89** D3 51 49N 4 08E
Hellifield North Yorkshire England **64** C3 54 01N 2 12W
Hellín Spain **90** B2 38 31N 1 43W
Helmand *r.* Afghanistan **107** J5 30 30N 62 30E
Helmond Netherlands **89** E3 51 28N 5 40E
Helmsdale Highland Scotland **59** F3 58 07N 3 40W
Helmsdale *r.* Highland Scotland **59** F3 58 10N 3 50W
Helmsley North Yorkshire England **65** D3 54 14N 1 04W
Helsingborg Sweden **97** C2 56 03N 12 43E
Helsinki *(Helsingfors)* Finland **97** E3 60 08N 25 00E
Helston Cornwall England **72** B3 50 05N 5 16W
Helvellyn *mt.* Cumbria England **64** B3 54 32N 3 02W
Hemel Hempstead Hertfordshire England **70** D2 51 46N 0 28W
Hempstead New York U.S.A. **138** D1 40 41N 73 39W
Hemsworth West Yorkshire England **65** D2 53 38N 1 21W
Henares *r.* Spain **90** B3 40 45N 3 10W
Henderson Kentucky U.S.A. **136** C1 37 49N 87 36W
Henderson Nevada U.S.A. **134** D4 36 01N 115 00W
Henfield West Sussex England **70** D1 50 56N 0 17W
Hengelo Netherlands **89** F4 52 16N 6 46E
Hengyang China **113** M4 26 58N 112 31E
Henley-in-Arden Warwickshire England **67** F2 52 17N 1 46W
Henley-on-Thames Oxfordshire England **70** D2 51 32N 0 56W
Hennigsdorf *admin.* Germany **87** F2 52 39N 13 08E
Henrietta Maria, Cape Canada **133** S4 55 00N 82 30W
Henryetta Oklahoma U.S.A. **135** G4 35 27N 96 00W
Henzada Myanmar **109** H3 17 36N 95 26E
Heraklia *hist. site* Syria **95** L1 36 00 38 58E
Herāt Afghanistan **107** J5 34 20N 62 12E
Hérault *r.* France **91** C1 43 50N 3 30E
Herbertstown Limerick Rep. of Ireland **75** C2 52 32N 8 28W
Herblay France **87** A2 48 59N 2 10E
Hereford Hereford and Worcester England **67** E2 52 04N 2 43W
Hereford and Worcester *co.* England **67** E2 52 10N 3 05W
Herentals Belgium **89** D3 51 11N 4 50E
Herford Germany **93** A2 52 07N 8 40E
Herisau Switzerland **93** A1 47 23N 9 17E
Herm *i.* Channel Is. British Isles **73** E2 49 28N 2 27W
Herma Ness *c.* Shetland Islands Scotland **57** F3 60 50N 0 54W
Hermel Lebanon **106** P12 34 25N 36 23E
Hermon, Mount Lebanon/Syria **106** O11 33 24N 35 50E
Hermosillo Mexico **140** B5 29 15N 110 59W
Herne Germany **86** C3 51 32N 7 12E
Herne Bay *tn.* Kent England **71** F2 51 23N 1 08E
Herning Denmark **97** B2 56 08N 8 59E
Hernodorf Germany **87** F2 52 38N 13 18E
Heron Point Khulna Bangladesh **110** G2 21 50N 89 28E
Herstal Belgium **89** E2 50 40N 5 38E
Herten Germany **86** C3 51 36N 7 08E
Hertfordshire *co.* England **70** D2 51 50N 0 05W
Hesadi Bihar India **110** C3 22 47N 85 16E
Hessen *admin.* Germany **93** A2 50 00N 9 00E
Hessle City of Kingston upon Hull England **65** E2 53 44N 0 26W
Hetton-le-Hole Tyne and Wear England **65** D3 54 50N 1 27W
Hexham Northumberland England **61** G2 54 58N 2 06W
Heysham Lancashire England **64** C3 54 02N 2 54W
Heywood Greater Manchester England **64** C2 53 36N 2 13W
Hibbing Minnesota U.S.A. **136** B3 47 25N 92 55W
Hickory North Carolina U.S.A. **135** J4 35 44N 81 23W
Hidaka Japan **114** F2 35 29N 134 44E
Hidalgo Mexico **140** E4 24 16N 99 28W
Hidalgo del Parral Mexico **140** C5 26 50N 105 40W
Higashi-Murayama Japan **115** A4 35 46N 139 28E
Higashi-Ōsaka Japan **114** G1 34 40N 135 35E
Higashi-suidō *sd.* Japan **114** A1 34 10N 130 00E
Higham Ferrers Northamptonshire England **70** D3 52 18N 0 36W
High Bentham North Yorkshire England **64** C3 54 08N 2 30W
Higher Walton Lancashire England **64** C2 53 45N 2 37W
Highgate Jamaica **141** R8 18 16N 76 53W
High Island Hong Kong China **112** D2 22 21N 114 21E
High Island Reservoir H.K. China **112** D2 22 22N 114 20E
Highland *u.a.* Scotland **59** E2 57 00N 5 00W
High Level *tn.* Alberta Canada **132** L4 50 10N 117 20W
High Point *tn.* U.S.A. **135** K4 35 58N 80 00W
High Veld *mts.* Rep. of South Africa **125** E2 28 00S 28 00E
Highworth Thamesdown England **70** C2 51 38N 1 43W
High Wycombe Buckinghamshire England **70** D2 51 38N 0 46W
Hiiumaa *i.* Estonia **104** A6 58 55N 22 30E
Hikami Japan **114** F2 35 12N 135 00E
Hikone Japan **114** H2 35 17N 136 13E
Hilden Germany **86** B1 51 10N 6 56E
Hildesheim Germany **93** A2 52 09N 9 58E
Hillaby, Mount Barbados **141** V12 13 12N 59 35W
Hillegom Netherlands **88** C3 52 18N 4 35E
Hilli West Bengal India **110** F6 25 17N 88 58E
Hillingdon Greater London England **70** D2 51 32N 0 27W
Hillsboro Ohio U.S.A. **137** D1 39 12N 83 37W
Hillsborough Lisburn Northern Ireland **60** C2 54 28N 6 05W
Hilo Hawaiian Islands **151** Z17 19 42N 155 04W
Hilversum Netherlands **89** E4 52 14N 5 10E
Himachal Pradesh *admin.* India **109** D6 32 00N 77 30E
Himalaya *mts.* Asia **109** D6/G5
Himarë Albania **94** A4 40 08N 19 43E
Himeji Japan **114** B1 34 50N 134 40E
Ḩimş Syria **106** E5 34 42N 36 40E
Hinckley Leicestershire England **67** F2 52 33N 1 21W
Hindhead Surrey England **70** D2 51 07N 0 44W
Hindley Greater Manchester England **64** C2 53 32N 2 35W
Hindu Kush *mts.* Afghanistan **107** K6 35 00N 70 00E
Hinis Turkey **95** M3 39 22N 41 43E
Hinnøya *i.* Norway **97** D4 68 35N 15 50E
Hirakata Japan **114** G1 34 45N 135 35E
Hirakud Reservoir Orissa India **109** E4 21 40N 83 40E
Hiratsuka Japan **114** L2 35 20N 139 19E
Hirfanli Baraji *l.* Turkey **95** H3 39 15N 33 35E
Hirosaki Japan **114** D3 40 34N 140 28E
Hiroshima Japan **114** B1 34 23N 132 27E
Hirson France **91** C2 49 56N 4 05E
Hirwaun Rhondda Cynon Taff Wales **66** D1 51 45N 3 30W
Hisai Japan **114** H1 34 42N 136 28E
Hisar India **109** D5 29 10N 75 45E
Hispaniola *i.* West Indies **141** J3 18 00N 70 00W
Histon Cambridgeshire England **71** E3 52 15N 0 06E
Hitachi Japan **114** D2 36 35N 140 40E
Hitchin Hertfordshire England **70** D2 51 57N 0 17W
Hitra *i.* Norway **97** B3 63 37N 8 46E
Hjørring Denmark **97** B2 57 28N 9 59E
Ho Ghana **127** F4 6 38N 0 38E
Hobart Australia **118** H1 42 54S 147 18E
Hoboken New Jersey U.S.A. **138** B1 40 44N 74 02W
Hobyo Somalia **124** I9 5 20N 48 30E
Ho Chi Minh *(Saigon)* Vietnam **111** D6 10 46N 106 43E
Ho Chung Hong Kong China **112** C2 22 22N 114 14E
Hockley Essex England **71** E2 51 35N 0 39E
Hodder *r.* Lancashire England **64** C2 53 55N 2 30W
Hoddesdon Hertfordshire England **70** D2 51 46N 0 01W
Hódmezővásárhely Hungary **96** C3 46 26N 20 21E
Hodnet Shropshire England **67** E2 52 51N 2 35W
Hodogaya Japan **115** B2 35 26N 139 36E
Hoek van Holland Netherlands **89** D4 51 59N 4 08E
Hof Germany **93** B2 50 19N 11 56E
Höfn Iceland **97** I6 64 16N 15 10W
Hofsjökull *ice cap* Iceland **97** I6 64 45N 18 45W
Hofu Japan **114** B1 34 02N 131 34E
Hoggar *mts.* Algeria **127** G7 23 45N 6 00E
Hohe Acht *mt.* Germany **89** G2 50 22N 7 00E
Hohe Rhön *hills* Germany **93** A2/B2 50 00N 10 00E
Hohe Tauern *mts.* Austria **93** B1 47 00N 13 00E
Hohhot China **113** M7 40 49N 117 37E
Hoi Ha Hong Kong China **112** C2 22 28N 114 20E
Hokisaku Japan **115** C2 35 18N 139 56E
Hokitika N.Z. **119** B2 42 43S 170 58E
Hokkaidō *i.* Japan **114** D3 43 30N 143 00E
Hokota Japan **114** M3 36 10N 141 30E
Hola Prystan' Ukraine **95** H7 46 30N 32 32E
Holbeach Lincolnshire England **65** F1 52 49N 0 01E
Holderness *p.* East Riding of Yorkshire England **65** E2 53 45N 0 05W
Holetown Barbados **141** V12 13 11N 59 38W
Holguín Cuba **141** I4 20 54N 76 15W
Holland *tn.* Michigan U.S.A. **136** C2 42 46N 86 06W
Hollandse IJssel *r.* Netherlands **88** D2 52 02N 4 52E
Hollick-Kenyon Plateau Antarctica **149** 77 00S 100 00W
Hollis Reservoir Trinidad and Tobago **141** T10 10 42N 61 11W
Hollyford Tipperary Rep. of Ireland **75** C2 52 38N 8 06W
Hollywood Wicklow Rep. of Ireland **75** E3 53 06N 6 35W
Hollywood California U.S.A. **139** A3 34 05N 118 21W
Hollywood Reservoir U.S.A. **139** A3 34 07N 118 20W
Holmes Chapel *tn.* Cheshire England **64** C2 53 12N 2 22W
Holme-on-Spalding-Moor East Riding of Yorkshire England **65** E2 53 49N 0 46W
Holmfirth West Yorkshire England **64** D2 53 35N 1 46W
Holmhead East Ayrshire Scotland **61** E3 55 29N 4 17W
Holsteinsborg *see* Sisimiut
Holston *r.* U.S.A. **135** J4 37 00N 82 00W
Holsworthy Devon England **72** C3 50 49N 4 21W
Holt Norfolk England **71** F3 52 55N 1 05E
Holy Cross Alaska U.S.A. **132** D5 62 10N 159 53W
Holycross Limerick Rep. of Ireland **75** C2 52 38N 7 52W
Holycross Tipperary Rep. of Ireland **75** D2 52 38N 7 52W
Holyhead Isle of Anglesey Wales **66** C3 53 19N 4 38W
Holy Island Isle of Anglesey Wales **66** C3 53 16N 4 39W
Holy Island *(Lindisfarne)* Northumberland England **61** H3 55 41N 1 48W
Holyoke Massachusetts U.S.A. **137** F2 42 12N 72 37W
Holywell Flintshire Wales **66** D3 53 17N 3 13W
Holywood North Down Northern Ireland **60** D2 54 38N 5 50W
Ho Man Tin Hong Kong China **112** B1 22 19N 114 10E
Homberg Germany **86** A2 51 27N 6 41E
Homburg Germany **93** A1 49 20N 7 20E
Home Bay N.W.T. Canada **133** V6 69 00N 67 00W
Homer Alaska U.S.A. **132** E4 59 40N 151 37W
Homestead Florida U.S.A. **135** J2 25 29N 80 29W
Homyel' *(Gomel')* Belarus **102** F6 52 25N 31 00E
Honda Colombia **146** C14 5 15N 74 50W
Honddu *r.* Wales **66** D1 51 50N 2 50W
Hondschoote France **71** G1 50 59N 2 35E
HONDURAS **140/141** G2
Hone Manitoba Canada **133** O4 56 20N 101 16W
Hong *see* Song-koi
Hong Kong *Spec. Admin.* China **150** D10 23 00N 114 00E
Hong Kong *i.* H.K. China **112** B1/C1 22 10N 114 10E
Hong Lok Yuen H.K. China **112** D2 22 27N 114 00E
Honguedo Passage *(Détroit d'Honguedo)* *sd.* Québec Canada **133** W2 49 30N 64 20W
Honiara Solomon Islands **118** J8 9 28S 159 57E
Honiton Devon England **73** D3 50 48N 3 13W
Honjō Japan **114** L3 36 16N 139 09E
Honokaa Hawaiian Islands **151** Z18 20 04N 155 27W
Honolulu Hawaiian Islands **151** Y18 21 19N 157 50W
Honshū *i.* Japan **114** C2 37 15N 139 00E
Hoo Kent England **71** E2 51 26N 0 34E
Hood, Mount Oregon U.S.A. **134** B6 45 24N 121 41W
Hoofddorp Netherlands **88** C3 52 18N 4 41E
Hoogeveen Netherlands **89** F4 52 43N 6 29E
Hoogezand Netherlands **89** F5 53 10N 6 45E
Hook Hampshire England **70** D2 51 17N 0 58W
Hook Head Rep. of Ireland **75** E2 52 10N 6 55W
Hoolehua Hawaiian Islands **151** Y18 21 11N 157 06W
Hooper Bay *tn.* Alaska U.S.A. **132** D5 61 20N 166 10W
Hoorn Netherlands **89** E4 52 38N 5 03E
Hopa Turkey **95** M4 41 26N 41 22E
Hope Barbados **141** V13 13 20N 59 36W
Hope B.C. Canada **132** K2 49 21N 121 28W
Hope Flintshire Wales **66** D3 53 07N 3 03W
Hopes Advance, Cape Canada **133** V5 61 00N 69 40W

I

Itarsi India 109 D4 22 39N 77 48W
Itchen *r.* Hampshire England 70 C2 51 05N 1 15W
Ithaca New York U.S.A. 137 E2 42 26N 76 30W
Ithaki *i.* Greece 94 B3 38 35N 20 40E
Ithon *r.* Powys Wales 66 D2 52 20N 3 25W
Ito Japan 114 I1 34 58N 139 04E
Itui *r.* Brazil 146 C11 5 30S 71 00W
Itzehoe Germany 93 A2 53 56N 9 32E
Ivano-Frankivs'k *(Ivano-Frankovsk)* Ukraine 96 C3 48 40N 24 40E
Ivanovo Russia 102 G7 57 00N 41 00E
Ivdel' Russia 102 I8 60 45N 60 30E
IVORY COAST *see* CÔTE D'IVOIRE
Ivry-sur-Seine France 87 B2 48 48N 2 24E
Ivujivik Québec Canada 133 T5 62 25N 77 54W
Ivybridge Devon England 72 D3 50 23N 3 56W
Iwai Japan 114 L3 36 02N 139 53E
Iwaki Japan 114 D2 37 03N 140 58E
Iwakuni Japan 114 B1 34 10N 132 09E
Iwamizawa Japan 114 D3 43 12N 141 47E
Iwanai Japan 114 D3 43 01N 140 32E
Iwo Nigeria 127 F4 7 38N 4 11E
Ixtaccihuati *mt.* Mexico 140 E3 19 11N 98 38W
Ixtepec Mexico 140 E3 16 32N 95 10W
Ixworth Suffolk England 71 E3 52 18N 0 50E
Iyo-nada *b.* Japan 114 B1 33 50N 132 00E
Izegem Belgium 89 C2 50 55N 3 13E
Izhevsk *(Ustinov)* Russia 102 H7 56 49N 53 11E
Izhma *r.* Russia 102 H8 64 00N 54 00E
Izmayil Ukraine 96 D3 45 20N 28 48E
Izmaylovoskiy Park Russia 102 N2 55 46N 37 46E
Izmir Turkey 106 C6 38 25N 27 10E
Izmit *see* Kocaeli
Iznik Turkey 94 F4 40 27N 29 43E
Iznik Gölu *l.* Turkey 94 F4 40 27N 29 40E
Izra' Syria 106 P11 32 52N 36 15E
Iztacalco Mexico 140 P1 19 23N 99 07W
Iztapalapa Mexico 140 P1 19 21N 99 05W
Izumi Japan 114 G1 34 29N 135 25E
Izu-shotō *is.* Japan 114 C1 34 20N 139 20E

J

Jabal Akhdar *mt.* Oman 107 I3 24 00N 56 30E
Jabal al Akhdar *mts.* Libya 124 D14 33 00N 22 00E
Jābal as Sawdāā *mts.* Libya 124 B13/C13 29 00N 15 00E
Jabalpur India 109 D4 23 10N 79 59E
Jablah Syria 95 J1 35 22N 35 56E
Jablonec Czech Republic 96 B4 50 44N 15 10E
Jaboatão Brazil 146 J11 8 05S 35 00W
Jaca Spain 90 B3 42 34N 0 33W
Jacarepagua Brazil 147 P2 22 57S 43 21W
Jackman Maine U.S.A. 137 F3 45 37N 70 16W
Jackson Barbados 141 V12 13 09N 59 36W
Jackson Michigan U.S.A. 137 D2 42 15N 84 24W
Jackson Mississippi U.S.A. 135 H3 32 20N 90 11W
Jackson Ohio U.S.A. 137 D1 39 03N 82 40W
Jackson Tennessee U.S.A. 135 I4 35 37N 88 50W
Jackson Wyoming U.S.A. 134 D5 43 28N 110 45W
Jackson Head N.Z. 119 A2 43 58S 168 37E
Jackson Heights *tn.* U.S.A. 138 B2 40 45N 73 52W
Jacksonville Florida U.S.A. 135 J3 30 20N 81 40W
Jacksonville Illinois U.S.A. 136 B1 39 44N 90 14W
Jacksonville North Carolina U.S.A. 135 K3 34 45N 77 26W
Jacksonville Beach *tn.* U.S.A. 135 J3 30 18N 81 24W
Jacmel Haiti 141 J3 18 18N 72 32W
Jacobabad Pakistan 108 B5 28 16N 68 30E
Jacobina Brazil 146 I10 11 13S 40 30W
Jacques-Cartier Passage *sd.* Québec Canada 133 W3 50 00N 64 00W
Jaén Spain 90 B2 37 46N 3 48W
Jaffna Sri Lanka 109 D1 9 40N 80 01E
Jagdalpur India 109 E3 19 04N 82 05E
Jagst *r.* Germany 93 A1 49 00N 9 00E
Jahrom Iran 107 H4 28 29N 53 32E
Jaintiapur Bangladesh 110 K6 25 06N 92 08E
Jaipur India 109 D5 26 53N 75 50E
Jaipurhat Rajshahi Bangladesh 110 G6 25 04N 89 06E
Jaisalmer India 107 L4 26 52N 70 55E
Jajapur Orissa India 110 D1 20 53N 86 22E
Jakarta Indonesia 111 D2 6 08S 106 45E
Jakobshavn *see* Ilulissat
Jakobstad Finland 97 E3 63 40N 22 42E
Jalālabād Afghanistan 107 L5 34 26N 70 25E
Jalandhar India 109 D6 31 18N 75 40E
Jalangi Khulna Bangladesh 110 F5 24 05N 88 40E
Jalapa Enriquez Mexico 140 E3 19 32N 96 56W
Jaleswar Orissa India 110 E2 21 48N 87 14E
Jalgaon India 109 D4 21 01N 75 39E
Jalna India 109 D3 19 50N 75 58E
Jalón *r.* Spain 90 B3 41 30N 1 35W
Jalpaiguri West Bengal India 110 F7 26 26N 88 45E
Jālū Libya 124 D13 29 02N 21 33E
JAMAICA 141 I3
Jamaica New York U.S.A. 138 C1 40 42N 73 48W
Jamaica Bay New York U.S.A. 138 C1 40 37N 73 50W
Jamaica Bay Wildlife Refuge New York U.S.A. 138 C1 40 37N 73 46W
Jamalpur Dhaka Bangladesh 110 G5 24 54N 89 57E
Jamalpur Bihar India 110 D6 25 19N 86 30E
Jambi Indonesia 111 C3 1 34S 103 37E
James *r.* South Dakota U.S.A. 135 G6 47 00N 98 00W
James *r.* Virginia U.S.A. 137 E1 37 00N 77 00W
James Bay Canada 133 S3 53 45N 81 00W
Jameson Land *p.* Greenland 133 EE7 71 30N 23 00W
Jamestown New York U.S.A. 137 E2 42 05N 79 15W
Jamestown North Dakota U.S.A. 136 A3 46 54N 98 42W
Jamiltepec Mexico 140 E3 16 18N 97 51W
Jammu Jammu & Kashmir 109 D6 32 43N 74 54E
Jammu & Kashmir *state* Southern Asia 109 D6 29 40N 76 30E
Jamnagar India 108 C4 22 28N 70 06E
Jamshedpur Bihar India 109 F4 22 47N 86 12E
Jamtara Bihar India 110 D4 23 58N 86 49E
Jamui Bihar India 110 D5 24 57N 86 14E
Jamuna *r.* Bangladesh 110 G6 25 00N 89 40E
Jamuwa Bihar India 110 D5 24 23N 86 08E
Janesville Wisconsin U.S.A. 136 C2 42 42N 89 02W
Jangipur West Bengal India 110 F5 24 28N 88 08E
Jan Mayen *i.* Arctic Ocean 148 71 00N 9 00W
Janput West Bengal India 110 E2 21 42N 87 45E
Januária Brazil 146 I9 15 28S 44 23W
JAPAN 114
Japan, Sea of 113 Q6/R7 39 00N 137 00E
Japan Trench Pacific Ocean 150 E11 35 00N 143 00E
Jarābulus Syria 95 L2 36 49N 38 01E
Jarocin Poland 96 B4 51 59N 17 30E
Jarrow Tyne and Wear England 65 D3 54 59N 1 29W
Jarú Brazil 146 E10 10 24S 62 45W
Jashipur Orissa India 110 D2 21 58N 86 03E
Jashpurnagar India 110 B3 22 53N 84 12E
Jāsk Iran 107 I4 25 40N 57 46E
Jasło Poland 96 C3 49 45N 21 28E
Jason Islands Falkland Islands 152 L16 51 05S 61 00W
Jasper Alberta Canada 132 L3 52 55N 118 05W
Jasper Indiana U.S.A. 136 C1 38 22N 86 58W
Jasper National Park Canada 132 L3 53 00N 118 00W
Jastrowie Poland 96 B4 53 25N 16 50E
Jaunpur India 109 E5 25 44N 82 41E
Java Sea Indonesia 111 E2 5 00S 112 00E
Java Trench Indian Ocean 150 B6 10 00S 110 00E
Jawa *i.* Indonesia 111 D2/E2 7 00S 110 00E
Jayapura Indonesia 118 G9 2 37S 140 39E
Jaynagar Bihar India 110 D7 26 36N 86 08E
Jaynagar Manzilpur India 110 F3 22 10N 88 21E
Jazāāir Farasān *is.* Saudi Arabia 106 F2 16 45N 42 10E
Jdaide Syria 95 L1 35 49N 3918E
Jebel Abyad Plateau Sudan 124 E11 18 00N 28 00E
Jebel Marra *mts.* Sudan 124 D10 13 00N 24 00E
Jedburgh Scottish Borders Scotland 61 G3 55 29N 2 34W
Jeetze *r.* Germany 93 B2 53 00N 11 00E
Jefferson Wisconsin U.S.A. 136 C2 43 01N 88 48W
Jefferson City Missouri U.S.A. 136 B1 38 33N 92 10W
Jeffersonville Indiana U.S.A. 136 C1 38 16N 85 45W
Jeffort Point Khulna Bangladesh 110 G2 21 89
Jēkabpils Latvia 97 F2 56 22N 25 50E
Jelenia Góra Poland 96 B4 50 55N 15 45E
Jelgava Latvia 97 E2 56 39N 23 40E
Jemeppe Belgium 89 E2 50 37N 5 30E
Jena Germany 93 B2 50 56N 11 35E
Jenin Jordan 106 O11 32 28N 35 18E
Jequié Brazil 146 I10 13 52S 40 06W
Jérémie Haiti 141 J3 18 40N 74 09W
Jerez de la Frontera Spain 90 A2 36 41N 6 08W
Jerez de los Caballeros Spain 90 A2 38 20N 6 45W
Jericho Middle East 106 O10 31 51N 35 27E
Jersey *i.* Channel Is. British Isles 73 E2 49 13N 2 07W
Jersey City New Jersey U.S.A. 138 B1 40 44N 74 06W
Jerusalem Israel/Jordan 106 O10 31 47N 35 13E
Jessore Khulna Bangladesh 110 G4 23 10N 89 12E
Jezioro Sniardwy *l.* Poland 96 C4 53 00N 21 00E
Jhajha Bihar India 110 D5 24 47N 86 23E
Jhalakati Khulna Bangladesh 110 H3 22 38N 90 10E
Jhalida West Bengal India 110 C4 23 21N 85 58E
Jhang Pakistan 109 C6 31 19N 72 22E
Jhanjharpur Bihar India 110 D7 26 16N 86 17E
Jhansi India 109 D5 25 27N 78 34E
Jhargram West Bengal India 110 D3 22 30N 86 57E
Jharsuguda Orissa India 110 B2 21 56N 84 04E
Jhelum Pakistan 109 C6 32 58N 73 45E
Jhelum *r.* Pakistan 109 C6 32 30N 72 30E
Jhenida Khulna Bangladesh 110 G4 23 32N 89 09E
Jhinkpani Bihar India 110 C3 22 27N 85 46E
Jhumri Tilaiya Bihar India 110 C5 24 18N 85 33E
Jiamusi China 113 Q8 46 59N 130 29E
Ji'an China 113 N4 27 08N 115 00E
Jianganj-Azimganj India 110 F5 24 15N 88 20E
Jiangmen China 113 M3 22 40N 113 05E
Jiaxing China 113 O5 30 15N 120 52E
Jiayuguan China 113 J0 39 47N 90 14E
Jiddah Saudi Arabia 106 E3 21 30N 39 10E
Ješjavree *l.* Norway 97 E4 69 40N 24 10E
Jihlavá Czech Republic 96 B3 49 24N 15 34E
Jihočesky *admin.* Czech Republic 93 B1 49 00N 14 00E
Jilin China 113 P7 43 53N 126 35E
Jiloca *r.* Spain 90 B3 41 08N 1 45W
Jīma Ethiopia 124 G9 7 39N 36 47E
Jiménez Mexico 134 F2 29 05N 100 40W
Jinan China 113 N6 36 41N 117 00E
Jingdezhen China 113 N4 29 17N 117 12E
Jinhua China 113 N4 29 06N 119 40E
Jining Nei Mongol Zizhiqu China 113 M7 40 58N 113 01E
Jining Shandong China 113 N6 35 25N 116 40E
Jinja Uganda 124 F8 0 27N 33 14E
Jinsha Jiang *(Yangtze) r.* China 113 K4 27 30N 103 00E
Jinxi China 113 O7 40 46N 120 47E
Jinzhou China 113 O7 41 07N 121 06E
Jiparaná *r.* Brazil 146 E11 8 00S 62 30W
Jisr ash Shughūr Syria 95 K1 35 48N 36 20E
Jiu *r.* Romania 96 C2 44 00N 24 00E
Jiujiang China 113 N4 29 41N 116 03E
Jixi China 113 Q8 45 17N 131 00E
Jīzān Saudi Arabia 106 F2 16 56N 42 33E
João Pessoa Brazil 146 J11 7 06S 34 53W
Jodhpur India 109 C5 26 18N 73 08E
Joensuu Finland 97 F3 62 35N 29 46E
Jōetsu Japan 114 C2 37 06N 138 15E
Jogighopa Assam India 110 I7 26 14N 90 35E
Johannesburg Rep. of South Africa 125 E2 26 10S 28 02E
John Day *r.* Oregon U.S.A. 134 B5 45 00N 120 00W
John H. Kerr Reservoir U.S.A. 135 K4 37 00N 78 00W
John o'Groats Highland Scotland 59 F3 58 38N 3 05W
John Redmond Reservoir U.S.A. 136 A1 38 00N 96 00W
Johnson City Tennessee U.S.A. 135 J4 36 20N 82 23W
Johnstone Renfrewshire Scotland 61 E3 55 50N 4 31W
Johnstown U.S.A. 137 E2 40 20N 78 56W
Johor Bharu Malaysia 111 C4 1 27N 103 45E
Joinville Brazil 147 H7 26 20S 48 55W
Joinville Island Antarctica 149 63 00S 56 00W
Jokkmokk Sweden 97 D4 66 37N 19 50E
Joliet Illinois U.S.A. 136 C2 41 32N 88 05W
Joliette Québec Canada 137 F3 46 02N 73 27W
Jonesboro Arkansas U.S.A. 135 H4 35 50N 90 41W
Jones Sound N.W.T. Canada 133 R8 76 00N 88 00W
Jönköping Sweden 97 C2 57 45N 14 10E
Jonquière Québec Canada 137 F3 48 25N 71 16W
Joplin Missouri U.S.A. 136 B1 37 04N 94 31W
JORDAN 106 E5
Jordan *r.* Middle East 106 O11 32 15N 32 10E
Jordan Valley *tn.* H.K. China 112 C1 22 19N 114 13E
Joseph Bonaparte Gulf Australia 118 D7 14 00S 128 30E
Jos Plateau Nigeria 127 G4/5 9 30N 8 55E
Jostedalsbreen *glacier* Norway 97 B3 61 40N 7 00E
Jotunheimen *mts.* Norway 97 B3 61 40N 8 00E
Joūnié Lebanon 106 O11 33 58N 35 38E
Jowai Meghalaya India 110 K6 25 26N 92 14E
Joyce Country Galway Rep. of Ireland 74 B3 53 32N 9 33W
Juan de Fuca Strait North America 134 B6 48 00N 124 00W
Juázeiro Brazil 146 I11 9 25S 40 30W
Juázeiro do Norte Brazil 146 J11 7 10S 39 18W
Juba Sudan 124 F8 4 50N 31 35E
Jubany *r.s.* Antarctica 149 62 14S 58 40W
Jubba *r.* Somalia 124 H8 3 00N 42 30E
Jubilee Reservoir H.K. China 112 B2 22 24N 114 08E
Júcar *r.* Spain 90 B2 39 08N 1 50W
Juchitán Mexico 140 E3 16 27N 95 05W
Juist *i.* Germany 93 A2 53 00N 7 00E
Juiz de Fora Brazil 147 I8 21 47S 43 23W
Juliaca Peru 146 C9 15 29S 70 09W
Julianehåb *see* Qaqortoq
Jülich Germany 89 F2 50 55N 6 21E
Julijske Alpe *mts.* Europe 92 B3 46 00N 13 00E
Jumet Belgium 89 D2 50 27N 4 26E
Junagadh India 108 C4 21 32N 70 32E
Junction City Kansas U.S.A. 135 G4 39 02N 96 51W
Jundiaí Brazil 147 H8 23 10S 46 54W
Juneau Alaska U.S.A. 132 I4 58 20N 134 20W
Jungfernheide Germany 87 F2 52 35N 13 16E
Jungfrau *mt.* Switzerland 91 D2 46 33N 7 58E
Junggar Pendi *(Dzungarian Basin)* China 112 G7 44 00N 07 30E
Junk Bay Hong Kong China 112 C1 22 18N 114 15E
Junsele Sweden 97 D3 63 40N 16 55E
Jur *r.* Sudan 124 E9 8 00N 28 00E
Jura *mts.* France/Switzerland 91 D2 46 30N 6 00E
Jura *i.* Argyll & Bute Scotland 60 C3/D3 55 55N 6 00W
Jura Krakowska *mts.* Poland 96 B4 50 00N 20 00E
Jura, Sound of Argyll & Bute Scotland 60 D3 55 45N 5 55W
Jurby Head Isle of Man British Isles 64 A3 54 21N 4 31W
Jūrmala Latvia 97 E2 56 59N 23 35E
Juru Juba *pt.* Brazil 147 Q2 22 56S 43 08W
Jutphaas Netherlands 89 E2 52 02N 5 04E
Juvisy-sur-Orge France 87 B1 48 42N 2 22E
Jylland *p.* Denmark 97 B2 55 00N 9 00E
Jyväskylä Finland 97 F3 62 16N 25 50E

K

K2 *(Qogir Feng, Godwin Austen) mt.* China/India 112 E6 35 47N 76 30E
Kābul Afghanistan 107 K5 34 30N 69 10E
Kabul *r.* Afghanistan 107 K5 34 40N 69 30E
Kabwe Zambia 125 E5 14 29S 28 25E
Kachchh, Gulf of India 108 B4 22 40N 69 30E
Kaçkar Daği *mt.* Turkey 95 M4 40 50N 41 09E
Kadinhani Turkey 94 H3 38 15N 32 14E
Kadirli Turkey 95 K2 37 22N 36 05E
Kadmat Island India 109 C2 11 08N 72 46E
Kadoma Zimbabwe 125 E4 18 21N 29 55E
Kaduna Nigeria 127 G5 10 28N 7 25E
Kaduna *r.* Nigeria 127 G5 10 00N 6 30E
Kaédi Mauritania 127 C6 16 12N 13 32W
Kaesŏng South Korea 113 P6 37 59N 126 30E
Kafue Zambia 125 E4 15 44S 28 10E
Kafue *r.* Zambia 125 E4 16 00S 27 00E
Kafue National Park Zambia 125 E4 15 00S 25 30E
Kagan Uzbekistan 105 J2 39 45N 64 32E
Kagerplassen *l.* Netherlands 88 B2 52 14N 4 31E
Kağizman Turkey 95 N4 40 08N 43 07E
Kagoshima Japan 114 B1 31 37N 130 32E
Kahoolawe *i.* Hawaiian Is. 151 Y18 20 30N 156 40W
Kahramanmaraş Turkey 95 K2 37 34N 36 54E
Kâhta Turkey 95 K2 37 48N 38 35E
Kahuku Point Hawaiian Is. 151 Y18 21 42N 158 00W
Kaiapoi N.Z. 119 B2 43 23S 172 39E
Kaifeng China 113 M5 34 47N 114 20E
Kaikohe N.Z. 119 B3 35 25S 173 48E
Kaikoura N.Z. 119 B2 42 24S 173 41E
Kailash India 108 M4 28 33N 77 15E
Kailua Hawaiian Islands 151 Z17 19 43N 155 59W
Kaimana Indonesia 111 I3 3 39S 133 44E
Kainan Japan 114 G1 34 09N 135 12E
Kainji Reservoir Nigeria 127 F5 10 25N 4 56E
Kaipara Harbour N.Z. 119 B3 30 12S 174 00E
Kairouan Tunisia 127 H10 35 42N 10 01E
Kaiserslautern Germany 93 A1 49 27N 7 47E
Kaitaia N.Z. 119 B3 35 07S 173 16E
Kaiwi Channel *sd.* Hawaiian Is. 151 Y18 21 20N 157 30W
Kajaani Finland 97 F3 64 14N 27 37E
Kakabeka Falls *tn.* Canada 136 C3 48 24N 89 40W
Kakamigahara Japan 114 H2 35 23N 136 52E
Kakhovka Ukraine 95 H7 46 50N 33 30E
Kakhovs'ke Vodoskhovyshche *res.* Ukraine 104 C4 47 30N 35 00E
Kākināda India 109 E3 16 59N 82 20E
Kakogawa Japan 114 F1 34 49N 134 52E
Kakwip West Bengal India 110 F2 21 53N 88 20E
Kalachinsk Russia 105 L6 55 02N 74 40E
Kaladan *r.* India/Myanmar 110 K2 21 10N 93 00E
Kaladar Ontario Canada 137 E2 44 39N 77 07W
Kalae *(South Cape)* Hawaiian Is. 151 Z17 18 58N 155 24W
Kalahari Desert Southern Africa 125 D3 23 30S 23 00E
Kalahari Gemsbok National Park Rep. of South Africa 125 D2 26 00S 20 30E
Kalaigaon Assam India 110 K7 26 31N 92 00E
Kalamaria Greece 94 C4 40 36N 22 59E
Kalamáta Greece 94 C2 37 02N 22 07E
Kalamazoo Michigan U.S.A. 136 C2 42 17N 85 36W
Kalambo Falls Tanzania/Zambia 125 F6 8 35S 31 13E
Kalampáka Greece 94 B3 39 43N 21 38E
Kalanchak Ukraine 95 H7 46 14N 33 18E
Kalat Pakistan 108 B5 29 01N 66 38E
Kalaus *r.* Russia 95 N6 45 50N 43 15E
Kale Turkey 94 F2 37 27N 28 21E
Kalémié Congo (D.R.) 125 E6 5 57S 29 10E
Kaletwa Myanmar 110 K2 21 45N 92 45E
Kalevala Russia 97 G4 65 15N 31 08E
Kalgoorlie-Boulder Australia 118 C3 30 49S 121 29E
Kaliaganj Bangladesh 110 F6 25 35N 88 19E
Kaliavesi *l.* Finland 97 F3 63 00N 27 20E
Kalihati Dhaka Bangladesh 110 H5 24 23N 90 00E
Kalimantan *admin.* Indonesia 111 E3 0 00 115 00E
Kalimpang West Bengal India 110 F8 27 04N 88 35E
Kalindri *r.* Bihar India 110 E6 25 50N 87 50E
Kalinin *see* Tver'
Kaliningrad Russia 96 C4 54 40N 20 30E
Kaliningrad *reg.* Russia 96 C4 54 40N 21 00E
Kaliningrad *tn* Russia 104 D6 55 56N 37 55E
Kaliningrad *admin.* Russia 104 A5 54 40N 20 30E
Kalinkavichy Belarus 96 52 08N 29 19E
Kalispell Montana U.S.A. 134 D6 48 12N 114 19W
Kalisz Poland 96 B4 51 46N 18 02E
Kalix älv *r.* Sweden 97 E4 66 40N 22 30E
Kalkaji India 108 M4 28 32N 77 16E
Kalkan Turkey 94 F2 36 16N 29 25E
Kallsjön *l.* Sweden 97 C3 63 30N 13 05E
Kalmar Sweden 97 D2 56 39N 16 20E
Kal'mius *r.* Ukraine 95 K7 47 20N 37 50E
Kalmthout Belgium 89 D3 51 23N 4 29E
Kalna West Bengal India 110 F4 23 13N 88 23E
Kalni *r.* Bangladesh 110 J5 24 45N 91 15E
Kalomo Zambia 125 E4 17 02S 26 29E
Kaló Neró Greece 94 B2 37 18N 21 42E
Kalpeni Island India 109 C2 10 05N 73 15E
Kaluga Russia 102 F6 54 31N 36 16E
Kalutara Sri Lanka 109 D1 6 35N 79 59E
Kálymnos Greece 94 E2 36 56N 26 59E
Kama *r.* Russia 105 H6 58 00N 55 30E
Kamaishi Japan 114 D2 39 18N 141 52E
Kamakura Japan 114 L2 35 19N 139 33E
Kaman Turkey 95 H3 39 22N 33 43E
Kamarān *i.* Yemen Republic 106 F2 15 21N 42 40E
Kamarhati India 108 K2 22 40N 88 22E
Kambara *i.* Fiji 150 V15 18 57S 178 58W
Kamchatka *p.* Russia 103 R7 57 30N 160 00E
Kamchatka Bay Russia 103 S7 55 00N 164 00E
Kamchiya *r.* Bulgaria 96 D2 43 00N 27 00E
Kamdara Bihar India 110 B3 22 55N 84 56E
Kamensk-Ural'skiy Russia 102 I7 56 29N 61 49E
Kameoka Japan 114 G2 35 02N 135 35E
Kames Argyll & Bute Scotland 60 D3 55 54N 5 15W
Kamet *mt.* India 109 D6 30 55N 79 36E
Kamina Congo (D.R.) 125 D6 8 46S 25 00E
Kamkhyanagar Orissa India 110 C1 20 59N 85 30E
Kamla *r.* Bihar India 110 D6 25 40N 86 30E
Kamloops B.C. Canada 132 K3 50 39N 120 24W
Kamogawa Japan 114 M2 35 06N 140 09E
Kampala Uganda 124 F8 0 19N 32 35E
Kampen Netherlands 89 E4 52 33N 5 55E
Kamp-Lintfort Germany 89 F3 51 30N 6 33E
Kamskoye Vodokhranilische *res.* Russia 105 H6 58 30N 56 00E
Kam''yanets'-Podil's'kyy Ukraine 96 D3 48 40N 26 36E
Kam''yanka-Dniprovs'ka Ukraine 95 J7 47 29N 34 25E
Kamyshevatskaya Russia 95 K7 46 25N 37 57E
Kamyshin Russia 102 G6 50 05N 45 24E
Kamyshlov Russia 105 J6 56 55N 62 41E
Kan *r.* Russia 105 P6 56 30N 95 00E
Kanagawa Japan 115 B2 35 29N 139 38E
Kanagawa *pref.* Japan 114 L2 35 29N 139 38E
Kananga Congo (D.R.) 125 D6 5 53S 22 26E
Kanawha *r.* U.S.A. 137 D1 38 00N 82 00W
Kanazawa Japan 114 C2 36 35N 136 38E
Kanbe Myanmar 111 B7 16 45N 96 04E
Kanchanpur Nepal 110 D7 26 42N 86 55E
Kanchipuram India 109 D2 12 50N 79 44E
Kānchrāpāra India 108 K3 22 56N 88 26E
Kandahār Afghanistan 107 K5 31 35N 65 45E
Kandalaksha Russia 97 G4 67 09N 32 31E
Kandarakshskiy Zaliv *(White Sea)* Russia 97 G4 66 00N 37 30E
Kandavu *i.* Fiji 150 U15 19 10S 178 30E
Kandavu Passage *sd.* Fiji 150 T15/U15 18 50S 178 00E
Kandi Benin 127 F5 11 05N 2 59E
Kandi West Bengal India 110 F4 23 57N 88 04E
Kandirat Turkey 94 G4 41 05N 30 08E
Kandla India 107 L3 23 03N 70 11E
Kandy Sri Lanka 109 E1 7 17N 80 40E
Kane Pennsylvania U.S.A. 137 E2 41 40N 78 48W
Kaneohe Hawaiian Islands 151 Y18 21 25N 157 48W
Kangān Iran 107 H4 27 51N 52 07E
Kangar Malaysia 111 C5 6 27N 100 11E
Kangaroo Island Australia 118 F2 35 50S 137 50E
Kangerlussuaq *(Søndre Strømfjord) fj.* Greenland 133 Y6 67 00N 50 59W
Kangertittivaq *(Scoresbysund) sd.* Greenland 133 70 25N 23 00W
Kangilinnguit *(Grønnedal)* Greenland 133 Z5 61 20N 48 00W
Kangnŭng South Korea 113 P6 37 48N 127 52E
Kanhar *r.* India 110 A4 23 55N 83 40E
Kanin, Cape Russia 76 P9 68 38N 43 20E
Kanin Peninsula Russia 102 G9 68 00N 45 00E
Kansas *r.* Kansas U.S.A. 136 A1 39 00N 95 00W
Kansas City Missouri U.S.A. 136 B1 39 02N 94 33W
Kansk Russia 103 L7 56 11N 95 48E
Kanthi West Bengal India 110 E2 21 49N 87 44E
Kanturk Cork Rep. of Ireland 75 C2 52 10N 8 55W
Kanye Botswana 125 D3 24 59S 25 19E
Kao-hsiung Taiwan 113 O3 22 36N 120 17E
Kaolack Senegal 127 B5 14 09N 16 08W
Kapaa Hawaiian Islands 151 X10 22 04N 160 20W
Kap Bismarck *c.* Greenland 148 77 00N 18 00W
Kap Broer Ruys *c.* Greenland 148 73 30N 20 20W
Kapchagayskoye Vodokhranilishche *res.* Kazakhstan 105 M3 44 00N 78 00E
Kap Farvel *see* Nunap Isua
Kapfenberg Austria 92 C3 47 27N 15 18E
Kapingamarangi Rise Pacific Ocean 150 F8 3 00N 154 00E
Kap Morris Jesup *c.* Greenland 148 83 20N 33 00W
Kaposvár Hungary 96 B3 46 21N 17 49E
Kapsukas *see* Marijampole
Kaptai Chittagong Bangladesh 110 22 21N 92 17E
Kapukasing Ontario Canada 137 D3 49 25N 82 26W
Kara Bogaz Gol, Zaliv *b.* Turkmenistan 102 H4 42 00N 53 00E
Karabük Turkey 95 h4 41 12N 32 36E
Karaburun Turkey 94 E3 38 38N 26 30E
Karacabey Turkey 94 F4 40 14N 28 22E
Karachayevsk Russia 95 M5 43 44N 41 57E
Karāchi Pakistan 108 B4 24 51N 67 02E
Karaganda Kazakhstan 105 L4 49 53N 73 07E
Karaginskiy *i.* Russia 103 S7 58 00N 164 00E
Karahalli Turkey 94 F3 38 20N 29 33E
Karaikkudi India 109 D2 10 04N 78 46E
Karaisalı Turkey 95 J2 37 16N 35 02
Karaj Iran 107 H6 35 48N 50 58E
Karak Jordan 106 O10 31 11N 35 42E
Karakaya Baraji *l.* Turkey 95 L3 38 35N 38 25E
Karakeçi Turkey 95 K2 37 25N 39 26E
Karakoram Pass China/Jammu & Kashmir 109 D7 35 33N 77 51E
Kara Kum *geog. reg.* Turkmenistan 105 H2/J2 40 00N 60 00E
Karakumskiy Kanal *can.* Turkmenistan 105 J2 37 30N 62 30E
Karama Jordan 106 O10 31 58N 35 34E
Karaman Turkey 95 H2 37 11N 33 13E
Karanjia Orissa India 110 C2 21 52N 85 59E
Karapinar Turkey 95 H2 37 44N 33 34E
Karasburg Namibia 125 C2 28 00S 18 43E
Kara Sea Russia 103 I11/J10 75 00N 70 00E
Karasjok Norway 97 F4 69 27N 25 30E
Karaşu Turkey 94 G4 41 07N 30 35E
Karatal *r.* Kazakhstan 105 M4 45 00N 78 00E
Karatas Turkey 95 J2 36 32N 35 22E
Karatau *mts.* Kazakhstan 105 K3 43 00N 70 00E
Karatoya *r.* Bangladesh 110 G6 25 15N 8915E
Karaturgay *r.* Kazakhstan 105 J5/K5 50 00N 65 00E
Karbalāā Iraq 106 F5 32 37N 44 03E
Karcag Hungary 96 C3 47 19N 20 53E
Kárditsa Greece 94 B3 39 22N 21 55E
Kargi Turkey 95 J4 41 09N 34 32E
Kariba Dam Zambia/Zimbabwe 125 E4 16 31S 28 50E
Kariba, Lake Zambia/Zimbabwe 125 E4 17 00S 28 00E
Karibib Namibia 125 C3 21 59S 15 51E
Karimganj Bangladesh 110 K5 24 52N 92 20E
Karisimbi, Mount Rwanda/Congo (D.R.) 124 E7 1 32S 29 27E
Kariya Japan 114 J1 35 00N 137 00E
Karkai India 110 D3 22 30N 86 00E
Karkinits'ka Zatoka *g.* Ukraine 95 H6 45 50N 32 20E
Karkinitskiy Zaliv *g.* Ukraine 104 C4 46 00N 32 50E
Karlino Poland 96 B4 54 02N 15 52E
Karliova Turkey 95 M3 39 17N 41 02E
Karl-Marx Stadt *see* Chemnitz
Karlovac Croatia 92 C3 45 30N 15 34E
Karlovo Bulgaria 94 D5 42 30N 24 49E
Karlovy Vary Czech Republic 96 A4 50 13N 12 52E
Karlshorst Germany 87 G1 52 28N 13 32E
Karlskoga Sweden 97 C2 59 19N 14 33E
Karlskrona Sweden 97 D2 56 10N 15 35E
Karlsruhe Germany 93 A1 49 00N 8 24E
Karlstad Sweden 97 C2 59 24N 13 32E
Karnafuli Reservoir Bangladesh 110 K3 22 30N 92 20E
Karnal India 109 D5 29 41N 76 58E
Karnataka *admin.* India 109 D2 14 40N 75 30E
Karnobat Bulgaria 96 D2 42 39N 26 59E
Karol Bagh India 108 L4 28 39N 77 11E
Karow Germany 87 F2 52 38N 13 28E
Kárpathos Greece 94 E2 35 31N 27 13E
Kárpathos *i.* Greece 94 E2 35 30N 27 12E
Karpenísi Greece 94 B3 38 55N 21 47E
Kars Turkey 95 N4 40 35N 43 05E
Karsakpay Kazakhstan 102 I5 47 47N 66 43E
Karshi Uzbekistan 105 K2 38 53N 65 45E
Kartal Turkey 94 F4 40 54N 29 12E
Kartaly Russia 105 J5 53 06N 60 37E
Karwar India 109 C2 14 50N 74 09E
Kaş Turkey 94 F2 36 12N 29 40E
Kasai *r.* Angola/Congo (D.R.) 125 C7 4 00S 19 00E
Kasai *r.* West Bengal India 110 D4 23 20N 86 20E
Kasai Japan 114 F1 34 56N 134 50E

Klarälven r. Sweden 97 C3 60 45N 13 00E
Klatovy Czech Republic 96 A3 49 24N 13 17E
Kleine Emscher can. Germany 86 B3 51 35N 6 45E
Kleinmachnow Germany 87 E1/F1 52 24N 13 13E
Klerksdorp Rep. of South Africa 125 E2 26 52S 26 39E
Kleve Germany 93 A2 51 47N 6 11E
Kłodzko Poland 96 B4 50 28N 16 40E
Klöfta Norway 97 C3 60 04N 11 06E
Klosterneuburg Austria 92 C3 48 19N 16 20E
Kluane National Park Canada 132 H5 60 30N 139 00W
Klyazma r. Russia 104 E6 56 00N 42 00E
Klyuchevskaya Sopka mt. Russia 103 S7 56 03N 160 38E
Knapdale Argyll & Bute Scotland 60 D3 55 52N 5 31W
Knaresborough North Yorkshire England 65 D3 54 00N 1 27W
Knighton Powys England 66 D2 52 21N 3 03W
Knock Mayo Rep. of Ireland 74 C3 53 47N 8 55W
Knockadoon Head c. Cork Rep. of Ireland 75 D1 51 50N 7 50W
Knockanevin Cork Rep. of Ireland 75 C2 52 17N 8 21W
Knockboy mt. Kerry Rep. of Ireland 75 B1 51 48N 9 27W
Knockdrislagh Cork Rep. of Ireland 75 C2 52 03N 8 41W
Knockmealdown Mountains mts. Tipperary/Waterford Rep. of Ireland 75 D2 52 13N 7 57W
Knocktopher Kilkenny Rep. of Ireland 75 D2 52 29N 7 13W
Knokke-Heist Belgium 89 C3 51 21N 3 19E
Knossós hist. site Greece 94 D1 35 18N 25 10E
Knottingley West Yorkshire England 65 D2 53 43N 1 14W
Knowle West Midlands England 67 F2 52 23N 1 43W
Knox Indiana U.S.A. 136 C2 41 17N 86 37W
Knoxville Iowa U.S.A. 136 B2 41 26N 93 05W
Knoxville Tennessee U.S.A. 135 J4 36 00N 83 57W
Knutsford Cheshire England 64 C2 53 18N 2 23W
Kōbe Japan 114 G1 34 40N 135 12E
København (Copenhagen) Denmark 97 C2 55 43N 12 34E
Koblenz Germany 93 A2 50 21N 7 36E
Kobleve Ukraine 94 G7 46 40N 31 14E
Kobrin Belarus 96 C4 52 16N 24 22E
Kobuk r. Alaska U.S.A. 132 D6 67 00N 157 30W
K'obulet'i Georgia 95 M4 41 49N 41 46E
Koca r. Turkey 94 F2 36 20N 29 15E
Kocaeli (Izmit) Turkey 94 F4 40 47N 29 55E
Kočani FYROM 94 C4 41 55N 22 25E
Koch Bihār West Bengal India 110 G7 26 20N 89 29E
Kōchi Japan 114 B1 33 33N 133 32E
Kochubey Russia 104 F3 44 25N 46 33E
Kodaira Japan 115 A3 35 44N 139 28E
Kodarma Bihar India 110 C5 24 28N 85 36E
Kodiak Alaska U.S.A. 132 E4 57 49N 152 30W
Kodiak Island Alaska U.S.A. 132 E4 57 20N 153 40W
Kodok Sudan 124 F9 9 51N 32 07E
Koel r. India 110 A5 24 25N 83 50E
Koforidua Ghana 127 E4 6 01N 0 12W
Kofu Japan 114 C2 35 42N 138 34E
Koga Japan 114 L3 36 12N 139 42E
Koganei Japan 115 B3 35 42N 139 30E
Kohat Pakistan 109 C6 33 37N 71 30E
Kohima India 109 G5 25 40N 94 08E
Koh-i-Mazar mt. Afghanistan 107 K5 32 30N 66 23E
Kohoku Japan 115 B3 35 30N 139 39E
Kohtla-Järve Estonia 97 F2 59 28N 27 20E
Koira Orissa India 110 C2 21 55N 85 14E
Koito r. Japan 115 C2 35 19N 139 54E
Kokand Uzbekistan 102 J4 40 33N 70 55E
Kokand Uzbekistan 105 L3 40 33N 70 55E
Kokawa Japan 114 G1 34 16N 135 24E
Kokkola Finland 97 E3 62 45N 30 06E
Kokomo Indiana U.S.A. 136 C2 40 30N 86 09W
Kokrajhar Assam India 110 H7 26 23N 90 20E
Kokshetau Kazakhstan 105 K5 53 18N 69 25E
Koksoak r. Québec Canada 133 V4 50 00N 69 00W
Kola Peninsula Russia 102 F9 67 30N 37 30E
Kolar Gold Fields tn. India 109 D2 12 54N 78 16E
Kolding Denmark 97 B2 55 29N 9 30E
Kolebira Bihar India 110 B3 22 42N 84 42E
Kolguyev i. Russia 102 G9 69 00N 49 30E
Kolhapur India 109 C3 16 40N 74 20E
Kolín Czech Republic 96 B4 50 02N 15 11E
Köln (Cologne) Germany 93 A2 50 56N 6 57E
Koło Poland 96 B4 52 12N 18 37E
Kołobrzeg Poland 97 D1 54 10N 15 35E
Kolomyya Ukraine 104 A4 48 31N 25 00E
Kolosib Mizoram India 110 K5 24 15N 92 45E
Kolpashevo Russia 103 K7 58 21N 82 59E
Kolpino Russia 104 C6 59 44N 30 39E
Kólpos Agíou Órous g. Greece 94 C4 40 10N 24 00E
Kólpos Kassándras g. Greece 94 C4 40 10N 23 30E
Kolvereid Norway 97 C3 64 53N 11 35E
Kolwezi Congo (D.R.) 125 E5 10 45S 25 25E
Kolyma r. Russia 103 R9 66 30N 152 00E
Kolyma (Gydan) Range Russia 103 R8 63 00N 160 00E
Kolyma Lowland Russia 103 R9 69 00N 155 00E
Komae Japan 114 L2 35 38N 139 36E
Komaki Japan 114 H2 35 18N 136 54E
Komandorskiye Ostrova is. Russia 150 G13 55 00N 166 30E
Komárno Slovakia 96 B3 47 46N 18 05E
Komatsu Japan 114 C2 36 25N 136 27E
Komotiní Greece 94 D4 41 06N 25 25E
Kompong Cham Cambodia 111 D6 11 59N 105 26E
Kompong Chhnang Cambodia 111 C6 12 16N 104 39E
Kompong Som Cambodia 111 C6 10 38N 103 28E
Komsomol'sk-na-Amure Russia 103 P6 50 32N 136 59E
Konda r. Russia 105 K7 60 00N 65 00E
Kondūz Afghanistan 107 K6 36 45N 68 51E
Kong Christian X Land geog. reg. Greenland 133 CC8 75 00N 27 30W
Kongolo Congo (D.R.) 125 E6 5 20S 27 00E
Kong Oscar Fjord Greenland 133 EE7 72 30N 23 00W
Kongur Shan mt. China 105 M2 39 00N 75 10E
Königswinter Germany 89 G2 50 41N 7 11E
Konin Poland 96 B4 52 12N 18 12E
Kónitsa Greece 94 B4 40 03N 20 45E
Köniz Switzerland 92 A3 46 56N 7 25E
Konnagar India 108 K2 22 42N 88 20E
Konosha Russia 102 G8 60 58N 40 08E
Konotop Ukraine 104 C5 51 15N 33 14E
Konstanz Germany 92 A3 47 40N 9 10E
Konya Turkey 95 H2 37 51N 32 30E
Konz Germany 89 F1 49 42N 6 35E
Kootenay Lake B.C. Canada 132 L3 50 00N 117 15W
Köpenick Germany 87 G1 52 27N 13 36E
Koper Slovenia 92 B3 45 31N 13 44E
Kopeysk Russia 105 J6 55 08N 61 39E
Köprü r. Turkey 94 G2 37 15N 31 10E
Kopychintsy Ukraine 96 D3 49 10N 25 58E
Korbach Germany 93 A2 51 16N 8 53E
Korçë Albania 94 B4 40 38N 20 44E
Korčula i. Croatia 92 C2 43 00N 17 00E
Korea Bay China/North Korea 113 O6 39 00N 124 00E
Korea Strait Japan/South Korea 113 P7/Q7 33 00N 129 00E
Korenovsk Russia 95 L6 45 29N 39 28E
Korhogo Côte d'Ivoire 127 D4 9 22N 5 31W
Korinthiakós Kólpos g. Greece 94 C3 30 00N 22 00E
Kórinthos Greece 94 C2 37 56N 22 55E
Kōriyama Japan 114 D2 37 23N 140 22E
Korkuteli Turkey 94 G2 37 07N 30 11E
Korla China 112 G7 41 48N 86 10E
Kormakiti, Cape Cyprus 95 H1 35 24N 32 56E
Koro i. Fiji 150 U16 17 20S 179 25E
Koróni Greece 94 B2 36 48N 21 57E
Koro Sea Fiji 150 U16/V16 17 35S 180 00
Korosten' Ukraine 104 B5 51 00N 28 30E
Korsakov Russia 103 Q5 46 36N 142 50E
Kortemark Belgium 71 H2 51 02N 3 03E
Kortrijk (Courtrai) Belgium 89 C2 50 50N 3 17E
Koryak Range mts. Russia 103 T8 62 00N 170 00E
Kós Greece 94 E2 36 53N 27 19E
Kós i. Greece 94 E2 36 45N 27 10E
Kościan Poland 96 B4 52 05N 16 38E
Kosciusko, Mount Australia 118 H2 36 28S 148 17E
Koshigaya Japan 114 L2 35 54N 139 47E
Kosi r. Nepal 110 D7/E7 26 45N 87 00E
Košice Slovakia 96 C3 48 44N 21 15E
Kosi Reservoir Nepal 110 D8 27 00N 86 45E
Kosovska Mitrovica Serbia Yugoslavia 94 B5 42 54N 20 52E
Kostenets Bulgaria 94 C5 42 17N 23 51E
Kosti Sudan 124 F10 13 11N 32 28E
Kostinbrod Bulgaria 94 C5 42 48N 23 11E
Kostroma Russia 102 G7 57 46N 40 59E
Kostrzyn Poland 96 A4 52 35N 14 40E
Kostyantynivka Ukraine 104 D4 48 33N 37 45E
Kostyantynivka Ukraine 95 J7 46 52N 35 25E
Koszalin Poland 96 B4 54 10N 16 10E
Kota India 109 D5 25 11N 75 58E
Kota Bharu Malaysia 111 C5 6 08N 102 14E
Kota Kinabalu Malaysia 111 F5 5 59N 116 04E
Köthen Germany 93 B2 51 46N 11 59E
Kotka Finland 97 F3 60 26N 26 55E
Kotlas Russia 102 G8 61 15N 46 35E
Kōtō Japan 115 C3 35 40N 139 49E
Kotri Pakistan 108 B5 25 22N 68 18E
Kotto r. Central African Rep. 124 D9 7 00N 22 30E
Kotuy r. Russia 103 M9 67 30N 102 00E
Kotzebue Alaska U.S.A. 132 C6 66 51N 162 40W
Kotzebue Sound U.S.A. 132 C6 66 40N 162 20W
Koudougou Burkina 127 E5 12 15N 2 23W
Koulamoutou Gabon 127 H2 1 12S 12 29E
Koulikoro Mali 127 D5 12 55N 7 31W
Koumra Chad 124 C9 8 56N 17 32E
Kounradskiy Kazakhstan 105 L4 46 58N 74 59E
Kourou French Guiana 146 G14 5 08N 52 37W
Kouvola Finland 97 F3 60 54N 26 45E
Kovel' Ukraine 104 A5 51 12N 24 48E
Kovrov Russia 104 E6 56 23N 41 21E
Kovzha r. Russia 104 D7 61 00N 37 00E
Kowloon Hong Kong China 112 B1 22 19N 114 11E
Kowloon Tong H.K. China 112 C2 22 20N 114 11E
Köyceğiz Turkey 94 F2 36 57N 28 40E
Koyukuk r. Alaska U.S.A. 132 E6 66 00N 154 00W
Koyulhisar Turkey 95 K4 40 27N 37 51E
Kozan Turkey 95 J2 37 27N 35 47E
Kozáni Greece 94 B4 40 18N 21 48E
Kozlu Turkey 94 G4 41 23N 31 44E
Kozlu Turkey 95 K4 40 35N 36 27E
Kpalimé Togo 127 F4 6 55N 0 44E
Kragujevac Serbia Yugoslavia 96 C2 44 01N 20 55E
Kraków Poland 96 B4 50 03N 19 55E
Kraljevo Serbia Yugoslavia 96 C2 43 44N 20 41E
Kramators'k Ukraine 104 D4 48 43N 37 33E
Kranj Slovenia 92 B3 46 15N 14 20E
Krasnodar Russia 102 F5 45 02N 39 00E
Krasnogvardeyskoye Russia 95 M6 45 51N 41 31E
Krasnohvardiys'ke Ukraine 95 J6 45 31N 34 16E
Krasnoperekops'k Ukraine 95 H6 45 56N 33 47E
Krasnovodsk Turkmenistan 102 H4 40 01N 53 00E
Krasnoyarsk Russia 103 L7 56 05N 92 46E
Krasnoyarskoye Vodokhranilishche res. Russia 105 P5/6 55 00N 91 00E
Krasny Stroitel Russia 102 M1 55 31N 37 00E
Krasnyy Kut Russia 104 F5 50 58N 47 00E
Krasnyy Luch Ukraine 104 D4 48 10N 39 00E
Krefeld Germany 93 A2 51 20N 6 32E
Kremenchuk Ukraine 104 C4 49 03N 33 25E
Kremenchuts'ke Vodokranilishche res. Ukraine 104 C4 49 30N 32 30E
Kremenets Ukraine 96 D4 50 05N 25 48E
Krems Austria 96 B3 48 25N 15 36E
Kreuzberg Germany 87 F2 52 30N 13 24E
Kribi Cameroon 127 G3 2 56N 9 56E
Krim (Crimea) p. Ukraine 77 M5 46 00N 34 00E
Krimpen Netherlands 88 C1 51 54N 4 35E
Krishna r. India 109 D3 16 00N 79 00E
Krishnanagar West Bengal India 110 F4 23 22N 88 32E
Kristiansand Norway 97 B2 58 08N 8 01E
Kristianstad Sweden 97 C2 56 02N 14 10E
Kristiansund Norway 97 B3 63 06N 7 58E
Kríti (Crete) i. Greece 94 D2 35 00N 25 00E
Krk i. Croatia 92 B2/3 45 00N 14 00E
Kronshtadt Russia 97 F3 60 00N 29 40E
Kropotkin Russia 95 M6 45 26N 40 36E
Krosno Poland 96 C3 49 40N 21 46E
Krotoszyn Poland 96 B4 51 41N 17 27E
Kruger National Park Rep. of South Africa 125 F2/F3 24 00S 32 00E
Krugersdorp Rep. of South Africa 125 E2 26 06S 27 46E
Krujë Albania 94 A4 41 31N 19 35E
Krung Thep see Bangkok
Kruševac Serbia Yugoslavia 96 C2 43 34N 21 20E
Krušnéhory see Erzbebirge
Krym' (Crimea) p. Ukraine 95 H6/J6 46 00N 34 00E
Krymsk Russia 95 K6 44 56N 38 00E
Kryvy Rih (Krivoy Rog) Ukraine 77 M5 47 55N 33 24E
Ksar El Boukhari Algeria 127 F10 35 55N 2 47E
Ksar-el-Kebir Morocco 90 A1 35 04N 5 56W
Kuala Lumpur Malaysia 111 C4 3 09N 101 42E
Kuala Terengganu Malaysia 111 C5 5 20N 103 09E
Kuantan Malaysia 111 C4 3 48N 103 19E
Kuban' r. Russia 95 K6 45 05N 38 00E
Kubiri Japan 115 B1 35 13N 139 42E
Kuchinda Orissa India 110 B2 21 45N 84 42E
Kuching Malaysia 111 F4 1 35N 110 21E
Kuçovë Albania 94 A4 40 49N 19 56E
Kudat Malaysia 111 F5 6 54N 116 50E
Kufstein Austria 92 B3 47 36N 12 11E
Kugluktuk (Coppermine) Canada 132 L6 67 49N 115 12W
Kuhmo Finland 97 F3 64 04N 29 30E
Kuito Angola 125 C5 12 25S 16 56E
Kujūkuri-hama beach Japan 114 M2 35 30N 140 30E
Kujū-san mt. Japan 114 B1 33 07N 131 14E
Kukës Albania 94 B5 42 05N 20 24E
Kuki Japan 114 L3 36 03N 139 41E
Kula Turkey 94 F3 38 33N 28 40E
Kulaura Chittagong Bangladesh 110 K5 24 32N 92 02E
Kuldiga Latvia 97 E2 56 58N 21 58E
Kulmbach Germany 93 B2 50 06N 11 28E
Kulpi West Bengal India 110 F3 22 04N 88 14E
Kulti West Bengal India 110 D4 23 45N 86 50E
Kulu Turkey 95 H3 39 06N 33 02E
Kulundinskaya Step' geog. reg. Kazakhstan/Russia 105 M5/N5 52 00N 80 00E
Kuma r. Russia 102 G4 45 00N 45 00E
Kumagaya Japan 114 L3 36 09N 139 22E
Kumamoto Japan 114 B1 32 50N 130 42E
Kumanovo FYROM 94 B5 42 07N 21 40E
Kumasi Ghana 127 E4 6 45N 1 35W
Kumba Cameroon 127 G3 4 39N 9 26E
Kumbakonam India 109 D2 10 59N 79 24E
Kumluca Turkey 94 G2 36 23N 30 17E
Kumukahi, Cape Hawaiian Is. 151 Z17 19 30N 154 50W
Kumul see Hami
Kunar r. Asia 107 L5 35 30N 71 20E
Kunashir i. Russia 114 E3 44 30N 146 20E
Kungrad Uzbekistan 105 H3 43 06N 58 54E
Kunlun Shan mts. China 112 F6/G6 36 30N 85 00E
Kunming China 113 K4 25 04N 102 41E
Kunsan South Korea 113 P6 35 57N 126 42E
Kunti, River India 108 K3 22 55N 88 20E
Kuntsevo Russia 102 L1 55 43N 37 25E
Kununurra Australia 118 D6 15 42S 128 50E
Kuolayarvi Russia 97 F4 67 07N 28 50E
Kuopio Finland 97 F3 62 54N 27 40E
Kupa r. Croatia 92 C3 45 30N 15 00E
Kupang Indonesia 111 G1 10 13S 123 38E
Kupferdreh Germany 86 C2 51 24N 7 06E
Kür r. Azerbaijan 95 P4 41 10N 45 40E
Kura r. Azerbaijan 104 E3 42 00N 47 30E
Kurashiki Japan 114 B1 34 36N 133 43E
Kurchum r. Kazakhstan 105 N4 49 00N 85 00E
Kŭrdzhali Bulgaria 94 D4 41 38N 25 21E
Kure Japan 114 B1 34 14N 132 32E
Kuressaare (Kingissepp) Estonia 97 E2 59 22N 28 40E
Kureyka r. Russia 103 L9 67 30N 91 00E
Kurgan Russia 102 I7 55 30N 65 20E
Kuria Muria Islands Oman 107 I2 17 30N 56 00E
Kurigram Rajshahi Bangladesh 110 G6 25 49N 89 39E
Kurihama Japan 115 B1 35 12N 139 41E
Kurikka Finland 97 E3 62 36N 22 25E
Kuril Islands Russia 103 R5/R6 50 00N 155 00E
Kuril Ridge Pacific Ocean 150 F12 47 50N 152 00E
Kuril Trench Pacific Ocean 150 F12 45 40N 154 00E
Ku-ring-gai Chase National Park Australia 119 G3 33 40S 151 00E
Kurnell Australia 119 G1 34 01S 151 12E
Kurnool India 109 D3 15 51N 78 01E
Kurseong West Bengal India 110 F7 26 54N 88 21E
Kursk Russia 102 F6 51 45N 36 14E
Kurskiy Zaliv g. Russia 96 C5 55 00N 21 00E
Kurşunlu Turkey 95 H4 40 49N 33 17E
Kurtalan Turkey 95 K4 37 58N 41 36E
Kurtun Turkey 95 L4 40 40N 39 06E
Kuru Bihar India 110 B4 23 30N 84 49E
Kurucaşile Turkey 95 H4 41 50N 32 42E
Kuruçay r. Turkey/Georgia 95 N4 41 15N 43 00E
Kurume Japan 114 B1 33 20N 130 29E
Kuşadasi Turkey 94 E2 37 52N 27 15E
Kusatsu Japan 114 G2 35 02N 135 59E
Kushchevskaya Russia 95 L7 46 34N 39 39E
Kushida-gawa r. Japan 114 H1 34 23N 136 15E
Kushiro Japan 114 D3 42 58N 144 24E
Kushka Turkmenistan 107 J6 35 14N 62 15E
Kushtia Khulna Bangladesh 110 G4 23 54N 89 07E
Kushva Russia 105 H6 58 20N 59 48E
Kuskokwim r. Alaska U.S.A. 132 C5 61 30N 160 45W
Kuskokwim Bay Alaska U.S.A. 132 C4 58 50N 164 00W
Kuskokwim Mountains U.S.A. 132 D5 62 00N 158 00W
Kustanay Kazakhstan 105 J5 53 15N 63 40E
Kütahya Turkey 94 F3 39 25N 29 56E
K'ut'aisi Georgia 95 N5 42 15N 42 44E
Kutno Poland 96 B4 52 13N 19 20E
Kutubdia Island Bangladesh 110 J2 21 50N 91 52E
Kuujjuaq Québec Canada 133 V4 58 25N 68 55W
Kuujjuarapik Québec Canada 133 T4 55 15N 77 41W
Kuusamo Finland 97 F4 65 57N 29 15E
Kuvango Angola 125 C5 14 27S 16 20E
KUWAIT 107 G4
Kuwana Japan 114 H2 35 04N 136 40E
Kuybyshev Forest Russia 102 M2 55 50N 37 45E
Kuytun China 112 F7 44 30N 85 00E
Kuyucuk Turkey 94 F2 37 53N 28 30E
Kuzbass geog. reg. Russia 105 O5/6 55 00N 87 00E
Kuz'minki Russia 102 M1/N1 55 41N 37 45E
Kwai Chung Hong Kong China 112 B2 22 22N 114 07E
Kwangju South Korea 113 P6 35 07N 126 52E
Kwango (Cuango) r. Congo (D.R.)/Angola 125 C6 6 00S 17 00E
Kwekwe (Que Que) Zimbabwe 125 E4 18 55S 29 49E
Kwethluk Alaska U.S.A. 132 C5 60 46N 161 34W
Kwigillingok Alaska U.S.A. 132 C4 59 50N 163 10W
Kwilu r. Congo (D.R.) 125 C6 6 00S 19 00E
Kwun Tong Hong Kong China 112 C1 22 18N 114 13E
Kwu Tung Hong Kong China 112 B3 22 30N 114 06E
Kyauktaw Myanmar 110 L1 20 48N 93 00E
Kyklades (Cyclades) is. Greece 106 B6 37 00N 25 00E
Kyleakin Highland Scotland 58 D2 57 16N 5 44W
Kyle of Durness Highland Scotland 59 E3 58 31N 4 50W
Kyle of Lochalsh Highland Scotland 58 D2 57 17N 5 43W
Kyle of Tongue b. Highland Scotland 59 E3 58 40N 4 25W
Kyles of Bute sd. Argyll & Bute Scotland 60 D3 55 52N 5 13W
Kylestrome Highland Scotland 59 D3 58 16N 5 02W
Kyllíni mt. Greece 94 C2 37 56N 22 24E
Kými Greece 94 D3 38 38N 24 06E
Kyoga, Lake Uganda 124 F8 2 00N 34 00E
Kyoga-misaki c. Japan 114 C2 35 48N 135 12E
Kyōto Japan 114 G2 35 02N 135 45E
Kyōto pref. Japan 114 G2 35 00N 135 30E
Kyparissiakós Kólpos g. Greece 94 B2 37 00N 21 00E
Kyrenia Cyprus 95 H1 35 20N 33 20E
Kyronjöki r. Finland 97 E3 63 00N 21 30E
Kýthira i. Greece 94 C2 36 00N 23 00E
Kýthnos i. Greece 94 D2 37 25N 24 25E
Kyūshū i. Japan 114 B1 32 20N 131 00E
Kyūshū-Palau Ridge Pacific Ocean 150 D9/D10 15 00N 135 00E
Kyustendil Bulgaria 96 C2 42 26N 22 40E
Kyyiv (Kiev) Ukraine 104 C5 50 25N 30 30E
Kyzyl Russia 103 L6 51 45N 94 28E
Kyzyl Kum d. Asia 105 I3/K3 43 00N 65 00E
Kzyl-Orda Kazakhstan 105 K3 44 25N 65 28E

L

Laascaanood Somalia 124 I9 8 35N 46 55E
La Asunción Venezuela 141 L2 11 06N 63 53W
Laayoune (El Aaiún) Western Sahara 127 C8 27 10N 13 11W
Laba r. Russia 95 M6 44 55N 40 30 E
la Baule-Escoublac France 91 B2 47 18N 2 22W
Labé Guinea 127 C5 11 17N 12 11W
Labe (Elbe) r. Europe 93 B2 50 20N 14 10E
Labinsk Russia 95 M6 44 39N 40 44E
Labrador geog. reg. Canada 133 W3 54 00N 63 00W
Labrador Basin Atlantic Ocean 152 B12/C12 58 00N 50 00W
Labrador City Canada 133 V3 52 54N 66 50W
Labrador Sea Canada/Greenland 133 X4 59 00N 56 00W
La Brea Trinidad and Tobago 141 S9 10 14N 61 37W
Lábrea Brazil 146 E11 7 20S 64 46W
Labytnangi Russia 103 I9 66 43N 66 28E
Lac Alaotra l. Madagascar 125 I4 17 30S 54 00E
Lac à l'Eau Claire l. Canada 133 U4 56 20N 74 30W
La Canada California U.S.A. 139 B3 34 12N 118 12W
Lac Bienville l. Québec Canada 133 U4 55 30N 73 00W
Lac de la Fôret d'Orient l. France 91 C2 48 15N 4 20E
Lac de Neuchâtel l. Switzerland 91 D2 46 45N 6 40E
Lac du Bonnet tn. Canada 136 A4 50 16N 96 03W
Lac du Der-Chantecoq l. France 91 C2 48 35N 4 45E
La Ceiba Honduras 141 G3 15 45N 86 45W
Lac Fitri l. Chad 124 C10 13 00N 17 30E
la Chaux-de-Fonds Switzerland 92 A3 47 07N 6 51E
Lachlan r. Australia 118 G3 34 00S 145 00E
Lachute Québec Canada 137 F3 45 39N 74 21W
la Ciotat France 91 D1 43 10N 5 36E
Lac Joseph l. Canada 133 V3 52 30N 65 15W
Lackawanna New York U.S.A. 137 E2 42 49N 78 49W
Lac la Martre see Wha Ti
Lac la Ronge l. Canada 132 N4 55 10N 105 00W
Lac Léman (Lake Geneva) Switzerland 92 A3 46 20N 6 20E
Lac Mai-Ndombe l. Congo (D.R.) 124 C7 2 00S 18 20E
Lac Manouané l. Canada 137 F4 51 00N 71 00W
Lac Mattagami l. Canada 137 E3 47 54N 81 35W
Lac Minto l. Canada 133 T4 57 35N 75 00W
Lac Mistassini l. Canada 133 U3 51 00N 73 20W
Lac Moero see Mweru, Lake
Lacolle Québec Canada 137 F3 45 04N 73 22W
La Coruña (Corunna) Spain 90 A3 43 22N 8 24W
Lac Payne l. Québec Canada 133 U4 59 25N 74 00W
La Cresenta California U.S.A. 139 B3 34 13N 118 14W
La Crosse Wisconsin U.S.A. 136 B2 43 48N 91 04W
Lac Saint-Jean l. Canada 133 L6 48 35N 72 00W
Lac St.-Jean l. Québec Canada 137 F3 48 00N 72 00W
Lac St. Joseph Ontario Canada 134 H7 51 30N 91 40W
Lac Seul l. Ontario Canada 133 Q3 50 20N 92 00W
Lacul Razim lagoon Romania 94 F6 44 50N 29 00E
Lacul Sinoie lagoon Romania 94 F6 44 35N 28 50E
Ladakh Range mts. Jammu & Kashmir 109 D6 34 30N 78 30E
la Défense France 87 A2 48 53N 2 14E
Ladoga, Lake see Ladozhskoye Ozero
Ladozhskoye Ozero (Lake Ladoga) l. Russia 102 F8 61 00N 30 00E
Ladybank Fife Scotland 59 F1 56 17N 3 08W
Ladybower Reservoir Derbyshire England 67 F3 53 23N 1 42W
Ladysmith B.C. Canada 132 K2 48 57N 123 50W
Ladysmith Rep. of South Africa 125 E2 28 34S 29 47E
Ladysmith Wisconsin U.S.A. 136 B3 45 27N 91 07W
Laedalsøyri Norway 97 B3 61 05N 7 15E
La Esmeralda Venezuela 146 D13 3 11N 65 33W
Lafayette Indiana U.S.A. 136 C2 40 25N 86 54W
Lafayette Louisiana U.S.A. 135 H3 30 12N 92 18W
La Fé Cuba 141 H4 22 02N 84 15W
la Flèche France 91 B2 47 42N 0 04W
Lagan r. Northern Ireland 60 C2 54 30N 6 05W
Lågen r. Norway 97 B3 61 40N 9 45E
Laggan Bay Argyll & Bute Scotland 60 C3 55 38N 6 17W
Laghouat Algeria 127 F9 33 49N 2 55E
Lagoa Brazil 147 Q2 22 58S 43 13W
Lago Argentino l. Argentina 147 C2 50 10S 72 30W
Lago da Tijuca l. Brazil 147 P2 22 59S 43 22W
Lago de Chapala l. Mexico 140 D4 20 05N 103 00W
Lago de Maracaibo l. Venezuela 146 C14 9 50N 71 30W
Lago de Marapendi l. Brazil 147 Q2 23 00S 43 20W
Lago de Nicaragua l. Nicaragua 141 G2 11 50N 86 00W
Lago de Piratininga l. Brazil 147 Q2 22 57S 43 05W
Lago de Poopó l. Bolivia 146 D9 18 30S 67 20W
Lago di Bolsena l. Italy 92 B2 42 00N 12 00E
Lago di Como l. Italy 92 A3 46 00N 9 00E
Lago di Garda l. Italy 92 B3 45 00N 10 00E
Lago d'Iseo l. Italy 92 A3 46 00N 10 00E
Lago do Jacarepaguá l. Brazil 147 P2 22 58S 43 23W
Lago Maggiore l. Italy 92 A3 46 00N 8 00E
Lago Rodrigo de Freitas l. Brazil 147 Q2 22 58S 43 13W
Lágos Greece 94 D4 41 00N 25 07E
Lagos Nigeria 127 F4 6 27N 3 20E
Lagos Portugal 90 A2 37 05N 8 40W
Lago Titicaca l. Peru/Bolivia 146 C9/D9 16 00S 69 30W
Lago Trasimeno l. Italy 92 B2 43 00N 12 02E
La Grande Oregon U.S.A. 134 C6 45 21N 118 05W
La Grande 2, Réservoir Canada 133 T3 54 00N 77 00W
La Grande 3, Réservoir Canada 133 U3 54 10N 72 30W
La Grande Rivière r. Canada 133 U3 54 00N 74 00W
La Grange Georgia U.S.A. 135 I3 33 02N 85 02W
La Guaira Venezuela 146 D15 10 38N 66 55W
Laguna Brazil 147 H7 28 29S 48 45W
Laguna Caratasca l. Honduras 141 H3 15 05N 84 00W
Laguna de Perlas l. Nicaragua 141 H2 12 30N 83 30W
Laguna Madre l. Mexico 140 E4 25 00N 98 00W
Laguna Mar Chiquita l. Argentina 147 E6 30 30S 62 30W
Lagunillas Venezuela 146 C15 10 07N 71 16W
La Habana (Havana) Cuba 141 H4 23 07N 82 25W
La Habra California U.S.A. 139 C2 33 56N 117 59W
Lahaina Hawaiian Islands 151 Y18 20 23N 156 40W
la Haye-du-Puits France 73 F2 49 17N 1 33W
Lahn r. Germany 93 A2 50 00N 8 00E
Lahore Pakistan 109 C6 31 34N 74 22E
Lahr Germany 93 A1 48 21N 7 52E
Lahti Finland 97 F3 61 00N 25 40E
Lai Chi Chong H.K. China 112 C2 22 27N 114 17E
Lai Chi Wo Hong Kong China 112 C3 22 32N 114 15E
Laine r. France 71 F1 50 43N 1 52E
Lairg Highland Scotland 59 E3 58 01N 4 25W
Lajes Brazil 147 G7 27 48S 50 20W
Lajpat Nagar India 108 M4 28 34N 77 15E
La Junta Colorado U.S.A. 134 F4 37 59N 103 34W
Lake Charles tn. U.S.A. 135 H3 30 13N 93 13W
Lake City Michigan U.S.A. 136 C2 44 22N 85 12W
Lake District National Park Cumbria England 64 B3/C3 54 30N 3 15W
Lake Harbour see Kimminit
Lakeland Florida U.S.A. 135 J2 28 02N 81 59W
Lakemba i. Fiji 150 V15 18 10S 178 49W
Lakemba Passage sd. Fiji 150 V15/16 18 10S 179 00W
Lakenheath Suffolk England 70 E3 52 25N 0 31E
Lakeport California U.S.A. 134 B4 39 04N 122 56W
Lake River tn. Ontario Canada 133 S3 54 30N 82 30W
Lakeview Oregon U.S.A. 134 B5 42 13N 120 21W
Lake Vrynwy see Llyn Efyrnwy
Lakewood California U.S.A. 139 B2 33 49N 118 08W
Lakewood Ohio U.S.A. 137 D2 41 29N 81 50W
Lakhisarai Bihar India 110 D6 25 12N 86 06E
Lakonikós Kólpos g. Greece 94 C2 36 30N 22 45E
Lakota North Dakota U.S.A. 136 A3 48 02N 98 20W
Laksefjord fj. Norway 97 F5 70 40N 26 30E
Lakselv Norway 97 E5 70 03N 24 55E
Lakshadweep admin. India 109 C1 9 30N 73 00E
Laksham Bangladesh 110 J4 23 15N 91 08E
Lakshimpur Bangladesh 110 H3 22 57N 90 50E
La Línea de la Concepción Spain 90 A2 36 10N 5 21W
Lalitpur India 109 D4 24 42N 78 24E
Lalmanir Hat Bangladesh 110 G6 25 51N 89 34E
la Louvière Belgium 89 D2 50 29N 4 12E
Lalpur Rajshahi Bangladesh 110 F5 24 12N 89 00E
Lama Chittagong Bangladesh 110 K2 21 46N 92 12E
La Maddalena Italy 92 A2 41 13N 9 25E
La Mancha admin. Spain 90 B2 39 10N 2 45W
La Manche see English Channel
Lamar Colorado U.S.A. 134 F4 38 04N 102 37W
Lamas Turkey 95 H2/J2 36 50N 34 20E
Lambasa Fiji 150 U16 16 25S 179 24E
Lambay Island Dublin Rep. of Ireland 74 E3 53 29N 6 01W
Lambaréné Gabon 127 H2 0 41S 10 13E
Lambert Glacier Antarctica 149 73 00S 70 00E
Lambourn Berkshire England 70 C2 51 31N 1 31W
Lambourn r. Berkshire England 70 C2 51 27N 1 28W
Lamego Portugal 90 A3 41 05N 7 49W

Mbuji-Mayi Congo (D.R.) **125** D6 6 10S 23 39E
Mead, Lake U.S.A. **134** D4 36 10N 114 25W
Meadville Pennsylvania U.S.A. **137** D2 41 38N 80 10W
Meaford Ontario Canada **137** D2 44 36N 80 35W
Meath *co.* Rep. of Ireland **74** E3 35 35N 6 30W
Meaux France **91** C2 48 58N 2 54E
Mecca *see* Makkah
Mechelen *(Malines)* Belgium **89** D3 51 02N 4 29E
Mecheria Algeria **127** E9 33 31N 0 20W
Mechernich Germany **89** F2 50 35N 6 39E
Mecklenburg Bay Europe **93** B2 54 00N 12 00E
Mecklenburg-Vorpommern *admin.* Germany **93** B2 53 30N 12 30E
Medan Indonesia **111** B4 3 35N 98 39E
Médéa Algeria **127** F10 36 15N 2 48E
Medellín Colombia **146** B14 6 15N 75 36W
Medemblik Netherlands **89** E4 52 47N 5 06E
Medenine Tunisia **127** H9 33 24N 10 25E
Medford Oregon U.S.A. **134** B5 42 20N 122 52W
Medgidia Romania **94** F6 44 15N 28 16E
Medias Romania **96** C3 46 10N 24 21E
Medicine Hat Alberta Canada **132** M3 50 03N 110 41W
Medina del Campo Spain **90** B3 41 18N 4 55W
Medinipur West Bengal India **110** E3 22 25N 87 24E
Mediterranean Sea Africa/Europe **76/77** E3/M2 35 00N 15 00E
Medvedkovo Russia **102** M2 55 55N 37 08E
Medvezh'yegorsk Russia **102** F8 62 56N 34 28E
Medway *r.* Kent England **71** E2 51 24N 0 40E
Meekatharra Australia **118** B4 26 30S 118 30E
Meerut India **109** D5 29 00N 77 42E
Mēga Ethiopia **124** G8 4 02N 38 19E
Mégantic Québec Canada **137** F3 46 10N 71 40W
Mégara Greece **94** C3 38 00N 23 20E
Megget Resevoir *res.* Scottish Borders Scotland **61** F3 55 27N 3 15W
Meghalaya *admin.* India **109** G5 25 30N 91 00E
Meguro Japan **115** B3 35 36N 139 43E
Meherpur Khulna Bangladesh **110** F4 23 47N 88 40E
Meig *r.* Highland Scotland **59** E2 57 35N 4 50W
Meiningen Germany **93** B2 50 34N 10 25E
Meissen Germany **93** B2 51 10N 13 28E
Mei Xian China **113** N3 24 19N 116 13E
Mejerda *r.* Tunisia **92** A1 36 30N 9 00E
Mek'ele Ethiopia **124** G10 13 32N 39 33E
Meknès Morocco **127** D9 33 53N 5 37W
Mekong *(Lancang Jiang, Mae Nam Khong) r.* Asia **111** D7 16 00N 105 00E
Mekong, Mouths of the *est.* Vietnam **111** D5 9 30N 106 45E
Melaka Malaysia **111** C4 2 11N 102 14E
Melanesia *geog. reg.* Pacific Ocean **150** F7 0 00 150 00E
Melbourn Cambridgeshire England **70** E3 52 05N 0 01E
Melbourne Australia **118** H2 37 45S 144 58E
Melbourne Derbyshire England **67** F2 52 49N 1 25W
Melbourne Florida U.S.A. **135** J2 28 04N 80 38W
Melfort Saskatchewan Canada **132** O3 52 52N 104 38W
Melilla *territory* Spain **90** B2 35 17N 2 57W
Melitopol' Ukraine **104** D4 46 51N 35 22E
Melksham Wiltshire England **70** B2 51 23N 2 09W
Mellégue *r.* Tunisia **92** A1 36 00N 8 00E
Melo Uruguay **147** G6 32 22S 54 10W
Melrose Scottish Borders Scotland **61** G3 55 36N 2 44W
Meltham West Yorkshire England **64** D2 53 36N 1 52W
Melton Mowbray Leicestershire England **67** G2 52 46N 0 53W
Melun France **91** C2 48 32N 2 40E
Melun-Senart *admin.* France **87** C1 48 35N 20 35E
Melvich Highland Scotland **59** F3 58 33N 3 55W
Melville Saskatchewan Canada **133** O3 50 57N 102 49W
Melville Bugt *see* Qimusseriarsuaq
Melville, Cape Australia **118** G7 14 08S 144 31E
Melville Hills N.W.T. Canada **132** K6 69 00N 121 00W
Melville Island Australia **118** E7 11 30S 131 00E
Melville Island N.W.T. Canada **132** M8 75 30N 112 00W
Melville, Lake Canada **133** X3 53 45N 59 00W
Melville Peninsula N.W.T. Canada **133** S6 68 00N 84 00W
Memari West Bengal India **110** F4 23 10N 88 07E
Memmingen Germany **93** B1 47 59N 10 11E
Memphis *hist. site* Egypt **106** D4 29 52N 31 12E
Memphis Tennessee U.S.A. **135** I4 35 10N 90 00W
Menai Australia **119** G1 34 01S 151 01E
Menai Bridge *tn.* Isle of Anglesey Wales **66** C3 53 14N 4 10W
Menai Strait Wales **66** C3 53 14N 4 10W
Mende France **91** C1 44 32N 3 30E
Mendebo Mountains Ethiopia **124** G9/H9 7 00N 40 00E
Menderes *r.* Turkey **106** C6 37 50N 28 10E
Mendi Papua New Guinea **118** G8 6 13S 143 39E
Mendip Hills Somerset England **73** E4 51 18N 2 45W
Mendocino Seascarp Pacific Ocean **151** L12 41 00N 145 00W
Mendota Illinois U.S.A. **136** C2 41 33N 89 09W
Mendoza Argentina **147** D6 32 48S 68 52W
Menen Belgium **89** C2 50 48N 3 07E
Mengdingjie China **113** J3 23 03N 99 03E
Menominee Michigan U.S.A. **136** C3 45 07N 87 37W
Menongue Angola **125** C5 14 36S 17 48E
Menorca *(Minorca) i.* Balearic Is. **90** F4/F4 39 45N 4 15E
Menteith, Lake of Stirling Scotland **59** E1 56 10N 4 18W
Menton France **91** D1 43 47N 7 30E
Mentor Ohio U.S.A. **135** J5 41 42N 81 22W
Meon *r.* Hampshire England **70** C2 51 00N 1 10W
Meoqui Mexico **134** E2 28 18N 105 30W
Meppel Netherlands **89** F4 52 42N 6 12E
Meppen Germany **93** A2 52 41N 7 18E
Mera Japan **114** L1 34 56N 139 50E
Merah *see* Song-koi
Merano Italy **92** B3 46 41N 11 10E
Merauke Indonesia **118** G8 8 30S 140 22E
Merced California U.S.A. **134** B4 37 17N 120 29W
Mercedes Argentina **147** D6 33 41S 65 28W
Mercedes Uruguay **147** F6 34 15S 58 02W
Mere Wiltshire England **70** B2 51 06N 2 16W
Meredith, Cape Falkland Is. **152** L15 52 15S 60 40W
Mergui Myanmar **111** B6 12 26N 98 34E
Mergui Archipelago Myanmar **111** B6 11 00N 97 40E
Mérida Mexico **140** G4 20 59N 89 39W
Mérida Spain **90** A2 38 55N 6 20W
Mérida Venezuela **146** C14 8 24N 71 08W
Meriden Connecticut U.S.A. **137** F2 41 32N 72 48W
Meridian Mississippi U.S.A. **135** I3 32 21N 88 42W
Mérignac France **91** B1 44 50N 0 36W
Merowe Sudan **124** F11 18 30N 31 49E
Merrick *mt.* Dumfries & Galloway Scotland **61** E3 55 08N 4 29W
Merrill Wisconsin U.S.A. **136** C3 45 12N 89 43W
Merriott Somerset England **73** E3 50 55N 2 49W
Merritt B.C. Canada **132** K3 50 09N 120 49W
Merrylands Australia **119** F2/G2 33 50S 150 59E
Mersea Island *i.* Essex England **71** E2 51 46N 0 57E
Merseburg Germany **93** B2 51 22N 12 00E
Mersey *r.* North West England **64** C2 53 20N 2 53W
Merseyside *co.* England **64** C2 53 30N 3 20W
Mersin *see* Icel
Merthyr Tydfil Morthyr Tydfil Wales **66** D1 51 46N 3 23W
Merthyr Tydfil *u.a.* Wales **66** D1 51 48N 3 20W
Merton *bor.* Greater London England **70** D2 51 25N 0 12W
Mertz Glacier Antarctica **149** 68 00S 145 00E
Merwede-kanaal *can.* Netherlands **89** E1 51 50N 5 03E
Merzifon Turkey **95** J4 40 52N 35 28E
Merzig Germany **93** A1 49 26N 6 39E
Mesa Arizona U.S.A. **134** D3 33 25N 115 50W
Mesolóngi Greece **94** B3 38 21N 21 26E
Mesopotamia *geog. reg.* Middle East **106** F5/F6 35 00N 42 00E
Messina Italy **92** C1 38 13N 15 33E
Messina Rep. of South Africa **125** E3 22 23S 30 00E
Messiniakós Kólpos *g.* Greece **94** C2 36 40N 22 05E
Mesudiye Turkey **95** K4 40 28N 37 45E
Meta Icognita Peninsula Canada **133** U5 63 30N 70 00W
Metheringham Lincolnshire England **65** E2 53 08N 0 25W
Methil Fife Scotland **59** F1 56 12N 3 01W
Metković Bosnia-Herzgovina **92** C2 43 02N 17 39E
Mettmann Germany **86** B2 51 15N 6 58E
Metz France **91** D2 49 07N 6 11E
Meu *r.* France **91** B2 48 05N 2 07W
Meudon France **87** A2 48 48N 2 15E
Meurthe-Moselle *admin.* France **89** E1 49 15N 5 50E
Meuse *r.* Belgium/France **89** E2 50 03N 4 40E
Meuse *admin.* France **89** E1 49 15N 5 30E
Mevagissey Cornwall England **72** C3 50 16N 4 48W
Mew Island North Down Northern Ireland **60** D2 54 41N 5 31W
Mexborough South Yorkshire England **65** D2 53 30N 1 17W
Mexicali Mexico **140** A6 32 36N 115 30W
MEXICO 140 D4 19 31N 99 09W
Mexico *admin.* Mexico **140** P2 19 31N 99 09W
México City Mexico **140** E3 19 25N 99 10W
Mexico, Gulf of Mexico **140/141** F4/G4 25 00N 90 00W
Meymaneh Afghanistan **107** J6 35 55N 64 47E
Mezada *(Masada) hist. site* Israel **106** O10 31 17N 35 20E
Mezen' Russia **102** G9 65 50N 44 20E
Mezhdurechensk Russia **105** O5 53 43N 88 11E
Mezraa Turkey **95** J4 41 13N 35 07E
Miami Florida U.S.A. **135** J2 25 45N 80 15W
Miami Oklahoma U.S.A. **136** B1 36 53N 94 54W
Mīāneh Iran **107** G6 37 23N 47 45E
Mianwali Pakistan **109** C6 32 32N 71 33E
Miass Russia **102** I6 55 00N 60 08E
Michigan *state* U.S.A. **136/137** C3/D2 45 00N 85 00W
Michigan City Indiana U.S.A. **136** C2 41 43N 86 54W
Michigan, Lake Canada/U.S.A. **136** C2 45 00N 87 00W
Michipicoten Ontario Canada **133** S2 47 57N 84 55W
Michipicoten Island Canada **136** C3 48 00N 86 00W
Michurin Bulgaria **94** E5 42 09N 27 51E
Michurinsk Russia **104** E5 52 54N 40 30E
Mickle Fell *mt.* Durham England **64** C3 54 38N 2 18W
Micronesia *geog. reg.* Pacific Ocean **150** G8 10 00N 160 00E
Mid-Atlantic Ridge Atlantic Ocean **152** D8/F11
Middelburg Netherlands **89** C3 51 30N 3 36E
Middle America Trench Pacific Ocean **151** P9/Q9 16 30N 99 00W
Middle Andaman *i.* Andaman Islands **109** G2 12 30N 93 00E
Middleburg Rep. of South Africa **125** E2 31 28S 25 01E
Middlebury Vermont U.S.A. **137** F2 44 02N 73 11W
Middle Harbour Australia **119** G2 33 48S 151 14E
Middle Loup *r.* Nebraska U.S.A. **134** F5 42 00N 101 00W
Middlesbrough *u.a.* England **65** D3 54 33N 1 04W
Middlesbrough Middlesbrough England **65** D3 54 35N 1 14W
Middlesex County *admin.* New Jersey U.S.A. **138** A1
Middleton Greater Manchester England **64** C2 53 33N 2 12W
Middleton-in-Teesdale Durham England **64** C3 54 38N 2 04W
Middleton-on-the-Wolds East Riding of Yorkshire England **65** E2 53 56N 0 33W
Middletown Connecticut U.S.A. **137** F2 41 34N 72 39W
Middletown New York U.S.A. **137** F2 41 26N 74 26W
Middletown Ohio U.S.A. **137** D1 39 31N 84 13W
Middlewich Cheshire England **64** C2 53 11N 2 27W
Midhurst West Sussex England **70** D1 50 59N 0 45W
Midland Ontario Canada **137** E2 44 45N 79 53W
Midland Michigan U.S.A. **137** D2 43 38N 84 14W
Midland Texas U.S.A. **134** F3 32 00N 102 09W
Midland Beach New York U.S.A. **138** B1 40 34N 74 07W
Midleton Cork Rep. of Ireland **75** C1 51 55N 8 10W
Midlothian *u.a.* Scotland **61** F3 55 50N 3 05W
Midori Japan **115** B3 35 33N 139 39E
Midouze *r.* France **91** B1 44 00N 0 45E
Mid-Pacific Mountains Pacific Ocean **150** F10/H10 21 00N 160 00E
Midsomer Norton Bath and North East Somerset England **70** B2 51 17N 2 30W
Midway Islands Pacific Ocean **150** I10 28 15N 177 25W
Midyat Turkey **95** M2 37 25N 41 20E
Mie *pref.* Japan **114** H1 34 35N 136 20E
Międzyrzecz Poland **96** B4 52 27N 15 34E
Miercurea-Ciuc Romania **96** D3 46 21N 25 48E
Mieres Spain **90** A3 43 15N 5 46W
Mijares *r.* Spain **90** B3 40 03N 0 30W
Mijdrecht Netherlands **88** D2 52 12N 4 52E
Mikhaylovgrad *see* Montana
Miki Japan **114** F1 34 50N 134 59E
Mikiwa-wan *b.* Japan **114** J1 34 42N 137 10E
Mikkeli Finland **97** F3 61 44N 27 15E
Milagro Ecuador **146** B12 2 11S 79 36W
Milan *see* Milano
Milano *(Milan)* Italy **92** A3 45 28N 9 12E
Milas Turkey **94** E2 37 19N 27 48E
Milborne Port Somerset England **73** E3 50 58N 2 29W
Mildenhall Suffolk England **71** E3 52 21N 0 30E
Mildura Australia **118** G3 34 14S 142 13E
Miles City Montana U.S.A. **134** E6 46 24N 105 48W
Milestone Tipperary Rep. of Ireland **75** C2 52 40N 8 05W
Milet *hist. site* Turkey **94** E2 37 31N 27 17E
Milford Donegal Rep. of Ireland **74** D5 55 07N 7 43W
Milford Pennsylvania U.S.A. **137** F2 41 19N 74 48W
Milford Utah U.S.A. **134** D4 38 22N 113 00W
Milford Haven Pembrokeshire Wales **66** B1 51 44N 5 02W
Milford Sound *tn.* N.Z. **119** A2 44 36S 167 49E
Miliana Algeria **90** C2 36 20N 2 15E
Milk *r.* Canada/U.S.A. **134** D6 49 00N 112 00W
Millau France **91** C1 44 06N 3 05E
Millbank South Dakota U.S.A. **136** A3 45 14N 96 38W
Mille Lacs *l.* Minnesota U.S.A. **136** B3 46 00N 94 00W
Millinocket Maine U.S.A. **137** G3 45 42N 68 43W
Millisle Ards Northern Ireland **60** D2 54 37N 5 30W
Millom Cumbria England **64** B3 54 13N 3 18W
Millport North Ayrshire Scotland **60** E3 55 46N 4 55W
Millstreet Cork Rep. of Ireland **75** B2 52 03N 9 04W
Milltown Malbay Clare Rep. of Ireland **75** B2 52 52N 9 23W
Milngavie East Dunbartonshire Scotland **61** E3 55 57N 4 19W
Milnthorpe Cumbria England **64** C3 54 14N 2 46W
Milos *i.* Greece **94** D2 36 00N 24 00E
Milton Ontario Canada **137** E2 43 31N 79 53W
Milton N.Z. **119** A1 46 07S 169 58E
Milton Pennsylvania U.S.A. **137** E2 41 01N 76 52W
Milton Keynes *u.a.* England **70** D3 52 02N 0 42W
Milton Keynes Milton Keynes England **70** D3 52 02N 0 42W
Milton Ness *c.* Aberdeenshire Scotland **59** G1 56 40N 2 20W
Milverton Somerset England **73** D4 51 02N 3 16W
Milwaukee Wisconsin U.S.A. **136** C2 43 03N 87 56W
Mimizan France **91** B1 44 12N 1 14W
Mina *r.* Algeria **90** C2 35 30N 1 00E
Minahassa Peninsula Indonesia **111** G4 0 30N 123 00E
Minaki Ontario Canada **136** B3 50 00N 94 40W
Minamata Japan **114** B1 32 13N 130 23E
Minami-Ashigara Japan **114** L2 35 20N 139 06E
Minas Uruguay **147** F6 34 20S 55 15W
Minas Gerais *admin.* Brazil **146** I9 17 30S 45 00W
Minatitlán Mexico **140** F3 17 59N 94 32W
Minato Japan **115** C1 35 13N 139 52E
Minch, The *sd.* Western Isles/Highland Scotland **58** C3/D3 58 00N 6 00W
Mindanao *i.* The Philippines **111** G5/H5 8 00N 125 00E
Mindel *r.* Germany **93** B1 48 00N 10 00E
Minden Ontario Canada **137** E2 44 56N 78 44W
Minden Germany **93** A2 52 18N 8 54E
Minden Louisiana U.S.A. **135** H3 32 26N 93 17W
Mindoro *i.* The Philippines **111** G6 13 00N 121 00E
Mine Head *c.* Waterford Rep. of Ireland **75** D2 52 00N 7 35W
Minehead Somerset England **72** D4 51 13N 3 29W
Mineral'nyye Vody Russia **95** N6 44 14N 43 10E
Mingäçevir Azerbaijan **104** F3 40 45N 47 03E
Mingan Québec Canada **133** W3 50 19N 64 02W
Mingulay *i.* Western Isles Scotland **58** B1 56 49N 7 38W
Minho *see* Miño
Minicoy Island India **109** C1 8 29N 73 01E
Minneapolis Minnesota U.S.A. **136** B2 45 00N 93 15W
Minnedosa Manitoba Canada **133** P3 50 14N 99 50W
Minnesota *state* U.S.A. **136** A3/B3 47 00N 95 00W
Minnesota *r.* Minnesota U.S.A. **136** G5 44 00N 95 00W
Minnitaki Lake Ontario Canada **136** B3 50 00N 92 00W
Mino Japan **114** H2 35 43N 136 56E
Miño *(Minho) r.* Spain/Portugal **90** A3 42 00N 8 40W
Mino-Kamo Japan **114** J2 35 29N 137 01E
Minorca *see* Menorca
Minot North Dakota U.S.A. **134** F6 48 16N 101 19W
Minsk Belarus **104** B5 53 51N 27 30E
Minster Isle of Sheppey, Kent England **71** E2 51 26N 0 49E
Minster Kent England **71** F2 51 20N 1 19E
Minsterley Shropshire England **66** E2 52 39N 2 55W
Mintlaw Aberdeenshire Scotland **59** H2 57 31N 2 00W
Minusinsk Russia **103** L6 53 43N 91 45E
Miraj India **109** C3 16 51N 74 42E
Miramichi New Brunswick Canada **133** V2 47 02N 65 30W
Miranda de Ebro Spain **90** B3 42 41N 2 57W
Miran Shah Pakistan **107** L5 33 00N 70 05E
Mirfield West Yorkshire England **64** D2 53 41N 1 42W
Miri Malaysia **111** F4 4 23N 114 00E
Mirnyy *r.s.* Antarctica **149** 66 33S 93 01E
Mirnyy Russia **103** N8 62 30N 113 58E
Mirpur Khas Pakistan **108** B5 25 33N 69 05E
Mirs Bay Hong Kong China **112** D3 22 33N 114 24E
Mirtoan Sea Greece **94** C2 37 00N 23 00E
Mirzapur Dhaka Bangladesh **110** H5 24 06N 90 06E
Mirzapur India **109** E5 25 09N 82 34E
Misaki Japan **114** G1 34 19N 135 09E
Misawa Japan **114** D3 40 42N 141 26E
Misfaq Egypt **106** N10 31 01N 33 11E
Mishima Japan **114** K2 35 08N 138 54E
Miskolc Hungary **96** C3 48 07N 20 47E
Misoöl *i.* Irian Jaya Indonesia **111** I3 1 50S 129 55E
Misrātah *(Misurata)* Libya **124** C14 32 23N 15 06E
Missinaibi River Ontario Canada **137** D4 49 30N 83 20W
Mississauga Ontario Canada **137** E2 43 38N 79 36W
Mississippi *r.* U.S.A. **135** H3 35 00N 90 00W
Mississippi *state* U.S.A. **135** H3 32 00N 90 00W
Mississippi Delta Louisiana U.S.A. **135** I2 30 00N 90 00W
Missoula Montana U.S.A. **134** D6 46 52N 114 00W
Missouri *r.* U.S.A. **135** H4 39 00N 93 00W
Missouri *state* U.S.A. **135** H4 38 00N 93 00W
Mistassini Québec Canada **137** F3 48 54N 72 13W
Mitaka Japan **114** L2 35 41N 139 35E
Mitchell Australia **118** H4 26 30S 147 56E
Mitchell *r.* Australia **118** G6 16 00S 142 30E
Mitchell South Dakota U.S.A. **136** A2 43 40N 98 01W
Mitchelstown Cork Rep. of Ireland **75** C2 52 16N 8 16W
Mitino Russia **102** L1 55 53N 37 24E
Mito Japan **114** D2 36 22N 140 29E
Mitry-Mory France **87** C2 48 58N 2 38E
Massawa Eritrea **106** E2 15 42N 39 25E
Mitsukaidō Japan **114** L3 36 03N 139 59E
Mitú Colombia **146** C13 1 07N 70 05W
Mitumba Mountains *see* Chaine des Mitumba
Miura Japan **114** L2 35 08N 139 37E
Miura-hantō *p.* Japan **114** L2 35 14N 139 40E
Mixcoac Mexico **140** P1 19 23N 99 11W
Miya-gawa *r.* Japan **114** H1 34 20N 136 16E
Miyako Japan **114** D2 39 38N 141 59E
Miyakonojō Japan **114** B1 31 43N 131 02E
Miyama Japan **114** G2 35 17N 135 32E
Miyazaki Japan **114** B1 31 56N 131 27E
Miyazu Japan **114** G2 35 33N 135 12E
Mizen Head Cork Rep. of Ireland **75** B1 51 30N 9 50W
Mizen Head Wicklow Rep. of Ireland **75** E2 52 52N 6 03W
Mizoram *admin.* India **109** G4 23 40N 93 30E
Mizunami Japan **114** J2 35 25N 137 16E
Mjøsa *l.* Norway **97** C3 60 40N 10 40E
Mladá Boleslav Czech Republic **96** A4 50 26N 14 55E
Mława Poland **96** C4 53 08N 20 20E
Mnevniki Russia **102** L2 55 46N 37 29E
Moala *i.* Fiji **150** U15 18 34S 179 56E
Moate Westmeath Rep. of Ireland **74** D3 53 24N 7 58W
Mobara Japan **114** M2 35 26N 140 20E
Mobaye Central African Rep. **124** D8 4 19N 21 11E
Mobile Alabama U.S.A. **135** I3 30 40N 88 05W
Moçambique Mozambique **125** H4 15 03S 40 45E
Mocuba Mozambique **125** G4 16 52S 36 57E
Modbury Devon England **72** D3 50 21N 3 53W
Módena Italy **92** B2 44 39N 10 55E
Modesto California U.S.A. **134** B4 37 37N 121 00W
Mödling Austria **92** C3 48 06N 16 18E
Moe Australia **118** H2 38 09S 146 22E
Moelfre Isle of Anglesey Wales **66** C3 53 21N 4 14W
Moel Hebog *mt.* Gwynedd Wales **66** C2 53 00N 4 09W
Moers Germany **89** F3 51 27N 6 36E
Moffat Dumfries & Galloway Scotland **61** F3 55 20N 3 27W
Moffat Water *r.* Dumfries & Galloway Scotland **61** F3 55 22N 3 21W
Mogadishu *see* Muqdisho
Mogilev *see* Mahilyow
Mogocha Russia **103** N6 53 44N 119 45E
Mogollon Rim *plat.* U.S.A. **134** D3 34 00N 111 00W
Mohammadia Algeria **90** C2 35 35N 0 05E
Mohe China **113** O9 52 55N 122 20E
Mohill Leitrim Rep. of Ireland **74** D3 53 54N 7 52W
Mohyliv-Podil's'kyy Ukraine **104** B4 48 29N 27 49E
Moinești Romania **94** E7 46 27N 26 31E
Mo-i-Rana Norway **97** C4 66 18N 14 00E
Mojave California U.S.A. **134** C4 35 02N 118 11W
Mokolo Cameroon **127** H5 10 49N 13 54E
Mokp'o South Korea **113** P5 34 50N 126 25E
Moksha *r.* Russia **104** E5 54 30N 43 00E
Mol Belgium **89** E3 51 11N 5 07E
Molango Mexico **140** E4 20 48N 98 44W
Mold Flintshire Wales **66** D3 53 10N 3 08W
Moldova *r.* Romania **96** D3 47 00N 26 00E
MOLDOVA *(MOLDAVIA)* **94** F7
Mole *r.* Surrey England **70** D2 51 15N 0 20W
Molepolole Botswana **125** E3 24 25S 25 30E
Molfetta Italy **92** C2 41 12N 16 36E
Moline Illinois U.S.A. **136** B2 41 31N 90 26W
Mollendo Peru **146** C9 17 00S 72 00W
Mölndal Sweden **97** C2 57 40N 12 00E
Molodezhnaya *r.s.* Antarctica **149** 67 40S 45 51E
Molokai *i.* Hawaiian Islands **151** Y18 21 40N 155 55W
Molopo *r.* Southern Africa **125** D2 26 30S 22 30E
Moluccas *see* Maluku
Molucca Sea Indonesia **111** G3/H4 0 30S 125 30E
Mombasa Kenya **125** G7 4 04S 39 40E
Mombetsu Japan **114** D3 42 28N 142 10E
Momchilgrad Bulgaria **94** D4 41 32N 25 24E
Møn *i.* Denmark **93** B2 55 00N 12 00E
MONACO 91 D1
Monadhliath Mountains Highland Scotland **59** E2 57 10N 4 00W
Monaghan *co.* Rep. of Ireland **74** D4/E4 54 10N 7 00W
Monaghan Monaghan Rep. of Ireland **74** E4 54 15N 6 58W
Monahans Texas U.S.A. **134** F3 31 35N 102 54W
Monarch, Sound of Western Isles Scotland **58** B2 57 35N 7 30W
Monasterevin Kildare Rep. of Ireland **75** D3 53 07N 7 02W
Monastir Tunisia **92** B1 35 46N 10 59E
Mona Vale Australia **119** H3 33 41S 151 18E
Monavullagh Mountains *mts.* Waterford Rep. of Ireland **75** D2 52 13N 7 35W
Monbetsu Japan **114** D3 44 23N 143 22E
Monçaó Brazil **146** H12 3 30S 45 15W
Monchegorsk Russia **97** G4 67 55N 33 01E
Mönchengladbach Germany **93** A2 51 12N 6 25E
Monclova Mexico **140** D5 26 55N 101 25W
Moncton New Brunswick Canada **133** V2 46 04N 64 50W
Mondego *r.* Portugal **90** A3 40 30N 0 15W
Mondovi Italy **92** A2 44 23N 7 49E
Moneen Galway Rep. of Ireland **74** C3 53 26N 8 54W
Monemvasia Greece **94** C2 36 41N 23 03E
Moneró Brazil **147** Q2 22 48S 43 11W
Moneymore Cookstown Northern Ireland **60** C2 54 42N 6 40W
Monfalcone Italy **92** B3 45 49N 13 32E
Mong Kok Hong Kong China **112** B1 22 09N 114 09E
MONGOLIA 112/113 H8/M8
Mongu Zambia **125** D4 15 13S 23 09E
Moniaive Dumfries & Galloway Scotland **61** F3 55 12N 3 55W
Monifieth Angus Scotland **59** G1 56 29N 2 49W
Monmouth Monmouthshire Wales **67** E1 51 50N 2 43W
Monmouthshire *u.a.* Wales **67** E1 51 47N 2 55W
Monnikendam Netherlands **88** D3 52 27N 5 02E
Mono *r.* Togo **127** F4 7 30N 1 30E
Monopoli Italy **92** C2 40 57N 17 18E
Monos *i.* Trinidad & Tobago **141** S10 10 42N 61 42W
Monroe Louisiana U.S.A. **135** H3 32 31N 92 06W
Monroe Michigan U.S.A. **137** D2 41 56N 83 21W
Monroe Reservoir Indiana U.S.A. **136** C1 39 00N 86 00W
Monrovia Liberia **127** C4 6 20N 10 46W
Mons Belgium **89** C2 50 28N 3 58E
Monster Netherlands **88** A2 52 01N 4 10E
Montagnes de la Margeride *mts.* France **91** C1 44 50N 3 15E
Montagnes Noires *mts.* France **91** B2 48 00N 3 30W
Montana *state* U.S.A. **134** E0 47 00N 111 00W
Montana *(Mikhaylovgrad)* Bulgaria **96** C2 43 25N 23 11E
Montañas de León *mts.* Spain **90** A3 42 30N 6 15E
Montargis France **91** C2 48 00N 2 44E
Montauban France **91** C1 44 01N 1 20E
Montauk Point New York U.S.A. **137** F2 41 04N 71 51W
Montbéliard France **91** D2 47 31N 6 48E
Mont Blanc *mt.* France/Italy **91** D2 45 50N 6 52E
Mont Cameroun *mt.* Cameroon **127** G3 4 13N 9 10E
Montceau-les-Mines France **91** C2 46 40N 4 23E
Montclair New Jersey U.S.A. **138** B2 40 48N 74 12W
Mont-de-Marsan France **91** B1 43 54N 0 30W
Montdidier France **91** C2 49 39N 2 35E
Montebello California U.S.A. **139** B3 34 01N 118 07W
Monte Binga *mt.* Zimbabwe/Mozambique **125** F4 19 47S 33 03E
Montebourg France **73** F2 49 29N 1 22W
Monte Carlo Monaco **91** D1 43 44N 7 25E
Monte Cinto *mt.* Corsica **91** D1 42 23N 8 57E
Montego Bay *tn.* Jamaica **141** Q8 18 27N 77 56W
Montélimar France **91** C1 44 33N 4 45E
Montemor-o-Novo Portugal **90** A2 38 38N 8 13W
Montenegro *admin.* Yugoslavia **96** B2 43 00N 19 30E
Montepulciano Italy **92** B2 43 0 5N 11 46E
Monterey California U.S.A. **134** B4 36 35N 121 55W
Monterey Park *tn.* U.S.A. **139** B3 34 03N 118 08W
Montería Colombia **146** B14 8 45N 75 54W
Montero Bolivia **146** E9 17 20S 63 15W
Monte Roraima *mt.* Guyana **146** E14 5 14N 60 44W
Monterrey Mexico **140** D5 25 40N 100 20W
Montes Claros *tn.* Brazil **146** I9 16 45S 43 52W
Montes de Toledo *mts.* Spain **90** B2 39 35N 4 30W
Montevideo Uruguay **147** F6 34 55S 56 10W
Mont Forel *mt.* Greenland **133** BB6 67 00N 37 00W
Montgeron France **87** B1 48 42N 2 27E
Montgomery Alabama U.S.A. **135** I3 32 22N 86 20W
Montgomery Powys Wales **66** D2 52 34N 3 10W
Monti del Gennargentu *mts.* Italy **92** A1/2 40 00N 9 30E
Monti Nebrodi *mts.* Italy **92** B1/C1 37 00N 14 00E
Mont-Joli Québec Canada **137** G3 48 36N 68 14W
Mont-Laurier *tn.* Québec Canada **137** E3 46 33N 75 31W
Montluçon France **91** C2 46 20N 2 36E
Montmagny Québec Canada **137** F3 46 50N 70 33W
Montmartin-sur-Mer France **73** F1 45 59N 1 32W
Montmirail France **91** C2 48 52N 3 34E
Montmorency France **87** B2 48 59N 2 19E
Montmorillon France **91** C2 46 26N 0 52E
Monto Australia **118** I5 24 53S 151 06E
Montoro Spain **90** B2 38 02N 4 23W
Montpelier Clare Rep. of Ireland **75** C2 52 45N 8 30W
Montpelier Vermont U.S.A. **137** F2 44 16N 72 34W
Montpellier France **91** C1 43 36N 3 53E
Montréal Québec Canada **137** F3 45 32N 73 36W
Montreux Switzerland **92** A3 46 27N 6 55E
Montrose Angus Scotland **59** G1 56 43N 2 29W
Montrose Colorado U.S.A. **134** E4 38 29N 107 53W
Montrose Basin Angus Scotland **59** G1 56 44N 2 30W
Montrouge France **87** B2 48 49N 2 19E
Monts d'Ambaza *mts.* France **91** C2 46 00N 1 30E
Monts d'Arrés *mts.* France **91** B2 48 20N 3 50W
Monts d'Auvergne *mts.* France **91** C2 45 30N 2 50E
Monts de Medjerda *mts.* Algeria/Tunisia **92** A1 36 50N 8 00E
Monts du Cantal *mts.* France **91** C2 45 04N 2 45E
Montserrat *i.* Lesser Antilles **141** L3 16 45N 62 14W
Monts Nimba *mts.* Guinea/Liberia **127** D4 7 39N 8 30W
Monts Otish *mts.* Québec Canada **133** U3 52 30N 70 20W
Monywa Myanmar **109** H4 22 05N 95 12E
Monza Italy **92** A3 45 35N 9 16E
Mooncoin Kilkenny Rep. of Ireland **75** D2 52 17N 7 15W
Moone Kildare Rep. of Ireland **75** E2 52 58N 6 49W
Moora Australia **118** B3 30 40S 116 01E
Moore, Lake Australia **118** B4 30 00S 117 30E

Nene *r.* Cambridgeshire England **71** E3 52 45N 0 10E
Nen Jiang *r.* China **113** P9 50 00N 125 00E
Nenjiang China **113** O8 49 10N 125 15E
Néo Monastíri Greece **94** C3 39 15N 22 17E
Neosho *r.* U.S.A. **136** A1 37 00N 95 00W
NEPAL 109 E5
Nepean Canada **137** E3 45 16N 75 48W
Nephin *mt.* Mayo Rep. of Ireland **74** B4 54 01N 9 22W
Nephin Beg Range *mts.* Mayo Rep. of Ireland **74** B4 54 00N 9 34W
Nerchinsk Russia **103** N6 52 02N 116 38E
Neretva *r.* Bosnia-Herzegovina **92** C2 43 30N 15 18E
Nerva Spain **90** A2 37 41N 6 33W
Neryungri Russia **103** O7 56 39N 124 38E
Nes Netherlands **89** E5 53 27N 5 46E
Neskaupstadur Iceland **97** J7 65 10N 13 43W
Neste *r.* France **91** C1 43 00N 0 15E
Neston Cheshire England **64** B2 53 18N 3 03W
Nestor Trinidad & Tobago **141** T10 10 31N 61 09W
Nestor Falls *tn.* Canada **136** B3 49 06N 93 55W
Néstos *r.* Greece **94** D4 41 20N 24 30E
Netanya Israel **106** O11 32 20N 34 51E
Netarhat Bihar India **110** B4 23 28N 84 18E
NETHERLANDS 93 A2
Nether Stowey Somerset England **73** D4 51 09N 3 10W
Nettetal Germany **89** F3 51 20N 6 14E
Nettilling Lake Canada **133** U6 66 30N 71 10W
Netzahualcóyotl Mexico **140** E3 19 24N 99 02W
Neubrandenburg Germany **93** B2 53 33N 13 16E
Neuburg Germany **93** B1 48 44N 11 12E
Neuchâtel Switzerland **92** A3 46 55N 6 56E
Neuenhagen Germany **87** G2 52 32N 13 41E
Neufchâteau Belgium **89** E1 49 51N 5 26E
Neufchâteau France **91** D2 48 21N 5 42E
Neufchâtel-en-Bray France **91** C2 49 44N 1 26E
Neufchâtel-sur-Aisne France **89** D1 49 27N 4 02E
Neuilly France **87** B2 48 53N 2 17E
Neuilly Plaisance France **87** C2 48 51N 2 31E
Neukölln Germany **87** F1 52 29N 13 28E
Neumarkt Germany **93** B1 49 17N 11 29E
Neumünster Germany **93** A2 54 05N 9 59E
Neunkirchen Germany **93** A1 49 21N 7 12E
Neuquén Argentina **147** D5 38 55N 68 05W
Neuruppin Germany **93** B2 52 56N 12 49E
Neusiedler See *l.* Austria **92** C3 48 00N 16 00E
Neuss Germany **93** A2 51 12N 6 42E
Neustadt Germany **93** A1 49 21N 8 09E
Neustrelitz Germany **93** B2 53 22N 13 05E
Neu-Ulm Germany **93** B1 48 23N 10 01E
Neuwied Germany **93** A2 50 26N 7 28E
Nevada *state* U.S.A. **134** C4 39 00N 118 00W
Nevada Missouri U.S.A. **136** B1 37 51N 94 22W
Nevers France **91** C2 47 00N 3 09E
Neves Brazil **147** Q2 22 51S 43 05W
Nevinnomyssk Russia **104** E3 44 38N 41 59E
Neviot Egypt **106** O9 28 58N 34 38E
Nevşehir Turkey **95** J3 38 38N 34 43E
New *r.* U.S.A. **137** D1 37 00N 81 00W
New Abbey Dumfries & Galloway Scotland **61** F2 54 59N 3 38W
New Albany Indiana U.S.A. **136** C1 38 17N 85 50W
New Alresford Hampshire England **70** C2 51 06N 1 10W
New Amsterdam Guyana **146** F14 6 18N 57 30W
Newark U.S.A. **138** B2 40 43N 74 11W
Newark Ohio U.S.A. **137** D2 40 03N 82 25W
Newark Bay U.S.A. **138** B1 40 40N 74 08W
Newark-on-Trent Nottinghamshire England **65** E2 53 05N 0 49W
New Ash Green Kent England **71** E2 51 21N 0 18E
New Bedford U.S.A. **137** F2 41 38N 70 55W
New Bern U.S.A. **135** K4 35 05N 77 04W
Newberry Michigan U.S.A. **136** C3 46 22N 85 30W
Newbiggin-by-the-Sea Northumberland England **61** H3 55 11N 1 30W
New Braunfels Texas U.S.A. **135** G2 29 43N 98 09W
Newbridge *tn* Caerphilly Wales **66** D1 51 41N 3 09W
Newbridge-on-Wye Powys Wales **66** D2 52 13N 3 27W
New Brighton U.S.A. **138** B1 40 48N 74 06W
New Britain *i.* Papua New Guinea **118** H8/I8 4 45S 150 30E
New Britain Connecticut U.S.A. **137** F2 41 40N 72 47W
New Brunswick *province* Canada **133** V2 47 30N 66 00W
New Buffalo Michigan U.S.A. **136** C2 41 48N 86 44W
New Buildings Londonderry Northern Ireland **60** B2 54 56N 7 21W
Newburgh Fife Scotland **59** F1 56 21N 3 15W
Newburgh U.S.A. **135** L5 41 30N 74 00W
Newburn Tyne & Wear England **64** D3 54 59N 1 43W
Newbury Berkshire England **70** C2 51 25N 1 20W
New Caledonia *i.* Pacific Ocean **118** K5/L5 22 00S 165 00E
New Castle Pennsylvania U.S.A. **137** D2 41 00N 80 22W
Newcastle Australia **118** I3 32 55S 151 46E
Newcastle Canada **137** E2 43 55N 78 35W
Newcastle Down Northern Ireland **60** D2 54 12N 5 54W
Newcastle Wyoming U.S.A. **134** F5 43 52N 104 14W
Newcastle Emlyn Carmarthenshire Wales **66** C2 52 02N 4 28W
Newcastle-under-Lyme Staffordshire England **67** E3 53 00N 2 14W
Newcastle upon Tyne Tyne & Wear England **64** D3 54 59N 1 35W
Newcastle West Limerick Rep. of Ireland **75** B2 52 27N 9 03W
New Cumnock East Ayrshire Scotland **61** E3 55 24N 4 12W
New Deer Aberdeenshire Scotland **59** G2 57 30N 2 12W
New Delhi India **109** D5 28 37N 77 14E
New Dorp U.S.A. **138** B1 40 34N 74 06W
New Forest *nat. park* Hampshire England **70** C1 50 50N 1 40W
Newfoundland *province* Canada **133** W4/Y2 52 30N 62 30W
Newfoundland *i.* Canada **133** X2 48 15N 57 00W
Newfoundland Basin Atlantic Ocean **152** D11/E11 44 00N 40 00W
New Galloway Dumfries & Galloway Scotland **61** E3 55 05N 4 10W
New Georgia Islands Solomon Is. **118** J8 8 00S 157 30E
New Grant Trinidad & Tobago **141** T9 10 17N 61 19W
New Guinea *i.* Pacific Ocean **118** E9/H8 5 00S 141 00E
New Hampshire *state* U.S.A. **137** F2 43 00N 72 00W
New Haven Connecticut U.S.A. **137** F2 41 18N 72 55W
New Hebrides Trench Pacific Ocean **150** G6 15 00S 169 00E
New Holland North Lincolnshire England **65** E2 53 42N 0 22W
New Hyde Park U.S.A. **138** D1 40 44N 73 42W
New Iberia Louisiana U.S.A. **135** H2 30 00N 91 51W
Newick East Sussex England **70** E1 50 58N 0 01E
Newinn Tipperary Rep. of Ireland **75** D2 52 26N 7 53W
New Ireland *i.* Papua New Guinea **118** I9 3 15S 152 30E
New Jersey *state* U.S.A. **137** F1 40 00N 75 00W
New Jersey Turnpike *road* U.S.A. **138** B2 40 50N 74 05W
New Liskeard Canada **137** E3 47 31N 79 41W
New London Connecticut U.S.A. **137** F2 41 21N 72 06W
Newlyn Cornwall England **72** B3 50 06N 5 34W
Newmachar Aberdeenshire Scotland **59** G2 57 16N 2 10W
Newmains North Lanarkshire Scotland **61** F3 55 47N 3 53W
Newman Australia **118** B5 23 20S 119 34E
Newmarket Suffolk England **71** E3 52 15N 0 25E
Newmarket Cork Rep. of Ireland **75** C2 52 13N 9 00W
Newmarket-on-Fergus Clare Rep. of Ireland **75** C2 52 45N 8 53W
New Mexico *state* U.S.A. **134** E3 35 00N 107 00W
New Milford U.S.A. **137** E2 41 52N 75 44W
New Milton Hampshire England **70** C1 50 46N 1 40W
New Orleans Louisiana U.S.A. **135** H2 30 00N 90 03W
New Philadelphia Ohio U.S.A. **137** D2 40 31N 81 28W
Newport Australia **119** H3 33 39S 151 19E
Newport Essex England **71** E2 51 58N 0 13E
Newport Isle of Wight England **70** C1 50 42N 1 18W
Newport Shropshire England **67** E2 52 47N 2 22W
Newport Mayo Rep. of Ireland **74** B3 53 53N 9 32W
Newport Tipperary Rep. of Ireland **75** C2 52 43N 8 25W
Newport Maine U.S.A. **137** G2 44 50N 69 17W
Newport Rhode Island U.S.A. **137** F2 41 30N 71 19W
Newport Vermont U.S.A. **137** F2 44 56N 72 18W
Newport *u.a.* Wales **66** D1/E1 51 33N 3 00W
Newport Newport Wales **66** D1 51 35N 3 00W
Newport Pembrokeshire Wales **66** C2 52 01N 4 50W
Newport Bay *b.* Mayo Rep. of Ireland **74** B3 53 51N 9 41W
Newport News Virginia U.S.A. **137** E1 36 59N 76 26W
Newport-on-Tay Fife Scotland **59** G1 56 27N 2 56W
Newport Pagnell Milton Keynes England **70** D3 52 05N 0 44W
New Providence *i.* The Bahamas **141** I5 25 00N 77 30W
New Quay Ceredigion Wales **66** C2 52 13N 4 22W
Newquay Cornwall England **72** B3 50 25N 5 05W
New Radnor Powys Wales **66** D2 52 15N 3 10W
New Rochelle U.S.A. **138** B2 40 55N 73 46W
New Romney Kent England **71** E1 50 59N 0 57E
New Ross Wexford Rep. of Ireland **75** E2 52 24N 6 56W
New Rossington South Yorkshire England **65** D2 53 29N 1 04W
Newry Newry & Mourne Northern Ireland **60** C2 54 11N 6 20W
Newry and Mourne *district* Northern Ireland **60** C2 54 10N 6 35W
New Sauchie Clackmannanshire Scotland **61** F4 56 08N 3 41W
New Scone Perth & Kinross Scotland **59** F1 56 25N 3 25W
New Siberian Islands *see* Novosibirskiye Ostrova
New South Wales *state* Australia **118** G3/I3 32 00S 145 00E
New Springville U.S.A. **138** B1 40 35N 74 10W
New Territories *admin.* H.K. China **112** B2 22 20N 114 00E
Newton Abbot Devon England **72** D3 50 32N 3 36W
Newton Aycliffe Durham England **64** D3 54 37N 1 34W
Newton Mearns East Renfrewshire Scotland **61** E3 55 45N 4 18W
Newtonmore Highland Scotland **59** E2 57 04N 4 08W
Newton Stewart Dumfries & Galloway Scotland **61** E2 54 57N 4 29W
Newtown Laois Rep. of Ireland **75** D2 52 52N 7 07W
Newtown Powys Wales **66** D2 52 32N 3 19W
Newtownabbey *co.* Northern Ireland **60** C2/D2 54 40N 6 05W
Newtownabbey Newtownabbey Northern Ireland **60** D2 54 40N 5 54W
Newtownards Ards Northern Ireland **60** D2 54 36N 5 41W
Newtown Cunningham Donegal Rep. of Ireland **74** D4 54 59N 7 31W
Newtownhamilton Newry & Mourne Northern Ireland **60** C2 54 12N 6 35W
Newtownmountkennedy Wicklow Rep. of Ireland **75** E3 53 06N 6 07W
Newtown St. Boswells Scottish Borders Scotland **61** G3 55 34N 2 40W
Newtownstewart Strabane Northern Ireland **60** B2 54 43N 7 24W
New Tredegar Caerphilly Wales **66** D1 51 44N 3 15W
New Ulm Minnesota U.S.A. **136** B2 44 19N 94 28W
New Westminster Canada **132** K2 49 10N 122 58W
New York *state* U.S.A. **137** E2/F2 43 00N 76 00W
New York U.S.A. **137** F2 40 40N 73 50W
NEW ZEALAND 150 H3/4
Neyagawa Japan **114** G1 34 45N 135 36E
Neyland Pembrokeshire Wales **66** C1 51 43N 4 57W
Neyrīz Iran **107** H4 29 14N 54 18E
Neyshābūr Iran **107** I6 36 13N 58 49E
Nez de Jobourg *c.* France **73** F2 49 32N 1 53W
Ngami, Lake Botswana **125** D3 21 00S 23 00E
Ngangla Ringco *l.* China **109** E6 31 40N 83 00E
Nganze Co *l.* China **109** F6 31 00N 87 00E
Ngaoundére Cameroon **127** H4 7 20N 13 35E
Ngau *i.* Fiji **150** U15/16 18 00S 179 16E
Ngau Chi Wan H.K. China **112** C2 22 25N 114 10E
Ngau Kwu Long H.K. China **112** A1 22 18N 113 58E
Ngauruhoe, Mount N.Z. **119** C3 39 10S 175 38E
Ngau Tam Mei H.K. China **112** B2 22 28N 114 04E
Ngong Ping H.K. China **112** A1 22 15N 113 54E
Nguigmi Niger **127** H5 14 19N 13 06E
Nguru Nigeria **127** H5 12 53N 10 30E
Nha Trang Vietnam **111** D6 12 15N 109 10E
Nhulunbuy Australia **118** F7 12 30S 136 56E
Niagara Falls *tn.* Canada **137** E2 43 05N 79 06W
Niagara Falls *tn.*U.S.A. **137** E2 43 06N 79 04W
Niamey Niger **127** F5 13 32N 2 05E
Niangara Congo (D.R.) **124** F8 3 45N 27 54E
Nibra India **108** K2 22 35N 88 15E
NICARAGUA 141 G2
Nicastro Italy **92** C1 38 59N 16 20E
Nice France **91** D1 43 42N 7 16E
Nicobar Islands India **109** G1 8 30N 94 00E
Nicosia Cyprus **95** H1 35 11N 33 23E
Nidd *r.* North Yorkshire England **64** D3 54 02N 1 30W
Nied *r.* France **89** F1 49 15N 6 30E
Niedere Tauern *mts.* Austria **92** B3 47 00N 14 00E
Niedersachsen *admin.* Germany **93** A2 52 00N 9 00E
Nienburg Germany **93** A2 52 38N 9 13E
Nieppe France **71** G1 50 42N 2 50E
Niers *r.* Germany **89** F3 51 00N 6 00E
Niesse *see* Nysa
Nieuwegein Netherlands **89** E4 52 00N 5 05E
Nieuwe Maas *r.* Netherlands **88** B1 51 54N 4 23E
Nieuwendam Netherlands **88** D3 52 23N 4 57E
Nieuwerkerk aan den IJssel Netherlands **88** C1 51 58N 4 37E
Nieuwe Waterweg Scheur *can.* Netherlands **88** A1 51 55N 4 10E
Nieuwkoopsche Plassen *l.* Netherlands **88** D2 52 08N 4 46E
Nieuw Nickerie Suriname **146** F14 5 52N 57 00W
Nieuwpoort Belgium **89** B3 51 08N 2 45E
Nieuwpoort Belgium **71** G2 51 08N 2 45E
Nieuw-Vennep Netherlands **88** C3 52 15N 4 39E
Nigde Turkey **95** J2 37 58N 34 42E
NIGER 127 G6/H6
Niger *r.* West Africa **127** G4 5 30N 6 15E
NIGERIA 127 F4/H5
Nigg Aberdeen City Scotland **59** G2 57 08N 2 03W
Nigg Bay Aberdeen City Scotland **59** G2 57 08N 2 03W
Nigg Bay Highland Scotland **59** E2 57 42N 4 01W
Nihoa *i.* Hawaiian Is. **151** J10 23 03N 161 55W
Niigata Japan **114** C2 37 58N 139 02E
Niihama Japan **114** B1 33 57N 133 15E
Niihau *i.* Hawaiian Is. **151** W18 21 50N 160 11W
Nii-jima *i.* Japan **114** C1 34 20N 139 15E
Niiza Japan **115** B4 35 48N 139 35E
Nijkerk Netherlands **89** E4 52 12N 5 30E
Nijmegen Netherlands **89** E3 51 50N 5 52E
Nikko Japan **114** C2 36 45N 139 37E
Nikolayev *see* Mykolayiv
Nikolayevsk-na-Amure Russia **103** Q6 53 10N 140 44E
Nikol'skiy *see* Satlayev
Nikopol' Ukraine **104** C4 45 34N 34 25E
Niksar Turkey **95** K4 40 35N 36 59E
Nikšić Montenegro Yugoslavia **96** B2 42 48N 18 56E
Nile *r.* Sudan/Egypt **124** F13 28 30N 30 40E
Niles Michigan U.S.A. **136** C2 41 51N 86 15W
Nilgiri Hills India **109** D2 11 00N 76 30E
Nilphamari Rajshahi Bangladesh **110** F6 25 58N 88 57E
Nîmes France **91** C1 43 50N 4 21E
Nimule Sudan **124** F8 3 35N 32 03E
Nim Wan H.K. China **112** A2 22 25N 113 56E
9 de Julio *(Nueve de Julio) tn.* Argentina **147** E5 35 28S 60 58W
Ninepin Group H.K. China **112** C1 22 15N 114 20E
Ninety Mile Beach N.Z. **119** B4 34 45S 172 58E
Nineveh *hist. site* Iraq **106** F6 36 24N 43 08E
Ningbo China **113** O4 29 54N 121 33E
Ninh Binh Vietnam **113** L3 20 14N 106 00E
Ninove Belgium **89** D2 50 50N 4 02E
Niobrara *r.* U.S.A. **134** F5 42 00N 102 00W
Nioro du Sahel Mali **127** D6 15 12N 9 35W
Niort France **91** B2 46 19N 0 27W
Nipigon Canada **136** C3 49 02N 88 26W
Nipigon *r.* Canada **136** C3 49 02N 88 26W
Nipigon, Lake Canada **136** C3/4 49 50N 88 30W
Nirmali Bihar India **110** D7 26 18N 86 35E
Niš Serbia Yugoslavia **96** C2 43 20N 21 54E
Nishi Japan **115** B2 35 26N 139 37E
Nishinomiya Japan **114** G1 34 44N 135 22E
Nishio Japan **114** J1 34 52N 137 02E
Nishiwaki Japan **114** F2 35 00N 134 58E
Nistru *(Dnestr) r.* Moldova **96** D3 47 30N 28 30E
Nísyros *i.* Greece **94** E2 36 33N 27 10E
Niteroí Brazil **147** I8 22 54S 43 06W
Nith *r.* Dumfries & Galloway Scotland **61** F3 55 20N 3 50W
Nithsdale *v.* Dumfries & Galloway Scotland **61** F3 55 15N 3 50W
Nitra Slovakia **96** B3 48 19N 18 04E
Niue *i.* Pacific Ocean **151** J6 19 02S 169 55W
Nive *r.* France **91** B1 43 00N 1 30W
Nivelles Belgium **89** D2 50 36N 4 20E
Nizamabad India **109** D3 18 40N 78 05E
Nizhneangarsk Russia **103** M7 55 48N 109 35E
Nizhnekamsk Russia **104** G6 55 38N 51 49E
Nizhnekamskoye Vodokhranilishche *res.* Russia **105** G6 56 00N 53 30E
Nizhnekolymsk Russia **103** S9 68 34N 160 58E
Nizhnevartovsk Russia **105** M7 60 57N 76 40E
Nizhniy Novgorod *(Gork'iy)* Russia **102** G7 56 20N 44 00E
Nizhniy Novgorod Vodokhranilishche *(Gor'kovskoye) res.* Russia **104** E6 57 00N 43 30E
Nizhniy Tagil Russia **102** I7 58 00N 59 58E
Nizhnocartovsk Russia **103** J8 60 57N 76 40E
Nizhnyaya (Lower) Tunguska *r.* Russia **103** L8/M8 64 00N 95 00E
Nizip Turkey **95** K2 37 02N 37 47E
Nízké Tatry *mts.* Slovakia **96** B3 49 00N 19 00E
Nkongsamba Cameroon **127** G3 4 59N 9 53E
Noabanki Khulna Bangladesh **110** G3 22 25N 89 12E
Noakhali Bangladesh **110** J3 22 52N 91 03E
Noamundi Orissa India **110** C3 22 11N 86 28E
Noatak U.S.A. **132** C6 67 33N 163 10W
Noatak *r.* U.S.A. **132** C6 67 33N 163 10W
Nobeoka Japan **114** B1 32 36N 131 40E
Nobi Japan **115** B1 35 11N 139 41E
Noda Japan **114** L2 35 57N 139 52E
Nogales Mexico **140** B6 31 20N 111 00W
Nogales Arizona U.S.A. **134** D3 31 20N 110 56W
Nogent France **87** C2 48 50N 2 30E
Noguera Ribagorzana *r.* Spain **90** C3 42 25N 0 45E
Noisy-le-Sec France **87** B2 48 53N 2 27E
Nojima-zaki *c.* Japan **114** L1 34 54N 139 54E
Nokrek Peak Meghalaya India **110** H6 25 29N 90 19E
Nola Central African Rep. **124** C8 3 28N 16 08E
Nome U.S.A. **132** B5 64 30N 165 30W
Nong Khai Thailand **113** K2 17 52N 102 44E
Nongstoin Meghalaya India **110** J6 25 30N 91 16E
Noord Beveland *i.* Netherlands **89** C3 51 35N 3 45E
Noord-Brabant *admin.* Netherlands **89** D3/E3 51 29N 5 00E
Noord-Holland *admin.* Netherlands **89** D4 52 30N 4 45E
Noordoost Polder Netherlands **89** E4 52 47N 5 45E
Noordwijk Netherlands **89** D4 52 15N 4 25E
Noordwijk aan Zee Netherlands **88** B2 52 14N 4 27E
Noordwijkerhout Netherlands **88** B3 52 15N 4 30E
Noordzeekanaal *can.* Netherlands **88** C3 52 25N 4 45E
Noorvik U.S.A. **132** C6 66 50N 161 14W
Nord-pas-de Calais *admin.* France **89** C2/D2 50 13N 4 03E
Norden Germany **93** A2 53 36N 7 13E
Nordenham Germany **93** A2 53 30N 8 29E
Norderney *i.* Germany **93** A2 53 00N 7 00E
Norderstedt Germany **93** A2 53 41N 9 58E
Nordfjord *fj.* Norway **97** B3 62 00N 5 15E
Nordfold Norway **97** D4 67 48N 15 20E
Nordfriesische Inseln *(North Frisian Islands) is.* Germany **93** A2 54 00N 8 00E
Nordhafen Walsum *harbour* Germany **86** A3 51 33N 6 43E
Nordhausen Germany **93** B2 51 31N 10 48E
Nordhorn Germany **93** A2 52 27N 7 05E
Nordkapp *(North Cape)* Norway **97** E5 71 11N 25 40E
admin. France **71** G1 50 49N 2 00E
Nordrhein-Westfalen *admin.* Germany **93** A2 52 00N 7 00E
Nordstrand *i.* Germany **93** A2 54 00N 8 00E
Nordvik Russia **103** N10 74 01N 111 30E
Nore *r.* Kilkenny Rep. of Ireland **75** D2 52 26N 7 02W
Nore *r.* Loais Rep. of Ireland **75** D2 52 57N 7 35W
Norfolk *co.* England **71** E3/F3 52 45N 1 00E
Norfolk Nebraska U.S.A. **135** G5 42 01N 97 25W
Norfolk Virginia U.S.A. **137** E1 36 54N 76 18W
Norfolk Island Pacific Ocean **150** G5 29 05S 167 59E
Norfolk Island Trough Pacific Ocean **150** G5 27 30S 166 00E
Norfolk Lake Arkansas U.S.A. **135** H4 36 00N 92 00W
Norham Northumberland England **61** G3 55 43N 2 10W
Noril'sk Russia **103** K9 69 21N 88 02E
Normanton Australia **118** G6 17 40S 141 05E
Normanton West Yorkshire England **65** D2 53 42N 1 25W
Norman Wells *tn.* Canada **132** J6 65 19N 126 46W
Norris Lake Tennessee U.S.A. **135** J4 36 00N 84 00W
Norristown U.S.A. **137** E2 40 07N 75 20W
Norrköping Sweden **97** D2 58 35N 16 10E
Norseman Australia **118** C3 32 15S 121 47E
North Adams U.S.A. **137** F2 42 42N 73 07W
Northallerton North Yorkshire England **65** D3 54 20N 1 26W
Northam Australia **118** B3 31 40S 116 40E
Northam Devon England **72** C4 51 02N 4 14W
North American Basin Atlantic Ocean **152** C10 34 00N 55 00W
Northampton Australia **118** A4 28 27S 114 37E
Northampton Northamptonshire England **70** D3 52 14N 0 54W
Northampton U.S.A. **137** F2 42 19N 72 38W
Northamptonshire *co.* England **70** C3/D3 52 20N 1 00W
North Andaman *i.* Andaman Is. **109** G2 13 00N 93 00E
North Anna *r.* Virginia U.S.A. **137** E1 38 00N 77 00W
North Atlantic Ocean 152 D7/D11
North Australian Basin Indian Ocean **150** B6 15 00S 115 00E
North Ayrshire *u.a.* Scotland **60** D3/E3 55 30N 5 05W
North Baddesley Hampshire England **70** C1 50 58N 1 27W
North Ballachulish Highland Scotland **58** D1 56 42N 5 11W
North Barrackpore India **108** K3 22 46N 88 21E
North Battleford Canada **132** N3 52 47N 108 17W
North Bay *tn.* Canada **137** E3 46 20N 79 28W
North Bergen U.S.A. **138** B2 40 46N 74 02W
North Berwick East Lothian Scotland **61** G4 56 04N 2 44W
North Canadian *r.* U.S.A. **134** F4 36 00N 100 00W
North Cape N.Z. **119** B4 34 25S 173 03E
North Cape Norway *see* Nordkapp
North Carolina *state* U.S.A. **135** K4 36 00N 80 00W
North Channel British Isles **60** D3/D2 55 20N 5 50W
North Channel Canada **137** D3 46 00N 83 00W
North Dakota *state* U.S.A. **134** F6 47 00N 102 00W
North Dorset Downs *hills* Dorset England **73** E3 50 40N 2 30W
North Down *co.* Northern Ireland **60** D2 54 40N 5 40W
North Downs *hills* Surrey/Kent England **70** D2 51 13N 0 30W
North Dvina *r.* Russia **77** P8 63 00N 43 00E
North East Lincolnshire *u.a.* England **65** E2 53 30N 0 10W
Northeim Germany **93** A2 51 43N 9 59E
Northern Ireland 60 B2/C2
NORTHERN MARIANAS 150 E9
Northern Range *mts.* Trinidad & Tobago **141** T10 10 47N 61 27W
Northern Sporades *see* Vóreioi Sporádes
Northern Territory *territory* Australia **118** E6/F5 19 00S 132 00E
North Esk *r.* Angus Scotland **59** G1 56 50N 2 50W
North European Plain Europe **76** J6/K6 54 00N 20 00E
North Fiji Basin Pacific Ocean **150** H6 18 00S 173 00E
North Foreland *c.* Kent England **71** F2 51 23N 1 27E
North Frisian Islands *see* Nordfriesische Inseln
North Guwahati Assam India **110** J7 26 15N 91 38E
North Head Australia **119** H2 33 49S 151 18E
North Hollywood U.S.A. **139** A3 34 10N 118 22W
North Hykeham Lincolnshire England **65** E2 53 12N 0 34W
Northiam East Sussex England **71** E1 50 59N 0 36E
North Island New Zealand **119** B3/C3 36 40S 177 00E
North Kessock Highland Scotland **59** E2 57 30N 4 15W
North Koel *r.* India **110** B4 23 20N 84 20E
NORTH KOREA 113 P6/7
North Lanarkshire *u.a.* Scotland **61** E3/F3 55 50N 3 55W
North Land *see* Severnaya Zemlya
Northleach Gloucestershire England **70** C2 51 51N 1 50W
North Lincolnshire *u.a.* England **65** E2 53 40N 0 40W
North Little Rock U.S.A. **135** H3 34 46N 92 16W
North Loup *r.* U.S.A. **134** F5 42 00N 100 00W
North Pacific Ocean 150
North Petherton Somerset England **73** D4 51 06N 3 01W
North Platte *r.* U.S.A. **132** O1 42 00N 104 00W
North Platte Nebraska U.S.A. **134** F5 41 09N 100 45W
North Point Barbados **141** V13 13 20N 59 37W
North Point *tn.* H.K. China **112** C1 22 18N 114 12E
North Pole Arctic Ocean **148** 90 00N
North Port Russia **102** L2 55 50N 37 29E
North River *tn.* Canada **133** Q4 58 55N 94 30W
North Ronaldsay *i.* Orkney Islands Scotland **57** C2 59 23N 2 26W
North Ronaldsay Firth Orkney Islands Scotland **57** C2 59 20N 2 30W
North Sea Atlantic Ocean **76** F7 57 00N 4 00E
North Shields Tyne & Wear England **65** D4 55 01N 1 26W
North Somercotes Lincolnshire England **65** F2 53 28N 0 08E
North Somerset *u.a.* England **70** B2 51 15N 2 50W
North Sound Galway Rep. of Ireland **74** B3 53 11N 9 43W
North Sound, The Orkney Islands Scotland **57** C2 59 17N 2 45W
North Tawton Devon England **72** D3 50 48N 3 53W
North Tidworth Wiltshire England **70** C2 51 16N 1 40W
North Tyne *r.* Northumberland England **61** G3 55 05N 2 10W
North Uist *i.* Western Isles Scotland **58** B2 57 04N 7 15W
Northumberland *co.* England **61** G3/H3 55 10N 2 05W
Northumberland National Park Northumberland England **61** G3 55 15N 2 10W
North Walsham Norfolk England **71** F3 52 50N 1 24E
North West Cape Australia **118** A5 21 48S 114 10E
North West Christmas Island Ridge Pacific Ocean **151** J8 9 30N 170 00W
Northwestern Atlantic Basin Atlantic Ocean **152** B10 33 00N 70 00W
Northwest Highlands Highland Scotland **58/9** D2/E3 58 00N 5 00W
Northwest Pacific Basin Pacific Ocean **150** F11 35 00N 150 00E
Northwest Territories *territory* Canada **132/133** M6 65 15N 115 00W
North Wheatley Nottinghamshire England **65** E2 53 22N 0 52W
Northwich Cheshire England **64** C2 53 16N 2 32W
North Wingfield Derbyshire England **67** F3 53 09N 1 24W
North York Moors North Yorkshire England **65** E3 55 22N 0 45W
North York Moors National Park North Yorkshire England **65** D3/E3 54 22N 0 45W
North Yorkshire *co.* England **64** C3/D3 54 10N 2 10W
Norton North Yorkshire England **65** E3 54 08N 0 48W
Norton Kansas U.S.A. **134** G4 39 51N 99 53W
Norton Sound U.S.A. **132** C5 64 00N 162 30W
Norvegia, Cape Antarctica **149** 71 28S 122 25W
Norwalk California U.S.A. **139** B2 33 56N 118 04W
Norwalk Connecticut U.S.A. **137** F2 41 07N 73 25W
NORWAY 97 B3
Norway House *tn.* Canada **133** P3 53 59N 97 50W
Norwegian Basin Arctic Ocean **152** H13 67 00N 0 00
Norwegian Sea Arctic Ocean **148** 70 00N 5 00E
Norwich Norfolk England **71** F3 52 38N 1 18E
Norwich Connecticut U.S.A. **137** F2 41 32N 72 05W
Nos Emine *pt.* Bulgaria **94** E5 42 40N 27 56E
Noshiro Japan **114** D3 40 13N 140 00E
Nos Kaliakra *pt.* Bulgaria **94** F5 43 21N 28 30E
Nosop *r.* Southern Africa **125** D2 25 00S 20 30E
Noss Head Highland Scotland **59** F3 58 28N 3 04W
Nosy Bé *i.* Madagascar **125** I5 13 00S 47 00E
Notéc *r.* Poland **96** B4 53 00N 17 00E
Notre Dame Bay Canada **133** X2 49 40N 55 00W
Notre-Dame du Lac *tn.* Canada **137** G3 47 38N 68 49W

Nottaway River Canada 137 E4 51 00N 78 00W
Nottingham Nottinghamshire England 65 D1 52 58N 1 10W
Nottingham Island Canada 133 T5 62 15N 77 30W
Nottinghamshire co. England 65 D2/E2 53 20N 1 00W
Nouadhibou Mauritania 127 B7 20 54N 17 01W
Nouakchott Mauritania 127 B6 18 09N 15 58W
Nouméa New Caledonia 118 L5 22 16S 166 26E
Nouzonville France 89 D1 49 49N 4 45E
Nova Friburgo Brazil 147 I8 22 16S 42 34W
Nova Iguaçu Brazil 147 I8 22 46S 43 23W
Nova Iguaçu admin. Brazil 147 P3 22 41S 43 20W
Nova Kakhovka Ukraine 95 H7 46 45N 33 20E
Nova Odesa Ukraine 94 G7 47 19N 31 45E
Novara Italy 92 A3 45 27N 8 37E
Nova Scotia province Canada 133 W1 44 30N 65 00W
Nova Scotia Basin Atlantic Ocean 152 C10 39 00N 55 00W
Novaya Zemlya is. Russia 103 H10 74 00N 55 00E
Nova Zagora Bulgaria 94 E5 42 29N 26 00E
Novgorod Russia 102 F7 58 30N 31 20E
Novi Iskŭr Bulgaria 94 C5 42 46N 23 19E
Novi Pazar Bulgaria 94 E5 43 20N 27 12E
Novi Pazar Serbia Yugoslavia 96 C2 43 09N 20 29E
Novi Sad Serbia Yugoslavia 96 B3 45 15N 19 51E
Novoazovs'k Ukraine 95 L7 47 07N 38 05E
Novocheboksarsk Russia 104 F6 56 05N 47 27E
Novocherkassk Russia 104 E4 47 25N 40 05E
Novo Hamburgo Brazil 147 G7 29 37S 51 07W
Novokazalinsk Kazakhstan 105 J4 45 48N 62 06E
Novokuybyshevsk Russia 104 G5 53 05N 49 59E
Novokuznetsk Russia 103 K6 53 45N 87 12E
Novolazarevskaya r.s. Antarctica 149 70 46S 11 50E
Novomikhaylovskiy Russia 95 L6 44 15N 38 53E
Novomoskovsk Russia 104 D5 54 06N 38 15E
Novooleksiyivka Ukraine 95 J7 46 14N 34 36E
Novopokrovskaya Russia 95 M6 45 56N 40 42E
Novorossiysk Russia 102 F4 44 44N 37 46E
Novoshakhtinsk Russia 104 D4 47 46N 39 55E
Novosibirsk Russia 103 K7 55 04N 83 05E
Novosibirskiye Ostrova (New Siberian Islands) is. Russia 148 75 00N 145 00E
Novotroitsk Russia 105 H5 51 11N 58 16E
Novotroyits'ke Ukraine 95 J7 46 21N 34 21E
Novvy Port Russia 103 J9 67 38N 72 33E
Novvy Urengoy Russia 103 J9 66 00N 77 20E
Nowai r. India 108 K2 22 39N 88 28E
Nowa Sól Poland 96 B4 51 49N 15 41E
Nowen Hill hill Cork Rep. of Ireland 75 B1 51 43N 9 11W
Nowgong India 109 G5 26 20N 92 41E
Nowy Dwor Mazowiecki Poland 96 C4 52 27N 20 41E
Nowy Sącz Poland 96 C3 49 39N 20 40E
Nubian Desert Sudan 124 F12 21 00N 33 00E
Nueces r. Texas U.S.A. 134 G2 28 00N 99 00W
Nueltin Lake Canada 133 P5 60 30N 99 00W
Nueva Rosita Mexico 140 D5 27 58N 101 11W
Nueva San Salvador El Salvador 140 G2 13 40N 89 18W
Nuevitas Cuba 141 I4 21 34N 77 18W
Nuevo Casas Grandes Mexico 140 C6 30 22N 107 53W
Nuevo Laredo Mexico 140 E5 27 39N 99 30W
Nuevo Leon admin. Mexico 134 F2 25 30N 100 00W
Nu Jiang (Salween) r. China/Myanmar 113 J4 25 00N 99 00E
Nuku'alofa Tonga 150 I5 21 09S 175 14W
Nukus Uzbekistan 105 H3 42 28N 59 07E
Nullarbor Plain Australia 118 D3 32 00S 128 00E
Numazu Japan 114 K2 35 08N 138 50E
Numedal geog. reg. Norway 97 B3 60 40N 9 00E
Nunap Isua (Kap Farvel) c. Greenland 133 AA4 60 00N 44 00W
Nuneaton Warwickshire England 67 F2 52 32N 1 28W
Nunivak Island U.S.A. 132 B5 60 00N 166 00W
Nunspeet Netherlands 89 E4 52 22N 5 47E
Nuoro Italy 92 A2 40 20N 9 21E
Nura r. Kazakhstan 105 L5 51 00N 71 00E
Nürnberg (Nuremberg) Germany 93 B2 49 27N 11 05E
Nürtingen Germany 93 A1 48 37N 9 20E
Nusaybin Turkey 95 M2 37 05N 41 11E
Nushki Pakistan 108 B5 29 33N 66 01E
Nutak Newfoundland Canada 133 W4 57 30N 61 59W
Nuthe r. Germany 87 E1 52 21N 13 07E
Nuuk (Godthåb) Greenland 133 Y5 64 10N 51 40W
Nuussuaq p. Greenland 133 Y7 70 50N 53 00W
Nyainqêntênglha Shan mts. China 112 G4/H5 30 00N 90 00E
Nyala Sudan 124 D10 12 01N 24 50E
Nyasa, Lake (Lake Malawi) Southern Africa 125 F5 12 00S 35 00E
Nyíregyháza Hungary 96 C3 47 57N 21 43E
Nykøbing Denmark 97 C1 54 47N 11 53E
Nyköping Sweden 97 D2 58 45N 17 03E
Nyngan Australia 118 H3 31 34S 147 14E
Nyoman r. Lithuania/Russia 104 55 00N 22 00E
Nyons France 91 D1 44 22N 5 08E
Nysa Poland 96 B4 50 30N 17 20E
Nysa (Niesse) r. Poland 96 A4 52 00N 14 00E
Nyūdō-zaki c. Japan 114 C2 40 00N 139 42E

O

Oadby Leicestershire England 67 F2 52 36N 1 04W
Oahe, Lake U.S.A. 134 F6 45 00N 100 00W
Oahu i. Hawaiian Is. 151 X18-Y18 21 30N 158 10W
Oakengates Shropshire England 67 E2 52 42N 2 28W
Oakes North Dakota U.S.A. 136 A3 46 08N 98 07W
Oakham Rutland England 70 D3 52 40N 0 43W
Oak Hill tn. U.S.A. 137 D1 37 58N 81 11W
Oakland California U.S.A. 134 B4 37 50N 122 15W
Oakland City Indiana U.S.A. 136 C1 38 21N 87 19W
Oakley Hampshire England 70 C2 51 15N 1 11W
Oakley Fife Scotland 61 F4 56 05N 3 35W
Oak Ridge tn. U.S.A. 135 J4 36 02N 84 12W
Oakville Canada 137 E2 43 27N 79 41W
Oamaru N.Z. 119 B1 45 06S 170 58E
Oano Islands Pitcairn Is. 151 N5 23 32S 125 00W
Ōarai Japan 114 M3 36 18N 140 35E
Oates Land geog. reg. Antarctica 149 70 00S 150 00E
Oaxaca Mexico 140 E3 17 05N 96 41W
Ob' r. Russia 103 I9 65 30N 66 00E
Oba Canada 133 S2 48 38N 84 17W
Obama Japan 114 G2 35 25N 135 45E
Oban Argyll & Bute Scotland 58 D1 56 25N 5 29W
Oberhausen Germany 93 A2 51 27N 6 50E
Ober Österreich admin. Austria 93 B1 48 00N 14 00E
Oberursel Germany 93 A2 50 12N 8 35E
Ob', Gulf of Russia 103 J9 68 00N 74 00E
Obidos Brazil 146 F12 1 52S 55 30W
Obihiro Japan 114 D3 42 56N 143 10E
Obitsu r. Japan 115 C2 35 25N 139 53E
O'Briensbridge Clare Rep. of Ireland 75 C2 52 45N 8 30W
Ocala Florida U.S.A. 135 J2 29 11N 82 09W
Ocaña Colombia 146 C14 8 16N 73 21W
Ocatlán Mexico 140 D4 20 21N 102 42W
Ocean City Maryland U.S.A. 137 E1 38 21N 75 06W
Ochakiv Ukraine 94 G7 46 37N 31 33E
Och'amch'ire Georgia 95 M5 42 44N 41 30E
Ochil Hills Perth & Kinross Scotland 59 F1 56 15N 3 30W
Ochokovo Russia 102 L1 55 39N 37 30E
Ocho Rios Jamaica 141 Q8 18 24N 77 06W
Ock r. Oxfordshire England 70 C2 51 38N 1 26W
Oconto U.S.A. 136 C2 44 55N 87 52W
Octeville France 73 F2 49 37N 1 39W
Ōda Japan 114 B2 35 10N 132 29E
Odate Japan 114 D3 40 18N 140 32E
Odawara Japan 114 L2 35 15N 139 08E
Odda Norway 97 B3 60 03N 6 34E
Oddsta Shetland Islands Scotland 57 F3 60 37N 0 59W
Ödemis Turkey 94 E3 38 11N 27 58E
Odense Denmark 97 C2 55 24N 10 25E
Odenwald mts. Germany 93 A1 49 00N 9 00E
Oder (Odra) r. Europe 93 B2 53 00N 14 00E
Oder-Spree Kanal can. Germany 87 G1 52 21N 13 43E
Odesa (Odessa) Ukraine 104 C4 46 30N 30 46E
Odessa Delaware U.S.A. 137 E1 39 27N 75 40W
Odessa Texas U.S.A. 134 F3 31 50N 102 23W
Odiel r. Spain 90 A2 37 32N 7 00W
Odon r. France 73 G2 49 06N 0 16W
Odra (Oder) r. Europe 93 B2 53 00N 14 00E
Oegstgeest Netherlands 88 B2 52 10N 4 29E
Oekusi see Dili
Ofanto r. Italy 92 C2 41 00N 15 00E
Offaly co. Rep. of Ireland 74/75 D3 53 15N 7 35W
Offenbach am Main Germany 93 A2 50 06N 8 46E
Offenburg Germany 93 A1 48 29N 7 57E
Ofuna Japan 115 B2 53 21N 139 32E
Ofunato Japan 114 D2 39 04N 141 43E
Ogaden geog. reg. Africa 124 I9 7 00N 51 00E
Ōgaki Japan 114 H2 35 22N 136 36E
Ogano Japan 114 L2 35 55N 139 11E
Ogasawara Guntō i. Pacific Ocean 150 E10 27 30N 43 00E
Ogawa Japan 115 A3 35 43N 135 29E
Ogbomoso Nigeria 127 F4 8 05N 4 11E
Ogden Utah U.S.A. 134 D5 41 14N 111 59W
Ogdensburg U.S.A. 137 E2 44 42N 75 31W
Ogilvie Mountains Canada 132 H6 65 05N 139 00W
Ogoki r. Canada 133 R3 51 00N 87 00W
Ogooué r. Gabon 127 G2 0 50S 9 50E
Ōhara Japan 114 M2 35 16N 140 22E
Ōhata Japan 114 D3 41 22N 141 11E
Ohio r. U.S.A. 136 C1 38 00N 85 00W
Ohio state U.S.A. 137 D2 40 00N 83 00W
Ohio River Pennsylvania U.S.A. 135 I4 40 30N 80 05W
Ohori Japan 115 C2 35 22N 139 52E
Ohře r. Czech Rep. 93 B2 50 00N 14 00E
Ohre r. Germany 93 B2 52 00N 11 00E
Ohrid FYROM 94 B4 41 06N 20 49E
Ohridsko Ezero l. Europe 94 B4 41 00N 21 00E
Oil City Pennsylvania U.S.A. 137 E2 41 26N 79 44W
Oilgate Wexford Rep. of Ireland 75 E2 52 25N 6 32W
Oise r. France 91 C2 49 10N 2 10E
Oistins Barbados 141 V12 13 04N 59 35W
Oistins Bay Barbados 141 V12 13 03N 59 34W
Ōita Japan 114 B1 33 15N 131 36E
Ojinaga Mexico 140 D5 29 35N 104 26W
Oka r. Russia 104 E5/6 55 00N 42 00E
Okanagan r. North America 134 C6 49 00N 119 00W
Okara Pakistan 107 L5 30 49N 73 31E
Okavango r. Southern Africa 125 C4 17 50S 20 00E
Okavango Basin Botswana 125 D4 19 00S 23 00E
Okaya Japan 114 C2 36 03N 138 00E
Okayama Japan 114 B1 34 40N 133 54E
Okazaki Japan 114 J1 34 58N 137 10E
Okeechobee, Lake U.S.A. 135 J2 27 00N 81 00W
Okehampton Devon England 72 C3 50 44N 4 00W
Okene Nigeria 127 G4 7 31N 6 14E
Okha Russia 103 Q6 53 35N 143 01E
Okhla India 108 M4 28 33N 77 16E
Okhotsk Russia 103 Q7 59 20N 143 15E
Okhotsk, Sea of Russia 103 Q7 55 00N 148 00E
Oki is. Japan 114 B2 36 05N 133 00E
Okinawa i. Japan 113 P4 26 30N 128 00E
Oklahoma state U.S.A. 135 G4 36 00N 98 00W
Oklahoma City U.S.A. 135 G4 35 28N 97 33W
Oktyabr'skiy Russia 103 R6 52 43N 156 14E
Okushiri-tō i. Japan 114 C3 42 15N 139 30E
Öland i. Sweden 97 D2 56 45N 51 50E
Olbia Italy 92 A2 40 56N 9 30E
Oldbury West Midlands England 67 E2 52 30N 2 00W
Oldcastle Meath Rep. of Ireland 74 D3 53 46N 7 10W
Old Crow Yukon Canada 132 H6 67 34N 139 43W
Oldenburg Germany 93 A2 53 08N 8 13E
Oldenzaal Netherlands 89 F4 52 19N 6 55E
Old Fletton Cambridgeshire England 70 D3 52 34N 0 12W
Oldham Greater Manchester England 64 C2 53 33N 2 07W
Old Harbour tn. Jamaica 141 Q7 17 56N 77 07W
Old Harbour Bay tn. Jamaica 141 Q7 17 54N 77 06W
Old Head c. Mayo Rep. of Ireland 74 B3 53 47N 9 46W
Old Head of Kinsale c. Cork Rep. of Ireland 75 C1 51 40N 8 30W
Oldmeldrum Aberdeenshire Scotland 59 G2 57 20N 2 20W
Olds Canada 132 M3 51 50N 114 06W
Old Town Maine U.S.A. 137 G2 44 55N 68 41W
Olean U.S.A. 137 E2 42 05N 78 26W
Olekma r. Russia 103 O7 59 00N 121 00E
Olekminsk Russia 103 O8 60 25N 120 25E
Olenëk Russia 103 N9 68 28N 112 18E
Olenëk r. Russia 103 O10 72 00N 122 00E
Olhão Portugal 90 A2 37 01N 7 50W
Olinda Brazil 146 J11 8 00S 34 51W
Olivia Minnesota U.S.A. 136 B2 44 47N 94 58W
Ollerton Nottinghamshire England 65 D2 53 12N 1 00W
Olney Milton Keynes England 70 D3 52 09N 0 43W
Olomouc Czech Rep. 96 B3 49 38N 17 15E
Olongapo The Philippines 111 G6 14 49N 120 17E
Olsztyn Poland 96 C4 53 48N 20 29E
Olten Switzerland 92 A3 47 22N 7 55E
Olteniţa Romania 96 D2 44 05N 26 40E
Olympia Washington U.S.A. 134 B6 47 03N 122 53W
Olympus mt. Greece 94 C4 40 05N 22 21E
Olympus mt. Cyprus 95 H1 34 55N 32 52E
Olympus, Mount U.S.A. 134 B6 47 49N 123 42W
Om' r. Russia 103 J7 55 30N 79 00E
Omagh district Northern Ireland 60 B2 54 30N 7 30W
Omagh Omagh Northern Ireland 60 B2 54 36N 7 18W
Omaha Nebraska U.S.A. 135 G5 41 15N 96 00W
OMAN 107 I2
Oman, Gulf of Iran/Oman 107 I3 24 30N 58 30E
Omboué Gabon 127 G2 1 38S 9 20E
Omdurman Sudan 124 F11 15 37N 32 29E
Ome Japan 114 L2 35 48N 139 17E
Omeath Louth Rep. of Ireland 74 E4 54 06N 6 17W
Omihachiman Japan 114 H2 35 08N 136 04E
Ōmiya Japan 114 L2 35 54N 139 39E
Omo r. Ethiopia 124 G9 7 00N 37 00E
Omolon r. Russia 103 R9/S9 65 00N 160 00E
Omoloy r. Russia 103 P9 70 00N 132 00E
Omsk Russia 103 J7 55 00N 73 22E
Ōmuta Japan 114 B1 33 02N 130 26E
Omutinskiy Russia 105 K6 56 30N 67 40E
Ondal West Bengal India 110 E4 23 36N 87 12E
Ondo Nigeria 127 F4 7 05N 4 55E
Onega, Lake see Ozero Onezhskoy
Oneonta U.S.A. 137 E2 42 28N 75 04W
Oneşti Romania 96 D3 46 15N 26 45E
Onezhskoye Ozero (Lake Onega) l. Russia 102 F8 62 00N 40 00E
Ongea Levu i. Fiji 150 V15 19 11S 178 28W
Onitsha Nigeria 127 G4 6 10N 6 47E
Ono Japan 114 F1 34 52N 134 55E
Onomichi Japan 114 B1 34 25N 33 11E
Onon r. Russia/Mongolia 113 M9 51 00N 114 00E
Onslow Australia 118 B5 21 41S 115 12E
Ontario province Canada 135 I7 51 00N 91 00W
Ontario California U.S.A. 134 C3 34 04N 117 38W
Ontario, Lake Canada/U.S.A. 137 E2 43 45N 78 00W
Ontonagon Michigan U.S.A. 136 C3 46 52N 89 18W
Onuki Japan 115 C2 35 17N 139 53E
Oola Limerick Rep. of Ireland 75 C2 52 33N 8 16W
Oologah Lake U.S.A. 136 A1 36 00N 95 00W
Oostelijk Flevoland geog. reg. Netherlands 89 E4 52 30N 5 40E
Oostende Belgium 89 B3 51 13N 2 55E
Oosterhout Netherlands 89 D3 51 39N 4 52E
Oosterschelde sd. Netherlands 89 C3 51 30N 3 58E
Oost-Vlaanderen admin. Belgium 89 C3 51 10N 3 45E
Oostvoorne Netherlands 88 A1 51 55N 4 06E
Opala Congo (D.R.) 124 D7 0 40S 24 20E
Opava Czech Rep. 96 B3 49 58N 17 55E
Opochka Russia 97 F2 56 41N 28 42E
Opole Poland 96 B4 50 40N 17 56E
Oporto see Porto
Opotiki N.Z. 119 C3 38 01S 177 17E
Optic Lake tn. Canada 133 O3 54 47N 101 15W
Oradea Romania 96 C3 47 03N 21 55E
Oradell Reservoir U.S.A. 138 B2 40 58N 74 00W
Orai India 109 D5 26 00N 79 26E
Oran Algeria 127 E10 35 45N 0 38W
Orán Argentina 147 E8 23 07S 64 16W
Orange Australia 118 H3 33 19S 149 10E
Orange France 91 C1 44 08N 4 48E
Orange r. Southern Africa 125 C2 28 30S 17 30E
Orange California U.S.A. 139 C2 33 43N 117 54W
Orange New Jersey U.S.A. 138 B2 40 45N 74 14W
Orange Texas U.S.A. 135 H3 30 05N 93 43W
Orangeburg U.S.A. 135 J3 33 28N 80 53W
Orange County admin. California U.S.A. 139 C2
Orange Free State admin. Rep. of South Africa 125 E2 27 30S 27 30E
Oranienburg Germany 93 B2 52 46N 13 15E
Oranmore Galway Rep. of Ireland 74 C3 53 16N 8 54W
Oraviţa Romania 96 C3 45 02N 21 43E
Orbetello Italy 92 B2 42 27N 11 07E
Orbigo r. Spain 90 A3 42 15N 5 45W
Orcadas r.s. Antarctica 149 60 44S 44 44W
Orchies France 89 C2 50 28N 3 15E
Orchy r. Argyll & Bute Scotland 59 E1 56 25N 4 50W
Orcia r. Italy 92 B2 42 00N 11 00E
Ordu Turkey 95 K4 41 00N 37 52E
Ordzhonikidze see Vladikavkaz
Örebro Sweden 97 D2 59 17N 15 13E
Oregon state U.S.A. 134 B5/C5 44 00N 120 00W
Oregon City Oregon U.S.A. 134 B6 45 21N 122 36W
Orekhovo-Zuyevo Russia 104 D6 55 47N 39 00E
Orël Russia 102 F6 52 58N 36 04E
Orem Utah U.S.A. 134 D5 40 20N 111 45W
Orenburg Russia 102 H6 51 50N 55 00E
Orense Spain 90 A3 42 20N 7 52W
Orestiáda Greece 94 E4 41 30N 26 33E
Orford Suffolk England 71 F3 52 06N 1 31E
Orford Ness c. Suffolk England 71 F3 52 05N 1 34E
Orge r. France 87 B1 48 40N 2 22E
Orhei Moldova 94 F7 47 23N 28 49E
Orient Bay tn. Canada 136 C3 49 23N 88 08W
Orihuela Spain 90 B2 38 05N 0 56W
Orillia Canada 137 E2 44 36N 79 26W
Orinoco r. Venezuela/Colombia 151 T8 8 00N 64 00W
Orissa admin. India 109 E4 20 20N 83 00E
Oristano Italy 92 A1 39 54N 8 36E
Orizaba Mexico 140 E3 18 51N 97 08W
Orkney Islands u.a. Scotland 57 B1/C2 59 00N 3 00W
Orlando Florida U.S.A. 135 J2 28 33N 81 21W
Orléans France 91 C2 47 54N 1 54E
Orly France 87 B1 48 44N 2 24E
Ormskirk Lancashire England 64 C2 53 35N 2 54W
Orne r. France 91 B2 48 50N 0 16W
Örnsköldsvik Sweden 97 D3 63 19N 18 45E
Oronsay i. Argyll & Bute Scotland 60 C4 56 00N 6 15W
Orontes see Asi
Oropucha r. Trinidad & Tobago 141 T10 10 36N 61 05W
Orrell Greater Manchester England 64 C2 53 33N 2 45W
Orrin Reservoir Highland Scotland 59 E2 57 30N 4 45W
Orsay France 87 A1 48 42N 2 11E
Orsha Belarus 104 C5 54 30N 30 23E
Orsk Russia 102 H6 51 13N 58 35E
Orşova Romania 96 C2 44 42N 22 22E
Orta Turkey 95 H4 40 37N 33 04E
Ortaköy Turkey 95 J4 40 17N 35 17E
Orthez France 91 B1 43 29N 0 46W
Ortigueira Spain 90 A3 43 43N 8 13W
Ortoire r. Trinidad & Tobago 141 T9 10 16N 61 15W
Ortona Italy 92 B2 42 21N 14 24E
Ortonville Minnesota U.S.A. 136 A3 45 18N 96 28W
Ortze r. Germany 93 B2 53 00N 10 00E
Orūmīyeh Iran 106 F6 37 40N 45 00E
Oruro Bolivia 146 D9 17 59S 67 08W
Orvieto Italy 92 B2 42 43N 12 06E
Orwell r. Suffolk England 71 F3 52 00N 1 15E
Osage r. U.S.A. 136 B1 38 00N 93 00W
Ōsaka Japan 114 G1 34 40N 135 30E
Ōsaka pref. Japan 114 G1 34 30N 135 10E
Ōsaka-wan b. Japan 114 G1 34 30N 135 10E
Osceola Iowa U.S.A. 136 B2 41 02N 93 46W
Osh Kirgyzstan 105 L3 40 37N 72 49E
Oshawa Canada 137 E2 43 53N 78 51W
Ō-shima i. Japan 114 C1 34 45N 139 25E
Oshkosh U.S.A. 136 C2 44 01N 88 32W
Oshogbo Nigeria 127 F4 7 50N 4 35E
Osijek Croatia 92 C3 45 33N 18 41E
Oskaloosa Iowa U.S.A. 136 B2 41 16N 92 40W
Oslo Norway 97 C2 59 56N 10 45E
Oslofjorden fj. Norway 97 C2 59 20N 10 37E
Osmaneli Turkey 94 F4 40 22N 30 00E
Osmaniye Turkey 106 E6 37 04N 36 15E
Osnabrück Germany 93 A2 52 17N 8 03E
Osorno Chile 147 C4 40 35S 73 14W
Oss Netherlands 89 E3 51 46N 5 31E
Ossa, Mount Australia 118 H1 41 52S 146 04E
Ossett West Yorkshire England 64 D2 53 41N 1 35W
Ostankino Russia 102 M2 55 50N 37 37E
Österdalälven r. Sweden 97 C3 61 40N 13 30E
Østerdalen geog. reg. Norway 97 C3 62 00N 10 30E
Osterode Germany 93 B2 51 44N 10 15E
Östersund Sweden 97 C3 63 10N 14 40E
Östervall Sweden 97 D3 62 20N 15 20E
Ostfriesische Inseln (East Frisian Islands) is. Germany 93 A2 53 00N 7 00E
Ostrava Czech Rep. 96 B3 49 50N 18 15E
Ostróda Poland 96 B4 53 42N 19 59E
Ostrołęka Poland 96 C4 53 05N 21 32E
Ostrov Russia 97 F2 57 52N 28 20E
Ostrowiec Swietokrzyski Poland 96 C4 50 58N 21 22E
Ostrów Mazowiecka Poland 96 C4 52 50N 21 51E
Ostrów Wielkopolski Poland 96 B4 51 39N 17 50E
Oswaldtwistle Lancashire England 64 C2 53 44N 2 24W
Oswego U.S.A. 137 E2 43 27N 76 31W
Oswestry Shropshire England 66 D2 52 52N 3 03W
Ōta Japan 115 B3 33 15N 131 36E
Otaheite Bay Trinidad & Tobago 141 S9 10 15N 61 30W
Otaki N.Z. 119 C2 40 46S 175 09E
Otaru Japan 114 D3 43 14N 140 59E
Otava r. Czech Rep. 93 B1 49 00N 13 00E
Otavalo Ecuador 146 B13 0 13N 78 15W
Otford Kent England 71 E2 51 19N 0 12E
O'The Cherokees, Lake Oklahoma U.S.A. 136 B1 37 00N 95 00W
Otley West Yorkshire England 64 D2 53 54N 1 41W
Otra r. Norway 97 B2 56 17N 7 30E
Otranto Italy 92 C2 40 08N 18 30E
Otranto, Strait of Adriatic Sea 92 C1/2 40 00N 19 00E
Otsego Michigan U.S.A. 136 C2 42 46N 85 42W
Ōtsu Japan 114 G2 35 00N 135 50E
Otsuki Japan 114 K2 35 38N 138 53E
Ottawa Canada 137 E3 45 24N 75 38W
Ottawa r. /Québec Canada 137 E3 46 00N 77 00W
Ottawa Illinois U.S.A. 136 C2 41 21N 88 51W
Ottawa Kansas U.S.A. 136 A1 38 35N 95 16W
Ottawa Islands Canada 133 S4 59 10N 80 25W
Otter r. Devon England 73 D3 50 51N 3 08W
Otterburn Northumberland England 61 G3 55 14N 2 10W
Otter Rapids tn. Canada 137 D4 50 12N 81 40W
Ottery r. Cornwall England 72 C3 50 40N 4 27W
Ottery St. Mary Devon England 73 D3 50 45N 3 17W
Ottumwa Iowa U.S.A. 136 B2 41 02N 92 26W
Ouachita Mountains U.S.A. 135 G3/H3 34 00N 95 00W
Ouadda Central African Rep. 124 D9 8 09N 22 20E
Ouagadougou Burkina 127 E5 12 20N 1 40W
Ouahigouya Burkina 127 E5 13 31N 2 20W
Ouargla Algeria 127 G9 32 00N 5 16E
Ouassel r. Algeria 90 C2 35 30N 2 00E
Oubangui r. Central Africa 127 I3 0 00 17 30E
Oude Mass r. Netherlands 88 B1/C1 52 06N 4 46E
Oudenaarde Belgium 89 C2 50 50N 3 37E
Oude Rijn r. Netherlands 89 D4 52 06N 4 46E
Oudtshoorn Rep. of South Africa 125 D1 33 35S 22 12E
Oued Dra r. Morocco 127 C8 28 10N 11 00W
Oued Zem Morocco 127 D9 32 55N 6 33W
Ouerrha r. Morocco 90 A1 34 00N 6 00W
Ouesso Congo 127 I3 1 38N 16 03E
Ouezzane Morocco 90 A1 34 25N 5 35W
Oughterard Galway Rep. of Ireland 74 B3 53 26N 9 19W
Ouham r. Central African Rep. 124 C9 7 00N 17 30E
Ouichita r. U.S.A. 135 H3 34 00N 93 00W
Oujda Morocco 127 E9 34 41N 1 45W
Oulart Wexford Rep. of Ireland 75 E2 53 30N 6 23W
Oulu Finland 97 F4 65 02N 25 27E
Oulu järvi l. Finland 97 F3 64 20N 27 00E
Oulujöki r. Finland 97 F3 64 50N 26 00E
Oundle Northamptonshire England 70 D3 52 29N 0 29W
Our r. Luxembourg/Germany 89 F1 50 00N 6 00E
Ourthe r. Belgium 89 E2 50 20N 5 50E
Ōu-sanmyaku mts. Japan 114 D2 39 20N 141 00E
Ouse r. East Sussex England 70 E1 50 55N 0 03E
Ouse r. North Yorkshire/York/East Riding of Yorkshire England 65 E2 53 45N 1 00W
Oust r. France 91 B2 47 50N 2 30W
Outer Hebrides is. Western Isles Scotland 58 B2/3 58 00N 7 00W
Outreau France 89 A2 50 42N 1 36E
Out Skerries is. Shetland Islands Scotland 57 F3 60 25N 0 46W
Outwell Norfolk England 71 E3 52 37N 0 14E
Ovalau i. Fiji 150 U16 17 40S 178 47E
Ovalle Chile 147 C6 30 33S 71 16W
Overflakkee i. Netherlands 89 D3 51 45N 4 10E
Overijssel admin. Netherlands 89 F4 52 23N 6 28E
Overton Hampshire England 70 C2 51 15N 1 15W
Overton Wrexham Wales 66 E2 52 58N 2 56W
Övertorneå Sweden 97 E4 66 22N 23 40E
Ovidiopol' Ukraine 94 G7 46 15N 30 25E
Oviedo Spain 90 A3 43 21N 7 18W
Owando Congo 127 I2 0 27S 15 44E
Owatonna Minnesota U.S.A. 136 B2 44 06N 93 10W
Owenboy r. Cork Rep. of Ireland 75 C1 51 49N 8 29W
Owenduff r. Mayo Rep. of Ireland 74 B4 54 03N 9 45W
Owenea r. Donegal Rep. of Ireland 74 C4 54 47N 8 22W
Owen Falls Dam Uganda 124 F8 0 29N 33 11E
Oweniny r. Mayo Rep. of Ireland 74 B4 54 11N 9 33W
Owenkillew r. Omagh Northern Ireland 60 B2 54 44N 7 09W
Owenmore r. Mayo Rep. of Ireland 74 B4 54 08N 9 40W
Owenmore r. Sligo Rep. of Ireland 74 C4 54 10N 8 30W
Owen, Mount N.Z. 119 B2 41 33S 172 33E
Owensboro Kentucky U.S.A. 136 C1 37 45N 87 05W
Owens Lake California U.S.A. 134 C4 36 25N 117 56W
Owen Sound tn. Canada 137 D2 44 3N 80 56W
Owen Stanley Range Papua New Guinea 118 H8 9 15S 148 30E
Owo Nigeria 127 G4 7 10N 5 39E
Owosso Michigan U.S.A. 137 D2 43 00N 84 11W
Owyhee r. U.S.A. 134 C5 43 00N 117 00W
Oxford Oxfordshire England 70 C2 51 46N 1 15W
Oxfordshire co. England 70 C2 51 50N 1 25W
Oxnard California U.S.A. 134 C3 34 11N 119 10W
Oxted Surrey England 70 D2 51 15N 0 01W
Oyama Japan 114 C2 36 18N 139 48E
Oyapock r. Brazil 146 G13 3 00N 52 30W
Oyem Gabon 127 H3 1 34N 11 31E
Oykel r. Highland Scotland 59 E2 57 58N 4 40W
Oyo Nigeria 127 F4 7 50N 3 55E
Oysterhaven Cork Rep. of Ireland 75 C1 51 41N 8 26W
Ozark Plateau Missouri U.S.A. 135 H4 37 00N 93 00W
Ozarks, Lake of the Missouri U.S.A. 136 B1 38 00N 93 00W
Ozero Alakol' salt l. Kazakhstan 105 N4 46 00N 82 00E
Ozero Aydarkul' l. Kazakhstan 105 K3 41 00N 68 00E
Ozero Balkhash (Lake Balkhash) l. Kazakhstan 105 L4/M4 46 00N 75 00E
Ozero Baykal (Lake Baykal) l. Russia 103 M6 54 00N 109 00E
Ozero Bol'shaya Imandra l. Russia 97 G4 67 45N 33 00E
Ozero Chany salt l. Russia 103 J6 55 00N 77 30E
Ozero Il'men' l. Russia 102 F7 58 00N 31 30E
Ozero Issyk-Kul' salt l. Kirgyzstan 105 M3 42 30N 77 30E
Ozero Khanka l. Asia 103 P5 45 00N 132 30E
Ozero Kulundinskoye l. Russia 105 M5 53 00N 80 00E
Ozero Leksozero l. Russia 97 G3 64 00N 31 20E
Ozero Manych Gudilo l. Russia 104 E4 46 30N 43 00E
Ozero Nyuk l. Russia 97 G3 64 30N 31 50E
Ozero Pskovskoye l. Estonia/Russia 97 F2 58 00N 28 00E
Ozero Pyaozero l. Russia 97 G4 66 00N 31 15E
Ozero Seletyteniz l. Kazakhstan 105 L5 53 30N 73 00E
Ozero Sevan l. Armenia 104 F3 40 00N 45 00E
Ozero Sredneye Kuyto l. Russia 97 G4 65 00N 31 15E
Ozero Taymyr l. Russia 103 M10 74 00N 102 30E
Ozero Teletskoye l. Russia 105 O5 52 00N 88 00E
Ozero Tengiz salt l. Kazakhstan 105 K5 51 00N 69 00E
Ozero Topozero l. Russia 97 G4 65 45N 32 10E
Ozero Zaysan l. Kazakhstan 105 N4 48 00N 84 00E
Ozieri Italy 92 A1 40 35N 9 01E

P

Paamiut (Frederikshåb) Greenland 133 Z5 62 05N 49 30W
Pabbay i. Western Isles Scotland 58 B2 57 47N 7 14W
Pabbay i. Western Isles Scotland 58 B1 56 51N 7 35W
Pabianice Poland 96 B4 51 40N 19 20E
Pabna Rajshahi Bangladesh 110 G5 24 00N 89 15E
Pacasmayo Peru 146 B11 7 27S 79 33W

Samer France **71** G1 50 38N 1 45E
Samkir Azerbaijan **95** P4 40 50N 45 58E
SAMOA *(WESTERN SAMOA)* **150** I6/J6
Sámos Greece **94** E2 37 45N 26 58E
Sámos *i.* Greece **94** E2 37 45N 26 45E
Samothráki Greece **94** D4 40 28N 25 32E
Samothráki *i.* Greece **94** D4 40 00N 25 00E
Samsun Turkey **95** K4 41 17N 36 22E
Samtredia Georgia **95** M5 42 10N 42 22E
San Mali **127** D5 13 21N 4 57W
San'ā Yemen Rep. **106** F2 15 23N 44 14E
SANAE *(South African National Expedition) r.s.* Antarctica **149** 70 18S 2 25W
Sanaga *r.* Cameroon **127** H3 4 30N 12 20E
Sanak Islands U.S.A. **132** C3 54 26N 162 40W
Sanandaj Iran **107** G6 35 18N 47 01E
San Andrés Tuxtla Mexico **140** E3 18 28N 95 15W
San Angelo Texas U.S.A. **134** F3 31 28N 100 28W
San Antonio Chile **147** C6 33 35S 71 39W
San Antonio Texas U.S.A. **134** G2 29 25N 98 30W
San Antonio *r.* Texas U.S.A. **135** G2 29 00N 97 00W
San Antonio Abad Balearic Is. **90** D4 38 59N 1 19E
San Antonio Oeste Argentina **147** E4 40 45S 64 58W
San Benedetto del Tronto Italy **92** B2 42 57N 13 53E
San Bernardino U.S.A. **134** C3 34 07N 117 18W
San Bernardino Freeway U.S.A. **139** C3 34 05N 117 58W
San Bernardo Chile **147** C6 33 37S 70 45W
San Carlos Falkland Is. **152** M16 51 00S 58 50W
San Carlos Luzon The Philippines **111** G7 15 59N 120 22E
San Carlos Negros The Philippines **111** G6 10 30N 123 29E
San Carlos Venezuela **146** D14 9 39N 68 35W
San Carlos de Bariloche Argentina **147** C4 41 11S 71 23W
San Carlos del Zulia Venezuela **146** C14 9 01N 71 58W
San Clemente Island California U.S.A. **134** C3 33 26N 117 36W
San Cristóbal Argentina **147** E6 30 20S 61 14W
San Cristóbal Mexico **140** F3 16 45N 92 40W
San Cristobal *i.* Solomon Is. **118** K7 11 00S 162 00E
San Cristóbal Venezuela **146** C14 7 46N 72 15W
Sancti Spíritus Cuba **141** I4 21 55N 79 28W
Sanda Japan **114** G1 34 54N 135 12E
Sanda Island Argyll & Bute Scotland **60** D3 55 18N 5 35W
Sandakan Malaysia **111** F5 5 52N 118 04E
Sanday *i.* Highland Scotland **58** C2 57 05N 6 30W
Sanday *i.* Orkney Islands Scotland **57** C2 59 15N 2 30W
Sanday Sound Orkney Islands Scotland **57** C2 59 11N 2 30W
Sandbach Cheshire England **64** C2 53 09N 2 22W
Sandhead Dumfries & Galloway Scotland **60** E2 54 48N 4 58W
Sandhurst Berkshire England **70** D2 51 21N 0 48W
San Diego U.S.A. **134** C3 32 45N 117 10W
San Diego Freeway U.S.A. **139** C1 33 44N 117 59W
Sandikli Turkey **94** G3 38 28N 30 16E
Sandown Isle of Wight England **70** C1 50 39N 1 09W
Sandpoint *tn.* U.S.A. **134** C6 48 17N 116 34W
Sandray *i.* Western Isles Scotland **58** B1 56 53N 7 30W
Sandringham Norfolk England **71** E3 52 50N 0 31E
Sandspit B.C. Canada **132** I3 53 14N 131 50W
Sandusky Ohio U.S.A. **137** D2 41 27N 82 42W
Sandwich Kent England **71** F2 51 17N 1 20E
Sandwip Chittagong Bangladesh **110** J3 22 30N 91 26E
Sandwip Island Bangladesh **110** J3 22 30N 91 25E
Sandy Bedfordshire England **70** D3 52 08N 0 18W
Sandy Lake Canada **133** Q3 52 45N 93 00W
San Felipe Mexico **140** B6 31 03N 114 52W
San Felipe Venezuela **146** D15 10 25N 68 40W
San Feliú de Guixols Spain **90** C3 41 47N 3 02E
San Fernando Mexico **140** A5 29 59N 115 10W
San Fernando Spain **90** A2 36 28N 6 12W
San Fernando Trinidad & Tobago **141** T9 10 16N 61 28W
San Fernando U.S.A. **139** A4 34 17N 118 27W
San Fernando de Apure Venezuela **146** D14 7 53N 67 15W
San Fernando Valley California U.S.A. **139** A3 34 14N 118 25W
Sanford Florida U.S.A. **135** J2 28 49N 81 17W
San Francique Trinidad & Tobago **141** S9 10 05N 61 39W
San Francisco Argentina **147** E6 31 29S 62 06W
San Francisco Dominican Rep. **141** J3 19 19N 70 15W
San Francisco U.S.A. **134** B4 37 45N 122 27W
San Francisco del Oro Mexico **140** C5 26 52N 105 50W
San Francisco Javier Balearic Is. **90** D4 38 43N 1 26E
San Gabriel California U.S.A. **139** B3 34 06N 118 06W
San Gabriel Moutains U.S.A. **139** B4/C3 34 18N 118 05W
San Gabriel Reservoir U.S.A. **139** C3 34 12N 117 52W
San Gabriel River U.S.A. **139** B2 33 58N 118 06W
San Gabriel River Freeway U.S.A. **139** B2 33 59N 118 03W
Sangar Russia **103** O8 64 02N 127 30E
Sangerhausen Germany **93** B2 51 29N 11 18E
Sangha *r.* Africa **127** I3 2 00N 17 00E
Sangli India **109** C3 16 55N 74 37E
Sangmélima Cameroon **127** H3 2 57N 11 56E
Sangre de Cristo Mountains U.S.A. **134** E4 37 00N 105 00W
Sangre Grande Trinidad & Tobago **141** T10 10 35N 61 08W
Sangu *r.* Chittagong Bangladesh **110** K3 22 10N 92 15E
San Javier Bolivia **146** E9 16 22S 62 38W
San Joaquin *r.* U.S.A. **134** B4 37 00N 120 00W
San José Balearic Is. **90** D4 38 55N 1 18E
San José Costa Rica **141** H1 9 59N 84 04W
San José California U.S.A. **134** B4 37 20N 121 55W
San José Uruguay **147** F6 34 27S 56 40W
San José del Cabo Mexico **140** C4 23 01N 109 40W
San Juan Argentina **147** D6 31 33S 68 31W
San Juán Peru **146** B9 15 22S 75 07W
San Juan Puerto Rico **141** K3 18 29N 66 08W
San Juan Trinidad & Tobago **141** T10 10 39N 61 27W
San Juan *r.* U.S.A. **134** D4 37 00N 110 00W
San Juan Bautista Balearic Is. **90** D4 39 05N 1 31E
San Juan de los Morros Venezuela **141** K1 9 53N 67 23W
San Juan Mountains U.S.A. **134** E4 37 50N 107 50W
San Julián Argentina **147** D3 49 17S 67 45W
Sankh *r.* India **110** B3 22 30N 84 20E
Sankosh *r.* Bhutan **110** H7/8 27 00N 90 00E
Sānkrāil India **108** J2 22 33N 88 14E
Sankt-Peterburg *(Leningrad, St. Petersburg)* Russia **100** F7 59 55N 30 25E
Sankuru *r.* Congo (D.R.) **125** D7 4 00S 23 30E
Sanliurfa *(Urfa)* Turkey **95** L2 37 08N 38 45E
Sanlúcar de Barrameda Spain **90** A2 36 46N 6 21W
San Lucas Mexico **140** C4 22 50N 109 52W
San Luis Argentina **147** D6 33 20S 66 23W
San Luis Obispo U.S.A. **134** B4 35 16N 120 40W
San Luis Potosí Mexico **140** D4 22 10N 101 00W
San Marcos Texas U.S.A. **135** G2 29 54N 97 57W
SAN MARINO 92 B2 44 00N 12 00E
Sanmenxia China **113** M5 34 46N 111 17E
San Miguel El Salvador **140** G2 13 28N 88 10W
San Miguel de Tucumán Argentina **147** D7 26 47S 65 15W
Sanming China **113** N4 26 16N 117 35E
Sannan Japan **114** G2 35 05N 135 03E
San Nicolas de los Arroyos Argentina **147** E6 33 25S 60 15W
Sannox North Ayrshire Scotland **60** D3 56 41N 5 08W
San Pablo The Philippines **111** G6 14 03N 121 19E
San Pedro Argentina **147** E8 24 12S 64 55W
San Pedro Côte d'Ivoire **127** D3 4 45N 6 37W
San Pedro Dominican Rep. **141** K3 18 30N 69 18W
San Pedro California U.S.A. **139** A1 33 45N 118 19W
San Pedro Bay U.S.A. **139** B1 33 43N 118 12W
San Pedro Channel U.S.A. **139** A1 33 43N 118 22W
San Pedro de las Colonias Mexico **140** D5 25 50N 102 59W
San Pedro Sula Honduras **140** G3 15 26N 88 01W
Sanquhar Dumfries & Galloway Scotland **61** F3 55 22N 3 56W
San Rafael Argentina **147** D6 34 35S 68 24W
San Rafael California U.S.A. **134** B4 37 58N 122 30W
San Remo Italy **92** A2 43 48N 7 46E
San Salvador El Salvador **140** G2 13 40N 89 10W
San Salvador *i.* The Bahamas **141** J4 24 00N 74 32W
San Salvador de Jujuy Argentina **147** D8 24 10S 65 48W
San Sebastián Spain **90** B3 43 19N 1 59W
San Severo Italy **92** C2 41 41N 15 23E
Santa Ana Bolivia **146** D10 13 46S 65 37W
Santa Ana El Salvador **140** G2 14 00N 89 31W
Santa Ana Mexico **134** D3 30 31N 111 08W
Santa Ana California U.S.A. **139** C2 33 44N 117 54W
Santa Ana Freeway U.S.A. **139** B2 33 53N 118 01W
Santa Ana River U.S.A. **139** C2 33 46N 117 54W
Santa Barbara Mexico **140** C5 26 48N 105 50W
Santa Barbara U.S.A. **134** C3 33 29N 119 01W
Santa Catalina Island U.S.A. **134** C3 33 25N 118 25W
Santa Catarina *admin.* Brazil **147** G7 27 00S 51 00W
Santa Clara Cuba **141** I4 22 25N 79 58W
Santa Clara Mexico **140** P2 19 32N 99 03W
Santa Cruz *r.* Argentina **147** D2 50 00S 70 00W
Santa Cruz Bolivia **146** E9 17 50S 63 10W
Santa Cruz Canary Islands **127** B8 28 28N 16 15W
Santa Cruz Jamaica **141** Q8 18 03N 77 43W
Santa Cruz California U.S.A. **134** B4 36 58N 122 03W
Santa Cruz Island U.S.A. **134** C3 34 00N 119 40W
Santa Cruz Islands Solomon Is. **118** L7 11 00S 167 00E
Santa Eulalia del Rio Balearic Is. **90** D4 38 59N 1 33E
Santa Fé Argentina **147** E6 31 35S 60 50W
Santa Fe New Mexico U.S.A. **134** E4 35 41N 105 57W
Santa Fe Dam Flood Control Basin California U.S.A. **139** C3 34 07N 117 58W
Santa Isabel *i.* Solomon Is. **118** J8 7 30S 158 30E
Santa Maria Brazil **147** G7 29 45S 53 40W
Santa Maria California U.S.A. **134** B3 34 56N 120 25W
Santa Marta Colombia **146** C15 11 18N 74 10W
Santa Monica U.S.A. **139** A3 34 00N 118 25W
Santa Monica Freeway U.S.A. **139** A3 34 02N 118 20W
Santa Monica Moutains U.S.A. **139** A3 33 07N 118 27W
Santana do Livramento Brazil **147** F6 30 52S 55 30W
Santander Spain **90** B3 43 28N 3 48W
Santander Colombia **146** B13 3 00N 76 25W
Sant'Antioco Italy **92** A1 39 04N 8 27E
Santañy Balearic Is. **90** E4 39 22N 3 07E
Santarém Brazil **146** G12 2 26S 54 41W
Santarém Portugal **90** A2 39 14N 8 40W
Santa Rosa Argentina **147** E5 36 37S 64 17W
Santa Rosa Honduras **140** G2 14 48N 88 43W
Santa Rosa California U.S.A. **134** B4 38 26N 122 43W
Santa Rosa New Mexico U.S.A. **134** F3 34 56N 104 42W
Santa Rosa Island U.S.A. **134** B3 34 00N 120 05W
Santa Rosalia Mexico **140** B5 27 20N 112 20W
Santa Teresa Brazil **147** Q2 22 57S 43 12W
Santa Teresa Gallura Italy **92** A1 41 14N 9 12E
Santiago Chile **147** C6 33 30S 70 40W
Santiago Panama **141** H2 8 08N 80 59W
Santiago de Compostela Spain **90** A3 42 52N 8 33W
Santiago de Cuba Cuba **141** I4 20 00N 75 49W
Santiago del Estero Argentina **147** E7 27 47S 64 15W
Santiago Ixcuintla Mexico **140** C4 21 50N 105 11W
San Tin H.K. China **112** B3 22 30N 114 04E
Santi Nagar India **108** L4 28 40N 77 10E
Santipur West Bengal India **110** F4 23 14N 88 29E
Santo Andre Brazil **147** H8 23 39S 46 29W
Santo Domingo Dominican Rep. **141** K3 18 30N 69 57W
Santo Domingo de los Colorados Ecuador **146** B12 0 13S 79 09W
Santoña Spain **90** B3 43 27N 3 26W
Santorini *see* Thíra
Santos Brazil **147** H8 23 56S 46 22W
Santpoort Netherlands **88** C3 52 26N 4 38E
San Uk Ha H.K. China **112** C3 22 30N 114 14E
Sanuki Japan **115** C2 35 16N 139 53E
San Vicente El Salvador **140** G2 13 38N 88 42W
Sanya *(Ya Xian)* China **113** L2 18 25N 109 27E
São Bernardo do Campo Brazil **147** H8 23 45S 46 34W
São Borja Brazil **147** F7 28 35S 56 01W
São Cristovão Brazil **147** Q2 22 52S 43 15S
São Gonçalo Brazil **147** Q2 22 48S 43 08W
São João de Meriti Brazil **147** P2 22 47S 43 22W
São João de Meriti *admin.* Brazil **147** P2 22 46S 43 22W
São José Brazil **147** H7 27 35S 48 40W
São José do Rio Prêto Brazil **146** H8 20 50S 49 20W
São José dos Campos Brazil **147** H8 23 07S 45 52W
São Luís Brazil **146** I12 2 34S 44 16W
Saône *r.* France **91** C2 46 28N 4 55E
São Paulo Brazil **147** H8 23 33S 46 39W
São Paulo *admin.* Brazil **146** G8/H8 21 30S 50 00W
São Paulo de Olivença Brazil **146** D12 3 34S 68 55W
São Tomé *i.* Gulf of Guinea **127** G3 0 25N 6 35E
SÃO TOMÉ AND PRINCIPE 127 G3
São Vicente Brazil **147** H8 23 57S 46 23W
Sapanca Turkey **94** G4 40 41N 30 15E
Sapatgram Assam India **110** H7 26 18N 90 08E
Sappemeer Netherlands **89** F5 53 10N 6 47E
Sapporo Japan **114** D3 43 05N 141 21E
Saqqez Iran **107** G6 36 14N 46 15E
Sarajevo Bosnia-Herzegovina **92** C2 43 52N 18 26E
Sarakhs Iran **107** J6 36 32N 61 07E
Saranac Lake *tn.* U.S.A. **137** F2 44 19N 74 10W
Sarandë Greece **94** A3 39 53N 20 00E
Saransk Russia **102** G6 54 12N 45 10E
Sarapali Orissa India **110** B2 21 16N 84 38E
Sarapui *r.* Brazil **147** P3 22 44S 43 17W
Sarapul Russia **105** G6 56 30N 53 49E
Sarasota Florida U.S.A. **135** J2 27 20N 82 32W
Saraswati, River India **108** K3 22 56N 88 22E
Saratov Russia **102** G6 51 30N 45 55E
Saravan Iran **107** J4 27 25N 62 17E
Sarawak *admin.* Malaysia **111** F4 1 00N 111 00E
Saraykoy Turkey **94** F2 37 54N 28 55E
Sarbhang Bhutan **110** H7 26 52N 90 16E
Sarcelles France **87** B2 48 59N 2 22E
Sardegna *(Sardinia) i.* Italy **92** A1/2 40 00N 9 00E
Sardindida Plain Kenya **124** G8/H8 2 00N 40 00E
Sardinia *see* Sardegna
Sar-e Pol Afghanistan **107** K6 36 13N 65 55E
Sargasso Sea Atlantic Ocean **152** B9 27 00N 60 00W
Sargeant Barbados **141** V12 13 05N 59 35W
Sargodha Pakistan **109** C6 32 01N 72 40E
Sarh Chad **124** C9 9 08N 18 22E
Saricakaya Turkey **94** G4 40 01N 30 41E
Sarigöl Turkey **94** F3 38 15N 28 42E
Sarikamiş Turkey **95** N4 40 19N 42 35E
Sarikaya Turkey **95** J3 39 27N 36 09E
Sarir Calanscio *d.* Libya **124** D13 26 00N 22 00E
Sariyar Baraji *r.* Turkey **94** G4 40 00N 31 30E
Sariyer Turkey **94** F4 41 11N 29 03E
Sark *i.* Channel Is. British Isles **73** E2 49 26N 2 22W
Sarkişla Turkey **95** K3 39 21N 36 27E
Sarmiento Argentina **147** D3 45 35S 69 08W
Sarnia Canada **137** D2 42 58N 82 23W
Sarny Ukraine **96** D4 51 21N 26 31E
Saros Körfezi *b.* Turkey **94** E4 40 30 26 30E
Sarpsborg Norway **97** C2 59 17N 11 06E
Sarrebourg France **91** D2 48 43N 7 03E
Sarreguemines France **91** D2 49 06N 6 55E
Sartène Corsica **91** D1 41 37N 8 58E
Sarthe *r.* France **91** B2 47 45N 0 30W
Sartrou-ville France **87** A2 48 56N 2 11E
Sarur Azerbaijan **95** P3 39 32N 45 56E
Sary Ishikotrau *d.* Kazakhstan **105** M3/4 45 00N 77 00E
Sarysu *r.* Kazakhstan **105** K4 47 00N 67 30E
Sasayama Japan **114** G2 35 03N 135 12E
Sasebo Japan **114** A1 33 10N 129 42E
Saskatchewan *province* Canada **132** N3 53 50N 109 00W
Saskatchewan *r.* Canada **151** P13 52 00N 110 00W
Saskatoon Canada **132** N3 52 10N 106 40W
Sassandra Côte d'Ivoire **127** D3 4 58N 6 08W
Sassandra *r.* Côte d'Ivoire **127** D4 5 50N 6 55W
Sassari Italy **92** A2 40 43N 8 34E
Sassenheim Netherlands **88** B2 52 13N 4 31E
Sassnitz Germany **97** C1 54 32N 13 40E
Sassuolo Italy **92** B2 44 32N 10 47E
Satkhira Khulna Bangladesh **110** G3 22 43N 89 06E
Satlayev *(Nikol'skiy)* Kazakhstan **105** K4 47 54N 67 25E
Satna India **109** E4 24 33N 80 50E
Satpura Range *mts.* India **109** C4/D4 21 40N 75 00E
Sattahip Thailand **111** C6 12 36N 100 56E
Satu Mare Romania **96** C3 47 48N 22 52E
SAUDI ARABIA 106 F3
Sauer *(Sûre) r.* Europe **89** F1 49 45N 6 30E
Sault Ste. Marie Canada **137** D3 46 31N 84 20W
Sault Ste. Marie U.S.A. **137** D3 46 29N 84 22W
Saumur France **91** B2 47 16N 0 05W
Saundersfoot Pembrokeshire Wales **66** C1 51 43N 4 43W
Saurimo Angola **125** D6 9 39S 20 24E
Sava *r.* Europe **76** J5 45 00N 18 00E
Savanna Illinois U.S.A. **136** B2 42 06N 90 07W
Savannah *r.* U.S.A. **135** J3 33 00N 82 00W
Savannah Georgia U.S.A. **135** J3 32 04N 81 07W
Savannakhet Laos **111** C7 16 34N 104 45E
Savanna la Mar Jamaica **141** P8 18 13N 78 08W
Savaştepe Turkey **94** E3 39 20N 27 38E
Saverne France **93** A1 48 45N 7 22E
Savona Italy **92** A2 44 18N 8 28E
Savur Turkey **95** M2 37 34N 40 53E
Sawahlunto Indonesia **111** C3 0 41S 100 52E
Sawankhalok Thailand **113** J2 17 19N 99 50E
Sawara Japan **114** M2 35 52N 140 31E
Sawbridgeworth Hertfordshire England **71** E2 51 50N 0 09E
Sawel *mt.* Northern Ireland **60** B2 54 49N 7 02W
Shawinigan Québec Canada **133** U2 46 33N 72 45W
Sawpit Canyon Reservoir U.S.A. **139** C3 34 10N 117 59W
Sawston Cambridgeshire England **71** E3 52 07N 0 10E
Sawu Sea Indonesia **111** G2 9 00S 122 00E
Saxilby Lincolnshire England **65** E2 53 17N 0 40W
Saxmundham Suffolk England **71** F3 52 13N 1 29E
Saxthorpe Norfolk England **71** F3 52 50N 1 09E
Sayabec Québec Canada **137** G3 48 35N 67 41W
Sayanogorsk Russia **103** L6 53 00N 91 26E
Sayano-Shushenskoya Vodokhranilishche *res.* Russia **105** P5 52 00N 92 00E
Saylac Somalia **124** H10 11 21N 43 30E
Saynshand Mongolia **113** M7 44 58N 111 10E
Sayrām Hu *l.* China **105** N3 44 45N 80 30E
Say'ūn Yemen Rep. **107** G2 15 59N 48 44E
Scafell Pike *mt.* Cumbria England **64** B3 54 27N 3 14W
Scalasaig Argyll & Bute Scotland **60** C4 56 04N 6 12W
Scalby North Yorkshire England **65** E3 54 18N 0 27W
Scalloway Shetland Islands Scotland **57** D3 60 08N 1 17W
Scalpay *i.* Highland Scotland **58** D2 57 15N 6 00W
Scalpay *i.* Western Isles Scotland **58** C2 57 52N 6 40W
Scandinavia *geog. reg.* Europe **76** H8/J9 64 00N 15 00E
Scapa Orkney Islands Scotland **57** C1 58 58N 2 59W
Scapa Flow *sd.* Orkney Islands Scotland **57** B1 58 55N 3 00W
Scarba *i.* Argyll & Bute Scotland **58** D1 56 45N 5 50W
Scarborough North Yorkshire England **65** E3 54 17N 0 24W
Scariff Island *i.* Kerry Rep. of Ireland **75** A1 51 44N 10 15W
Scarinish Argyll & Bute Scotland **58** C1 56 29N 6 48W
Scarp *i.* Western Isles Scotland **58** B3 58 02N 7 08W
Scarriff Clare Rep. of Ireland **75** C2 52 55N 8 37W
Scarsdale U.S.A. **138** D2 40 59N 73 49W
Scartaglin Kerry Rep. of Ireland **75** B2 52 10N 9 26W
Sceaux France **87** B2 48 46N 218E
Schaerbeek Belgium **89** D2 50 52N 4 22E
Schaffhausen Switzerland **92** A3 47 42N 8 38E
Schagen Netherlands **89** D4 52 47N 4 47E
Schefferville *(Kawawachikamach)* Canada **133** V3 54 50N 67 00W
Schelde *(Scheldt) r.* Netherlands **89** D3 51 15N 4 16E
Scheldt *see* Schelde
Scheldt Estuary Europe **76** F6 51 30N 3 30E
Schenectady U.S.A. **137** F2 42 48N 73 57W
Scheveningen Netherlands **88** B2 52 06N 4 18E
Schiedam Netherlands **89** D3 51 55N 4 25E
Schiermonnikoog *i.* Netherlands **89** F5 53 28N 6 10E
Schildow Germany **87** F2 52 40N 13 21E
Schleswig Germany **93** A2 54 32N 9 34E
Schleswig-Holstein *admin.* Germany **93** A2/B2 54 00N 10 00E
Schönebeck Germany **93** B2 52 01N 11 45E
Schöneberg Germany **87** F1 52 24N 13 22E
Schöneiche Germany **87** G1 52 28N 13 43E
Schönwalde Frankfurt Germany **87** F2 52 43N 13 26E
Schönwalde Potsdam Germany **87** E2 52 41N 13 27E
Schoonhoven Netherlands **88** D1 51 56N 4 51E
Schorndorf Germany **93** A1 48 48N 9 33E
Schoten Belgium **89** D3 51 15N 4 30E
Schouwen *i.* Netherlands **89** C3 51 40N 3 50E
Schreiber Canada **136** C3 48 48N 87 17W
Schulzendorf Germany **87** G1 52 20N 13 34E
Schwäbische Alb *mts.* Germany **93** A1/B1 48 00N 9 00E
Schwäbisch Gmünd Germany **93** A1 48 49N 9 48E
Schwäbisch Hall Germany **93** A1 49 07N 9 45E
Schwandorf Germany **93** B1 49 20N 12 07E
Schwanebeck Germany **87** F2 52 40N 13 27E
Schwarze Elster *r.* Germany **93** B2 52 00N 13 00E
Schwarzwald *(Black Forest) mts.* Germany **93** A1 47 00N 8 00E
Schwarzwälder Hochwald *mts.* Germany **89** F1 49 00N 7 00E
Schwaz Austria **92** B3 47 21N 11 44E
Schwechat Austria **92** C3 48 09N 16 27E
Schwedt Germany **93** B2 53 04N 14 17E
Schweinfurt Germany **93** B2 50 03N 10 16E
Schwelm Germany **86** D2 51 17N 7 18E
Schwerin Germany **93** B2 53 38N 11 25E
Schwielowsee *l.* Germany **87** D1 52 19N 13 57E
Schwyz Switzerland **92** A3 47 02N 8 34E
Sciacca Italy **92** B1 37 31N 13 05E
Scilly, Isles of England **72** A2 49 56N 6 20W
Scioto *r.* Ohio U.S.A. **137** D1 40 00N 83 00W
Sconser Highland Scotland **58** C2 57 18N 6 07W
Scoresbysund *tn. see* Ittoqqortoormiit
Scoresbysund *sd. see* Kangertittivaq
Scotia Ridge Atlantic Ocean **152** C1 53 00S 50 00W
Scotia Sea Atlantic Ocean **152** C1 56 30N 50 00W
Scotland 56 F8
Scott Base *r.s.* Antarctica **149** 77 51S 166 45E
Scottish Borders *u.a.* Scotland **61** G3 55 30N 2 55W
Scott Island Southern Ocean **150** H1 66 35S 180 00
Scottsbluff Nebraska U.S.A. **134** F5 41 52N 103 40W
Scourie Highland Scotland **58** D3 58 20N 5 08W
Scrabster Highland Scotland **59** F3 58 37N 3 34W
Scranton Pennsylvania U.S.A. **137** E2 41 25N 75 40W
Scunthorpe North Lincolnshire England **65** E2 53 35N 0 39W
Scye *r.* France **73** F2 49 27N 1 42W
Seaford East Sussex England **71** E1 50 46N 0 06E
Seaham Durham England **65** D3 54 50N 1 20W
Seahouses Northumberland England **61** H3 55 35N 1 38W
Sealdah India **108** K2 22 32N 88 22E
Seal River Canada **133** P4 59 10N 97 00W
Seascale Cumbria England **64** B3 54 24N 3 29W
Seaton Cumbria England **64** B3 54 40N 3 30W
Seaton Devon England **72** D3 50 43N 3 05W
Seaton Delaval Northumberland England **61** H3 55 04N 1 31W
Seattle Washington U.S.A. **134** B6 47 35N 122 20W
Seben Turkey **94** G4 40 25N 31 36E
Sebeş Romania **96** C3 45 58N 23 34E
Sedalia Missouri U.S.A. **136** B1 38 42N 93 15W
Sedan France **91** C2 49 42N 4 57E
Sedbergh Cumbria England **64** C3 54 20N 2 31W
Seddinsee *l.* Germany **87** G1 52 23N 13 42E
Seferihisar Turkey **94** E3 38 11N 26 50E
Ségou Mali **127** D5 13 28N 6 18W
Segovia Spain **90** B3 40 57N 4 07W
Segre *r.* Spain **90** C3 42 00N 1 10E
Segura *r.* Spain **90** B2 38 00N 1 00W
Seine *r.* France **91** C2 49 15N 1 15E
Seine-et-Marne *admin.* France **87** C1 48 44N 2 38E
Seine-St-Denis *admin.* France **87** C2 48 55N 2 35E
Seki Japan **114** H2 35 30N 136 54E
Sekijiri Japan **115** C1 35 15N 139 56E
Sekondi Takoradi Ghana **127** E3 4 59N 1 43W
Selat Melaka *see* Malacca, Strait of
Selat Sunda *sd.* Indonesia **111** D2 5 50S 105 30E
Selborne Hampshire England **70** D2 51 06N 0 56W
Selby North Yorkshire England **65** D2 53 48N 1 04W
Seldovia U.S.A. **132** E4 59 29N 151 45W
Selemdzha *r.* Russia **103** P6 53 00N 132 00E
Selendi Turkey **94** F3 38 45N 28 53E
Selenge *r.* Mongolia **113** K8 49 00N 102 00E
Sélestat France **91** D2 48 16N 7 28E
Selety *r.* Kazakhstan **105** L5 52 50N 73 00E
Selima Oasis Sudan **124** E12 21 22N 29 19E
Selkirk Canada **136** A4 50 10N 96 52W
Selkirk Scottish Borders Scotland **61** G3 55 33N 2 50W
Selma Alabama U.S.A. **135** I3 32 24N 87 01W
Selsey West Sussex England **70** D1 50 44N 0 48W
Selsey Bill *p.* West Sussex England **70** D1 50 43N 0 48W
Sélune *r.* France **91** B2 48 40N 1 15W
Selwyn Mountains B.C. Canada **132** I5 63 00N 131 00W
Semarang Indonesia **111** E2 6 58S 110 29E
Semenovskoye Russia **102** M1 56 39N 37 32E
Seminoe Reservoir U.S.A. **134** E5 42 00N 106 00W
Seminole Oklahoma U.S.A. **135** G4 35 15N 96 40W
Semiozernoye Kazakhstan **105** J5 52 22N 64 06E
Semipalatinsk Kazakhstan **103** K6 50 26N 80 16E
Semnān Iran **107** H6 35 30N 53 25E
Semois *r.* Belgium **89** E1 49 40N 5 30E
Senart-Ville-Nouvelle France **87** C1 48 36N 2 35E
Sendai Honshu Japan **114** D2 38 16N 140 52E
Sendai Kyūshū Japan **114** B1 31 50N 130 17E
Seneca Lake U.S.A. **137** E2 43 00N 77 00W
SENEGAL 127 B5/C6
Sénégal *r.* Senegal/Mauritania **127** C6 16 45N 14 45W
Senftenberg Germany **93** B2 51 31N 14 01E
Senhor do Bonfim Brazil **146** I10 10 28S 40 11W
Senj Croatia **96** A3 45 00N 14 55E
Senja *i.* Norway **97** D4 69 15N 17 20E
Senlis France **91** C2 49 12N 2 35E
Sennar Sudan **124** F10 13 31N 33 38E
Sennar Dam Sudan **106** D1 13 20N 33 45E
Sennen Cornwall England **72** B3 50 03N 5 42W
Sennybridge Powys Wales **66** D1 51 57N 3 34W
Senobe Japan **114** G2 35 09N 135 25E
Sens France **91** C2 48 12N 3 18E
Senyavin Islands Pacific Ocean **150** G8 7 00N 161 30E
Seoul *see* So'ul
Sepik *r.* Papua New Guinea **118** G9 4 15S 143 00E
Sept-Iles Québec Canada **133** V3 50 10N 66 00W
Sepulveda Dam Recreational Area U.S.A. **139** A3 34 10N 118 25W
Seraing Belgium **89** E2 50 37N 5 31E
Seram *(Ceram) i.* Indonesia **118** D9 3 30S 129 30E
Seram Sea Indonesia **111** H3 2 30S 130 00E
Serang Indonesia **111** D2 6 07S 106 09E
Serbia *admin.* Yugoslavia **96** C2 43 00N 21 00E
Serchhip Mizoram India **110** K4 23 18N 92 48E
Serdan Mexico **140** C5 28 40N 105 57W
Sereflikoçhisar Turkey **95** H3 38 56N 33 31E
Seremban Malaysia **111** C4 2 43N 102 57E
Serengeti National Park Tanzania **124** F7 2 30S 35 00E
Serenje Zambia **125** F5 13 12S 30 15E
Sergino Russia **103** I8 62 30N 65 40E
Sergipe *admin.* Brazil **146** J10 11 00S 38 00W
Sergiyev Posad *(Zagorsk)* Russia **102** F7 56 20N 38 10E
Seria Brunei Darussalam **111** E4 4 39N 114 23E
Serian Malaysia **111** F4 1 10N 110 35E
Sérifos *i.* Greece **94** D2 3710N 24 25E
Serik Turkey **94** G2 36 55N 31 06E
Serov Russia **102** I7 59 42N 60 32E
Serowe Botswana **125** E3 22 25S 26 44E
Serpukhov Russia **104** D5 54 53N 37 25E
Serra Brazil **146** I9 20 06S 40 16W
Serra do Mar *mts.* Brazil **147** H7 27 30S 49 00W
Serra do Navio Brazil **146** G13 1 00N 52 05W
Serra Grande *mts.* Brazil **147** Q2 22 55S 43 02W
Serrania de Cuenca *mts.* Spain **90** B3 40 30N 2 15W
Serra Tumucumaque *mts.* Brazil **146** F13/G13 2 00N 55 00W
Serre *r.* France **89** C1 49 40N 3 52E
Sérres Greece **94** C4 41 03N 23 33E
Setagaya Japan **115** B3 35 37N 139 38E
Sète France **91** C1 43 25N 3 43E
Sete Lagoas Brazil **146** I9 19 29S 44 15W
Sete Pontes Brazil **147** Q2 22 51S 43 04W
Setesdal *geog. reg.* Norway **97** B2 59 30N 7 10E
Sétif Algeria **76** G3 36 11N 5 24E
Setit *r.* Sudan **124** G10 14 20N 36 15E
Seto Japan **114** J2 35 14N 137 06E
Seto-Naikai *sd.* Japan **114** B1 34 00N 132 30E
Settat Morocco **127** D9 33 04N 7 37W
Settle North Yorkshire England **64** C3 54 04N 2 16W
Setúbal Portugal **90** A2 38 31N 8 54W
Sevan Armenia **95** P4 40 33N 44 56E
Sevastopol' Ukraine **104** C3 44 36N 33 31E
Seven Head *c.* Cork Rep. of Ireland **75** C1 51 34N 8 42W
Severn *r.* Canada **133** R4 55 10N 89 00W
Severn *r.* England/Wales **67** E2 52 25N 2 25W
Severnaya (North) Dvina *r.* Russia **102** G8 63 00N 43 00E
Severnaya Sos'va *r.* Russia **102** I8 62 30N 62 00E

Tiffin Ohio U.S.A. **137** D2 41 07N 83 11W
Tiflis *see* T'bilisi
Tighina Moldova **96** D3 46 50N 29 29E
Tighnabruaich Argyll & Bute Scotland **60** D3 55 56N 5 14W
Tigris *r.* Turkey/Iraq **107** G5 32 00N 46 00E
Tikrit Iraq **106** F5 34 36N 43 42E
Tijuana Mexico **140** A6 32 29N 117 10W
Tijuca Brazil **147** P2 22 56S 43 16W
Tijuca National Park Brazil **147** P2 22 58S 43 17W
Tikarpara Orissa India **110** B1 20 36N 84 47E
Tikhoretsk Russia **104** E4 45 52N 40 07E
Tikra *r.* Orissa India **110** B2 21 10N 84 55E
Tiksi Russia **103** O10 71 40N 128 45E
Tilaiya Reservoir *res.* Bihar India **110** C5 24 20N 85 25E
Tilak Nagar India **108** L4 28 38N 77 07E
Tilburg Netherlands **89** E3 51 34N 5 05E
Tilbury Essex England **71** E2 51 28N 0 23E
Till *r.* Lincolnshire England **65** E2 53 20N 0 40W
Till *r.* Northumberland England **61** G3 55 38N 2 08W
Tillicoultry Clackmannanshire Scotland **59** F1 56 09N 2 45W
Tillsonburg Canada **137** D2 42 53N 80 44W
Tílos *i.* Greece **94** E2 36 25N 27 20E
Tilt *r.* Perth & Kinross Scotland **59** F1 56 52N 3 44W
Timaru N.Z. **119** B2 44 24S 171 15E
Timashevsk Russia **95** L6 45 38N 38 56E
Timbira *r.* Brazil **147** Q3 22 40S 43 12W
Timbuktu *see* Tombouctou
Timimoun Algeria **127** F8 29 15N 0 14E
Timiryazev Park Russia **102** M2 55 50N 37 32E
Timişoara Romania **96** C3 45 45N 21 15E
Timişul *r.* Romania/Yugoslavia **96** C3 45 00N 21 00E
Timmins Canada **133** S2 48 30N 81 20W
Timon Brazil **146** I11 5 08S 42 52W
Timor *i.* Indonesia **111** G1/H2 9 00S 125 00E
Timor Sea Indonesia **111** H1/H2 10 45S 126 00E
Tinahely Wicklow Rep. of Ireland **75** E2 52 48N 6 28W
Tindouf Algeria **127** D8 27 42N 8 10W
Tingwall Orkney Islands Scotland **57** B2 59 04N 3 03W
Tinos *i.* Greece **94** D2 37 00N 25 00E
Tintagel Cornwall England **72** C3 50 40N 4 45W
Tintagel Head *c.* Cornwall England **72** C3 50 41N 4 46W
Tipperary *co.* Rep. of Ireland **75** C2/D2 52 30N 8 00W
Tipperary Tipperary Rep. of Ireland **75** C2 52 29N 8 10W
Tiptree Essex England **71** E2 51 49N 0 45E
Tiranë *(Tirana)* Albania **94** A4 41 20N 19 49E
Tiraspol' Moldova **76** L5 46 50N 29 38E
Tiraz Mountains Namibia **125** C2 25 30S 16 30E
Tire Turkey **94** E3 38 04N 27 45E
Tirebolu Turkey **95** L4 40 02N 38 49E
Tiree *i.* Argyll & Bute Scotland **58** C1 56 30N 6 55W
Tírnavos Greece **94** C3 39 45N 22 18E
Tirol *admin.* Austria **92** B3 47 00N 11 00E
Tirso *r.* Italy **91** D1 40 00N 9 00E
Tiruchchirāppalli India **109** D2 10 50N 78 41E
Tirunelveli India **109** D1 8 45N 77 43E
Tirupati India **109** D2 13 39N 79 25E
Tiruppur India **109** D2 11 05N 77 20E
Tisdale Canada **132** O3 52 51N 104 01W
Tisza *r.* Hungary/Yugoslavia **96** C3 46 00N 20 00E
Titāgarh India **108** K2 22 44N 88 22E
Titograd *see* Podgorica
Titovo Uzice Serbia Yugoslavia **96** B2 43 52N 19 50E
Titov Veles FYROM **94** B4 41 43N 21 49E
Titu Romania **96** D2 44 40N 25 32E
Tiu Chung Chau *i.* H.K. China **112** C1/2 22 20N 114 19E
Tiumpan Head Western Isles Scotland **58** C3 58 15N 6 10W
Tiverton Devon England **72** D3 50 55N 3 29W
Tiverton Rhode Island U.S.A. **137** F2 41 38N 71 13W
Tivoli Italy **92** B2 41 58N 12 48E
Tizimín Mexico **140** G4 21 10N 88 09W
Tizi Ouzou Algeria **127** F10 36 44N 4 05E
Tiznit Morocco **127** D8 29 43N 9 44W
Tlalnepantla Mexico **140** P2 19 32N 99 12W
Tlaltenco Mexico **140** P1 19 17N 99 01W
Tlemcen Algeria **127** E9 34 53N 1 21W
Toad River *tn.* B.C. Canada **132** J4 59 00N 125 10W
Toamasina Madagascar **125** I4 18 10S 49 23E
Toba Japan **114** H1 34 29N 136 51E
Tobago *i.* Trinidad & Tobago **141** L2 11 15N 60 40W
Tobercurry Sligo Rep. of Ireland **74** C4 54 03N 8 43W
Tobermore Magherafelt Northern Ireland **60** C2 54 48N 6 42W
Tobermory Canada **137** D3 45 15N 81 39W
Tobermory Argyll & Bute Scotland **58** C1 56 37N 6 05W
Tobi-shima *i.* Japan **114** C2 39 12N 139 32E
Tobol *r.* Russia **103** I7 57 00N 67 30E
Tobol'sk Russia **103** I7 58 15N 68 12E
Tocantins *admin.* Brazil **146** H10 12 00S 47 00W
Tochigi *pref.* Japan **114** L3 36 20N 139 40E
Toco Trinidad & Tobago **141** U10 10 49N 60 57W
Tocopilla Chile **147** C8 22 05S 70 10W
Todmorden West Yorkshire England **64** C2 53 43N 2 05W
Toe Head *c.* Cork Rep. of Ireland **75** B1 51 30N 9 12W
Toe Head Western Isles Scotland **58** B2 57 50N 7 07W
Tōgane Japan **114** M2 35 34N 140 22E
TOGO 127 F4
Tokat Turkey **95** K4 40 20N 36 35E
Tokelau Islands Pacific Ocean **150** I7 9 00S 168 00W
Toki Japan **114** J2 35 25N 137 12E
Tokmak Ukraine **95** J7 47 13N 35 43E
Tokoname Japan **114** H1 34 50N 136 50E
Tokorozawa Japan **114** L2 35 47N 139 28E
Tokrau *r.* Kazakhstan **105** M4 48 00N 75 00E
Tokushima Japan **114** B1 34 03N 134 34E
Tokuyama Japan **114** B1 34 03N 131 40E
Tōkyō Japan **115** C3 35 35N 139 40E
Tōkyō *pref.* Japan **114** L2 35 35N 139 40E
Tōkyō-wan *b.* Japan **114** L2 35 30N 139 50E
Tôlanaro Madagascar **125** I2 25 01S 47 00E
Tolbukhin *see* Dobrich
Toledo Spain **90** B2 39 52N 4 02W
Toledo Ohio U.S.A. **137** D2 41 40N 83 35W
Toliara Madagascar **125** H3 23 20S 43 41E
Tollygunge India **108** K2 22 30N 88 19E
Tolly's Nullah *r.* India **108** K1 22 28N 88 24E
Tolmezzo Italy **92** B3 46 24N 13 01E
Tolo Channel H.K. China **112** C2 22 28N 114 17E
Tolo Harbour H.K. China **112** C2 22 26N 114 14E
Tolosa Spain **90** B3 43 09N 2 04W
Tolsta Head Western Isles Scotland **58** C3 58 20N 6 10W
Toluca Mexico **140** E3 19 20N 99 40W
Tol'yatti Russia **102** G6 53 32N 49 24E
Tom' *r.* Russia **105** O5 54 00N 87 30E
Tomakomai Japan **114** D3 42 39N 141 33E
Tomaniivi *mt.* Fiji **150** U16 17 37S 178 01E
Tomar Portugal **90** A2 39 36N 8 25W
Tomaszów Mazowiecki Poland **96** B4 51 33N 20 00E
Tomatin Highland Scotland **59** F2 57 20N 3 59W
Tomatlán Mexico **140** C3 19 54N 105 18W
Tombigbee *r.* U.S.A. **135** I3 32 00N 88 00W
Tombouctou *(Timbuktu)* Mali **127** E6 16 49N 2 59W
Tombua Angola **125** B4 15 49S 11 53E
Tomelloso Spain **90** B2 39 09N 3 01W
Tomintoul Moray Scotland **59** F2 57 14N 3 22W
Tomioka Japan **114** K3 36 14N 138 45E
Tomogashima-suidō *sd.* Japan **114** F1/G1 34 15N 134 00E
Tom Price, Mount Australia **118** B5 22 49S 117 51E
Tomsk Russia **103** K7 56 30N 85 05E
Tomuzlovka *r.* Russia **95** N6 44 45N 43 15E
Tonalá Mexico **140** F3 16 08N 93 41W
Tonawanda U.S.A. **137** E2 43 01N 78 54W
Tonbridge Kent England **71** E2 51 12N 0 16E
Tønder Denmark **93** A2 54 57N 8 53E
Tone *r.* Somerset England **73** D4/E4 51 00N 3 00W
Tone-gawa *r.* Japan **114** M2 35 51N 140 09E
TONGA 150 I5
Tonga Trench Pacific Ocean **150** I5 20 00S 173 00W
Tongchuan China **113** L6 35 05N 109 02E
Tongeren Belgium **89** E2 50 47N 5 28E
Tong Fuk H.K. China **112** A1 22 14N 113 56E
Tonghai China **113** K3 24 07N 104 45E
Tonghua China **113** P7 41 42N 125 45E
Tongking, Gulf of China/Vietnam **113** L2 19 00N 107 00E
Tongling China **113** N5 30 58N 117 48E
Tongsa *r.* Bhutan **110** H8 27 10N 90 40E
Tongue Highland Scotland **59** E3 58 28N 4 25W
Tonle Sap *l.* Cambodia **111** C6 12 00N 103 50E
Tonopah Nevada U.S.A. **134** C4 38 05N 117 15W
Tønsberg Norway **97** C2 59 16N 10 25E
Tonyrefail Rhondda Cynon Taff Wales **66** D1 51 36N 3 25W
Tooele Utah U.S.A. **134** D5 40 32N 112 18W
Toomyvara Tipperary Rep. of Ireland **75** C2 52 51N 8 02W
Toowoomba Australia **118** I4 27 35S 151 54E
Topeka Kansas U.S.A. **136** A1 39 02N 95 41W
Toplita Romania **96** D3 46 56N 25 20E
Topsham Devon England **72** D3 50 42N 3 27W
Torbali Turkey **94** E3 38 07N 27 08E
Tor Bay *b.* Devon England **72** D3 50 27N 3 30W
Torbay Devon England **72** D3 50 27N 3 30W
Tordesillas Spain **90** A3 41 30N 5 00W
Tore Highland Scotland **59** E2 57 27N 4 21W
Torfaen *u.a.* Wales **66** D1 51 38N 3 04W
Torhout Belgium **89** C3 51 04N 3 06E
Toride Japan **114** M2 35 54N 140 07E
Torigni-sur-Vire France **73** G2 49 02N 0 59W
Torino *(Turin)* Italy **91** D2 45 04N 7 40E
Tormes *r.* Spain **90** A3 41 03N 5 58W
Torne *see* Torneälven
Torneälven *(Tornionjoki)* *r.* Sweden/Finland **97** E4 67 03N 23 02E
Torne-träsk *l.* Sweden **97** D4 68 14N 19 40E
Torngat Mountains Canada **133** W4 59 00N 64 15W
Tornio Finland **97** E4 65 50N 24 10E
Tornionjoki *(Torneälven)* *r.* Finland/Sweden **97** F4 67 03N 23 02E
Toronto Canada **137** E2 43 42N 79 46W
Tororo Uganda **124** F8 0 42N 34 12E
Toros Dağlari *mts.* Turkey **94/95** G2/J2 37 10N 33 10E
Torpoint *tn.* Cornwall England **72** C3 50 22N 4 11W
Torquay Devon England **91** B3 50 28N 3 30W
Torrance California U.S.A. **139** A2 33 50N 118 20W
Torre del Greco Italy **92** B2 40 46N 14 22E
Torrelavega Spain **90** B3 43 21N 4 03W
Torremolinos Spain **90** B2 36 38N 4 30W
Torrens, Lake Australia **118** F3 31 00S 137 50E
Torrente Spain **90** B2 39 27N 0 28W
Torreón Mexico **140** D5 25 34N 103 25W
Torres Strait Australia **118** G7/8 10 00S 142 30E
Torres Vedras Portugal **90** A2 39 05N 9 15W
Torrevieja Spain **90** B2 37 59N 0 40W
Torridge *r.* Devon England **72** C3 50 56N 4 22W
Torridon Highland Scotland **58** D2 57 33N 5 31W
Torrington Connecticut U.S.A. **137** F2 41 48N 73 08W
Tortosa Spain **90** C3 40 49N 0 31E
Toruń Poland **96** B4 53 01N 18 35E
Tory Island *i.* Donegal Rep. of Ireland **74** C5 55 16N 8 14W
Tory Sound *sd.* Donegal Rep. of Ireland **74** C5 55 15N 8 05W
Tosa-wan *b.* Japan **114** B1 33 20N 133 40E
Toshima Japan **115** B3 35 43N 139 41E
Tosya Turkey **95** J4 41 02N 34 02E
Totland Isle of Wight England **70** C1 50 40N 1 32W
Totnes Devon England **72** D3 50 25N 3 41W
Totoya *i.* Fiji **150** U15 18 56S 179 50W
Totsuka Japan **115** B2 35 23N 139 32E
Tottington Greater Manchester England **64** C2 53 37N 2 20W
Totton Hampshire England **70** C1 50 56N 1 29W
Tottori Japan **114** B2 35 32N 134 12E
Touggourt Algeria **127** G9 33 08N 6 04E
Toul France **91** D2 48 41N 5 54E
Toulon France **91** D1 43 07N 5 55E
Toulouse France **91** C1 43 33N 1 24E
Toungoo Myanmar **111** B7 18 57N 96 26E
Tourcoing France **73** C2 50 44N 3 10E
Tournai Belgium **89** C2 50 36N 3 24E
Tours France **91** C2 47 23N 0 42E
Tovuz Azerbaijan **95** P4 40 55N 45 23E
Toward Argyll & Bute Scotland **60** E3 55 54N 4 58W
Towcester Northamptonshire England **70** D3 52 08N 1 00W
Tow Law *sum.* Durham England **64** D3 54 45N 1 49W
Town Island H.K. China **112** D2 22 20N 114 21E
Townsville Australia **118** H6 19 13S 146 48E
Toyama Japan **114** C2 36 42N 137 14E
Toyoake Japan **114** H2 35 02N 136 55E
Toyohashi Japan **114** J1 34 46N 137 22E
Toyokawa Japan **114** J1 34 47N 137 24E
Toyonaka Japan **114** G1 34 48N 135 35E
Toyooka Japan **114** F2 35 35N 134 48E
Toyota Japan **114** J2 35 05N 137 09E
Tozeur Tunisia **127** G9 33 55N 8 07E
Trâblous *(Tripoli)* Lebanon **106** O12 34 27N 35 50E
Trabotiviste FYROM **94** C4 41 54N 22 49E
Trabzon Turkey **95** L4 41 00N 39 43E
Tracy Québec Canada **137** F3 45 59N 73 04W
Trail B.C. Canada **132** L2 49 04N 111 39W
Tralee Kerry Rep. of Ireland **75** B2 52 16N 9 42W
Tralee Bay *b.* Kerry Rep. of Ireland **75** B2 52 20N 9 55W
Tramore Waterford Rep. of Ireland **75** D2 52 10N 7 10W
Tramore Bay Waterford Rep. of Ireland **75** D2 52 08N 7 08W
Tranent East Lothian Scotland **61** G3 55 57N 2 57W
Trani Italy **92** C2 41 17N 16 25E
Transantarctic Mountains Antarctica **149**
Trans-Canada Highway Canada **132** M3 50 00N 110 00W
Transvaal *province* Rep. of South Africa **125** E3/F3 24 30S 28 00E
Trápani Italy **92** B1 38 02N 12 32E
Traun Austria **92** B3 48 14N 14 15E
Traunstein Germany **93** B1 47 52N 12 39E
Traverse City Michigan U.S.A. **136** C2 44 46N 85 38W
Travers, Mount N.Z. **119** B2 42 01S 172 44E
Trawsfynydd Gwynedd Wales **66** D2 52 54N 3 55W
Trebinje Bosnia-Herzegovina **96** B2 42 44N 18 20E
Tredegar Blaenau Gwent Wales **66** D1 51 47N 3 16W
Tregaron Ceredigion Wales **66** D2 52 13N 3 55W
Tregony Cornwall England **72** C3 50 16N 4 55W
Treinta-y-Tres Uruguay **147** G6 33 16S 54 17W
Trelew Chile **147** D4 43 13S 65 15W
Tremadog Bay Gwynedd Wales **66** C2 52 54N 4 15W
Tremplinersee *l.* Germany **87** E1 52 21N 13 02E
Trencín Slovakia **96** B3 48 53N 18 00E
Trenque Lauquen Argentina **147** E5 35 56S 62 43W
Trent *r.* Derbyshire/Nottinghamshire/North Lincolnshire England **67** F2 52 45N 1 40W
Trent and Mersey Canal England **67** E2/F2 52 25N 1 40W
Trento Italy **92** B3 46 04N 11 08E
Trenton Canada **137** E2 44 07N 77 34W
Trenton U.S.A. **137** F2 40 15N 74 43W
Trepassey Canada **133** Y2 46 45N 53 20W
Treptow Germany **87** F1 52 29N 13 27E
Tres Arroyos Argentina **147** E5 38 26S 60 17W
Tresco *i.* Isles of Scilly England **72** A2 49 57N 6 20W
Treshnish Isles Western Isles Scotland **58** C1 56 30N 6 25W
Três Lagoas Brazil **146** G8 20 46S 51 43W
Treviso Italy **92** B3 45 40N 12 15E
Trevose Head *c.* Cornwall England **72** B3 50 33N 5 01W
Trichur India **109** D2 10 32N 76 14E
Trier Germany **93** A1 49 45N 6 39E
Trieste Italy **92** B3 45 39N 13 47E
Trikala Greece **94** B3 39 33N 21 46E
Trim Meath Rep. of Ireland **74** E3 53 34N 6 47W
Trincomalee Sri Lanka **109** E1 8 34N 81 13E
Trindade *i.* Atlantic Ocean **152** F4 20 30S 29 20W
Tring Hertfordshire England **70** D2 51 48N 0 40W
Trinidad Bolivia **146** E10 14 46S 64 50W
Trinidad Cuba **141** H4 21 48N 80 00W
Trinidad *i.* Trinidad & Tobago **141** L2 11 00N 61 30W
Trinidad Colorado U.S.A. **134** F4 37 11N 104 31W
TRINIDAD AND TOBAGO 141 L2
Trinity *r.* U.S.A. **135** G3 32 00N 96 00W
Trinity Hills Trinidad & Tobago **141** T9 10 07N 61 07W
Trinity Islands U.S.A. **132** E4 56 45N 154 15W
Trípoli Greece **94** C2 37 31N 22 22E
Tripoli Lebanon *see* Trâblous
Tripoli Libya *see* Tarābulus
Tripura *admin.* India **109** G4 23 40N 92 00E
Tristan da Cunha *i.* Atlantic Ocean **152** G2 37 15S 12 30W
Trivandrum India **109** D1 8 30N 76 57E
Trnava Slovakia **96** B3 48 23N 17 35E
Troisdorf Germany **93** A2 50 49N 7 09E
Trois-Pistoles Québec Canada **137** G3 48 08N 69 10W
Trois-Rivières *tn.* Canada **137** F3 46 21N 72 34W
Troitsk Russia **105** J5 54 08N 61 33E
Troitsko Pechorsk Russia **105** H7 62 40N 56 08E
Trollhätten Sweden **97** C2 58 17N 12 20E
Trollheimen *mts.* Norway **97** B3 63 00N 9 00E
Tromsø Norway **97** D4 69 42N 19 00E
Trondheim Norway **97** C3 63 36N 10 23E
Trondheimsfjorden *fj.* Norway **97** C3 63 40N 10 30E
Troon South Ayrshire Scotland **61** E3 55 32N 4 40W
Trotternish *p.* Skye Scotland **58** C2 57 00N 6 00W
Troup Head Aberdeenshire Scotland **59** G2 57 42N 2 18W
Trout Lake Canada **132** K5 61 00N 121 30W
Trouville France **91** C2 49 22N 0 05E
Trowbridge Wiltshire England **70** B2 51 20N 2 13W
Troy *hist. site* Turkey **94** E3 39 55N 26 17E
Troy Alabama U.S.A. **135** I3 31 49N 86 00W
Troy New York U.S.A. **135** L5 42 43N 73 43W
Troyes France **91** C2 48 18N 4 05E
Trujillo Peru **146** B11 8 06S 79 00W
Trujillo Spain **90** A2 39 28N 5 53W
Trujillo Venezuela **146** C14 9 20N 70 38W
Truk Islands Caroline Islands **150** F8 7 30N 152 30E
Truro Cornwall England **72** B3 50 16N 5 03W
Truro Nova Scotia Canada **133** W2 45 24N 63 18W
Truyère *r.* France **91** C1 44 55N 2 47E
Tsangpo *see* Yarlung Zangbo Jiang
Tsarskoye Selo Russia **104** B6 59 43N 30 22E
Tsavo National Park Kenya **124** G7 3 30S 38 00E
Tseung Kwan O H.K. China **112** C1 22 19N 114 14E
Tshane Botswana **125** D3 24 05S 21 54E
Tshchikskoye Vodokhranilishche *r.* Russia **95** L6/M6 45 00N 40 00E
Tshuapa *r.* Congo (D.R.) **124** D7 1 00S 23 00E
Tsimlyanskoye Vodokhranilishche *res.* Russia **104** E4 47 30N 43 00E
Tsimlyansk Reservoir Russia **77** P6 47 30N 43 00E
Tsing Chau Tsai H.K. China **112** B2 22 20N 114 02E
Tsing Yi H.K. China **112** B2 22 21N 114 06E
Tsing Yi *i.* H.K. China **112** B2 22 10N 114 00E
Tsin Shui Wan H.K. China **112** C1 22 14N 114 12E
Ts'khinvali Georgia **95** N5 42 14N 43 58E
Tsu Japan **114** H1 34 41N 136 30E
Tsuchiura Japan **114** M3 36 05N 140 11E
Tsuen Wan H.K. China **112** B2 22 22N 114 06E
Tsugaru-kaikyō *sd.* Japan **114** D3 41 30N 140 30E
Tsumeb Namibia **125** C4 19 13S 17 42E
Tsuna Japan **114** F1 34 26N 134 53E
Tsunashima Japan **115** B3 35 13N 139 38E
Tsuru Japan **114** K2 35 36N 138 54E
Tsuruga Japan **114** C2 35 40N 136 05E
Tsurugi-zaki Japan **114** L2 35 08N 139 37E
Tsuruoka Japan **114** C2 38 42N 139 50E
Tsushima Japan **114** H2 35 10N 136 45E
Tsushima *i.* Japan **114** A1 34 30N 129 20E
Tsuyama Japan **114** B2 35 04N 134 01E
Tsz Wan Shan H.K. China **112** C2 22 21N 114 12E
Tua *r.* Portugal **90** A3 41 20N 7 30W
Tuam Galway Rep. of Ireland **74** C3 53 31N 8 50W
Tuamotu Archipelago *is.* Pacific Ocean **151** M6 15 00S 145 00W
Tuamotu Ridge Pacific Ocean **151** L6 19 00S 144 00W
Tuapse Russia **95** L6 44 06N 39 08E
Tuba *r.* Russia **105** P5 54 00N 93 00E
Tubize Belgium **89** D2 50 42N 4 12E
Tübingen Germany **93** A1 48 32N 9 04E
Tubruq Libya **124** D14 32 05N 23 59E
Tubuai Islands Pacific Ocean **151** L5 23 23S 149 27W
Tuchitua Yukon Canada **132** J5 61 20N 129 00W
Tucson Arizona U.S.A. **134** D3 32 15N 110 57W
Tucumcari U.S.A. **134** F4 35 11N 103 44W
Tucupita Venezuela **146** E14 9 02N 62 04W
Tucuruí Brazil **146** H12 3 42S 49 44W
Tudela Spain **90** B3 42 04N 1 37W
Tudweiliog Gwynedd Wales [illegible] 52 55N 4 [illegible]W
Tuen Mun H.K. China **112** A2 22 23N 113 57E
Tufanbeyli Turkey **95** K3 38 15N 36 13E
Tugaske Canada **132** N3 50 54N 106 15W
Tujunga California U.S.A. **139** B3 34 14N 118 16W
Tuktoyaktuk Canada **132** I6 69 24N 133 01W
Tukums Latvia **97** E2 56 58N 23 10E
Tula Hidalgo Mexico **140** E4 20 01N 99 21W
Tula Tamaulipas Mexico **140** E4 23 00N 99 41W
Tula Russia **102** F6 54 11N 37 38E
Tulcán Ecuador **146** B13 0 50N 77 48W
Tulcea Romania **96** D3 45 10N 28 50E
Tulita *(Fort Norman)* Canada **132** J5 64 55N 125 29W
Tulkarm Jordan **106** O11 32 19N 35 02E
Tulla Clare Rep. of Ireland **75** C2 52 52N 8 45W
Tullamore Offaly Rep. of Ireland **74** D3 53 16N 7 30W
Tulle France **91** C2 45 16N 1 46E
Tullow Carlow Rep. of Ireland **75** E2 52 48N 6 44W
Tuloma *r.* Russia **97** G4 69 00N 32 00E
Tulsa Oklahoma U.S.A. **135** G4 36 07N 95 58W
Tulsk Roscommon Rep. of Ireland **74** C3 53 47N 8 15W
Tuluá Colombia **146** B13 4 05N 76 12W
Tulun Russia **103** M6 54 32N 100 35E
Tumaco Colombia **146** B13 1 51N 78 46W
Tumbes Peru **146** A12 3 37S 80 27W
Tumkur India **109** D2 13 20N 77 06E
Tummel *r.* Perth & Kinross Scotland **59** E1/F1 56 40N 4 00W
Tummel Bridge Perth & Kinross Scotland **59** F1 56 43N 3 58W
Tunapuna Trinidad & Tobago **141** T10 10 38N 61 23W
Tunceli Turkey **95** L3 39 07N 39 34E
Tunduru Tanzania **125** G5 11 08S 27 21E
Tundzha *r.* Bulgaria **96** D2 42 00N 25 00E
Tungabhadra *r.* India **109** D3 16 00N 77 00E
Tung Lung Chau *i.* H.K. China **112** C1 22 15N 114 17E
Tungsten Canada **132** J5 62 25N 128 40W
Tunis Tunisia **127** H10 36 50N 10 13E
TUNISIA 127 G9/H9
Tunja Colombia **146** C14 5 33N 73 23W
Tunnsjøen *l.* Norway **97** C3 64 45N 13 25E
Tupelo Mississippi U.S.A. **135** I3 34 15N 88 43W
Tupiza Bolivia **146** D8 21 27S 65 45W
Tupper Lake *tn.* U.S.A. **137** F2 44 14N 74 29W
Túquerres Colombia **146** B13 1 06N 77 37W
Tura Meghalaya India **110** H6 25 32N 90 14E
Tura Russia **103** M8 64 20N 100 17E
Tura *r.* Russia **105** J6 58 00N 63 00E
Turda Romania **96** C3 46 35N 23 50E
Turfan *see* Turpan
Turfan Depression China **112** G7 42 40N 89 30E
Turgay *r.* Kazakhstan **105** J4 49 30N 63 30E
Tŭrgovishte Bulgaria **94** E5 43 14N 26 37E
Turgutlu Turkey **94** E3 38 30N 27 43E
Turhal Turkey **95** K4 40 23N 36 05E
Turia *r.* Spain **90** B2 39 45N 0 55W
Turin *see* Torino
Turkana, Lake Ethiopia/Kenya **124** G8 4 00N 36 00E
Turkeli Turkey **95** J4 41 57N 34 26E
Turkestan Kazakhstan **105** K3 43 17N 68 16E
TURKEY 94/95 G3/M3
TURKMENISTAN *(TURKMENIA)* **105** H3/J2
Turks and Caicos Islands West Indies **141** J4 21 30N 72 00W
Turks Island Passage West Indies **141** J4 21 30N 71 30W
Turku Finland **97** E3 60 27N 22 15E
Turnberry South Ayrshire Scotland **61** E3 55 20N 4 50W
Turnhout Belgium **89** C3 51 19N 4 57E
Turnu Măgurele Romania **96** C2 43 44N 24 53E
Turpan *(Turfan)* China **112** G7 42 55N 89 06E
Turramurra Australia **119** G3 33 44S 151 07E
Turriff Aberdeenshire Scotland **59** G2 57 32N 2 28W
Turtle Creek Lake U.S.A. **136** A1 39 00N 96 00W
Turukhansk Russia **103** K9 65 49N 88 00E
Tuscaloosa Alabama U.S.A. **135** I3 33 12N 87 33W
Tushino Russia **102** L2 55 52N 37 37 26E
Tutbury Staffordshire England **67** F2 52 52N 1 40W
Tuticorin India **109** D1 8 48N 78 10E
Tuttlingen Germany **93** A1 47 59N 8 49E
TUVALU 150 H7
Tuxpan Nayarit Mexico **140** C4 21 58N 105 20W
Tuxpan Veracruz Mexico **140** E4 20 58N 97 23W
Tuxtla Gutierrez Mexico **140** F3 16 45N 93 09W
Túy Spain **90** A3 42 03N 8 39W
Tuz Gölü *(Lake Tuz)* *l.* Turkey **95** H3 38 40N 33 35E
Tuzi Montenegro Yugoslavia **94** A5 42 22N 19 20E
Tuzla Bosnia-Herzegovina **96** B2 44 33N 18 41E
Tuz, Lake *see* Tuz Gölü
Tver' *(Kalinin)* Russia **102** F7 56 49N 35 57E
Tweed *r.* Scottish Borders/Northumberland Scotland/England **61** G3 55 45N 2 10W
Tweedmouth Northumberland England **61** G3 55 47N 2 00W
24 Parganas *admin.* India **108** K1 22 27N 88 19E
Twin Falls *tn.* U.S.A. **134** D5 42 34N 114 30W
Twin Lakes *tn.* Canada **132** L4 60 40N 154 00W
Twyford Berkshire England **70** D2 51 29N 0 53W
Twyford Hampshire England **70** C2 51 01N 1 19W
Tyan Shan *(Tian Shan')* *mts.* China **105** M3/N3 41 00N 76 00E
Tyldesley Greater Manchester England **64** C2 53 32N 2 29W
Tyler Texas U.S.A. **135** G3 32 22N 95 18W
Tylers Green Buckinghamshire England **70** D2 51 37N 0 42W
Tylihul *r.* Ukraine **94** G7 47 20N 30 45E
Tym *r.* Russia **103** K7 59 00N 82 30E
Tympáki Greece **94** D2 35 04N 24 45E
Tynda Russia **103** O7 55 10N 124 35E
Tyndrum Stirling Scotland **59** E1 57 27N 4 44W
Tyne *r.* Northumberland/Tyne & Wear England **61** H2 54 55N 1 50W
Tyne *r.* East Lothian Scotland **61** G3 55 58N 2 43W
Tyne and Wear *co.* England **64/65** D3 55 00N 1 10W
Tynemouth *tn* Tyne & Wear England **65** D4 55 01N 1 24W
Tynset Norway **97** C3 62 17N 10 47E
Tyre *see* Soûr
Tyrrhenian Sea Europe **92** B1/2 40 00N 12 00E
Tyumen' Russia **105** K6 57 11N 65 29E
Tyung *r.* Russia **103** N8 65 00N 119 00E
Tywi *r.* Carmarthenshire Wales **66** C1 51 50N 4 25W
Tywyn Gwynedd Wales **66** C2 52 35N 4 05W

U

U.A.E. *see* UNITED ARAB EMIRATES
Uaupés Brazil **146** D12 0 07S 67 05W
Ubagan *r.* Kazakhstan **106** J5/K5 54 00N 65 00E
Ubangi *r.* Central African Rep. **124** C8 4 00N 18 00E
Ube Japan **114** B1 33 57N 131 16E
Uberaba Brazil **146** H9 19 47S 47 57W
Uberlândia Brazil **146** H9 18 57S 48 17W
Ubon Ratchathani Thailand **111** C7 15 15N 104 50E
Ubundu Congo (D.R.) **124** E7 0 24S 25 30E
Uchiura-wan *b.* Japan **114** D3 42 30N 140 40E
Uckfield East Sussex England **71** E1 50 58N 0 05E
Uda *r.* Russia **103** P6 54 00N 134 00E
Udaipur Rajasthan India **109** C4 24 36N 73 47E
Udaipur Tripura India **110** J4 23 31N 91 31E
Udalguri Assam India **110** J7 26 46N 91 58E
Uddevalla Sweden **97** C2 58 20N 11 56E
Uddjaur *l.* Sweden **97** D4 65 55N 17 50E
Uden Netherlands **89** E3 51 40N 5 37E
Udgir India **109** D3 18 26N 77 11E
Udine Italy **92** B3 46 04N 13 14E
Udon Thani Thailand **111** C7 17 25N 102 45E
Ueda Japan **114** C2 36 27N 138 13E
Uele *r.* Congo (D.R.) **124** E8 4 00N 27 00E
Uelen Russia **103** U9 66 13N 169 48W
Uelzen Germany **93** B2 52 58N 10 34E
Ueno Japan **114** H1 34 45N 136 08E
Ufa Russia **102** H6 54 45N 55 58E
Ufa *r.* Russia **105** H6 55 30N 56 30E
Uffculme Devon England **73** D3 50 54N 3 21W
Ugab *r.* Namibia **125** C3 21 00S 15 00E
UGANDA 124 F8
Ugie *r.* Aberdeenshire Scotland **59** H2 57 33N 1 55W
Ugra *r.* Russia **104** C5 54 30N 34 00E
Uig Highland Scotland **58** C2 57 35N 6 22W
Uinta Mountains Utah U.S.A. **134** D5 40 00N 111 00W
Uitenhage Rep. of South Africa **125** E1 33 46S 25 25E
Uithoorn Netherlands **89** D4 52 14N 4 49E
Uithuizen Netherlands **89** F5 53 24N 6 41E
Uji Japan **114** G1 34 54N 135 48E
Ujjain India **109** D4 23 11N 75 50E

W

Wa Ghana **127** E5 10 07N 2 28W
Waal *r.* Netherlands **89** E3 51 50N 5 07E
Waalwijk Netherlands **89** E3 51 42N 5 04E
Wabana Newfoundland Canada **133** Y2 47 40N 52 58W
Wabash *r.* North America **135** I4 38 00N 87 30W
Wabash Indiana U.S.A. **136** C2 40 47N 85 48W
Wabowden Canada **133** P3 54 57N 98 38W
Wabush Newfoundland Canada **133** V3 52 45N 66 50W
Waco Texas U.S.A. **135** G3 31 33N 97 10W
Wadayama Japan **114** F2 35 22N 134 49E
Waddeneilanden *(West Frisian Islands)* Netherlands **89** D5/E5 53 25N 5 15E
Waddenzee *sea* Netherlands **89** D5/E5 53 15N 5 15E
Waddesdon Buckinghamshire England **70** D2 51 51N 0 56W
Waddington Lincolnshire England **65** E2 53 10N 0 32W
Waddington, Mount B.C. Canada **132** J3 51 22N 125 14W
Wadebridge Cornwall England **72** C3 50 32N 4 50W
Wadhurst East Sussex England **71** E2 51 04N 0 21E
Wādī al Masīlah *r.* Yemen Rep. **107** H2 16 00N 50 00E
Wadi Araba *r.* Israel **106** O10 30 30N 35 10E
Wādī ath Tharthār *r.* Iraq **95** N1 35 40N 42 50E
Wadi el 'Arish *r.* Egypt **106** N9/10 30 05N 33 50E
Wadi Halfa Sudan **124** F12 21 55N 31 20E
Wadinxveen Netherlands **88** C2 52 02N 4 39E
Wad Medani Sudan **124** F10 14 24N 33 30E
Waesch, Mount Antarctica **149** 77 00S 127 30W
Wageningen Netherlands **89** E3 51 58N 5 40E
Wager Bay Canada **133** R6 66 00N 89 00W
Wagga Wagga Australia **118** H2 35 07S 147 24E
Wagin Australia **118** B3 33 20S 117 15E
Waglan Island H.K. China **112** C1 22 10N 114 18E
Wah Pakistan **109** C6 33 50N 72 44E
Waha Libya **124** C13 28 10N 19 57E
Wahiawa Hawaiian Is. **151** X18 21 36N 158 05W
Wahpeton North Dakota U.S.A. **136** A3 46 16N 96 36W
Waialua Hawaiian Is. **151** X18 21 35N 158 08W
Waigeo *i.* Irian Jaya Indonesia **111** I3 0 15S 130 45E
Waihi N.Z. **119** C3 37 57S 175 44E
Waikaremoana, Lake N.Z. **119** C3 38 46S 177 06E
Waikato *r.* N.Z. **119** C3 37 25S 175 45E
Wailuku Hawaiian Is. **151** Y18 20 54N 156 30W
Waimate N.Z. **119** B2 44 44S 171 03E
Wainfleet All Saints Lincolnshire England **65** F2 53 06N 0 15E
Wainwright Canada **132** M3 52 49N 110 52W
Wainwright U.S.A. **132** D7 70 39N 160 10W
Waipawa N.Z. **119** C3 39 57S 176 35E
Wairoa N.Z. **119** C3 39 03S 177 25E
Waitaki *r.* N.Z. **119** B2 44 45S 170 30E
Waitara N.Z. **119** B3 39 00S 174 14E
Wajima Japan **114** C2 37 23N 136 53E
Wajir Kenya **124** H8 1 46N 40 05E
Wakasa-wan *b.* Japan **114** C2 35 40N 135 30E
Wakatipu, Lake N.Z. **119** A1 45 06S 168 31E
Wakayama Japan **114** G1 34 12N 135 10E
Wakefield West Yorkshire England **65** D2 53 42N 1 29W
Wakefield Rhode Island U.S.A. **137** F2 41 26N 71 30W
Wake Island Pacific Ocean **150** G10 19 18N 166 36E
Wakkanai Japan **114** D4 45 26N 141 43E
Wako Japan **115** B4 35 46N 139 37E
Wałbrzych Poland **96** B4 50 48N 16 19E
Walbury Hill *mt.* Berkshire England **70** C2 51 25N 1 35W
Walcheren *i.* Netherlands **89** C3 51 30N 3 30E
Wałcz Poland **96** B4 53 17N 16 29E
Waldorf Maryland U.S.A. **137** E1 38 38N 76 56W
Wales U.S.A. **132** B6 65 38N 168 09W
Wales 00
Walker Lake Nevada U.S.A. **134** C4 38 40N 118 43W
Walkerton Canada **137** D2 44 08N 81 10W
Wallaceburg Canada **137** D2 42 34N 82 22W
Wallaroo Australia **118** F3 33 57S 137 36E
Wallasey Merseyside England **64** B2 53 26N 3 03W
Walla Walla Washington U.S.A. **134** C6 46 05N 118 18W
Wallingford Oxfordshire England **70** C2 51 37N 1 08W
Walls Shetland Islands Scotland **57** D3 60 14N 1 34W
Wallsend Tyne & Wear England **64** D3 55 00N 1 31W
Walney, Isle of Cumbria England **64** B3 54 05N 3 10W
Walnut California U.S.A. **139** C3 34 01N 117 50W
Walsall West Midlands England **67** F2 52 35N 1 58W
Walsenburg Colorado U.S.A. **134** F4 37 36N 104 48W
Walsum Germany **86** A3 51 32N 6 41E
Waltham Abbey Essex England **70** E2 51 41N 0 00
Waltham Forest Greater London England **70** D2 51 30N 0 00
Waltham on the Wolds Leicestershire England **67** G2 52 49N 0 49W
Walton-le-Dale Lancashire England **64** C2 53 45N 2 41W
Walton-on-the-Naze Essex England **71** F2 51 51N 1 16E
Waltrop Germany **86** D3 51 37N 7 25E
Walvis Bay *tn.* Namibia **125** B3 22 59S 14 31E
Walvis Ridge Atlantic Ocean **152** I3/4 30 00S 3 00E
Walyevo Fiji **150** V16 17 35S 179 58W
Wamba *r.* Congo (D.R.) **125** C6 6 30S 17 30E
Wanaka, Lake N.Z. **119** A2 44 28S 169 09E
Wanganui N.Z. **119** C3 39 56S 175 03E
Wanganui *r.* N.Z. **119** C3 39 30S 175 06E
Wang Chau *i.* H.K. China **112** C1 22 20N 114 22E
Wangerooge *i.* Germany **93** A2 53 47N 7 54E
Wang Toi Shan H.K. China **112** B2 22 26N 114 05E
Wanheimerort Germany **86** B2 51 23N 6 45E
Wanlockhead Dumfries & Galloway Scotland **61** F3 55 24N 3 47W
Wanne-Eickel Germany **86** C3 51 31N 7 09E
Wansbeck *r.* Northumberland England **61** H3 55 10N 1 50W
Wansee Germany **87** E1 52 24N 13 09E
Wantage Oxfordshire England **70** C2 51 36N 1 25W
Wanxian China **113** L5 30 54N 108 20E
Warangal India **109** D3 18 00N 79 35E
Warboys Cambridgeshire England **70** D3 52 24N 0 06W
Warburg Germany **93** A2 51 28N 9 10E
Wardha *r.* India **109** D4 20 30N 79 00E
Ward Hill Orkney Islands Scotland **57** B1 58 54N 3 20W
Ward's Stone *hill* Lancashire England **64** C3 54 03N 2 38W
Ware Hertfordshire England **70** D2 51 49N 0 02W
Waregem Belgium **89** C2 50 53N 3 26E
Wareham Dorset England **73** E3 50 41N 2 07W
Waremme Belgium **89** E2 50 42N 5 15E
Waren Germany **93** B2 53 32N 12 42E
Warendorf Germany **93** A2 51 57N 8 00E
Warley West Midlands England **67** F2 52 30N 1 59W
Warlingham Surrey England **70** D2 51 19N 0 04W
Warminster Wiltshire England **70** B2 51 13N 2 12W
Warnow *r.* Germany **93** B2 53 00N 12 00E
Warrego *r.* Australia **118** H4 27 30S 146 00E
Warren Michigan U.S.A. **137** D2 42 30N 83 02W
Warren Ohio U.S.A. **137** D2 41 15N 80 49W
Warren Pennsylvania U.S.A. **137** E2 41 52N 79 09W
Warrenpoint *tn.* Newry & Mourne Northern Ireland **60** C2 54 06N 6 15W
Warrensburg Missouri U.S.A. **136** B1 38 46N 93 44W
Warrington Cheshire England **64** C2 53 24N 2 37W
Warrnambool Australia **118** G2 38 23S 142 03E
Warroad Minnesota U.S.A. **136** A3 48 54N 95 20W
Warsaw *see* Warszawa
Warsop Nottinghamshire England **65** D2 53 13N 1 10W
Warszawa *(Warsaw)* Poland **96** C4 52 15N 21 00E
Warta *r.* Poland **96** B4 52 00N 17 00E
Warton Lancashire England **64** C2 53 46N 2 54W
Warwick Australia **118** I4 28 12S 152 00E
Warwick Warwickshire England **67** F2 52 17N 1 34W
Warwick Rhode Island U.S.A. **137** F2 41 42N 71 23W
Warwickshire *co.* England **67** F2 52 15N 1 40W
Wasaga Beach *tn.* Canada **137** D2 44 31N 80 02W
Washburn U.S.A. **136** B3 46 41N 90 53W
Washingborough Lincolnshire England **65** E2 53 14N 0 28W
Washington Tyne & Wear England **64** D3 54 54N 1 31W
Washington *state* U.S.A. **134** B6/C6 47 00N 120 00W
Washington Pennsylvania U.S.A. **137** D2 40 11N 80 16W
Washington D.C. District of Columbia U.S.A. **137** E1 38 55N 77 00W
Wash, The *b.* Lincolnshire England **65** F1 52 55N 0 10E
Waskaganish *(Fort Rupert)* Québec Canada **137** E4 51 30N 79 45W
Wasmes Belgium **89** C2 50 25N 3 51E
Wassenaar Netherlands **89** D4 52 07N 4 23E
Wast Water *l.* Cumbria England **64** B3 54 26N 3 18W
Watampone Indonesia **111** G3 4 33S 120 20E
Watchet Somerset England **73** D4 51 12N 3 20W
Waterbeach Cambridgeshire England **71** E3 52 16N 0 11E
Waterbury Connecticut U.S.A. **137** F2 41 33N 73 03W
Waterbury Vermont U.S.A. **137** F2 44 21N 72 46W
Waterfall *tn.* Australia **119** G1 34 08S 151 00E
Waterford *co.* Rep. of Ireland **75** D2 52 10N 7 30W
Waterford Waterford Rep. of Ireland **75** D2 52 15N 7 06W
Waterford Harbour *b.* Waterford/Wexford Rep. of Ireland **75** E2 52 10N 7 00W
Watergrasshill Cork Rep. of Ireland **75** C2 52 00N 8 20W
Waterloo Belgium **89** D2 50 43N 4 24E
Waterloo Trinidad & Tobago **141** T9 10 28N 61 28W
Waterloo Iowa U.S.A. **136** B2 42 30N 92 20W
Waterlooville Hampshire England **70** C1 50 53N 1 02W
Waternish Point Highland Scotland **58** C2 57 38N 6 38W
Water of Feugh *r.* Aberdeenshire Scotland **59** G2 57 00N 2 40W
Water of Girvan *r.* South Ayrshire Scotland **61** E3 55 15N 4 45W
Water of Leith *r.* City of Edinburgh Scotland **61** F3 55 53N 3 21W
Water of Luce *r.* Dumfries & Galloway Scotland **60** E2 54 55N 4 53W
Waterton Lakes National Park Canada **134** D6 49 00N 114 00W
Watertown New York U.S.A. **137** E2 43 57N 75 56W
Watertown South Dakota U.S.A. **136** A2 44 54N 97 08W
Waterville Kerry Rep. of Ireland **75** A1 51 50N 10 10W
Waterville Maine U.S.A. **137** G2 44 34N 69 41W
Watford Hertfordshire England **70** D2 51 39N 0 24W
Wath upon Dearne South Yorkshire England **65** D2 53 31N 1 21W
Watkins Glen U.S.A. **137** E2 42 23N 76 53W
Watlington Oxfordshire England **70** D2 51 39N 1 00W
Watseka Illinois U.S.A. **136** C2 40 46N 87 45W
Watson Lake *tn.* Yukon Canada **132** J5 60 07N 128 49W
Watten France **89** B2 50 50N 2 13E
Wattenscheid Germany **86** C2 51 27N 7 07E
Watton Norfolk England **71** E3 52 34N 0 50E
Wattrelos Belgium **89** C2 50 40N 3 14E
Wau Papua New Guinea **118** H8 7 22S 146 40E
Wau Sudan **124** E9 7 40N 28 04E
Waukegan Illinois U.S.A. **136** C2 42 21N 87 52W
Waukesha U.S.A. **136** C2 43 01N 88 14W
Wausau U.S.A. **136** C2 44 58N 89 40W
Wauwatosa U.S.A. **136** C2 43 04N 88 02W
Waveney *r.* Suffolk/Norfolk England **71** F3 52 30N 1 30E
Wavre Belgium **89** D2 50 43N 4 37E
Wawa Canada **137** D3 48 04N 84 49W
Waycross Georgia U.S.A. **135** J3 31 12N 82 22W
Wayne U.S.A. **138** A2 40 55N 74 15W
Waynesboro Virginia U.S.A. **137** E1 38 04N 78 54W
Weald, The *geog. reg.* East Sussex/Kent England **71** E2 51 05N 0 25E
Wear *r.* Durham England **64** C3 54 45N 2 05W
Weardale *v.* Durham England **64** C3 54 45N 2 10W
Weaver *r.* Cheshire England **64** C2 53 20N 2 40W
Weaverham Cheshire England **64** C2 53 16N 2 35W
Webster City Iowa U.S.A. **136** B2 42 30N 93 50W
Weddell Island Falkland Is. **152** L16 51 55S 61 30W
Weddell Sea Southern Ocean **149** 71 00S 40 00W
Wedding Germany **87** F2 52 33N 13 21E
Wedmore Somerset England **73** E4 51 14N 2 49W
Weedon Bec Northamptonshire England **70** C3 52 14N 1 05W
Weert Netherlands **89** E3 51 15N 5 42E
Weesp Netherlands **89** E4 52 19N 5 02E
Weiden Germany **93** B1 49 40N 12 10E
Weifang China **113** N6 36 44N 119 10E
Wei He *r.* China **113** L5 34 00N 106 00E
Weimar Germany **93** B2 50 59N 11 20E
Weipa Australia **118** G7 12 35S 141 56E
Weirton West Virginia U.S.A. **135** J5 40 24N 80 37W
Weissensee Germany **87** F2 51 12N 11 05E
Weisse Elster *r.* Germany **93** B2 51 00N 12 00E
Weissenfels Germany **93** B2 51 12N 11 58E
Weisswasser *tn.* Germany **93** B2 51 31N 14 38E
Wejherowo Poland **96** B4 54 36N 18 12E
Welland Canada **137** E2 45 59N 79 14W
Welland *r.* Rutland/Northamptonshire England **70** D3 52 30N 0 50W
Wellesley Islands Australia **118** F6 16 30S 139 00E
Wellingborough Northamptonshire England **70** D3 52 19N 0 42W
Wellington Shropshire England **67** E2 52 43N 2 31W
Wellington Somerset England **73** D3 50 59N 3 15W
Wellington N.Z. **119** B2 41 17S 174 46E
Wellington *admin.* N.Z. **150** H3 40 10S 175 00E
Wellington Kansas U.S.A. **135** G4 37 17N 97 25W
Wells Somerset England **73** E4 51 13N 2 39W
Wellsboro Pennsylvania U.S.A. **137** E2 41 45N 77 18W
Wellsford N.Z. **119** B3 36 18S 174 31E
Wells-next-the-Sea Norfolk England **71** E3 52 58N 0 51E
Wels Austria **93** B1 48 10N 14 02E
Welshpool Powys Wales **66** D2 52 40N 3 09W
Welton East Riding of Yorkshire England **65** E2 54 47N 3 00W
Welwyn Garden City Hertfordshire England **70** D2 51 48N 0 13W
Wem Shropshire England **67** E2 52 51N 2 44W
Wemyss Bay Inverclyde Scotland **60** E3 55 55N 4 53W
Wendover Buckinghamshire England **70** D2 51 46N 0 46W
Wenlock Edge *hills* Shropshire England **67** E2 52 30N 2 45W
Wensleydale *v.* North Yorkshire England **64** C3 54 15N 2 00W
Wensum *r.* Norfolk England **71** F3 52 45N 1 10E
Wenzhou China **113** O4 28 02N 120 40E
Werder Germany **87** D1 52 23N 12 56E
Wernigerode Germany **93** B2 51 51N 10 48E
Werra *r.* Germany **93** B2 51 00N 10 00E
Wertach *r.* Germany **93** B1 48 00N 10 00E
Wesel Germany **93** A2 51 39N 6 37E
Weser *est.* Germany **93** A2 53 00N 8 00E
Weser *r.* Germany **93** A2 53 00N 8 00E
West Allis U.S.A. **136** C2 43 01N 88 00W
West Antarctica *geog. reg.* Antarctica **149** 80 00S 120 00W
West Bank *territory* Israel **106** O11 32 00N 35 00E
West Bay *c.* Dorset England **73** E3 50 33N 2 30W
West Bengal *admin.* India **109** F4 22 00N 88 00E
Westbourne Canada **136** A4 50 08N 98 33W
West Bridgford Nottinghamshire England **65** D1 52 56N 1 08W
West Bromwich West Midlands England **67** F2 52 31N 1 59W
Westbrook *tn.* Maine U.S.A. **137** F2 43 41N 70 22W
West Burra *i.* Shetland Islands Scotland **57** D3 60 05N 1 21W
Westbury Wiltshire England **70** B2 51 16N 2 11W
West Caroline Basin Pacific Ocean **150** D8 3 00N 136 00E
West Chester Pennsylvania U.S.A. **137** E1 39 58N 75 37W
Westchester County *admin.* U.S.A. **138** D2 40 55N 73 42W
West Covina California U.S.A. **139** C3 34 04N 117 56W
West Dunbartonshire *u.a.* Scotland **61** E4 56 02N 4 39W
Westeinder Plas *l.* Netherlands **88** C2 52 15N 4 44E
Westerham Kent England **71** E2 51 16N 0 05E
Westerland Germany **93** A2 54 54N 8 19E
Western Australia *state* Australia **118** A5/D3 25 00S 117 00E
Western Ghats *mts.* India **109** C2/3 15 30N 74 00E
Western Isles *u.a.* Scotland **58** B2 57 45N 7 30W
WESTERN SAHARA 127 C7/8
WESTERN SAMOA *see* SAMOA
Western Sayan *mts.* Russia **105** O5/P5 52 30N 92 30E
Western Yamuna Canal India **108** L4 28 40N 77 08E
Westerschelde *sd.* Netherlands **89** C3 51 20N 3 45E
Westerwald *geog. reg.* Germany **93** A2 50 00N 8 00E
West European Basin Atlantic Ocean **152** G11 47 00N 18 00W
West Falkland *i.* Falkland Is. **152** L16 51 00S 60 40W
West Felton Shropshire England **66** D2 52 49N 2 58W
Westfield U.S.A. **137** F2 42 07N 72 45W
West Fork White River Indiana U.S.A. **136** C1 39 00N 87 00W
West Frisian Islands *see* Waddeneilanden
West Haddon Northamptonshire England **70** C3 52 20N 1 04W
Westhill Aberdeenshire Scotland **59** G2 57 11N 2 16W
West Horsley Surrey England **70** D2 51 16N 0 26W
West Ice Shelf Antarctica **149** 66 00S 85 00E
West Indies *is.* Caribbean Sea **141** J4/K4 22 00N 69 00W
West Kilbride North Ayrshire Scotland **60** E3 55 42N 4 51W
West Kirby Merseyside England **64** B2 53 22N 3 10W
West Lamma Channel H.K. China **112** B1 22 10N 114 00E
West Loch Tarbert *b.* Argyll & Bute Scotland **60** D3 55 48N 5 31W
West Loch Tarbert Western Isles Scotland **58** B2/C2 57 57N 7 00W
West Los Angeles California U.S.A. **139** A3 34 02N 118 25W
West Lothian *u.a.* Scotland **61** F3 55 50N 3 36W
West Marianas Basin Pacific Ocean **150** D9 16 00N 137 30E
Westmeath *co.* Rep. of Ireland **74** D3 53 30N 7 30W
West Memphis Arkansas U.S.A. **135** H4 35 09N 90 11W
West Mersea Essex England **71** E2 51 47N 0 55E
West Midlands *co.* England **67** E2 52 35N 2 00W
Westminster California U.S.A. **139** C2 33 45N 117 59W
Weston West Virginia U.S.A. **137** D1 39 02N 80 28W
Weston-super-Mare North Somerset England **70** B2 51 21N 2 59W
West Palm Beach *tn.* Florida U.S.A. **135** J2 26 42N 80 05W
West Plains *tn.* Missouri U.S.A. **136** B1 36 44N 91 51W
West Port Russia **102** L1 55 45N 37 30E
Westport Mayo Rep. of Ireland **74** B3 53 48N 9 32W
Westport Connecticut U.S.A. **137** F2 41 09N 73 22W
Westport Bay Mayo Rep. of Ireland **74** B3 53 49N 9 37W
Westray *i.* Orkney Islands Scotland **57** B2 59 18N 3 00W
Westray Firth *sd.* Orkney Islands Scotland **57** B2/C1 59 15N 3 00W
West Siberian Lowland Russia **103** J7/J8 60 00N 75 00E
West Sussex *co.* England **70** D1/2 51 00N 0 25W
West Terschelling Netherlands **89** E5 53 22N 5 13E
West Thurrock Essex England **71** E2 51 28N 0 20E
West Virginia *state* U.S.A. **137** D1 39 00N 81 00W
West-Vlaanderen *admin.* Belgium **89** B3 51 10N 3 00E
Westward Ho! Devon England **72** C4 51 02N 4 15W
West Wittering West Sussex England **70** D1 50 47N 0 54W
West Yorkshire *co.* England **64** D2 53 50N 1 30W
Wetar *i.* Indonesia **111** H2 7 15S 126 45E
Wetaskiwin Canada **132** M3 52 57N 113 20W
Wetherby West Yorkshire England **65** D2 53 56N 1 23W
Wetzlar Germany **93** A2 50 33N 8 30E
Wevelgem Belgium **89** C2 50 48N 3 12E
Wewak Papua New Guinea **118** G9 3 35S 143 35E
Wexford *co.* Rep. of Ireland **75** E2 52 25N 6 35W
Wexford Wexford Rep. of Ireland **75** E2 52 20N 6 27W
Wexford Bay Wexford Rep. of Ireland **75** E2 52 25N 6 10W
Wexford Harbour *b.* Wexford Rep. of Ireland **75** E2 52 20N 6 25W
Wey *r.* Surrey England **70** D2 51 18N 0 30W
Weybridge Surrey England **70** D2 51 22N 0 28W
Weyburn Saskatchewan Canada **132** O2 49 39N 103 51W
Weymouth Dorset England **73** E3 50 37N 2 25W
Weymouth U.S.A. **137** F2 42 14N 70 58W
Whakatane N.Z. **119** C3 37 58S 176 59E
Whaley Bridge Derbyshire England **67** F3 53 20N 1 59W
Whalley Lancashire England **64** C2 53 50N 2 24W
Whalsay *i.* Shetland Islands Scotland **57** F3 60 22N 0 59W
Whangarei N.Z. **119** B3 35 43S 174 19E
Wharfe *r.* North Yorkshire England **65** D2 53 55N 1 30W
Wharfedale *v.* North Yorkshire England **64** C3 54 05N 2 00W
Wha Ti *(Lac la Martre)* Canada **132** L5 63 00N 117 30W
Wheatley Oxfordshire England **70** C2 53 22N 0 52W
Wheaton Minnesota U.S.A. **136** A3 45 49N 96 30W
Wheeler Lake Alabama U.S.A. **135** I3 34 00N 87 00W
Wheeling West Virginia U.S.A. **137** D2 40 05N 80 43W
Whernside *sum.* North Yorkshire England **64** C3 54 14N 2 23W
Whickham Tyne & Wear England **64** D3 54 57N 1 40W
Whiddy Island Cork Rep. of Ireland **75** B1 51 41N 9 30W
Whitburn Tyne & Wear England **65** D3 54 57N 1 21W
Whitburn West Lothian Scotland **61** F3 55 52N 3 42W
Whitby Canada **137** E2 43 52N 78 56W
Whitby North Yorkshire England **65** E3 54 29N 0 37W
Whitchurch Buckinghamshire England **70** D2 51 53N 0 51W
Whitchurch Hampshire England **70** C2 51 14N 1 20W
Whitchurch Shropshire England **67** E2 52 58N 2 41W
White *r.* U.S.A. **135** H4 35 00N 92 00W
Whiteadder Water *r.* Scottish Borders/Northumberland Scotland/England **61** G3 55 50N 2 10W
White Bay Canada **133** X3 50 30N 55 50W
Whitecourt Canada **132** L3 54 10N 115 38W
Whitefield Greater Manchester England **64** C2 53 34N 2 18W
Whitegate Cork Rep. of Ireland **75** C1 51 50N 8 14W
Whitehaven Cumbria England **64** B3 54 33N 3 35W
Whitehead Carrickfergus Northern Ireland **60** D2 54 45N 5 43W
Whitehills Aberdeenshire Scotland **59** G2 57 40N 2 35W
Whitehorse Yukon Canada **132** H5 60 41N 135 08W
Whitehorse Hill *mt.* Oxfordshire England **70** C2 51 37N 1 35W
White Horse, Vale of Thamesdown/Oxfordshire England **70** C2 51 35N 1 30W
Whiteland Indiana U.S.A. **136** C1 39 32N 86 05W
White Mountains New Hampshire U.S.A. **137** F2 44 00N 72 00W
Whiten Head Highland Scotland **59** E3 58 34N 4 32W
White Nile *see* Bahr el Abiad
White Nile Dam Sudan **124** F11 14 18N 32 20E
Whiteparish Wiltshire England **70** C2 51 01N 1 39W
White River *tn.* Canada **136** C3 48 35N 85 16W
White Sea Russia **102** F9 66 00N 37 30E
White Strand *c.* Clare Rep. of Ireland **75** B2 52 46N 9 32W
White Volta *r.* Ghana **127** E4/5 9 30N 1 30W
Whitfield Kent England **71** F2 51 09N 1 17E
Whithorn Dumfries & Galloway Scotland **61** E2 54 44N 4 25W
Whitland Carmarthenshire Wales **66** C1 51 50N 4 37W
Whitley Bay *tn.* Tyne & Wear England **65** D4 55 03N 1 25W
Whitney Canada **137** E3 45 29N 78 15W
Whitney, Mount California U.S.A. **134** C4 36 35N 118 17W
Whitsand Bay Cornwall England **72** C3 50 20N 4 25W
Whitstable Kent England **71** F2 51 22N 1 02E
Whittier California U.S.A. **139** B2 33 58N 118 02W
Whittier Narrows Dam Reservoir Area California U.S.A. **139** B3 34 02N 118 02W
Whittington Shropshire England **66** D2 52 52N 3 00W
Whittlesey Cambridgeshire England **70** D3 52 34N 0 08W
Whitton North Lincolnshire England **65** E2 53 43N 0 38W
Whitworth Lancashire England **64** C2 53 40N 2 10W
Whyalla Australia **118** F3 33 04S 137 34E
Wiarton Canada **137** D2 44 44N 81 10W
Wiay *i.* Western Isles Scotland **58** B2 57 23N 7 13W
Wichita Kansas U.S.A. **135** G4 37 43N 97 20W
Wichita *r.* Texas U.S.A. **134** F3 33 00N 100 00W
Wichita Falls *tn.* Texas U.S.A. **134** G3 33 55N 98 30W
Wick Highland Scotland **59** F3 58 26N 3 06W
Wick *r.* Highland Scotland **57** B1 58 26N 3 10W
Wickford Essex England **71** E2 51 38N 0 31E
Wickham Hampshire England **70** C1 50 54N 1 10W
Wickham Market Suffolk England **71** F3 52 09N 1 22E
Wicklow *co.* Rep. of Ireland **74/75** E2 52 55N 6 25W
Wicklow Wicklow Rep. of Ireland **75** E2 52 59N 6 03W
Wicklow Head *c.* Wicklow Rep. of Ireland **75** E2 52 58N 6 00W
Wicklow Mountains Wicklow Rep. of Ireland **75** E2 53 00N 6 20W
Wide Firth Orkney Islands Scotland **57** B2/C2 59 02N 3 00W
Widnes Cheshire England **64** C2 53 22N 2 44W
Wien *(Vienna)* Austria **92** C3 48 13N 16 22E
Wiener Neustadt Austria **92** C3 47 49N 16 15E
Wieprz *r.* Poland **96** C4 51 00N 23 00E
Wierden Netherlands **89** F4 52 21N 6 35E
Wiesbaden Germany **93** A2 50 05N 8 15E
Wigan Greater Manchester England **64** C2 53 33N 2 38W
Wigston Leicestershire England **67** F2 52 36N 1 05W
Wigton Cumbria England **64** B3 54 49N 3 09W
Wigtown Dumfries & Galloway Scotland **61** E2 54 52N 4 26W
Wigtown Bay Dumfries & Galloway Scotland **61** E2 54 45N 4 20W
Wijchen Netherlands **89** E3 51 48N 5 44E
Wijde Blik *l.* Netherlands **89** E2 52 13N 5 04E
Wil Switzerland **92** A3 47 28N 9 03E
Wilberfoss East Riding of Yorkshire England **65** E2 53 57N 0 53W
Wildau Germany **87** G1 52 18N 13 38E
Wilhelm II Land *geog. reg.* Antarctica **149** 70 00S 90 00E
Wilhelmshaven Germany **93** A2 53 32N 8 07E
Wilkes-Barre U.S.A. **137** E2 41 15N 75 50W
Wilkes Land *geog. reg.* Antarctica **149** 68 00S 105 00E
Willemstad Curaçao **141** K2 12 12N 68 56W
Willebroek Belgium **89** D3 51 04N 4 22E
Williamnagar Meghalaya India **110** H6 25 90
Williams Bridge U.S.A. **138** C2 40 53N 73 51W
Williamsburg Virginia U.S.A. **137** E1 37 17N 79 43W
Williams Lake *tn.* B.C. Canada **132** K3 52 08N 122 09W
Williamson U.S.A. **137** D1 37 42N 82 16W
Williamsport U.S.A. **135** K5 41 16N 77 03W
Williamstown Kentucky U.S.A. **137** D1 38 39N 84 32W
Willington Durham England **64** D3 54 43N 1 41W
Williston North Dakota U.S.A. **134** F6 48 09N 103 39W
Williston Lake B.C. Canada **132** K4 49 27N 80 37W
Williton Somerset England **73** D4 51 10N 3 20W
Willmar Minnesota U.S.A. **136** A3 45 06N 95 03W
Willow Springs *tn.* U.S.A. **136** D1 36 59N 91 59W
Wilmersdorf Germany **87** F1 52 28N 13 16E
Wilmington Delaware U.S.A. **137** E1 39 46N 75 31W
Wilmington North Carolina U.S.A. **135** K3 34 14N 77 55W
Wilmslow Cheshire England **64** C2 53 20N 2 15W
Wilson U.S.A. **135** K4 35 43N 77 56W
Wilton Wiltshire England **70** C2 51 05N 1 52W
Wiltshire *co.* England **70** B2/C2 51 30N 2 00W
Wiluna Australia **118** C4 26 37S 120 12E
Wimborne Minster Dorset England **73** F3 50 48N 1 59W
Wimereux France **89** A2 50 46N 1 37E
Wincanton Somerset England **73** E4 51 04N 2 25W
Winchelsea East Sussex England **71** E1 50 55N 0 42E
Winchester Hampshire England **70** A2 51 04N 1 19W
Winchester Virginia U.S.A. **135** K4 39 11N 78 12W
Windermere *l.* Cumbria England **64** B3 54 20N 3 10W
Windermere *tn* Cumbria England **64** C3 54 23N 2 54W
Windhoek Namibia **125** C3 22 34S 17 06E
Windlestraw Law *mt.* Scottish Borders Scotland **61** F3 55 40N 3 01W
Wind River Range *mts.* U.S.A. **134** E5 43 00N 109 00W
Windrush *r.* Oxfordshire/Gloucestershire England **70** C2 51 48N 1 34W
Windsor Canada **137** D2 42 18N 83 00W
Windsor Berkshire England **70** D2 51 29N 0 38W
Windward Islands Lesser Antilles **141** L2 12 30N 62 00W
Windward Passage *sd.* Cuba/Haiti **141** J3/J4 20 00N 73 00W
Wingate Durham England **65** D3 54 55N 1 23W
Wingerworth Derbyshire England **67** F3 53 13N 1 28W
Wingham Canada **137** D2 43 46N 81 19W
Winisk Lake Canada **133** R3 52 30N 87 30W
Winisk River Canada **133** R4 54 50N 87 00W
Winkleigh Devon England **72** D3 50 51N 3 56W
Winkler Canada **136** A3 49 12N 97 55W
Winnebago, Lake U.S.A. **136** C2 44 00N 88 00W
Winnemucca Nevada U.S.A. **134** C5 40 58N 117 45W
Winnipeg Canada **136** A3 49 53N 97 10W
Winnipeg, Lake Canada **133** P3 52 30N 97 00W
Winnipegosis, Lake Canada **133** O3 52 10N 100 00W
Winnipesaukee, Lake U.S.A. **137** F2 43 00N 72 00W
Winona Minnesota U.S.A. **136** B2 44 02N 91 37W
Winschoten Netherlands **89** G5 53 07N 7 02E
Winscombe North Somerset England **70** B2 51 28N 2 52W
Winsford Cheshire England **64** C2 53 11N 2 31W
Winslow Buckinghamshire England **70** D2 51 57N 0 54W
Winslow Arizona U.S.A. **134** D4 35 01N 110 43W
Winston-Salem U.S.A. **135** J4 36 05N 80 18W